环球雅思学校雅思（IELTS）考试
培生教育集团旗下品牌

环球教育

IELTS

雅思全真模拟试题

环球雅思教学研究中心 (GTRC) ◎编著

南京大学出版社

图书在版编目（CIP）数据

雅思全真模拟试题 / 环球雅思教学研究中心(GTRC)
编著. -- 南京：南京大学出版社, 2014.5
ISBN 978-7-305-13073-1

Ⅰ.①雅… Ⅱ.①环… Ⅲ.①IELTS－习题集 Ⅳ.
①H319.6

中国版本图书馆CIP数据核字(2014)第074053号

出版发行 南京大学出版社
社　　址 南京市汉口路22号　　邮　　编 210093
网　　址 http://www.NjupCo.com
出 版 人 左　健

书　　名 雅思全真模拟试题
编　　著 环球雅思教学研究中心(GTRC)
责任编辑 李晟月　于春艳　裴维维　　编辑热线 010-62127297
审读编辑 陈颖隽　张　静

印　　刷 北京合众伟业印刷有限公司
开　　本 787×1092　1/16　　印张　36.5　　字数　1072千
版　　次 2014年5月第1版　　2014年5月第1次印刷
印　　数 0001—4000
ISBN 978-7-305-13073-1
定　　价 59.80 元（内附MP3光盘）

发行热线 010-62127297
电子邮箱 Press@NjupCo.com
Sales@NjupCo.com（市场部）

环球雅思图书编委会核心小组

前　言

剑桥真题系列截止到目前共有九本，从剑桥1到剑桥9，是由剑桥大学出版社出版的，书中所包含的全真试题资料由剑桥大学考试委员会提供，极具权威性和实用性，是所有备考雅思的资料中最重要的参考书！每本真题的发布都是万众瞩目的，因为每次剑桥真题的发布，都会预示未来雅思考试的命题方向和考试趋势。为了帮助考生全面、深刻地理解剑桥最新的考试，掌握最新的考试题型，从而在考试中以高分取胜，环球雅思学校一线名师和外籍雅思专家组联袂震撼出击，依据剑桥真题的题型、考题难度精心编写了这本《雅思全真模拟试题》。一线名师学术底蕴深厚，从事雅思培训工作多年，无一不是在业界声望卓著的金牌培训师、优秀作者和著名语言测试专家，其培养的学员数以万计，在考生中口碑甚佳。外籍雅思专家组为本书提供了高质量的雅思口语范例、写作范文，确保了本书的专业性和实用性，为雅思考生提供了具有极强针对性和指导性的复习建议。

全书内含15套剑桥雅思全真模拟试题，并附有详细、精准的答案解析。本书最大的特色如下：

1. 含15套剑桥全真模拟试题，其中A类10套和G类5套。模拟训练强度之高、力度之大，是市面上其他同类书籍无法比拟的，完全符合考生对试题数量的需求。本书不仅适用于所有雅思学术类考生，还同时适用一般移民类的考生。
2. 试题的设计、编写完全以测试理论为指导，以剑桥大学考试委员会制订的Test Specifications为依据，以雅思真题为蓝本，紧扣命题思路，总结归纳考试命题规律，为考生备考指引方向，真正实现从题型到试题难度都达到了理论性和科学性的统一，“知己知彼，百战不殆”。
3. 15套模考试题均由外籍雅思专家组提供口语测试回答样本及写作范文，且对所选试题进行了严格审定，进一步提升了试题的质量。
4. 试题材料均选自与真题同源的网站或国外期刊，并按真题形式做相应的调整或修改。所有题型及难度与剑桥雅思真题高度贴近，仿真度极高，真正做到“一书在手，全部拥有”。
5. 题目解析精准，考点全面，归纳到位。听力和阅读试题解析包括【答案速查】和【解题思路】两大模块。【答案速查】呈现最终答案，让考生迅速为自己的答题评分；【解题思路】详细呈现每道题的解题过程，提供考题精解和考点分析，以帮助考生更透彻地理解考题和关键信息点。

6 重现真题场景、题型，使考生能够“身临其境”。对于复习时间有限的考生而言，试题完全遵照真题考点和场景编写，可以起到很好的指南作用。

通过《雅思全真模拟试题》的测试，考生既可以全方位地提高雅思英语水平，又可以熟悉并掌握雅思最新考试内容、考试形式、命题方向、试题类型等。相信本书中极具实战价值的试题定能成为考生在短期内迅速提高成绩、获得实战经验的制胜法宝。

本书篇幅之大、题量之多、选材之精、要求之高、耗时之长，可以说是编者们之前未曾经历的。由于工作量大，时间紧迫，同时水平有限，书中难免存在不足之处，恳请读者和同仁批评和指正。

编者

2014年4月

目录 Contents

解析篇

题目篇

Test 1

Test 2

Test 3

Test 4

Test 5

Test 6

Test 7

Test 8

Test 9

Test 10

General Training Reading and Writing TEST A

General Training Reading and Writing TEST B

General Training Reading and Writing TEST C

General Training Reading and Writing TEST D

General Training Reading and Writing TEST E

Test 1

LISTENING

SECTION 1 *Questions 1–10*

Questions 1–4

Complete the notes below.

Write ***NO MORE THAN TWO WORDS AND/OR A NUMBER*** *for each answer.*

White Cloud Adventures
Length of tour: 1 ....
Maximum group size: Up to **2** .... on the boat
Next available tour date: 3 ....
Hotel name: The **4** ....

Questions 5 and 6

Choose ***TWO*** *letters from* ***A–E****.*

Which **TWO** things are included in the price of the tour?

A overnight accommodation
B evening meal
C drinks and lunch
D use of kayaks
E sauna and gym

Questions 7–10

Complete the sentences below.

Write ***NO MORE THAN THREE WORDS AND/OR A NUMBER*** *for each answer.*

7 For a booking of three or more, the tour costs .... per person.

8 A .... deposit is required when you book.

9 The coach leaves at ....

10 The booking number is ....

SECTION 2 *Questions 11–20*

Questions 11–14

*Choose the correct letter, **A**, **B** or **C**.*

11 According to the speaker, the bus pick-up service

A runs on a number of different routes.
B departs approximately every hour and a half.
C has to be booked in advance.

12 What information is given about the Croc Express?

A There is one return trip to the zoo each day.
B The ticket price includes the services of a tour guide at the zoo.
C Tourists must make arrangements for the coach to come to their hotel.

13 When visiting the zoo, which of the following is probably necessary at a certain time of the year only?

A a jumper
B rainwear
C sun protection

14 Which facility must zoo visitors pay extra for?

A car parking
B a locker
C Internet connection

Questions 15–20

Label the map below.

*Write the correct letter, **A–I**, next to questions 15–20.*

The Australian Zoo

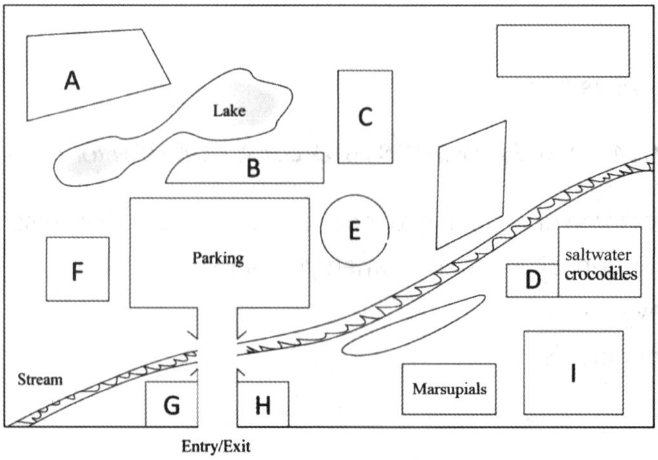

15 Gift shop ....

16 Tigers ....

17 Museum of hunting ....

18 Australian snakes ....

19 Kids' Zoo ....

20 African savannah exhibition ....

SECTION 3 *Questions 21–30*

Questions 21–23

Complete the summary below.

Write ***NO MORE THAN THREE WORDS AND/OR A NUMBER*** *for each answer.*

Mediterranean-style food has proven to be good for health and can increase likelihood of a longer life by **21** .... As our lifestyles are hectic, it can be difficult to find time for the gym or **22** .... However, keeping active is important and experts claim we should aim to take 10,000 **23** .... every day.

Questions 24 and 25

Choose ***TWO*** *letters from* ***A–E.***

Which **TWO** benefits of practising yoga are mentioned?

A It protects the heart.
B It lowers blood pressure.
C It detoxifies the body.
D It helps to prevent disease.
E It strengthens the mind.

Questions 26–28

Which factor in our lifestyle is related to the following effects?

Choose your answers from the box and write the correct letter, ***A–F,*** *next to questions 26–28.*

A	can have a negative impact on other parts of our lives
B	significantly increased risk of death from a prominent disease
C	increases cancer risk
D	may cause problems with immune system
E	speeds circulation
F	is the most significant contributor to ill health

26 Lack of sleep ....
27 A negative attitude ....
28 Work-related stress ....

Questions 29 and 30

*List the **TWO** possible reasons why people living in the countryside in the UK live longer.*

*Write **NO MORE THAN THREE WORDS** for each answer.*

29 ....

30 ....

SECTION 4 *Questions 31–40*

Questions 31–34

Which action does each type of penguin do?

*Choose your answers from the box and write the letters, **A–G**, next to Questions 31–34.*

A	lean forward when making sound
B	often hesitate before jumping
C	walk with its flippers pointing downwards
D	always use their bills when climbing
E	like to come about at night
F	timid to go somewhere steep
G	usually think twice before they leap

31 Gentoos ....

32 Pockhoppers ....

33 Magellanics ....

34 King penguins ....

Questions 35–37

Answer the questions below.

*Write **NO MORE THAN THREE WORDS** for each answer.*

35 When do Emperor penguins breed?

....

36 Which penguin is the least similar to Emperor penguin in appearance and size?

....

37 Write down things that Emperor Penguins mainly eat.

....

Questions 38–40

Complete the summary below.

Write ***NO MORE THAN THREE WORDS*** *for each answer.*

A father Emperor penguin withstands the Antarctic cold for **38** .... to protect his egg. He keeps it on his feet, covered with a feathered flap,which is called **39** .... During this entire time he doesn't eat a thing. Most father penguins lose about **40** .... of his body weight while they wait for their babies to hatch. When the mother penguins return to care for the young, the fathers go to sea to eat and rest.

READING

READING PASSAGE 1

*You should spend about 20 minutes on **Questions 1–13**, which are based on Reading Passage 1 below.*

Personal Time Management

Since the early work of Halberg (1960), the existence of human "circadian rhythms" has been well-known to biologists and psychologists. Circadian rhythms dictate that there are certain times of the day when we are at our best both physically and psychologically. At its simplest, the majority of us feel more alive and creative in the mornings, while come the evenings we are fit only for collapsing with a good book or in front of the television. Others of us note that in the morning we take a great deal of time to get going physically and mentally, but by the evening are full of energy and bright ideas, while a very few of us feel most alert and vigorous in the late afternoon.

Irrespective of our personal rhythms, most of us have a productive period between 10am and noon, when the stomach, pancreas, spleen and heart all appear to be in their most active phases. Conversely, the majority of us experience a low period in the hour or two after lunch (a time when people in some societies sensibly take a rest), as most of our energy is devoted to the process of digestion. The simple rules here are: don't waste too much prime time having a coffee break around 11 am when you should be doing some of your best work, and don't make the after-lunch period even less productive by overloading your digestion. A short coffee or tea break is, in fact, best taken on arrival at the office, when it helps us start the day in a positive mood, rather than mid-morning when it interrupts the flow of our activities. Lunch is best taken early, when we are just beginning to feel hungry, and we are likely to eat less than if we leave it until later. An early lunch also means that we can get back into our productive stride earlier in the afternoon.

Changes in one's attitude can also enhance personal time management. For example, the notion of pro-action is eminently preferable to reaction. To pro-act means to anticipate events and be in a position to take appropriate action as soon as the right moment arrives. To react, on the other hand, means to have little anticipation and do something only when events force you to do so. Pro-actors tend to be the people who are always one step ahead of other people, who always seem to be in the right place at the right time, and who are always better informed than anyone else. Many of us like an easy life, and so we end to be reactors. This means that we aren't alert to the challenges and opportunities coming our way, with the consequence that challenges bother us or opportunities pass us by before we're even properly aware they're upon us. We can train ourselves in pro-action by regularly taking the time to sit down and appraise the likely immediate future, just as we sit down and review the immediate past.

Psychologists recognise that we differ in the way in which we characteristically attribute responsibility for the various things that happen to us in life. One of the ways in which we do this is known as locus of control (Weiner, 1979), which refers to assigning responsibility. At its simplest, some individuals have a predominantly external locus of control, attributing responsibility to outside causes (for example, the faults of others or the help given by them), while with other individuals the locus of control is predominantly internal, in which responsibility is attributed to oneself (for example, one's own abilities or lack of them, hard work, etc.).

However, the picture usually isn't as simple as this. Many people's locus of control is more likely to be specific to a particular situation, for example internal in certain areas, such as their social lives, and external in others, such as their working lives. Or, to take another example, they may attribute certain kinds of results to themselves, such as their successes, and certain kinds of results to other people, such as their failures. Obviously the best kind of locus of control is one that is realistic and able to attribute every effect to its appropriate cause, and this is particularly important when it comes to time management. Certainly, there are occasions when other people are more responsible for our time loss than we are, but for most of us, and for most of the time, the blame must fall fairly and squarely upon ourselves.

Questions 1–6

*Choose **ONE** feature, **A–J**, from the list in the box below to complete each key point below.*

*Write the correct letters, **A–J**, in boxes 1–6 on your answer sheet.*

NB *You may use any phrase more than once.*

Example	***Answer***
Our patterns of circadian rhythms	G

1 A pro-active person ....

2 A reactive person ....

3 Analysing circadian rhythms ....

4 The idea that the best time to work is in the morning ....

5 The notion of feeling alert in the late afternoon ....

6 Productivity appears to be enhanced ....

List of features

A agrees with the circadian rhythms of most people.

B makes us feel alive and creative.

C conforms to the circadian rhythms of a minority of people.

D if our energy is in a low phase.

E is more able to take advantage of events when they happen.

F enables one to gauge physical potential at particular times throughout the day.

G can affect us physically and mentally.

H when several specific internal organs are active.

I takes a more passive attitude towards events.

J when we eat lunch early.

Questions 7–13

Complete the sentences below.

Choose ***NO MORE THAN THREE WORDS*** *from the passage for each answer.*

Write your answers in boxes 7–13 on your answer sheet.

7 Our .... influence our physical and mental performance.

8 We are more likely to be productive in the afternoon if we have ....

9 A person who reacts tends not to see .... when they are approaching.

10 Assessing the .... aids us in becoming pro-active.

11 A person with a mainly internal locus of control would be likely to direct blame towards ....

12 A person with a mainly external locus of control would likely direct failure towards ....

13 A person with a healthy and balanced locus of control would attribute a result, whether negative or positive, to ....

READING PASSAGE 2

*You should spend about 20 minutes on **Questions 14–26**, which are based on Reading Passage 2 below.*

Ambergris

A Ambergris (Ambra grisea, Ambre gris, ambergrease, or grey amber) is a solid, waxy, flammable substance of a dull gray or blackish colour produced in the digestive system of sperm whales. Ambergris has a peculiar sweet, earthy odor. The principal historical use of ambergris was as a fixative in perfumery, though it has now been largely displaced by synthetics.

B Ambergris occurs as a biliary secretion of the intestines of the sperm whale, and can be found floating upon the sea, or in the sand near the coast. It is also sometimes found in the abdomens of whales. Because giant squids' beaks have been found embedded within lumps of ambergris, scientists have theorized that the whale's intestine produces the substance as a means of easing the passage of hard, sharp objects that the whale might have inadvertently eaten. Ambergris is usually passed in the fecal matter. Ambergris that forms a mass too large to exit via the anus is expelled via the mouth, leading to the reputation of ambergris as primarily coming from whale vomit.

C Ambergris can be found in the Atlantic Ocean; on the coasts of Brazil and Madagascar; and on the coast of Africa, of the East Indies, the Maldives, China, Japan, India, Australia, New Zealand and the Molucca islands. Most commercially collected ambergris comes from the Bahama Islands and Providence Island in the Caribbean.

D Ambergris is found in lumps of various shapes and sizes, weighing from 15g (½ oz) to 50kg (100 pounds) or more. When initially expelled by or removed from the whale, the fatty precursor of ambergris is pale white in colour (sometimes streaked with black), soft, with a strong fecal smell. Following months to years of photo-degradation and oxidation in the ocean, this precursor gradually hardens, developing a somewhat black colour, a crusty and waxy texture, and a peculiar odor that is at once sweet, earthy, marine, and animalic. Its smell has been generally described as a vastly richer and smoother version of isopropanol without its stinging harshness. In this developed condition, ambergris has a specific gravity ranging from 0.780 to 0.926. It melts at about 62 °C to a fatty, yellow resinous liquid; and at 100 °C it is volatilized into a white vapour. It is soluble in ether, and in volatile and fixed oils.

E Ambergris is relatively noncreative to acid. White crystals of a substance called Ambrein can be separated from ambergris by heating raw ambergris in alcohol, then allowing the resulting solution to cool.

F Historically, the primary commercial use of ambergris was in fragrance chemistry, although it has also been used for medicinal and flavouring purposes. Ambergris has historically been an important perfume odorant and is highly sought. However, it is difficult to get a consistent and reliable supply of high quality ambergris. Due to demand for ambergris and its high price, replacement compounds have been sought out by the fragrance industry and chemically synthesized. The most important of these are ambroxan, ambrox and its stereoisomer, which has largely taken its place and is the most widely used ambergris-replacement odorant in perfume manufacturing. The oldest and most commercially significant synthesis of ambrox is from sclareol (primarily extracted from clarysage), although syntheses have been devised from a variety of other natural products, including cisabienol and thujone. Procedures for the microbial production of ambrox have also been devised.

G As of 2006, raw ambergris fetched approximately US $10 per gram, with much higher prices possible for particularly high-quality samples. In the United States, importing, buying, or selling ambergris — including ambergris that had washed ashore — was considered a violation of *the Marine Mammal Protection Act* of 1972. In 2001 this ruling was overturned, and ambergris was deemed not to be a byproduct of the whaling industry, since the whale expels this substance naturally.

H Ambergris has been mostly known for its use in creating perfume and fragrance much like musk. While perfumes can still be found with ambergris around the world, American perfumers usually avoid it due to legal ambiguities. Ancient Egyptians burned ambergris as incense, while in modern Egypt ambergris is used for scenting cigarettes. The ancient Chinese called the substance "dragon's spittle fragrance". During the Black Death in Europe, people believed that carrying a ball of ambergris could help prevent them from getting the plague. This was because the fragrance covered the smell of the air which was believed to be the cause of plague. This substance has also been used historically as a flavouring for food, and some people consider it an aphrodisiac. During the Middle Ages, Europeans used ambergris as a medication for headaches, colds, epilepsy, and other ailments.

Questions 14–20

Reading Passage 2 has eight paragraphs, **A–H**.

Which paragraph contains the following information?

*Write the correct letter, **A–H**, in boxes 14–20 on your answer sheet.*

NB *You can use any letter more than once.*

14 what is the cost of Ambergris
15 physical properties of Ambergris
16 historical and cross-cultural uses of Ambergris
17 various sources of Ambergris
18 chemical properties of Ambergris
19 distributing areas of Ambergris
20 replacing compounds of Ambergris

Questions 21–25

*Complete the summary of sections **D** and **E** below.*

*Choose **NO MORE THAN TWO WORDS** for each answer.*

Write your answers in boxes 21–25 on your answer sheet.

At first, Ambergris is expelled from the whale. At this time, the fatty excretion is soft, smelly and pale white in colour. Gradually, through **21** .... and **22** .... in the salty condition, the precursor becomes hard and changes into **23** .... It is usually vapourized to a **24** .... when heated and is soluble in air.

In industry, people usually use **25** .... to abstract Ambrein from the precursor.

Question 26

*Choose the correct letter **A**, **B**, **C** or **D**.*

Which field has Ambergris **NOT** been used widely throughout the whole world?

Write the correct letter in box 26 on your answer sheet.

A medication
B toiletry
C weapon
D amulet

READING PASSAGE 3

*You should spend about 20 minutes on **Questions 27–40**, which are based on Reading Passage 3 below.*

When Your Carpet Calls Your Doctor

The coming convergence of wireless communications, social networking and medicine will transform health care.

Is it possible that amid all the hoopla about Apple's iPad, one potential use has been overlooked? Larry Nathanson, head of emergency-medicine "informatics" at one of Harvard Medical School's hospitals, has experimented with using the device in the casualty ward. He writes that "initial tests with our clinical applications went amazingly well...the EKGs look better on screen than on paper. It was great having all of the clinical information right at the bedside to discuss with the patient. "

Dr Nathanson's enthusiasm hints at the potential of wireless gadgets to improve health care, and to ensure more personalised treatment in particular. Pundits have long predicted that advances in genetics will usher in a golden age of individually tailored therapies. But in fact it is much lower-tech wireless devices and Internet-based health software that are precipitating the mass customisation of health care, and creating entirely new business models in the process.

Wireless health is "becoming omnipresent" in hospitals, according to Kalorama Information, a market-research firm. It estimates that the market for such devices and services in America alone will grow from $2.7 billion in 2007 to $9.6 billion in 2013. Don Jones of Qualcomm, a maker of networking technology, argues that the trend speeds diagnosis and treatment, and saves doctors' and nurses' time. GE, an industrial giant, and Sprint, an American mobile operator, have joined forces to offer hospitals such services. GE's Carescape software allows the secure monitoring of patients' health via mobile phones, as does rival software from Airstrip.

Doctors are an obvious early target for wireless health. A forthcoming report by the California Health Care Foundation (CHCF), a think tank, estimates that two-thirds of American physicians already have smart-phones. Over one third of American doctors use Epocrates, a programme for mobiles and laptops which offers instant information on drug-to-drug interactions, treatment recommendations and so on. The software will soon be able to access electronic health records (EHRs) via mobiles—which the authour of the CHCF's report thinks could be "the killer application" of wireless health.

The hope is that nimble new technologies, from smart-phones to EHRs to health monitoring devices, will empower patients and doctors, and thus improve outcomes while cutting costs. The near ubiquity of mobile phones is the chief reason to think this optimistic scenario may come true. Patients with fancy smart phones can certainly benefit from interactive "wellness" applications that track diet, exercise and vital signs. Apple's AppStore, for example, offers thousands of health-related applications. Jitterbug, an American mobile operator that offers easy-to-use phones for the elderly, recently added more health services; rival mobile carriers are doing much the same.

But Carolyn Buck-Luce of Ernst & Young, a consultancy, points out that "mHealth" is transforming health care in poor countries as well as rich ones. Medical Home, a Mexican outfit that provides medical consultations by mobile, already has millions of customers. Paul Meyer of Voxiva, an American technology firm that has set up mHealth systems in Rwanda and Peru, among other places, says that such schemes have been so successful in the developing world that they are now being adopted in the rich world too. His firm has helped the American government with its recent launch of Text 4 Baby, a public-health campaign to educate pregnant mothers (they receive free text messages with medical advice) that will soon become the biggest such effort in the world.

What is more, mobile phones are but one part of a broader wireless trend in health care that McKinsey, a consultancy, estimates may soon be worth up to $60 billion globally. Many companies are coming up with "home health" devices embedded with wireless technology. Some are overtly clinical in nature: Medtronic, a devices giant, is developing a bedside monitor that wirelessly tracks the blood sugar levels in diabetic children sleeping nearby. GE has come up with "body sensor networks", tiny wireless devices that track the vital signs of those who wear them.

The most successful gadgets may be, as Eric Dishman of Intel puts it, "surreptitious". His firm, a big chipmaker, is investing in devices to track the health of the elderly, such as "magic carpets" that sense erratic movements and thus can predict a fall. Continua, an industry coalition, is developing shared standards so that blood-pressure monitors and scales can wirelessly transfer readings to doctors' offices or personal EHR services like Google Health.

All these devices and services do not just allow doctors to make more accurate diagnoses, prescribe more effective treatments and keep better track of patients' conditions. They also allow health services to tailor treatments depending on patients' personal preferences and behavioural foibles. Studies show, for example, that although some patients with chronic conditions are fastidious about taking pills or insulin properly, others are careless or forgetful. Some prefer efficient electronic reminders, where as others respond best when a nurse calls home. A global consumer survey released on April 6th by Price

Waterhouse Coopers (PWC), a consultancy, finds that the elderly prefer high-quality care with lots of personal attention, whereas younger types prefer low-cost care and wellness schemes.

Many health systems, PWC's accompanying report finds, are beginning to divide customers into different categories and customise treatments accordingly. For example, Discovery Health, a South African insurer, uses a variety of different methods to get patients with chronic diseases to follow through on their treatments, from text messages reminding them to take their pills to rewards for good behaviour.

A similar scheme run by Health Media, a wellness firm owned by Johnson & Johnson, a big drugs firm, uses online tools (it calls them "digital health coaches") to help patients manage diabetes and lose weight. Its studies suggest that half of the digitally coached do lose weight, and the improved health of those with chronic conditions is worth $1,000 a year to their employers.

Virgin Health Miles, an American rival, has taken the same idea a step further, using online social networks, through which co-workers or family members can cheer on or nag patients electronically, in order to encourage exercise or weight loss. Patients seem to like this kind of thing: one patient who suffers from ulcerative colitis, for example, has created a forum for fellow sufferers that can be accessed through an iPhone application.

All these initiatives are particularly promising because they help bring about behavioural change, normally the hardest element of any treatment. Patients often ignore doctors' lectures, but are more inclined to listen to supportive friends and family. By the same token, doctors and nurses are not always on hand to encourage healthy behaviour, but mobile phones and other wireless gadgets can be. That is something that even personalised genetic therapies could not offer.

Questions 27–31

The following questions are based on Reading Passage 3.

Use the information in the passage to match the people or the organisations with the achievements or statements listed below.

*Write the appropriate letter, **A–H**, in boxes 27–31 on your answer sheet.*

NB *You can use any letter more than once.*

27 There is a great potential of wireless devices to better health condition.
28 He foretold the coming of customised therapies.
29 Wireless health will be time-saving for doctors.
30 They provided the smart phones for the old.
31 They track the blood sugar level in children wirelessly.

A	Don Jones
B	Pundits
C	Jitterbug
D	Medical Home
E	Dr Nathanson
F	Medtronic
G	HealthMedia
H	Larry Nathanson

Questions 32–36

Do the following statements agree with the information given in Reading Passage 3?

In boxes 32–36 on your answer sheet, write

TRUE	*if the statement agrees with the information*
FALSE	*if the statement contradicts the information*
NOT GIVEN	*if there is no information on this*

32 It is predicted that American wireless health services will go beyond $9 billion in 2013.
33 More than half of American doctors obtain quick information through Epocrates.
34 Both the poor countries and rich ones are equally served by "mHealth" practices.
35 Though very beneficial, wireless medical services can not produce accurate diagnoses or effective prescription.

36 According to Price Waterhouse Coopers, young people don't care about individual treatment.

Questions 37–40

Complete the sentences below.

Choose **NO MORE THAN TWO WORDS** *from the passage for each answer.*

Write your answers in boxes 37–40 on your answer sheet.

37 .... are regarded as the first group of customers for initiative wireless devices in medical care.

38 Patients tend to regard .... and family as the most trustworthy when they are in need of behavioural change.

39 HealthMedia made a scheme, using .... to help patients cope with diabetes and obesity.

40 .... and other wireless appliances can always remind the patient to keep good behaviour.

WRITING

WRITING TASK 1

You should spend about 20 minutes on this task.

The pie charts below show a survey about the students' satisfaction for facilities in a UK university in 2013. It involves three aspects: university café, study facilities in bedroom and social facilities in two groups—undergraduates and postgraduates.

Summarise the information by selecting and reporting the main features, and make comparisons where relevant.

Write at least 150 words.

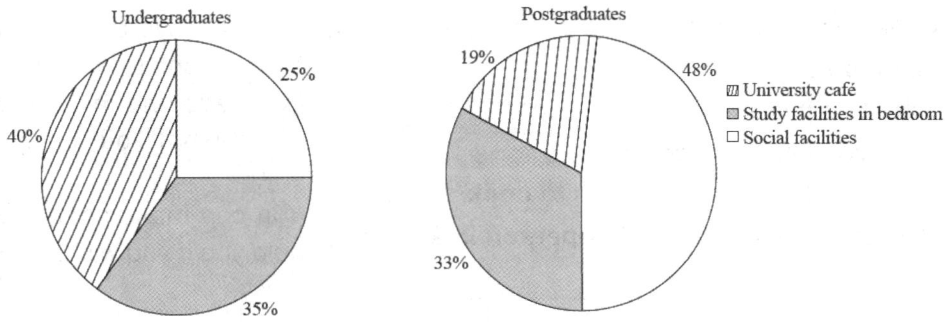

WRITING TASK 2

You should spend about 40 minutes on this task.

Write about the following topic:

Young people in the modern world seem to have more power and influence than any previous young generation.

Why is this the case?
What impact does this have on the relationship between old and young people?

Give reasons for your answer and include any relevant examples from your own knowledge or experience.

Write at least 250 words.

SPEAKING

PART 1

The examiner asks the candidate about him/herself, his/her home, work or studies and other familiar topics.

EXAMPLE

Concentration

- How important is concentration?
- In what situations is it particularly important to focus on what you do?
- What can people do to avoid distractions?

PART 2

Describe someone who is good at cooking.

You should say:

who this person is

how you know the person

what foods the person likes to cook

and explain why you think this person is a good cook.

You will have to talk about the topic for one to two minutes.
You have one minute to think about what you are going to say.
You can make some notes to help you if you wish.

PART 3

Discussion topics:

Cooking

Example questions:

Who normally does the cooking in families in your country?
Is home cooking always better than food cooked in other places?
Why do people like to have dinner at restaurants, instead of at home?

Cooking different dishes

Example questions:

Is it better to learn to cook traditional dishes or dishes from around the world?
How easy is it to buy unusual ingredients for cooking where you live?
Have international restaurants increased in popularity where you live?

Test 2

LISTENING

SECTION 1 *Questions 1–10*

Questions 1–6

*Choose the correct letter **A**, **B**, or **C**.*

1 What does the woman need to do to join the library?

A to write down her name and address
B to show some kind of identification
C to show something with her old address

2 What's the woman's problem?

A There is no address on her letters.
B Her bankbook is old.
C Everything she has now has her old address.

3 How is the woman finally able to join the library?

A by showing her husband's driving licence
B by showing her air ticket
C by showing her passport

4 How many records can she take out?

A four
B two
C five

5 Where is the catalogue?

A to the right
B around the corner
C on the second floor

6 How long can she keep the books?

A three weeks
B four weeks
C two weeks

Questions 7–10

Complete the notes below.

Write ***NO MORE THAN THREE WORDS AND/OR A NUMBER*** *for each answer.*

Application Form

Name: 7 ....

Telephone No.: 8 ....

Address: 9 .... Road, Hanwell

Passport No.: 10 ....

SECTION 2 *Questions 11–20*

Questions 11–15

For which reason does the speaker recommend each of the following rental properties?

*Write the correct letter, **A**, **B** or **C**, next to questions 11–15.*

NB *You may use any letter more than once.*

A	one of its features
B	its location
C	its size

Rental properties

11 Pennington ....

12 Hillsboro ....

13 Westfield ....

14 Lennox Village ....

15 Covenant Crossing ....

Questions 16–20

Label the plan below.

*Write the correct letter, **A–H**, next to questions 16–20.*

Single-family House: Second Level

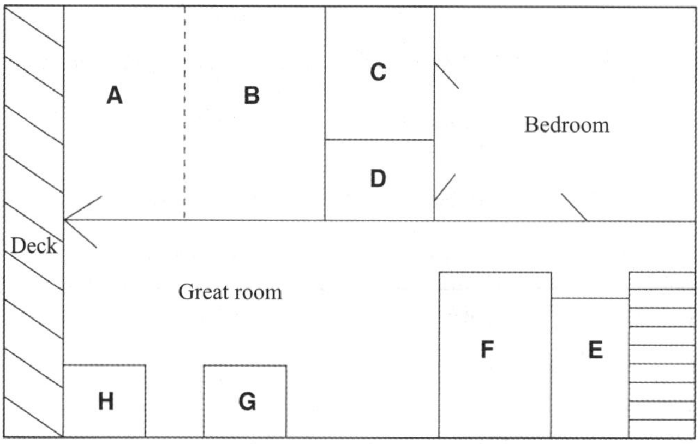

16 Storage area ....

17 Dressing room ....

18 Office ....

19 Dining area ....

20 Stove ....

SECTION 3 *Questions 21–30*

Questions 21–24

Complete the notes below.

Write ***NO MORE THAN THREE WORDS*** *for each answer.*

Notes

- People think the process originated from **21** .... about 8,000 years ago.
- The two main kinds of cheeses were called **22** .... and .... cheeses.

  23 .... were great pioneers in cheese-making.
- The new skills began to spread between **24** .... and ....

Questions 25–30

Complete the table below.

Write ***NO MORE THAN THREE WORDS*** *for each answer.*

Time	People's Knowledge About Cheese-making
Early stage	It was known cheeses' tastes were related to **25** .... and ....
19th century	The knowledge about **26** .... increased. It was possible to **27** .... the process.
At present	Cheeses began being made largely in **28** .... , but **29** .... still plays an essential role. Despite the scale of production, **30** .... and .... can still develop.

SECTION 4 *Questions 31–40*

Question 31

Choose the correct letter, ***A, B*** *or* ***C.***

31 The speaker says that

A ten of the seventeen sorts of penguins have died out.

B the regulation on Terrestrial Wild Animal Conservation was issued in 1982.

C the regulation aims to protect wild animals and manage wild animas hunting, etc.

Questions 32–34

Choose ***THREE*** *letters,* ***A–E.***

What are the direct causes of the penguins' decrease?

A the shortage of fish and other food

B people's hunting

C higher temperatures of the water

D the heating of the air

E the oil leaks

Questions 35–40

Complete the notes below.

Write NO MORE THAN TWO WORDS *for each answer.*

In Galapagos, many adult penguins die of **35** ....

In 1990, penguins in New Zealand died because of a **36** ....

Penguins also have natural enemies, including **37** .... , **38** .... ,

39 .... and **40** ....

READING

READING PASSAGE 1

You should spend about 20 minutes on ***Questions 1–13****, which are based on Reading Passage 1 below.*

Test 2

Signs of Life

As the search for alien life turns 50, its practitioners find new methods.

Frank Drake, who was born in Chicago, Illinois, graduated in 1952 from Cornell University and obtained his PhD in 1958 from Harvard. He worked initially at the National Radio Astronomy Observatory (NRAO), West Virginia (1958–1963) and at the Jet Propulsion Laboratory, California (1963–1964) before returning to Cornell and serving as professor of astronomy from 1964. He was appointed professor of astronomy at the University of California in 1984.

A Half a century ago a radio astronomer called Frank Drake thought of a way to calculate the likelihood of establishing contact with aliens. He suggested the following figures should be multiplied: how many stars are formed in the galaxy in a year; what fraction of these have planets and thus form solar systems; the average number of planets per solar system that have the potential to support life; on what percentage of those where it is possible do such biospheres actually form; what percentage of such biospheres give rise to intelligent species; what percentage of intelligent life is able to transmit signals into space; and for how long could such intelligence keep sending signals.

B This calculation became celebrated as the Drake equation–perhaps the best attempt so far to tame a wild guess. Most of the terms remain hard to tie down, although there is a consensus that about ten stars are formed per year in the galaxy. Also, recent searches for extra solar planets have concluded that planets are not rare.

C At the AAAS, Dr Drake reflected on his search for alien signals. One reason this is hard is that radio telescopes must chop the spectrum into fine portions to study it, like tuning into a signal on a car radio. Another is the trade off between a telescope's field of view and its magnification. Small telescopes see a lot of sky but can detect only strong signals. Large ones, which can detect weak signals, have a narrow focus. Astronomers therefore have difficulty looking both carefully and comprehensively.

D Dr Drake said there may be another difficulty. Researchers tend to look for signals similar to those now made by humanity. The Earth, though, is getting quieter because the rise of spread-spectrum communication makes stray emissions less likely than in the past.

E Spread-spectrum works by smearing a message across a wide range of frequencies. That has the advantages of combating noise and allowing many signals to be sent at once. But it also makes those signals hard for eavesdroppers to hear (which is why spread-spectrum is beloved by military men). If technologically sophisticated aliens came to the same conclusions, and thus used spread spectrum technology, humans would have a hard time hearing them. Dr Drake suggests, therefore, that there might be only a narrow window of time in the development of civilisations, analogous to the past 50 years on Earth, during which noisy electromagnetic signals are generated in large amounts. It is, however, also possible that someone is actively trying to send signals to the Earth. If that were the case, the best way to do this, reckons Paul Horowitz, a physicist at Harvard, is with a laser.

F Although radio power has changed little over the decades, the power of lasers has grown exponentially. Today's most powerful versions can shine ten thousand times brighter than the sun, though only for a billionth of a second. If aliens have made similar progress, and point a laser towards the Earth's solar system, such brief flashes would be detectable at a distance of many light-years. Dr Horowitz has already set up one suitable detector and this, because no huge magnification is involved, is capable of looking at broad swathes of sky.

G There is also potential for improvement on the radio side. For many years, the Arecibo telescope in Puerto Rico, which is 300 metres across, has led the search for alien life. Now the Chinese are building a 500-metre telescope, known as FAST, in Guizhou Province, and an international collaboration called the Square Kilometre Array is trying, as its name suggests, to build a grid of radio telescopes over a square kilometre of land in either South Africa or Australia. Both may be helpful. As indeed many a large new telescope in northern California were built by Paul Allen, a co-founder of Microsoft.

H Many of the terms in the Drake equation are likely to remain elusive, so it is still impossible to predict how likely such efforts are to succeed. But even after 50 fruitless years–if the eagerness in the eyes of Dr. Drake and his colleagues is any guide–it still is fun looking. It may be that the laws of physics absolutely preclude any intelligent civilisation from making physical contact with another one. Perhaps it simply takes too long and costs too much to go anywhere, and perhaps there is no "warp drive" shortcut.

Questions 1–5

Reading Passage 1 has eight paragraphs, **A–H**.

Which paragraph contains the following information?

Write the correct letter, ***A–H****, in boxes 1–5 on your answer sheet.*

NB *You may use any letter more than once.*

1 the superiority of laser power

2 the discussion of ways to send signals

3 the improvement of radio telescope

4 the calculation for the possibility of intelligent life

5 reasons why the search for alien signals is difficult

Questions 6–10

Complete the summary of the first ***FOUR*** *paragraphs below.*

Choose ***NO MORE THAN TWO WORDS*** *from the passage for each answer.*

Write your answers in boxes 6 –10 on your answer sheet.

A well-known equation invented by Frank Drake, a radio astronomer, was used to calculate the possibility of the human contact with **6** ……………………… .The scientist came up with a number of figures to suggest the situation in which potential intelligent life might be able to **7** ……………………… into space. However, the job of searching for alien signals is not easy at all. On the one hand, **8** ……………………… must be split by the radio telescope into delicate parts as for the humans to study it. On the other hand, there is a contradiction between a telescope's field of view and **9** ……………………… . Moreover, the difficulty may be complicated when researchers focus their attention on **10** ……………………… made by both humans and other potential intelligent life.

Questions 11–13

Complete the sentences below.

Choose ***ONE WORD ONLY*** *from the passage for each answer.*

Write your answers in boxes 11–13 on your answer sheet.

11 Spread-spectrum technique is considered an advantageous method which can be applied in reducing .... and sending signals in a second.

12 The power of lasers has increased so rapidly that the strongest lasers send off lights much .... than the sun.

13 The results of the research for alien signals are unpredictable since many .... terms are used in the Drake equation.

READING PASSAGE 2

*You should spend about 20 minutes on **Questions 14–25**, which are based on Reading Passage 2 below.*

Changing the Channel

Television is adapting better to technological change than any other media business.

A ONE evening Steve Purdham noticed something odd. The flow of data into and out of We7, a British music-streaming website he runs, had abruptly slowed. An hour later it returned to normal. Such a sharp fluctuation usually means a server is malfunctioning — a potentially ruinous problem. But when engineers checked the computer system they found nothing wrong. So what could have happened between 8pm and 9pm on a Saturday night to cause such a sudden drop in use? Suddenly it dawned on Mr Purdham: "Britain's Got Talent" was on television.

B There are now hundreds of channels. A channel-surf through a basic cable-TV package in America turns up a history of the civil war, a melodrama, a college basketball game, a Hispanic talent show, European football and a documentary. Many more options are available on demand with a few clicks of the remote control. The offerings are decidedly mixed, but there is always something on. "There are not many genres that are not addressed any more," says Philippe Dauman, CEO of Viacom, a media company. "We try to think of new ones all the time." Japan is a country that leads many technological trends. Last year Tokyo residents spent an average of 60 minutes a day at home consuming media on the Internet or a mobile phone, up from just six minutes in 2000. But they also spent more time in front of the television: an average of 216 minutes. Among young women, the group that advertisers most want to reach, television-watching went up more steeply. Admittedly their attention was not always fixed on the box. Many teenage girls send text messages on their mobile phones while watching television.

C Distinctions between television sets, computers and mobile phones are gradually disappearing. Televisions' monitors have double-sized and recently they became digital wireless connected with the Internet. Now high-end televisions can obtain all sorts of things, from stock quotes to weather forecasts. At the same time TV is moving beyond the living room. Many programmes can be viewed on computers, mobile phones and so on. Video-streaming websites are becoming more professional, meaning they are both better designed and contain more proper television programmes. Every media business that the Internet has touched so far has come off badly. Recorded music sales have fallen steeply in value since Napster, a file-sharing website, appeared in 1999. The Internet has drawn classified advertising away from local newspapers. Book publishers have watched helplessly as online retailers and e-readers have driven down prices.

D The Internet tends to decompose media products, breaking music albums into tracks and splitting magazines into their constituent articles. It also brings content directly to consumers, sometimes by means of piracy. Online, people can pick and choose the content that interests them without paying much for it. One of the most harmful things about the Internet as it has evolved in the past few years, says Jeff Bewkes, the boss of Time Warner, is the assumption that charging for content is hostile to the consumer. As the saying goes, content wants to be free — or, at least, paid for only by advertising.

E In 1961 America had three broadcast networks, which operated on the principle that the least objectionable shows would draw the biggest audiences and the most advertising revenue. However competition improved matters. In the 1970s cable and satellite television began to spread. The result, beginning in the late 1990s and continuing today, has been a golden age for television. It can be argued that Hollywood makes less impressive films these days than it did in the 1970s (or the 1930s), but that is not true of television. Modern TV shows are so superior to what went before — so much better written, better acted and better shot — that they almost seem to belong to a different medium.

F Howard Stringer, Sony's boss, fears television will return to the wasteland. The danger is not lack of choice but a surfeit of choice. So much content will be available on so many digital platforms that audiences will become too small to pay for good TV programmes. The Internet already competes strongly for advertising. In Britain more money is now spent online than on television, although some of this can be blamed on artificial restrictions on TV advertising rates.

G Television is not about to suffer the fate of music or newspapers, yet the next few years will be dangerous nonetheless. A handful of upstart websites, with audiences smaller than many channels at the bottom of the programme guides, have already rattled the giant TV industry. In 1990 George Gilder, an American writer, claimed that by the end of the 20th century traditional television would be extinct because technology would enable consumers to track down programmes that catered to their particular interests. Even the technological futurists found it hard to imagine the explosion of websites, social networking and mobile phones that was to come. Yet these things have not displaced television.

H The TV set has also evolved. Televisions used to be seen as squat cubes. Gradually they have flattened and turned into panels, and their screens have become sharper and brighter. They have spread to bedrooms, kitchens and even bathrooms (with heated screens to ward off condensation). The latest devices are as thin as laptop computers. Television has gone online and become mobile. Much sooner it will expand into the three dimension.

Questions 14–17

*Choose **FOUR** letters, **A–H**.*

Write your answers in boxes 14–17 on your answer sheet.

Which **FOUR** of the following statements are true of the Reading Passage 2?

NB *Your answers may be given in any order.*

A There are surveys on the amount of time spending on the Internet or in watching TV.

B The Internet has drawn all advertising completely.

C There is a great variety of offerings on TV programmes.

D At present TV programmes are limited within the living room.

E The explosion of websites is displacing the television.

F TV industry makes more impressive works these days.

G The gap between television sets and computers are gradually expanding.

H A few emergent Internet businesses have threatened the TV industry.

Questions 18–22

Look at the following people and the list of statements below.

Match each person with the correct statement.

*Write the correct letter, **A–H**, in boxes 18–22 on your answer sheet.*

18 Steve Purdham ....

19 Philippe Dauman ....

20 Jeff Bewkes ....

21 Howard Stringer ....

22 George Gilder ....

List of Statements	
A	supported the idea that consumers should denounce the means of piracy.
B	There are already too many channels on TV.
C	predicts the shrinkage on investment in the TV programmes when more people turn to the Internet.
D	believed that the conventional TV would die out.
E	confused by the unstable flow of data.
F	thinks that the readers are dislike to pay for the contents online.
G	TV industry is developing and soaring quickly.
H	figured that a server was malfunctioning.

Questions 23–25

*Complete the summary of the **LAST** paragraph of Reading Passage 2.*

*Write the correct letter, **A–H**, in boxes 23–25 on your answer sheet.*

Following the **23** .... of the TV set, the **24** .... televisions have emerged with **25** .... screen. The up-to-date TV set is getting much thinner and more mobile. It is predicted that three dimension TV will come into our life in the near future.

A	three dimension	**B**	degrade	**C**	development	**D**	drab
E	fresher	**F**	cube	**G**	more vivid	**H**	panel

READING PASSAGE 3

*You should spend about 20 minutes on **Questions 26–40**, which are based on Reading Passage 3 below.*

Sleeping

Sleep medicine is a relatively young field in the UK, with only a couple of centres until the 1980s. In the last decade a number of centres have sprouted, often led by chest physicians and ENT surgeons with an interest in obstructive sleep apnoea, forcing neurologists and neurophysiologists to wake up and contribute to the non-respiratory aspect of this neglected subject.

Within sleep, two states are recognised-non rapid eye movement (NREM) and rapid eye movement (REM). These alternate cyclically through the night with cycle time of 90 minutes (50–60 minutes in the newborn). NREM sleep is divided into four stages: stages 1 and 2 (considered light sleep), and stages 3 and 4 (deep sleep with high arousal threshold).

REM is onto genically primitive with EEG activity closer to wake state, intermittent bursts of REMs and muscle atonia interrupted by phasic bursts producing asynchronous twitching. The atonia of REM sleep prevents acting out of dreams and is lost in REM behaviour disorder when dream content becomes violent and patients act out their dream, often resulting in injury. REM behaviour disorder can be a precursor of neurodegenerative disease including Parkinsons. Dream content (pleasant/unpleasant) will be remembered on waking from REM sleep but there is often little memory of the preceding mental activity on arousals from NREM sleep, even when associated with complex behaviours and autonomic disturbance as occurs in night terrors or sleep walking.

In the newborn 50 percent of total sleep time is occupied by REM sleep, progressively shrinking to 25 percent in the adult, the first block of REM sleep occurring about 90 minutes after sleep onset. Abrupt withdrawal of alcohol and many centrally acting recreational and non-recreational drugs can cause REM sleep to occur at sleep onset. This can also increase total REM sleep, leading to intense, vivid, often frightening dreams (hypnogogic-sleep onset/hypnopompic or, on waking, hallucinations), similar to that experienced by patients with narcolepsy.

The NREM/REM sleep states are interrupted by brief arousals and transient awakenings. The frequency of the arousals may increase with emotional disturbance or environmental discomfort but also in many intrinsic sleep disorders such as periodic leg movements in sleep, obstructive sleep apnoea and narcolepsy.

A basic rest-activity cycle originates in fetal life. The newborn sleeps an equal amount during the day and night, the sleep-wake cycle organised around three to four-hourly feeds. By the second month favouring of sleep towards night-time occurs and by six months the baby will have about 12 hours of sleep at night in addition to a couple of daytime naps. In general, children born prematurely have a tendency to be awake more at night in the first year and breast-fed babies wake more frequently, but the difference disappears by the second year. Persistent night awakenings in infants and toddlers usually reflect the child's inability to self-soothe back to sleep without parental attention and will respond to a well-supported behavioural programme.

The establishment of a consolidated night sleep pattern in children reflects brain maturation and may be disrupted in children with developmental problems. Even in this group success is possible by persisting with behavioural work, though many paediatricians prescribe melatonin for these children with some success. But as the long-term safety of melatonin remains unknown it should be used as a last resort. There are now good studies looking at short-term use of melatonin in sleep-wake cycle disorders such as delayed sleep phase syndrome. Its use as a hypnotic should be discouraged, especially in the developing child as there is uncertainty on other cycles, such as menstrual.

In addition to the NREM/REM cycles, there is a circadian (24 hours) sleep-wake cycle entrained by intrinsic rhythms (melatonin and body temperature) and extrinsic factors (light and social cues such as mealtimes, school/work times). The pineal hormone melatonin plays a role in entraining the sleep-wake cycle to the light-dark cycle. Melatonin secretion is high in darkness and low in daylight hours, the process beginning in the retina with the suprachiasmatic nucleus playing a major role as a sleep regulator via melatonin. Blind people may lose this entrainment and develop a free running sleep-wake cycle with progressive advancement of sleep onset time.

Polymorphism of the circadian clock gene has now been identified with the population divided between morning types (larks) and evening types (owls). Those predisposed to later sleep onset time (evening types) are susceptible to developing delayed sleep phase syndrome especially during adolescence when sleep requirement increases and there is a tendency towards later time for sleeping and waking. In delayed sleep phase syndrome, sleep onset is delayed to the early hours of the morning with consequent difficulty in waking in time for school/work. Once established, advancing sleep onset time is difficult and requires treatment with appropriately timed melatonin or bright light therapy-advancing sleep onset progressively forwards until the desired sleep time is reached.

In contrast the elderly who are more susceptible to perturbation in their sleep-wake schedule can develop advanced sleep phase syndrome with sleep onset occurring early in the evening. Shift workers often struggle to cope with shift patterns as they grow older due to difficulty in re-adjusting their circadian clock. In general, morning bright light exposure is a more powerful synchroniser of the circadian rhythm than melatonin.

Questions 26–28

*Choose the correct letter, **A**, **B**, **C** or **D**.*

Write the correct letter in boxes 26–28 on your answer sheet.

26 According to the passage,

A the growing concern on sleep medicine from physicians and ENT surgeons contributed to the boom of this domain.

B neurologists and neurophysiologists have neglected the study of obstructive sleep apnoea.

C the infants have the cycle of NREM and REM every 90 minutes.

D NREM and REM alternate periodically in four stages.

27 About the REM and NREM sleep,

A people cannot recall the dream content when they are waking from REM sleep.

B the atonia remains when the content of dream is violent.

C REM is accompanied by the EEG activity.

D the REM will make people act out their dream content.

28 According to the passage,

A the infants have to sleep three to four hours during the daytime.

B babies would rather sleep during the daytime in the second month.

C the newborn sleep a dozen of hours during the day.

D the difference between prematured and breast-fed babies will cease to exist in the second year.

Questions 29–33

Complete the sentences below.

*Choose **NO MORE THAN TWO WORDS** from the passage for each answer.*

Write your answers in boxes 29–33 on your answer sheet.

29 REM behaviour disorder is thought as one kind of predecessor of ....

30 People almost have no .... of what they dreamed when they wake up from NREM sleep even though they have undergone night terrors or sleep walking.

31 The dreams those patients with narcolepsy have are vivid even ....

32 How often the .... happen depends on the many factors involving emotional and environmental effects and intrinsic sleep disorders.

33 The infants may have the night awakening problems that it is difficult for them to return to sleep when there is no ....

Questions 34–40

Complete the summary below.

Choose ***NO MORE THAN THREE WORDS*** *for each answer.*

Write your answers in boxes 34–40 on your answer sheet.

The Use of Melatonin

Some developmental problems could influence the sleeping pattern of children negatively and accordingly **34** .... is prescribed by doctors to children though the behavioural practice works better. The use of melatonin is just suggested as the last resort not as a **35** .... for it may do harm to some **36** .... of the developing child. There is an important cycle called the sleep-wake cycle in people, in which with the participation of melatonin secretion the **37** .... is regulated. People are categorised into two groups, larks and owls. The owl type is easily developing into the delayed sleep phase syndrome, in which the **38** .... will be postponed but melatonin and more natural treatment like **39** .... can be used to reach the desired sleep time. The senior citizens always suffer from another syndrome by which they fall asleep **40** .... at night and shift workers similarly must try to adapt themselves to the shift patterns.

Test 2

WRITING

WRITING TASK 1

You should spend about 20 minutes on this task.

Plan A below shows a health centre in 2008. Plan B shows the same place in the present day.

Summarise the information by selecting and reporting the main features, and make comparisons where relevant.

Write at least 150 words.

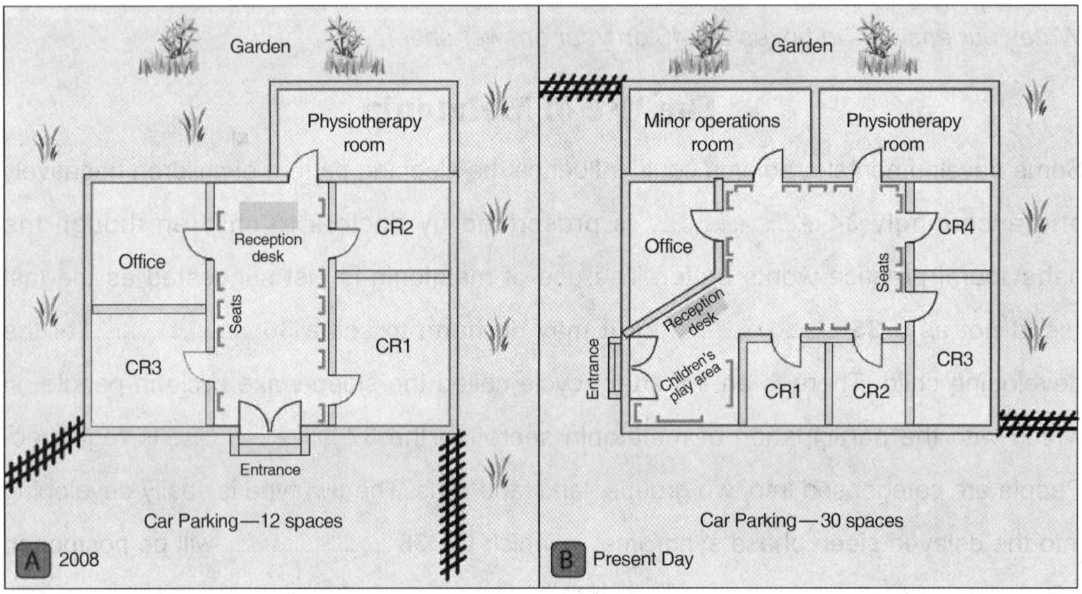

CR—Consulting room

WRITING TASK 2

You should spend about 40 minutes on this task.

Write about the following topic:

> ***Some say that it would be better if the majority of employees worked from home instead of travelling to a workplace every day.***
>
> ***Do you think the advantages of working from home outweigh the disadvantages?***

Give reasons for your answer and include any relevant examples from your own knowledge or experience.

Write at least 250 words.

SPEAKING

PART 1

The examiner asks the candidate about him/herself, his/her home, work or studies and other familiar topics.

EXAMPLE

Family

- How big is your family?
- How often do you spend time together?
- What do you enjoy doing as a family?
- How do you keep in touch with members of your family?

PART 2

Describe something you bought that you were not happy with.
You should say:
what you bought
why you were not happy with it
what you did with it
and explain how you felt about the situation.

You will have to talk about the topic for one to two minutes. You have one minute to think about what you are going to say. You can make some notes to help you if you wish.

PART 3

Discussion topics:

Products people buy in your country

Example questions:

Are there more goods available in shops now than in the past? Why/Why not?
Do people generally prefer to buy products from their own or from other countries?
What kinds of products are most affected by fashions from other countries?
Will overseas trends and fashions have more or less impact on what people buy in the future?

Protecting consumers

Example questions:

What kind of techniques do advertisers use to persuade people to buy more?
Who should be responsible for the quality of products: producers, shops or customers?
How could governments protect the rights of consumers?

Test 3

LISTENING

SECTION 1 *Questions 1–10*

Questions 1–8

Complete the form below.

Write ***NO MORE THAN THREE WORDS AND/OR A NUMBER*** *for each answer.*

SPCA Application for Dog Adoption

Example ***Answer***

Name: Helen Morgan

- Date of interview: **1** .... September
- Address: 12 Towley Avenue Meadowlea
- Telephone: 443 5421

Lifestyle details

- Work schedule: at home apart from Wed/Fri. between 10am and **2** ....
- Reason for adopting a dog: as a **3** ....
- Number of people permanently living in household: **4** ....
- Ages of children who visit regularly: **5** ....
- Allergies to dogs: none
- Main carer: applicant and **6** ....

Property details

- Home owned or rented: rented
- Landlord's contact number: 0795 **7** ....
- Fenced yard/garden: Yes
- Height of fence: **8** ....

Questions 9 and 10

Complete the form below.

*Write **NO MORE THAN TWO WORDS** for each answer.*

Previous Ownership		
Breed	Time owned	What happened?
9	**10**	died from old age

SECTION 2 *Questions 11–20*

Questions 11 and 12

*Choose **TWO** letters, **A–E**.*

Which **TWO** things does the speaker say about use of the bank's debit card abroad?

A There is a fixed charge for buying something with the card.
B The bank's charge for each cash withdrawal is at least £4.50.
C The card is accepted in most European countries.
D The bank does not accept responsibility for any losses due to fraud.
E The bank is willing to text customers whenever their card is used.

Questions 13 and 14

*Choose **TWO** letters, **A–E**.*

Which **TWO** pieces of information does the speaker give about buying foreign currency in the UK?

A The bank's charge for currency is equal to the amount being charged by UK post offices.
B Customers can collect their currency at any branch if they have ordered it the previous day.
C There is no administration charge if a customer's debit card is used in payment.
D Certain currencies are immediately available at all of the bank's branches.
E There is a limit to the amount of foreign currency that can be bought at one time.

Questions 15–20

Complete the flow-chart below.

*Choose **SIX** answers from the box and write the correct letter, **A–I**, next to questions 15–20.*

A Provide personal details
B Decide on type of cover
C Download application form
D Check terms of existing policy
E Make online payment
F Go to bank's website
G Make card payment
H Provide travel details
I Provide bank's overall information

How to Buy the Bank's Travel Insurance

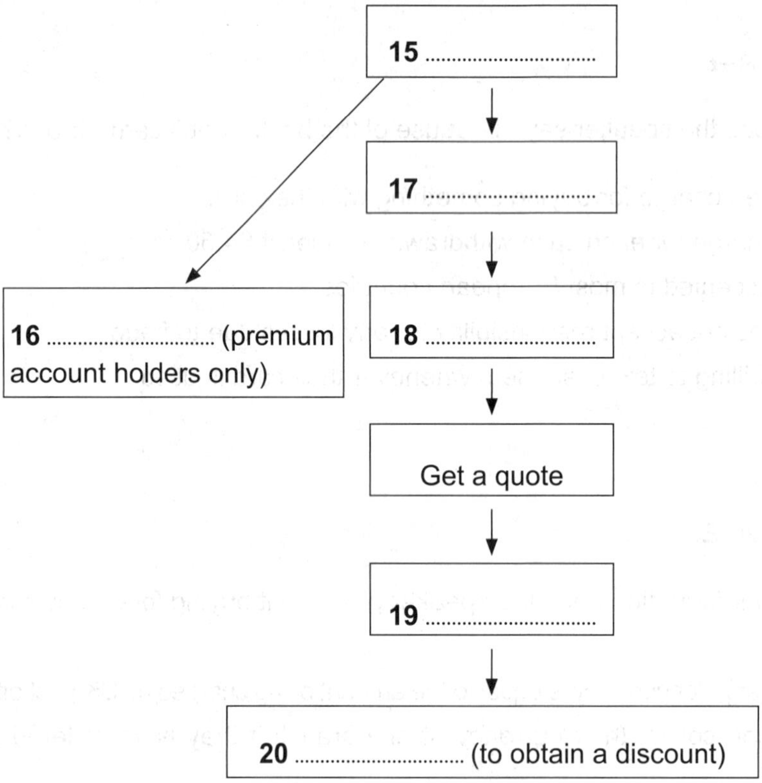

SECTION 3 *Questions 21–30*

Questions 21–25

What do the students think about their reading?

*Write the correct letter, **A–H**, next to questions 21–25.*

A	It is poorly translated.
B	Its index is inadequate.
C	Its illustrations are uncommon.
D	It is badly organized.
E	It omits essential facts.
F	It contains clear arguments and is easy to understand.
G	It offers us useful background information.
H	It is not suitable for freshmen to read.

21 *The Puzzling Failure of Economics* ....

22 *Decay of the Dismal Science* ....

23 *Economists and the Economy* ....

24 *History of Economic Thought* ....

25 *The Evolution of Economic Ideas* ....

Questions 26–30

Complete the notes below.

*Write **NO MORE THAN THREE WORDS** for each answer.*

Michael's Programme

- **26** .... on IMF policies.
- **27** .... to download useful information.
- Go to libraries to borrow reference books, **28** .... and non-print materials.
- See Dr Forbes to agree on the **29** ....
- Work on the **30** ....

SECTION 4 *Questions 31–35*

Answer the questions below.

Write ***NO MORE THAN TWO WORDS AND/OR A NUMBER*** *for each answer.*

31 What is the main environmental problem at the moment?

....

32 In which continent have large amounts of trees been cut down?

....

33 Which group of countries is responsible for using the most resources?

....

34 Which group of people is increasing the depletion of resources in China?

....

35 What is the term used to describe the divide between the rich and the poor?

....

Questions 36–40

Which country uses the highest proportion of each method of pollution prevention?

A Canada
B France
C Germany
D England
E Norway
F Thailand
G United States

36 Energy conservation ....
37 Recycling ....
38 Waste management ....
39 Education ....
40 Punishments ....

READING

READING PASSAGE 1

*You should spend about 20 minutes on **Questions 1–12**, which are based on Reading Passage 1 below.*

Charles Darwin: A Natural Selection

Of the many books marking the 200th anniversary of the birth of the father of modern evolutionary theory, two contrasting volumes stand out.

Charles Darwin is known to the world for one book. *On the Origin of Species by Means of Natural Selection,* or *The Preservation of Favored Races in the Struggle for Life*, to give it its full, long-winded Victorian title, was published a century and a half ago this year. In truth Darwin was a prolific authour. Like a 19th-century David Attenborough, he churned out volume after bestselling volume on earthworms, coral reefs, emotion, orchids, insectivorous plants and, of course, human origins.

Darwin would probably forgive the avalanche of books celebrating this anniversary and his 200th birthday, even if it leaves the modern reviewer reeling. There is an edited edition of his letters from his trip round the world on HMS Beagle, an effort to connect his life with that of Abraham Lincoln (who was born on the same day, February 12th 1809), an attempt (surely redundant for supporters and futile for opponents) to explain "Why Evolution is True", and even a collection of essays on Alfred Russel Wallace, who came up with the idea of natural selection at the same time as Darwin, and bounced him into publishing before he was really ready. *On the Origin of Species*, too, has been republished, complete with a trendy cover by Damien Hirst, a trendy British artist. But in the search for a new angle to tempt the jaded public, the most successful offerings are those of Steve Jones, a geneticist, and Adrian Desmond and James Moore, two historians of science.

Darwin's Island, Mr Jones's book, is not, actually, all that much about Darwin. Instead, each chapter uses one of the naturalist's other books as a point of departure for a meandering, but ultimately enlightening, natural-history lesson. *Insectivorous Plants*, published in 1875, inspires chapter called *The Green Tyrannosaurs* that shows, using modern genetics, how insect ivory has evolved many times in unrelated groups of vegetables in response to a lack of nitrogen in the soil. *The Movements and Habits of Climbing Plants* (also published in 1875) gives rise to an exploration of how similar the problems faced by plants are to those faced by animals, and how the former deal with them without being able to move. The four-volume treatise on barnacles (1851–1854), is used to investigate the central question of how species originate. And *The Descent of Man, and Selection in Relation to Sex* (1871) is the point of departure for the inevitable chapter on human evolution.

Mr Desmond and Mr Moore, by contrast, have written very precisely about the man himself. *Darwin's Sacred Cause* is an exhaustive tome by the authours of an earlier biography, *Darwin* (1992). Their thesis is that, far from arriving at the idea of human evolution from his studies of natural history, Darwin took as one of his starting points the diversification of humanity into "races".

There are many interesting twists here. That humanity is one and indivisible would have been taken for granted until about the time of Darwin's birth. Christians, at least, would have believed that everyone was descended from Adam and Eve, with what biologists would now refer to as a genetic "bottleneck" at the time of Noah. By the time Darwin was a student in Edinburgh and Cambridge, though, this was being questioned. The idea that the different races had different origins (from different types of monkey, or from different acts of divine creation, depending on the views of the proposer), began as a convenient piece of slave-traders' propaganda, intended to denigrate the humanity of Africans. It rapidly became a matter of scientific debate, challenging the literalist interpretation of *The Bible* in a manner reminiscent of the questioning of the early geologists with their antediluvian fossils.

Darwin, brought up among Whiggish abolitionists and then exposed during his circumnavigation both to the horrors of slavery and to people from almost every one of the races into which Victorian science was dividing mankind, became convinced of the opposite. He saw humanity as the product of common descent. The different races were, in his view, branches of a single tree, or, more accurately, twigs of a single branch, for the tree itself was not just the human family tree, but the tree of life. According to Mr Desmond and Mr Moore, it was the unity he saw in humanity's diversity as much as that visible in the different breeds of domestic animals (fancy pigeons, for example), which helped him understand what was going on.

Reader, beware: this book is as much about the anti-slavery movement as it is about the genesis of a scientific idea. It also, unlike Mr Jones's book, presents itself as a work of scholarship; there are 79 pages of notes and bibliography while *Darwin's Island* has none. But, if nothing else, *Darwin's Sacred Cause* shows that there is still new material to be gleaned from the life of a man much picked over, and who turned the world upside down.

Questions 1–6

Look at the following statements (Questions 1–6) and the list of editions, books or treatises below.

Match the correct letter, ***A–F****, in boxes 1–6 on your answer sheet.*

1 It is in purpose of explaining the reason for the reality of evolution.

2 It eventually gave rise to the thinking of natural history.

3 It boosted the further exploration of the problems both plants and animals face.

4 From here, the authour unfolded the chapter focusing on human evolution.

5 The evolution of humanity into "races" was considered as one of the starting points of Darwin.

6 It adopted the current genetic researching method.

A	*Darwin's Sacred Cause*
B	The edition of Darwin's letters on HMS Beagle
C	*Darwin's Island*
D	*The Green Tyrannosaurs*
E	*The Movements and Habits of Climbing Plants* (published in 1875)
F	*The Descent of Man, and Selection in Relation to Sex* (1871)

Questions 7–12

Choose the correct letter, ***A****,* ***B****,* ***C*** *or* ***D****.*

Write the correct letter in boxes 7–12 on your answer sheet.

7 What was referred to as a genetic "bottleneck" at the time of Noah?

A People believed religious explanation of human origins.

B People couldn't figure out human origins.

C Various people who held contradictory opinions about human origins couldn't reach an agreement.

D The idea that God created the first man was being questioned.

8 What was the idea that different races had different origins used for?

A It was used to advocate that white people are inferior to other races.

B It was applied to explain difference among the tribes.

C It was used as a proof taken advantage by slave-traders.

D It was applied to force a matter of scientific debate.

9 How did early geologists challenge the literalist?

A By holding public debate.
B By accumulating archaeological evidence.
C By publishing treatises.
D By opposing the slave trade.

10 What was Darwin's idea about different races?

A Some were worse developed than others.
B They shared some physical characteristics.
C They had the same origin.
D They had different religions.

11 Why did Mr Desmond and Mr Moore mention different species of domestic animals?

A To reveal the source of Darwin's inspiration.
B To compare the evolutionary process of humans with that of domestic animals.
C To contrast the evolutionary process of humans and domestic animals.
D To show the long and difficult evolutionary process of humans.

12 What is the book *Darwin's Sacred Cause* like?

A It shows Darwin had accumulated to prove his theory.
B It focuses on both anti-slavery movement and scientific study.
C It is a work of professional research.
D It mainly tells the notes and bibliography.

READING PASSAGE 2

You should spend about 20 minutes on ***Questions 13–26****, which are based on Reading Passage 2 below.*

Revolutionary Buildings

Engineering: Clever construction techniques could usher in a new architectural era in which entire buildings are capable of rotating.

In biology almost nothing revolves freely. An owl's head, for example, can twist so far round that it faces backward, but when the bird wants to look forward again, it must turn its head back the way it came. There is a reason for this. Animals are wired up internally by blood vessels, nerves, intestines, and so on. Evolution has not yet come up with a way of keeping these links intact while allowing different parts of the body to revolve independently of one another. And this is not just a biological problem. Even human engineers have difficulty with it, which is one reason why revolving buildings—with their need for water, sewerage, gas and electrical connections—are so rare. But that could now be changing.

The simplest approach to such a building is what might be called the owl solution—in other words, incomplete rotation. This allows fixed but flexible connections to be used. Some years ago Bill Butler, an amateur architect, used this trick in a house in Snow Creek, California. Water and gas are delivered, and sewage removed, via vertical steel pipes in the non-rotating base. Rubber hoses connect the uprights to their mates in the mobile part of the building. The house's ability to rotate is thus limited only by the length of the hoses at full stretch. In the case of Mr Butler's dwelling, that allows it to sweep out an arc of 120°.

Two other Californians, Al and Janet Johnstone, however, have gone the whole hog. Their house, designed by Technology of Henderson, Nevada (of which Mr Johnstone is a director) and built in the aptly named neighbourhood of Mountain Helix, revolves completely, once an hour.

Rather than using rubber hoses to connect the stationary and moving parts of the building, 3 sixty's ingenious plumbing system employs horizontal ring-shaped pipes made of steel. Or, rather, it employs two ring-shaped half-pipes that rotate with respect to one another (the lower one remaining fixed while the upper one revolves along with the building). The joints between the half-pipes have rubber seals to stop the contents leaking, and each half-pipe has a vertical pipe connected to it, to introduce or dispose of the fluid concerned. Electricity, meanwhile, is delivered via a conductive brush that sweeps around a metal ring in the stationary base.

Electricity, of course, is needed to turn a revolving building. But if the building is well pivoted to reduce friction that requires surprisingly little power. The motor that moves Mr Butler's house consumes about 370 watts; the Johnstones' — which is solar-powered — a bit over a kilowatt.

A couple of bespoke houses does not amount to a trend. But larger commercial developments are under construction, too. In April, for example, the world's first owners of revolving flats will begin moving into the Suite Vollard in Curitiba, Brazil, built by Moro Construções Civis. Each of the 11 apartments occupies an entire circular floor, costs about $550,000 and revolves at the occupant's command, in either direction, once an hour. (Moro has sidestepped the plumbing problem: the kitchens and bathrooms are located in the building's stationary central core.) Rogério Kffuri, Moro's head of sales, says the firm has signed contracts with developers in America, Canada, Japan, Portugal and the United Arab Emirates (UAE).

The UAE, in particular, seems keen on this sort of novelty. Dubai Property Ring, a local developer, plans to build a 30-storey block of flats called 55° Time Dubai. Instead of revolving platforms or individual floors, the entire structure will turn once a week, a pace that Tav Singh, the project's manager, calls "dignified". The owl problem, meanwhile, will be solved using a system similar to 3 sixty's. The most ambitious proposal yet comes from David Fisher, an architect based in Italy. He wants to build a skyscraper called the Dynamic Tower in Dubai. It would have 80 independently rotating, non-circular floors. This would give the tower a continuously changing shape. Solar panels and horizontal wind turbines between the floors would generate the power needed to turn it.

Mr Fisher has provided few details. But Antony Wood, head of the Council on Tall Buildings and Urban Habitat, an industry association based in Chicago, says technological limitations no longer rule out such towers. If the Dynamic Tower is not built, Mr Wood says, the explanation will not be an unavoidable lack of know-how, but an old-fashioned lack of money.

Questions 13–20

Complete the summary below.

Choose ***NO MORE THAN THREE WORDS*** *from the passage for each answer.*

Write your answers in boxes 13–20 on your answer sheet.

When designing the architectures, human engineers used to face the problem similar to biological problem. However, they come up with a solution named **13** .... Bill Butler, an amateur architect, adopted **14** .... to deal with water, gas and sewage. However, when the hoses are at full stretch, the building's ability **15** .... is restricted. Of the examples of the revolving buildings, the masterpiece of David Fisher is the most remarkable. The Dynamic Tower in Dubai can change its shape unstoppably because of eighty self-rotating **16** .... The power comes from **17** .... and **18** .... According to Antony Wood, people's desires to build such buildings are not confined by **19** .... any more, but by insufficiency of **20** ....

Questions 21–26

Look at the following statements (Questions 21–26) and the list of architects below.

Match the correct letter, ***A–E****, in boxes 21–26 on your answer sheet.*

NB *You may use any letter more than once.*

21 designed a building which can alter its appearance at any moment

22 designed a house that can revolve at a certain frequency

23 used rubber hoses to link the stationary and moving parts of the building

24 works for a company which has a great market

25 designed a tower whose rotating capability is limited

26 designed the masterpiece with a motor driven by clean energy

A	Rogério Kffuri
B	David Fisher
C	Bill Butler
D	Antony Wood
E	Al and Janet Johnstone

Test 3

READING PASSAGE 3

*You should spend about 20 minutes on **Questions 27–40**, which are based on Reading Passage 3 below.*

Fair Comment

The Internet: Books and other products sold by online retailers can attract thousands of reviews. Why are they worth reading or writing?

A If a book on *Amazon.com*, the leading online retailer, already has hundreds of reviews, is it worth bothering to add another? Evidently some people think it is. Peter Hoflich, a financial journalist based in Singapore, recently wrote the 3,250th review of *Harry Potter and the Deathly Hallows*, for example. "I wonder if anyone will benefit from my review, especially since there are so many," he muses. Oddly enough, somebody might. That is because the raw number of reviews or comments, and the proportion of positive and negative ones, send useful signals to other people, even if they do not trawl through all of them. Accordingly, websites make it as easy as possible for people to add their comments.

B Amazon was a pioneer in this regard: it has allowed customers to post reviews of books and other products for many years. Initially, publishers and authours were worried that allowing negative reviews would hurt sales. Online retailers have generally been reluctant to allow users to leave comments, says John McAteer, Google's retail industry director, who runs *shopping.google.com*, the Internet giant's comparison-shopping site. But a handful of bad reviews, it seems, are worth having. "No one trusts all positive reviews," he says. So a small proportion of negative comments — "just enough to acknowledge that the product couldn't be perfect" — can actually make an item more attractive to prospective buyers.

C The sheer volume of reviews makes far more difference, according to Google's analysis of clicks and sales referrals. "Single digits didn't seem to move the needle at all," says Mr McAteer. "It wasn't enough to get people comfortable with making that purchase decision." But after about 20 reviews of a product are posted, "We start to see more reviews — it starts to accelerate," says Sam Decker, the chief marketing officer of Bazaar voice, a firm that powers review systems for online retailers.

D His company's research shows that visitors are more reluctant to buy until a product attracts a reasonable number of reviews and picks up momentum. In a test with Kingston, a maker of computer memory, Bazaar voice collected reviews of Kingston products from the firm's website and syndicated them to the website of Office Depot, a retailer. As a result there were more than ten reviews per product, compared with one or two for competitors' offerings. The result was a "drastically" higher conversion rate, which extended even to other Kingston products that lacked the additional reviews.

E Yet even when a product has attracted hundreds or even thousands of reviews, they keep coming in. Five reviews of the first book in the popular "twilight" series, which was published in October 2005, were posted on *Amazon.com* on a typical day recently. Most retailers and comparison sites try to strike a balance between recent reviews and helpful ones. Allowing visitors to rate reviews allows the most informative to rise to the top. And displaying recent reviews indicates that people are still interested in the product.

F "Most people only look at the most recent — they don't go back and look at the first review," says Mr McAteer. Clay Shirky, a consultant on social media, points out that reverse-chronological sorting, which is how blog posts, comments and reviews are generally displayed on the web, "Gives people a latent expectation that recency matters." People like to read recent reviews, but why does anyone post new ones? Mr Shirk suggests that in many cases, writing a review is more like writing fan mail (or hate mail) for a product, and the people who post them do not really expect it to be read.

G But Daphne Durham, book editor at Amazon, says some reviewers really do want to shape others' opinions. "Someone out there is reading *Harry Potter* for the first time," she says. This prompts other readers who feel strongly about it "to debunk the hype, or to validate it." On Amazon, indeed, the most prolific reviewers are promoted almost as celebrities in their own right. This prompts reviewers to focus on quantity, not quality, however, so Amazon recently changed its ranking system. Now the "helpfulness" of reviews is taken into account, causing Harriet Klausner, the most prolific reviewer with over 18,000 reviews to her credit, to drop below 500th place in the rankings. Readers rated her reviews as helpful 71% of the time, compared with 95% for the new number one reviewer, "mark", who has written fewer than 500 reviews.

H What is true for reviews does not appear to apply to comments left on news stories or blogs, however. "You can probably have a decent discussion until you get to about 350 comments," says Markos Moulitsas, the founder of Daily Kos, a popular left-leaning political site. But after that, he says, "Most outside people will stay away from the thread, and further growth will come from people already inside that thread carrying forth a discussion, debate, or argument." Such discussion threads are more of a conversation, and the page they inhabit usually has a limited lifespan during which people continue to post — unlike the Amazon pages for the *Harry Potter* books, which continue to attract reviews even today, years after the books' publication.

Questions 27–34

Reading Passage 3 has eight paragraphs, **A–H**.

Which paragraph contains the following information?

*Write the correct letter, **A–H**, in boxes 27–34 on your answer sheet.*

27 People who post the reviews care more about their own feelings, rather than whether others read their reviews.

28 The best-selling products always have more reviews than those of their competitors.

29 The reviews of some books have a long lifespan.

30 When the reviews reach a certain number, the rate of posting will be increasing.

31 When the reviews reach a certain number, the posting can't be stopped.

32 The value of adding another review has been heatedly discussed.

33 A small proportion of negative reviews do have effect on potential customers.

34 Harriet Klausner is one of the example of the famous reviewers.

Questions 35–38

Do the following statements agree with the information given in Reading Passage 3?

In boxes 35–38 on your answer sheet, write

TRUE	*if the statement agrees with the information*
FALSE	*if the statement contradicts the information*
NOT GIVEN	*if there is no information on this*

35 Peter Hoflich recently wrote the 3,250th review of *Harry Potter and the Deathly Hallows* because he wanted to express his own feelings.

36 Publishers and authours supported allowing the negative reviews at the beginning.

37 Visitors are likely to buy something when its reviews accumulate to a certain amount.

38 Few people go back to see the past reviews.

Questions 39 and 40

*Choose the correct letter, **A**, **B**, **C** or **D**.*

39 How do most retailers balance the recent reviews and helpful ones?

A They reduce the number of total reviews.

B They give high scores to the helpful ones.

C They give the helpful ones preferential position.

D They cancel the past reviews and bad ones.

40 Why does Amazon change its ranking system?

A Some reviewers focus on quantities, rather than qualities.

B Some reviewers don't give fair comments about the products.

C Some reviewers are becoming celebrities and get economic benefits.

D Some reviewers complained about Amazon's ranking system.

WRITING

WRITING TASK 1

You should spend about 20 minutes on this task.

The table below shows the results of a survey to find out what members of a city sports club think about the club's activities, facilities and opening hours.

Summarise the information by selecting and reporting the main features, and make any comparisons where relevant.

Write at least 150 words.

Range of activities	**Very satisfied**	**Satisfied**	**Not satisfied**
Female members	35%	35%	30%
Male members	55%	40%	5%
Club facilities			
Female members	64%	22%	14%
Male members	63%	27%	10%
Opening hours			
Female members	72%	25%	3%
Male members	44%	19%	37%

WRITING TASK 2

You should spend about 40 minutes on this task.

Write about the following topic:

In recent years some countries have experienced very rapid economic development. This has resulted in much higher standards of living in urban areas but not in the countryside. This situation may bring some problems for the country as a whole.

What are these problems?
How might they be reduced?

Give reasons for your answer and include any relevant examples from your own knowledge or experience.

Write at least 250 words.

SPEAKING

PART 1

The examiner asks the candidate about him/herself, his/her home, work or studies and other familiar topics.

EXAMPLE

Collections

- Do you like to collect things?
- What do Chinese people like to collect?
- What did you collect when you were young?
- What can people get from their collections?

PART 2

Describe a family event you are looking forward to.
You should say:
what the event is
where it will be held
what you will do at this event
and explain why you are looking forward to this family event.

You will have to talk about the topic for one to two minutes. You have one minute to think about what you are going to say. You can make some notes to help you if you wish.

PART 3

Discussion topics:

Family celebrations

Example questions:

What type of special occasions are generally celebrated in your country?
How important is it for families to celebrate occasions together? Why?
Are family occasions as important today as they were for former generations?

Social changes

Example questions:

How has the role of elderly people in the family changed in recent times?
Who has more power and influence in the family today, young people or grandparents?
What impact have modern lifestyles had on neighbourhood communities?Why?

Test 4

LISTENING

SECTION 1 *Questions 1–10*

Questions 1–5

Complete the notes below.

*Write **NO MORE THAN TWO WORDS AND/OR A NUMBER** for each answer.*

- The cheapest accommodation is in **1** .... flat.
- Look on **2** .... for studio flats.
- New requirement from landlords—show documents about your **3** ....
- Check if **4** .... and .... are included in rent.
- Best to buy **5** .... bus pass.

Questions 6–10

Complete the table below.

*Write **NO MORE THAN THREE WORDS** for each answer.*

	Blooms leisure centre	**Good life centre**
For non-members	guided tour available	**6** .... for free
Café	**7** .... members get 10% discount	closed at present
Equipment	wide range of machines	machines arranged for doing **8** ....
Facilities	full-sized swimming pool is now **9**	all-weather tennis courts; small pool
Support	personal trainers are always available	consult qualified trainers **10** .... only

SECTION 2 *Questions 11–20*

Questions 11–16

Choose the correct letter, ***A***, ***B*** *or* ***C***.

11 Mr Griffin has been to the Sunrise Hotel

A once previously.

B twice previously.

C three times previously.

12 Mr Griffin is from

A Melbourne.

B Sydney.

C Perth.

13 Mr Griffin's passport number is

A 87647489.

B 87637289.

C 87637489.

14 Mr Griffin wants to book

A a single room for two nights.

B a double room for two nights.

C a single room for one night.

15 Mr Griffin will arrive at the Sunrise Hotel at

A 9.15pm.

B 10pm.

C 9.35pm.

16 When he gets to the Sunrise Hotel, the food Mr Griffin will find in his room will be

A a cake.

B a sandwich.

C a burger.

Questions 17–20

Answer the questions below.

Write ***NO MORE THAN TWO WORDS AND/OR A NUMBER*** *for each answer.*

17 Which room will Mr Griffin be in at the Sunrise Hotel?

....

18 How much will Mr Griffin pay per night at the Sunrise Hotel?

....

19 Who will take Mr Griffin's food to his room?

....

20 How much will Mr Griffin pay for his food?

....

SECTION 3 *Questions 21–30*

Questions 21 and 22

*Choose **TWO** letters, **A–E**.*

Which **TWO** courses had Jill considered to be interesting when choosing a course?

A archaeology
B architecture
C business administration
D industrial design
E information management

Questions 23 and 24

*Choose **TWO** letters, **A–E**.*

Which **TWO** aspects of student life does Desmond find difficult?

A prioritising tasks
B controlling finances
C getting information from lectures
D working silently in the library
E getting to know other students

Questions 25–30

Who will do the following tasks?

*Write the correct letter, **A**, **B** or **C** next to questions 25–30.*

A	Desmond
B	Jill
C	both Desmond and Jill

25 design experiment structure ....
26 get advice from statistics tutor ....
27 compare examples of previous research ....
28 investigate possible support from IT section ....
29 organise focus groups ....
30 speak at presentation ....

SECTION 4 *Questions 31–40*

Questions 31–40

Complete the sentences below.

Write ***NO MORE THAN TWO WORDS AND/OR A NUMBER*** *for each answer.*

River Turtles

Nesting habits

31 The arrau turtle's shell is approximately .... long.

32 A female arrau deposits at least .... every night.

33 River terrapins make a noise similar to ....

34 Male river terrapins' heads change .... in the breeding season.

Threats

35 Alexander von Humboldt estimated that .... jars of oil were produced at Orinoco River.

36 River terrapins used to be protected by a system of .... for egg collectors.

37 River turtles are used in traditional .... in Asia.

38 River turtles can reproduce for several .... if they are unharmed.

Farming as a solution

39 Turtle farmers are encouraged not to sell turtles until they are ....

40 It is uncertain whether turtle farming will be successful in .... terms.

READING

READING PASSAGE 1

*You should spend about 20 minutes on **Questions 1–13**, which are based on Reading Passage 1 below.*

Malaria: Resistance Is Useless

Evolutionary theory may help to fight a fatal disease.

Like many other activities, global health has fashions. For the past couple of decades AIDS has captured both the imagination and the research dollars. Recently, though, the focus has shifted towards malaria, which kills a million people a year, most of them children, and debilitates hundreds of millions more. Insecticide-impregnated bed nets designed to stop people being bitten by infected mosquitoes are being scattered throughout Africa. New drugs based on a Chinese herb called Artemisia have been introduced. And researchers are vying with one another to be the first to devise an effective vaccine. But the traditional first line of attack on malaria, killing the mosquitoes themselves, has yet to have a serious makeover.

One reason is that time and again chemical insecticides have produced the same dreary pattern. They prove wonderfully effective at first, only to dwindle into uselessness. This is because evolution quickly throws up resistant strains. Indeed, spraying campaigns, which generally aim to kill mosquitoes before they can breed, might have been devised as textbook examples of how to provoke an evolutionary response. With their competitors all dead, the progeny of a mosquito carrying a mutation that can neutralise the insecticide in question have the world to themselves.

The upshot is that discovering a way to retain the anti-malarial benefits of insecticides without provoking an evolutionary response would be a significant breakthrough. And that is what Andrew Read of Pennsylvania State University and his colleagues think they have done. They have rethought the logic of insecticides, putting evolutionary theory at the centre, instead of a simple desire to destroy the enemy. The result is a modest proposal to deal with the problem of resistance.

Euthanasia for mosquitoes

Dr Read started from the observation that it is old, rather than young, mosquitoes that are infectious. Only females can transmit malaria (males suck plant juices, not blood) but they are not born with the parasites inside their bodies. They have instead to acquire them from humans already carrying the disease, and that takes time. Once a female does feed on infected blood, the parasites she ingests require a further 10 to 14 days to mature and migrate to her salivary glands, whence they can be transmitted to another host when she next feeds. In theory, then, killing only the oldest female mosquitoes–those at significant risk of being infectious–could stop the transmission of the disease. Since these females would have had plenty of time to reproduce before they died, the evolutionary pressure imposed by killing them would be much lower.

To test this insight, the researchers constructed a mathematical model of the mosquito's lifecycle. They then plugged in data, collected from malaria hotspots in Africa and Papua New Guinea that describe the insect's lifespan and egg-laying cycles in those parts of the world and the way that malaria parasites grow inside mosquitoes. The model, which they have just published in the Public *Library of Science*, reveals that selectively killing elderly mosquitoes would reduce the number of infectious bites by 95% and that resistance to such a tactic would spread very slowly, if it spread at all, because mosquitoes vulnerable to a post-breeding insecticide would have had a chance to pass on their vulnerable genes to future generations.

The problem, of course, is to find an insecticide that kills only the elderly. One option is to use existing chemicals, but at greater dilutions. That could work because older mosquitoes are more vulnerable to insecticides than younger ones.

A more radical answer, though, may be to use a completely different sort of insecticide: a fungus. The team is working with fungi that take 10 to 12 days to become lethal. That is short enough to kill parasite-infected insects before they become infectious, but long enough to allow them to breed. A trial of this idea, spraying fungal spores on to bed nets and house walls in Tanzania, is being set up at the moment. If it works, it will be a good example of the value of thinking about biological problems from an evolutionary perspective. People will still get bitten, but the bites will merely be irritating, not life-threatening.

Questions 1–3

*Choose the correct letter, **A**, **B**, **C** or **D**.*

Write the correct letter in boxes 1–3 on your answer sheet.

1 Why does the authour mention AIDS?

A to illustrate the history of the topics of global health
B to emphasise the change of the topics of global health
C to show the importance of caring for AIDS
D to introduce Artemisia from a Chinese herb

2 Why have chemical insecticides produced dreary pattern?

A They can kill the limited number of insects.
B They can kill the limited species of insects.
C Resistant strains appear soon.
D They can kill a large number of insects.

3 What do Andrew Read and his colleagues focus on?

A the evolutionary theory

B the aim to annihilate the enemy

C the environmental effects

D the demonstration of their ability

Questions 4–13

Complete the table below.

*Write **NO MORE THAN TWO WORDS** for each answer.*

Write your answers in boxes 4–13 on your answer sheet.

	Dr Read's method	**A more radical answer**
Method	Kill solely **4** .... mosquitoes	Use **5** ....
Theoretical grounds	**6** .... that female mosquitoes infect can transmit the disease	Annihilate parasite-infected insects before they become **7** ....
Ways to practice	• Set up a **8** .... • Use **9**	**10** .... fungal spores on to bed nets and **11** ....
Result	**12** .... the number of infectious bites	The bites will not be **13** ....

READING PASSAGE 2

You should spend about 20 minutes on ***Questions 14–26****, which are based on Reading Passage 2 below.*

Second Life

Biologists debate the scale of extinction in the world's tropical forests.

A rare piece of good news from the world of conservation: the global extinction crisis may have been overstated. The world is unlikely to lose 100 species a day, or half of all species in the lifetime of people now alive, as some have claimed. The bad news, though, is that the lucky survivors are tiny tropical insects that few people care about. The species that are being lost rapidly are the large vertebrates that conservationists were worried about in the first place.

This new view of the prospects for biodiversity emerged from a symposium held this week at the Smithsonian Institution in Washington, DC, but the controversy over how bad things really are has been brewing since 2006. That was when Joseph Wright of the Smithsonian Tropical Research Institute in Panama and Helene Muller-Landau of the University of Minnesota first suggested that the damage might not be as grim as some feared. They reasoned that because population growth is slowing in many tropical countries, and people are moving to cities, the pressure to cut down primary rainforest is falling and agriculturally marginal land is being abandoned, allowing trees to grow.

This regrown "secondary" forest is crucial to the pair's analysis. Within a few decades of land being abandoned, half of the original biomass has returned. Depending on what else is nearby, these new forests may then be colonized by animals and additional plants, and thus support many of the species found in the original forest.

Dr Wright and Dr Muller-Landau therefore reckon that in 2030 reasonably unbroken tropical forest will still cover more than a third of its natural range, and after that date its area — at least in Latin America and Asia — could increase. Much of this woodland will be secondary forest, but even so they suggest that in Africa only 16–35% of tropical-forest species will become extinct by 2030, in Asia, 21–24% and, in Latin America, fewer still. Once forest cover does start increasing, the rate of extinction should dwindle.

There are, however, two criticisms of this analysis. The first questions whether the raw data about forest cover are a good indicator of biodiversity, at least for big animals. William Laurance, a colleague of Dr Wright's, pointed out to the symposium that birds and mammals are more vulnerable to alterations in their habitat than are insects and other small animals. His data suggest that even in some of the world's best-protected primary forests, these species face severe pressures.

Elizabeth Bennett, of the Wildlife Conservation Society, an American conservation group, agreed and mentioned that for large birds and mammals, uncontrolled hunting for food and for trade is causing a phenomenon known as "empty-forest syndrome". She said that although many forests look healthy when viewed from a satellite, they are actually falling silent because many of their large animals have been removed for subsistence or profit.

Nonetheless, the symposium's participants agreed that the number of species of large animals may no longer be reliable indicators of the status of the millions of other species that live in a forest, and about which far less is known. Most species, as Nigel Stork of the University of Melbourne pointed out, are insects—and these are more resilient and much less threatened.

A diversity of opinion

The second criticism of Dr Wright's and Dr Muller-Landau's view questions their interpretation of the link between a country's population and its rate of deforestation. Dr Laurance suggested this link may not be as strong in the future as it once was. In the past two decades, he said, many parts of the tropics have seen a rise in industrial forms of land use such soya-bean farming, oil-palm plantations, and oil and gas development, together with the road-building and other construction projects that these bring in their wake. Such activities vary with the demands of international markets, not the size of the local population. In particular, Dr Laurance is worried that the liberalisation of agricultural trade and the rise of biofuels could lead to a huge increase in demand for land in the tropics.

What everyone agreed, though, was that climate change is a threat. Even the optimistic Dr Wright is worried. He warned the meeting that because many tropical species evolved in an environment that has very little temperature variation, they are not equipped to cope with an increase of as little as 3°C, which is the sort of change that many climate scientists predict. Such species may thus have to migrate long distances if they are to survive. He said that by the end of the century, 75% of tropical forests will be warmer than today, and what will remain in these hot, wet places is unknown.

Questions 14–18

Do the following statements agree with the information given in Reading Passage 2?

In boxes 14–18 on your answer sheet, write

TRUE *if the statement agrees with the information*
FALSE *if the statement contradicts the information*
NOT GIVEN *if there is no information on this*

14 In the analysis of Joseph Wright and Helene Muller-Landau, the secondary forest plays an important part.

15 The rate of extinction increases accordingly as forest cover increases.

16 Whether the forests can provide habitats for big animals is controversial.

17 Not everyone reaches the agreement on the matter of climate change.

18 Tropical species will die out if the temperature increases as little as 3°C.

Questions 19–26

Look at the following statements (Questions 19–26) and the list of researchers below.

Match each statement with the corect researcher, ***A–E****.*

Write the cerrect letter, ***A–E****, in boxes 19–26 on your answer sheet.*

NB *You may use any letter more than once.*

19 Tropical species have to change their habitats in order to adapt to the new environment.

20 The link between a country's population and the rate of deforestation was stronger in the past.

21 In fact, we can have an optimistic attitude towards the damage.

22 The demand on land will increase because of some factors.

23 Many forests are not as healthy as they are viewed from the satellite.

24 The insects are less vulnerable to environmental changes.

25 Tropical forests, including secondary forest, will cover a certain proportion of natural range.

26 It is harder for birds and mammals to get used to alterations in their habitat.

List of researchers

A Joseph Wright and Helene Muller-Landau
B Joseph Wright
C William Laurance
D Elizabeth Bennett
E Nigel Stork

READING PASSAGE 3

*You should spend about 20 minutes on **Questions 27–40**, which are based on Reading Passage 3 below.*

Salmon Breeding Comes Ashore

The environmentally friendly Danish model fish farms are to be expanded from the current freshwater farms to also include saltwater fish farms. This requires new technological solutions, which in itself could become something of an export bonanza.

Fish farming is currently one of the world's fastest growing food industries. Denmark has a long tradition of fish farming and today is among the world leaders in equipment for green production, thanks to the development of so-called model fish farms. The high-tech and environmentally friendly model fish farms use water from boreholes, rather than from rivers, and are based on water recirculation technology. This means that the fish farm recycles as much as 95 percent of the water instead of merely letting it drain away into the countryside.

Now DTU Aqua and several of the key players in the industry are joining forces to take Danish fish farming a stage further. In order to put large rainbow trout and salmon on the menu as well, the so-called model fish farms are to be expanded to include the breeding of saltwater fish as well as freshwater fish and it is to take place inland. The project is being supported by the Ministry of Food, Agriculture and Fisheries' Green Development and Demonstration Programme (GUDP).

"The global salmon market is huge. The production of fish in the aquaculture industry is increasing in several countries, but so far Denmark has not increased production significantly, mainly because of environmental restrictions. But why should the Norwegians produce our salmon if we can do it just as well-and without compromising the environment?" asks technical project manager Per Bovbjerg Pedersen, from DTU Aqua in Hirtshals.

In order to increase production in a sustainable and profitable manner, we need cross-disciplinary collaboration on new technological solutions for breeding fish in salt water to complement those solutions that DTU Aqua has already helped to develop within the field of freshwater fish breeding.

"The goal is to produce more fish, but with the same or even lower emissions of nitrogen out into the environment. This will be done partly through applying a known technique in freshwater farming, whereby bio-filters are used to convert the ammonia excreted by the fish into nitrate. Now the goal is to develop the technology to do the same with salt water, in order to convert this nitrate into nitrogen which can be released as a harmless gas. In this way the nitrogen is removed safely from the water," explains Per Bovbjerg Pedersen.

In a four-year project supported by the Ministry of Food, Agriculture and Fisheries' Green Development and Demonstration Programme (GUDP), DTU Aqua, in collaboration with key industry players, is to develop technology to enable large rainbow trout to be farmed inland in salt water. After two years, the project will be expanded to test the feasibility of farming Atlantic salmon in inland saltwater fish farms.

DTU Aqua is responsible for the professional management of the project, in particular the environmental impact, water quality parameters and the development and optimisation of cleaning technologies. The work is being carried out at the North Sea Science Park in Hirtshals in collaboration with representatives from all relevant parts of industry including the leading Danish food producer Biomar and the largest breeding, processing and sales company AquaPri.

The goal in the long term is not only to create a basis for the Danish production and export of sustainably produced saltwater fish: the actual technology itself will have equally strong export potential, Per Bovbjerg believes.

"Denmark is already a world leader in water recirculation technology and model fish farms, thanks to our unique composition of components drawn from our experience in water recirculation techniques. The aim is to further exploit and expand the Danish position in the field of water recirculation by combining it with breeding techniques, equipment and complete plant solutions for saltwater fish farming," says the technical project manager from DTU Aqua.

What is a model fish farm? The high-tech and environmentally friendly model fish farms for breeding fish use water from boreholes and are based on water recirculation technology. This means that a farm recycles as much as 95 percent of its water. A comprehensive measurement and documentation project to monitor the environmental impact of model fish farms was started in 2005. The project was based among other things on DTU Aqua's know-how about fish farming systems, including water recirculation technology.

Today, model fish farms are located in large concrete plants on the traditional fish farms sites. But as the model fish farms do not need the water from the streams, the streams are now free of obstacles such as dams and barriers. This also provides free passage for the wild fish on their way to and from spawning grounds and the sea, which is beneficial for wild fish stocks.

Today the aquaculture industry—both inland and sea-based fish farms—is the world's fastest growing food industry.

Questions 27–35

Complete the summary below.

Choose ***NO MORE THAN THREE WORDS*** *from the passage for each answer.*

Write your answers in boxes 27–35 on your answer sheet.

Fish farming is booming these years and Denmark becomes the leader in the environmentally friendly field due to **27** .... This practice chooses water from **28** .... not **29** .... In order to improve the fish industry, companies like **30** .... decide to stretch this high technology to somewhere **31** ....

However, the output in Denmark is not satisfactory because of **32** .... Therefore, Danish players use a new technology for breeding more fish as well as protecting the environment. Through this approach, the **33** .... emitted from fish can be transferred into **34** .... , and then to the harmless **35** ....

Test 4

Questions 36–40

Do the following statements agree with the information given in Reading Passage 3?

In boxes 36–40 on your answer sheet, write

TRUE	*if the statement agrees with the information*
FALSE	*if the statement contradicts the information*
NOT GIVEN	*if there is no information on this*

36 The GUDP project aims to guarantee that saltwater fish can be farmed inland.

37 Water quality parameters are more important than cleaning technologies in the management of the GUDP project.

38 The long-term target is to satisfy the export market of saltwater fish.

39 Dams built in streams improve wild fish stocks.

40 Model fish farms are the reason for the rapid progress of aquaculture industry.

WRITING

WRITING TASK 1

You should spend about 20 minutes on this task.

The graphs below indicate the effect of treatment for two types of cancer in females.

Using the information in the graphs, describe and compare the situation with and without treatment for the two types of cancer.

Write at least 150 words.

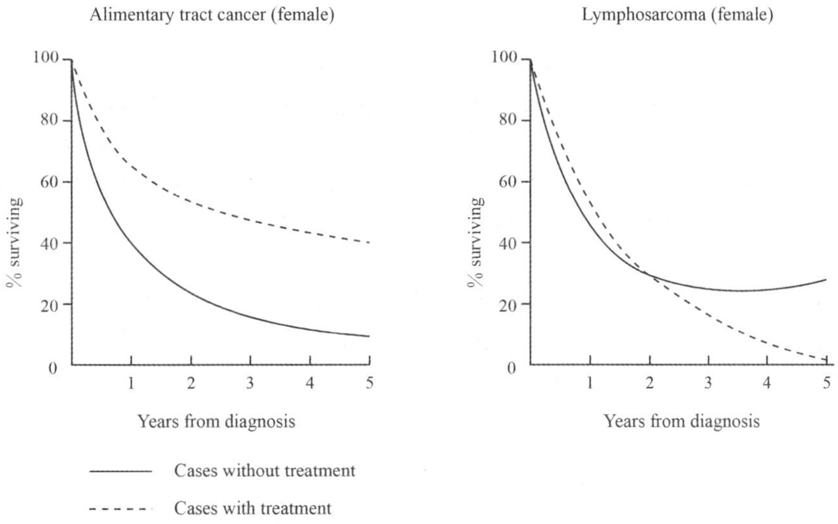

WRITING TASK 2

You should spend about 40 minutes on this task.

Write about the following topic:

Some people think that old people should be taken care of at home, while others think they should be placed in old people's house.

What is your opinion?

Give reasons for your answer and include any relevant examples from your own knowledge or experience.

Write at least 250 words.

SPEAKING

PART 1

The examiner asks the candidate about him/herself, his/her home, work or studies and other familiar topics.

EXAMPLE

Friends

- Do you often spend time with friends?
- Did you meet most of friends through school/work?
- Do you and your friends have similar hobbies and interests?
- Do you spend more of your free time with friends or family?

PART 2

Describe a TV or radio programme you enjoyed when you were a child.

You should say:

what the programme was about

when it was on

where you watched or listenned to it

and explain why you enjoyed this programme when you were a child.

You will have to talk about the topic for one to two minutes.
You have one minute to think about what you are going to say.
You can make some notes to help you if you wish.

PART 3

Discussion topics:

TV and radio in your country

Example questions:

In your country, which do people prefer, watching TV or listening to radio? Why?

What kind of programmes are most popular?

Do men and women tend to like the same kind of programmes? Why/Why not?

The effects of TV

Example questions:

Some people think that watching TV can be a negative influence. Would you agree?

What benefits can TV bring people?

What priorities do you think TV stations should have?

Test 5

LISTENING

SECTION 1 *Questions 1–10*

Complete the notes below.

Write ***NO MORE THAN THREE WORDS AND/OR A NUMBER*** *for each answer.*

Architecture 21 Conference

Conference dates: 1 ....

Conference venue: 2 ....

Reservations phone No.: 3 ....

- Cost $300 for three days
- Student rate $150 for three days or **4** .... a day

Contact person: 5 ....

Must act fast!

Closing day for talks: 6 ....

The outline of talk should include **7** ....

The maximum length of outline: 8 ....

Also send: 9 ....

E-mail address: 10 .... *edu.au*

SECTION 2 *Questions 11–20*

Complete the notes below.

Write ***NO MORE THAN TWO WORDS AND/OR A NUMBER*** *for each answer.*

Arrangements for Stopover in London

Accommodation

- Bedford Hotel (in **11** .... London)
  Family room, no special facilities. Close to the **12** ....
- Premier Hotel (west London, very close to airport)
  13 .... rooms (hotel has a swimming pool and a **14** ....)
- Airline will give us a voucher for room(s), evening meal and breakfast.
- Airline will give us **15** .... in cash to cover incidental expenses.
- Airline will refund other essential expenses over £20 e.g. taxis, overseas phone calls (we must keep **16** ....) .
- Airline will not reimburse non-essential expenses, e.g. **17** .... , shopping, refreshments.

Onward Flight

- Call free phone number (**18** ....) to find out about flights tomorrow. Between 9 and 10am.
- Ask for Mr Philip **19** ....
- If the flight is cancelled again a **20** .... will drop additional vouchers off at the hotel.

Test 5

SECTION 3 *Questions 21–30*

Questions 21 and 22

*Choose the correct letter, **A**, **B** or **C**.*

21 Where was Louis Braille blinded when he was a child?

A in restaurant
B in college
C in his father's workshop

22 When did Braille invent the writing system?

A in 1823
B in 1824
C in 1825

Questions 23 and 24

Complete the sentences below.

*Write **NO MORE THAN TWO WORDS** for each answer.*

23 An early writing system for the blind used ....

24 A military system using dots was called ....

Questions 25–27

*Choose the correct letter, **A**, **B** or **C**.*

25 What can the combined dots represent?

A both letters and words
B only individual words
C only letters of the alphabet

26 When was Braille system officially adopted?

A two years after it was invented
B after Louis Braille had died
C as soon as it was invented

27 In what way was the Braille system officially adopted?

A The texts have to be read backwards.

B It can only be written using a machine.

C Hand written Braille is created in reverse.

Questions 28–30

*Choose **THREE** letters, **A–G**.*

*Choose **THREE** subjects that also use a Braille code:*

A Mathematics

B Biology

C Statistics

D Science

E Music

F Physics

G Psychics

SECTION 4 *Questions 31–40*

Questions 31–35

*Choose the correct letter, **A**, **B** or **C**.*

31 Hong Kong universities are adopting the IELTS test as

A an entrance test.

B a progress test.

C an exit test.

32 To show good English competency, students should achieve at least

A band 5.

B band 6.

C band 7.

33 The three main things to consider about the test are

A timing, format and question types.

B timing, formality and section types.

C testing, functionality and topics.

34 Currently, on Mondays 2.30 to 4.30 in the CILL, you can attend

A a complete IELTS course.

B a discussion about IELTS practice materials.

C an introductory workshop.

35 Also in the CILL you can take advantage of

A the Speaking and Writing Assistance programmes.

B practice materials: books, tapes, tests and online materials.

C both of the above.

Questions 36–40

Choose **FIVE** items which the speaker says candidates "must" do to prepare thoroughly for the IELTS test from the list below.

36 ....

37 ....

38 ....

39 ....

40 ....

A Understand the format

B Eat well and get plenty of sleep before the test

C Understand what you are being asked or tested on

D Prioritize IELTS preparation over course work

E Apply for a Master's degree abroad

F Do as many test papers as possible

G Do as much speaking practice as possible

H Delay preparation until a week or so before the test so it will be fresh in your mind

I Stop listening to English TV or radio as the language is too informal for the test

J Start preparing as early as possible

READING

READING PASSAGE 1

*You should spend about 20 minutes on **Questions 1–13**, which are based on Reading Passage 1 below.*

Rainforest Burning Issues

A new experiment is setting the Amazon on fire.

This month Jennifer Balch will head into the Amazon rainforest of Mato Grosso state, in Brazil. She intends to set fire to it and find out what happens. When Dr Balch, who is based at Woods Hole Research Centre, in Massachusetts, and her 30 helpers have finished their weeklong task, 50 hectares will have been torched. "It's pretty darn exciting and a bit crazy," she says, "to see a bunch of researchers running around burning down a forest."

The questions that prompt all this destruction are important. The first is: Will tropical forests survive the increasing occurrence of wildfires as the climate changes and people move in, or will the landscape shift from one ruled by trees to one dominated by grassland? The second is: How much carbon do such wildfires release into the atmosphere?

Wildfires are certainly a problem in Brazil. During the droughts of 1997 and 1998, which were linked to El Niño, an irregular warming of the Pacific Ocean, 39,000 square kilometres of Amazonian forest were burned by such fires. That is twice the area deliberately cut down in Brazil each year between 1988 and 2005. Similar fires occurred all over South-East Asia and Latin America, causing $19 billion–24 billion of damage through loss of timber, destruction of property and the effect of the smoke on human health.

Tropical wildfires are different from the ones that happen in temperate woodlands, for example in the western United States. Temperate-forest fires burn hot and fast, and sometimes all the way up to the crown of a tree. Tropical forest is wetter and usually supports only knee-high fires that spread slowly through the understory. Indeed, they are slow enough to be outrun—which is convenient for Dr Balch and her associates.

Tropical fires are, nevertheless, a significant source of carbon dioxidc. And their increasing frequency is an important part of the degradation of the Amazon forest—and could be an indicator of large-scale environmental change. To find out more about what such fires presage, Dr Balch has been conducting experimental burns like the one now planned since 2004.

At the start of each experiment the group cuts a fire break along the perimeter of the area. This means removing all vegetation, right down to the soil. Then researchers ran out across the forest measuring the temperature and the humidity of the air (two of the factors that determine how a fire will behave), and recording the amount of woody fuel in the forest and the moisture in that fuel. Five minutes after that come the fire-raisers, who light 10km of "fire line" using drip torches (devices that drop flaming paraffin at a constant rate). Five minutes after them it is the turn of the unfortunate team charged with measuring the height of the flames and mapping the fire line in order to calculate how fast it is moving—all without inhaling too much smoke as they go.

The results so far are worrying. Though many of the largest trees in the Amazon can survive repeated fires, smaller plants do less well. In those areas that have had three or four periods of experimental burning only half the number of species of tree seedlings originally found are still there. Grasses, by contrast, are doing well. So far, they have invaded as far as 200 metres from the edge of the forest.

That is worrying for those who prefer forest to savannah. Global warming alone is predicted to favour the conversion of woodland to grassland, and Dr Balch thinks her work shows that wildfires may accelerate the process. Grasses are well adapted to fire, being able to resprout quickly from their roots and thus outcompete tree seedlings.

The goal, then, is to encourage landowners to do more to prevent wildfires from starting and spreading. Those landowners, however, are in it for the money. At the moment, standing forest is of little commercial value, and much of it continues to exist only because of laws intended to prevent total clearance of the land. But talk of financial incentives for forest-owners to preserve their trees is in the air, and a deal may be struck at the United Nations climate-change meeting being held in Copenhagen in December.

Intriguingly, Dr Balch's experimental area is part of an 80,000-hectare holding owned by the family of Blairo Maggi, a soybean magnate who is the governor of Mato Grosso. In 2005 Mr Maggi "won" the Greenpeace "golden chainsaw" award for deforestation. But if money to preserve trees were on the table his views might change. Dr Balch has done a back-of-the-envelope calculation. Assuming a conservative value of $5 per ton of carbon locked up by trees, she calculates that a wildfire which spread through half of the landholding that Mr Maggi is legally required to keep as forest would cost him $16m. That would make intact rainforest hot property indeed.

Questions 1–8

Complete the summary below.

Choose ***NO MORE THAN TWO WORDS*** *from the passage for each answer.*

Write your answers in boxes in 1–8 on your answer sheet.

Jennifer Balch and her 30 helpers ran around to burn down a forest. The aims are very vital: one is to check whether the landscape will shift from one dominated by trees to one ruled by **1** .... ; the other one is to calculate the quantity of **2** .... released into the environment. The forest damaged by **3** .... is twice that is cut down in Brazil annually between 1998 and 2005. Through the loss of timber, **4** .... was destroyed while **5** .... was threatened. While **6** .... fires spread hot and fast, **7** .... is humid enough to support **8** .... fires.

Questions 9–11

Choose ***THREE*** *letters,* ***A–G****.*

Write the correct letter, ***A–G****, in boxes 9–11 on your answer sheet.*

Why do we need to pay attention to tropical fires?

A They lead to the increase in lung cancer suffers.

B They lead to the increase in carbon dioxide.

C They can reveal large-scale environmental change.

D They do harm to local agriculture.

E They degrade the tropical forests.

F They endanger animals' lives.

G They can change the climate.

Questions 12 and 13

Choose the correct letter, ***A****,* ***B****,* ***C*** *or* ***D****.*

Write the correct letter, ***A****,* ***B****,* ***C*** *or* ***D****, in boxes 12 and 13 on your answer sheet.*

12 What conclusions do scientists get?

A Smaller plants are more easily to be burnt.

B Grasses are more adaptable to the fire.

C Tree seedlings need a long time to recover.

D Tree seedlings can protect the grassland.

13 What are the attitudes of landowners towards standing forests?

A They are willing to protect them.

B They think standing forests have little value.

C They call for the laws to forbid chopping down the forests.

D They lack financial incentives to protect them.

READING PASSAGE 2

You should spend about 20 minutes on ***Questions 14–25****, which are based on Reading Passage 2 below.*

The Fad for Functional Foods

Over the past decade, the biggest trend in food marketing has been the shift towards organic, "natural" and even "whole" foods. Consumers in wealthier markets worldwide have demanded foods with minimal processing, in a state as close as possible to their natural one, in the fervent (and often mistaken) belief that such food is healthier for their bodies and for the planet. Ironically, this success is now prompting multinational food giants to accelerate investments in "functional" foods that are intentionally modified to make them healthier or more nutritious.

Consumers are swallowing such products, and the marketing claims that come with them, enthusiastically. Price Waterhouse Coopers, a consultancy, expects the global market for functional foods to mushroom from $78 billion in 2007 to $128 billion in 2013. One example of this approach is the enrichment of eggs with omega-3 fatty acids to combat hypertension. Another is the addition of chemicals called sterols to margarines to impede the absorption of cholesterol. The best example is the recent boom in bacteria-enriched yogurts, such as Danone's blockbuster brand Activia, which are supposed to fight "bloating" (code for constipation).

Functional foods are nothing new, observes Bernard Hours of Danone. He says that his firm, a French dairy giant, was selling yogurt in pharmacies in Barcelona as long ago as 1919. Public-health campaigners have long added vitamin B to flour to fight pellagra and vitamin D to milk to defeat rickets. Adding iodine to salt has also helped in the battle against goiter. The modern craze for functional foods began much more recently—and it started in Asia, not Europe. Long before Activia came Yakult, a bioactive yogurt-like drink from Japan that is now available worldwide. Encouraged by a government keen to improve public health, Japanese manufacturers have long tinkered with packaged foods to allow them to make health claims. On average, the Japanese spend twice as much per person on functional foods as Americans and nearly three times as much as Europeans. When Coca-Cola wanted to experiment with a supposedly healthy green-tea-flavoured drink, it targeted young Japanese women first.

The trend is now spreading most rapidly in America. Firms selling everything from energy drinks to breakfast foods to artificial sweeteners (Splenda now comes with added fiber) are rushing to add miracle ingredients to their wares in the hope that the supposed benefits will entice customers. A number of rival food giants have even banded together into a coalition (dubbed "smart Choices") to agree on common labeling standards for functional foods.

All this sounds impressive, but there are two factors that could yet trip things up: consumer skepticism and regulatory disapproval. There is reason to think that punters are growing wary of the notion that they can eat their way to fighting fitness. Earlier this year, Coca-Cola was sued by a consumer group over health claims made for its Vitamin Water brand. Danone also faced a similar class-action lawsuit over its yogurts. On September 18th the firm settled that case, admitting no wrongdoing but agreeing to set up a $35m fund to reimburse unhappy yogurt-eaters.

The over-exuberance of some marketers has also irked regulators. When Cheerios, a popular cereal brand owned by General Mills, tried earlier this year to claim on its box that it was "clinically proven to reduce cholesterol", America's Food and Drug Administration (FDA) decided that it had gone too far. More recently, the decision by the Smart Choices coalition to endorse sugary cereals such as Froot Loops has attracted criticism. On September 21st an American Congresswoman, Rosa DeLauro, sent an angry letter to the FDA demanding an investigation to see whether unhealthy products were being "misbranded". If the only real function behind such labels is to bolster profits, consumers and regulators will eventually see through the hype.

Questions 14–19

Do the following statements agree with the claims of the writer in Reading Passage 2?

In boxes 14–19 on your answer sheet, write

YES	*if the statement agrees with the claims of the writer*
NO	*if the statement contradicts the claims of the writer*
NOT GIVEN	*if it is impossible to say what the writer thinks about this*

14 Over the past decade, the customers prefer functional foods.

15 Multifunctional food giants think that functional foods are healthier or more nutritious.

16 People can improve the absorption of cholesterol by adding chemicals.

17 On the average, Japanese are the people who spend most on functional foods.

18 Not all customers are happy with functional foods.

19 Consumers and regulators will believe in advocates when the food giants can supply the convincing medical evidence.

Questions 20–25

Look at the following statements (Questions 20–25) and the choices below.

*Write the correct letter, **A–E**, in boxes 20–25 on your answer sheet.*

NB *You may use any letter more than once.*

20 It agrees to compensate its unhappy customers.
21 It targets at Asian market.
22 It has shorter history in making yogurt than some Japanese competitors.
23 It now adds some fiber to cater for customers.
24 It believes that the functional foods have a long history.
25 It agrees on the common labeling and advertising standards for functional foods.

A Danone
B Activia
C Coca-Cola
D Splenda
E "Smart Choices"

READING PASSAGE 3

*You should spend about 20 minutes on **Questions 26–40**, which are based on Reading Passage 3 below.*

The Research on Self-esteem

A Self-esteem is generally considered the evaluative component of the self-concept, a broader representation of the self that includes cognitive and behavioural aspects as well as evaluative or affective ones. While the construct is most often used to refer to a global sense of self-worth, narrower concepts such as self-confidence or body-esteem are used to imply a sense of self-esteem in more specific domains. It is also widely assumed that self-esteem functions as a trait, that is, it is stable across time within individuals.

B Self-esteem is an extremely popular construct within psychology, and has been related to virtually every other psychological concept or domain, including personality (e.g., shyness), behavioural (e.g., task performance), cognitive (e.g., attributional bias), and clinical concepts (e.g., anxiety and depression). While some researchers have been particularly concerned with understanding the nuances of the self-esteem construct, others have focused on the adaptive and self-protective functions of self-esteem. Self-esteem has been related both to socioeconomic status and to various aspects of health and health-related behaviours, as has a related construct, self-efficacy. Self-efficacy, a term associated with the work of Bandura, refers to an individual's sense of competence or ability in general or in particular domains.

C Low self-esteem is the universal common denominator among literally all people suffering from addictions to any and all mind altering substances such as alcohol — not genes. In the book *Alcoholism: A False Stigma: Low Self-esteem the True Disease* (1996), Candito reports, "Those who have identified themselves as 'recovered alcoholics' indicate that low self esteem is the most significant problem in their lives. Low self-esteem is the true problem and the true disease. Alcohol is but a symptom of an alcoholic's disease." Studies have found that 18-year-olds who used drugs frequently were using them as early as age seven, already more psychologically troubled than their peers. They were already anxious and unhappy, alienated from their family and peers, and overly impulsive. Low self-esteem, lack of conformity, poor academic achievement and poor parental-child relationships are also indicators of young children likely to end up using drugs.

D Candito comes to the conclusion that low self-esteem is the underlying origin of all problematic behaviours, and the true disease that plagues the world, resulting in alcohol abuse, drug abuse, and all other obsessive behaviours including criminal behaviour. This conclusion is also shared by Andrew Keegan (1987), who maintains that low self-esteem either causes or contributes to neurosis, anxiety, defensiveness, and ultimately alcohol and drug abuse. The reason why some become alcoholic while others do not is dependent upon their ability to contend with low self-esteem.

E However, many of the positive outcomes attributed to high self-esteem are not substantiated by research, according to Brown psychologist Joachim I. Krueger associate professor of psychology, and faculty from three other universities formed that conclusion after reviewing more than two decades of objective research studies on self-esteem at the invitation of the American Psychological Society. Their report appears in this month's issue of *Psychological Science* in the *Public Interest*, a supplement to *Psychological Science*. "Across most measures—school and job performance, violence and crime, and health—there were few consistent links between the level of self-esteem and the quality of outcomes," said Krueger. High self-esteem does not prevent children from smoking, drinking, taking drugs or engaging in early sex, the task force reported. If anything, high self-esteem fosters experimentation, which may increase early sexual activity or drinking. The exception was a connection between high self-esteem and reduced chances of the eating disorder bulimia in females. In adults, according to the task force, occupational success may boost self-esteem rather than the reverse. And neither high nor low self-esteem is a direct cause of violence.

F In fact, pleasant feelings and enhanced initiative were the two benefits of high self-esteem found by the task force within the body of research. High self-esteem has a strong relationship to happiness and low self-esteem is more likely than high to lead to depression under some circumstances. Those with high self-esteem were also found to exhibit more persistence at tasks. Yet the task force also noted that there are basically two types of high self-esteem-that which is realistic, and that which is out of touch with reality. People who fall into the former category accept their good qualities. Those in the latter are characterised as narcissistic, defensive or conceited individuals. In some studies, narcissism led to some negative qualities such as increased aggression in retaliation for wounded pride.

G The self-esteem movement began in California during the 1980s with the idea that many of society's problems were related to low self-esteem. The California legislature financed a task force to increase self-esteem in an effort to reduce welfare dependency, unwanted pregnancy, school failure, crime, drug addiction and other problems, with the goal of saving taxpayer dollars, according to the task force. Since then, there has been a nationwide proliferation of techniques to raise self-esteem—particularly in schools—and a proliferation of books marketed to people helping themselves. Yet, "after a quarter of a century of research, the high hopes of the self-esteem movement have not been realised, and customers of the self-help industry should not look to heightened self-esteem as a panacea," said Krueger.

Questions 26–30

Reading Passage 3 has seven paragraphs, **A–G**.

Which paragraph contains the following information?

Write the correct letter, ***A–G****, in boxes 26–30 on your answer sheet.*

26 Researchers focused their studies on varied aspects of self-esteem.

27 Some researchers related problematic drink behaviours to self-esteem.

28 The reason of violence seems not related to the quality of self-esteem.

29 Scientists have agreed with each other on the results of low self-esteem.

30 Many inventions of methods are stimulated to increase the self-esteem.

Questions 31–35

Complete the summary below.

Choose ***NO MORE THAN TWO WORDS*** *from the passage for each answer.*

Write your answers in boxes 31–35 on your answer sheet.

The conception of self-esteem includes broader sense and **31** ………………… one in certain fields. One the other hand, it is regarded as a **32** ………………… of people themselves. Some researchers focused more on the relationship between self-esteem and **33** ………………… from different domains. While other researchers claimed upon their study that most problematic behaviours originated from **34** ………………… , some researchers insisted that though **35** ………………… brought about kinds of results positively, it could not stop the youth from smoking and early sex.

Questions 36–40

Do the following statements agree with the information given in Reading Passage 3?

In boxes 36–40 on your answer sheet, write

TRUE	*if the statement agrees with the information*
FALSE	*if the statement contradicts the information*
NOT GIVEN	*if there is no information on this*

36 Some studies showed that some 18-year-olds having used drugs were troubled more from psychological depression than their same olds.

37 High self-esteem is more unlikely to incur depression under some conditions.

38 Any types of high self-esteem will have good qualities.

39 The self-esteem campaign started in California in 1996.

40 Krueger believed self-esteem would have been improved to cure all kinds of difficulties.

WRITING

WRITING TASK 1

You should spend about 20 minutes on this task.

The table below gives information on the marriage in Australia between 1970 and 2010.

Summarise the information by selecting and reporting the main features, and make comparisons where relevant.

Write at least 150 words.

Year	Religion marriage	Civil marriage	Average age of bride	Average age of bridegroom
1970	22,000	8,000	21	24
1980	44,000	12,000	25	26
1990	50,000	16,000	23	28
2000	32,000	30,000	27	30
2010	34,000	40,000	30	32

WRITING TASK 2

You should spend about 40 minutes on this task.

Write about the following topic:

Some people believe that personal happiness is directly related to economic success. Others believe there are other factors.

What do you think?

Give reasons for your answer and include any relevant examples from your own knowledge or experience.

Write at least 250 words.

SPEAKING

PART 1

The examiner asks the candidate about him/herself, his/her home, work or studies and other familiar topics.

EXAMPLE

Media

- How do you get the latest news?
- Do many people in your country listen to the radio?
- Do you like to read newspapers?

PART 2

Describe a part of the world you would like to visit.

You should say:

where it is

how and what you know about it

what you would like to do there

and explain why you would like to visit this part of the world.

You will have to talk about the topic for one to two minutes.
You have one minute to think about what you are going to say.
You can make some notes to help you if you wish.

PART 3

Discussion topics:

Tourism

Example questions:

Why do you think people want to visit other countries?
What makes some places very attractive to tourists?
Will international tourism increase or decrease in the future? Why?

The effects of tourism

Example questions:

How can tourism benefit local people and places?
Are there any drawbacks of tourism?
Does tourism help to promote international understanding? Why/Why not?
How reliable is tourism as an industry?

Test 6

LISTENING

SECTION 1 *Questions 1–10*

Questions 1–7

Complete the form below.

*Write **NO MORE THAN THREE WORDS AND/OR A NUMBER** for each answer.*

Personal Information Form

Holiday booked: 1 .... in Egypt

Customer's name: 2 ....

Current address: 18 **3** ....Street, Melford

Postcode: 4 ....

Work number: 5 ....

Insurance: 6 ....

Total tour price: 7 ....

Questions 8–10

Complete the notes below.

*Write **NO MORE THAN TWO WORDS** for each answer.*

What things does the travel agent recommend to bring?

- Suitcases
- Bags e.g. hiking bags, **8** ....
- Comfortable shoes
- **9** ....
- **10** ....
- Camera

SECTION 2 *Questions 11–20*

Questions 11–13

*Choose the correct letter, **A**, **B** or **C**.*

11 Mary Golding is

A a college lecturer.
B a student officer.
C a tour guide.

12 The trip begins on

A Wednesday 4th, April.
B Saturday 31st, March.
C Wednesday 31st, March.

13 They will travel by

A a minibus with 16 places.
B a medium-sized coach with 45 seats.
C a medium-sized bus with 54 seats.

Questions 14–18

Will you have to pay for these activities?

In boxes 14–18 on your answer sheet, write

F *if it is free*
I *if it is included in the cost of the trip*
P *if you have to pay for it yourself*

14 a boat ride ....

15 The London Eye ....

16 Big Ben ....

17 Westminster Abbey ....

18 British Museum ....

Questions 19 and 20

Complete the table below.

Write ***NO MORE THAN THREE WORDS AND/OR A NUMBER*** *for each answer.*

Spots	**Main Attractions**
British Museum	Newly constructed £100 million Great Court
Natural History Museum	**19** .... million specimens, including the Blue Whale exhibit, rainforest gallery, etc.
Globe Theatre	Rebuilt with the same **20** .... as in the 16th century

SECTION 3 *Questions 21–30*

Questions 21–25

*Choose the correct letter, **A**, **B** or **C**.*

21 What did Sarah say about the last two questions?

A She had read them both.

B There were too many questions.

C She didn't answer them.

22 John thought the exam was

A extremely easy.

B five minutes long.

C more difficult than the management exam.

23 The subject of Marketing Communication was

A particularly challenging.

B not covered on the course.

C written by Cutler.

24 What was the word limit for rebranding in the exam?

A a minimum of 200 words

B a maximum of 450 words

C exactly 300 words

25 What effect has "viral marketing" had on customers?

A They are consistently engaged by the adverts.

B They perceive the advertised products as modern.

C They have become accustomed to it.

Questions 26–30

Who did the following types of revision?

A	John
B	Sarah
C	Ken
D	All

*Write the correct letter, **A**, **B**, **C** or **D** next to questions 26–30.*

26 Reread the course notes ....

27 Used revision websites ....

28 Participated in a revision group ....

29 Completed past exam papers ....

30 Visited the learning support department ....

SECTION 4 *Questions 31–40*

Complete the notes below.

Write ***NO MORE THAN THREE WORDS AND/OR A NUMBER*** *for each answer.*

Facts About MSG

What is MSG?

- It is a commonly used **31** .... to add flavours to food.
- Long before glutamate was identified in 1908, **32** .... cooks used it to flavour food.
- Two forms: bound and **33** .... , which is .... in improving the food's flavour.

How is it used?

- It can draw out a special taste, as the **34** .... basic taste, which can be found all around the world, including the soy sauces of **35** ....
- Despite contributing a lot to salty and sour tastes, it is less effective to **36** .... foods.
- To a pound of meat or **37** .... vegetables, half a teaspoon of MSG is sufficient.

A self-limiting substance

Overuse of MSG damages the flavour.

What's the harm of MSG?

- It may kill **38** .... and lead to plenty of mild illness.
- Food industry-sponsored studies show **39** .... people are sensitive to MSG.
- Despite the potential harm, it's still widely used as an **40** .... way to enhance the flavour.

READING

READING PASSAGE 1

*You should spend about 20 minutes on **Questions 1–13**, which are based on Reading Passage 1 below.*

Worms Put New Life into Derelict Site

Poisoned soil at an old steelworks is being cleansed by thousands of worms

A Thousands of deep-burrowing earthworms are to help turn the long-derelict site of a steelworks into woodland and a renewable energy park.

B As part of a pioneering low-cost plan to reclaim the site of the former Hallside Steelworks at Cambuslang near Glasgow, worms are being used to accelerate the process of soil regeneration and to transform the land, over time, into an attractive and financially productive site.

C Hallside's closure in 1979 put an end to more than 100 years of steel production. The surrounding land had become heavily compacted and was too contaminated with heavy metals such as chromium, cadmium and led to support any kind of brick and mortar development.

D The site's 30 hectares were left abandoned until 1990, when a rescue plan put together by local landscaping and earthmoving company, HL Banks, and the regional developer, Scottish Greenbelt, was approved by local authourities.

E Now the site has been covered by a two-metre layer of partially treated sewage material which has been mixed with colliery waste. This will be converted into usable soil by about 21,000 Lumbricus terrestris (garden lobworms) and Aporrectodea longa (black headed worms) that have been let loose on the site.

F The specially raised hermaphrodites, which are self-impregnating, will spend the next five to ten years chewing their way through the topping layer to create a soil structure able to sustain long-term plant growth. Without them, the process could take up to 60 years.

G Researchers at Bell College of Technology in nearby Hamilton examined the use of earthworms in land regarding, and found that even in the hostile mixture of coal-tip waste and partially treated sewage, earthworms were able to speed up the process of soil recomposition.

H They selected different varieties of deeper burrowing earthworm species, whose bulk feeding and casting actions, as well as their ability to improve the mineral content of soil, would increase the rate of reformulation much faster than the natural processes.

I Sean Ince, of Bell's department of biology, says, "The idea is that earthworms will contribute in a cumulative way to further soil binding, and that they will aerate and add nitrogen to the soil covering the Hallside site."

J At the same time, Scottish Greenbelt has begun planting the area with 250,000 trees including willow and alder specially selected for their ability to grow on degraded land.

K These will have the dual function of extracting contaminants from the soil through their root systems, and burning or chipboard manufacture.

L By using the cash raised from wood harvesting, David Craven, director of Scottish Greenbelt, says he expects Hallside to be self-financing.

M "The first tranche of trees was planted in April and they are now over six feet tall, despite dry weather through the summer," he says. The fields are being planted on a four-year rotation basis and will be used to help us meet our costs.

N Craven says the cost of land bio-remediation—the labour intensive process of removing soil for chemical and bacterial cleansing—could have been more than £30m.

O At Bell College, Ince says "There's a whole legacy of toxic soil contamination going back many years. There is physical degradation of the soil as well as contamination from metals, including lead, chromium and arsenic."

P Sampling of the soil at regular intervals over the next few years will give an indication of the level of contaminants. Within less than 20 years the land could be re-integrated into the community.

Q Hopes of a successful outcome at Hallside have paved the way for similar regeneration plans for the nearby Gartoosh steelworks and at Glengarnock in Ayrshire.

Questions 1–5

Choose the correct letter, ***A****,* ***B****,* ***C*** *or* ***D****.*

Write the correct letter in boxes 1–5 on your answer sheet.

1 The Hallside site has been

A turned into a steelworks from a woodland and an energy park.
B in use as an energy park.
C disused for a long period of time.
D out of use for a short period of time.

2 After more than one hundred years of steel production at Hallside,

A the land could not be used for anything.
B it was impossible to use the land to build on.
C the land could then be built on.
D the land could be used for any purpose.

3 The plan to reclaim Hallside was proposed by

A Scottish Greenbelt and the regional developer.
B local authorities and Scottish Greenbelt.
C a local landscaping company and authorities.
D Scottish Greenbelt and HL Banks.

4 In the conversion of the soil at the Hallside site,

A two types of worms are being used.
B three types of worms are being used.
C many types of worms are being used.
D thousands of different types of worms are being used.

5 The soil regeneration at the Hallside site will take

A 60 years.
B between 5 and 10 years.
C over 60 years.
D less than five years.

Questions 6–9

Complete the sentences below.

Choose ***NO MORE THAN THREE WORDS*** *from the passage for each answer.*

Write your answers in boxes 6–9 on your answer sheet.

6 In the research of Bell College, worms were used to quicken ....

7 The Bell researchers chose worms that would convert contaminated soil more rapidly than the ....

8 The soil at Hallside will be enriched by adding air and ....

9 Contaminants will be removed from the soil by ....

Questions 10–13

Choose ***ONE*** *phrase from the list of phrases,* ***A–H****, below to complete each of the following sentences 10–13.*

Write the appropriate letters in boxes 10–13 on your answer sheet.

10 The Hallside site is expected to ....

11 Bio-remediation at Hallside could ....

12 Within 20 years, the land at Hallside could ....

13 Similar regeneration plans may ....

A	be contaminated
B	be in use again by the community
C	work everywhere
D	take place at other steelworks
E	have cost millions of pounds
F	have been proved intensive
G	pay for itself
H	cost more than bio-remediation

Test 6

READING PASSAGE 2

*You should spend about 20 minutes on **Questions 14–26**, which are based on Reading Passage 2 below.*

A If it weren't for nicotine, people wouldn't smoke tobacco. Why? Because of the more than 4,000 chemicals in tobacco smoke, nicotine is the primary one that acts on the brain, altering people's moods, appetites and alertness in ways they find pleasant and beneficial. Unfortunately, as it is widely known, nicotine has a dark side: it is highly addictive. Once smokers become hooked on it, they must get their fix of it regularly, sometimes several dozen times a day. Cigarette smoke contains 43 known carcinogens, which means that long-term smoking can amount to a death sentence. In the US alone, 420,000 Americans die every year from tobacco-related illnesses.

B Breaking nicotine addiction is not easy. Each year, nearly 35 million people make a concerted effort to quit smoking. Sadly, less than 7 percent succeed in abstaining for more than a year; most start smoking again within days. So what is nicotine and how does it insinuate itself into the smoker's brain and very being?

C The nicotine found in tobacco is a potent drug and smokers, and even some scientists, say it offers certain benefits. One is enhancing performance. One study found that non-smokers given doses of nicotine typed about 5 percent faster than they did without it. To greater or lesser degrees, users also say nicotine helps them to maintain concentration, reduce anxiety, relieve pain, and even dampen their appetites (thus helping in weight control). Unfortunately, nicotine can also produce deleterious effects beyond addiction. At high doses, as are achieved from tobacco products, it can cause high blood pressure, distress in the respiratory and gastrointestinal systems and an increase in susceptibility to seizures and hypothermia.

D First isolated as a compound in 1828, in its pure form nicotine is a clear liquid that turns brown when burned and smells like tobacco when exposed to air. It is found in several species of plants, including tobacco and, perhaps surprisingly, in tomatoes, potatoes, and eggplant (though in extremely low quantifies that are pharmacologically insignificant for humans).

E As simple as it looks, the cigarette is highly engineered nicotine delivery device. For instance, when tobacco researchers found that much of the nicotine in a cigarette wasn't released when burned but rather remained chemically bound within the tobacco leaf, they began adding substances such as ammonia to cigarette tobacco to release more nicotine. Ammonia helps keep nicotine in its basic form, which is more readily vapourised by the intense heat of the burning cigarette than the acidic form. Most cigarettes for sale in the US today contain 10 milligrams or more of nicotine. By inhaling smoke from a lighted cigarette, the average smoker takes 1 or 2 milligrams of vapourised nicotine per cigarette.

F Today we know that only a miniscule amount of nicotine is needed to fuel addiction. Research shows that manufacturers would have to cut nicotine levels in a typical cigarette by 95% to forestall its power to addict. When a smoker puffs on a lighted cigarette, smoke, including vapourised nicotine, is drawn into the mouth. The skin and lining of the mouth immediately absorb some nicotine, but the remainder flows straight down into the lungs, where it easily diffuses into the blood vessels lining the lung walls. The blood vessels carry the nicotine to the heart, which then pumps it directly to the brain. While most of the effects a smoker seeks occur in the brain, the heart takes a hit as well. Studies have shown that a smoker's first cigarette of the day can increase his or her heart rate by 10 to 20 beats a minute. Scientists have found that a smoked substance reaches the brain more quickly than one swallowed, snorted (such as cocaine powder) or even injected. Indeed, a nicotine molecule that hides in smoke will reach the brain within 10 seconds. The nicotine travels through blood vessels, which branch out into capillaries within the brain. Capillaries normally carry nutrients but they readily accommodate nicotine molecules as well. Once inside the brain, nicotine, like most addictive drugs, triggers the release of chemicals associated with euphoria and pleasure.

G Just as it moves rapidly from the lungs into the bloodstream, nicotine also easily diffuses through capillary walls. It then migrates to the spaces surrounding neurons-ganglion cells that transmit nerve impulses throughout the nervous system. These impulses are the basis for our thoughts, feelings, and moods. To transmit nerve impulses to its neighbour, a neurone releases chemical messengers known as neurotransmitters. Like nicotine molecules, the neurotransmitters drift into the so-called synaptic space between neurones, ready to latch onto the receiving neurone and thus deliver a chemical "message" that triggers an electrical impulse.

H The neurotransmitters bind onto receptors on the surface of the recipient neurone. This opens channels in the cell surface through which enter ions, or charged atoms, of sodium. This generates a current across the membrane of the receiving cell, which completes delivery of the "message". An accomplished mimic, nicotine competes with the neurotransmitters to bind to the receptors. It wins and, like the vanquished chemical, opens ion channels that let sodium ions into the cell. However, there's a lot more nicotine around than the original transmitter, so a much larger current spreads across the membrane. This bigger current causes increased electrical impulses to travel along certain neurones. With repeated smoking, the neurones adapt to this increased electrical activity, and the smoker becomes dependent on the nicotine.

Questions 14–20

Do the following statements agree with the claims of the writer in Reading Passage 2?

In boxes 14–20 on your answer sheet, write:

YES	*if the statement agrees with the claims of the writer*
NO	*if the statement contradicts the claims of the writer*
NOT GIVEN	*if it is impossible to say what the writer thinks about this*

14 Although nicotine is probably the well-known chemical in cigarettes, it is not necessarily the one that changes the psyche of the smoker when cigarettes are smoked.

15 In spite of the difficulties, more than 35 million people a year give up smoking.

16 It has been shown that nicotine in cigarettes can improve people's abilities to perform some actions more quickly.

17 Added ammonia in cigarettes allows smokers to inhale more nicotine.

18 Snorted substances reach the brain faster than injected substances.

19 Nicotine dilates the blood vessels that carry it around the body.

20 Nicotine molecules allow greater electrical charges to pass between neurones.

Questions 21–25

Answer the questions below.

Choose ***NO MORE THAN THREE WORDS AND/OR A NUMBER*** *from the passage for each answer.*

Write your answers in boxes 21–25 on your answer sheet.

21 What is the natural colour of nicotine?

22 By how much would cigarette companies have to cut the nicotine content in cigarettes to prevent them from being addictive?

23 Name ONE thing that first takes nicotine into a smoker's body.

24 By how many beats a minute can the smoker's first cigarette of the day raise his heart rate?

25 What type of cell in the human body encloses neurones?

Question 26

Choose the most suitable title for Reading Passage 2.

Write your answer in box 26 on your answer sheet.

26 ....

A How to Quit Smoking
B The Dangers of Smoking
C Cell Biology
D Why Smoking Is Addictive
E Nicotine Is a Poison

READING PASSAGE 3

*You should spend about 20 minutes on **Questions 27–40**, which are based on Reading Passage 3 below.*

Cleaning up the Thames

A The River Thames, which was biologically "dead" as recently as the 1960s, is now the cleanest metropolitan river in the world, according to the Thames Water Company. The company says that thanks to major investment in better sewage treatment in London and the Thames Valley, the river that flows through the United Kingdom capital and the Thames Estuary into the North Sea is cleaner now than it has been for 130 years. The Fisheries Department, who is responsible for monitoring fish levels in the River Thames, has reported that the river has again become the home to 115 species of fish including sea bass, flounder, salmon, smelt, and shad. Recently, a porpoise was spotted cavorting in the river near central London.

B But things were not always so rosy. In the 1950s, sewer outflows and industrial effluent had killed the river. It was starved of oxygen and could no longer support aquatic life. Until the early 1970s, if you fell into the Thames you would have had to be rushed to hospital to get your stomach pumped. A clean-up operation began in the 1960s. Several Parliamentary Committees and Royal Commissions were set up, and, over time, legislation has been introduced that puts the onus on polluters—effluent-producing premises and businesses—to dispose of waste responsibly. In 1964 the Greater London Council (GLC) began work on greatly enlarged sewage works, which were completed in 1974.

C The Thames clean up is not over though. It is still going on, and it involves many disparate arms of government and a wide range of non-government stakeholder groups, all representing a necessary aspect of the task. In London's case, the urban and non-urban London boroughs that flank the river's course each has its own reasons for keeping "their" river nice. And if their own reasons do not hold out a sufficiently attractive carrot, the government also wields a compelling stick. The *2000 Local Government Act* requires each local borough to "prepare a community strategy for promoting or improving the economic, social and environmental well-being of their area". And if your area includes a stretch of river, that means a sustainable river development strategy.

D Further legislation aimed at improving and sustaining the river's viability has been proposed. There is now legislation that protects the River Thames, either specifically or as part of a general environmental clause, in *the Local Government Act, the London Acts*, and the law that created the post of the mayor of London. And these are only the tip of an iceberg that includes industrial, public health and environmental protection regulations. The result is a wide range of bodies officially charged, in one way or another, with maintaining the Thames as a public amenity. For example, Transport for London—the agency responsible for transport in the capital—plays a role in regulating river use and river users. They now are responsible for controlling the effluents and rubbish coming from

Test 6

craft using the Thames. This is done by officers on official vessels regularly inspecting fling craft and doing spot checks. Another example is how Thames Water (TW) has now been charged to reduce the amount of litter that finds its way into the tidal river and its tributaries. TW's environment and quality manager, Dr Peter Spillett, said: "This project will build on our investment which has dramatically improved the water quality of the river. London should not be spoiled by litter which belongs in the bin not the river." Thousands of tons of rubbish end up in the river each year, from badly stored waste, people throwing litter off boats, and rubbish in the street being blown or washed into the river. Once litter hits the water it becomes too heavy to be blown away again and therefore the rivers act as a sink in the system. While the Port of London already collects up to 3,000 tons of solid waste from the tideway every year, Thames Water now plans to introduce a new device to capture more rubbish floating down the river. It consists of a huge cage that sits in the flow of water and gathers the passing rubbish. Moored just offshore in front of the Royal Naval College at Greenwich, south-east London, the device is expected to capture up to 20 tons of floating litter each year. If washed out to sea, this rubbish can kill marine mammals, fish and birds. This machine, known as the Rubbish Muncher, is hoped to be the first of many, as the TW is now looking for sponsors to pay for more cages elsewhere along the Thames.

E Monitoring of the cleanliness of the River Thames in the past was the responsibility of a welter of agencies—British Waterways, Port of London Authourity, the Environment Agency, the Health and Safety Commission, Thames Water—as well as academic departments and national and local environment groups. If something was not right someone was bound to call foul and hold somebody to account, whether it was the local authourity, an individual polluter or any of the many public and private sector bodies that bore a share of the responsibility for maintaining the River Thames as a public amenity. Although they will all still have their part to play, there is now a central department in the Environment Agency, which has the remit of monitoring the Thames. This centralisation of accountability will, it is hoped, lead to more efficient control and enforcement.

Questions 27–32

Look at the following actions and the names of the agencies (Questions 27–32) below.

Match each action with the agency responsible for doing it.

*Write the appropriate letters, **A–G**, in boxes 27–32 on your answer sheet.*

Actions to Clean up the River Thames

A Operating the Rubbish Muncher
B Creating community strategies
C Monitoring the cleanliness of the River Thames
D Monitoring fish levels
E Collecting solid waste from the tideway
F Creating enlarged sewage works
G Controlling the River Thames' traffic

Example	***Answer***
The Fisheries Department	D

27 The Environment Agency ....

28 Transport for London ....

29 The Greater London Council ....

30 Thames Water ....

31 Port of London ....

32 Local Boroughs ....

Questions 33–40

Do the following statements agree with the claims of the writer in Reading Passage 3?

In boxes 33–40 on your answer sheet, write

YES	*if the statement agrees with the claims of the writer*
NO	*if the statement contradicts the claims of the writer*
NOT GIVEN	*if it is impossible to say what the writer thinks about this*

33 The Thames is now cleaner than it was in 1900.

34 Swimming in the Thames now poses no health hazards.

35 It is now mainly the responsibility of those who pollute the Thames to clean their waste up.

36 All local London boroughs are now partly responsible for keeping the Thames clean.

37 Transport for London now employs a type of River Police to enforce control of their regulations.

38 Rubbish Munchers are now situated at various locations on the Thames.

39 Previously no one department had overall responsibility or control for monitoring the cleanliness of the Thames.

40 British Waterways will no longer have any part in keeping the Thames clean.

WRITING

WRITING TASK 1

You should spend about 20 minutes on this task.

The diagrams below show the development of the village of Kelsbey between 1700 and 2000.

Summarize the information by selecting and reporting the main features, and make comparisons where relevant.

Write at least 150 words.

1700

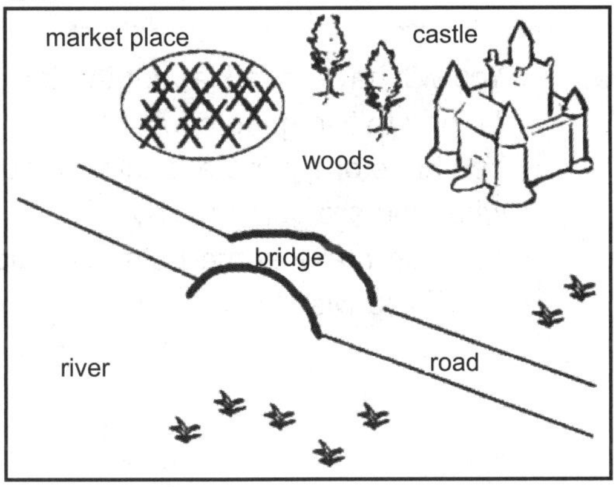

2000

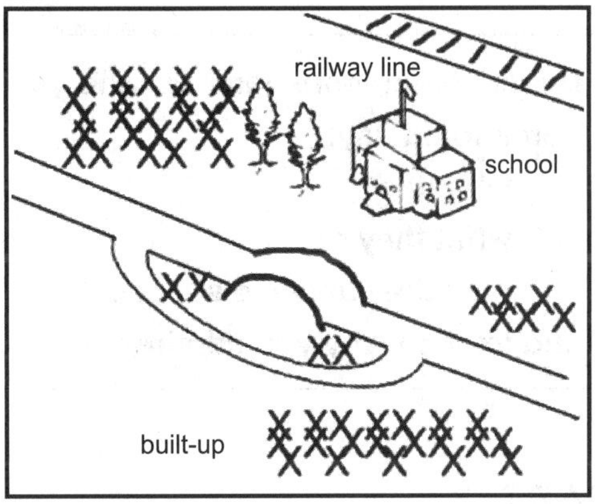

WRITING TASK 2

You should spend about 40 minutes on this task.

Write about the following topic:

Nowadays, nurseries and kindergartens take care of children from an early age, so women can return to their work and children can get used to the society early.

Is this a good thing? What's your opinion?

Give reasons for your answer and include any relevant examples from your own knowledge or experience.

Write at least 250 words.

SPEAKING

PART 1

The examiner asks the candidate about him/herself, his/her home, work or studies and other familiar topics.

EXAMPLE

Places of Interest

- Which places in your city or province would you suggest a tourist visit?
- Why are they significant?
- Do you often visit such places?

PART 2

Describe someone famous who you admire. **You should say:** **who it is** **what they do** **how they became successful** **and explain why you admire them.**

You will have to talk about the topic for one to two minutes.
You have one minute to think about what you are going to say.
You can make some notes to help you if you wish.

PART 3

Discussion topics:

Fame

Example questions:

Can you evaluate the pros and cons of being famous?
Can you comment on whether the media should be allowed to report on the private lives of celebrities?
Can you outline the responsibilities celebrities have to our society?

Success

Example questions:

Talk about which element is more important for success: luck or hard work?
Define how success is measured.
How can success change a person?

Test 7

LISTENING

SECTION 1 *Questions 1–10*

Complete the notes below.

*Write **ONE WORD AND/OR A NUMBER** for each answer.*

Volunteering in the USA

Summer camp programmes:

- for non-USA residents only
- working directly with children or working as support staff (must be a full time **1** ....)
- May/June–August
- work for a minimum of **2** ....

Participants must:

- like children
- be outgoing, flexible and **3** ....
- be at least **4** .... of age

Benefits for participants:

- work in a **5** .... environment
- become familiar with American **6** ....
- get free meals and accommodation
- make international **7** ....
- enjoy up to 30 days' travel in the USA with free **8** ....
- enhances their **9** ....

Application process:

- complete an online form
- attend an interview
- apply for a **10** ....
- attend an orientation programme

SECTION 2 *Questions 11–20*

Questions 11–14

Label the map below.

*Choose **FOUR** answers from the box and write the correct letter, **A–G**, next to questions 11–14.*

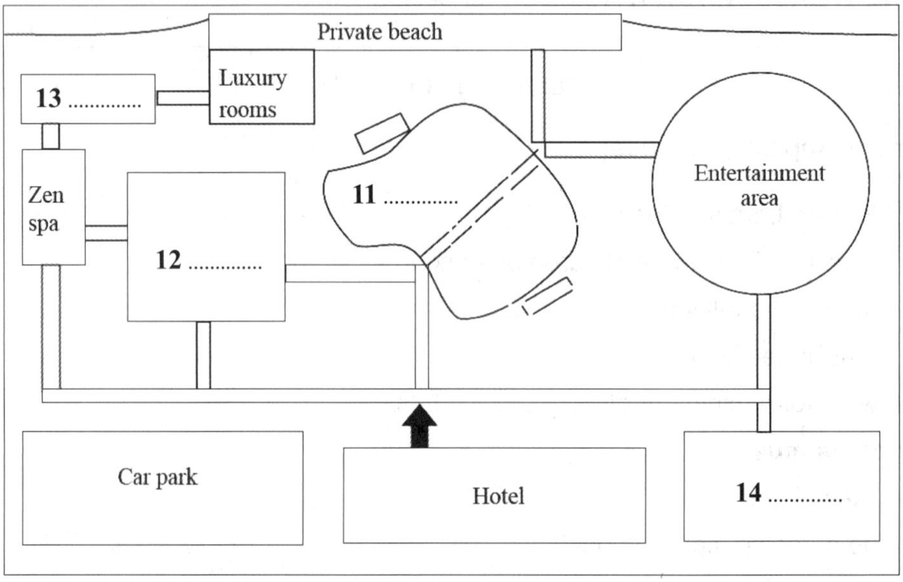

A	Café restaurant
B	Swimming pool
C	Reception
D	Family rooms
E	Bar
F	Sports centre
G	Gym

11 ....

12 ....

13 ....

14 ....

Questions 15 and 16

*Choose **TWO** letters from **A–E**.*

Which **TWO** activities are offered at the aquarium?

A Fishing
B Children's shows
C Swimming with the fish
D Feeding the animals
E Afternoon tea

Questions 17–20

Complete the table below.

*Write **NO MORE THAN TWO WORDS AND/OR A NUMBER** for each answer.*

Day	Departure time	Attraction	Notes
Monday	8am	land's end	**17** ....
Tuesday	7.30am	**18**	includes lunch
Wednesday	**19**	train to Bowman	famous for cider
Friday	1.35pm	**20**	sells Cornish biscuits

SECTION 3 *Questions 21–30*

Complete the form below.

Write ***NO MORE THAN THREE WORDS AND/OR A NUMBER*** *for each answer.*

Client Survey Form		
Membership number: 21 .... **Start date: 22** .... **Length of membership:** six months		
Type of class	**Instructors score: 1–5 (5 being the best)**	**Suggestions for improvement**
Yoga	**23**	The club could run **24** .... in the evenings.
Pilates	n/a	n/a
Aerobics	4	More opportunities for **25** ....
Facilities	**Rated: excellent, good, average, poor**	**Suggestions for improvement**
Swimming pool	**26**	Could be repainted
Changing rooms	**27**	Make complementary products such as **28** .... and body creams available to clients.

Relaxation facilities	**Frequency of use**	**Rated: excellent, good, average, poor**	**Suggestions for improvement**
Café	**29**	Average	Reduce waiting time and **30** .... selection

SECTION 4 *Questions 31–40*

Questions 31–35

*Choose the correct letter **A**, **B** or **C**.*

31 The purpose of the Orientation is to

A give an overview of procedures and allow staff to become familiar with each other.

B familiarise staff with the centre's procedures and Health and Safety policies.

C ensure staff are informed of the policies and procedures of the Learning Support Centre.

32 The Learning Support Centre

A was the last department to be established and focuses on enhancing support services for students.

B focuses on assisting non-native English speakers with language issues they face in their studies.

C is one of the more recent additions to literacy and numeracy services at the polytechnic.

33 Staff cannot generally plan lessons in advance

A as students are not required to make an appointment.

B as students may change their minds at what they wish to discuss.

C because many clients are coming for the first time.

34 The Learning Support Centre encourages limited and short-term use by individual students as

A the staff's workload is very high.

B independence indicates success.

C students only visit with specific questions.

35 Staff are required to be flexible as

A they need a broad knowledge of mathematics, business, science and English language.

B they may need to work outside of usual working hours.

C they may need to advise in areas outside of their field.

Questions 36–40

Which departments of the polytechnic help students in the following ways?

A the library

B the Learning Support Centre

C the department the student is studying their course under

D the Academic Office

Write the correct letter ***A, B, C*** *or* ***D*** *next to questions 36–40.*

36 Requests for remarking of submitted work

37 Requests for recognition of prior learning

38 Orientation of library resources

39 Ordering of additional academic resources

40 Arrangement of Student ID cards

READING

READING PASSAGE 1

*You should spend about 20 minutes on **Questions 1–12**, which are based on Reading Passage 1 below.*

A Science proceeds by trial and error. The successes are trumpeted. The errors are often regarded with embarrassment by subsequent generations, and locked away in attic rooms of the subject's mansion like mad relatives in a Victorian novel. Usually, they stay there. Craniology, phrenology and eugenics, once-respectable fields of endeavour that are now regarded with a shudder, may shriek from time to time, but few sane people pay attention to them. One, however, has escaped recently, and is trying to rehabilitate itself. For years physiognomy—the idea that a person's face is a reflection of his character—was sneered at. Now, it is making a comeback.

B Appearances certainly count. Women, for instance, judge men by their faces. Testosterone levels are reflected in the face, and who is seen as a one-night stand and who as a potential husband depends in part on this physical feature. Similarly, a male face betrays the owner's underlying aggressiveness and even his business acumen. Facial beauty in either sex is also associated with higher incomes. The latest research, though, cuts to the moral quick. For Jefferson Duarte of Rice University in Houston, Texas, and his colleagues are suggesting that one of a person's most telling moral features, his creditworthiness, can also be seen in his face.

C Dr Duarte's research was enabled by the Internet. Once, if you wanted to borrow money, you had either to visit a bank or to tap a rich friend or relative. Now it is possible to do business directly with a stranger, using a peer-to-peer lending site. The needy advertise themselves, and how much they want. Those flush with cash assess potential borrowers and decide who to lend to, and at what rate of interest.

D The borrowers themselves have to disclose their financial positions, credit histories, jobs and education. Often, though this is not required, they also post photographs of themselves. That means it might be possible to assess the effects of appearance on the outcome. And the process is an open auction, which means that all offers, acceptances and rejections are in the public domain.

E For his research, Dr Duarte chose a site called *Prosper.com*. His intention was twofold: to see if physiognomy-based prejudices about creditworthiness existed and, if they did, whether they were justified. To do so he used another peer-to-peer website to subcontract the job of assessing creditworthiness to a number of ordinary people. The site in question (which is run by Amazon) is called Mechanical Turk. In this case the people it matches are those who have a task that needs doing, and those willing to perform it.

F The team recruited 25 Mechanical Turk workers and asked them to assess pictures of potential borrowers that had been posted on *Prosper.com*. In particular, they were asked to rate, on a scale of one to five, how trustworthy these people looked, and to estimate the percentage probability that each individual would repay a $100 loan. They were also asked to make several other assessments, such as the individual's sex, race, age, attractiveness and obesity. The 25 results for each photograph were then averaged and analysed.

G The researchers looked at 6,821 loan applications, 733 of which were successful. Their first finding was that the assessments of trustworthiness, and of likelihood to repay a loan, that were made by Mechanical Turk workers did indeed correlate with potential borrowers' credit ratings based on their credit history. That continued to be so when the other variables, from beauty to race to obesity, were controlled for statistically. Shifty physiognomy, it seems, is independent of these things.

H That shiftiness was also recognised by those whose money was actually at stake. People flagged as untrustworthy by the Mechanical Turks were less likely than others to be offered a loan at all. To have the same chance of getting one as those deemed most trustworthy they were required to pay an interest rate that was, on average, 1.82 percentage points higher, even when the effects of historical creditworthiness were statistically eliminated.

I For trustworthiness, then, physiognomy works. Unfortunately, Dr Duarte's method was not designed to find out which features label someone as trustworthy. But credit-rating agencies are no doubt working on that question even now.

Questions 1–8

Reading Passage 1 has nine paragraphs, **A–I**.

Which paragraph contains the following information?

*Write the correct letter, **A–I**, in boxes 1–8 on your answer sheet.*

1 The researchers adopted a large scale of samples.

2 One web-site offers the opportunities of borrowing money from strangers.

3 The process of loaning can be seen in public field.

4 The factors which contribute to trustworthiness are still unknown.

5 The participants were asked to forecast the creditworthiness of the potential borrowers.

6 In order to get the loan, the borrowers who seemed untrustworthy have to pay for higher interest rates.

7 Women can decide whether to have a further relationship with men according to appearance.

8 The researcher wanted to find out whether the prejudice based on physiognomy could be reasonable.

Questions 9–11

*Choose the correct letter, **A**, **B**, **C** or **D**.*

Write the correct letter in boxes 9–11 on your answer sheet.

9 Why does the authour mention the mad relatives in a Victorian novel?

A To compare the different ways we treat our relatives in the past and today.

B To illustrate the way we treat our errors.

C To show our progress in regarding errors.

D To reveal the significance of success.

10 What did people think of physiognomy in the past?

A People didn't take it seriously.

B People didn't know its existence.

C People used to be convinced of it.

D People used to be hostile to it.

11 What do Jefferson Duarte and his colleagues suggest?

A It can be seen whether a person's appearance is the same with his heart.

B It can be seen whether a person tells a lie.

C It can be seen whether a person is worth trusting.

D It can be seen whether a person is aggressive.

Question 12

*Choose the correct letter, **A**, **B**, **C** or **D**.*

Write the correct letter in box 12 on your answer sheet.

Which is the most suitable title for the passage?

A About Face: Creditworthiness Can Be Seen in the Face

B About Face: Self-Discipline Can Be Seen from Appearances

C About Face: Marital Status Can Be Seen in the Face

D About Face: Happiness Can Be Seen from Appearances

READING PASSAGE 2

*You should spend about 20 minutes on **Questions 13–25**, which are based on Reading Passage 2 below.*

A Vitelio Menza has been dependent on coffee in Colombia all his life. Now at 43 he is still unable to finish building his house due to lack of funds and is struggling to keep his family together. The fortunes of Vitelio, his wife Maria Enith and their four children have fluctuated dramatically along with the price of coffee.

B Over the years the family has suffered illness brought by malnutrition. In other parts of the same area, some families have turned to growing drugs in order to survive; higher prices are paid for coca leaf (the raw material for cocaine). The Menzas have stayed loyal to the coffee crop but not without great personal sacrifices.

C Coffee is grown in 80 countries in a band around the equator and provides a living for nearly 10 million farmers. Altogether, more than 25 million people worldwide depend on growing, processing, trading and retailing coffee for their livelihood.

D Coffee is the second most valuable commodity after oil. Not surprisingly, it is the most valuable agricultural commodity in world trade. Its total value — $ 8,000 million per year — is twice the value of exports of tea and cocoa put together. But the journey from the Menzas' farm in Colombia to the supermarket shelf is a long and tortuous one with a succession of people taking their cut along the way.

E From tree to supermarket shelf it has been estimated the Menzas' coffee beans can change hands as many as 150 times, whilst the Menzas, like millions of other coffee growers, retain only a tiny share of the price consumers pay for the crop.

F Between 1989 and 1993 there was a 50% reduction in the world market price of coffee. An examination of the price paid to a farmer like Menza and the cost to a shopper in the supermarket reveals that both have lost out while many of the players in between have still managed to make gains.

G When the world price fell by 50% during 1989, farmers suffered an immediate fall in their incomes yet there was no noticeable reduction in the supermarket price of coffee. Retail prices remained stable for four more years before there was a fall of 20% in 1993. Yet when the market picked up in 1994 and the market price of coffee rose by 50%, the retail price rose immediately and sustained its price even when the market fell again the following year.

H For the farmers, this meant that the price of coffee had dropped below the cost of producing it for several years in a row. This had a devastating impact on their already precarious existence, forcing some farmers to abandon their land and go in search of work in the cities. Apart from the consequences for already overcrowded cities, this created a vicious circle in which the lack of labour for crop maintenance reduced the quality and value of the coffee, further reducing the price.

I But for small farmers the world price is only one of the factors undermining their ability to make a decent living. Indeed, if they were able to get a reasonable share of this price, they would be pleased. Without the means to process or transport their crop to market, limited knowledge of the frequently changing world price and a debt driven necessity to sell their coffee the moment it is ripe (when prices are lowest), small independent farmers find themselves in a weak negotiating position. They are prey to local dealers who buy the coffee and sell it on to international markets. With only one major harvest a year, farmers are desperate for cash by the time their crop is ripe and are keen to sell at whatever price they can get. Not surprisingly, local dealers are quick to exploit this.

J The farmers' need for a quick sale is a symptom of their inability to get loans at a fair rate from banks, pushing them into the arms of loan sharks to pay for fertilisers, harvest labour and basic living costs prior to harvest. Many farmers have got together to set up cooperative marketing ventures which enable them to bypass the middlemen. All too often, however, even the coop cannot get finance to buy the crop, and members still sell to local traders for cash, rather than wait for a better price. Evidence of low and declining living standards is clear. The Fairtrade Foundation's research shows that reduced spending on housing, children's education, health and food.

Questions 13–19

Do the following statements agree with the claims of the writer in Reading Passage 2?

In boxes 13–19 on your answer sheet, write:

YES	*if the statement agrees with the claims of the writer*
NO	*if the statement contradicts the claims of the writer*
NOT GIVEN	*if it is impossible to say what the writer thinks about this*

13 The Menzas have tried growing coca leaf instead of coffee.

14 In trade, only oil is more important than coffee.

15 The Menzas receive 50% of the supermarket price for their coffee.

16 The production of cocoa is less exploitative than coffee.

17 In 1989 both world and supermarket prices dropped.

18 Setting up a cooperative is always an effective solution for farmers.

19 The farmers have less and less money to spend on their families.

Questions 20–24

Complete the sentences below.

Choose ***NO MORE THAN TWO WORDS*** *from the passage for each answer.*

Write your answers in boxes 20–24 on your answer sheet

20 Coffee is worth .... as much value as tea and cocoa.

21 Coffee farmers only keep a .... of the final retail value.

22 If there is only one coffee crop each year, farmers have very little .... by the time it is ready to harvest.

23 Although farmers suffered a lot from the world price fall in 1989, the supermarket price of coffee didn't experience a .... drop.

24 It is impossible for farmers to borrow money at a ....

Question 25

25 What is the purpose of the passage on Fairtrade?

A To advise readers against buying non-Fairtrade coffee.

B To explain how coffee farmers like the Menzas are exploited by international markets.

C To advise coffee farmers like the Menzas how to make a good living.

D To encourage readers to protest about the current situation.

READING PASSAGE 3

*You should spend about 20 minutes on **Questions 26–40**, which are based on Reading Passage 3 below.*

Software Aims to Put Your Life on a Disk

A Engineers are working on software to load every photo you take, every letter you write—in fact your every memory and experience—into a surrogate brain that never forgets anything, New Scientist can reveal.

B It is part of a curious venture dubbed the MyLifeBits project, in which engineers at Microsoft's Media Presence lab in San Francisco are aiming to build multimedia databases that chronicle people's life events and make them searchable. "Imagine being able to run a Google-like search on your life," says Gordon Bell, one of the developers.

C The motivation? Microsoft argues that our memories often deceive us: experiences get exaggerated, we muddle the timing of events and simply forget stuff. Much better, says the firm, to junk such unreliable interpretations and instead build a faithful memory on that most reliable of entities, the PC.

D Bell and his colleagues developed MyLifeBits as a surrogate brain to solve what they call the "giant shoebox problem". "In a giant shoebox full of photos, it's hard to find what you are looking for," says Microsoft's Jim Gemmell. Add to this the reels of home movies, videotapes, bundles of letters and documents we file away, and remembering what we have, let alone finding it, becomes a major headache.

E Before he speaks at December's Association for Computing Machinery Multimedia Conference in Juan Les Pins, France, Bell is going to log everything he possibly can onto his MyLifeBits database.

F Apart from official documents like his passport, he is hoping to post everything from letters and photos, to home videos and work documents. All his email is automatically saved on the system, as is anything he reads or buys online. He has also started recording phone conversations and meetings to store as audio files. The privacy and corporate security risks are clear.

G Of course the system takes up a huge amount of memory. But Bell calculates that within five years, a 1,000-gigabyte hard drive will cost less than $300 and that is enough to store four hours of video every day for a year. Each media file saved in MyLifeBits can be tagged with a written or spoken commentary and linked to other files. Spoken annotations are also converted into text, so the speech is searchable, too.

H To recall a period in his past, Bell just types in the dates he is interested in. MyLifeBits then calls up a timeline of phone and email conversations, things he has read on the Web and any images he recorded.

I The system can also be used to build narratives involving other people, events or places. Searching for a friend's name would bring together a chronological set of files describing when you both did things together, for instance.

J Although MyLifeBits is essentially a large database, it may gradually become a repository for many of our experiences. Now that many mobile devices contain photomessaging cameras, you could save everyday events onto the system. "Users will eventually be able to keep every document they read, every picture they view, all the audio they hear and a good portion of what they see," says Gemmell. Bell believes that for some people, especially those with memory problems, MyLifeBits will become a surrogate memory that is able to recall past experiences in a way not possible with the familiar but disparate records like photo albums and scrapbooks. "You'll begin to rely on it more and more," he believes.

K A really accuate searchable store of events could also help us preserve our experiences more vividly for posterity. Doug de Groot, who works on computer generated human beings called avatars and other types of digital "life" at Lelden University in the Netherlands, says Bell's system could eventually form the basis for "meet the ancestor" style educational tools, where people will quiz their ancestors on what happened in their lifetimes.

L A system like MyLifeBits was first suggested in 1945, when presidential technology adviser Vannevar Bush hatched the then farsighted idea of an infinite personal archive based on the emerging digital computer. His ideas also inspired the Internet archive website.

Questions 26–30

Classify the following opinions as expressed by:

A	Doug de Groot
B	Gordon Bell
C	Jim Gemmell
D	Vannevar Bush

26 In the future we will be able to save most of what we see and hear.

27 MyLifeBits will be especially helpful for people whose memories are not very good.

28 Conventional ways of keeping photos are not good because the memories aren't all kept in one place.

29 Our descendants will be able to learn about our lives through systems like MyLifeBits.

30 The price of storing information will go down in the near future.

Questions 31–35

Complete the summary below.

*Choose **NO MORE THAN THREE WORDS** from the Reading Passage 3.*

Write your answers in boxes 31–35 on your answer sheet.

Bell is saving **31** .... onto his MyLifeBits database: letters, photos, home videos, work documents, emails and his online shopping or whatever he **32** .... online and on audio he is saving **33** .... and meetings.

Bell can remember what happened at a particular time in his life by keying in the **34** .... Or he could look for **35** .... and find all the files that tell him what they did together.

Questions 36–38

*Choose **THREE** letters, **A–G**.*

Write the correct letters in boxes 36–38 on your answer sheet.

Which **THREE** of the following are problems with conventional ways of storing our memories?

A We forget when things happened.

B It can be difficult to find a suitable shoebox to keep things in.

C It can be difficult to find where we have stored our photo, letters, etc.

D We forget what records of our past we have.

E We accidentally throw away important documents.

F We tend to keep too much stuff.

G We tend to clear all the documents.

Questions 39 and 40

*Choose **TWO** letters, **A–E**.*

Write the correct letters in boxes 39 and 40 on your answer sheet.

Which **TWO** of the following are possible disadvantages of the MyLifeBits project?

A It can be unreliable.

B It may not be very secure.

C It can be very time consuming.

D It requires a very large amount of computer memory.

E It is very complicated to use.

WRITING

WRITING TASK 1

You should spend about 20 minutes on this task.

> ***The graph and bar chart below show the average monthly rainfall and temperature for one region of East Africa.***
>
> ***Summarise the information by selecting and reporting the main features, and making comparisons where relevant.***

Write at least 150 words.

Average Monthly Rainfall and Temperatures

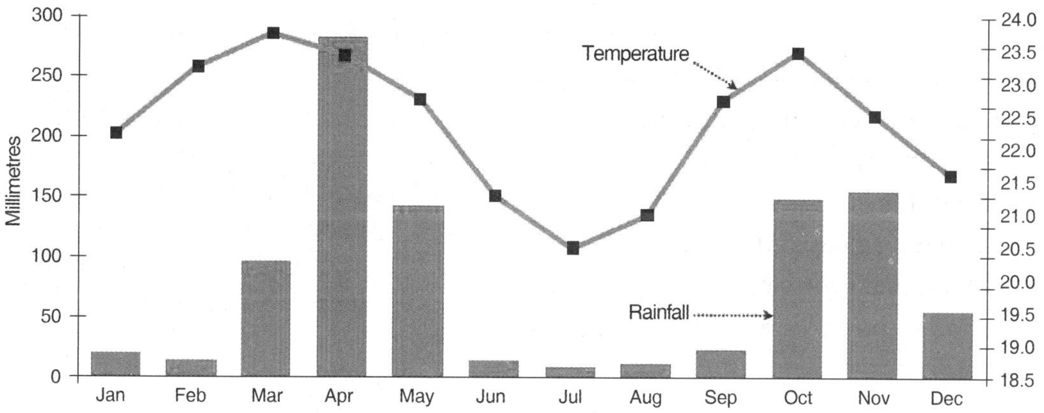

WRITING TASK 2

You should spend about 40 minutes on this task.

Write about the following topic:

> ***Meat production requires relatively more land than crop production. Some people think that as land is becoming scarce, the world's meat consumption should be reduced.***
> ***What measures could be taken to reduce the world's meat consumption? What kinds of problem might such measures cause?***

Give reasons for your answer and include any relevant examples from your own knowledge or experience.

Write at least 250 words.

Test 7

SPEAKING

PART 1

The examiner asks the candidate about him/herself, his/her home, work or studies and other familiar topics.

EXAMPLE

Transport

- What form of transport do you prefer to use? Why?
- What's the most common means of/form of transport in your hometown?
- What do you think of the transport conditions in your hometown?
- How has the transport system in your hometown changed in the past few decades?

PART 2

Describe a problem in your city.
You should say:
what it is
how it was caused
why it is a problem
and offer some solutions to the problem.

You will have to talk about the topic for one to two minutes. You have one minute to think about what you are going to say. You can make some notes to help you if you wish.

PART 3

Discussion topics:

The development of cities

Example questions:

Can you discuss the causes of urbanization?
Can you explain how the overcrowding of cities affects our lives?
Can you predict how cities will develop in the future?

Global issues

Example questions:

Can you evaluate the problem of overpopulation in your country?
How obvious is the gap between rich and poor in your country?
Can you talk about how worried you are about rising world temperatures?

Test 8

LISTENING

SECTION 1 *Questions 1–10*

Complete the notes below.

Write ***NO MORE THAN THREE WORDS AND/OR A NUMBER*** *for each answer.*

Name: 1 ....

Address: 2 .... Road, Flat **3** ....

Telephone number: 4 ....

Date of pictures taken: 5 ....

Location of pictures taken: 6 ....

Occasion of pictures taken: 7 ....

Serial number of film: 8 ....

Compensation: 9 ....

Customer satisfied? 10 ....

SECTION 2 *Questions 11–20*

Questions 11–14

Label the map below.

*write the correct letter, **A–F**, next to questions 11–14.*

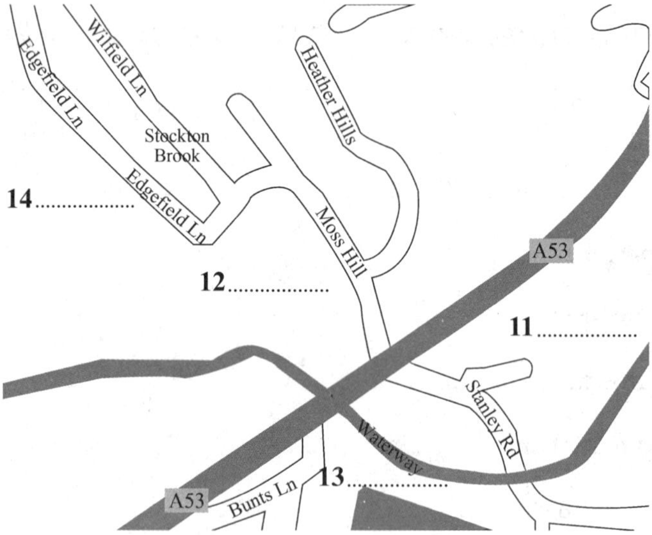

A	family restaurant
B	new housing estate
C	existing primary school
D	conservation area
E	new primary school
F	new recreation area

Questions 15–18

Complete the summary below.

*Write **NO MORE THAN THREE WORDS AND/OR A NUMBER** for each answer.*

Although the development of the area is a necessity, the council assures that residents' **15** .... will be maintained. The council intends to allow the building of **16** .... new 4-bedroomed houses, all of high quality which they believe will **17** .... to the area. Building is scheduled to finish in July of next year. Once new residents have moved into the area, Stockton's population will be around **18** ....

Questions 19 and 20

List the **TWO** reasons why people living in Stockton are worried about the development plan.

*Write **NO MORE THAN THREE WORDS** for each answer.*

19 ....

20 ....

SECTION 3 *Questions 21–30*

Questions 21–24

Complete the sentences below.

*Write **NO MORE THAN THREE WORDS** for each answer.*

21 Dormouse numbers have fallen .... as well as in the UK.
22 Dormice are about as heavy as two ....
23 You are most likely to have seen a dormouse in a ....
24 In the UK, dormice probably live in hedges and woods, and next to ....

Questions 25–27

Label the identification sheet below.

*Write the correct letter, **A–E**, next to questions 25–27.*

A	a hole in the shell with an even and regular edge
B	a hole with orderly marks on the inner rim
C	half shells with rough edges
D	a tiny hole of no more than 2 millimetres across
E	a hole with parallel marks on the inner rim

25 opened by woodmice ....
26 opened by voles ....
27 opened by dormice ....

Questions 28–30

Complete the summary below.

*Write **ONE WORD ONLY** for each answer.*

If you find nuts opened by dormice, **28** .... where you found them. Put them into some kind of **29** .... and **30** .... them (name and address). Post them to Action for Wildlife.

SECTION 4 *Questions 31–40*

Questions 31–35

Complete the table below.

Write ***ONE WORD ONLY*** *for each answer.*

Time Perspectives

Time Zone	Outlook	Features & Consequences
Past	Positive	Remember good times, e.g. birthdays Keep family records, photo albums, etc.
	31	Focus on disappointments, failures, bad decisions
Present	Hedonistic	Live for **32** ....; seek sensation; avoid pain
	Fatalistic	Life is governed by **33** ...., religious beliefs, social conditions. Life's path can't be changed.
Future	**34**	Prefer work to play. Don't give in to temptation.
	Fatalistic	Have a strong belief in life after death and importance of **35** .... in life

Questions 36–40

Choose the correct letter ***A, B*** *or* ***C***.

36 We are all present hedonists

A at school.

B at birth.

C while eating and drinking.

37 American boys drop out of school at a higher rate than girls because

A they need to be in control of the way they learn.

B they play video games instead of doing school work.

C they are not as intelligent as girls.

38 Present-orientated children

A do not realise present actions can have negative future effects.

B are unable to learn lessons from past mistakes.

C know what could happen if they do something bad, but do it anyway.

39 If Americans had an extra day per week, they would spend it

A working harder.

B building relationships.

C sharing family meals.

40 Understanding how people think about time can help us

A become more virtuous.

B work together better.

C identify careless or ambitious people.

READING

READING PASSAGE 1

*You should spend about 20 minutes on **Questions 1–14**, which are based on Reading Passage 1 below.*

Spider Silk Cuts Weight of Bridges

A strong, light bio-material made by genes from spiders could transform construction and industry.

A Scientists have succeeded in copying the silk-producing genes of the Golden Orb Weaver spider and using them to create a synthetic material which they believe is the model for a new generation of advanced bio-materials. The new material, biosilk, which has been spun for the first time by researchers at DuPont, has an enormous range of potential uses in construction and manufacturing.

B The attraction of the silk spun by the spider is a combination of great strength and enormous elasticity, which man-made fibres have been unable to replicate. On an equal-weight basis, spider silk is far stronger than steel and it is estimated that if a single strand could be made about 10m in diameter, it would be strong enough to stop a jumbo jet in flight. A third important factor is that it is extremely light. Army scientists are already looking at the possibilities of using it for lightweight, bullet-proof vests and parachutes.

C For some time, biochemists have been trying to synthesise the drag-line silk of the Golden Orb Weaver. The drag-line silk, which forms the radial arms of the web, is stronger than the other parts of the web and some biochemists believe a synthetic version could prove to be as important a material as nylon, which has been around for 50 years, since the discoveries of Wallace Carothers and his team ushered in the age of polymers.

D To recreate the material, scientists, including Randolph Lewis at the University of Wyoming, first examined the silk-producing gland of the spider. "We took out the glands that produce the silk and looked at the coding for the protein material they make, which is spun into a web. We then went looking for clones with the right DNA," he says.

E At DuPont, researchers have used both yeast and bacteria as hosts to grow the raw material, which they have spun into fibres. Robert Dorsch, Dupont's director of biochemical development, says the globules of protein, comparable with marbles in an egg, are harvested and processed. "We break open the bacteria, separate out the globules of protein and use them as the row starting material. With yeast, the gene system can be designed so that the material excretes the protein outside the yeast for better access," he says.

F "The bacteria and the yeast produce the same protein, equivalent to that the spider uses in the drag lines of the web. The spider mixes the protein into a water-based solution and then spins it into a solid fibre in one go. Since we are not as clever as the spider and we are not using such sophisticated organisms, we substituted man-made approaches and dissolved the protein in chemical solvents, which are then spun to push the material through small holes to form the solid fiber."

G Researchers at DuPont say they envisage many possible uses for a new biosilk material. They say that earthquake-resistant suspension bridges hung from cables of synthetic spider silk fibres may become a reality. Stronger ropes, safer seat belts, shoe soles that do not wear out so quickly and tough new clothing are among the other applications. Biochemists such as Lewis see the potential range of uses of biosilk as almost limitless. "It is very strong and retains elasticity; there are no man-made materials that can mimic both these properties. It is also a biological material with all the advantages that has over petrochemicals," he says.

H At DuPont's laboratories, Dorsch is excited by the prospect of new super-strong materials but he warns they are many years away. "We are at an early stage but theoretical predictions are that we will wind up with a very strong, tough material, with an ability to absorb shock, which is stronger and tougher than the man-made materials that are conventionally available to us," he says.

I The spider is not the only creature that has aroused the interest of material scientists. They have also become envious of the natural adhesive secreted by the sea mussel. It produces a protein adhesive to attach itself to rocks. It is tedious and expensive to extract the protein from the mussel, so researchers have already produced a synthetic gene for use in surrogate bacteria.

Questions 1–5

Reading Passage 1 has nine paragraphs, **A–I**.

Which paragraph contains the following information?

*Write the correct letter, **A–I**, in boxes 1–5 on your answer sheet.*

1 a comparison of the ways that two materials are used to replace silk-producing glands

2 predictions regarding the availability of the synthetic silk

3 on-going research into other synthetic materials

4 the research into the part of the spider that manufactures silk

5 the possible application of the silk in civil engineering

Questions 6–11

Complete the flow-chart below.

Choose ***NO MORE THAN TWO WORDS*** *from the passage for each answer.*

Write your answers in boxes 6–11 on your answer sheet.

Synthetic gene growth in **6** .... or **7** ....

↓

globules of **8** ....

↓

dissolved in **9** ....

↓

passed through **10** ....

↓

to produce **11** ....

Questions 12–14

Do the following statements agree with the information given in Reading Passage 1?

In boxes 12–14 on your answer sheet, write

TRUE	*if the statement agrees with the information*
FALSE	*if the statement contradicts the information*
NOT GIVEN	*if there is no information on this*

12 Biosilk has already replaced nylon in parachute manufacture.

13 The spider produces silk of varying strengths.

14 Lewis and Dorsch co-operated in the synthetic production of silk.

READING PASSAGE 2

*You should spend about 20 minutes on **Questions 15–27**, which are based on Reading Passage 2 below.*

Carbolic Smoke Ball: Fake or Cure?

The curious case of the carbolic smoke ball forced companies to treat customers honestly and openly and still has impact today.

The 1892 case of Carlill and the Carbolic Smoke Ball Company is an odd tale set against the backdrop of the swirling mists and fog of Victorian London, a terrifying Russian flu pandemic, and a forest of unregulated quack medicines offering cures for just about everything.

It is a case known to legal students the world over. It is also seen by some as the birth of modern consumer protection as it helped to define in law the trading relationship between a company and its customers.

The carbolic smoke ball was a peculiar device marketed as a cure for various ailments including influenza. It consisted of a rubber ball, filled with powdered carbolic acid. You squeezed the ball sending a puff of acidic smoke right up a tube inserted into your nose. The idea was that your nose would run and the cold would be flushed out.

The company making the ball advertised it in the *Pall Mall Gazette* offering a £100 reward to anyone using it correctly who then contracted influenza. They deposited £1,000 in the Alliance Bank in Regent Street to show the money was there. The advertisement also contained testimonials from a raft of aristocrats and clergy — the Victorian equivalent of today's celebrity endorsement.

It was seen by one Mrs Louisa Elizabeth Carlill. She bought a ball and used it, as directed, three times daily for nearly two months, then promptly caught the flu. Not surprisingly she claimed her reward from the company.

The manufacturers ignored two letters from her husband who had trained as a solicitor. They finally replied saying that if used properly they had total confidence in their product. In order to protect themselves against a fraudulent claim they stated Mrs Carlill would have to attend their offices at 27 Princess Street, Hanover Square, London each day and have her use of the ball checked by their secretary.

Mrs Carlill sued, claiming there was a contract between her and the company. The company denied there was one. She won her case in the High Court. The company and its proprietor, Mr Frederick Rowe, appealed. He raised almost every conceivable reason why there was no contract between his company and Mrs Carlill. Among their arguments were the following: First, they said the advertisement was "mere puff", like a modern toothpaste which claims to leave your teeth "whiter than white". Claims like these are not meant to have any legal consequences and are understood not to by the public. The company failed largely because they had deposited £1,000 to show that they were serious. Second, they maintained there was no way of knowing whether Mrs Carlill had followed the instructions correctly. That would have been a good argument that had the court not simply dismissed it out of hand. Next they said an offer could not be understood to have been made to the entire world.

Again the court disagreed. It said that if the offer was clear and to a group, anyone fulfilling the terms could be deemed to have accepted it. There was no need for those accepting to say who they were when they accepted the offer.

One of the judges, Lord Bowen, put it like this: "If I advertise to the world that my dog is lost, and that anybody who brings the dog to a particular place will be paid some money, are all the police or other persons whose business it is to find lost dogs to be expected to sit down and write me a note saying that they have accepted my proposal?" The company also argued there was no "consideration" or "thing of value" passing between Mrs Carlill and themselves. To be valid all contracts must have consideration. The court decided any use of the smoke ball would be likely to promote sales, and would thus be of value to the company. Mrs Carlill's use of the smoke ball was therefore deemed to be good or "valuable" consideration.

Mrs Carlill won the appeal, and so significantly helped to define the relationship between companies, their products and their customers. However, it was not until the Thalidomide scandal in 1961, which led to the *Medicines Act of 1968* and the *Trade Descriptions Act* of the same year, that there was a clear statutory improvement in consumer rights.

The carbolic smoke ball case helped ordinary people to fight big companies. In 1992, Hoover came unstuck when it offered customers free flights — initially to Europe and then to the United States — if they bought over £100 worth of its appliances. Thousands of people took up the offer.

The company simply could not keep up with demand. Customers claimed Hoover was not keeping its promises. Hoover found itself fighting legal battles up and down the country and ended up losing nearly £50 million. It was one of the biggest marketing disasters of all time.

And what of Mrs Carlill who set the consumer rights ball rolling? She died on 10 March 1942 at the age of 96. Clearly her considerable age contributed to her death. But on the death certificate, there was only one cause stated: influenza.

Questions 15–20

Do the following statements agree with the information given in Reading Passage 2?

In boxes 15–20 on your answer sheet, write

TRUE	*if the statement agrees with the information*
FALSE	*if the statement contradicts the information*
NOT GIVEN	*if there is no information on this*

15 Carbolic smoke ball case set an example for the consumer law, especially for the relationship between customers and companies.

16 In the advertisement, those who contracted influenza after using the ball correctly would get the deposited money as a reward.

17 The company turned down Mrs Carlill's request for no reason.

18 In the first trial, Mrs Carlill won her suit in the High Court.

19 The toothpaste company said the advert was just a marketing strategy and the public should understand it.

20 The Thalidomide scandal in 1961 contributed to the enactment of *Medicines Act* of 1968 because the customer won the case again.

Questions 21–24

Complete the summary below.

Choose ***NO MORE THAN THREE WORDS*** *from the passage for each answer.*

Write your answers in boxes 21–24 on your answer sheet.

The Carbolic Smoke Ball Company made a product called the "smoke ball". It claimed to be a cure for **21** .... and a number of other diseases. The smoke ball was a **22** .... ball, which was filled with **23** .... A **24** .... was then inserted into the user's nose. It was squeezed at the bottom to release a puff of acidic smoke into the nose of the user. This would cause the nose to run, and hopefully flush out the viral infection.

Questions 25–27

Complete each sentence with the correct ending, ***A–E****, below.*

Write the correct letter, ***A–E****, in boxes 25–27 on your answer sheet.*

25 Mrs Louisa Elizabeth Carlill's husband ....

26 Mr Frederick Rowe ....

27 Lord Bowen ....

A	bought the carbolic smoke ball and then contracted influenza.
B	sent letters to the carbolic smoke ball company.
C	doomed Mrs Carlill's case to a failure in the High Court.
D	appealed and put forward several reasons to prove his ideas.
E	quoted an example to turn the company down.

READING PASSAGE 3

*You should spend about 20 minutes on **Questions 28–40**, which are based on Reading Passage 3 below.*

Questions 28–30

Reading Passage 3 has three sections **A–C**.

Choose the correct heading for each section from the list of headings below.

*Write the correct number, **i–vi**, in boxes 28–30 on your answer sheet.*

List of Headings

i	the pilgrimage into the bucolic paddy fields
ii	the existence of heart of rice
iii	the decreasing population in the village Tochikubo
iv	the possible solutions to increase the productivity of rice
v	the dilemma the country confronts
vi	the reasons for the symptoms in the village Tochibuko

28 Section **A** ....

29 Section **B** ....

30 Section **C** ....

You Are What You Eat

Can a country as modern as Japan cling onto a culture as ancient as rice?

Section A

In early autumn a pilgrimage takes place in Japan. People ride the bullet train from Tokyo, pass through a long tunnel in the mountains west of the capital and emerge in Niigata, one of the richest rice-growing regions in the country. They travel to see the harvest, which takes place as the leaves on the trees are turning red. But it is not as bucolic as it could be.

Even on a trip to rural Japan, you rarely lose sight of the speed of that change. This awareness of time is closely associated with a rice-growing calendar that has helped to shape Japan's identity since 2,400 years ago. The Japanese take great pride in the quality taste and stickiness of their rice. After each harvest each farmer's crop is checked by gruff inspectors. Anything below grade two is considered unfit for the table and the price plummets accordingly.

Test 8

But the obsession goes deeper yet, as if in the grains of polished rice the Japanese see a reflection of themselves and of their blemishes. Recently, that image has been more troubling than uplifting. Among the many rice-growing nations of Asia, there is none as rich, efficient and modern as Japan. Among grains, few are so steeped in tradition and mystique as rice. Despite a rush to modernity, Japan still clings to its ancient rice culture as if losing it would destroy its soul. Yet its farmers are literally dying out. Almost half of them are over 65. If they take rice's rich heritage to the grave, what will that do to Japan?

Section B

The village of Tochikubo sits halfway up a mountain. It is, at first glance, a prosperous looking place; there are new cars and an attractive school built. But there is a disconcerting fact about the school. A few decades ago there were 120 pupils. Now there are only 11, of such a variety of ages that they need seven teachers.

The shortage of children is symptomatic of chronic affliction: young families have abandoned places like Tochikubo, unable to make a living. The hollowing out of such communities is a source of deep anxiety in Japan. Tochikubo is on the brink of the aging precipice when more than half of the community is over 65. It is not quite there yet (40% are over 65), but according to the OECD, 18,775 such communities will lose their traditional character over the next decade. Will Tochikubo be one?

What is worse, no one has a clue what to do about it. Ask Akira Fueki, president of the local farming co-operative, how to reverse the abandonment of rural areas, and he says: "It is a tough life, even those have grown up in the village don't want their children to work in the rice fields. You should only work in the fields if you are willing to do so and it is only when people are over 50 that they are willing."

It is not just the physical effort that is discouraging. The economics are too. In Tochikubo, each of 60 households owns about one hectare. They produce on average, 4,060kg sacks per hectare. A sack sells for about 20,000 yen ($230). That amounts to a yearly income of only about 800,000 yen, which barely covers the costs of machinery.

These were glorious times for farmers, whose mission was to return Japan to rice self-sufficiency. It coincided with Japan's industrial renaissance, and with a rising demand for labour in factories that were beginning to lead the world in production of high-tech goods. Yukie Kuwabara, who travels around the rice fields she has farmed for the past 50 years, recalls how her sons left Tochikubo to work as "salary men". That helped generate cash. But it all came at a cost, she laments.

Section C

A The more the young left the villages, the more they were gripped by the fever of modernization. Even as rice crops grew, Japanese people were eating less rice. They turned increasingly to bread and meat, much of it imported. Today each of Japanese consumes, on average, about 60kg of rice a year, roughly half the amount of the early 1960s. Self-sufficiency in rice quickly turned to surplus, and from the 1970s onwards the government has paid people not to produce. In a country that had always yearned for more rice, farmers suddenly felt that, like their crops, they were superfluous.

B For all the lyricism, many Japanese are also disturbingly nationalistic over the food stuff. They ignore the fact that rice, in various forms is eaten by 3 billion people across Asia, and that the reverence for it is shared by many cultures. Such perceptions hold sway at the national level, and governments have done little to change them. That helps explain the extraordinary protectionism in Japanese agriculture. The Japanese may grumble at how taxes are used to support farmers. But it is not just farmers who resist free trade.

C In polls, ordinary people say that they are opposed to imports, even if prices would drop. The irony is that if the government did not protect farmers quite so assiduously, then lower prices might encourage people to eat more rice.

D But Japanese agriculture is paralyzed, the farmers are unable to think clearly, as if fearing that market forces were unleashed, paddies would be forever lost, changing both the landscape and the traditional orderliness of the Japanese psyche. It need not be like that. Hearteningly, in villages such as Tochikubo, a small flame of private enterprises is being lit. On a Sunday morning in October, 35 students, environmentalists and businessmen, as well as a couple of foreigners, gathered in Tochikubo with sickles in hand to harvest something very rare in Japan: an organic rice field. They cut the stalks, bound them with straw and hung them on iron poles to dry in the autumn sun. Then, adopting the age-old thriftiness common to farmers worldwide, they gleaned every inch of the paddy for the last grains.

E It could all have been done much more quickly by combine harvester. And the villagers were bemused to see city folk trying to twist rice into sheaves. But there was a sense of purpose to the shared endeavour, and the farmers sold their rice to the visitors for good prices.

F "It's rare to find people in their 60s and 70s trying to be entrepreneurs. But there's only us left." said Mr Fueki, the co-operative president. That is the sort of spirit rice-growing needs, and there are faint signs of it emerging in parcels of land across Japan. Farmers say that using their initiative lets them bring enthusiasm back to a job that is in danger of becoming as depressingly obsolete as Soviet-style collective farming. If farmers — for so long part of the Japanese bone marrow — recover some self-esteem, perhaps Japan might too.

Questions 31–34

Do the following statements agree with the claims of the writer in Reading Passage 3?

In boxes 31–34 on your answer sheet, write

YES	*if the statement agrees with the claims of writer*
NO	*if the statement contradicts the claims of writer*
NOT GIVEN	*if it is impossible to say what the writer thinks about this*

31 The pilgrimage, after a trip, is eager to see the scene of harvest.

32 Thousands of years ago, the schedule of agriculture in rice played a part in forming the country' self-awareness.

33 Any rice below grade two is the main source of food for the living stock.

34 The young families abandon the village Tochikubo only because of the physical exhaustion.

Questions 35–40

Section **C** has six paragraphs, **A–F**.

Which paragraph contains the following information?

Write the correct letter, ***A–F****, in boxes 35–40 on your answer sheet.*

35 Without inappropriate policy, the consumption of rice would mount.

36 There are still hopes in the elderly people.

37 The authourity had persuaded the peasants to cut the productivity.

38 Farmers participated in the efforts as well.

39 Some personally-owned firms have adopted some actions.

40 The citizens would rather stick to eating nationally-produced rice.

WRITING

WRITING TASK 1

You should spend about 20 minutes on this task.

The charts below show the percentage of monthly household income spent on various items by two different groups in one European country.

Summarise the information by selecting and reporting the main features, and make comparisons where relevant.

Write at least 150 words.

Percentage of Household Income Spent on Different Items*

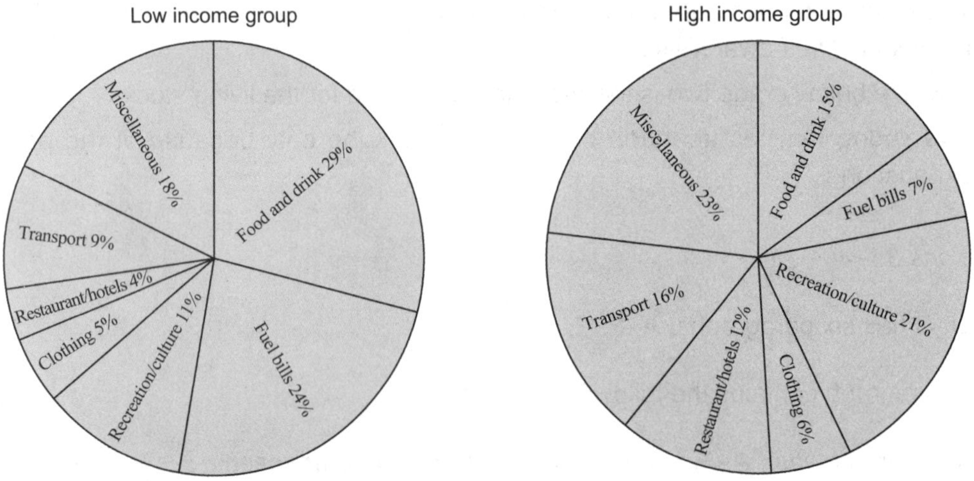

* Earnings excluding house rent/purchase

WRITING TASK 2

You should spend about 40 minutes on this task.

Write about the following topic:

What do you imagine are the advantages and disadvantages of working abroad, as far as individuals and countries are concerned?

Give reasons for your answer and include any relevant examples from your own knowledge or experience.

Write at least 250 words.

Test 8

SPEAKING

PART 1

The examiner asks the candidate about him/herself, his/her home, work or studies and other familiar topics.

EXAMPLE

Noise

- Do you mind noises?/Do any noises bother you?
- What types of noise do you come across in your daily life?
- Are cities becoming noisier?
- Would you like to work in a noisy place? Why/Why not?

PART 2

Describe an electronic device you own.
You should say:
what it is
what it looks like
what functions it has
and explain why you like it.

You will have to talk about the topic for one to two minutes.
You have one minute to think about what you are going to say.
You can make some notes to help you if you wish.

PART 3

Discussion topics:

The Internet

Example questions:

Is online shopping popular in your country?
Can you suggest several ways to make the Internet safer for children?
Can you summarise the pros and cons of e-learning?

Information technology

Example questions:

Has technology made our lives simpler or more complex?
Can you predict how technology will change our daily lives?
Can you justify the amount of money spent on developing technology?

Test 9

LISTENING

SECTION 1 *Questions 1–10*

Complete the notes below.

Write ***ONE WORD AND/OR A NUMBER*** *for each answer.*

Portman Air Lost Luggage Report	
Passenger details	
Name:	John **1** ....
Address:	**2** .... View, Takapuna, Auckland
Telephone:	9712170
Passport number:	**3** ....
Flight details	
Number:	PA980
Departure from:	Medan
Stopover(s):	**4** ....
Luggage details	
Item description:	**5** ....
Colour:	Blue and **6** ....
Material:	Canvas
Approximate size:	60 × **7** ....
Distinctive features:	
	Picture of a **8** .... on the front
	Striped **9** ....
Contents:	
	Clothing
	Books
	Cash
	10 ....

SECTION 2 *Questions 11–20*

Questions 11 and 12

*Choose **TWO** letters, **A–E**.*

Which **TWO** of the following rules apply to participation in the charity race?

A It is possible to book a place at certain shops.
B People can register up to one hour before the race starts.
C Men are not allowed to take part.
D There is no registration fee.
E Children must be over five years of age.

Questions 13 and 14

*Choose **TWO** letters, **A–E**.*

Which **TWO** of the following must all race participants wear?

A clothing of a standard style
B a running number
C trainers
D a hat
E a back sign

Questions 15–20

Label the map below.

*Write the correct letter, **A–I**, next to questions 15–20.*

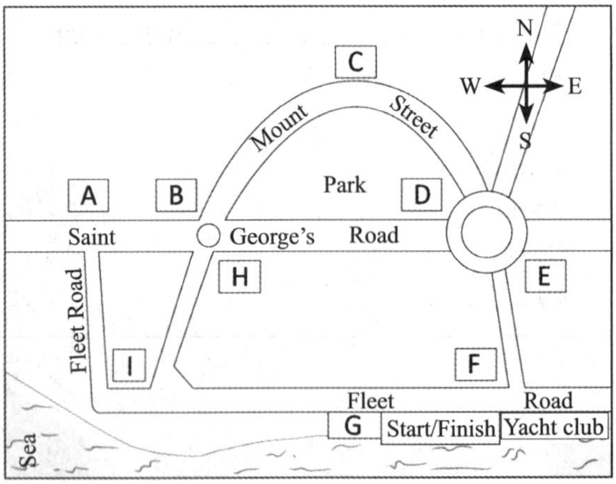

The Route

15 Ferry stop ……………………………

16 Children's playground ……………………………

17 Grand Hotel ……………………………

18 Swimming pool ……………………………

19 Library ……………………………

20 Police station ……………………………

SECTION 3 *Questions 21–30*

Questions 21–24

*Choose the correct letter, **A**, **B** or **C**.*

21 In terms of prices, the cheapest area is in

- **A** the east.
- **B** the north.
- **C** the west and south.

22 Many people enjoy living in the east because of

- **A** the low rental price.
- **B** the prosperous business.
- **C** the pretty hills and parks.

23 The price of some flats in the east is as high as $1,100 because

- **A** they are on the hills.
- **B** rivers run through them.
- **C** they've got the best views.

24 The lowest price of flats in the north is

- **A** from $650.
- **B** from $170.
- **C** from $400.

Questions 25–30

Fill in the table below.

*Write **NO MORE THAN THREE WORDS** for each answer.*

	East	**South**	**West**	**North**
Advantage	pretty scenes	**26**	**27**	
Disadvantage	**25**	much industry	**28** **29**	**30** ....

SECTION 4 *Questions 31–40*

Questions 31–35

Complete the table below.

Write ***NO MORE THAN THREE WORDS*** *for each answer.*

Home Security	
Item	**Suggestion**
windows	fit **31** …………………………
doors	install a good quality **32** …………………………
33 …………………………	locked away in a safe
newspaper, **35** …………………………	cancel the **34** ………………………… , contact post office

Questions 36–40

Complete the sentences.

Write ***NO MORE THAN THREE WORDS*** *for each answer.*

36 Inform your neighbours when you go on holiday, then they can keep an eye on your ………………………… .

37 Call the police station if you see someone ………………………… or showing a particular interest in others' property.

38 Don't leave valuable items in your car, such as mobile phones, laptop computers, cash, and ………………………… .

39 Always remove the ………………………… and lock all doors when you leave your car.

40 The information pack contains a ………………………… .

READING

READING PASSAGE 1

You should spend about 20 minutes on ***Questions 1–13*** *which are based on Reading Passage 1 below.*

Questions 1–6

Reading Passage 1 has six paragraphs, **A–F**.

Choose the correct heading for each paragraph from the list of headings below.

Write the correct number, ***i–ix****, in boxes 1–6 on your answer sheet.*

List of Headings

- **i** Disinterring impact of cyber-bullying
- **ii** Approaches to solving cyber-bullying
- **iii** An example of cyber-bullying for warning
- **iv** Fears of cyber-bullying from inhabitants
- **v** Harder to obstruct cyber-bullying than real-world one
- **vi** Kinds of punishment of cyber-bullying
- **vii** Other groups who are facing cyber-bullying
- **viii** The role of governments in preventing cyber-bullying
- **ix** Inevitability even for the grown-ups

1 Paragraph **A**
2 Paragraph **B**
3 Paragraph **C**
4 Paragraph **D**
5 Paragraph **E**
6 Paragraph **F**

The Rise of Cyber-Bullying

A Gail Jones, a 15-year-old girl from Tranmere near Liverpool in the UK took her life after receiving, at one point, 20 silent calls on her cellphone every 30 minutes. Her father, Glyn, suspects a final call in the middle of the night pushed her over the edge.This is extreme but far from unique example of the devastation wrought by cyber-bullying. Since Jones died in 2000, more and more children are logging onto the Internet, so it's likely that online bullying, including sending threatening messages, displaying private messages and posting embarrassing video and photos online, is also increasing. A study last month by the Pew Internet & American Life Project based in Washington DC found that one-third of US teenage Internet users have been targets of cyber-bullying. Meanwhile, as online communication evolves from instant messaging and chatrooms to social networking sites and YouTube, the venues where bullying occurs are becoming both more central to young people's lives, and more public.

B Research into the causes and effects of cyber-bullying is still in its infancy. But it is becoming clear that aspects of online communication encourage people to act aggressively, prompting them to do things they wouldn't dare to try in real life.What's more, the ability to reach more people and the always-on culture of the Internet, mean that cyber-bullying can have an even more detrimental effect on the victim than conventional playground bullying. "It's school-yard bullying taken to the next level," says Justin Patchin, a criminologist at the University of Wisconsin, Eau Claire. A study by UK-based Internet market research firm YouGov in 2006 found that for one in eight young people cyber-bullying is even worse than physical bullying. One reason for this is the sheer number of people who can view something that is posted online. "It would be bad enough to be cyber-bullied by one kid and nobody else knew about it, but a video seen by hundreds or thousands of your peers could be devastating," says Robin Kowalski, a psychologist at Clemson University in South Carolina and co-authour of the book *Cyber-Bullying: Bullying in the Digital Age*, which will be published in October. Ghyslain Raza, also known as the "Star Wars Kid", learned this in the hard way. In 2002, the somewhat overweight and slightly awkward Canadian adolescent made a video of himself playing with a pretend light sabre and left it lying around at school. When his classmates found the video in 2003, they posted it online as a joke. Raza was so upset he finished the school year from a psychiatric ward. Unfortunately for him, it wasn't just his friends who found the video amusing. According to UK marketing firm—The Viral Factory, it became the Internet's most downloaded video of 2006.

C "Another reason why cyber-bullying is so harmful is its relentlessness," says John Carr, chair of the Children's Charities' Coalition for Internet Safety in London. "When I was a kid, playground bullying stopped when the bell rang and you went back inside or when you went home at the end of the day," he says. "With cyber-bullying it is 24/7, 365 days a year. There is no escape." While an adult could simply turn off the computer, that's not really an option for today's teens, who are dependent on the Internet for communicating with their peers. "This is the always-on generation," says Kowalski. "This is how they communicate." A 2007 Pew study found that 93 percent of US teens use the Internet and 61 percent go online daily. The Internet doesn't just amplify the effect of bullying, however. The many options to remain anonymous when online, by using pseudonyms for instant messaging, say, means people can write things they would not dare to if their identity was known. Anonymity can amplify bullying's negative effect on the victim. "The psychological ramifications of not knowing who's attacking you can be maddening," says Kowalski. "The bully could be your best friend, a sibling, or half the school." In a recent, as yet unpublished survey she carried out, nearly half of the children she interviewed didn't know who their cyber-bully was. The lack of face-to-face contact might tempt bullies to new levels of cruelty. "On the playground, seeing the stress and pain of the victim face to face can act as an inhibitor to some degree," explains Carr. "In cyberspace, where there is no visual contact, you get more extreme behaviour." Kowalski says the effect is unique to computer-mediated communication. "There is a distancing of the self and immediacy in response that we don't have in any other form of communication," she says. "On the computer, it's like it's not really you."

D Led by Ruth Aylett of Heriot-Watt University in Edinburgh, UK, a consortium of European researchers recently developed role-playing software called Fear Not!, which gets children to empathise with a victim of bullying. After watching a short animation of a child being bullied either in the playground or online, the viewer is asked to help the victim by typing advice into the computer. The software will be tested in schools in the UK and Germany later this year. Meanwhile, some governments have taken legislative action. In January 2006, the US Congress passed a law making it a federal crime to "annoy, abuse, threaten or harass" another person over the Internet. Approximately 36 states have enacted similar legislation. And in South Korea, the "Internet real-name system", introduced last month, forces online portals and news websites to record the identities of people who post content and to disclose their contact details if someone wants to sue them for libel or infringement of privacy. However, it can be difficult to persuade people to take these laws seriously, and in the US they only apply to over-18s. "Many jurisdictions don't want to investigate or prosecute these cases," says Al Kush of WiredSafety.org, an Internet safety advocacy group based in Seattle, Washington. "They are short-staffed and busy pursuing what they call 'real crime'." John Halligan, the father of a boy who killed himself after being harassed online, continues to lobby for cyber-bullying legislation that specifically targets children. He also talks to school groups and runs a website recounting the events that led to his son's death. "It won't bring Ryan back," he says. "But it is helping a lot of Ryans out there that are still alive and don't know where to turn."

E Known best as a problem facing teens, cyber-bullying affects adults too. Inhabitants of virtual worlds, from film stars to teachers have all been victims. Second Life is designed for adults and to access most locations you are supposed to be at least 18 years old. Yet nearly 2,000 abuse reports are filed each day, says Linden Labs of San Francisco, who created Second Life. "It's adults hassling other adults," says Thomas Chesney of the University of Nottingham, UK, who has encountered pushing, swearing and shooting there. Chesney and colleagues recently set up an office in Second Life where they interviewed more than 100 inhabitants about bullying. Chesney says that because many people come to Second Life with a background in gaming, they bring preconceived notions of violence and aggression with them. "They're playing games like *World of Warcraft*—where the aim is to kill everybody—and they take that attitude into Second Life," he says. "It's a bit depressing that we haven't progressed beyond hassling one other, but not surprising given all we know about workplace bullying."

F Teachers have also been victims. Tired of insults from students on websites such as *Rate My Teachers.co.uk*, the UK Association of Teachers and Lecturers said earlier this year that it is ready to go to court in support of teachers who have been libelled online. The union would target publishers of websites directly, not the children who post disparaging comments. Meanwhile in South Korea, celebrities have been the high-profile victims of anonymous cyber-bullying attacks, reportedly including TV star Jeong Da-Bin and pop singer Yuni, who both later committed suicide.

Questions 7–13

Do the following statements agree with the views of the writer in Reading Passage 1?

In boxes 7–13 on your answer sheet, write

YES	*if the statement agrees with the views of the writer*
NO	*if the statement contradicts the views of the writer*
NOT GIVEN	*if it is impossible to say what the writer thinks about this*

7 The reasons and impacts of cyber-bullying have been well-researched by scientists.

8 A young boy committed suicide in 2003 when his classmates put his video online.

9 Unlike playground bullying, cyber-bullying happens all the time.

10 There is nothing to restrain playground bullying.

11 Some authourities aim to prevent cyber-bullying through law.

12 Mortals from all walks of life may be influenced by cyber-bullying.

13 Teachers have been bullied by students from their own classes.

READING PASSAGE 2

You should spend about 20 minutes on ***Questions 14–26****, which are based on Reading Passage 2 on the following pages.*

Questions 14–20

Reading Passage 2 has eight paragraphs, **A–H**.

Choose the correct heading for each paragraph from the list of headings below.

Write the correct number, ***i–xii****, in boxes 14–20 on your answer sheet.*

List of Headings

i Research on earphones' harm
ii Earphones' most alarming danger
iii The maximum noise level of the "Walkman"
iv Harmful noise pollution
v Noise everywhere
vi Reasons for harm of earphones
vii The maximum safe noise dosage
viii The curse of silence
ix A cure for "tinnitus"
x Alarming statistical evidence
xi A chronic hearing loss impairment
xii The danger of falling asleep

14 Paragraph **A**
15 Paragraph **B**
16 Paragraph **C**
17 Paragraph **D**
18 Paragraph **E**
19 Paragraph **F**
20 Paragraph **G**

Example	***Answer***
Paragraph **H**	vii

Test 9

A It is by old saying that the virtue of silence by claiming it is golden, yet experience tells us that silence is as hard to come by as the precious metal itself. The benefit of silence to the human ear is scientifically demonstrable. Less superfluous noise; less impairment to the hearing. Yet this precious commodity is no longer valued. Noise is ever present in modern life and is an accumulative experience. The ill effects of noise pollution are of two kinds: acute-exposure to an individual instance of a very loud noise, such as a gunshot or explosion; and chronic—the experience of too much noise over an extended period of time.

B City and urban dwellers exist in an increasingly noise-ridden environment, and it is now almost impossible to escape exposure to high noise levels. Even if we exclude the more obvious sources of noise pollution such as jet plane engines, road works, power tools, loud music at dance parties and so on, it is clear that noise is a constant and often unwelcome companion. We have only to walk through a suburban shopping mall or department store, or catch a bus or train to be subjected to noise levels that a few decades ago would have been considered beyond human endurance. The popular practice of "layering" sound, by adding a louder source of noise to that which already exists in order to mask it, merely compounds the problem. Because of the accumulative nature of noise abuse, constant noise is worse than noisy periods interspersed with silence.

C Our noise level acceptance threshold is rising in step with the number of persons developing hearing problems. Data available from a recent survey conducted by the Australian Bureau of Statistics show that 7.4% of people over 14 years of age have some discernible hearing problem. According to the survey, 24.6% of the 7.4% of persons with affected hearing have problems caused by subjection to a constant barrage of noise, either at work, in the everyday living environment, or as the result of a particular choice of leisure activity. The problem is most severe for males aged between 25 and 64 years of age, 9.1% of whom have a hearing disability, and for which the cause is constant noise in 44.4% of cases.

D Of current concern to acoustical engineers and psychologists at the National Acoustics Laboratories in Sydney, Australia, is the potential for damage to the eardrum caused by the transmission of loud sound through earphones placed directly into the ear canal. An almost universal fad among young people, the pocket-sized radio-cassette player (commonly known by the brand name "Walkman") may be exposing its owner to greater than the maximum safe dosage of noise recommended for industrial workers—90 decibels over a period of eight hours. This dosage, called Dose 1, can be achieved much sooner by exposing the ear to only slightly more than 90 decibels. Increases to the decibel level logarithmically shorten the exposure time required to reach a given dose. For instance, to achieve Dose 1 in four hours, it is necessary to raise the decibel exposure level by a mere three decibels.

E One danger posed to young ears is that the peak sound level from these radio-cassette players is often far too great; at high volume it is all too easy to receive Dose 1 in a short period of time. Any further noise heard above 90 decibels that day and the recipient is causing measurable damage to his or her ears. Another danger is the likelihood of a change in the pain threshold of noise resulting in users compensating by increasing the volume to levels way above what is considered safe. Finally, insertable earphones block the ear canal, thereby further increasing the noise level absorbed.

F But perhaps the most alarming potential for danger caused by insertable earphones is the ease with which the listener can exceed the safe time length of exposure to noise. The small earphones can be comfortably worn for extended periods of time. What is more, there is the danger of falling asleep with the earphones inserted, leading to an accumulation of excess noise while unconscious.

G Noise abuse soon leads to varying degrees of hearing loss. What may begin as an acute temporary condition, in time becomes a chronic and irreversible disability. A common complaint is "tinnitus", or a "ringing in the ears" which fails to subside after the ears are subjected to a short but extreme dose of noise. It is an exhausting condition that can seriously threaten the composure of the sufferer who can be driven to near madness. It is believed the composer Beethoven was particularly aggravated by this malady. At present, there is little that can be done in the majority of cases, although the victim might be able to obtain some temporary relief by using an asking device which blocks out the offending frequencies of sound with other, less annoying frequencies.

H Inevitably, though, years of excessive noise accumulation take their toll and partial or complete deafness results. If silence is the cure for ailing ears (or, at least, the best way to prevent further deterioration of one's hearing), it is sobering to realise that it is also the unfortunate and permanent curse of a lifetime of noise abuse caused by ignoring the warnings.

Questions 21–26

Do the following statements agree with the information given in Reading Passage 2?

In boxes 21–26 on your answer sheet, write:

TRUE	*if the statement agrees with the information*
FALSE	*if the statement contradicts the information*
NOT GIVEN	*if there is no information on this*

21 It is not easy to achieve silence as usual in the past.

22 Gunshot or explosion will be bracketed with long-time noise experience in one category of noise pollution.

23 "Layering" sound reduces the overall amount of sound by masking it.

24 Australian Bureau of Statistics surveyed that less than 20 percent people over 14 years old affected hearing have problems caused by constant barrage of noise at work or in the everyday living environment.

25 To achieve Dose 1 in four hours, the ear needs to be exposed to 93 decibels for that period of time.

26 Beethoven ever believed that his ability to compose music was threatened by his "tinnitus".

READING PASSAGE 3

*You should spend about 20 minutes on **Questions 27–40**, which are based on Reading Passage 3 below.*

Tidal Power on the Cheap?

A The startup, located on the Orkney Islands, way north of Scotland, has raised £62 million to build a working prototype of a floating tidal turbine that it says will be cheaper to install and maintain than others being tested now. The 8-metre-long prototype, ideally, will go into the water at the European Marine Energy Centre (EMEC) Tidal Test Site that sits just down the road from ScotRenewables in 2010. Commercial versions of the turbine will measure up to 40 metres long and weigh 250 tons, but generate 1.2 megawatts of power.

B "That's quite impressive when you compare it to others," said CEO Barry Johnston. "We want to be competitive with offshore wind." Rather than anchoring a permanent turbine on the ocean floor, ScotRenewables will build a floating turbine that is slack moored with chains to an anchor on the sea floor. The body of the turbine-a long 40-metre tube of metal with a point at the end-will face directly into the tide. Below, two turbines attached to fins will convert the power of the tides into electricity. Johnston explained "A1-metre prototype ScotRenewables is experimenting with in the wave tank is built. It looks like a model rocket with two fins with propellers attached to the ends of the fins."

C Tidal is the potentially most predictable, reliable form of renewable energy. With a tide table and computer, ScotRenewables can calculate the power output of a turbine decades in advance. You can't do that with intermittent, variable sources like wind, solar or wave. Unfortunately, harnessing tidal power is quite difficult. Some of the prototypes that have been tested in the decades are quickly destroyed by rushing tides. Pulling those turbines up from the sea bed and taking them into the shop consumes time and money. Taking the ScotRenewables turbine in for repairs should be easy: maintenance workers would just have to take a boat out, unhook it, and put another in its place while the first is being entangled.

D Tidal power is also 50 percent stronger at the surface than at the seabed so these turbines should be capable of generating more power. Other companies have tried to create surface tidal turbines before. The difficulty has been keeping the turbine pointed in the direction of the tide. Some get washed away. Other times, the creators build large superstructures around the turbine, which costs money. ScotRenewables says it will come up with control mechanisms and advanced hydrodynamics (i.e., aerodynamics in water) to keep the turbines pointed in the right direction.

E Scotland is betting heavily on wind and wave power. The notoriously harsh waves and currents of the Pentland Firth, a channel which separates the main body of the UK with the Orkneys that is often referred to as the Saudi Arabia of Marine Energy by locals. By 2020, Scotland wants to get half of its power from renewable sources, including large hydroelectric dams. Hydroelectric constitutes about 11 percent of the country's power now and 9 percent comes from wind and other renewables. A large portion of the new renewable sources of power will come from wind, tidal and wave. Marine energy could provide up to 35 terawatt hours of power to the UK by 2020 and 84 terawatt hours of power by 2050, according to Edwina Cook, business development officer at EMEC. The UK in 2004 consumed 340 terawatt hours of power. The EMEC has created tidal and wave testing centres for companies to build and validate prototypes. (The Pelamis-that sea snake-looking wave power device-was tested at EMEC before commercial rollouts in Portugal.) The government has also passed exceptionally large credits for power providers that put tidal and wave power on the grid. (Prototypes participating in the EMEC test beds are actually connected to the grid and selling small amounts of power.) The hope is that the programme will create jobs, exports and green energy. Offshore, the Dublin-Based Open Hydro Power is already testing a large tidal device that looks like a big rotating fan.

F Talking about the prototype and commercial power production, however, is easier said than done. ScotRenewables did not like the software simulation tools it found when it first set out. Some software focused on tidal changes; others focused on waves. To build an effective surface tidal turbine, Johnston realised that both tidal and wave power should be taken into account. Thus, it had to build its own tools, which cost several thousands. It also built its own wave tank. It was easier than trying to book time at an EMEC wave tank. The company now hopes to lease time on the tank to other wave companies to generate revenue. And, because ships to deploy tidal and wave devices are in short supply, it is contemplating buying or building its own multi-purpose vessel.

Questions 27–30

Reading Passage 3 has six paragraphs, **A–F**.

Which paragraph contains the following information?

*Write the correct letter, **A–F**, in boxes 27–30 on your answer sheet.*

27 New plan has been made to involve a new factor besides tidal power.

28 Damages have happened to the models in the past years.

29 A detailed structure of a model is demonstrated.

30 The immature model is expected to apply at the beginning of the 21st century after further development.

Questions 31–35

Complete the summary below.

Choose **NO MORE THAN TWO WORDS** *from the passage for each answer.*

Write your answers in boxes 31–35 on your answer sheet.

The experiment ScotRenewables does is taking advantages of tidal power rather than those sources such as **31** .... .The turbine output can be counted by use of **32** .... as well as computer. Upon the past failure, some companies found it hard to keep the turbine pointed to the **33** .... , but ScotRenewables had the confidence to cope with such problems by building up **34** .... and advanced hydrodynamics in water. The EMEC has developed tidal and wave testing centres to validate prototypes. Also, **35** .... are passed by government aiming to put tidal and wave power on the grid.

Questions 36–40

Do the following statements agree with the information given in Reading Passage 3?

In boxes 36–40 on your answer sheet, write

TRUE	*if the statement agrees with the information*
FALSE	*if the statement contradicts the information*
NOT GIVEN	*if there is no information on this*

36 Floating turbine is not good enough because it could not be anchored to the ocean floor forever.

37 Tidal has proved to be forecasted upon the renewable energy.

38 ScotRenewables model is easier to repair because it will take less time to replace.

39 Scientists have enough experience to design and modify the prototype so as to put it into commercial use.

40 Booking time at an EMEC wave tank is more difficult than the ScotRenewables.

WRITING

WRITING TASK 1

You should spend about 20 minutes on this task.

The graph below shows radio and television audiences throughout one day in 1992. (percentage of UK population over 4 years old)

Write a report to a university lecturer describing the information shown below.

Write at least 150 words.

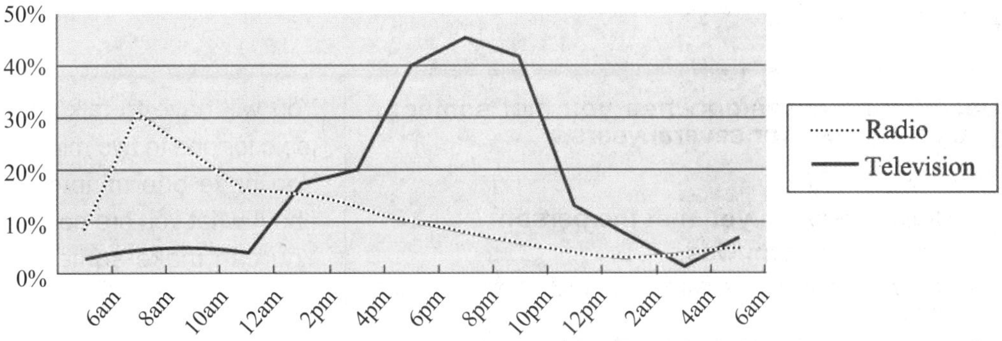

WRITING TASK 2

You should spend about 40 minutes on this task.

Write about the following topic:

Some people argue that national governments should use large projects to provide jobs and economic growth. Others argue that this wastes money and leads to corruption.

Discuss both these views and give your own opinon.

Give reasons for your answer and include any relevant examples from your own knowledge or experience.

Write at least 250 words.

SPEAKING

PART 1

The examiner asks the candidate about him/herself, his/her home, work or studies and other familiar topics.

EXAMPLE

Shops

- Do you enjoy going shopping? Why?
- In your country, what time do shops generally open?
- What would you recommend visitors to your country to buy? Why?
- How are shops changing in your country? Why?

PART 2

Describe an occasion when you met someone you hadn't seen for several years.

You should say:

how and when you met the person
who the person was
how long it was since you had last seen him or her

and explain how you felt about meeting this person again.

You will have to talk about the topic for one to two minutes.
You have one minute to think about what you are going to say.
You can make some notes to help you if you wish.

PART 3

Discussion topics:

Keeping in contact

Example questions:

In what different ways can people keep in touch with each other?
How important do you think it is to keep in touch with friends? Why/Why not?
Which way of keeping in touch do you think is most popular with young people?

Long-term relationships

Example questions:

How valuable do you think long-term friendships are compared with new relationships? Why/Why not?
Do you agree that maintaining long-term relationships sometimes requires effort? Why/Why not?

Test 10

LISTENING

SECTION 1 *Questions 1–10*

Complete the form below.

Write ***ONE WORD AND/OR A NUMBER*** *for each answer.*

Employment Registration Form

Job sector: Retail or **1** ……………………

Geographical area: North London

Salary required: **2** …………………… wage or more

Hours: Daytimes or evenings (no **3** ……………………)

Start date: 1st March

Applicant's personal details

Name: Alison **4** ……………………

Date of birth: 08, 10, 1992

Address: **5** …………………… St, London

Phone number: **6** ……………………

Qualifications and skills

Educational level: College diploma (in basic **7** ……………………)

Skills: Fluent in **8** …………………… ; full driving licence

Previous work experience: **9** …………………… ; sales assistant

Additional notes (if any)

Applicant prefers to be contacted by **10** …………………… .

Is not available for interview on Wednesdays.

SECTION 2 *Questions 11–20*

Questions 11–15

Which characteristic does the tour manager mention for each of the following restaurants?

*Choose **FIVE** answers from the box and write the correct letter, **A–G**, next to questions 11–15.*

Characteristics

A It only serves vegetarian food.
B It is always necessary to book a table.
C It is relatively expensive.
D There is a very good view.
E All the ingredients are produced locally.
F It operates on a self-service basis.
G There is a wide choice of food.

Restaurants

11 Benidentes ....

12 Jingjing ....

13 Paul and Lenny's ....

14 Primera ....

15 Torreminos ....

Questions16–20

Label the map below.

*Write the correct letter, **A–H**, next to questions 16–20.*

Town map

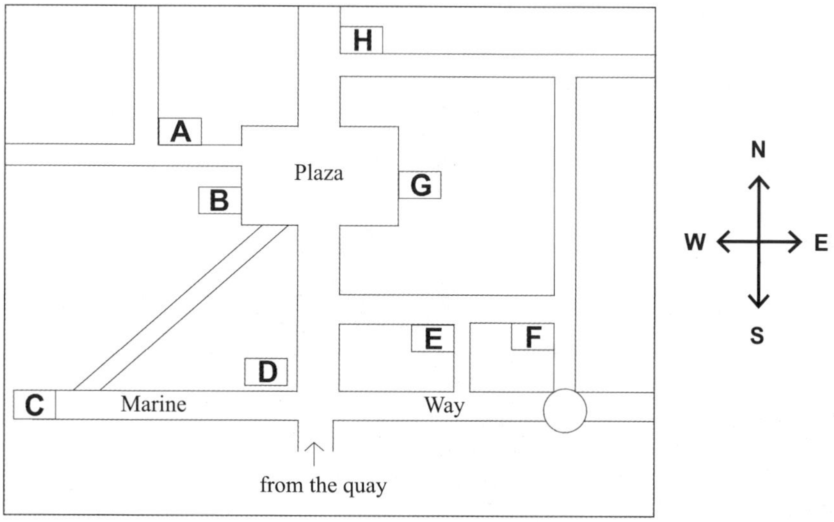

16 cathedral ....

17 museum ....

18 tour bus office ....

19 bike hire company ....

20 market ....

SECTION 3 *Questions 21–30*

Question 21

*Choose the correct letter, **A**, **B**, or **C**.*

21 When is the appointment with Dr Johnson?

A 10 o'clock in the morning
B 10.30 in the morning
C 12 o'clock in the morning

Questions 22 and 23

*Choose **TWO** letters, **A–E**.*

What **TWO** things does Dr Johnson recommend to use?

A spiral notebook
B three-ring binder
C bound book
D highlighters
E reference books

Questions 24–30

Complete the notes below.

*Write **NO MORE THAN THREE WORDS** for each answer.*

Developing a note-taking method
Start each new lecture on a new page.
Set them out side-by-side for **24** ....
Leave blank spaces to add comments or note questions.
Develop a system of **25** ....
Contents included in notes
26 ....
Details, facts, or explanations
27 .... or lists of things that are discussed
Taking better notes
Use a **28** .... to capture the whole lecture.
29 .... your notes right away when they are still fresh.
30 .... your note within 24 hours since memory fades quickly.

SECTION 4 *Questions 31–40*

Questions 31 and 32

Complete the sentences below.

*Write **NO MORE THAN THREE WORDS** for each answer.*

31 Besides sporting injuries, sports medicine doctors deal more with .... problems of common individuals.

32 The total care offered by sports medicine doctors includes workouts, instant care and ....

Questions 33–37

Complete the notes below.

*Write **NO MORE THAN THREE WORDS** for each answer.*

Injuries and Treatment

Injuries of bones, muscles and ligaments

Problem

- The damages of tissues can cause the joints to **33** .... and ....

Preventive measures

- X-rays to determine potential **34** ....

Joints

- The repetition of motions can cause **35** .... of the soft tissue.
- Losing balance even causes bone fracture.

Treatment

- Use ice pack to reduce the swelling and pain.

New treatment

- The injured joints receive the **36** .... of mixture of healing protein and blood.

Advantage

- convenience
- without **37** ....

Questions 38–40

Choose ***THREE*** *letters,* ***A–G****.*

Write the correct letters in boxes 38–40 on your answer sheet.

What is the advice for preventing sports injuries?

A lighten the training load

B practice constant fitness-training activities

C perform enough fitness exercises

D do enough preparatory exercises before training

E stop doing exercises when you don't feel well

F use homemade medicines

G take regular rests every 30 minutes

READING

READING PASSAGE 1

You should spend about 20 minutes on ***Questions 1–14****, which are based on Reading Passage 1 below.*

Of Ducks and Duck Eggs

For people who like to keep poultry, ducks offer certain advantages over hens. Ducks are immune to some common diseases found in hens and are less vulnerable to others. Some breeds of duck produce bigger eggs than those of hens. In addition, ducks lay eggs over a longer season than hens do.

Poultry keepers with gardens have less to worry about if they keep ducks rather than hens because the former are less apt to dig up plants and destroy roots. While both hens and ducks benefit the garden by eating pests, hens are known to damage herb and grass beds. Ducks, on the other hand, will search for insects and snails more carefully. Only very delicate plants are at risk from the broad, webbed feet of ducks.

Like all waterbirds, ducks need access to water, and duck keepers typically provide this by building a pond. Something this large is not absolutely necessary; however, ducks need only to be able to dip their heads in the water to keep their nostrils clean. If a pond is provided though it is important to keep ducklings away from it until they are old enough to withstand the cool temperature of the water—about eight weeks.

When keeping ducks, one has to consider just how many the land will support. Generally the rule is 100 ducks per half hectare. If more than this proportion is introduced, there is a risk of compacting the soil, which can lead to muddy conditions for long periods as the rain is not easily absorbed into the ground.

While ducks offer many advantages over hens, they must be given greater quantity of food, especially if regular eggs are desired. An adult duck will eat between 170 to 200 grams of food a day. If the ducks have access to grass and a pond, they will be able to find for themselves approximately 70% of their daily dietary, requirements in warmer months but less than half that in colder times. Therefore, it is important that they are fed enough food, such as grain, every day.

Experienced duck keepers raise ducklings every three years or so because it is after this period of time that ducks' egg-laying powers begin to seriously weaken. If the aim is to hatch duckling, keepers should be aware that not all ducks make good mothers, and that certain breeds of duck appear to be worse than others. The poor mothers abandon their eggs a few days after laying them.

A sure way of making sure the rejected eggs hatch is to place them next to chicken eggs under a hen.

The eggs of ducks as food for humans have a mixed reputation. This is because of a number of cases of salmonella food poisoning in Europe in the 1970s. Although it was never conclusively shown that duck eggs were to blame, the egg-eating public stopped buying and many duck egg producers went bankrupt. Indeed, there is a risk of salmonella poisoning when ducks lay their eggs in damp conditions, such as on ground that is constantly wet but the same can be said for the eggs of hens. And commercial duck egg production in France and England, where the outbreaks of salmonella poisoning took place, followed the same standards as those used in the hen egg industry, which experienced no salmonella problems. (Storage of eggs, whether those of hen or duck, can also be a factor in contamination. Studies have found that bacterial growth reaches potentially dangerous levels at storage temperatures of 5°C or greater.)

The salmonella scare was over by the early 1980s, but, at least in smaller markets like Australia and New Zealand, few producers wished to risk investment in ducks for fear of problems. No large-scale commercial duck egg production exists in these countries. It has thus been left to small producers, and, more commonly, home duck keepers.

Questions 1–8

Classify the characteristics listed below as belonging to

D	Ducks
H	Hens
B	Both ducks and hens
NI	If there is no information in the reading passage

Write the appropriate letters in boxes 1–8 on your answer sheet.

1 lengthier laying period
2 better mothers
3 less likely to uproot plants
4 dangerous to grass
5 more eggs per week
6 eat more grain
7 beneficial to garden by eliminating pests
8 more vulnerable to illness

Questions 9–12

Complete the summary below.

Choose ***NO MORE THAN TWO WORDS*** *from the passage for each answer.*

Write your answers in boxes 9–12 on your answer sheet.

To prevent their **9** .... from getting dirty, ducks should have access to water. This may be provided by building a pond, but ducklings under **10** .... of age should be prevented from entering it because of the **11** .... of the water. If too many ducks are kept on a plot of land, the soil may eventually become **12** .... as a result of compaction. For this reason, it is advised that one should limit the number of ducks per half hectare of land to 100.

Questions 13 and 14

Choose the correct letter, ***A***, ***B***, ***C*** *or* ***D***.

Write the correct letter in boxes 13 and 14 on your answer sheet.

13 Salmonella food poisoning

A resulted from consumption of duck eggs.
B created difficulties for the duck egg business.
C occurred all over Europe.
D was found in both duck and hen eggs.

14 Duck eggs

A have been produced in large quantities in New Zealand since the early 1980s.
B are more at risk of salmonella contamination than hen egg.
C may be contaminated when laid in wet conditions.
D should be kept at 5℃ to prevent contamination.

READING PASSAGE 2

*You should spend about 20 minutes on **Questions 15–27**, which are based on Reading Passage 2 below.*

Questions 15–19

Reading Passage 2 has six paragraphs, **A–F**.

*Choose the correct heading for paragraphs, **B–F**, from the list of headings below.*

*Write the correct number, **i–ix**, in boxes 15–19 on your answer sheet.*

List of Headings

i	Responsibilities of responding police officers
ii	Perceived advantages of rapid response
iii	Police response to public satisfaction
iv	Communicating response time to people requesting help
v	When rapid response is and is not necessary
vi	Role of technology in improving police response
vii	Rapid response time and success of rapid response
viii	Public demand for catching criminals
ix	Not quickly contacting the police

Example	***Answer***
Paragraph **A**	vi

15 Paragraph **B**
16 Paragraph **C**
17 Paragraph **D**
18 Paragraph **E**
19 Paragraph **F**

Rapid Police Response

A Police departments in the United States and Canada see it as central to their role that they respond to calls for help as quickly as possible. This ability to react fast has been greatly improved with the aid of technology. The telephone and police radio, already long in use, assist greatly in the reduction of police response time. In more recent times there has been the introduction of the "911" emergency system, which allows the public easier and faster contact with police, and the use of police computer systems, which assist police in planning patrols and assigning emergency requests to the police officers nearest to the scene of the emergency.

B An important part of police strategy, rapid police response is seen by police officers and the public alike as offering tremendous benefits. The more obvious ones are the ability of police to apply first-aid life-saving techniques quickly and the greater likelihood of arresting people who may have participated in a crime. It aids in identifying those who witnessed an emergency or crime, as well as in collecting evidence. The overall reputation of a police department, too, is enhanced if rapid response is consistent, and this in itself promotes the prevention of crime. Needless to say, rapid response offers the public some degree of satisfaction in its police force.

C While these may be the desired consequences of rapid police response, actual research has not shown it to be so beneficial. For example, it has been demonstrated that rapid response leads to a greater likelihood of arrest only if responses are in the order of 1–2 minutes after a call is received by the police. When response times increase to 3–4 minutes — still quite a rapid response — the likelihood of an arrest is substantially reduced. Similarly, in identifying witnesses to emergencies or crimes, police are far more likely to be successful if they arrive at the scene no more than four minutes on average, after receiving a call for help. Yet both police officers and the public define "rapid response" as responding up to 10–12 minutes after calling the police for help.

D Should police assume all the responsibility for ensuring a rapid response? Studies have shown that people tend to delay after an incident occurs before contacting the police. A crime victim may be injured and thus unable to call for help, for example, or no telephone may be available at the scene of the incident. Often, however, there is no such physical barrier to calling the police. Indeed, it is very common for crime victims to call their parents, their minister, or even their insurance company first. When the police are finally called in such cases the effectiveness of even the most rapid of responses is greatly diminished.

E The effectiveness of rapid response also needs to be seen in light of the nature of the crime. For example, when someone rings the police after discovering their television set has been stolen from their home, there is little point, in terms of identifying those responsible for the crime, in ensuring a very rapid response. It is common in such burglary or theft cases that the victim discovers the crime hours, days, even weeks after it has occurred. When the victim is directly involved in the crime, however, as in the case of a robbery, rapid response, provided the victim was quickly able to contact the police, is more likely to be advantageous. Based on statistics comparing crimes that are discovered and those in which the victim is directly involved, Spelman and Brown (1981) suggest that three in four calls to police need not be met with rapid response.

F It becomes clear that the importance of response time in collecting evidence or catching criminals after a crime must be weighed against a variety of factors. Yet because police department officials assume the public strongly demands rapid response, they believe that every call to the police should be met with it. Studies have shown, however, that while the public wants quick response, more important is the information given by the police to the person asking for help. If a caller is told the police will arrive in five minutes but in fact it takes ten minutes or more. Waiting the extra time can be extremely frustrating. But if a caller is told he or she will have to wait 10 minutes and the police indeed arrive within that time, the caller is normally satisfied. Thus, rather than emphasize rapid response, the focus of energies should be on establishing realistic expectations in the caller and making every attempt to meet them.

Questions 20 and 21

What are the **TWO LATEST** technological developments that reduce police response time?

*Use **NO MORE THAN THREE WORDS** for each answer.*

Write your answers in boxes 20 and 21 on your answer sheet.

20 ....

21 ....

Questions 22–27

Do the following statements agree with the claims of the writer in Reading Passage 2?

In boxes 22–27 on your answer sheet, write

YES	*if the statement agrees with the claims of the writer*
NO	*if the statement contradicts the claims of the writer*
NOT GIVEN	*if it is impossible to say what the writer thinks about this*

22 Police believe there is a better chance of finding witnesses to a crime if response is rapid.

23 A response delay of 1–2 minutes may have substantial influence on whether or not a suspected criminal is caught.

24 The public and the police generally agree on the amount of time normally taken for a rapid response.

25 Physical barriers are the greatest cause of delay in contacting police.

26 Rapid response is considered desirable in handling cases of burglary.

27 Research shows that some 75% of crimes are discovered by victims after they have been committed.

READING PASSAGE 3

*You should spend about 20 minutes on **Question 28–40**, which are based on Reading Passage 3 below.*

The History of Early Cinema

The history of the cinema in its first thirty years is one of major and, to this day, unparalleled expansion and growth. Beginning as something unusual in a handful of big cities-New York, London, Paris and Berlin-the new medium quickly found its way across the world, attracting larger and larger audience wherever it was shown and replacing other forms of entertainment as it did so. As audiences grew, so did the places where films were shown, finishing up with the "great picture palaces" of the 1920s, which rivaled, and occasionally superseded, theatres and opera-houses in terms of opulence and splendor. Meanwhile, films themselves developed from being short "attractions" only a couple of minutes long, to the full length feature that has dominated the world's screens up to the present day.

Although French, German, American and British pioneers have all been credited with the invention of cinema, the British and the Germans played a relatively small role in its world-wide exploitation. It was above all the French, followed closely by the Americans, who were the most passionate exporters of the new invention, helping to start cinema in China, Japan, Latin America and Russia. In terms of artistic development it was again the French and the Americans who took the lead, though in the years before the First World War, Italy, Denmark and Russia also played a part.

In the end, it was the United States that was to become, and remain, the largest single market for films. By protecting their own market and pursuing a vigorous export policy, the Americans achieved a dominant position on the world market by the start of the First World War. The centre of film-making had moved westwards, to Hollywood, and it was films from these new Hollywood studios that flooded onto the World's film markets in the years after the First World War, and have done so ever since. Faced with total Hollywood domination, few film industries proved competitive. The Italian industry, which had pioneered the feature film with spectacular films like *Quo Vadis* (1913) and *Cabiria* (1914) almost collapsed. In Scandinavia, the Swedish cinema had a brief period of glory, notably with powerful epic films and comedies. Even the French cinema found itself in a difficult position. In Europe, only Germany proved industrially capable, while in the new Soviet Union and in Japan the development of the cinema took place in conditions of commercial isolation.

Hollywood took the lead artistically as well as industrially. Hollywood films appealed because they had better-constructed narratives, their special effects were more impressive, and the star system added a new dimension to screen acting. If Hollywood did not have enough of its own resources, it had a great deal of money to buy up artists and technical innovations from Europe to ensure its continued dominance over present or future competition.

The rest of the world survived partly by learning from Hollywood and partly because audiences continued to exist for a product which corresponded to needs which Hollywood could not supply. As well as popular audiences, there were also increasing audiences for films which were artistically more adventurous or which dealt with the issues in the outer world.

None of this would have happened without technology, and cinema is in fact unique as an art form. In the early years, this art form was quite primitive, similar to the original French idea of using a lantern and slides back in the seventeenth century. Early cinema programmers were a mixture of items, combining comic sketches, free-standing narratives, serial episodes and the occasional trick or animated film. With the arrival of the feature length narrative as the main attraction, other types of films became less important. The making of cartoons became a separate branch of film-making, generally practiced outside the major studios, and the same was true of serials. Together with newsreels, they tended to be shown as short items in a programme which led to the feature.

From early cinema, it was only American slapstick comedy that successfully developed in both short and feature format. However, during this "Silent Film" era, animation, comedy, serials and dramatic features continued to thrive, along with factual films or documentaries, which acquired an increasing distinctiveness as the period progressed. It was also at this time that the avant-garde film first achieved commercial success, this time thanks almost exclusively to the French and the occasional German film.

Of the countries which developed and maintained distinctive national cinemas in the silent period, the most important were France, Germany and the Soviet Union. Of these, the French displayed the most continuity, in spite of the war and post-war economic uncertainties. The German cinema, relatively insignificant in the pre-war years, exploded on to the world scene after 1919. Yet even they were both overshadowed by the Soviet after the 1917 Revolution. They turned their back on the past, leaving the style of the pre-war Russian cinema to the émigrés who fled westwards to escape the Revolution.

The other countries whose cinemas changed dramatically are: Britain, which had an interesting but undistinguished history in the silent period; Italy, which had a brief moment of international fame just before the war; the Scandinavian countries, particularly Denmark, which played a role in the development of silent cinema quite out of proportion to their small population; and Japan, where a cinema developed based primarily on traditional theatrical and, to a lesser extent, other art forms and only gradually adapted to Western influence.

Questions 28–30

*Choose **THREE** letters, **A–F**.*

Write the correct letters in boxes 28–30 on your answer sheet.

Which **THREE** possible reasons for American dominance of the film industry are given in the passage?

A plenty of capital to purchase what it didn't have
B making films dealing with serious issues
C being first to produce a feature film
D well-written narratives
E the effect of the First World War
F excellent special effects

Questions 31–33

Answer the questions below.

*Choose **NO MORE THAN THREE WORDS** from the passage for each answer.*

Write your answers in boxes 31–33 on your answer sheet.

31 Which **TWO** types of films were not generally made in major studios?
32 Which type of film did America develop in both short and feature films?
33 Which type of film started to become profitable in the "silent" period?

Questions 34–40

Look at the following statements (Question 34–40) and the list of countries below.

Match each statement with the correct country.

*Write the correct letter, **A–J**, in boxes 34–40 on your answer sheet.*

NB *You may use any letter more than once.*

34 It helped other countries develop their own film industry.
35 It was the biggest producer of films.
36 It was first to develop the "feature" film.
37 It was responsible for creating stars.
38 It made the most money from "avant-garde" films.

39 It made movies based more on its own culture than outside influences.

40 It had a great influence on silent movies, despite its size,

List of Countries	
A	France
B	Germany
C	USA
D	Denmark
E	Sweden
F	Japan
G	Soviet Union
H	Italy
I	Britain
J	China

WRITING

WRITING TASK 1

You should spend about 20 minutes on this task.

The diagram below show how leather goods are produced.
Summarise the information by selecting and reporting the main features, and making comparisons where relevant.

Write at least 150 words.

A Method of Producing Leather Goods

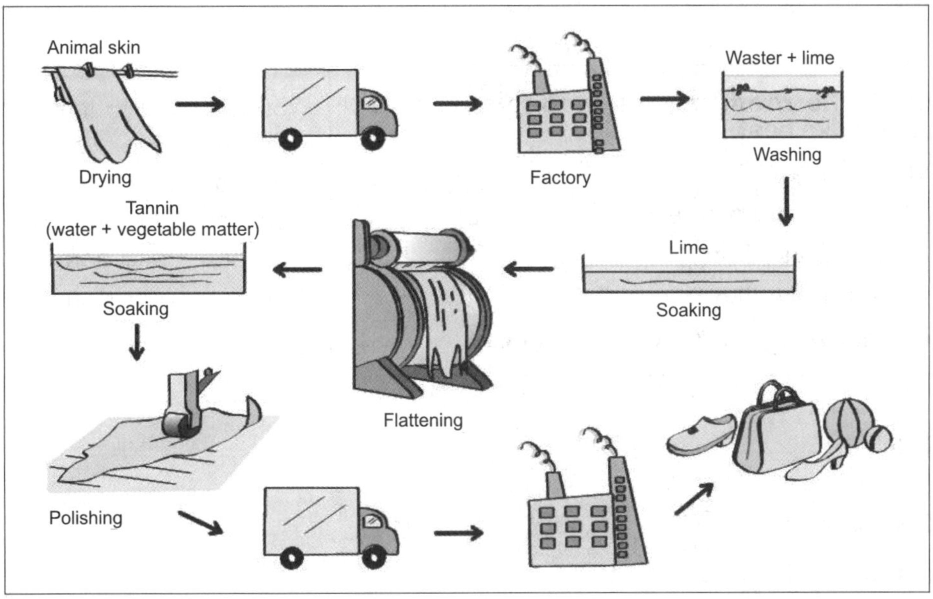

WRITING TASK 2

You should spend about 40 minutes on this task.

Write about the following topic:

Some people think that parents should spend more time with their children.
To what extent do you agree or disagree?

Give reasons for your answer and include any relevant examples from your own knowledge or experience.

Write at least 250 words.

SPEAKING

PART 1

The examiner asks the candidate about him/herself, his/her home, work or studies and other familiar topics.

EXAMPLE

Communication

- How do you usually keep in touch with members of your family?
- Do you prefer to speak to people by phone or by writing emails?
- Do you ever write letters by hand? Why/Why not?

PART 2

Describe the room in your house/apartment which you like best.

You should say:

where the room is

what it is used for

what it looks like

and explain why you like this room best.

You will have to talk about the topic for one to two minutes. You have one minute to think about what you are going to say. You can make some notes to help you if you wish.

PART 3

Discussion topics:

Rooms in general

Example questions:

Which room do families usually spend most time in? Why?

What types of thing do people usually put on the walls of their rooms?

Is it more important for a room to look nice, or to be comfortable? Why?

Interior design

Example questions:

How can different room colours affect the way people feel?

What is modern furniture like compared to older styles of furniture?

Do you think women are more interested than men in the way rooms are decorated? Why/Why not?

General Training Reading and Writing

TEST A

READING

SECTION 1 *Questions 1–14*

Read the text below and answer Questions 1–7.

A

Bookkeeper Required

A Major International Company Requires a Bookkeeper.

Essential:

3 years experience in a multi-national company.

Experience of computerised accounting.

Ability to work on own initiative.

A qualification in bookkeeping.

Desirable:

A university degree in business or a related subject.

5 years work experience.

Willingness to travel.

For an application form contact:

Kelly Smith

ERP electronics plc

02l-7274 3682

B

Foot-In-The Door Products

Successful members of our sales team earn in excess of £35,000 per year. Do you want to join them?

- Are you a team player?
- Do you have the motivation to succeed in an increasingly competitive marketplace?
- Are you result oriented?

If the answer to the above questions is "Yes" then you may be the person we are looking for.

Phone: 0737-2463

Don't delay, phone today! Your success is our success!

C

Manner Clinic Requires a Nursing Assistant

Manner Clinic was founded in 1901 to care for the elderly who otherwise had 110 relatives. It has since grown to become one of the biggest and best-known nursing homes in the UK.

As a nursing assistant you will be expected to assist in the day-to-day care of the elderly. You need to be an excellent communicator with a patient and caring disposition, willing to work with other members of staff and be prepared to work unsociable hours.

A GNVQ level IV in nursing is desirable although training will be given. Some travelling may be required within the Greater Manchester area.

Call in for an application form or call 666-5252 during office hours.

D

Teacher of Psychology

A qualified and experienced teacher of psychology required for a prestigious boys' school in the West of England.

In addition to the main curriculum area, the successful applicant will also be required to teach basic skills to boys with learning difficulties. Although a qualification in teaching basic skills is desirable, it is not necessary, as the opportunity to work towards a City and Guilds in the Teaching of Basic Skills will be provided.

Salary is paid in accordance to the national scale.

6462-8436

Questions 1–7

Complete the following answers by writing the appropriate letter, ***A–D****, against each question.*

Write the correct letter in boxes 1–7 on your answer sheet.

1 Which **TWO** jobs require you to travel?

2 Which **THREE** jobs require you to have studied the subject?

3 Which **TWO** jobs require you to work as a member of a team?

4 Which job requires you to work evenings?

5 Which **TWO** jobs exactly offer specialised training?

6 Which job exactly tells you how much you will earn?

7 Which **TWO** jobs specify that you must have experience?

Read the text below and anwer Questions 8–14.

Change of Company Policy

The management hereby gives notice of a change in smoking policy to take effect from Monday July 1st, 2002.

Due to in-house complaints and changes in social acceptance of smoking in general, a series of consultations have recently been held between the management and staff which has led to a revision in our smoking policy.

Smoking is now prohibited throughout the building, including all office space, adjoining corridors as well as toilets. Smoking is allowed in the work's canteen but only in the area designated for this purpose.

Following complaints from smokers, it has been decided that a smoking room is going to be built on each floor. Construction of the smoking rooms is due to begin next month. In the mean time, however, smokers are asked to leave the building during their coffee break if they wish to smoke.

The management will take any infringement of this regulation seriously, and any member of staff seen to be smoking on work premises, outside of the designated smoking areas, will receive a written warning that may lead to dismissal.

Issued: Friday June 28th, 2002

Questions 8–14

Do the following statements agree with the information given in the passage above?

In boxes 8–14 on your answer sheet, write

TRUE	*if the statement agrees with the information*
FALSE	*if the statement contradicts the information*
NOT GIVEN	*if there is no information on this*

8 Smoking on company premises is allowed for two days from the time the notice was issued.

9 Areas outside of the building have been designated for smoking.

10 Fewer areas are allowed for smoking now than in the past.

11 People complained about smoking in the office.

12 Smoking is only allowed in the company restaurant during lunch times.

13 Smoking rooms have been built on each floor.

14 Smoking in the office will result in the loss of one's job.

SECTION 2 *Questions 15–27*

Read the text below and answer Questions 15–21.

Capital Travel Cards

Any tour of any city is facilitated if your travel arrangements are made easy. And there is no better way of touring London than with a Capital Travel Card.

Capital Travel Cards allow you to travel around London using the buses, tube and trams. Unlike many other travel cards that restrict you to travelling between the hours of 10am and 4pm, a Capital Travel Card has no time restrictions: you are free to travel where and when you wish, even during peak times, saving you £30 on travel expenses.

A variety of cards are available from our Singles Travel Card, designed for individual people travelling independently, Couples Travel Card, for two people travelling together, and our Family Saver Card, which can be used by up to four people travelling in a group*. In addition, there is our Student Traveller which is available at a discounted price for students with a valid student union card but which comes with the same restrictions as a Singles Card.

For travel outside of London our Capital Travel Extra allows you to travel on any train service in the Southeast of England and provides you with a 10% discount on Train-travel to other parts of the country.

Type of card	One day	Weekend	Seven days
Singles	£4.10	£6.10	£19.30
Couples	£7.60	£11.40	£32.95
Family Saver	£10.40	£14.90	£39.64
Travel Extra	£17.30	£24.60	£52.10
Student Traveller	£3.61	£5.41	£17.27

The price of the cards vary according to the time for which they are valid (see table above), and can be purchased for one day, a weekend or seven days. Cards can be purchased from any train or tube station in the London area. In addition, they can be purchased from registered outlets which can be found in the capital's high streets. Simply look for the Capital Travel Card logo in shop windows. All Capital Travel Cards come with a free guide to London available in most major world languages.

* Two members of the group must be children under the age of 16.

Questions 15–21

Look at the Capital Travel Cards article below.

Complete the following answers with words taken from the passage.

*Use **NO MORE THAN THREE WORDS** from the passage for each answer.*

Write your answers in boxes 15–21 on your answer sheet.

15 A Family Saver Card must include ....

16 Compared with other travel cards, a Capital Travel Card has .... time restrictions.

17 With a Capital Travel Extra you can travel anywhere in ....

18 The cost of the cards depends on their .... periods.

19 Students are eligible for a ....

20 Travel cards can only be purchased in ....

21 A student with Student Traveller will spend .... one day if he/she travels in London.

Read the text below and answer Questions 22–27.

Scoring for Science

Learning has joined up with the Institute of Physics and the Royal Society of Chemistry to create a new science web portal, Secondary Online Science (SOS). The site features three games; Energy Quest; Fashion Victim; and Sound Park, developed in styles borrowed from the games console industry and targeted at both boys and girls. Secondary Online Science aims to bring high quality and innovative web design to the core of the secondary science curriculum.

The three games on SOS are highly interactive and provide a novel presentation of the science curriculum. The games are complex and challenge the students' game-playing skills, at the same time testing their understanding of science. Children of all abilities can enjoy the games. A good garner, who may not be academically successful, may do well in the game and achieve a top position in the high score league table. The style of SOS is motivational and supportive for individual learners.

- Energy Quest: Explore the three fun filled islands of Buzz Archipelago. The user has to solve the energy problems in time for the opening of the club 11–13.
- Fashion Victim: Hang out in the shopping village, buy clothes and play action games! The user has to buy the best clothes and learn about the fabrics they are made from.
- Sound Park: Hang out in Sound Park, play games and try to unlock the music samples trapped in the audio zones. The user learns about sound and makes music that can be published on the Channel 4 website.

"This has been a unique partnership between the three parties. Two scientific societies and a media company have joined forces to make science fun, multicultural and accessible to kids of all abilities," says Simon Fuller, Deputy Manager, for Learning. "Most children find computer games very absorbing. What we have tried to do with SOS is to combine the motivating aspects of game playing with suitable science content. The whole concept behind SOS is making science relevant and enjoyable."

The SOS portal also appeals to children by being relevant to their own lives and by using real world applications of science, such as DJ culture, fashion, sport and environment. The series of three games are based upon the same model and principles creating a consistent language for the user. The user can create their own characters in SOS by using different skin and hair tones and selecting different coloured clothes.

Questions 22–27

Choose the correct letter, ***A, B, C*** *or* ***D****, for each question.*

Write the correct letter in boxes 22–27 on your answer sheet.

22 Secondary Online Science has been designed for

A low ability students.

B mixed ability students.

C high ability students.

D no information given.

23 Secondary Online Science is designed to be

A educational.

B motivational.

C interesting and fun.

D motivating and educational.

24 Secondary Online Science has been designed as

A a set of teaching resources.
B a set of questions and answers.
C a web site.
D a set of games.

25 Secondary Online Science has mainly been designed for

A children.
B teenagers.
C adults.
D people of all ages and abilities.

26 Secondary Online Science has been designed to

A improve students' understanding of computers.
B improve students' understanding of science.
C improve students' understanding of fabrics and music.
D improve students' skills at playing computer games.

27 Secondary Online Science has been designed to be used by

A one player.
B two players.
C four players.
D more than four players.

SECTION 3 *Questions 28–40*

Read the text below and answer Questions 28–40.

The History of Tea

A Tea is believed to have originated in an area encompassing Southwest China and Northern India sometime before the last ice age, spreading to other parts of the land as the ice receded. Even so, when man first began drinking tea is unclear, although it is thought to have been first used as a medicine. Indeed, legend has it that China's father of agriculture and medicine, Shen Nong Shi, whose habit was to personally consume plants to assess their medicinal effects, recovered from a serious bout of accidental poisoning after eating tealeaves. From that time on tea was administered as a remedy for illnesses ranging from poisoning and digestive problems to common fatigue. And even today, tea is believed to help prevent certain types of cancer.

B When tea finally made the transition from purely medicinal use to a generally enjoyed beverage, it was unlike the drink that we know today. Instead tealeaves were processed and compressed into a cake. Tea was subsequently made by breaking off parts of the cake and boiling it in a container into which ingredients such as salt and fruit were added—a similar process is still observed by habitants of the Tibetan plateau today.

C As tea drinking gained popularity, it gradually necessitated a variety of utensils from which tea could be prepared and drunk. This in turn spurred on the ceramic industry, as well as the academic study of tea, and gave rise to the first tea masters who had great expertise in the variety of different teas as well as the best way to prepare them. Consequently, by the end of the Tang Dynasty teahouses were widespread throughout China. Tea became so prized, in fact, that it was even used as a form of exchange, in place of money, for horses bred by neighbouring tribes. Moreover, during the Song Dynasty tea was exported to Japan and sparked off a tea drinking culture there. Even today the traditional Japanese and tea making still reflects the tea making that predominated in China during the time of the Song Dynasty. Many of the traditional arts of tea preparation, however, were lost during the Mongol Empire, and only revived following the rise of the Ming Dynasty, some one hundred years later, albeit in a modified form.

D Tea eventually reached Western countries by way of the great trading routes, such as the Silk Road, and first became established as a national drink in Holland, and later England; most other European countries preferring to hold on to their coffee drinking traditions. The demand for tea became so great that ships known as tea clippers were specially designed and built for the sole purpose of transporting tea, stimulating the ship building industry in Glasgow, Scotland, and giving rise to famous Oceanic races when ships would challenge each other to be the first to reach the English coastline from the East China ports. Tea became so popular, in fact, that during the Victorian period (18th and early 19th centuries) ladies of leisure would spend their afternoons engaged in conversation and tea drinking, out of which grew numerous teashops. Thus, even today, alongside countries such as China and Japan, England remains a great tea-drinking nation.

E The wide varieties of teas available derive from two main facts: the region in which they are grown and the process by which the leaves are prepared. Generally, however, there are three main categories of tea: green tea, which is made from unfermented leaves, brown tea (Oolong) which is brewed from leaves that have undergone a process of semi-fermentation, and finally black tea for which full-fermented leaves are used. For many years, however, China jealously guarded the secrets of how to grow and cultivate tea as a way of holding onto their monopoly of the tea trade. This led to some Western botanists guessing wrongly that green and black teas originate from different plants, when in truth they are the same. Instead, tea leaves change their colour, from their natural green through to brown and eventually black through a process known as "oxidation", when the leaves are prepared by first being dried on racks to render them soft after which they are crashed by rollers and spread out in a fermentation room where they are allowed to oxidize. Finally, they are dried with hot air which stops the fermentation process and turns the leaves black.

F In modem times, tea is drunk in many countries throughout the world. And although tea has less commercial value than coffee, it still remains second only to water in being the world's most popular beverage.

Questions 28–32

Do the following statements agree with the information given in the text?

In boxes 28–32 on your answer sheet, write

TRUE *if the statement agrees with the information*
FALSE *if the statement contradicts the information*
NOT GIVEN *if there is no information on this*

28 According to legend, the founder of Chinese agriculture was accidentally poisoned after eating tealeaves.

29 Tea is sometimes used as a medicine.

30 The way of processing and preparing tea changed after the demise of the Mongol Empire.

31 Because of international trade routes tea became very important to the Chinese economy.

32 The tea clipper promoted the development of Glasgow, Scotland.

Questions 33–36

Complete the flow-chart below.

Use ***NO MORE THAN THREE WORDS*** *from the text for each answer.*

Write your answers in boxes 33–36 on your answer sheet.

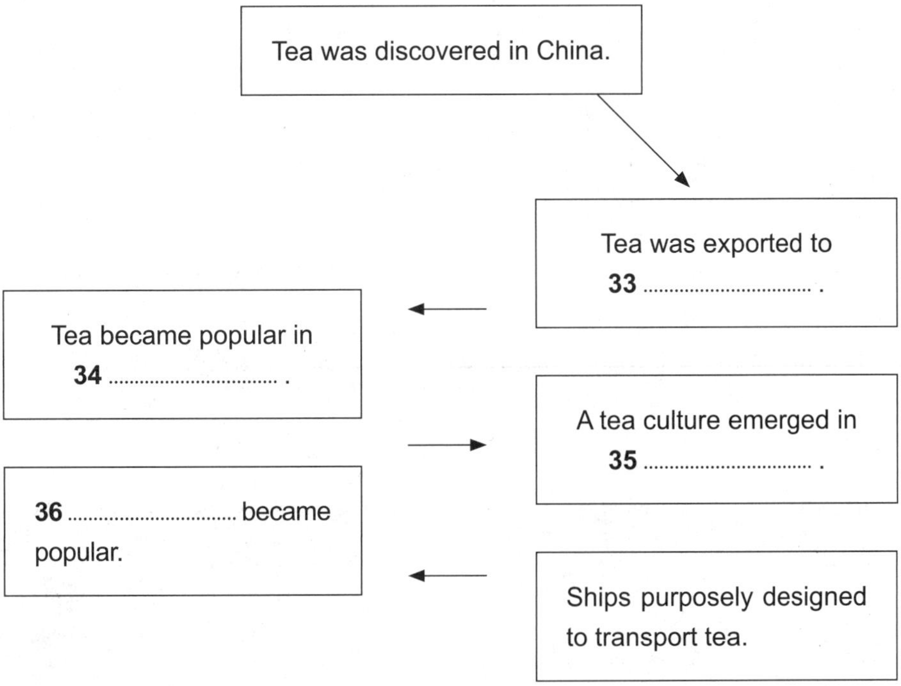

Questions 37–40

*Complete the summary using the list of words, **A–I**, below.*

*Write the correct letter, **A–I**, in boxes 37–40 on your answer sheet.*

NB *There are more words than spaces so you will not use them all.*

Following its discovery tea was admired for its **37** .... qualities, although it quickly emerged as a popular drink. As it spreaded to many other parts of the world it set in motion a **38** .... in both Eastern and Western countries. Moreover, the whole process of growing, refining and preparing tea spawned in its wake a whole host of different **39** .... And today tea has become one of the most popular **40** .... in the world, second only to water.

A tea culture	**B** medicinal	**C** trade route
D drink	**E** industries	**F** fatigue
G oceanic race	**H** poison	**I** stimulating

WRITING

WRITING TASK 1

You should spend about 20 minutes on this task.

You want something that you can't buy in your own country. You decide to ask an English friend to help you.

Write a letter to the friend. In your letter
- ***say what you want***
- ***explain why you want it***
- ***suggest how the friend could help***

Write at least 150 words.

You do **NOT** need to write any addresses.

Begin your letter as follows:

Dear .... ,

WRITING TASK 2

You should spend about 40 minutes on this task.

Write about the following topic:

Housing shortage in big cities can cause severe consequences. Only government action can solve this problem.

To what extent do you agree or disagree?

Give reasons for your answer and include any relevant examples from your own knowledge or experience.

Write at least 250 words.

General Training Reading and Writing

TEST B

READING

SECTION 1 *Questions 1–14*

Read the text below and answer Questions 1–9.

Citywide Power Company

Welcome

We are pleased to welcome you to Citywide.

We aim to make our customers' lives as simple as possible by offering a range of payment options and special discounts.

If you need to call us for any reason, freephone Customer Service on 1900 12 55 12.

Payment Options

Choose the option that suits your preference and rest assured that we offer everyone a 15% discount if the entire bill is paid before the due date.

Direct Debit

Set up a direct debit and your energy bill will be paid automatically each month (as long as you have sufficient funds in your chosen bank account).You qualify for a further 2% Prompt Pay Discount if you choose this method.

Internet Banking

Add Citywide Power to your bill payment options; receive your bill online; transfer the full amount owing before the due date and get a 2% Prompt Pay Discount. What could be easier?

Automatic Payment

If you want to pay your bills in smaller installments at regular intervals, say weekly or fortnightly, then set up an automatic payment with your bank. This option is more suitable for customers with regular energy usage, although you can change the amount and the interval at any time.

Telephone Transfer

Fast and easy bill payment at your fingertips. Make Citywide Power one of your telephone transfer options at the bank and you can just pick up the phone and pay straight from your bank account when you receive your energy bill. The 2% Prompt Pay Discount applies if accounts are paid in full on time.

Credit Card

Register your credit card details with us, and we'll automatically debit your monthly bill from your credit card. To set up this form of payment, you'll need to phone us with your credit card details, account number and ICP number. We accept most credit cards — all the major ones anyway.

Cheque

Yes, we know there are still customers who prefer to pay by cheque. If this is the case, simply write the cheque – being sure to note your account number on the back – and mail it in your pre-paid, reusable envelope in which you received your bill.

In Person

Got time to pay in person? Then pop into any branch of Citywide with your bill and the means to pay it.

Questions 1–9

Do the following statements agree with the information given in the text?

In boxes 1–9 on your answer sheet, write

TRUE	*if the statement agrees with the information*
FALSE	*if the statement contradicts the information*
NOT GIVEN	*if there is no information on this*

1 Calls that you make to Citywide Customer Service are not billed to you by the phone company.

2 Every Citywide customer receives a 15% discount.

3 If you do not have enough money in your bank account when the direct debit is due, a penalty of 2% is added to your bill.

4 With Internet banking, the bank does not automatically transfer the funds.

5 Automatic payment suits people on low incomes.

6 You should pay your bill straight away if you are using telephone transfer.

7 Citywide does not accept all credit cards.

8 There are no postage costs associated with sending a cheque to Citywide in the mail.

9 You should use cash to pay in person.

Questions 10–14

The following text has five paragraphs, **A–E**.

Choose the correct heading for each paragraphs *from the list of heading below.*

*Write the correct number, **i–viii**, in boxes 10–14 on your answer sheet.*

List of Headings

i	Add shine
ii	Return to original condition
iii	Avoid excessive wetness
iv	Prevent damage
v	Heat the straightening irons
vi	Move the irons through the hair
vii	Take only a second
viii	Remove moisture

10 Paragragh **A**

11 Paragragh **B**

12 Paragragh **C**

13 Paragragh **D**

14 Paragragh **E**

How to Use Your New Flemings Flat Irons

A Make sure to coat strands with a heat-protective spray before use. This will stop the straightening irons from causing excessive dehydration and frizz, which can sap the integrity of the hair shaft.

B Part hair into four or five large sections, and blow-dry each section using a paddle brush.

C Take a one or two inch section of hair and clamp the iron down as close to the roots as possible. Pull the iron down towards the tips with a firm, steady hand. Be careful to not to tug or jerk on the hair, and do not pause for more than a split-second.

D After straightening, smooth a serum gloss from mid-shaft to the tips. This creates a slightly reflective sheen, which gives a polished and healthy appearance to your hair.

E Your new hairdo can withstand some moisture such as misty rain or mild humidity, but take care not to get it saturated. This will counteract the effect of the straightening, and the hair will return to its natural curly or wavy state.

SECTION 2 *Questions 15–27*

Read the text below and answer Questions 15–23.

Employees and Contractors

An employee is someone who performs work under a contract of employment. Identifying who is, or is not, an employee has become an increasingly disputed area, with a number of different factors to be considered. Non-employees may be "independent contractors" or "sub-contractors" and are employed under a contract for services or even as agents representing a client business. The legal consequences of being an independent contractor are significantly different to those for employees. Only an "employee" can be covered by an award: something (e.g. a pay rise) given as a result of arbitration (process of resolving a dispute, e.g. between employers and a trade union) or make a workplace agreement. However, some cleaners, outworkers and some drivers of public passenger vehicles who might ordinarily be considered independent contractors are deemed to be employees under *the Fair Work Act*.

The rights and obligations of employees are very different to those who are self-employed. To distinguish between employees and independent contractors, the courts take into account a number of factors to determine what the real nature of a particular work relationship is. These factors may include: Control over work—generally an employee works as directed by the employer whereas a contractor has a greater say in how the work is to be done.

Payment—employees are usually paid on the basis of an hourly rate or a salary. Contractors are more often paid for a required outcome, with less regard for time.

Work injury–contractors are responsible to insure themselves against injury but employees are not.

Risk–employees generally do not bear in a direct way the risk of financial loss incurred by the business for which they work. Contractors have a chance of profit, and also the risk of loss.

Sub-contracting—an employee cannot assign or delegate the work to others whereas a contractor is typically permitted to do so.

Tools and equipment—contractors may supply special equipment or tools to do the job.

Income tax and superannuation—employers usually pay these for their employees whereas contractors make their own arrangements.

Questions 15–23

*Write the correct letter **A, B** or **C** in boxes 15–23 on your answer sheet.*

NB *You may use any letter more than once.*

Classify the following as

A contractors
B employees
C employers

15 People who work for wages or salary rather than profit
16 pay tax on behalf of others
17 have less responsibility for the way in which a job is carried out
18 do not provide their own work gear
19 pay by the hour
20 do not have the freedom to pay other people to do their job for them
21 do not benefit from belonging to a trade union
22 are paid for the end result rather than hours recorded
23 are required to sign an employment contract

Read the text below and answer Questions 24–27.

Paid Parental Leave

If you are a working parent expecting a child after July 31st, the information below about Paid Parental Leave concerns you. From 1st August, the first national Paid Parental Leave scheme will start. It's a new entitlement for working parents, funded by the government.

Why Paid Parental Leave?

Taking time away from work for a new baby is a common part of working life. Paid Parental Leave is designed to help parents spend time with a new baby and also to help employers retain skilled staff.

What Is Paid Parental Leave?

Eligible working parents of children born or adopted on or after 1st August may get 18 weeks government-funded pay at the National Minimum Wage to help them care for a new baby.

Am I Eligible?

Full-time, part-time, casual, seasonal, contract and self-employed workers may be eligible. You must have worked at least 330 hours (just over one day a week) for 10 of the 13 months before your new baby arrives. You can have up to an 8 week unpaid break between two working days and still be eligible. You can earn up to $100, 000 a year (individual salary) and still be eligible.

Is It for Both Parents?

Yes, usually the mother must apply for Paid Parental Leave. If you are eligible, you can transfer some or all of the pay to your partner (he needs to be eligible too). The scheme gives families more options to balance work and family.

When Can I Take It?

You can claim up to three months in advance, and your pay can start any time you choose from when your child is born or adopted. It will be paid in one continuous period from the start date and must all be taken with the first year after the birth or adoption. You are encouraged to apply early.

What About My Other Employer-provided Entitlements?

Eligible parents can receive Parental Leave pay at the same time, before or after other employer-provided paid leave or entitlements. The existing minimum entitlement to 12 months unpaid parental leave for long-term employees is unchanged.

From 1st August, employers must provide Government-funded Parental Leave pay through their usual pay cycle to eligible employees who have been with their business for at least 12 months. Other eligible parents will be paid through the Family Assistance Office.

For further information visit the website or call the appropriate number below:
www.ppl.govt.com
Parents 01800 4321
Employers 01800 1211

Questions 24 and 25

*Choose **TWO** letters, **A–E**.*

Write your answers in boxes 24 and 25 on your answer sheet.

Eligibility for Paid Parental Leave requires employees to have worked a certain number of hours in the months preceding the arrival of a baby. Of those, who is entitled to Paid Parental Leave?

A New parents only
B Working mothers only
C A couple who adopts a child
D A father earning less than $100,000
E All parents who work for the government

Questions 26 and 27

Do the following statements agree with the information given in the passage above?

In boxes 26 and 27 on your answer sheet, write

TRUE	*if the statement agrees with the information*
FALSE	*if the statement contradicts the information*
NOT GIVEN	*if there is no information on this*

26 Employees cannot receive the benefit once the child reaches the age of 12 months.

27 Employees who do not make a claim early may miss out on Paid Parental Leave.

SECTION 3 *Questions 28–40*

*Read the text below and answer Questions **28–40.***

Chickens

As pets and useful garden animals

Before making a decision whether to keep chickens either as pets or convenient egg-layers and insect-eaters, it would be wise to check with the local council. Regulations vary from region to region and, although some cities still allow residents to keep chickens, the practice is far from usual today. Some communities prohibit roosters because of their early morning crowing and only allow the much quieter hens. However, in most rural areas, there are generally no restrictions on keeping chickens either as ornamental or practical birds.

There are some Asian ornamental varieties with eye-catching plumage: the Cochin and Silkie from China have distinctive feathery feet and the Peacock from Sri Lanka has a strikingly long tail. These are examples of birds that have been imported by Western countries to serve mainly ornamental purposes, even appearing in exhibitions.

Chickens do not have to be especially beautiful to make loving and gentle companions and raising a few as garden pets is not at all difficult. The main concern is protection from predators—both domestic predators such as dogs and wild predators such as stoats and weasels. Backyard poultry need a secure place to roost at night. A cage or other structure which provides shelter, perches and nesting boxes with a lock-up door will suffice. Straw or non-toxic wood shavings can be spread on the floor and in the nesting boxes. Nocturnal predators are a danger and most chickens cannot flap their wings well enough to escape from peril. However, as they will naturally return to the same roost at night, they will enter the cage of their own volition as dusk falls and as long as the door is shut after them, they will remain secure till morning. If the birds are expected to stay in the chicken coop all day, a much larger structure is called for.

Chickens which are allowed to roam around the back garden during the day will prove to be safe, natural and effective methods of insect control. Not only that, but their constant scratching in search of insects will take care of unwanted weeds under bushes and other plants and even provide some beneficial soil cultivation. Chickens are great recyclers too and will eat almost any kind of kitchen scraps-leftovers and wastage are turned into usable, fresh, nutritious eggs! One of the benefits of free-ranging poultry is that they are exposed to the benefit of abundant sunshine which is a great health boost. On the other hand, wet weather can be perilous and make them more prone to disease. A planned approach to disease and parasite control is needed for the general health and well-being of backyard fowls. This may include a vaccination programme, health supplements in their feed, and keeping them in a clean, dry pen in times of extremely rainy weather. In dry weather, there is nothing more luxurious for a hen than a good dust bath to take care of mites and other problems. Young chicks are effortlessly turned into tame pets by hand feeding and simply spending time with them. Older hens also respond well to being fed by hand or they can be helped to forage for themselves if small rocks and other items are turned over allowing them access to the bugs and worms beneath. In both these cases, human presence is undoubtedly associated with food and will not only be tolerated but welcomed. Thus, companionship is assured and sought after! Chickens are said to be loyal, intelligent and even cheeky but it probably depends on the depth of their avian-human relationships.

Breeding chickens will obviously require a rooster to fertilise the hens' eggs. If local by-laws allow it, invest in a rooster and watch his fascinating courting behaviour. Typically, when he finds food, he clucks in a high pitch to attract the hens and lets them eat first. When he is courting a particular hen, he may circle her, dragging one wing on the ground-attracting her attention in this way is just part of the mating ritual.

When a hen goes "broody", she stops laying eggs and sits on the nest to incubate the clutch of eggs under her. She will rarely leave the nest during this stage, even to eat or drink, because she must keep the eggs at a constant temperature and humidity. Incubation takes approximately three weeks but the eggs do not hatch all at the same time so she will stay on the nest for a few more days. After the eggs have hatched, she will take care of the new chicks. This is a time when it is naturally important to keep predators away.

Raising chickens can be a satisfying and enjoyable hobby. They do not need as much care and attention as most pets and there is always the reward of wholesome and nourishing eggs to look forward to.

Questions 28–35

Do the following statements agree with the information given in the text?

In boxes 28–35 on your answer sheet, write

TRUE	*if the statement agrees with the information*
FALSE	*if the statement contradicts the information*
NOT GIVEN	*if there is no information on this*

28 Keeping chickens in some cities is common practice.

29 Male chickens make a lot of noise.

30 In the country many people keep chickens.

31 Some species of chickens are popular because they have beautiful feathers.

32 Certain tame, household animals may pose a threat to chickens.

33 At night chickens like to sleep on straw or other bedding scattered on the floor of the hen house.

34 Most chickens will manage to fly out of harm's way.

35 Free-range chickens do not need a large hen house.

Questions 36–40

Complete the sentences below.

Choose ***NO MORE THAN TWO WORDS*** *from the text for each answer.*

Write your answers in boxes 36–40 on your answer sheet.

36 Chickens in the garden are a good form of ....

37 Scratching in the dirt not only helps the soil but it also gets rid of ....

38 Hens prefer .... to rain.

39 Chickens can be successfully hand-reared and tamed easily if they learn to make a connection between people and ....

40 Incubating eggs must have a consistent level of warmth and ....

WRITING

WRITING TASK 1

You should spend about 20 minutes on this task.

You invited your family to have a special celebration dinner in a well-known restaurant, but you are unsatisfied with the meal.

Write a letter to make a complaint. In your letter

- ***tell what the situation is***
- ***describe what the problem is***
- ***explain what you want them to do***

Write at least 150 words.

You do **NOT** need to write any addresses.

Begin your letter as follows:

Dear .... ,

WRITING TASK 2

You should spend about 40 minutes on this task.

Write about the following topic:

Research suggests that the majority of criminals who are sent to prison would commit crimes when set free.

Why do you think this is the case?

What can be done to solve this problem?

Give reasons for your answer and include any relevant examples from your own knowledge or experience.

Write at least 250 words.

General Training Reading and Writing

TEST C

READING

SECTION 1 *Questions 1–14*

Read the text below and answer Questions 1–8.

Student Accommodation Guide

For students new to the city, here is a range of places you could stay.

A Halls of Residence

These are buildings owned by the university for the purpose of housing students. Due to their limited availability "halls" are generally only available to first year students. Living in halls gives students time to settle into their new environment and make friends before moving into private house. They rented accommodation in their second year.

As long as you are prepared to abide by the rules, halls of residence are an excellent option for first year students. They are generally located on campus or within easy reach of the university. Other benefits include having your linen washed once a week and the bathrooms cleaned regularly. Students will be asked to sign a Residence Agreement lasting approximately 40 weeks.

B House/Flat Share

This is the most common type of private rented accommodation for students and the main focus of this guide. Finding good quality accommodation to share is no easy task and as you will see as you read through this guide there are many hurdles to cross along the way.

C Room in a Private House

This may not be the type of accommodation that you had in mind when you imagined your wild student days ahead, but if you have left it later it may be preferable to some of the more squalid shared houses. At least with this type of accommodation you are generally guaranteed a well maintained property at a reasonable rent and no additional bills.

Resident landlords have greater freedom to bring your tenancy to an end because it is acknowledged that, should the relationship between the landlord and tenant break down, the landlord is more vulnerable in his or her own home.

D Private Flat

Having spent several months living with housemates, you may begin to dream of your own place. The trouble is that it's expensive and therefore out of reach for most students. Faced with a probable 100% increase in your accommodation costs it's easier to see the positives in sharing a house; the camaraderie, the solidarity, the thrill of never knowing if your food is still in the fridge!

E Private Sector, Halls of Residence

These are a fairly recent addition to the choices available to students. Developers were quick to see a way of cashing in on the rising number of students requiring inner city accommodation. These properties tend to be designed around the principles of a shared house with four or five single rooms grouped around a communal kitchen/diner.

They are generally new build multi-storey blocks and are fitted out to a similar standard of a three star hotel with en-suite bathrooms and large communal areas. They tend to be a bit more expensive than the universities' halls and as they are independent you will be sharing with a diverse mixture of people. This could be the option for you if you still get excited about staying in a single room in a cheap hotel !

F Parent Purchasers

This is a trend that started around the mid 1990s and has been gathering pace ever since. Rather than fork out for their student off-spring's rent, parents take the opportunity to become buy-to-let landlords. Their son or daughter invite three or four of their most trustworthy friends to become tenants and Mum and Dad can pay off the student loan with their capital growth. It sounds like a classic win-win situation but not always if you are the purchaser's child. Your fellow tenants will see you as the landlord's representative on the ground. Imagine the dilemmas: one of your housemates can't come on a night out with you because they've only just got enough money to pay their rent or your parents get a complaint about the noise and ask you to sort it out.

If your parents are proposing buying a property for you to live in, urge them to give it to a local agent to manage and collect the rent. Most agents will manage properties for a monthly fee even if they have not supplied the tenants.

Questions 1–8

Look at the accommodation options, ***A–F****.*

For which options are the following statements **TRUE**?

Write the correct letter, ***A–F****, in boxes 1–8 on your answer sheet.*

NB *You may use any letter more than once.*

1 Your tenancy could be ended easily by the resident landlord.
2 You will be considered the representative of the landlord.
3 It is better than some of the more squalid shared houses and has a reasonable rent.
4 The facilities of this accommodation are somewhat like those of a hotel.
5 This accommodation is possibly the most expensive kind listed here.
6 This kind of accommodation is for freshmen only.
7 Here you can have a single room but a shared kitchen.
8 You will probably have a cleaner living environment and is convenient for college life.

Read the text below and answer Questions 9–14.

NIS Extra-Curricular Activities

NIS offers a variety of extra-curricular activities for the students.

A After-School Activities (ASA)

In the pursuit of creating balanced lifestyles, NIS provides opportunities for students to participate in a range of after-school activities. The school believes that after-school activities are an integral part of the overall education process. Our programme aims to provide students with opportunities to cultivate and enrich existing skills, explore new areas of interest and to grow physically, socially and cognitively, and adjust to life in China. We seek to offer a broad range of activities over the course of the school year in an effort to cater to the varied interests of our students.

B NIS Community Activities (NISCA)

As an International school, NIS is well placed to benefit local communities by acting as a bridge between cultures. In this light, NIS seeks to increase the opportunities for local Chinese students and community members in the Ya Dong community to interact with NIS students and families and to use NIS facilities. Local members of the Ya Dong community are encouraged to contact NIS to discuss the possibility of developing joint activities with NIS or for utilising NIS facilities outside regular school hours.

The NISCA programme offers a wide range of interesting, educational and enriching activities on a cost-only basis. These activities are available for local community members. We hope that you will join our programme and share the many opportunities we offer to make life in Nanjing a more interesting and rewarding experience. Since NIS initiated this programme in 2006 the programme has developed and we look forward to offering more exciting activities this year.

Chinese Arts
Clay Making
Chinese Musical Instruments
Chinese Language
English Language for Adults
English Language for Primary School Children

C Inter-School Competitions and Activities

NIS is a member of both ACAMIS (Association of Chinese and Mongolian International Schools) and CISSA (Chinese International Schools Sports Association). Both these organizations provide opportunities for students to compete in a range of inter-school sports competitions and cultural activities. ACAMIS offers competitions in a range of sports for senior students as well as cultural activities and academic competitions, while CISSA provides sporting and cultural opportunities for Primary and Middle Year students within the Shanghai-Suzhou-Nanjing region. These activities often involve travel to another city, and have the added benefit of enabling students to make friends with their counterparts in other international schools in China. NIS also hosts ACAMIS and CISSA activities. Details of these events will be provided on the NIS website at the beginning of the academic year.

D Inter-House Competitions and Activities

NIS has a school wide inter-house competition that incorporates three houses—Wutaishan, Taiping and Xuanwu—named after three well-known places in Nanjing. Students from Pre-K to Grade 12 are placed into a House upon enrolment and are provided with a House T-shirt and sweatshirt to be worn during Inter-House activities, PE classes and other events.

Throughout the year various tournaments, competitions and activities are held in which students can earn points for their house. Regular points updates, given throughout the year, are displayed on the Inter-House notice board, in the School Bulletin and also announced in assemblies. The overall house winner is announced at the final presentation evening at the end of the school year.

Each house has a male and female house captain in MYP/DP and two representatives from Grade. House captains are elected by the students each year. These students are responsible for organizing teams for each event. For big events, outside school hours, teams often get bonus points for the biggest participation level or level of support.

Questions 9–14

Do the following statements agree with the information given in the text?

In boxes 9–14 on your answer sheet, write

TRUE	*if the statement agrees with the information*
FALSE	*if the statement contradicts the information*
NOT GIVEN	*if there is no information on this*

9 Programme of NIS is designed to help the students get more familiar with their life in China.

10 Local members of the Ya Dong community can use NIS facilities at any time.

11 The programme of NIS begins in 2006 and has become more complex.

12 This year, local members of the community can participate in such activities as English arts.

13 Both ACAMIS and CISSA offer competitions in a range of sports, culture and academic field for students of any grade.

14 Representatives are elected by the students each year.

SECTION 2 *Questions 15–27*

Read the text below and answer Questions 15–21.

Adams College Admission Requirements

Adams State College welcomes all applications for admission. Students should have an Index Score of 80 or higher, based on the Colorado Commission on Higher Education Admission Index. The Index combines your high school grade point average with your ACT or SAT scores. An 80 Index Score, for example, is equivalent to a 2.4 high school GPA combined with a 19 ACT or 900 composite SAT score. Lower ACT/SAT scores can be combined with higher GPAs in order to reach an 80 Index Score, and vice versa. Index Scores of less than 80 but higher than 70 will be considered on a case-by-case basis.

Adams State College does attract many high-quality students. As an example, the average GPA of a recent incoming class was 3.2, and the average enhanced ACT score was 20.8.

NOTE: If applying for scholarships or financial aid, prospective students must be admitted by March 15.

Freshman

First-time freshmen should complete the following steps for admission to Adams State College. Those needing clarification or any further assistance should call the Office of Admissions at (800)824-6494:

1 Send a completed application for admission, including the $30 application fee or complete our online application.

2 Ask your high school counselor to send your official high school transcript directly to the following address:
Adams State College
Office of Admissions
Alamosa, CO 81102

3 Notify the testing authourity to send official copies of your ACT or SAT scores directly to the Adams State College Office of Admissions. Our ACT code is 0496, and our SAT code is 4001.

Transfer Students

Transfer students entering from an accredited college or university are required to submit official transcripts with a minimum of 13 transferable credit hours and a 2.3 cumulative GPA or higher. For the complete transfer policy and additional transfer information, please visit the Transfer Page.

Graduate Students

For Graduate School requirements please visit the Graduate Student Page.

International Student Admission

Adams State College welcomes international students. To be considered for admission to ASC, international students need to submit the following:

1 Completed Online Application.
2 Provide verification of financial support.
3 $25 admission application fee.
4 Proof of English proficiency.
5 Academic transcripts translated into English.

A score of 550 or better on the TOEFL exam or successful completion of level 109 in an ESL programme will satisfy the English proficiency requirement. College or university level work completed outside the United States will be accepted directly in transfer only if the college or university is accredited by one of the US regional accrediting association.

Non-Degree Admission

A student who is interested in taking classes, but is not interested in a degree programme, may be accepted to Adams State College on a non-degree status. To be considered for non-degree admission, the student must complete a non-degree admission application and submit it to the Office of Admissions.

Non-degree students are not eligible for financial aid. If a non-degree student wishes to change his/her status to degree seeking, the student must provide complete academic information, test scores, and other required information to the Office of Admissions.

For more information contact the Office of Admissions, Adams State College, Alamosa, CO 81102.

Veterans

Adams State College welcomes the opportunity to assist qualified veterans with academic plans and preparation for the future. The college considers, on an individual basis, the needs, interests, and purposes of veterans who desire to continue their education. The College is authourized by the Colorado State Approving Agency for veterans education in accordance with federal law to educate students receiving benefits through the Veterans Administration. For further information regarding veterans benefits, see the Veterans Clerk in the Records Office, Richardson Hall room number 188.

Questions 15–21

Complete the sentences below.

Choose ***NO MORE THAN THREE WORDS AND/OR A NUMBER*** *from the text for each answer.*

Write your answer in boxes 15–21 on your answer sheet.

15 Based on the Colorado Commission on Higher Education Admission Index, an Index Score of .... is required to apply for admission.

16 If you want to apply for scholarship, you must be admitted by ....

17 As a freshman you should pay .... application fee.

18 At least .... transferable credit hours and a 2.3 cumulative GPA or higher are needed for transfer students.

19 English proficiency is required for admission of ....

20 If you don't have financial aid and is interested in taking class only, you should apply for ....

21 If a non-degree student wishes to change his/her status to degree seeking, the student must provide .... , test scores, and other required information to the Office of Admissions.

Read the text below and answer Questions 22–27.

Jobs in Arizona

A **Position Title:** Mortgage Loan Officer

Building Location: Code AZ007–Tucson, AZ

Job Type: Regular

Job Status: Full Time

Job Description: ☞

As an employee of PNC Financial Services Group, you become part of an organisation committed to customers, employees, investors, and the communities in which we do business. PNC is an established, growing and successful financial services company, with businesses organised around retail and commercial banking, asset management, and funds processing. Our branches are concentrated in thirteen states and the District of Columbia; additional offices are located nationwide and internationally. We are growing in size and through recent acquisitions have become the fifth largest bank by deposits in the US. We are also growing in reputation, as a leader in areas such as work/life family culture, "green" building design, frontier technology, and strong corporate social responsibility.

B **Position Title:** Business Analytics and Optimisation Consultant
Company: IBM
Work Country: USA
Job Type: Regular
Job Status: Full Time Job
Description:

IBM Global Business Services currently has immediate opportunities for experienced Business Analytics and Optimisation (BAO) Consultants in: BAO Strategy, Business Intelligence and Performance Management, Advanced Analytics and Optimisation, Enterprise Information Management, and Enterprise Content Management Initiatives.

As a part of IBM Global Business Services, you will:

* Develop innovative solutions to solve our clients' most complex business and technical issues.
* Have the opportunity to translate your expertise across 17 industries into integrated consulting services that help our clients transform their businesses and deliver bottom-line business value.
* Make a difference for top-tier global businesses and public sector clients, while also gaining valuable knowledge and skills and having access to resources and opportunities only a global leader like IBM can provide.

C **Job Title:** AVON Independent Sales Representative
Location: Work from home; work online
Job Description:

At a time when jobs are scarce and credit is tight, you can start an Avon business and take control of your finances. Avon offers hundreds of innovative beauty products created in our own state-of-the-art $100 million Research & Development Centre. Because Avon Independent Sales Representatives sell these products directly to customers, you can offer them at a smart value.

Becoming an Avon Independent Sales Representative offers unlimited opportunities. Even if you've never sold a product before, you can do it with Avon. As the world's leader in anti-aging skincare, fragrances and colour cosmetics, we make it easy for you to sell and succeed, right away. Avon is a proven path to success for millions of Representatives around the world, from all ages, cultures and walks of life.

Over 5 million Avon Representatives worldwide are enjoying these advantages and so can you:

* Flexible home-based business
* Minimum start-up investment—for a little more than the price of a lipstick, you can run your own Avon business.
* Set your own hours
* No inventory required
* Unlimited earning potential—sell and share the opportunity with those you recruit and mentor for greater financial rewards.
* Excellent opportunities in selling Avon—enjoy great rewards and incentives, access to preferred suppliers of health insurance, participation in the exclusive Avon Independent Sales Representative Savings Plan, training, scholarships, product discounts, and more.

D Quiznos Is Hiring a Restaurant Manager!

As a Quiznos Restaurant Manager, you will be managing new openings and re-openings of Quiznos restaurants. The Manager coordinates all aspects of an opening from working with contractors, service technicians and utilities to hiring staff, obtaining health permits and certificates of occupancy.

The Restaurant Manager is responsible for the execution of internal systems, training of operational procedures and managerial functions such as: customer experience, speed of service, cleanliness, product handling and spec management, food safety & sanitation, management checklists, equipment operation & maintenance, local store marketing, catering and quality assurance. The Restaurant Manager is expected to be an expert in all Quiznos operating standards.

Qualifications:

* Serve Safe Certification is preferred (If you do not have this certification you need to be willing to get it)
* Experience in restaurant management
* Strong understanding and experience with restaurant Profit & Loss (P&L) statements required
* Ability to train and coach crew members
* Ability to work independently and be flexible to change
* Must be proficient with Microsoft Office and the Internet

Requirements:

* Ability to work extensive hours during openings including nights and weekends
* 55+ hour work weeks
* Must be willing to travel as needed
* Valid Driver's License and must be insurable on rental vehicles required

Questions 22–27

Choose **NO MORE THAN THREE WORDS** *from the text for each answer.*

Write your answers in boxes 22–27 on your answer sheet.

22 Which job is concerned with finance and funds processing?

23 If you want to have a job in IBM, what is necessary to solve the clients' most complex and technical issues?

24 If you are particularly interested in working at home, which job will you apply for?

25 How many Avon Representatives worldwide are working for AVON?

26 In Quiznos Restaurant, who is responsible for the execution of internal systems, training of operational procedures and managerial functions?

27 Which job requires relatively long work hours when needed?

SECTION 3 *Questions 28–40*

Read the text below and answer Questions 28–40.

Human Noise May Disturb Whales' "Love Songs"

Whales belt out the loudest songs on Earth—the slow, low ballads of blue and fin whales can be heard for several thousand miles. Researchers tracked down bellowing bassist fin whales in the Sea of Cortez, and concluded that the songs were breeding displays to "serenade" females because all the singers were male. The finding raises concerns that rising levels of ocean noise caused by commercial vessels and military sonar could interfere with these communications.

"These creatures sing for days at a time trying to get a simple message out—I'm here, I'm available. Is anybody out there?" said Christopher Clark, co-authour of the study and a bioacoustics researcher at Cornell University, which boasts one of the world's major centres for the study of whale sounds.

"The finding that only male fin whales are singing provides strong evidence that these long vocal sequences are courtship songs," said Roger Payne, President of the Ocean Alliance but best known for his co-discovery of humpback whale songs in the late 1960s. He was also one of the first to suggest that blue and fin whale songs could be heard across oceans.

The discovery makes a lot of sense because fin whales, like blue whales, do not have breeding grounds, said Payne. But they don't need them because they can locate each other with these long-distance calls.

The whales belt out their songs at a frequency of about 20 hertz—just below the range of human hearing—and at an intensity equivalent to sitting in the front row of a rock concert.

Since the human contribution to ocean noise is also dominated by the low frequency sounds produced by shipping vessels, oil and gas exploration, and military activities, researchers fear the cacophony may disrupt or drown out the ocean banter of marine animals and could possibly damage their hearing.

Clark and his colleagues towed a hydrophone—an underwater microphone originally developed by the Navy to look for submarines—behind the research vessel to detect whale songs. The hydrophone fed into a converter box crafted by Clark to shift the whale songs to a higher pitch that humans could hear. A computer also analysed the sounds and allowed the researchers to pinpoint the location of the individual making the noise.

Each note in the song lasts only a second and sounds like a “gentle burp”, said Clark. Then there is a 14-second pause before the fin whale hits the next note. The entire song lasts about eight to ten minutes. Only when the composition is played at about 60 times its actual speed is the rhythm and pitch variation apparent. Blue whale songs can last up to twenty minutes with a two-minute interval between notes.

After locating a singing whale, Clark and his colleagues used a crossbow to get a sample of the whale’s skin for genetic analysis. In each case there was no ambiguity that the whales they sampled were indeed the performers. In all nine cases the singers were male.

Taking a small biopsy sample for analysis is necessary because it is difficult to determine the sex of a fin whale unless it rolls on its stomach—which it rarely does.

Clark’s team also surveyed all the fin whales in the area and found there were equal numbers of males and females—further supporting the idea that the singing was to attract females to the area. The research was published in the June 20th issue of the journal Nature.

While the Sea of Cortez, where the study took place, is relatively quiet, other waters, such as the Mediterranean sea, are polluted with the din of commercial vessels, ferries, and jet skis.

“In many places the oceans are filled with a generalised acoustic smog,” said Clark. “Commercial shipping lanes around major ports are as noisy as the tarmac at Kennedy Airport.”

But like people chatting in a crowded room, whales must have the ability to pick out signals from the rest of the noise, said Payne. The ocean is a very noisy place with the chatter of animals, the wind and storms, the grinding of the tides, and constant earthquakes.

Sonar initially generated concern when sixteen rare and elusive beaked whales beached themselves in the Bahamas after the Navy used a mid-range sonar in March 2000. There is still no conclusive evidence whether the Navy’s new low frequency sonar will cause problems for fin or blue whales.

"The frequency of the sonar is four octaves above those used for fin whale communication, but we don't know whether it will be bothersome to the fin whales or other marine life," said Payne. The same is true for increases in commercial traffic. "We are faced with real genuine ignorance."

One study published in Nature in 2000 showed that low-frequency active sonar altered the singing behaviour of humpback whales. Humpback songs were associated with reproduction but it is not clear whether the alterations would affect reproduction rates or were needed to compensate for the noise.

Questions 28–34

Do the following statements agree with the information given in the text?

In boxes 28–34 on your answer sheet, write

TRUE	*if the statement agrees with the information*
FALSE	*if the statement contradicts the information*
NOT GIVEN	*if there is no information on this*

28 The songs belt out by whales are about 20 hertz, but they can be heard by human at an intensity that equals to a rock concert.

29 Humans make noises in ocean mainly by making low frequency sounds.

30 Researchers were able to know where the whales exactly were by using the hydrophone.

31 The rhythm and pitch of the song changes clearly only when the composition is played at a higher speed.

32 The entire song lasts about eight to ten minutes and there are ten pauses in the song.

33 All of the nine whales analysed are males.

34 The noisy ocean makes it impossible for whales to pick out signals from others.

Questions 35–37

Choose the correct letter, ***A***, ***B***, ***C*** *or* ***D***.

Write the correct letter in boxes 35–37 on your answer sheet.

35 Researchers fear the cacophony can possibly damage the hearing of the marine animals because

A humans make great contributions to lower the frequency of the noises.

B the noises humans made are low frequency sounds.

C shipping vessels make noises.

D oil and gas exploration and military activities make noises.

36 Which statement is **NOT** true about hydrophone?

A Clark and his colleagues used it to detect whale songs.

B It is initially used by the Navy to locate submarines.

C Through hydrophone, humans could not hear the whales' songs.

D It is fed into a converter box.

37 What further supports the idea that the singing was to attract females to the area?

A In all nine cases the singers were male.

B The sex of the fin whale is determined by genetic analysis.

C There were equal numbers of males and females in the area.

D Fin whale seldom rolls on its stomach.

Questions 38–40

Look at the following statements (Questions 38–40) and the list of researchers below.

*Match each statement with the correct researchers, **A–D**.*

*Write the correct letter, **A–D**, in boxes 38–40 on your answer sheet.*

NB *You may use any letter more than once.*

38 change the whale songs to a higher pitch that humans could hear

39 whales must have the ability to pick out signals from the rest of the noise

40 have his research published in *Nature*

List of Researchers

A Christopher Clark

B Roger Payne

C None of the above

D The navy

WRITING

WRITING TASK 1

You should spend about 20 minutes on this task.

You would like to work overseas.   ***Write a letter to a job agency. In your letter:***   • ***tell what job you would like to apply***   • ***say what companies you are looking for***   • ***explain why do you want to work overseas***

Write at least 150 words.

You do **NOT** need to write any addresses.

Begin your letter as follows:

Dear .... ,

WRITING TASK 2

You should spend about 40 minutes on this task.

Write about the following topic:

Some people think the recent increase in cheap air travel brings benefits, while other people think it has drawbacks to the environment and the world's resources.   ***Discuss both views and give your own opinion.***

Give reasons for your answer and include any relevant examples from your own knowledge or experience.

Write at least 250 words.

General Training Reading and Writing

TEST D

READING

SECTION 1 *Questions 1–14*

Read the text below and answer Questions 1–9.

How to apply for admission

To be considered for freshman admission, complete the following application requirements. All items needed to complete an application must arrive in the Office of Admissions by the deadline. (If you plan to submit December test scores, visit the Testing and Test Scores page for details.)

Find out about the time needed to process documents submitted by mail and fax.

- Summer/Fall Deadline: December 1
- Spring Deadline: October 1

	Application Requirements
Application	• Submit your completed Apply Texas Application (the online application is preferred). The online summer/fall application opens on August 1. • Scholarship applicants must apply for admission using the online Apply Texas Application for Admission.
Essays	• Include two admissions essays; the easiest way to submit your essays is with your Apply Texas online application. • Visit the Essays page for prompts, options for submitting your essays, and tips on writing your essays.
Official high school transcript	• An official transcript includes the school's official seal or the signature of a school official, your class rank and size, and your high school coursework, usually through the end of the junior year. • Visit the Transcripts page for details.
High school coursework requirements (other items as needed)	• If you are on track to meet the state's high school coursework requirements, the transcript you submit should indicate that you will graduate under the Recommended or Distinguished/Advanced High School Programme. • You must also submit information about your senior-year coursework; visit the Transcripts page for details. • Some students may also need to submit an exemption form and complete other requirements. Visit the High School Coursework Requirements page for details.

Test scores	• Have official SAT Reasoning or ACT (including writing test) scores sent directly to UT Austin from the testing agency. • Scores on transcripts and student score reports don't fulfill this requirement. • Visit the Testing & Test Scores page for details.
Non-refundable $60 application processing fee ($90 for international applicants)	• Online payment preferred; pay by credit card (MasterCard or Visa) if paid while applying online. • If you believe that you may qualify for a fee waiver based on financial need, mail or fax us a copy of your SAT or ACT test fee waiver or a letter from your high school counselor or principal explaining your financial situation and reason for needing an admissions application fee waiver.
Additional requirements (if applicable)	• Programme-specific requirements: applicants may need to submit additional items to be considered for admission to certain majors. • International students who qualify for Texas residency (under HB 1403): submit a complete copy of the Residency Affidavit. • Permanent residents: submit a photocopy of the front of your permanent resident card. • Home-schooled students: submit any other credentials that reflect your academic potential (such as SAT Subject Test scores or dual credit coursework). • Completed college coursework—including dual credit coursework—while in high school: submit official transcripts of the credit issued by the college or university.
Recommended and optional items	• Resume • Letters of Recommendation • Special Circumstances

After you submit a complete application, the Office of Admissions will begin the process of making your admission decision.

Admission Decisions

Once you complete your application, an admissions professional in the Office of Admissions will review it. Using guidelines established by the state and the university, the reviewer will consider your academic achievement and personal achievement. Issues, such as whether applicants qualify for automatic admission, are Texas residents, or come from a non-ranking school, can also affect the final admission decision.

Questions 1–5

Do the following statements agree with the claims of the writer in the text?

In boxes 1–5 on your answer sheet, write

YES	*if the statement agrees with the claims of the writer*
NO	*if the statement contradicts the claims of the writer*
NOT GIVEN	*if it is impossible to say what the writer thinks about this*

1 The earliest date for summer application is October 1.

2 Scholarship applicants should use the online Apply Texas Application for Admission only when applying for admission.

3 An official transcript is also needed, which includes the signature of a school official, the size of the class, and high school coursework.

4 You should pay $60 as application processing fee and the money will be returned in the future.

5 A complete copy of the Residency Affidavit is needed for international students who qualify for Texas residency.

Questions 6–9

Choose ***NO MORE THAN THREE WORDS AND/OR A NUMBER*** *from the text for each answer.*

Write your answer in boxes 6–9 on your answer sheet.

6 When does the online summer/fall application end?

7 How many essays are needed?

8 What kind of applicant should submit a photocopy of the front of the permanent resident card?

9 What should a home-schooled student submit to indicate his academic ability?

Read the text below and answer Questions 10–14.

College Study Tips for Students

These college study tips are to help students learn how and when to study, and tips and tricks you can use to get ahead. Studying for college is no fun, but if you plan your time correctly and get your work done, you will have more time for fun such as college parties.

Create Mnemonics

Mnemonics are devices that can help you remember formulas, key concepts, definitions, etc. A really basic example of a mnemonic is "Please excuse my dear Aunt Sally" which stands for parenthesis, exponents, multiplication, division, addition, and subtraction.

Make a Study Guide

Whether or not your professor gives you a study guide for an exam, making a study guide is very helpful when studying for tests. Go through the textbook, notes, and any other material and write down any information that you think may be on the test such as important concepts, definitions, and formulas. Reading and writing the information will help you remember it faster. If your professor gives you a study guide, make sure to cover all the points listed.

Make Flash Cards

Making flash cards can be a bit time-consuming, but flash cards are helpful tools in remembering vocabulary, formulas, and key concepts. They are also easy to carry around with you so you can review them anytime.

Set Time Goals

Setting time goals for yourself will help make sure that you stay on track especially when you have time constraints. You're more likely to be productive if you have goals to achieve.

Don't Study Alone

Studying with other people is always easier, because you are all there and you know nothing else is going on. If possible convince your college friends to meet at the library at a specific time on a regular basis. If you and your friends have different schedules, do your best to find time when at least two of you are able to meet. This will also help you and your friends develop good study skills, keep tabs on your friends, and make sure they will be with you on graduation day.

Study During the Week

For those college students who like to party, studying during the week is the way to go. Typically studying Monday through Thursday is the way to go. When it's not football season, Sunday could also be a good day, but never count on it. If you have time between or after classes while you are still on campus, that is the best time to pop into the library for a quick hour of studying. This will allow you to enjoy your nights without worrying about studying later. Thursdays are notorious for being college party nights, so don't plan on studying late that night. College students that are big partiers will be hungover Friday, Saturday and Sunday, so the week is usually the best time. Having self-control and studying hard all week should allow students have the weekends free.

Avoid Studying on Coffee, Ritalin and Adderall

Since studying is no fun, students look for ways to enhance their ability to study and stay focused. Coffee has been used by college students to pull "all-nighters" or just to prevent falling asleep in an open book. If you choose to use coffee as a study aid, monitor your sleep patterns and how you feel throughout the day before making it a regular habit. Ritalin and Adderall are prescription drugs used to treat ADD (Attention Deficit Disorder) and ADHD (Attention Deficit Hyperactivity Disorder). These drugs are hard to predict because they are made for students with ADD/ADHD. Students without either disorder are advised not to take these if not prescribed, but there are always college students who choose to sell some or all of their prescribed medication. If you choose to go that route and try it (not recommended), be sure to try small doses at first (5mg) so you can see its effects. As always, students should only take things from those who are trusted.

Questions 10–14

Complete the sentences below.

*Choose **NO MORE THAN THREE WORDS** from the text for each answer.*

Write your answer in boxes 10–14 on your answer sheet.

10 The authour uses "Please excuse my dear Aunt Sally" to illustrate the importance of ....

11 Flash cards are helpful tools in remembering vocabulary, formulas and ....

12 One's productivity can possibly be improved if he has ....

13 .... are notorious for being college nights, so don't plan to study late that night.

14 If students want to use Ritalin and Adderall as a study aid, at first the doses should be ....

SECTION 2 *Questions 15–27*

Read the text below and answer Questions 15–22.

How to Improve Your Family's Web Security

Although no technology can be a replacement for parental involvement, there are ways to use Microsoft software to help protect your children from inappropriate content. Here are some tips for protecting your children's privacy and safety when they're using the computer.

Step 1 Decide where your child can and can't go on the Internet

It's a good idea to check out some sites for kids. Pay particular interest to sites that collect personal information. If you don't agree with the privacy statement of a particular site or if you don't want to give away any of your child's personal information, do a little searching and you may find a similar site that doesn't request any information at all.

- Windows vista parental controls

As a parent you have a unique opinion on what kind of content is appropriate for your child depending on his age, maturity, and your personal beliefs. Windows Vista introduces a rich and powerful set of parental control features to help parents monitor, manage, and administer their children's computer use and help keep them safe.

- Windows live one care family safety

Software that helps you filter information based on each child's age to help protect them from content you don't want them to see. You can also limit searches, block or allow certain Web sites, and monitor what your kids are doing online. You'll also have access to guidelines on how to help a child use online communications safely or how parents should talk to children about inappropriate Web browsing.

Step 2 Increase your security and privacy

- Create different user accounts

With Windows Vista and Windows XP, you can create multiple user accounts for your computer. Each user can log on separately and has a unique profile with his or her own Desktop and My Documents folder. As a parent you can give yourself an Administrator account with full control over the computer, and give your children Limited User accounts, with restricted controls. Limited Users cannot change system settings or install new hardware or software, including most games, media players, and chat programmes.

TEST D

- Adjust Web browser security settings

You can also help protect your child through your Web browser. Internet Explorer helps you control your security and privacy preferences by allowing you to assign security levels to Web sites. Internet Explorer also helps protect your privacy while you're on the Web by providing features that help control how Web sites track your activities.

Step 3 Remind kids not to talk to strangers online

Real-time chats and instant messaging can be a great way for children to discuss their interests and build friendships. But the anonymity of the Internet can also put children at risk of falling victim to imposters and predators. To help minimise your children's vulnerability, teach them to take precautions such as:

* Using only a first name or nickname to identify themselves.
* Never disclosing a phone number or address.
* Never sending photographs of themselves.
* Never agreeing to meet someone they met online without supervision.

- Set family rules for Internet use

Although software can help you protect your family from inappropriate content on the Web; there is no substitute for teaching your children a few basic rules. Talk to your children about the risks of going online, and teach them how to handle uncomfortable situations. And finally, set limits, and discuss them with your children. Together, you can create a fun and safer environment for your children online.

Questions 15–22

Complete the summary below.

Choose ***NO MORE THAN THREE WORDS*** *from the text for each answer.*

Write your answer in boxes 15–22 on your answer sheet.

It's necessary to protect children's privacy and safety when they are surfing on line. First of all, parents should decide where children can and can't go on the Internet. And particularly attention should be paid to Web sites that **15** .... Such elements as the child's age, **16** .... and parent's personal beliefs are considered in terms of what is appropriate for children. Windows Vista produces a rich and powerful set of **17** .... to help parents monitor, manage, and administer their children's computer use and help keep them safe. Software can be used to filter information based on each child's **18** .... to help protect them from some content. Creating different user accounts is also an effective method. Parents can give themselves an **19** .... with full control over the computer, and children have a limited user accounts. And **20** .... helps you control your security and privacy preferences by allowing you to assign security levels to Web sites. Real-time chats and instant messaging can be a great way for children to discuss their interests and build friendships. But the **21** .... of the Internet can also put children at risk of falling victim to imposters and predators. To help minimize your children's vulnerability, the authour suggests that **22** .... or nickname be used to identify themselves.

Read the text below and answer Questions 23–27.

College Scholarships

Financial aid bang for the buck, you can't beat the benefits of winning scholarship money. It's simple: scholarship money is free, usually with few strings attached. Whether you win $10,000 or $200, every little bit counts when it comes to college.

Types of scholarships

Truth is there are scholarships designed for almost every type of student. The key: take the time to search for the scholarships that best suit you.

* Academic scholarships abound and are based on GPA and performance in school. Other scholarships are based on athletics, skills or extra-curricular activities. Even your part-time job can be an opportunity for a scholarship.
* Many scholarships are designed for minority students and women. These awards offer financial opportunity to students traditionally underprivileged in higher education.
* You can even find scholarships for very unusual attributes such as scholarships just for left-handed people and scholarships for the best prom dress made out of tinfoil. Don't take scholarships like these lightly, the cash reward is very real.

Scholarship providers

Scholarships come from all types of sources, including:

* Institution specific scholarships, or academic scholarships, come directly from the college to which you are applying and often include both merit and need-based Programmes.
* Corporate scholarships may come from philanthropic companies such as Microsoft, McDonalds and Coca-Cola. Scholarships may be designed for minority students or based on field of study or interest, with further income and GPA qualifications. Big-name corporate scholarships are often very competitive.

* Charitable organisations nationally and locally based. Don't overlook your hometown organisations, such as the VFW, local garden club, or your church.
* Professional organisations and member–based groups make it part of their credo to support student endeavours. These often target students studying in a particular field, such as agriculture, technology, nursing and medicine, business or engineering, to name a few.
* Scholarships do not preclude you from applying for other financial aid. Always apply for federal student loans, no matter what. And in some cases scholarships require you have filed a FAFSA, especially college or institution–specific scholarships.

Where to search for scholarships

Want to know where to uncover the nearly $3 billion in scholarship money available each year?

One of the hands–down best resources for scholarships is the Internet. Here are some common online sources:

* Profile-based scholarship matching services.
* Scholarship search databases and indexes.
* College and university scholarship search tools.
* Search engines

You can also find scholarships offline. A good resource should be your high school guidance or career counselor, local teen centre or community centre. There are also many books on the topic of scholarships that offer comprehensive resources with current award listings.

Questions 23–27

Do the following statements agree with the information given in the text?

In boxes 23–27 on your answer sheet, write

TRUE *if the statement agree with the information*
FALSE *if the statement contradicts the information*
NOT GIVEN *if there is no information on this*

23 Every type of students can apply for a certain scholarship.

24 All scholarships are based on GPA and performance in school.

25 Academic scholarships come from the college and often include both merit and need-based programmes.

26 Applicants can get more scholarships from the college to which they are applying than some Charitable organisations.

27 High school guidance or career counselor are the best sources of scholarship.

SECTION 3 *Questions 28–40*

Read the text below and answer Questions 28–40.

Why do We Dream?

For centuries, we've tried to figure out just why our brains play these nightly shows for us. Early civilisations thought dream worlds were real, physical worlds that they could enter only from their dream state. Researchers continue to toss around many theories about dreaming. Those theories essentially fall into two categories:

- The idea that dreams are only physiological stimulations
- The idea that dreams are psychologically necessary

Physiological theories are based on the idea that we dream in order to exercise various neural connections that some researchers believe affect certain types of learning. Psychological theories are based on the idea that dreaming allows us to sort through problems, events of the day or things that are requiring a lot of our attention. Some of these theorists think dreams might be prophetic. Many researchers and scientists also believe that perhaps it is a combination of the two theories.

Dreaming and the brain

When we sleep, we go through five sleep stages. The first stage is a very light sleep from which it is easy to wake up. The second stage moves into a slightly deeper sleep, and stages three and four represent our deepest sleep. Our brain activity throughout these stages is gradually slowing down so that by deep sleep, we experience nothing but delta brain waves—the slowest brain waves. About 90 minutes after we go to sleep and after the fourth sleep stage, we begin REM sleep.

Rapid eye movement (REM) was discovered in 1953 by University of Chicago researchers Eugene Aserinsky, a graduate student in physiology, and Nathaniel Kleitman, Ph.D., chair of physiology. REM sleep is primarily characterised by movements of the eyes and is the fifth stage of sleep.

How to improve your dream recall

It is said that five minutes after the end of a dream, we have forgotten 50 percent of the dream's content. Ten minutes later, we've forgotten 90 percent of its content. Why is that? We don't forget our daily actions that quickly. The fact that they are so hard to remember makes their importance seem less.

There are many resources both on the Web and in print that will give you tips on how to improve your recall of dreams. Those who believe we have a lot to learn about ourselves from our dreams are big proponents of dream journals. Here are some steps you can take to increase your dream recall:

* When you go to bed, tell yourself you will remember your dreams.
* Set your alarm to go off every hour and half so you'll wake up around the times that you leave REM sleep when you're most likely to remember your dreams. (Or, drink a lot of water before you go to bed to ensure you have to wake up at least once in the middle of the night!)
* Keep a pad and pencil next to your bed.
* Try to wake up slowly to remain within the "mood" of your last dream.
* Common Dream Themes and Their Interpretations

Being naked in public

Most of us have had the dream at some point that we're at school, work or some social event, and we suddenly realise we forgot to put on clothes! Experts say this means:

* We're trying to hide something (and without clothes we have a hard time doing that).
* We're not prepared for something, like a presentation or test (and now everyone is going to know—we're exposed!).
* If we're naked but no one notices, then the interpretation is that whatever we're afraid of is unfounded. If we don't care that we're naked, the interpretation is that we're comfortable with whom we are.
* You're falling, falling, falling... and then you wake up. This is a very common dream and is said to symbolise insecurities and anxiety. Something in your life is essentially out of control and there is nothing you can do to stop it. Another interpretation is that you have a sense of failure about something. Maybe you're not doing well in school or at work and are afraid you're going to be fired or expelled. Again, you feel that you can't control the situation.

Being chased

The ever-popular chase dream can be extremely frightening. What it usually symbolises is that you're running away from your problems. What that problem is depends on who is chasing you. It may be a problem at work, or it may be something about yourself that you know is destructive. For example, you may be drinking too much, and your dream may be telling you that your drinking is becoming a real problem.

Taking an exam (or forgetting that you have one)

This is another very common dream. You suddenly realise you are supposed to be taking an exam at that very moment. You might be running through the hallways and can't find the classroom. This type of dream can have several variations that have similar meanings. (Maybe your pen won't write, so you can't finish writing your answers.) What experts say this may mean is that you're being scrutinised about something or feel you're being tested—maybe you're facing a challenge you don't think you're up to. You don't feel prepared or able to hold up to the scrutiny. It may also mean there is something you've neglected that you know needs your attention.

Flying

Many flying dreams are the result of lucid dreaming. Not all flying dreams are, however. Typically, dreaming that you are flying means you are on top of things. You are in control of the things that matter to you. Or, maybe you've just gained a new perspective on things. It may also mean you are strong-willed and feel like no one and nothing can defeat you. If you are having problems maintaining your flight, someone or something may be standing in the way of you having control. If you are afraid while flying, you may have challenges that you don't feel up to.

Running, but going nowhere

This theme can also be part of the chasing dream. You're trying to run, but either your legs won't move or you simply aren't going anywhere—as if you were on a treadmill. According to some, this dream means you have too much on your plate. You're trying to do too many things at once and can't catch up or ever get ahead.

Questions 28–31

*Choose the correct letter, **A**, **B**, **C** or **D**.*

Write the correct letter in boxes 28–31 on your answer sheet.

28 According to the passage, the deepest sleep happens

- **A** in the second stage.
- **B** when our brain waves are of the slowest type.
- **C** after REM sleep begins.
- **D** after we sleep for minutes.

29 What is the most distinguished characteristic of REM?

- **A** It is discovered in 1953 by a researcher of physiology.
- **B** It is the deepest sleep of the several stages.
- **C** It includes the movements of the eye.
- **D** It is the fifth stage of sleep.

30 We can remember the content of dreams more easily by

A having more REM sleep.
B telling yourself you will have a dream.
C avoiding getting up during sleep.
D waking up slowly to keep the mood of last dream.

31 The following statements are **TRUE** about the flying dreams **EXCEPT**

A dreaming that you are flying means you are in control of the things that matter to you.
B it may also mean you are decisive and feel like no one and nothing can defeat you.
C you've just gained a new perspective on things.
D the writer is afraid of flying.

Questions 32–34

Complete the sentences below.

Choose ***NO MORE THAN THREE WORDS*** *from the text for each answer.*

Write your answer in boxes 32–34 on your answer sheet.

32 You're falling, falling, falling in your dream, which is said to symbolise ....
33 Being chased in a dream usually means that you're running away from your ....
34 The dream of taking an examine means that you don't feel prepared for ....

Questions 35–40

Do the following statements agree with the claims of the writer in the text?

In boxes 35–40 on your answer sheet, write

YES	*if the statement agrees with the* claims of the writer
NO	*if the statement contradicts the* claims of the writer
NOT GIVEN	*if it is impossible to say what the writer thinks about this*

35 Early theories held that dreams were the reflection of people's real, physical worlds.
36 According to physiological theories, dreaming prevents us from sorting through problems or things that require our attention.
37 REM occurs at the third and fourth stage which is primarily characterised by movements of the eyes.
38 Dreams are very difficult to remember, so they do not seem important.
39 Trying to get recorded what you said or did in your dream can help increase your dream recall.
40 If a person dreams that he is naked and he doesn't care, it means that he is pleased with the current situation.

WRITING

WRITING TASK 1

You should spend about 20 minutes on this task.

> ***You have had an accident and are in hospital.***
>
> ***Write a letter to your college administration explaining why you will be absent from class for the next month. Ask for advice about how to continue your studies during this period.***

Write at least 150 words.

You do **NOT** need to write any addresses.

Begin your letter as follows:

Dear .... ,

WRITING TASK 2

You should spend about 40 minutes on this task.

Write about the following topic:

> ***Surveys show that in many countries, people are living longer but increased life expectancy has many implications for the aging individuals and for society as a whole.***
>
> ***What are the possible effects of longer living for individuals and society?***

Give reasons for your answer and include any relevant examples from your own knowledge or experience.

Write at least 250 words.

General Training Reading and Writing

TEST E

READING

SECTION 1 *Questions 1–14*

Read the text below and answer Questions 1–5.

A

The Authentic Taste of Thailand

Changtom Thai Restaurant and Hotel

12-3 6-12 Closed Sundays

- Set in 40 Acres of Scenic Woodland
- Outside Dining Area
- Fresh Produce Always Used
- Credit Cards Accepted
- Seating for up to 50
- Fully Licensed Bar
- Small Function Room Available for Hire
- Luxury Accommodation Available
- Easy Parking
- View over Beautiful Landscaped Gardens

FOR THE FINEST STANDARDS OF CUISINE & SERVICE

B

Jack's Traditional and American Restaurant

For a Family Treat or That Special Occasion...

- Superb Selection of Classic
- Fish & Chips & Vegetarian Plus Children's Menu
- Licensed Bar
- Wedding & Party Booking Welcome
- Takeaway Service

Lunchtimes
Tuesday–Saturday
Evening Wednesday–Saturday

C

Moghul Express
Indian Takeaway

- Enjoys Fine Indian Food in the Comfort of Your Home
- Open 7 Days a Week Including Public Holidays
- Good Parking Facilities
- Home Delivery Service Within a 4-mile Radius of Our Takeaway—Small Charge

Tel: Norwich 420988/588980

Top UK Takeaway Award & Hygiene & Quality Award for Two Years Running

D

The Marina Restaurant

Delicious International Cuisine at Local Prices
We Have a Constantly Changing Menu of Home-Produced Fresh Food
Using Only the Best Local Produce
Business Lunches *Anniversaries and Weddings *All Special
Occasions Snacks & Light Meals, Lunches & Dinners,
Full Bar & Extensive Wine List Dine in Style Aboard
The Marina in Relaxed & Informal Surroundings & Sample
The Pleasures of Norwich's Premier Restaurant

Open All Day, Mon.–Sat.

Large Video Scanned Car Park Opposite

E

Peking House
Restaurant and takeaway
Delicious high class
Chinese food
Experienced chefs
Own unique&ultra-modern
Kitchens
Free delivery-ample car park
Telephone orders welcome
Ask about our chef's
Specially

	Lunchtime	Evening
Sunday	Closed	5–11pm
Monday	Closed	5–11.30pm
Tuesday	Closed	5–11.30pm
Wednesday	Closed	5–11.30pm
Thursday	Closed	5–11.30pm
Friday	Closed	5–Midnight
Saturday	Closed	5–Midnight

Norwich (01603) 571122
40 Queen Street, Norwich

TEST E

Questions 1–5

Look at the five restaurant advertisements, ***A–E****, below.*

Match each description with proper restaurant, ***A–E****.*

Write the correct letter, ***A–E*** *, in boxes 1–5 on your answer sheet.*

NB *You may use any letter more than once.*

1 You can't eat at this restaurant on Monday evenings.

2 You can have a meal here in peaceful country surroundings.

3 You can eat here on a Sunday night.

4 You can have your order delivered for an extra fee.

5 You can have dinner here and then stay the night.

Read the text below and answer Questions 6–14.

A Richmond Experimental Theatre

Learn to act introduces people to a broad range of acting techniques. It is specially geared to those with little or no acting experience. The atmosphere is relaxed and unthreatening and great emphasis is placed on developing the confidence and abilities of the people who may initially be a little apprehensive!

B World Culture Day

Brazilian street percussion
2.30–4.30

Samba percussion workshop. Lift your spirits with the taste of carnival! It doesn't matter whether you're an experienced musician or a complete beginner. You'll be creating complex exotic rhythms in no time.

African story-telling
3.45–4.45

The magical African story-telling tradition of narration, poetry and proverbs (mainly from Ghana and Nigeria).
An event for all the family.

C Scottish Dancing

IT'S FUN
IT'S Good Exercise

We have classed foe dancers of all abilities.
Previous experience is not essential.
All you need to bring is a pair of soft shoes and enthusiasm.
Classes are held in a number of places and at different times.
We guarantee you a warm welcome.

D The Renaissance Singers

New singers are invited to join our choir, formed in 1993. It is to perform a wide variety of music in Cambridge. We meet every Wednesday evening from 7.30pm to 9.30pm. And this term we are rehearsing for a special concert with audience participation on Saturday 1st December.

An ability to sight-read and previous experience in choral singing is desirable, although not essential.

E Drawing with Colour

An intensive workshop for beginners
Saturday 13th and Sunday 14th October
This unusual workshop offers instruction in effective ways to draw in colour. Activities will include study of light and shade and ways to express mood and emotion in colour.

The small class (12 students) assures maximum attention for each student. Professional quality materials are included in the fee of $95.

Questions 6–14

The passage above has five sections, **A–E**.

Match each description with proper club, ***A–E****.*

Write the correct letter, ***A–E****, in boxes 6–14 on your answer sheet.*

NB *You may use any letter more than once.*

6 A friendly greeting awaits new members.
7 Some relevant skills are preferred.
8 This activity could cheer you up.
9 This activity is suitable for a variety of ages.
10 Individual guidance will be provided.
11 Participants can take part in a public performance.
12 This activity could help someone who wants to overcome shyness.
13 This activity promises rapid progress.
14 This activity is not held during the day.

SECTION 2 *Questions 15–27*

Read the text below and answer Questions 15–20.

Student Life at Canterbury College

Most of the courses at Canterbury College only take up four days of the week, leaving one day free for independent study.

The atmosphere at the college is that of an adult environment where a relationship of mutual respect is encouraged between students and tutors. Canterbury is a student city with several institutes of further and higher education. The city centre is just a five-minute walk from the college, easily accessible in lunch or study breaks.

Canterbury College has developed strong international links over the years and, as a result, many students have the opportunity of visiting and working in a European country in the course of their studies.

Students' Union and SRC

All students are automatically members of the Canterbury College Students' Union (CCSU) and can attend meetings. The Union is very active and is run by an Executive Committee elected by students in the Autumn Term. The President is elected every Summer Term to provide continuity for the next academic year. Representatives from each area of study form the Student Representative Council (SRC) which allows every student a say in Union affairs. In addition to representing students internally in the college on the Academic Board and with a sub-committee of the college corporation, the CCSU also belongs to the National Union of Students which represents the interests of students nationally. The Union also arranges and supports entertainments, sporting activities and trips.

Student Facilities

Learning Resources Centre (LRC)

The Carey Learning Resources Centre provides easy access to a wide range of printed and audiovisual learning materials which can help students with coursework. There is ample space for quiet independent study and there are also areas for group work. Resources provided include books, journals, audio and video cassettes and CD-ROMs. Inter-library loans are available locally and nationally via the British Library. All students are encouraged to use the Open Access Information Technology Centre situated on the first floor. This has a variety of computing, word processing and desktop publishing software.

Bookshop

A branch of Waterstone's bookshops is located on campus, where you can buy a range of stationery, drawing equipment, artists' materials and books, as well as many other useful items you may need.

Children's Centre

The College Children's Centre has places for under 5s with some subsidised places being available to students. Places are limited, so, if you are interested, apply early to reserve a place by contacting Linda Baker on the college telephone number.

Refectory

This provides refreshments between 08.30 and 19 with hot meals served three times a day.

Healthy eating options are available.

Crypt Restaurant

This restaurant offers good quality cuisine in pleasant surroundings. Meals are very reasonably priced and you are invited to sample the students' highly skilled dishes when the restaurant is open to the public during the week. Reservations can be made on 01227511244.

Chapel View Restaurant

This is another restaurant that is set up as a quick-service facility which offers a selection of snacks and main courses at a modest price.

Questions 15–20

Do the following statements agree with the information given in the passage?

In boxes 15–20 on your answer sheet, write

TRUE	*if the statement agrees with the information*
FALSE	*if the statement contradicts with the information*
NOT GIVEN	*if there is no information on this*

15 Many students are allocated a job experience placement abroad.

16 The elections for the Union President and Executive Committee are held together.

17 There are staffs in the LRC to help students use the facilities.

18 Nursery care is available on a first-come, first-served basis.

19 The Refectory serves fast-food options.

20 The Chapel View Restaurant is for students only.

Read the text below and answer Questions 21–27.

Canterbury College

List of Courses

Course A

This course will enable students to experience performing arts and the media at a basic level. It will give them the experience to decide if they wish to pursue an interest in this field and to develop their potential and adaptability for working in a performance company in either a performing or a technical role.

Course B

The aim of this course is to provide a thorough grounding in business—related skills and a comprehensive knowledge of business practice. It is for students with a business studies background who can manage a heavy workload that will contain a greater degree of academic study.

Course C

This course provides progression to a range of higher levels. Units will include maintaining employment standards, salon management duties, providing facial massage and skin care, instruction on make-up. Lash and brow treatments. Artificial nail structures and ear piercing.

Course D

This course is designed to develop skills used in leisure operations. It covers preparing for and conducting physical activities, maintenance of facility areas, building relationships with participants and colleagues, handing sports equipment and health and safety issues.

Course E

This course gives a foundation for a career in caring for children, the elderly or people with special needs. Core units are Numeracy, Communication and Information Technology. Work placements are an important part of the course.

Course F

This course is designed to provide a foundation in graphic and visual communication skills. Students complete units in picture composition and photographic design, and gain hands-on experience of desktop publishing and presentations.

Course G

This course is designed to provide an introduction to the construction industry. Units covered include Heat, Light and Sound, Introduction to the Urban Environment, Communication Processes and Techniques and Properties of Materials. All students complete vocational assignments which are integrated with work experience with reputable companies.

Course H

The qualifications gained and the skills developed on this course will provide a good basis for gaining employment in office work. In addition to word processing, the course also covers spreadsheets, computerised accounting, databases and desktop publishing. All students are given chances to develop their confidence, and advice and information is given on job search skills, presentation techniques and personal appearance.

Questions 21–27

Look at the list of courses at Canterbury College, ***A–H****.*

Which course would you recommend for people with the following career interests?

Write the correct letter, ***A–H****, in boxes 21–27 on your answer sheet.*

21 advertising

22 TV production

23 architecture

24 company management

25 working with the disabled

26 secretarial tasks

27 beauty therapy

SECTION 3 *Questions 28–40*

Read the text below and answer Questions 28–40.

Doesn't That Sound Terribly Yellow to You?

"I can't say. I'm colour blind", was my flatmate's response. And that was that for another twenty odd years, when by chance I came across an article in a newspaper on research into synaesthesia at a London hospital. At last, I understood my interpretation of the world through colour.

Synaesthesia is the subjective sensation of a sense other than the one being stimulated. For example, the sight of a word may evoke sensations of colour or the sound of music may also have a similar effect, as my taste. Or, to put it simply, synaesthetes, i.e. people with synaesthesia, have their senses held together, so that they experience several senses simultaneously.

To those not already aware of it, synaesthesia seems a new phenomenon. Yet, it is far from new. In 1690, John Locke, the philosopher, wrote of a blind man with synaesthetic capabilities. The first reference in the medical field was in 1710, by Thomas Woodhouse, an English ophthalmologist. In his *Theory of Colour*, the German writer, Goethe, talked about colour and the senses. The poet, Arthur Rimbaud, wrote about synaesthesia in his 1871 poem "Voyelles", as did another French poet Baudelaire, in "Correspondence". So, synaesthesia has a respectable history.

Synaesthesia is understandably met with a certain degree of scepticism, since it is something beyond the comprehension of the vast majority of people. Son et lumiere shows in the 19th century were an attempt at combining the senses in a public display, but such displays were not capable of conveying the sensations experienced by involuntary synaesthesia, as the ability which a synaesthete's experience is called. There has been a number of well-documented synaesthetes. Alexander Scriabin, the Russian composer(1871–1915), tried to express his own synaesthetic abilities in his symphony Prometheus, *the Poem of Fire*(1992). And another Russian, Rimsky-Korsakov, noted the colour associations musical keys possessed. For example, Scriabin saw C major as red, while to Rimsky-Korsakov it was white. Arthur Bliss, an English composer, based his *A Colour Symphony* in 1922 on the concept of synaesthesia. He did not claim to be a synaesthete; his colour choices were arbitrary and the project was an intellectual exercise.

In the field of the visual arts, probably the best-known artist with synaesthetic capabilities is the Russian artist, Wassily Kandinsky (1866—1944), credited with being the founder of abstract painting. It is said he experienced "sensory fusion" at a performance of Wagner's Lohengrin, with the music producing colours before his eyes. He did not see colours solely in terms of objects, but associated them with sounds. He even composed an opera, *Der Gelbe Klang* (The Yellow Sound), which was a mixture of colour, light, dance and sound.

For many people with synaesthesia, knowing that what they have been experiencing has both a name and a history and that they are among a number of notable sufferers is a revelation. Initially, they often feel that there is something wrong psychologically or mentally, or that everyone feels that way. Then they realise with a thud that other people do not. Suppression is an option, but unwittingly some people have managed to make use of the ability to their advantage. While the condition of synaesthesia may hamper many people because of its disorienting effects, it can also open up a range of new skills. It is not unusual for people who have synaesthesia to be creative and imaginative. As many studies have shown, memory is based to some extent on association. Synaesthetes find they are able to remember certain things with great ease. The person who associates the shape is able to remember a longer sequence of words; and the same goes for other areas where memory needs to be used.

But this condition like all gifts, has its drawbacks. Some people see words as colours; others even individual letters and syllables, so that a word becomes a kaleidoscope of colour. Beautiful though such a reading experience may be, synaesthesia can cause problems with both reading and writing. Reading can take longer, because one has to wade through all the colours, as well as the words! And, because the colour sequences as well as the words have to fit together, writing is then equally difficult.

Questions 28–32

Do the following statements agree with the information given in the text?

In boxes 28–32 on your answer sheet, write

TRUE	*if the statement agrees with the information*
FALSE	*if the statement contradicts the information*
NOT GIVEN	*if there is no information on this*

28 Newspaper articles and TV news reports about synaesthesia are appearing with monotonous regularity nowadays.

29 Synaesthetes experience several senses at the same time.

30 Synaesthesia is a new phenomenon.

31 Early description of synaesthesia can be traced back to the 17th century.

32 It is strange that many people are sceptical about synaesthesia.

Questions 33–36

*Choose the correct letter, **A**, **B**, **C** or **D**.*

Write the correct letter in boxes 33–36 on your answer sheet.

33 Son et lumiere shows

A attempted to combine public senses.
B were frequent in the 19th century.
C were both public and involuntary.
D did not reproduce the experiences of synaesthetes'.

34 Both Alexander Scriabin and Rimsky-Korsakov

A wanted to have synaesthetic abilities.
B created a lot of documents.
C linked music to colour.
D agreed with Bliss in 1922.

35 The Russian artist, Wassily Kandinsky

A performed Wagner's Lohengrin.
B found many abstract paintings.
C also composed music.
D saw objects.

36 At first, "sufferers" of synaesthesia believe that

A there is something wrong with them.
B they are revelation.
C they are psychologically or mentally superior.
D they are unique.

Questions 37–40

*Choose **FOUR** letters, **A–G**.*

Which **FOUR** of these statements are true about synaesthetes?

Write the correct letters in boxes 37–40 on your answer sheet.

NB *Your answers may be given in any order.*

A Some synaesthetes are disoriented by their abilities.
B Unusually, some synaesthetes have great creativity.

C Memory may be heightened by synaesthesia.

D They have more advantages than non-synaesthesia.

E Some synaesthetes use their ability to help themselves.

F Their ability can be an obstacle to them.

G Some synaesthetes write in colour.

WRITING

WRITING TASK 1

You should spend about 20 minutes on this task.

You have recently made a purchase from the local department store. However, when you used it, you found a fault with it.

Write a letter to the manager. In your letter
- ***say what the product is***
- ***explain the problem and***
- ***say what you'd like to be done about it***

Write at least 150 words.

You do **NOT** need to write any addresses.

Begin your letter as follows:

Dear .... ,

WRITING TASK 2

You should spend about 40 minutes on this task.

Write about the following topic:

When we seek a future career, what factors should we consider?

Whose suggestions should we consider?

Give reasons for your answer and include any relevant examples from your own knowledge or experience.

Write at least 250 words.

解析篇

Test 1

答案速查

LISTENING

Section 1, Questions 1–10

1 1.5 days
2 20 (people)
3 December 18th
4 Kaoriland Lodge
5&6 IN EITHER ORDER A C
7 $390
8 50%
9 8am
10 26591T

Section 2, Questions 11–20

11 C
12 A
13 A
14 B
15 G
16 B
17 D
18 E
19 I
20 A

Section 3, Questions 21–30

21 25%
22 an exercise class
23 steps
24&25 IN EITHER ORDER B D
26 D
27 B
28 A
29 cleaner air
30 more active lifestyles

Section 4, Questions 31–40

31 B
32 D
33 G
34 C
35 in winter
36 King penguin
37 fish, squid, crustaceans
38 9 weeks
39 brood pouch
40 a (one) third

READING

Reading Passage 1, Questions 1–13

1 E
2 I
3 F
4 A
5 C
6 H
7 circadian rhythms
8 an early lunch
9 challenges and opportunities
10 likely immediate future
11 oneself
12 outside causes
13 (its) appropriate cause

Reading Passage 2, Questions 14–26

14 G
15 D
16 H
17 B
18 E
19 C
20 F
21 photo-degradation
22 oxidation
23 black colour
24 white vapour
25 alcohol
26 C

Reading Passage 3, Questions 27–40

27 E
28 B
29 A
30 C
31 F
32 TRUE
33 FALSE
34 NOT GIVEN
35 FALSE
36 NOT GIVEN
37 Doctors
38 supportive friends
39 online tools
40 Mobile phones

名师解析

LISTENING

SECTION 1

主题场景	旅游信息咨询
主旨大意	一位客户向White Cloud Adventures（白云冒险）咨询短途旅行的相关信息。
考查题型	笔记填空题、选择题、句子填空题

名师解读

1　1.5 days　actually之后的信息为答案，短途旅行持续的时间为一天半，读作one and a half days，写作1.5 days。注意客户问的2 days为干扰项。

2　20 (people)　题干中的maximum表明此空需要填写最大的数字，一只船上最多20人。注意原文中的15为安排的旅行次数超过15次，而每组达到20人，故答案为20。

3　December 18th　题干考查的是下一个有效的旅行日期，题干要求next，应填写之后第一个出现的日期December 18th，而不是下一句中的December 23rd。

4　Kaoriland Lodge　此空需填写旅馆的名称。拼写旅馆名称，注意区分字母A与O，及Lodge中的最后一个字母e听起来接近a，不要混淆。

5&6　IN EITHER ORDER A C　5和6题为选择题，题干要求included in the price。原文出现the price includes时要迅速在对应的选项中做标记，听到overnight accommodation为答案，而其他项目未在选项中出现；之后的evening meal前有pay，不能选。之后drinks and lunch后有included，为答案。

7　$390　第一个出现的数字不是答案，转折词but之后的价钱$390为答案。正常情况一个人是$420，若超过3人预订，价格可以优惠到$390。

8　50%　若预订需要交50%的押金。考生不要和文中的其他几个百分数相混淆。

9　8am　题干要求是leave，即车离开的时间，文中的7点45分为干扰项，需要客户不要晚于7点45分到达本地点，而长途汽车上午8点准时出发。

10　26591T　此空需填写预订电话，号码为数字与字母组合。即使没有听清最后一个字母，也可从That's T for tango中获取信息。

SECTION 2

主题场景	旅游场景
主旨大意	介绍如何参观澳大利亚动物园以及动物园的布局
考查题型	选择题、地图题

名师解读

11　C　题干中的bus pick-up service为原文重现，原文中的Booking与选项C中的booked对应，同时原文中的essential（必要的）与has to（不得不）是同义表达。

12　A　选项B为干扰项，ticket price不仅包括zoo entry，还包括return transport。注意原文中与时间相关的表达是解答本题的关键。

13　A　根据题干中的时间关键词at a certain time与原文中的during the colder months, at those times对应来进行定位，题干中的is probably与原文中的might be对应，necessary为原文重现，故前面的a jumper即为答案。考生注意本题在听到necessary后才能确定答案，需要考生具有一定的短时记忆能力。

14　B　根据题干中的facility与原文中的facilities，为同一名词的单复数形式来定位答案，原文中的hire在这里是“租用”的意思，也就是需要付钱，与题干中的pay extra对应，故hire后的a locker即为答案。本题需要考生具备迅速捕捉信息的能力。

15 G 根据题干关键词Gift shop定位答案，接着后面对其的描述是on your left，也就是在entrance的左边。考生注意Presenter介绍zoo的起始位置。

16 B 考生注意situated后面的between...and...的表达为解题的关键，Tigers是在the car park和the artificial lake之间。park和lake的位置已经在图中给出，二者之间的B位置就是Tigers所在的位置。

17 D 原文中的adjoining一词说明这个Museum在the crocodile的旁边。这里的crocodile就是指图中saltwater crocodiles的位置，那么在其旁边的D位置就是Museum。

18 E 根据对这个景点建筑的描述为circular building，考生通过观察图中的建筑形状只有E位置的建筑是圆的，而且通过它紧挨着stream，可进一步确定答案。本题较为简单。

19 I 原文提到Kids' Zoo的位置是在角落处，紧挨着the marsupials, marsupials的位置图上已经给出，考生可以根据该信息，与图中的位置对应即可找到答案。

20 A 考生只要抓住原文对African savannah exhibition的地点描述是在湖的左边，the far side就可以确定答案。

SECTION 3

主题场景	专题场景
主旨大意	*Lifestyle*节目从多方面对更健康的生活方式进行介绍。
考查题型	摘要填空题、选择题、配对题

名师解读

21 25% 考生一定要读懂题干，介词by后应填写百分数，如果预测准确，就很容易定位答案的位置。研究表明如此饮食的人英年去世的可能性降低了25%。

22 an exercise class gym为关键词，之后的exercise class为答案。很多人发现很难安排出时间去健身房或者锻炼。set aside for...表示“为……留出”或“抽出……”。

23 steps 数字10,000为关键词，之后的steps为答案。在听力考试中，出现数字是非常普遍的，因此要注意培养对数字的敏感性。

24&25 IN EITHER ORDER B D 注意关键词yoga，选项的词汇在原文基本没有替换。yoga被证明能够减轻压力、降血压以及预防疾病。

26 D 本题的选项多且长，读题时划出关键词并尽量记住，但录音开始后以听为主，千万不要边听边看，极易错过重要信息。此题sleep为关键词，重点听之后的信息immune system，对应选项。

27 B 原文听到positive attitude，对应题干negative attitude，之后的内容为答案信息，原文听到die of..., such as heart disease，对应B项的death from。注意排除干扰项F，此选项有原文词汇significant，但ill health与原文不匹配。

28 A 原文employment-related stress对应题干work-related stress，之后听到personal relationship对应选项A中的other parts of our lives。

29&30 IN ORDER cleaner air, more active lifestyles 这两个题需填写两个表原因的名词，原文rural对应题干countryside，之后注意听名词，due to之后有明显的并列词and, cleaner air与more active lifestyles为答案。

SECTION 4

主题场景	专题讲座场景
主旨大意	介绍企鹅相关的信息
考查题型	选择题、简答题、摘要填空题

名师解读

31　B　原文中的jump与选项B中的jumping为同根词，原文中的if they have to, look carefully down与选项B中的often hesitate对应。考生注意本题的答案在转折词even之后，原文中表示转折处通常为考点。

32　D　根据原文中的grip与选项D中的climbing对应，选项D中的bills为原文重现。

33　G　原文中double-checked与选项G中的think twice对应，原文中的as if...until...与选项G中的before对应。

34　C　flippers为原文重现，原文中towards the ground与选项C中的pointing downwards对应。

35　in winter　根据题干中的关键词When判定，本题要求回答的是时间。题干中的breed与原文中的breeds是同根词，那词后面的in winter即为答案。本题简单，考生只要准确定位即可。

36　King penguin　题干中的appearance，size均为原文重现，由and连接，与原文对比，只是互换了位置。题干中的similar为原文重现，其前面的修饰词least与原文中的remotely对应，题干的句子是对原文句子的改写，故原文此句中的表语King penguin为答案。

37　IN ANY ORDER fish, squid, crustaceans　live on...（以……为生）与题干中的mainly eat对应，故原文on后的fish, squid, crustaceans为答案。

38　9 weeks　题干中的father与原文中的male对应，protect与原文中的ensure对应，his egg为原文重现。原文的9-week用来修饰后面的incubation period为形容词形式，考生将答案改写为名词复数形式即可。

39　brood pouch　题干中的keeps与原文的keep为同根词，on his feet为原文重现，题干中的feathered与原文中的feathers为同根词。题干中的定语从句which is called...是对原文后置定语动词called的过去分词形式的改写，故原文called后的brood pouch即为答案。

40　a (one) third　题干中的father penguins与原文中的male对应，题干中的lose与原文中的lost为同根词，his body weight为原文重现，故of前的a (one) third为答案。

READING

READING PASSAGE 1

体　裁　　说明文
题　材　　社会科学类
主　题　　个人时间管理
题　型　　配对题、句子填空题

Questions 1–6

题型　配对题(Matching Endings)

注意　可以采用这样的解题方法：划词读词，记词找词，文中寻词，回题干比词。这样的过程最为简洁。如果配对题题干中有两个词非常相似，可以并在一起记忆。选择时可以有的放矢，提高效率。

1	关键词	pro-active
	原文定位	第三段第三句To pro-act means to anticipate events and be in a position to take appropriate action as soon as the right moment arrives.
	题解	**答案E**　题干中pro-active（主动的）对应原文中pro-act（主动出击），是指能够在适当的时间采取适当的行动。选项E is more able to take advantage of events when they happen（在适当的时候，主动的人能更好地掌控这些事情），与原文相对应。

2	关键词	reactive
	原文定位	第三段第四句To react, on the other hand, means to have little anticipation and do something only when events force you to do so.
	题解	答案I　本题同第1小题，题干中reactive（被动的）对应原文中react（被动出击），是指对事情毫无预见性，被迫而已。选项I takes a more passive attitude towards events（对事件采取更被动的态度），与原文相对应。
3	关键词	circadian rhythms
	原文定位	首段第二句Circadian rhythms dictate that there are certain times of the day when we are at our best both physically and psychologically.
	题解	答案F　昼夜节律表明生理和心理都有各自最好的时间段，因此对昼夜节律进行分析，enables one to gauge physical potential at particular times throughout the day（能够在特定的时间衡量一整天的身体潜能），选项F所述符合原文昼夜节律的内容。
4	关键词	best time, work
	原文定位	第二段第三句The simple rules here are: don't waste too much prime time having a coffee break around 11am when you should be doing some of your best work.
	题解	答案A　题干考查的是最佳工作时间是在上午这一观点，而昼夜节律也表明在上午11点左右应该做最主要的工作，二者一致。这说明题干考查的观点同大部分人的昼夜节律一致，选项A agrees with the circadian rhythms of most people（符合大部分人的昼夜节律）与此相符。
5	关键词	alert
	原文定位	首段末句...while a very few of us feel most alert and vigorous in the late afternoon.
	题解	答案C　……在下午晚些时候，a very few of us（少数人）感到思维最敏捷，对应选项C conforms to the circadian rhythms of a minority of people（符合少数人的昼夜节律）。其中minority（少数人）对应原文中的a very few（少数）。
6	关键词	productivity, enhanced
	原文定位	第二段首句...most of us have a productive period between 10am and noon, when the stomach, pancreas, spleen and heart all appear to be in their most active phases.
	题解	答案H　……从10点到午时，大部分人的精力旺盛，选项H when several specific internal organs are active（几个具体的内脏处于活跃期），其中internal organs（内脏）对应原文中的stomach, pancreas, spleen and heart（胃、胰腺、脾脏以及心脏）。

Questions 7–13

题型 句子填空题(Sentence Completion)

注意 在定位到答案后，一定要注意是否符合句子题目的文法规则，避免即使找到了答案，但因为词的变形或时态的小问题而没有拿分。

7	关键词	physical and mental
	原文定位	首段第二句Circadian rhythms dictate that there are certain times of the day when we are at our best both physically and psychologically.
	题解	答案circadian rhythms　题干中physical and mental（身体和精神）对应原文中physically and psychologically（生理和心理），所以是circadian rhythms（昼夜节律）影响了生理和心理。
8	关键词	productive in the afternoon
	原文定位	第二段倒数第一句An early lunch also means that we can get back into our productive stride earlier in the afternoon.
	题解	答案an early lunch　题干中productive in the afternoon（下午精力旺盛）与原文get back into our productive stride（效率更高）相对应。
9	关键词	react
	原文定位	第三段倒数第二句This means that we aren't alert to the challenges and opportunities coming our way, with the consequence that challenges bother us or opportunities pass us...
	题解	答案challenges and opportunities　原文中this指代reactor（被动出击者），与题干中A person who reacts（被动出击者）相对应，结合原文"被动出击者"对即将发生的挑战和机遇没有警觉，即看不到挑战和机遇。
10	关键词	assessing, becoming pro-active
	原文定位	第三段末句We can train ourselves in pro-action...and appraise the likely immediate future, just as we sit down and review the immediate past.
	题解	答案likely immediate future　题干中assessing（评价）对应原文中appraise（评价），结合定位句可知，对将来进行预估有助于我们主动出击。
11	关键词	internal locus of control
	原文定位	第四段末句...while with other individuals the locus of control is predominantly internal, in which responsibility is attributed to oneself...
	题解	答案oneself　结合原文，题干中A person with a mainly internal locus of control（带有内控型人格的人）更倾向于责备自己本身。题干中的direct blame towards（归咎于……）对应原文的is attributed to（归因于……）。

12	关键词	external locus of control
	原文定位	第四段第三句...some individuals have a predominantly external locus of control, attributing responsibility to outside causes...
	题解	**答案outside causes** 本题对应11题，11题考查的是predominantly internal（主要为内部的），而12题考查的是predominantly external（主要为外部的）。前者将责任归因于自己，而题干中A person with a mainly external locus of control（带有外控型人格的人）更倾向于将失败归因于外界。
13	关键词	healthy and balanced locus of control
	原文定位	第五段第四句Obviously the best kind of locus of control is one that is realistic and able to attribute every effect to its appropriate cause, and this is particularly important when it comes to time management.
	题解	**答案(its) appropriate cause** 其中the best locus of control（最佳控制倾向）与题干中的a healthy and balanced locus of control（健康且平衡的控制倾向）相对应。最佳的控制倾向应把问题归因于appropriate cause（合理的原因）。

READING PASSAGE 2

体　裁　说明文
题　材　生物类
主　题　龙涎香
题　型　配对题、摘要填空题、选择题

Questions 14–20

题型 配对题(Matching Information)

注意 注意原文大写词语及数字的上下行通常为考点。

14	关键词	cost
	原文定位	G段首句As of 2006, raw ambergris fetched approximately US $10 per gram, with much higher prices possible for particularly high-quality samples.
	题解	**答案G** G段指出了ambergris（龙涎香）每克的价格，生龙涎质量越高，价格越高，题干cost of Ambergris（龙涎香的价格）与原文相对应。
15	关键词	physical properties
	原文定位	D段首句Ambergris is found in lumps of various shapes and sizes, weighing from 15g (½ oz) to 50kg (100 pounds) or more.
	题解	**答案D** D段指出龙涎香有不同形状、大小和重量。题干所述Physical properties（物理性质）与原文的shapes and sizes, weighing（形状、大小和重量）相对应。

16	关键词	historical and cross-cultural
	原文定位	H段首句Ambergris has been mostly known for its use in creating perfume and fragrance much like musk.
	题解	**答案H** 该段主要介绍了在不同国家，如America, ancient and modern Egypt, ancient China和Europe（美国、古埃及和现埃及、古代中国和欧洲）等，在不同时代，对龙涎香的使用情况。
17	关键词	various sources
	原文定位	B段首句及第二句Ambergris occurs as a biliary secretion of the intestines of the sperm whale, and can be found floating upon the sea, or in the sand near the coast. It is also sometimes found in the abdomens of whales.
	题解	**答案B** 该段主要介绍了龙涎香的不同来源。题干的Various sources（不同来源）与此相对应。
18	关键词	chemical properties
	原文定位	E段末句White crystals of a substance called Ambrein can be separated from ambergris by heating raw ambergris in alcohol, then allowing the resulting solution to cool.
	题解	**答案E** 该段主要介绍了可在酒精中加热生龙涎香提取龙涎香精，这属于龙涎香的Chemical properties（化学性质）。题干所述与原文相对应。
19	关键词	distributing
	原文定位	C段首句Ambergris can be found in the Atlantic Ocean; on the coasts of Brazil and Madagascar; and on the coast of Africa, of the East Indies, the Maldives, China, Japan, India, Australia, New Zealand and the Molucca islands.
	题解	**答案C** 该段主要介绍了龙涎香的不同分布地区，如Atlantic Ocean, Brazil, Madagascar, Africa（大西洋、巴西、马达加斯加、非洲）等等。该段的地名较多，可以较为容易地进行选择。
20	关键词	replacing compounds
	原文定位	F段第四句及第五句Due to demand for ambergris and its high price, replacement compounds have been sought out...and is the most widely used ambergris-replacement odorant in perfume manufacturing.
	题解	**答案F** 该段主要介绍了龙涎香的替代混合物的发现以及使用。题干中的Replacing compounds（替代化合物）与原文的replacement compounds（替代化合物）相对应。

Questions 21–25

题型 摘要填空题(Summary Completion)

注意 注意空格前后的词，到原文中去找这些词的对应词。对应词可能是原词，也可能发生词性或语态变化，或为同义词。

21 & 22	关键词	fatty excretion
	原文定位	原文D段第三句Following months to years of photo-degradation and oxidation in the ocean...
	题解	答案IN ORDER photo-degradation, oxidation　21题与22题的空格由and连接，应填入两个并列的名词。题干中through...（通过……）与原文中的following...（接下来的……）相对应，题干中in the salty condition（在含盐条件下）与原文in the ocean（在海洋中）相对应。
23	关键词	hard and changes into
	原文定位	D段第三句Following months to years of photo-degradation and oxidation in the ocean, this precursor gradually hardens, developing a somewhat black colour...earthy, marine, and animalic.
	题解	答案black colour　题干中的changes into...（变成……）与原文中developing（发展为）相对应。
24	关键词	vapourized to
	原文定位	D段倒数第二句It melts at about 62℃ to a fatty, yellow resinous liquid; and at 100℃ it is volatilized into a white vapour.
	题解	答案white vapour　龙涎香在100℃时蒸发成白色蒸汽。题干中的vapourized to（蒸发变成）与原文中的volatilized into（挥发形成）相对应。
25	关键词	Ambrein
	原文定位	E段第二句White crystals of a substance called Ambrein can be separated from ambergris by heating raw ambergris in alcohol, then allowing the resulting solution to cool.
	题解	答案alcohol　通过在酒精中加热龙涎香可以得到龙涎香精这种物质。题干中的abstract（提取）与原文中的separate from（分离）相对应。

Question 26

题型 选择题(Multiple Choice)

注意 选择题是一种简单题型。因为正确答案的数目是已知的，也就是在题目的要求中会告诉考生要选出几个选项。另外，题目要求中常有WHICH FOUR, WHICH THREE等字样。利用排除法逐一去除干扰项，最终确定答案。

26	关键词	used widely throughout the whole world
	原文定位	H段 Ambergris has been mostly known for its use in creating perfume and fragrance much like musk...During the Middle Ages, Europeans used ambergris as a medication for headaches, colds, epilepsy, and other ailments.
	题解	答案C 该段主要介绍了龙涎香的历史，及其在各个国家的应用，最熟知的是作为香料用于香水等化妆品，所以B项可排除；在欧洲发生黑死病时期，龙涎香被视为可以远离瘟疫的保护物，所以D项可排除；在中世纪，欧洲人认为龙涎香是治疗头痛感冒的药物，所以A项可排除；综上所述，并没有提及龙涎香在武器方面的应用，答案为C。

READING PASSAGE 3

体　裁　说明文
题　材　社会科学类
主　题　医疗保健服务改革
题　型　配对题、判断题、句子填空题

Questions 27–31

题型 配对题(Matching Information)

注意 注意用原文的意思验证题目，本末不可倒置。

27	关键词	potential of wireless devices
	原文定位	第二段首句Dr Nathanson's enthusiasm hints at the potential of wireless gadgets to improve health care, and to ensure more personalised treatment in particular.
	题解	答案E 观点配对题貌似是对全篇文章的考查，其实考查的就是文中几个人所说的几句话。故应先从文中找人名，再去找答案。Dr Nathanson的热衷显示出无线小装置在improve health care（改善医疗保健）方面的潜能，题干的better health condition（改善医疗条件）对应原文的improve health care。
28	关键词	customised therapies
	原文定位	第二段第二句Pundits have long predicted that advances in genetics will usher in a golden age of individually tailored therapies.
	题解	答案B 专家们预测“量体裁衣”式医疗服务将会到来。其中题干所述customised therapies（按客户特别订制）对应原文individually tailored therapies（量体裁衣）；foretold（预言）对应predicted（预测）。

29	关键词	time-saving
	原文定位	第三段第三句Don Jones of Qualcomm, a maker of networking technology, argues that the trend speeds diagnosis and treatment, and saves doctors' and nurses' time.
	题解	**答案A** Don Jones指出，无线医疗设备普及节省了医生和护士的时间。题干中的time-saving for doctors（对于医生来说，节省了时间）对应原文的saves doctors' and nurses' time（节省了医生、护士的时间）。
30	关键词	smart phones
	原文定位	第五段末句Jitterbug, an American mobile operator that offers easy-to-use phones for the elderly, recently added more health services; rival mobile carriers are doing much the same.
	题解	**答案C** Jitterbug为老年人提供便捷手机。其中题干中的smart phone（便捷电话）对应原文中的easy-to-use phones（便捷电话），题干中的the old（老年人）对应原文中the elderly（老年人）。
31	关键词	blood sugar level
	原文定位	第七段第三句Some are overtly clinical in nature: Medtronic, a devices giant, is developing a bedside monitor that wirelessly tracks the blood sugar levels in diabetic children sleeping nearby.
	题解	**答案F** Medtronic开发的检测器能够无线追踪血糖浓度变化。题干基本由原文简化而来。

Questions 32–36

题型 判断题(Identifying Information)

注意 判断题的思路是简单的单向思维，即从原文出发，以原文为基础，对题目进行是、非、无判断。

32	关键词	$9 billion, 2013
	原文定位	第三段首句...it estimates that the market for such devices and services in America alone will grow from $2.7 billion in 2007 to $9.6 billion in 2013.
	题解	**答案TRUE** ……美国的设备和服务市场将在2013年将增加到96亿美元。题干所述为beyond $9 billion in 2013（超过90亿），符合原文。
33	关键词	Epocrates
	原文定位	第四段第三句 Over one third of American doctors use Epocrates, a programme for mobiles and laptops which offers instant information on drug-to-drug interactions, treatment recommendations and so on.
	题解	**答案FALSE** 超过三分之一的美国医生使用Epocrates。而题干所说为超过一半的美国医生通过Epocrates获取信息，题干所述与原文不相对应。

34	关键词	mHealth
	原文定位	第六段首句But Carolyn Buck-Luce of Ernst & Young, a consultancy, points out that "mHealth" is transforming health care in poor countries as well as rich ones.
	题解	答案NOT GIVEN　mHealth在改变富国和贫国的医疗保健。题干所述为mHealth相同程度上服务贫国和富国，而原文并未有是否equally（平等地）的相应表述。
35	关键词	accurate diagnoses, effective prescription
	原文定位	第九段首句All these devices and services do not just allow doctors to make more accurate diagnoses, prescribe more effective treatments and keep better track of patients' conditions.
	题解	答案FALSE　题干中表现的是否定含义，而原文中出现的是more accurate（更精确的）、more effective（更有效的）及better（更好的），很明显这是肯定的含义。即题干所述与原文不相对应。
36	关键词	Price Waterhouse Coopers
	原文定位	第九段末句...Price Waterhouse Coopers...finds that the elderly prefer high-quality care with lots of personal attention, whereas younger types prefer low-cost care and wellness schemes.
	题解	答案NOT GIVEN　普华永道的调查表示年轻人更青睐于low-cost care（低成本的保健）方案。题干中指出年轻人不关注individual treatment（个人治疗），这点并未在原文中体现。

Questions 37–40

题型　句子填空题(Sentence Completion)

注意　找出题目中的关键词，先定位到原文的段落中，再对照原文查找题目中所缺信息。

37	关键词	initiative wireless devices
	原文定位	第四段首句Doctors are an obvious early target for wireless health.
	题解	答案Doctors　题干考查的是initiative wireless devices in medical care（最早在医疗护理中使用无线设备），原文指出无限设备早期是面向doctors的。
38	关键词	tend to, family
	原文定位	原文末段第二句Patients often ignore doctors' lectures, but are more inclined to listen to supportive friends and family.
	题解	答案supportive friends　题干考查的是在病人的行为变化中，他们将谁视做最信赖的人，而原文表示患者通常不理会医生的嘱咐，却倾向于听从朋友和家人的意见，可知病人最信赖的是家人和朋友。

39	关键词	HealthMedia
	原文定位	倒数第三段首句A similar scheme run by HealthMedia, a wellness firm owned by Johnson & Johnson, a big drugs firm, uses online tools (it calls them "digital health coaches") to help patients manage diabetes and lose weight.
	题解	答案online tools　HealthMedia公司使用online tools（网络工具）帮助病人控制糖尿病和体重。此题为题干cope with（应付）与原文manage（成功应付）的同义转换。
40	关键词	wireless appliances
	原文定位	末段第三句By the same token, doctors and nurses are not always on hand to encourage healthy behaviour, but mobile phones and other wireless gadgets can be.
	题解	答案mobile phones　此题为题干与原文的同义转换，题干中的wireless appliances替换原文的wireless gadgets。

WRITING

WRITING TASK 1

名师解读

本题为双饼图(pie charts)，两个饼图展示的是2013年英国大学学生对学校设施的满意度。两个饼图的元素基本相同，因此两个图之间存在横向比较关系，故不能独立写，必须合并写。

在具体写作的过程中要注意文章整体的布局：introduction开门见山；body paragraph(s)抓住饼图的关键词，适时making comparisons；结尾彰显出两组饼图的共性或相关性。另外，在body paragraph(s)和conclusion写作过程中，注意正确运用时态。

高分范文

The two pie charts below vividly **mirror** a fact that two types of students (undergraduates and postgraduates) **react** differently to the **facilities** provided by a UK university in the year 2013. Three kinds are concerned: university café, study facilities in bedroom and social facilities.

From these two pies we can see that only 25% undergraduates **were content with** the social facilities, while there are nearly half postgraduates showing satisfaction towards the same facilities with proportion standing at 48%. As to satisfaction towards university café, the percentage of undergraduates is up to 40% which is sharply higher than that of postgraduates arriving at 19%. While **in terms of** satisfaction towards study facilities in bedroom, the percentages of two groups of students are almost the same. The proportion of undergraduates shows **marginally** higher than that of postgraduates, with 35% and 33% respectively.

Overall, the most popular facility in the university for undergraduates goes to the university café. However, most postgraduates prefer its social facilities. (165 words)

WRITING TASK 2

文章结构

解释问题+原因、影响+措施

problem+cause 1+cause 2+solutions
第一段：引出话题
第二段：原因1+举例
第三段：原因2+影响
第四段：总结+建议

思路点拨

步骤一：审题（<3分钟）

Young people in the modern world seem to have more power and influence than any previous young generation. Why is this the case? What impact does this have on the relationship between old and young people?

→通读题目，了解大意。

现代的年轻人似乎比以前任何一代年轻人都具有权力和影响力。为什么会出现这样的情况呢？这种现象对于老年人和青年人之间的关系有什么影响呢？

→再读题目，辨别关键词，区分主题词和限定词，推测考官的出题意图。

主题词：Young people in the modern world, more power and influence

限定词：Why, impact

步骤二：列大纲（<3分钟）

英文提纲	Introduction: Agree (opinion)→young people today play a bigger role in society (topic) Body: Cause 1: large social and technological changes→better educated→better informed Cause 2: affected by globalisation→powerful consumers Impact: relationships with older people are often difficult Conclusion: Both have to make efforts→spend more time together
中文提纲	引出话题：同意（观点）→当今的年轻人在社会上发挥的作用更大（话题） 主体段： 原因1：社会和科技的巨大进步→受到更好的教育→更见多识广 原因2：全球化的影响→强大的消费者 影响：同老年人的关系紧张 总结：双方共同努力→多花时间相处

高分范文

I would agree that young people today play a bigger role in society than their parents' or grandparents' generation did.

This is mainly due to the large social and technological changes that have widened the experience gap between the generations. For instance, young people today are generally better educated, and because they have been trained from a young age to use computer technology, they have Internet **access to information** in a way that was **unimaginable** for earlier generations. This means that they are probably better **informed** than their parents or grandparents were at their age, and their high-tech skills give them confidence in dealing with the very rapid changes in technology that are so uncomfortable for older people.

In addition, younger people are often the most affected by **globalisation**. They follow fashions in clothes, music and social habits that are common among young people throughout the world. So they have become powerful consumers who influence big global markets today. As a result of all these developments, relationships with older people are often difficult. Teachers and parents are no longer treated with respect, and experience is **undervalued** because young people think they know everything, or at least can learn about everything from the Internet. In many cultures this has led to a lack of **discipline** in schools, family breakdowns and even serious social problems. However, the current generation gap is the responsibility of both younger and older generations.

Both have to **make efforts to** understand each other and a good starting point would be for families to spend more time together than they normally do today. (265 words)

SPEAKING

名师解读

Part 1的题目为注意力，话题与考生关系较大，可预测性高。

对于Part 2，很少有人能在没有准备的情况下出口成章。即使有人可以，也难回答得完美。因此准备素材就尤为重要。

Part 3是对Part 2提示卡内容的深化和拓展。考生可以将话题引到自身的经历。这会让考官觉得更加真实，从而赢得更多的好感。

无论是哪一个部分，要把握几个要点：逻辑严密，语言连贯，语调恰当，语速适中，时间利用充分。

高分示例

PART 1

Concentration

- How important is concentration?

Oh, it's very important! First, if we don't concentrate we cannot study well, so we will not get good grades as a result. Another thing is we can put our lives in danger if we are not aware of what we are doing. I heard about people who fell onto subway tracks while texting. It was because they were not paying attention.

- In what situations is it particularly important to focus on what you do?

Well, probably when we are studying for an important exam. Usually, we need to review a lot of materials, and we should really focus in order to remember all the details so we don't fail the exam later on.

- What can people do to avoid distractions?

I guess it depends on the situation. If we are at home and we need to study, we can turn off our phone and email notifications. However, if we are in the dormitory and there are other roommates around, we cannot do that. In this case, we can probably wear headphones to show others that we do not want to be disturbed. Unfortunately, it's not always possible.

PART 2

My aunt Jing's a wonderful cook. She lives just two streets away, so I was at her house very often when I was growing up. It became a sort of family joke that you could always find my aunt working in the kitchen, day or night. She used to have an office job, but she decided to give that up so she could spend all her time cooking.

People hire her to cook for their special celebrations. Aunt Jing makes just about every kind of food. She likes making traditional food, but she also likes trying new things. Lately, she learned to make a few western dishes and served them to our family. Last month she made pizza. I don't usually like western food, but my aunt's pizza was delicious.

Everything Aunt Jing prepares tastes really good, but her speciality is dumplings. She makes many different kinds. My favourite is steamed shrimp jiaozi. She also makes delicious sweet dumplings, especially for holidays.

Aunt Jing is very scientific about her cooking. When she tries a new recipe, she'll make it again and again. Sometimes she'll make two batches on the same day, each a little different. Then she'll ask us to taste both and tell her which ones we liked best. She'll keep testing and testing until it's perfect. Once she's satisfied with it, she'll write down the recipe and make it exactly the same way every time. I think this is why my aunt is such a good cook.

PART 3

Cooking

- Who normally does the cooking in families in your country?

Normally women still do the cooking, though this is changing. My mother and father are both excellent cooks, and they take turns making meals. In fact, I think they're both talented cooks, and I enjoy anything they make.

- Is home cooking always better than food cooked in other places?

No, it's not always better, but it usually is in my home. There are talented cooks and delicious dishes all over the world. Perhaps these are found in a restaurant. But we always think home cooking is best not just because of the food, but also the love that's served with it.

- Why do people like to have dinner at restaurants, instead of at home?

I think people eat out for a change of place. Sometimes you get tired of cooking, and sometimes you want to celebrate an event. Of course, it's a treat to have your birthday dinner at your favourite restaurant, too.

Cooking different dishes

- Is it better to learn to cook traditional dishes or dishes from around the world?

It's best to learn traditional dishes first. This gives you an appealing way to share your culture with others. Also, if you're in a foreign country you'll know how to make home-style food. This can be a skill you take with you wherever you go. But sometimes it's fun to research an unknown recipe from around the world and try it.

- How easy is it to buy unusual ingredients for cooking where you live?

We can buy many ingredients that Westerners would probably call unusual. I think Chinese people are happy to try more foods, especially southern Chinese! The things we think are unusual are Western things, and they're becoming increasingly available in China.

- Have international restaurants increased in popularity where you live?

Oh, yes! Many children love to go to Western restaurants. It used to be only KFC and McDonald's, but now there are so many choices: Subway, Dairy Queen, Papa John's, Pizza Hut, Starbucks, and so on. People used to go mostly for prestige, but nowadays they're going because they actually like the food.

重点词汇

LISTENING

excursion	[ɪk'skɜːʃn]	*n.*	短途旅行；远足
recommend	[ˌrekə'mend]	*v.*	推荐
dolphin	['dɒlfɪn]	*n.*	海豚
split	[splɪt]	*v.*	分离
unpredictable	[ˌʌnprɪ'dɪktəbl]	*adj.*	不可预知的；出乎预料的
discount	['dɪskaʊnt]	*n.*	折扣
accommodation	[əˌkɒmə'deɪʃn]	*n.*	住处，膳宿
lodge	[lɒdʒ]	*n.*	旅馆；门房
beachfront	['biːtʃfrʌnt]	*n.*	海滨地区
snorkel	['snɔːkl]	*n.*	（潜水者用的）呼吸管
kayak	['kaɪæk]	*n.*	皮艇
sauna	['sɔːnə]	*n.*	桑拿浴
floodlit	['flʌdlɪt]	*adj.*	照明的
refundable	[rɪ'fʌndəbl]	*adj.*	可退还的；可偿还的
departure	[dɪ'pɑːtʃə]	*n.*	出发；离开
cancellation	[ˌkænsə'leɪʃn]	*n.*	取消；删除
promptly	['prɒmptli]	*adv.*	迅速地；立即地
essential	[ɪ'senʃl]	*adj.*	基本的；必要的；本质的
luxury	['lʌkʃəri]	*n.*	奢侈，奢华；奢侈品；享受
automatically	[ˌɔːtə'mætɪkli]	*adv.*	自动地；机械地；无意识地
air-conditioned		*adj.*	备有空调装置的
approximately	[ə'prɒksɪmətli]	*adv.*	大约，近似地；近于
pensioner	['penʃənə]	*n.*	领养老金者；领取抚恤金者
outlet	['aʊtlet]	*n.*	出口，排放孔
skin cream		*n.*	护肤霜，面霜
waterproof	['wɔːtəpruːf]	*adj.*	防水的，不透水的
unpredictable	[ʌnprɪ'dɪktəbl]	*adj.*	不可预知的；不定的；出乎意料的
excellent	['eksələnt]	*adj.*	卓越的；极好的；杰出的
crocodile	['krɒkədaɪl]	*n.*	鳄鱼
enclosure	[ɪn'kləʊʒ]	*n.*	附件；围墙
disability	[ˌdɪsə'bɪləti]	*n.*	无资格；无能
diagonally	[daɪ'ægənəli]	*adv.*	对角地；斜对地
artificial	[ˌɑːtɪ'fɪʃl]	*adj.*	人造的；仿造的
adjoin	[ə'dʒɔɪn]	*v.*	邻接
supervision	[ˌsuːpə'vɪʒn]	*n.*	监督，管理
marsupial	[mɑː'suːpɪəl]	*n.*	有袋类动物
calf	[kɑːf]	*n.*	小牛；小腿
lamb	[læm]	*n.*	羔羊，小羊
piglet	['pɪglət]	*n.*	小猪（尤指乳猪）
continent	['kɒntɪnənt]	*n.*	大陆，洲，陆地
savannah	[sə'vænə]	*n.*	大草原，热带草原
giraffe	[dʒə'rɑːf]	*n.*	[脊椎] 长颈鹿
rhino	['raɪnəʊ]	*n.*	犀牛
zebra	['zebrə]	*n.*	[脊椎] 斑马
Mediterranean	[ˌmedɪtə'reɪnɪən]	*adj.*	地中海的
in moderation			适度地，有节制地
detoxify	[ˌdiː'tɒksɪfaɪ]	*v.*	（使）解毒

anti-oxidant		*n.*	抗氧化剂
pedometer	[pe'dɒmɪtə]	*n.*	步程计，计步器
robust	[rəʊ'bʌst]	*adj.*	强健的；健康的
enormously	[ɪ'nɔːməsli]	*adv.*	非常地；巨大地
irritable	['ɪrɪtəbl]	*adj.*	急躁的；易怒的
benchmark	['bentʃmaːk]	*n.*	基准
recuperate	[rɪ'kuːpəreɪt]	*v.*	恢复
detrimental	[ˌdetrɪ'mentl]	*adj.*	有害的
knock-on		*adj.*	有（必然且间接）影响的
spiraling	['spaɪrəlɪŋ]	*adj.*	螺旋上升的
depression	[dɪ'preʃn]	*n.*	沮丧
dweller	['dwelə]	*n.*	居民
metabolise	[mə'tæbəlaɪz]	*v.*	新陈代谢
antarctic	[æn'taːktɪk]	*adj.*	南极的
penguin	['peŋgwɪn]	*n.*	企鹅；空军地勤人员
graceful	['greɪsfl]	*adj.*	优雅的；优美的
comical	['kɒmɪkl]	*adj.*	滑稽的，好笑的
elegant	['elɪgənt]	*adj.*	高雅的，优雅的；讲究的
signature	['sɪgnətʃə(r)]	*n.*	署名；签名；信号
fascinating	['fæsɪneɪtɪŋ]	*adj.*	迷人的；吸引人的
Gentoo	['dʒentuː]	*n.*	巴布亚企鹅
landscape	['lændskeɪp]	*n.*	风景，景色；山水画
timid	['tɪmɪd]	*adj.*	胆小的；羞怯的
slightly	['slaɪtli]	*adv.*	些微地，轻微地；纤细地
Argentina	[ˌaːdʒən'tiːnə]	*n.*	阿根廷（位于拉丁美洲）
upright	['ʌpraɪt]	*adj.*	正直的，诚实的；垂直的
biologically	[baɪə'lɒdʒɪkli]	*adv.*	生物学上，生物学地
Princess Elizabeth Lands			伊丽莎白公主岛
Ross Sea			罗斯海（南太平洋深入南极洲的大海湾）
permanently	['pɜːmənəntli]	*adv.*	永久地，长期不变地
territory	['terətri]	*n.*	领土，领域；范围
incubate	['ɪŋkjubeɪt]	*v.*	孵化；培养；温育
predator	['predətə]	*n.*	捕食者；食肉动物；掠夺者
streamlined	['striːmlaɪnd]	*adj.*	流线型的；改进的；最新型的
blackish-blue		*n.*	黑蓝色
submerged	[səb'mɜːdʒd]	*adj.*	水下的，在水中的
insulate	['ɪnsjuleɪt]	*v.*	隔离，孤立；绝缘
huddle	['hʌdl]	*v.*	把……挤在一起；缩成一团
bunch	[bʌntʃ]	*n.*	群；串；突出物
hatch	[hætʃ]	*v.*	孵；策划
trek	[trek]	*n.*	艰苦跋涉
independently	[ˌɪndɪ'pendəntli]	*adv.*	独立地；自立地

READING

circadian	[sɜː'keɪdɪən]	*adj.*	全天的；生理节奏的
collapse	[kə'læps]	*v.*	（健康等）垮掉；累倒
irrespective	[ɪrɪ'spektɪv]	*adj.*	无关的
pancreas	['pæŋkrɪəs]	*n.*	胰腺
spleen	[spliːn]	*n.*	脾脏
stride	[straɪd]	*n.*	进展；（一）大步

eminently	['emɪnəntli]	*adv.*	突出地
appraise	[ə'preɪz]	*v.*	评定，评价
locus	['ləʊkəs]	*n.*	轨迹；地点
predominantly	[prɪ'dɒmɪnəntli]	*adv.*	占主导地位地；显著地
ambergris	['æmbəgriːs]	*n.*	龙涎香；鲸粪
flammable	['flæməbl]	*adj.*	易燃的，可燃的
fixative	['fɪksətɪv]	*n.*	固定剂；定色剂
biliary	['bɪlɪəri]	*adj.*	胆的；胆汁的；输送胆汁的
secretion	[sɪ'kriːʃn]	*n.*	分泌；分泌物
intestine	[ɪn'testɪn]	*n.*	肠
abdomen	['æbdəmən]	*n.*	腹部；下腹；腹腔
squid	[skwɪd]	*n.*	乌贼
beak	[biːk]	*n.*	鸟嘴；（鳖等的）喙状嘴
inadvertently	[ˌɪnəd'vɜːtəntli]	*adv.*	疏忽地；不注意地
fecal	['fiːkəl]	*adj.*	排泄物的；残渣的
anus	['eɪnəs]	*n.*	肛门
Madagascar	[ˌmædə'gæskə]	*n.*	马达加斯加岛
expel	[ɪk'spel]	*v.*	排出；排除
precursor	[priː'kɜːsə]	*n.*	先驱，前导
oxidation	[ɒksɪ'deɪʃn]	*n.*	氧化
crusty	['krʌsti]	*adj.*	执拗的；有壳的
stinging	['stɪŋɪŋ]	*adj.*	烈的；刺人的
resinous	['rezɪnəs]	*adj.*	树脂的；树脂质的
fragrance	['freɪgrəns]	*n.*	香味，芬芳
musk	[mʌsk]	*n.*	麝香；麝香鹿
ambiguity	[ˌæmbɪ'gjuːəti]	*n.*	含糊；不明确；暧昧
incense	['ɪnsens]	*n.*	香；奉承
spittle	['spɪtl]	*n.*	唾沫；吐出的泡沫
aphrodisiac	[ˌæfrə'dɪzɪæk]	*n.*	春药；催欲剂
epilepsy	['epɪlepsi]	*n.*	癫痫，癫痫症
ailment	['eɪlmənt]	*n.*	疾病；小病
amid	[ə'mɪd]	*prep.*	在其中
hoopla	['huːplaː]	*n.*	喧闹
omnipresent	[ˌɒmnɪ'preznt]	*adj.*	无所不在的
nimble	['nɪmbl]	*adj.*	聪明的
ubiquity	[juː'bɪkwəti]	*n.*	普遍存在
scenario	[sə'nɑːrɪəʊ]	*n.*	方案
outfit	['aʊtfɪt]	*n.*	机构
gadget	['gædʒɪt]	*n.*	小配件
surreptitious	[ˌsʌrəp'tɪʃəs]	*adj.*	秘密的，暗中的
erratic	[ɪ'rætɪk]	*adj.*	不稳定的
coalition	[ˌkəʊə'lɪʃn]	*n.*	联合
foible	['fɔɪbl]	*n.*	弱点
fastidious	[fæ'stɪdɪəs]	*adj.*	挑剔的
insulin	['ɪnsjəlɪn]	*n.*	胰岛素

WRITING

mirror	['mɪrə]	*v.*	反映；反射
react	[rɪ'ækt]	*v.*	反应；影响
facility	[fə'sɪləti]	*n.*	设施，设备

be content with...			对……感到满足
in terms of...			在……方面；按照……
marginally	['mɑːdʒɪnəli]	*adv.*	稍微地
access to information			信息获取途径
unimaginable	[ˌʌnɪ'mædʒɪnəbl]	*adj.*	不可思议的
informed	[ɪn'fɔːmd]	*adj.*	见多识广的；消息灵通的
globalisation	[ˌgləʊbəlaɪ'zeɪʃn]	*n.*	全球化
undervalue	[ˌʌndə'væljuː]	*v.*	低估，看轻
discipline	['dɪsəplɪn]	*n.*	纪律；学科
make efforts to			努力

SPEAKING

concentration	[ˌkɒnsn'treɪʃn]	*n.*	注意力，集中力
distraction	[dɪ'strækʃn]	*n.*	注意力分散
ingredient	[ɪn'griːdɪənt]	*n.*	（烹调的）原料
track	[træk]	*n.*	轨道
speciality	[ˌspeʃɪ'æləti]	*n.*	专长
shrimp	[ʃrɪmp]	*n.*	虾
batch	[bætʃ]	*n.*	一炉
prestige	[pre'stiːʒ]	*n.*	声望，声誉

Test 1

听力原文

SECTION 1

(CUSTOMER SERVICE REPRESENTATIVE=R; CUSTOMER=C)

R: Good morning, White Cloud Adventures. How can I help you?

C: Hi, I was wondering if you could help me. I'm trying to find out more about the excursions you offer in this region.

R: OK, well we offer a number of tours. Where were you thinking of going?

C: Well, my friend recommended the overnight trip that takes people to see dolphins. I quite like the sound of that one.

R: Yes, that's our Dolphin Watch Explorer. It's very popular so you usually need to book in advance.

C: All right, and how long does it last, I think my friend said it was two days?

R: It's actually Q1 1.5 days—and that includes the two-hour travel time each way from here.

C: That's perfect. So do we leave from this office and travel by minibus?

R: Yes, you leave from here, but you travel by coach, and then split into smaller groups for the boat trip. There are up to Q2 20 people on each boat, though we run tours for numbers over 15. The boats travel to different spots in the ocean, so we don't have too many people disturbing the dolphins.

C: OK, so how regular are the tours?

R: Well, because it's peak time now, there is a tour every day, though we run them once a month outside of peak season and at certain times of year, we close the tours down completely for a while.

C: So you said they get booked up really quickly, when is the next available date?

R: Just let me check on the computer. OK, well, the next available booking is six days from now on Q3 December 18th and then we don't have any free places on another tour until December 23rd.

C: OK, and is it a good time of year to see the dolphins? I hear sometimes groups might not actually get to see any at all.

R: That's actually quite unusual, though of course the dolphins can be unpredictable! Actually this is a very good time of the year to see them and we have a policy that if you don't get to see any dolphins throughout the 1.5 days, you will get a 50% discount on a second booking.

C: Really? That's great!

R: Yes, and you will get to stay in really nice accommodation too, I would say the majority of our customers rate the tour really highly. The hotel we use is called the Q4 Kaoriland Lodge, and it's right on the beachfront and has a lovely restaurant and gardens.

C: Sorry, what is the name of the hotel?

R: Kaoriland Lodge—that's K-A-O-R-I-L-A-N-D—all one word—lodge L-O-D-G-E. It's one of the oldest buildings in the area, it's very beautiful and has a long history.

C: Sounds good. So what is actually included in the tour price?

R: Almost everything! The price includes transportation to and from the hotel, the boat trip, Q5 & Q6 overnight accommodation, lunch on the boat and breakfast at the hotel the next day. You do need to pay for your evening meal though, that isn't included in the price. The hotel restaurant is quite reasonably priced and there are one or two nice eating places just a few minutes walk away too, if you feel like exploring.

C: OK, that's alright. What do I need to take with me for the boat trip?

R: Q5 & Q6 Well drinks and lunch are included in the package, so you really just need to take your swimwear, a towel and some warm clothing as it can get quite windy on the boat. Don't forget your camera and some sun screen. Oh, and I forgot to mention, you can hire snorkels and kayaks very cheaply while you're on the trip, so you can have fun in the water when the boat stops for lunch.

C: Are there many things to do once the boat trip is finished?

R: Well, you'll get back to the hotel at around 5.30pm. It has lovely hot pools and there is also a sauna and gym. You have to pay extra to use those. But there is also a floodlit tennis court and indoor swimming pool which are free to guests.

C: That all sounds great. So how much does the tour cost?

R: It is usually $420 dollars at this time of the year, but there is a discount for bookings of more than three people which brings the price down to Q7 $390 per person.

C: So do you have enough spaces for four people on the next tour?

R: Just let me check, I think that should be OK...yes that's fine, we have six places left at the moment.

C: OK, well, I'd like to book those places please.

R: Alright. Well, you need to pay a Q8 50% deposit at the time of booking; that is fully refundable if for any reason you have to cancel more than 48 hours before the departure date. The full amount must be paid at least two days before departure. If you cancel within 48 hours of the tour, you have to pay a 25% cancellation fee.

C: Yes, that's all fine. Can I pay by credit card? I might as well pay the full amount now.

R: Yes, credit card is fine. So I'll make a booking for four people for the 18th of December. You'll need to be here at this office by no later than 7.45am on the day of departure, the coach leaves promptly at Q9 8am.

C: OK, that's fine.

R: Well that's all booked for you now. Just sign here. Oh, write down this booking number too, just in case you lose your tickets or anything.

C: OK, what is it?

R: It's Q10 2-6-5-9-1-T. That's T for tango. That's all done for you. Wish you have a great trip.

C: Thanks very much, I'm sure we will.

SECTION 2

(PRESENTER=P)

P: Good day folks, and welcome to our weekly programme for visitors to Queensland. This week we're suggesting that you take a trip to Australia Zoo in Beerwah. There are plenty of easy ways to get there even if you don't have a car. First of all there's the bus pick-up service from the Gold Coast. This service is only $5 per person return, and you can board at any one of seven stops on the route. Q11 Booking is essential, and you can do it either by phone or on the internet. The journey takes between half an hour and an hour and a half, depending on where you board the bus, and the proceeds from the service go towards Australia Zoo Conservation Projects.

Then there's a luxury coach service called the Croc Express. It operates seven days a week, and it calls automatically at all the major hotels in Brisbane and the Gold Coast. Once you're aboard you can relax in air-conditioned comfort while a tour guide tells you about all the sights along the way. The tour departs the Gold Coast at approximately 8am, Q12 and arrives at Australia Zoo around 10.15am, in time for all the wildlife action. The day is then yours to spend exploring the zoo at your leisure, Q12 before departing at 4.30pm. The ticket includes return transport and zoo entry, and costs $126 per adult, or $121 for students and pensioners.

Then...what should you take with you? Well, there are lots of food outlets at the zoo, but if you want to bring a picnic, there are plenty of grassy areas where you can sit. The afternoons can get chilly in Beerwah during the colder months, and at those times Q13 a jumper might be necessary. But the sun can be fierce even during winter, so you should always take glasses and a hat as well as skin cream. You're also advised to carry a poncho or waterproof jacket as the rainfall can be unpredictable. And wear a watch! There are feeding times and scheduled talks throughout the day that you might not want to miss.

The zoo facilities are excellent. While you're at the zoo you can hire Q14 a locker to store anything you don't want to carry around everywhere, including your picnic lunch. If you've brought your smart phone you can share your experiences with friends and family by taking advantage of the zoo's free Wifi service. This is available in the food court, at the crocodile enclosure, and in front of the bird house. Other facilities which are included in the ticket price are the use of the car park, and disability scooters for disabled badge holders.

P: Now I'll just say a little bit about the layout of the zoo...Whether you're on foot or in a car there's always one public entrance to the zoo, and this is also the exit. As you go into the zoo the ticket office is on your right, and Q15 the gift shop is on your left. Take my advice and walk quickly past that building if you've got kids, or you might be persuaded to part with a small fortune there! Now there's a stream which runs diagonally through the zoo site, and there's also a man-made lake. If you're interested in big cats there's a Sumatran tiger enclosed situated Q16 between the car park and the artificial lake. I'd advise you to visit the tigers first, because they get sleepy as the day goes on and then you might not catch sight of them...Then perhaps you'd like to see something Australian. The saltwater crocodiles are very popular, and there's a museum about crocodile hunting Q17 adjoining the crocodile enclosure. This museum was originally set up by Australia's well-known conservationist and wildlife expert, Steve Irwin...You could also take a look at the collection of Australian snakes. These are in the Q18 circular building next to the stream, between the car park and the birds of prey. You might even get to handle some of these, under supervision of course! Now if you've got young kids I'd recommend the zoo within a zoo—the special Kids' Zoo. It's tucked away in the corner, Q19 next to the marsupials, and it's where children can hand feed baby farm animals, like calves, lambs and piglets...Then...switching continents again, why not visit the African savannah exhibition? Q20 That's in the left-hand corner on the far side of the lake. If you're lucky, you'll see giraffes, rhinos and zebras there. It's well worth a visit. And if you enjoy...[fade]

SECTION 3

Hello and welcome to *Lifestyle* today. In this programme we will be looking at ways of living a healthier life, many experts believe that adding some of the elements we will discuss today into your lifestyle can actually also lead to a longer life.

We'll start with the more familiar aspects of healthy living; these being diet and exercise. For some time now, experts have been advising us that incorporation of a Mediterranean-style diet into our eating habits can bring enormous benefits. Researches report that those following such diets are Q21 25% less likely to die at a young age—many of the advantages being attributed to the properties of olive oil. Red wine drunk in moderation can also allow the body to detoxify and protect the heart in particular, due to the high levels of anti-oxidants it contains.

Regarding exercise, many of us find it difficult to set time aside for visits to the gym or Q22 an exercise class; however, it is important not to under estimate the contribution that walking can make to our health. More people nowadays are buying a pedometre, which can count their steps as they go about their day to day business. Health experts say that we should aim to take 10,000 Q23 steps every day. This can be achieved more easily than you think, using stairs instead of lifts, walking to a bus stop further away than the one you may usually use if you travel to work by bus, and ditching the car altogether for shorter trips. Any type of exercise is beneficial; however, yoga in particular is thought to make a number of valuable contributions to health. It has proven to reduce stress, Q24 & Q25 lower blood pressure, and protect the body from diseases.

Also remember that it is not just important to exercise your body, but also your mind; like any muscle or body part, it becomes more robust through exercise and stimulation. Playing chess, reading books or completing puzzles challenges our mind and keeps it active and healthy. Use it or lose it, some might say.

The type of lifestyle we lead also impacts enormously on our health. Getting enough sleep is vital and getting too little can result in becoming stressed, irritable and can even speed up the aging process. What is "enough" varies from person to person; however, somewhere between six and eight hours per night is a good benchmark. Our bodies are given a chance to recuperate during sleep and it improves our concentration, appearance and Q26 boosts the immune system. More recent studies suggest that appropriate quantities of sleep can also help us burn calories and maintain a healthy weight.

Being happy during our waking hours is also important. Laughter is the body's natural way of reducing stress and it also improves blood circulation. Research conducted in the Netherlands indicates that there are close links between having a positive attitude and health. According to the study, Q27 optimists are 55% less likely to die of one of the most significant killer diseases of our time, such as heart disease, than someone with a negative attitude. In order to maintain happiness, it is also important to be able to leave work in the workplace. Employment-related stress is on the increase and Q28 is not only detrimental to health, but can also have a knock-on effect on our personal relationships, which can lead to a spiralling situation of unhappiness and high anxiety levels.

Human beings are naturally social animals and having someone close to share our lives with also contributes to good health. Researches suggest that being married increases a person's life expectancy; however, getting divorced can have the opposite effect, almost certainly due to the high levels of stress that are normally involved in the ending of a relationship. Pet ownership, dogs in particular, has also been observed to lower blood pressure and fight off depression.

Finally, recent studies from the UK revealed that people living in rural areas, on average, live six years longer than urban dwellers; these findings are likely to be due to the fact that the air is cleaner and those living in the countryside tend to have Q29 & Q30 more active lifestyles. There are enormous benefits to spending time outdoors in the fresh air. Although over-exposure to sun can be dangerous. Provided we protect ourselves from UV rays with sun screen, sunshine is extremely beneficial as it allows the body to metabolise vitamin D which contributes to bone strength.

Well, that's it for today, thanks for listening. After the break we will be opening our phone lines to hear what you think about our suggestions and to find out what ideas our listeners have for leading a healthier life.

SECTION 4

When one thinks of Antarctic wildlife, penguins are often the first animals that come to mind. Indeed these graceful yet comical, hardy yet elegant creatures are considered by many to be the signature species of the polar south. That is why we decided to create a separate section devoted to the many penguin species and their fascinating characteristics.

Take Gentoo for example. They are rather cautious. They don't like going about at night, maybe because they are scared of the dark, and if they climb over some rocky landscape, Q31 they'll only jump if they have to. And even then they will look carefully down and spend time deciding whether to do it or not.

However, Pockhopper, another type of penguins, is different. They will have a quick look if it's somewhere they haven't dropped down before. But they don't seem timid. In fact, Q32 they're pretty determined and if they're trying to get up somewhere, they grip onto the stones with their slightly hooked bills as well as their nails when the surface gets very steep. Nothing stops them.

The third type of penguin I'd like to talk about is Magellanic. If they come across something they haven't seen before, they cock their head first one side then the other, peering out of each eye in turn, Q33 as if they don't quite believe anything until they've double-checked it.

Whereas King penguin, another famous type you may be familiar with, stand very upright when they call. Q34 And they have the longest flippers, which they hold towards the ground, as if they are worried about falling over.

Sounds interesting. Right? Well, however, among all these penguins, the largest and the most biologically interesting one is the regal Emperor penguin. Concentrated in the Weddell Sea and Dronning Maud Land, Enderby, Princess Elizabeth Lands, and the Ross Sea, Emperors remain in Antarctica permanently, breeding on the sea ice in some of the coldest conditions on Earth. They do not build nests or defend a fixed territory, using their warm bodies instead to incubate and raise their young. This unique breeding behaviour—Emperors are the only Antarctic bird that breeds Q35 in winter—may have developed to allow chicks to grow to independence at a time when food is most plentiful and predators are few.

Emperor Penguins have a big head, a short, thick neck, a streamlined shape, a short, wedge-shaped tail, and tiny, flipper-like wings. The sexes are alike, with blue-grey upperparts and blackish-blue heads adorned with large white and yellow ear patches. Their underparts are mostly white but with the upper breast showing a pale yellow. The only penguin remotely similar in size and appearance is the Q36 King penguin which is smaller and more brightly marked. Like all penguins, Emperors have shiny, waterproof feathers that help keep their skin dry and webbed feet which they use for swimming.

Unlike most penguins, which feed on surface krill, Emperor penguins live on Q37 fish, squid, and crustaceans caught on long, deep pursuit dives. They will quite often reach depths of more than 700 feet and remain submerged for up to 18 minutes.

Emperor penguins establish loose breeding colonies on the pack ice surrounding the Antarctic continent. In May, female Emperors will lay a single egg after a 63-day gestation period, and then will pass the egg over to her mate while she goes off to sea to feed.

Male Emperors will be unable to eat during the ensuing Q38 9-week incubation period. Instead, he must keep his egg warm by balancing it on his feet, where it is insulated by a thick roll of skin and feathers called the Q39 "brood pouch". For added warmth and protection against the bitter winds and sub-zero temperatures, the males will huddle together in tight bunches. After the eggs have hatched, young chicks will remain in the "brood pouch" for a short time until they are able to regulate their own body temperatures.

By the time the female returns to take over feeding the chick, the male will have lost up to Q40 a third of his body weight. He must now make another long trek over the ice—up to 60 miles—to find food.

By January, as the sea-ice begins to break out, the chicks have lost most of their soft silvery-gray down, and are now able to head out independently for the open sea.

Test 2

答案速查

LISTENING

Section 1, Questions 1–10

1 B
2 C
3 C
4 B
5 B
6 A
7 Barbara Cooper
8 7236518
9 25 Saint Mary
10 G57980942

Section 2, Questions 11–20

11 A
12 A
13 C
14 B
15 B
16 E
17 D
18 F
19 A
20 H

Section 3, Questions 21–30

21 southwest Asia
22 fresh (and) ripened/fresh (and) salty
23 (The) Ancient Romans
24 60 BC (and) 300 AD
25 temperature (and) environment
26 micro-organisms
27 industrialise
28 factories
29 human judgment
30 art (and) technology

Section 4, Questions 31–40

31 C
32–34 **IN ANY ORDER** A C D
35 hunger
36 mysterious disease
37–40 **IN ANY ORDER** wild dogs, sharks, seals, sea lions

READING

Reading Passage 1, Questions 1–13

1 F
2 E
3 G
4 A
5 C
6 aliens
7 transmit signals
8 spectrum
9 its magnification
10 similar signals
11 noise
12 brighter
13 elusive

Reading Passage 2, Questions 14–25

14 A
15 C
16 F
17 H
18 E
19 B
20 F
21 C
22 D
23 C
24 H
25 G

Reading Passage 3, Questions 26–40

26 A
27 C
28 D
29 neurodegenerative disease/Parkinsons
30 memory
31 frightening
32 arousals
33 parental attention
34 melatonin
35 hypnotic
36 cycles
37 sleep
38 sleep onset
39 bright light therapy
40 early

名师解析

LISTENING

SECTION 1

主题场景	图书馆场景
主旨大意	办理图书馆会员证
考查题型	选择题、笔记填空题

名师解读

1 B 注意题干中的关键词need，女士要加入图书馆需要提供什么？图书管理员给出了all we need is..., 这时应该注意捕捉后面的信息。identification一词重读，是定位词，故答案是选项B。old address是与题干无关的干扰项。

2 C 因为everything has my old address，故答案是选项C。A和B选项中bankbook和letter均未在对话中出现，为干扰项。

3 C 注意定位文中信息：图书管理员先问What about your passport? 女士想起来护照上有他们的新地址，故答案是选项C。选项B中是用护照订到air ticket，为干扰项。

4 B 图书管理员说出了几个与数字相关的表述：four books, two cards, three magazines or periodicals, $5，但要注意题干中的关键词record，不要掉入这种“信息轰炸”的陷阱，真正的答案在后面：to take out two records at a time。

5 B 图书管理员提到几处地点，注意题干关键词catalogue，对话中出现的相关内容为you can look it up in the catalogue，但答案在其后的定语从句you'll find just around the corner中。

6 A 注意疑问词how long以及女士的问话how long am I allowed to keep the books for? 图书管理员回答的首句the normal loan period is three weeks即为答案。后面图书管理员又提到two weeks extension和four weeks，这些都是干扰信息。注意在听到多个相关信息时，应听清楚哪一个是题干所需要的。

7 Barbara Cooper 7至10题为个人信息表格题。本题要注意人名的拼写。

8 7236518 本题要准确听写数字。

9 25 Saint Mary 本题的地名要注意大写以及正确拼写。

10 G57980942 注意本题填写的是护照号，不要受到后面卡号M930123的干扰。

SECTION 2

主题场景	租房场景
主旨大意	介绍可以租房子的种类以及房间布局相关的信息
考查题型	配对题、地图题

名师解读

11 A 原文转折词but后提到几个优点single-family house, pretty standard in design和got two bedrooms等。考生注意原文中but, because后面的内容通常是考点。

12 A 原文中介绍Hillsboro时，提到了was built in 1969, two bedrooms, a thousand square feet, fairly standard design这几个特征。

13 C 原文中的square footage与题干中的size对应，都是对大小的描述，由原文后面的内容is considerably more than the others确定，Westfield的突出特征是size。

14 B 原文中的stand out与题干中的recommend对应，原文is后that引导的从句it's right in the heart of the city正是对Lennox Village的location的说明。

15 B 原文中的quite surprising与题干中的recommend对应，原文中的situated与location对应。

16 E 原文中的the room指代的是前文的storage area，它的位置是紧挨着the stairs。楼梯的位置在图中已标出。考生注意原文中与位置、方位有关的词语，以此确定位置。

17 D 注意原文的描述，the bathroom的描述与bigger对应，dressing room的描述与 slightly smaller对应，而这两个房间的位置是在前面提到的，它们紧挨着the bedroom, bedroom的位置图中已经给出，据此可以判定这两个房间就是图中的C和D位置，dressing room的位置就是略小一点的D位置。本题的位置和信息点的判定需要考生有一定的短时记忆能力。

18 F 原文后面提到office的位置是在the bedroom的对面opposite，紧挨着the great room的右面，great room的位置在图中已经给出，据此考生可以判定office即图中F的位置。

19 A 参照的物体为deck，描述图中A和B两个房间，其中的一个房间可以通向the dining area和great room，而且这个房间的右面是the kitchen，那么这个房间指的应该是B。所以dining area应该是房间A。

20 H 本题较为简单，对stove的位置定位是在great room的corner处。剩下的只有H的位置是在角落里。

SECTION 3

主题场景	专题讲座场景
主旨大意	奶酪的制作过程
考查题型	笔记填空题、表格填空题

名师解读

21 southwest Asia 注意题干中的关键词process和8,000 years，同时应注意听接下来的定位词came from，它与题干中的originated from同义，故其后紧跟的地点名词southwest Asia为正确答案。注意Asia首字母要大写。

22 fresh (and) ripened/fresh (and) salty 注意题干中的关键词two main kinds of，这里要填的是两种奶酪的名称，要注意听文中的mainly two types of，以便定位文中so-called后出现的答案fresh cheeses，另一个答案并没有紧接着出现，要集中注意听出现的another one。

23 (The) Ancient Romans 从上下文判断，此句缺少主语，主语可能是who, what或where，但文中关键词great pioneers出现在答案之后，要注意及时回忆上句的主语ancient Romans。

24 60 BC (and) 300 AD 此句需要填两个时间名词，当关键词spread在对话中出现后，要注意捕捉时间词。

25 temperature (and) environment 根据此句中的关键词cheeses' taste定位到原文中的relevant to something，但此时不能大意，要继续集中注意听，两个certain后的词应为答案，即temperature和environment。

26 micro-organisms 注意时间关键词19th century的出现就可以很容易听到答案，题干中的句子是对听力原文名词短语the increasing knowledge about micro-organism的改写，knowledge后为答案。

27 industrialise 此句需要填写的是动词，关键词possible后有两个动词introduce和industrialise，但要注意宾语是process。

28 factories 此句要填写的是地点名词，原文largely是对题干中a large scale的改写，紧接着就是本句的状语为in factories，故factories即为答案。

29 human judgment 本题较难，根据题干中的关键词an essential role，定位到听力原文important role for所在的这句。像although这样表示转折关系的句子多为考点，一般会包含答案信息。

30 art (and) technology 题干的句子是对原文Whatever the scale of production, there is still room for the development of art alongside the technology的改写，despite和alongside分别与whatever和and相对应，develop与原文development是同根词，把名词短语the development of art alongside the technology改写成句子，故答案为名词art和technology。要注意转折介词despite后一般为考查点。

SECTION 4

主题场景	学术场景
主旨大意	介绍企鹅处于濒危边缘
考查题型	选择题、笔记填空题

名师解读

31 C 原文中的regulations与选项C中的regulation为同根词。选项将原文的名词短语protection of wild animals和management of wild animal hunting分别改写为动词短语形式，原文中animal domestication and reproduction, sales and utilization of wild animals的信息用etc.省略。选项B的时间信息1982与原文中的时间1992不符。本题考查考生辨别原文细节信息的能力。

32–34 IN ANY ORDER A C D 本题要求考生选出导致penguins 减少的direct causes。原文中的a shortage of fish and other food内容完全是选项A的重现。原文中的water temperatures被题干改写为temperatures of the water，原文比较级higher与选项C中的higher对应。原文中的the heating of与选项D为重现，原文中的atmosphere与选项D中的air对应。

35 hunger 根据题干关键词Galapagos进行定位，题干中的many adult penguins die of与原文一一对应，故直接可以判定of后的hunger即为答案。

36 mysterious disease 根据地点名词New Zealand进行定位。died为原文重现，原文中of后的mysterious disease就是penguins的死因。

37–40 IN ANY ORDER wild dogs, sharks, seals, sea lions 题干中的Penguins also have natural enemies, including为原文重现，可以直接判定including后面的内容就是答案。考生注意本题确定答案位置简单，但要注意单词的拼写。

READING

READING PASSAGE 1

体　裁　说明文
题　材　科学研究
主　题　人类对外星生命信号的探寻
题　型　配对题、摘要填空题、句子填空题

题型 配对题(Matching Information)

注意 此种题型出题特点为无序，做法上不能按照题号顺序主动定位，否则会浪费大量时间。应以理解段落大意为主，兼顾细节提取，然后从题目当中选出段落的相应信息。

Questions 1–5

1	关键词	laser power
	原文定位	F段首句Although radio power has changed little over the decades, the power of lasers has grown exponentially.
	题解	**答案F** 从首句的although引导的让步状语从句获知，本段意在讨论laser（激光），在接着看本段落后面的内容，讨论的都是激光的优势，这与第一题信息the superiority of laser power（激光能量的优越性）相吻合。

2	关键词	ways to send signals
2	原文定位	E段首句Spread-spectrum works by smearing a message across a wide range of frequencies. 和末句If that were the case, the best way to do this, reckons Paul Horowitz, a physicist at Harvard, is with a laser.
2	题解	**答案E** smearing a message across...（通过……发射信息）与题干中的send signals（发射信号）相对应，而且末句中的the best way to（……最好的方式）更是起到了总结本段、点题的作用，根据此段的首末句可知此段是在讨论发射信号的方法，与第二题信息the discussion of ways to send signals（讨论发射信号的方式）对应。
3	关键词	improvement, radio
3	原文定位	G段首句There is also potential for improvement on the radio side.
3	题解	**答案G** 从首句可知本段主要讲述射电望远镜也仍然具有改进空间，接下来提到中国在建造直径为500米的射电望远镜以及一个名为“平方公里阵列”的国际组织即将建造巨型射电望远镜等，这些举措都是对望远镜进行改进的措施，与题干信息the improvement of radio telescope（改善无线望远镜）相对应。
4	关键词	calculation
4	原文定位	A段首句Half a century ago a radio astronomer called Frank Drake thought of a way to calculate the likelihood establishing contact with aliens.
4	题解	**答案A** 此段首句是主题句，可知此段是在讲述有关判断外星生命存在的可能性的方法，其中calculate（动词，计算）与calculation（名词，计算）是同根词，likelihood（可能性）与possibility（可能性）相对应，aliens（外星人）与intelligent life（智能生命）相对应，因此与本题信息相对应。
5	关键词	search, alien signals, difficult
5	原文定位	C段首句At the AAAS, Dr Drake reflected on his search for alien signals. 和第二句One reason this is hard is that radio telescopes must chop the spectrum into fine portions to study it, like tuning into a signal on a car radio.
5	题解	**答案C** Drake博士在AAAS回顾了他寻找外星人信号的历程，而且第二句是本段的主题句，讲述的就是寻找外星人信号有难度的原因，difficult（困难的）是原文第二句中hard（困难的）的同义转述。

Questions 6–10

题型 摘要填空题(Summary Completion)

注意 此种题型主要考查语言理解能力和归纳能力，宜找到归纳范围后边读边填。

6	关键词	Frank Drake, calculate, contact
	原文定位	A段首句Half a century ago a radio astronomer called Frank Drake thought of a way to calculate the likelihood of establishing contact with aliens.
	题解	答案aliens　先判断出本题所填单词应为名词。was used to（被用来……）与原文thought of a way to（想出一种方式……）相对应，the possibility of（可能性）与原文the likelihood of（可能性）是同义替换。Frank想方设法找出计算与外星人建立联系可能性的方法。
7	关键词	figures to suggest, intelligent life
	原文定位	A段第二句He suggested the following figures should be multiplied...what percentage of intelligent life is able to transmit signals into space; and for how long could such intelligence keeps sending signals.
	题解	答案transmit signals　本题考查对细节的把握能力。根据空前be able to（能够……）可推知该题所填单词应为动词原形，再根据figures定位可知智能生命会向宇宙transmit signals（传送信号）。
8	关键词	radio telescope
	原文定位	C段第二句One reason this is hard is that radio telescopes must chop the spectrum into fine portions to study it, like tuning into a signal on a car radio.
	题解	答案spectrum　此段主题就是为搜寻外星人信号困难的原因。题目中On the one hand（一方面）指代文中one reason（其中一个原因），这里split by（被……分离为……）与原文chop...into（砍成……）相对应，此处应填这个动作的主语，即spectrum（光谱）。
9	关键词	between a telescope's field of view
	原文定位	C段第三句Another is the trade-off between a telescope's field of view and its magnification.
	题解	答案its magnification　此题承接上一题，很明显，此题意在考查与上题相关的第二个原因。根据关键词on the other hand（另一方面）可定位在C段第三句another（另一个原因），根据结构可知此处应填名词，a contradiction（一个矛盾）与原文中the trade-off（一种权衡）相对应。
10	关键词	focus their attention on
	原文定位	D段第二句Researchers tend to look for signals similar to those now made by humanity.
	题解	答案similar signals　根据考点词focus...on（集中精力……），与原文tend to look for（倾向于寻找……）相对应，humanity（人类）对题干中的both humans and other potential intelligent life（人类及其他潜在智能生命）的概括，故此处应填入的词为similar signals（相似的信号）。

Questions 11–13

题型 句子填空题(Sentence Completion)

注意 此种题型要注意答案的字数要求。

11	关键词	advantageous
	原文定位	E段第二句That has the advantages of combating noise and allowing many signals to be sent at once.
	题解	**答案noise** E段提到了扩展频谱这一技术的优点，从中可知这个优点之一是combating noise（抗击噪声），即减少噪音，再根据句意可知此处应填名词作reducing的宾语。
12	关键词	power, increased, strongest
	原文定位	F段第二句Today's most powerful versions can shine ten thousand times brighter than the sun, though only for a billionth of a second.
	题解	**答案brighter** 通过题干可知此题考查激光在发光能力方面与太阳进行比较，所以此处应该填形容词的比较级；再根据关键词send off lights（发射的光）找到了代表比较级的词brighter（更明亮的）。
13	关键词	unpredictable
	原文定位	H段首句Many of the terms in the Drake equation are likely to remain elusive, so it is still impossible to predict how likely such efforts are to succeed.
	题解	**答案elusive** 根据题干可知此句是在探讨alien signals（外星人信号）研究结论仍未可知的原因，since在这里是因果连词，表"因为"。根据关键词results（结果）和unpredictable（不可预测的）可以把答案定位在H段，unpredictable（不可预测的）是原文impossible to predict（不可能预测）的同义替换，很明显so（因此）后面为提示信息"……未可知"，前面半句话为原因，空白处应填形容词。

READING PASSAGE 2

体　裁　议论文
题　材　媒体生活
主　题　有关于电视的特别报道
题　型　选择题、配对题、摘要填空题

Questions 14–17

题型 选择题(Multiple Choice)

注意 此种题型在寻找正确答案之前，一定要事先通读选项，因为选项提供了对原文正确或者是错误的同义转换。但是由于选项较长，不可能一次性全部记住，所以有必要把选项里的核心词划出来，这样可以减轻记忆负担，使做题更加有针对性。

14	关键词	amount of time, Internet or in watching TV
	原文定位	B段倒数第五句Last year Tokyo residents spent an average of 60 minutes a day at home consuming media on the Internet or a mobile phone, up from just six minutes in 2000. 和倒数第四句But they also spent more time in front of the television: an average of 216 minutes.
	题解	**答案A** 题干中the amount of time spending（花费在……上的时间）是对原文an average of 60 minutes a day（平均每天60分钟）和an average of 216 minutes（平均216分钟）的概括，本段的倒数第五句提到了在Internet（网络）上花费的时间，倒数第四句提到了在television（电视）上花费的时间。故A的陈述正确。
15	关键词	offerings
	原文定位	B段第三句Many more options are available on demand with a few clicks of the remote control. 和第四句The offerings are decidedly mixed, but there is always something on.
	题解	**答案C** 本段提到电视节目很丰富，电视可以提供更多的选择，这里TV programmes（电视节目）指代原文的remote control（遥控器），a great variety of（大量的）与are available on（……是可用的）为同义替换，点击几下遥控器，可以有更多的选择。虽然产品肯定是褒贬不一，但总有一些节目在上映，这与C选项的句意正好一致。
16	关键词	more impressive works
	原文定位	E段末句Modern TV shows are so superior to what went before—so much better written, better acted and better shot—that they almost seem to belong to a different medium.
	题解	**答案F** 根据关键词more impressive（更印象深刻的）定位到E段的末句，此处提到现代的电视节目是在各个方面都优于之前的情况，似乎属于不同的媒介，其中these days（这些日子）和more impressive（给人以更深刻印象的）分别与modern（现代的）和so superior（非常出众的）相对应，works（工作）是对much better written（更好的剧本），better acted（更好的表演）和better shot（更好的摄像）的概括。
17	关键词	TV industry
	原文定位	G段中的首句...yet the next few years will be dangerous nonetheless.和第二句 A handful of upstart websites, with audiences smaller than many channels at the bottom of the programme guides, have already rattled the giant TV industry.
	题解	**答案H** 本段首句中转折词yet后的内容是Television（电视）将要处于危险之中，也就是会受到威胁，后边紧接着提到少数的upstart websites（新生网站）已经在电视产业引起慌乱，这与H选项的句意正好一致，其中emergent Internets（出现的网络）和have threatened（已经威胁了）分别与upstart websites（新生的网站）和be dangerous（危险的）相对应。

Questions 18–22

题型 配对题(Matching Features)

注意 此种题型主要考查考生理解能力，先找到人名位置，读懂相应的观点。

18	关键词	Steve Purdham
	原文定位	A段首句ONE evening Steve Purdham noticed something odd. 和第二句The flow of data into and out of We7, a British music-streaming website he runs, had abruptly slowed.
	题解	**答案E** confused by（受困惑）与原文中noticed something odd（注意到奇异的情况）相对应，而unstable（不稳定的）与本段第二句的abruptly slowed（突然减慢）相对应，所以这两句内容正与E选项的信息相符。
19	关键词	Philippe Dauman
	原文定位	B段第五句"There are not many genres that are not addressed anymore,"says Philippe Dauman, CEO of Viacom, a media company. 和第六句"We try to think of new ones all the time."
	题解	**答案B** There are not many genres that are not addressed any more，这个句子含有双重否定，表达的是肯定的意思，说明电视节目和频道都非常多，这与B选项句意一致。
20	关键词	Jeff Bewkes
	原文定位	D段第三句Online, people can pick and choose the content that interests them without paying much for it. 和末句As the saying goes, content wants to be free—or, at least, paid for only by advertising.
	题解	**答案F** 只要能定位出这两句，可以理解出Jeff Bewkes认为人们想要的是网上的内容免费，也就是不愿意付费，这与F选项句意一致。
21	关键词	Howard Stringer
	原文定位	F段第三句So much content will be available on so many digital platforms that audiences will become too small to pay for good TV programmes.
	题解	**答案C** 本句后半部分的too...to...表示"太……而不能……"，也就是因为人们开始转向digital platforms（数字平台）导致audiences（电视观众）少了，这会使为good TV programmes（好节目）付费的人减少。the shrinkage on investment（投资缩水）是原文中too small to pay（太少而不能支付）的同义转述。
22	关键词	George Gilder
	原文定位	G段第三句In 1990 George Gilder, an American writer, claimed that by the end of the 20th century traditional television would be extinct because technology would enable consumers to track down programmes that catered to their particular interests.
	题解	**答案D** 选项D中的conventional TV（传统的电视）是原文中traditional television（传统的电视）的同义替换，die out（消失，灭绝）与形容词词组be extinct（灭绝的）的意思相同。

Questions 23–25

题型 摘要填空题(Summary Completion)

注意 答案可能是原文关键词的替换，也可能就是原文原词。

23	关键词	TV set
	原文定位	H段首句The TV set has also evolved.
	题解	**答案C** 原文evolved的意思是发展，进化，根据题干中的following引导的介词短语的意思，选项development（发展）是evolve（进化）的同义替换词。
24	关键词	have emerged with, screen
	原文定位	G段第二句Gradually they have flattened and turned into panels, and their screens have become sharper and brighter.
	题解	**答案H** 根据原文得知，24题答案为flatten（变平）或panel（嵌镶板）都可以，但是下面的选择项里只有panel（嵌镶板），所以选H。
25	关键词	have emerged with, screen
	原文定位	G段第二句Gradually they have flattened and turned into panels, and their screens have become sharper and brighter.
	题解	**答案G** become（变得）与have emerged with（出现）为同义转换，所以25题应选意义与sharper and brighter（更清晰和更明亮）相近选项。

READING PASSAGE 3

体　裁　说明文
题　材　社会生活
主　题　本文是关于人类睡眠研究的文章，主要了解两种睡眠形式和相关的研究成果。
题　型　选择题、句子填空题、摘要填空题

Questions 26–28

题型 选择题(Multiple Choice)

注意 选择题是阅读中的常规题型，答案通常在文中按顺序出现，每个题目均可以利用选项定位原文。

26	关键词	ENT surgeons
	原文定位	第一段末句In the last decade a number of centres have sprouted, often led by chest physicians and ENT surgeons with an interest in obstructive sleep apnoea...
	题解	**答案A** 选项中A的the growing concern（逐渐增加的关注）与原文sprouted（迅速生长）相对应，contributed to（归功于……）与原文led by（由……导致）为同义转换。选项B和第一段末句的后半部分矛盾，文中说的是wake up and contribute to（开始了解真相和促成……），显然和题目的neglect（忽视）相反。选项C中的90 minutes错误，文中第二段第二句说newborn（新生儿）是50–60分钟。选项D的主语不对，文中第二段末句说的是NREM is divided into four stages（NREM被分为四个阶段），没有提及REM。

27	关键词	EEG activity
	原文定位	第三段首句REM is onto genically primitive with EEG activity closer to wake state, intermittent bursts of REMs and muscle atonia interrupted by phasic bursts producing asynchronous twitching.
	题解	答案C 选项A cannot recall the dream content（不能回想起梦的内容）与第三段中的will be remembered on waking from REM sleep（从REM睡眠形式中醒来……将会被记住）矛盾；选项B与第三段第二句中The atonia...is lost in REM behaviour disorder when dreams content becomes violent相矛盾；选项C与第三段首句REM is onto genically primitive with EEG activity closer to wake state相符合，其中is accompanied by（由……伴随）与is onto genically primitive with（通常映射原始的……）相对应；选项D与第三段第二句中间部分矛盾，不是people（人们），而是patients（病人）。
28	关键词	breast-fed babies
	原文定位	第六段倒数第二句In general, children born prematurely have a tendency to be awake more at night in the first year and breast-fed babies wake more frequently, but the difference disappears by thesecond year.
	题解	答案D 选项A的判断中的during the daytime（在白天期间）与原文第六段第二句不相符；选项B与第六段倒数第二句中的but the difference disappears（消失）by the second year矛盾；选项C原文并未判断；第六段倒数第二句中the difference（区别）指代前面的children born prematurely（早产儿）和breast-fed babies（母乳喂养的婴儿）。

Questions 29–33

题型 句子填空题(Sentence Completion)

注意 该题型属于纯粹的填空题，答案一般为原文原词。

29	关键词	REM behaviour disorder
	原文定位	第三段第三句REM behaviour disorder can be a precursor of neurodegenerative disease including Parkinsons.
	题解	答案neurodegenerative disease/Parkinsons 题干中predecessor（前辈）与原文中的precursor（先驱）对应，与题干相比就可以得出答案。
30	关键词	night terrors, sleep walking
	原文定位	第三段末句Dream content (pleasant/unpleasant) will be remembered on waking from REM sleep but there is often little memory of the preceding mental activity on arousals from NREM sleep...
	题解	答案memory 注意本题考查的是but后面的内容，与NREM sleep有关，题干中的almost...no（大多数……都没）与little（完全不）是同义替换，what they dreamed（他们所梦见的是……）与原文中the preceding（在前的） mental activity（心理活动）相对应，undergone（经历）与原文中occurs（发生）的同义替换。

31	关键词	narcolepsy, vivid
	原文定位	第四段末句This can also increase total REM sleep, leading to intense vivid often frightening dreams (hypnogogic-sleep onset/hypnopompic or, on waking, hallucinations), similar to that experienced by patients with narcolepsy.
	题解	答案frightening　该题目较为简单，题干是对第四段末句的改写，similar to that experienced by patients with narcolepsy（嗜眠发作）改为主语，leading to（导致）用be作为谓语，显然要找到一个和vivid（生动的）所对应的词。文中信息只有frightening（令人恐惧的）满足要求。
32	关键词	emotional, environmental effects, intrinsic sleep disorders
	原文定位	第五段第二句The frequency of the arousals may increase with emotional disturbance or environmental discomfort but also in many intrinsic sleep disorders such as periodic leg movements in sleep, obstructive sleep apnoea and narcolepsy.
	题解	答案arousals　文中的frequency（频率）与题干中的how often（多久一次）是对应词，depends on（取决于）与原文中increase with（随着……增加）相对应，题干中many factors（很多因素）后接involving引导的现在分词，修饰factors（因素），将原文中的emotional disturbance or environmental discomfort but also in many intrinsic sleep disorders信息概括为emotional and environmental effects（情感和环境因素）和intrinsic sleep disorders（固有的睡眠紊乱）。
33	关键词	The infants, return to sleep
	原文定位	第六段末句Persistent night awakenings in infants and toddlers usually reflect the child's inability to self-soothe back to sleep without parental attention and will respond to a well-supported behavioural programme.
	题解	答案parental attention　题干the infants may have the night awakening problems是对原文persistent night awakenings in infants的改写，difficult（困难）与原文中inability（无能力）对应；题干中的no（没有）与原文中的without（没有）对应；return to sleep（重新入睡）与原文中back to sleep（再度入睡）对应。

Questions 34–40

题型　摘要填空题(Summary Completion)

注意　摘要题是一种综合性填空题，有的空格可能会有一定的归纳性，尤其是带选项的摘要题。

34	关键词	prescribed
	原文定位	倒数第四段第二句Even in this group success is possible by persisting with behavioural work, though many paediatricians prescribe melatonin for these children with some success.
	题解	答案melatonin　prescribed与原文中的prescribe（开处方）明显对应，而doctors（医生）与原文中paediatricians（小儿科医师）对应，题干是将原文中的主动句改为被动句。

35	关键词	the last resort
	原文定位	倒数第四段第三句But as the long-term safety of melatonin remains unknown it should be used as a last resort. 和末句Its use as a hypnot c should be discouraged, especially in the developing child as there is uncertainty on other cycles, such as menstrual.
	题解	**答案hypnotic** 第三句与题干对应，而第七句melatonion（褪黑激素）不该用做hypnotic（安眠药）。
36	关键词	developing child
	原文定位	倒数第四段末句Its use as a hypnotic should be discouraged, especially in the developing child as there is uncertainty on other cycles, such as menstrual.
	题解	**答案cycles** 题干中的the developing child为原词重现，as there is...（因为有）与for it may have harm...（因为它可能对……有害）对应。
37	关键词	melatonin secretion, regulated
	原文定位	倒数第三段第三句Melatonin secretion is high in darkness and low in daylight hours, the process beginning in the retina with the suprachiasmatic nucleus playing a major role as a sleep regulator via melatonin.
	题解	**答案sleep** 题干中的melatonin secretion（褪黑激素的分泌）为原文重现，题干中的important（重要的）与原文中playing a major role（起主要作用）对应，同时regulated（动词，规定）与原文中regulator（名词，规定者）是同根词。
38	关键词	delayed sleep phase syndrome, postponed
	原文定位	倒数第二段第三句In delayed sleep phase syndrome, sleep onset is delayed to the early hours of the morning with consequent difficulty in waking in time for school/work.
	题解	**答案sleep onset** 题干中的delayed sleep phase syndrome（延迟睡眠的综合症状）是原文重现；题干中postponed（推迟）与原文中的delayed（延迟）对应。
39	关键词	natural treatment, reach, sleep time
	原文定位	倒数第二段末句Once established, advancing sleep onset time is difficult and requires treatment with appropriately timed melatonin or br ght light therapy—advancing sleep onset progressively forwards until the desired sleep time is reached.
	题解	**答案bright light therapy** 题干的提示是一种天然的治疗方法，故对应bright light therapy（治疗），其中题干中be used to reach the desired sleep time（被用来达到期望的睡眠时间）是将原文对这种疗法的解释the desired sleep time is reached（已经达到了期望的睡眠时间）进行了改写。
40	关键词	senior citizens
	原文定位	末段首句In contrast the elderly who are more susceptible to perturbation in their sleep-wake schedule can develop advanced sleep phase syndrome with sleep onset occurring early in the evening.
	题解	**答案early** 题干中senior citizens（年长的人）是原文中the elderly（上了年纪的人）的同义替换；题干中的suffer from（承受）与原文are more susceptible to（易受……影响的）相对应；题干中的at night（在晚上）对应原文的in the evening（在晚上）。

Test 2

WRITING

WRITING TASK 1

名师解读

本题为变迁类地图题，属于对比说明型的文章，主要是让考生阐明健康中心过去和现在在建造结构上的一些变化。

考生首先需要花一点时间来解析图片，通过对比找到健康中心过去和现在各部分结构是如何分布以及两者之间的变化和差别。既然是对比说明型的文章，那么能够体现对比的词、短语、甚至是句型就显得尤其重要。此外，在这类地图的表述中，应重视描述的逻辑性和重点性，不可面面俱到。

地图题并不一定需要引言段和结尾段，但是为了文章结构上的完整，加上开头和结尾也是有必要的。切记小作文不是大作文，开头和结尾要尽量简单，只需要说明这幅图表示了什么即可。

高分范文

The plans show the changes of a health centre over the last six years. Since 2008, the centre has expanded in a number of different ways. Firstly, an extension has been added to accommodate a minor operation room. Also, the interior has been significantly remodeled.

In 2008, there was a large entrance area with wide doors and a lot of open space for waiting, with the reception desk in the middle. There were only three consulting rooms and a physiotherapy room. This room has stayed the same size but the consulting rooms have been made smaller and increased to four in number. The office has been made smaller and the reception desk has been put in front of it. A children's play area has been added in the corner near the entrance.

Outside there have also been changes. The car park has been expanded with room for 18 more cars. The garden is decreased in size to accommodate the extra parking space. (164 words)

WRITING TASK 2

文章结构

正反观点辩论+原因+立场

viewpoint +reason1+reason2+standpoint
第一段：背景句+引出话题+反方观点+理由
第二段：正方观点+理由
第三段：总结+立场

思路点拨

步骤一：审题（<3分钟）

Some say that it would be better if the majority of employees worked from home instead of travelling to a workplace every day. Do you think the advantages of working from home outweigh the disadvantages?

→通读题目，了解大意，判断题型。

本题的题型为议论文。题目的大意为：有人认为，如果大多数员工每天在家工作而不是去办公室办公会更好。你认为远程工作的优势多于劣势吗?

→细读题目，理解上下句表达的意思。

首句给出对于employees worked from home instead of travelling to a workplace这个问题的一种观点，第二句要求考生针对这个问题提出对此问题的看法。

→再读题目，辨别关键词，区分主题词和限定词，推测考官的出题意图。

主题词：employees worked from home

限定词：advantages, disadvantages

步骤二：列大纲（<3分钟）

英文提纲	Intro: more and more people are staying at home→opponent 1→opponent 2→opponent 3→ they don't believe Body：the advantages of working at home→many workers prefer home working→new technologies, much easier to do this→less travel, a smaller carbon footprint→enables many people to join the workforce Conclusion：believe strongly that working at home is the fairest and most efficient option
中文提纲	引出话题：越来越多的人在家工作→反方观点一→反方观点二→反方观点三→不相信远程工作 主体段落：在家工作的优势→许多人喜欢在家工作→新技术的发展使在家工作更容易→更少的交通，低碳生活→使更多的人加入到工作之中 总结：强烈支持在家工作

高分范文

In many parts of the world, and in many different sectors, more and more people are staying at home rather than commuting to work. **Opponents** of home-working say that being together in a workplace with colleagues is an important part of keeping people healthy and happy. Staying at home, never meeting people can lead to **depression**. They also say that, from a professional point of view, it is important to spend time in formal and less formal situations with co-workers. Although it is argued that **interaction** can happen via computers, especially with a visual element such as video conferencing, they do not believe this can ever replace face to face contact.

For me, the advantages of working at home **outweigh** the disadvantages. Firstly, many workers prefer home working, saying they function more effectively because they can relax, without the pressure and waste of the **long commute**. With new technologies placing people in the same room **metaphorically**, it is becoming much easier to do this. With less travel, there is a smaller **carbon footprint**. There is a claim that due to the fact that many people choose to live in remoter areas, car use is significantly reduced. Finally, what clinches the argument for me is the fact that working at home enables many people to join the workforce who would not otherwise be able to do so. This option is particularly liberating for women because they often have more caring responsibilities.

To sum up, I believe strongly that working at home is the fairest and most **efficient** option for most people. (263 words)

SPEAKING

名师解读

Part 1的题目属于家庭话题，此类题目一直都是口语考试当中最常见的一类，一般都与考生日常生活息息相关，所以考生会有话可说，但要出彩、吸引考官，还是不容易的。

Part 2属于口头作文，要认真审题，陈述的内容应包括所有考点，但不能面面俱到，要有重点。

Part 3购物是雅思口语考试中最常见的话题之一，考生在备考时要多积累与购物话题相关的词汇和素材。

高分示例

PART 1

Family

- How big is your family?

I have quite a big family. It includes my parents and my father's parents as well as my brother and me.

- How often do you spend time together?

We all spent a lot of time together and were very close, about once a week. The time we are together is really amazing.

- What do you enjoy doing as a family?

During the holidays I go home to visit them. My brother and his wife and son usually come too. **Other than** the holidays, my mother will sometimes come to Beijing to visit us.

We love to go for picnics and walks in the mountains. We also enjoy going to the zoo and the theatre.

- How do you keep in touch with members of your family?

While I am in Beijing, I call my mother once or twice per week to speak to her and my grandparents, but my brother and his family live near me so I see them more often.

PART 2

The other day my kettle broke, so I went to a shop to buy a new one. It was a really expensive one, but it had lots of **features** and went well with my other appliances.

Less than a week later though, it stopped working and I was really **upset**. I packed it back into its box and found the **receipt** to take it back to the store but they wouldn't refund it or give me a new one. I asked to speak to the manager or the **supervisor**, but they wouldn't fetch them and kept giving me excuses.

Eventually I just took down the name of the employee I spoke to and told him I was going to file a complaint with the headquarters. I e-mailed my complaint to the headquarters but it's been two weeks now and I've heard nothing from them.

I am really unhappy about what happened but I don't know what to do about it now. One thing is for sure, I will never go to that store again.

PART 3

Products people buy in your country

- Are there more goods available in shops now than in the past? Why/Why not?

If you compare shopping now to shopping ten years ago, I would say there are definitely more goods **available**, in every section of **grocery** stores. Not only are there more people to serve and more stores to choose from, but most of the stores are **specialty** stores that care specific products. This forces the customer to **seek out** different stores for different needs, instead of like in the past where there were maybe five different stores that people used for major shopping.

- Do people generally prefer to buy products from their own or from other countries?

When it comes to buying goods from other countries or your own, I believe it's personal preference. Some people prefer the food from their own country, but like the clothes or shoes from another. I know that **personally**, I prefer the food in Beijing to the food at home, but that is all dependant on the person. Some people prefer their home countries' goods because they make them **feel at ease** and comfortable.

- What kinds of products are most affected by fashions from other countries?

When it comes to fashions and trends, the world is heavily affected by other countries, mostly America, the UK and Europe. In these countries, the height of fashion is created and then shown to the rest of the world who try to copy it for their own needs. As a result, clothing and the like are most heavily affected.

- Will overseas trends and fashions have more or less impact on what people buy in the future?

Of course, importing and selling the original line would be too expensive for the general population, so new products are always made to look **somewhat** like the high fashion of the major countries. This is important to look at and to discuss with other people because most of the time, we don't even realise that we are being affected by trends and fashions from all around the world. All it takes is one person and the chain reaction will follow. As to if this will affect everyone more or less in their buying future, it is up to whether they can decide to follow the set trends for fashion or make their own.

Protecting consumers

- What kind of techniques do advertisers use to persuade people to buy more?

Advertisers use many tricks of the trade to persuade people to buy more of their products from **guilt** to power, **charity** to fellowship. They tell people that their lives would be better with certain items, or that they will be more desired if they wear this or that. They play on the emotions of each person at the same time to **cohere** them into buying their products.

- Who should be responsible for the quality of products: producers, shops or customers?

I think that everyone should be at least partly responsible, but the producers should ensure that their products are of high standards, that way the shop can offer quality products and the customers would not have to return faulty or wrong products.

- How could governments protect the rights of consumers?

I'm not too sure how the government could protect the rights of consumers, without removing the rights to sell certain things. However, I do believe that the government could make certain changes to the system that make sure that customers are refunded or the item replaced in case of mishap. Or they could go a step further and ensure all products sold **are up to** standard before it reaches the shops.

Test 2

重点词汇

LISTENING

district	['dɪstrɪkt]	*n.*	区域；地方
micro-organism		*n.*	微生物
biochemical	[ˌbaɪəʊ'kemɪkl]	*adj.*	生物化学的
deliberately	[dɪ'lɪbərətli]	*adv.*	故意地；谨慎地
criterion	[kraɪ'tɪərɪən]	*n.*	（批评判断的）标准；准则
Pennington			彭宁顿（英国城市）
slightly	['slaɪtli]	*adv.*	些微地，轻微地；纤细地
apartment	[ə'pɑːtmənt]	*n.*	公寓；房间
footage	['fʊtɪdʒ]	*n.*	英尺长度；连续镜头
considerably	[kən'sɪdərəbli]	*adv.*	相当地；非常地
compromise	['kɒmprəmaɪz]	*v.*	妥协；危害
waterfront	['wɔːtəfrʌnt]	*n.*	滩，海滨；水边
apparently	[ə'pærəntli]	*adv.*	显然地；似乎，表面上
completely	[kəm'pliːtli]	*adv.*	完全地，彻底地；完整地
radiator	['reɪdɪeɪtə]	*n.*	散热器；暖气片；辐射体
cosy	['kəʊzi]	*adj.*	舒适的；惬意的
endangered	[ɪn'deɪndʒəd]	*adj.*	濒临灭绝的；有生命危险的
terrestrial	[tə'restrɪəl]	*adj.*	地球的；陆地的
conservation	[ˌkɒnsə'veɪʃn]	*n.*	保存，保持；保护
domestication	[dəˌmestɪ'keɪʃn]	*n.*	驯养；教化
reproduction	[ˌriːprə'dʌkʃn]	*n.*	繁殖，生殖；复制品
utilization	[ˌjuːtəlaɪ'zeɪʃn]	*n.*	利用，使用
shrimp-like			像虾一样的
crustacean	[krʌ'steɪʃn]	*n.*	甲壳纲动物
krill	[krɪl]	*n.*	[无脊椎] 磷虾
poisonous	['pɔɪzənəs]	*adj.*	有毒的；恶毒的；讨厌的
organism	['ɔːgənɪzəm]	*n.*	有机体；生物体
responsible	[rɪ'spɒnsəbl]	*adj.*	负责的，可靠的；有责任的
mysterious	[mɪ'stɪərɪəs]	*adj.*	神秘的；不可思议的；难解的
shark	[ʃɑːk]	*n.*	鲨鱼；骗子
oil spill			漏油；浮油

READING

alien	['eɪlɪən]	*n.*	外星人
galaxy	['gæləksi]	*n.*	星系，银河系
biosphere	['baɪəʊsfɪə]	*n.*	生物圈
celebrated	['selɪbreɪtɪd]	*adj.*	有名的，著名的
tame	[teɪm]	*v.*	（使）服从，驯服
tie down			捆住，束缚
consensus	[kən'sensəs]	*n.*	（意见等）一致，一致同意
extrasolar	[ˌekstrə'səʊlə]	*adj.*	（存在于或来自于）太阳系以外的
spectrum	['spektrəm]	*n.*	光谱，波谱
magnification	[ˌmægnɪfɪ'keɪʃn]	*n.*	放大（率，倍数）
detect	[dɪ'tekt]	*v.*	探测
spread-spectrum		*n.*	扩展频谱

stray	[streɪ]	*adj.*	[物]（物理量）杂散的，分散的
emission	[ɪ'mɪʃn]	*n.*	发出物，发射物
eavesdropper	['iːvzdrɒpə]	*n.*	偷听者
analogous	[ə'næləgəs]	*adj.*	相似的，可比拟的
electromagnetic	[ɪˌlektrəʊmæg'netɪk]	*adj.*	电磁的
swathe	[sweɪð]	*n.*	长而宽的一条（或地带）
collaboration	[kəˌlæbə'reɪʃn]	*n.*	合作，协作
elusive	[ɪ'luːsɪv]	*adj.*	难以捉摸的
preclude	[prɪ'kluːd]	*v.*	阻止
warp	[wɔːp]	*v.*	弄弯，变歪
music-streaming		*adj.*	音乐主流（网站）的
abruptly	[ə'brʌptli]	*adv.*	突然地，意外地
fluctuation	[ˌflʌktʃʊ'eɪʃn]	*n.*	波动，涨落，起伏
malfunction	[ˌmæl'fʌŋkʃn]	*n.*	机器运转失常，出现故障
potentially	[pə'tenʃəli]	*adv.*	潜在地，可能地
ruinous	['ruːɪnəs]	*adj.*	破坏性的，灾难性的；严重受损的
channel-surf		*n.*	频道搜索
melodrama	['melədrɑːmə]	*n.*	情节剧
Hispanic	[hɪ'spænɪk]	*adj.*	西班牙的；说西班牙语国家的
documentary	[ˌdɒkju'mentri]	*n.*	纪录片
remote control			遥控器
decidedly	[dɪ'saɪdɪdli]	*adv.*	无疑地，显然地
genre	['ʒɒ̃rə]	*n.*	（文学、艺术等的）类型，体裁，风格
distinction	[dɪ'stɪŋkʃn]	*n.*	区别
quote	[kwəʊt]	*v.*	报价
video-streaming website			视频媒体网站
professional	[prə'feʃənl]	*adj.*	职业的，专业的
come off			表现
steeply	[stiːpli]	*adv.*	大坡度地
file-sharing website			文件共享网站
draw away			抽取；吸引走
drive down			驱使……下降
decompose	[ˌdiːkəm'pəʊz]	*v.*	腐烂，使分解
constituent	[kən'stɪtjuənt]	*adj.*	构成的，组成的
piracy	['paɪrəsi]	*n.*	盗版行为，非法复制
assumption	[ə'sʌmpʃn]	*n.*	假定
hostile	['hɒstaɪl]	*adj.*	怀有敌意的，敌方的
principle	['prɪnsəpl]	*n.*	原则，原理；准则
objectionable	[əb'dʒekʃənəbl]	*adj.*	令人不快的，讨厌的
revenue	['revənjuː]	*n.*	收入；税收
superior	[suː'pɪərɪə]	*adj.*	级别较高的；优良的，较好的，优秀的
wasteland	['weɪstlænd]	*n.*	荒原，荒地
surfeit	['sɜːfɪt]	*n.*	过量，过度
artificial	[ˌɑːtɪ'fɪʃl]	*adj.*	人造的，人工的，假的
restriction	[rɪ'strɪkʃn]	*n.*	约束，限制，限定
advertising rate			广告费率，广告价格
nonetheless	[ˌnʌnðə'les]	*adv.*	虽然如此，但是
a handful of			少许，一些
upstart websites			新兴起的网站
rattle	['rætl]	*v.*	摇动，使紧张，使恐惧
extinct	[ɪk'stɪŋkt]	*adj.*	灭绝的，绝种的

track down			追捕到，追查出
cater to			迎合
squat	[skwɒt]	*adj.*	矮胖，矮而宽的
squat cube			矮而宽的立方体，指电视机
flatten	['flætn]	*v.*	变平，使（某物）变平
ward off			避开，挡住
condensation	[ˌkɒnden'seɪʃn]	*n.*	冷凝，凝聚
dimension	[daɪ'menʃn]	*n.*	维（度）
sprout	[spraʊt]	*v.*	（使）萌芽
apnoea	[æp'niːə]	*n.*	呼吸暂停
neurologist	[njuə'rɒlədʒɪst]	*n.*	神经学者
alternate	[ɔːl'tɜːnət]	*adj.*	交替的
homeotherm	['həʊmɪəθɜːm]	*adj.*	恒温的；温血的
intermittent	[ˌɪntə'mɪtənt]	*adj.*	间歇的
disturbance	[dɪ'stɜːbəns]	*n.*	骚动，动乱，打扰，干扰
shrink	[ʃrɪŋk]	*v.*	（使）收缩
hypnopompic	[ˌhɪpnəʊ'pɒmpɪk]	*adj.*	半醒的
transient	['trænzɪənt]	*adj.*	短暂的，瞬时的 *n.* 瞬时现象
frequency	['friːkwənsi]	*n.*	频率
narcolepsy	['nɑːkəʊlepsi]	*n.*	嗜眠发作
infant	['ɪnfənt]	*n.*	婴儿，幼儿
toddler	['tɒdlə]	*n.*	初学走路的孩子
maturation	[ˌmætʃʊ'reɪʃn]	*n.*	成熟；化脓
paediatrician	[ˌpiːdɪə'trɪʃn]	*n.*	儿科医师
menstrual	['menstrʊəl]	*adj.*	[生理] 月经的
secretion	[sɪ'kriːʃn]	*n.*	分泌
retina	['retɪnə]	*n.*	视网膜
adolescence	[ˌædə'lesns]	*n.*	青春期（一般指成年以前13至15岁的发育期）
therapy	['θerəpi]	*n.*	治疗

WRITING

opponent	[ə'pəʊnənt]	*n.*	对手；竞争者
depression	[dɪ'preʃn]	*n.*	抑郁；沮丧
interaction	[ˌɪntər'ækʃn]	*n.*	相互作用
outweigh	[ˌaʊt'weɪ]	*v.*	大于；重于；超过
long commute			通勤路程很长
metaphorically	[ˌmetə'fɒrɪkli]	*adv.*	比喻性地
carbon footprint			碳排放量；碳足迹
efficient	[ɪ'fɪʃnt]	*adj.*	效率高的；有能力的

SPEAKING

other than			除了；不同于
feature	['fiːtʃə]	*n.*	特色，特征
upset	[ʌp'set]	*adj.*	心烦的；混乱的；弄翻的
receipt	[rɪ'siːt]	*n.*	收到；收据
supervisor	['suːpəvaɪzə]	*n.*	监督人
eventually	[ɪ'ventʃʊəli]	*adv.*	最后，终于
available	[ə'veɪləbl]	*adj.*	有效的，可得的

grocery	['grəʊsəri]	*n.*	食品杂货店
specialty	['speʃəlti]	*n.*	专业，专长；特产
seek out			找出；搜出
personally	['pɜːsənəli]	*adv.*	亲自地；当面
feel at ease			感到心安理得；感到轻松
somewhat	['sʌmwɒt]	*adv.*	有点；多少
guilt	[gɪlt]	*n.*	犯罪，过失；内疚
charity	['tʃærəti]	*n.*	慈善；施舍；慈善团体
cohere	[kəʊ'hɪə]	*v.*	凝聚；连贯
be up to			胜任；该由……负责

听力原文

SECTION 1

(WOMAN=W; LIBRARIAN= L)

W: Good morning.

L: Morning, can I help you?

W: Yes, I'd like to join the library. We're new to the district, you see.

L: Certainly. Well, all we need is Q1 some sort of identification with your name and address on it.

W: Oh dear. We just moved in, you see, and Q2 everything has my old address.

L: A driving licence, perhaps?

W: No, I don't drive.

L: Your husband's would do.

W: Yes, but his licence will still have the old address on it.

L: Perhaps you have a letter addressed to you at your new house?

W: No, I'm afraid not. We've only been there a few days, you see, and no one's written to us yet.

L: What about your bankbook?

W: That's just the same. Oh dear, and I did want to get some books out this weekend. We're going on holiday to relax after the move, you see, and I wanted to take something with me to read.

L: Well, I'm sorry, but we can't possibly issue cards without some form of identification. Q3 What about your passport?

W: What? Oh yes, how silly I am. I've just got a new one and it does have our new address. I've just been to book our air tickets, so I have it with me.

L: Well, that's all right. Your card will be ready soon.

W: OK. Er, how many books am I allowed to take out?

L: You can take four books out at a time and you also get two cards to take out three magazines or periodicals. Newspapers, I'm afraid, can't be taken out.

W: Oh that's fine. Do you have a record library? Some libraries do, I know.

L: Yes, we do. You have to pay a deposit of $5 in case you damage them. But that Q4 entitles you to take out two records at a time.

W: That's good. Could you show me where your history and biography sections are, please?

L: Yes, just over there to your right. If there's any particular book you want, you can look it up in the catalogue, which you'll find Q5 just around the corner. You can also find a touch screen information service on level two.

W: Thank you. Oh, and how long am I allowed to keep the books for?

L: Well, Q6 the normal loan period is three weeks with two weeks extension.

W: Oh dear. We're going away for four weeks. Can I renew them now?

L: I'm afraid not. You must do that at the end of three weeks.

W: I see. Thank you very much.

L: Well, let's go into some details. Your name, please, madam?

W: My name is Q7 Barbara. The surname is Cooper. It's spelt as C-O-O-P-E-R.

L: Fine. And what's your contact number? If we have new books coming, we can contact you in time.

W: Good. You can call Q8 7236518, but it's better after 5pm. You know I have to work during the daytime. Do you need the office number?

L: I don't think so. It's enough. Could you tell me the address?

W: I lived in King Road, but of course you need my new address. It is Q9 25 Saint Mary Road, Hanwell.

L: That's H-A-N-W-E-L-L. Is it right?

W: Yes. Do you need the passport number? I have it with me. Here you are.

L: Yes, thank you. The number of your passport is Q10 G57980942. OK. And your card is ready. The number is M930123.

W: Thank you. Could I take a look around and check out some books?

L: Of course. As you like.

SECTION 2

(WOMAN=W; MAN=M)

W: Hi. Nice to see you again! Have you found any suitable places for me to look at?

M: Yes ma'am, I have. I've arranged for you to

see five today, that all more or less match your search criteria. I know you're not familiar with this city and you aren't sure exactly which area you want to live in, so I've started by picking property in five different places. The first one's in Pennington. It's 900 square feet, which is slightly small compared to some of the others, and it's also in a rather out-of-the-way part of town, but I thought it might appeal to you because Q11 it's a single-family house rather than an apartment, and you said that you liked privacy. It's pretty standard in design—it was built in 1969 and it's got two bedrooms. Then...this next one is in Hillsboro. Q12 This one was built in 1969 as well. It's got two bedrooms and it's a thousand square feet altogether. It's a fairly standard design but it's the only one I've found so far with a fitness centre, and you did tell me that you and your husband like working out in the mornings. It's at the upper end of your price range, that one. Q13 The next one's in an area called Westfield. Its square footage is considerably more than the others, and I guessed you'd like to see the amount of space you could get within your budget if you were willing to compromise a bit on location and facilities. There's only a very small garden, for example. Then...there's an apartment in Lennox Village...It's average size, and the agent doesn't seem to know exactly when it was built. Q14 What makes it stand out is that it's right in heart of the city, so you'd have easy access to transport, nightlife and so on. There's even a hospital right opposite, and I know you said you were looking for work as a nurse. And the last one is at Covenant Crossing. This one's the smallest, but it's also the cheapest, which is quite surprising as Q15 it's situated near the waterfront, with easy access to the river. I guess you'd be interested in it because of that. Its decor is a bit tired—the apartment was built in the 1970s and nothing much has been done since then, but it's only superficial work that needs doing...Anyway, here are a few details of all five properties if you want to have a closer look.

M: OK...Well I thought we'd go to see the single-family house first, and I've printed off a floor plan for you. This one here is the plan of the second level...So you can see that on the left there's a covered deck, which runs along the whole of the side wall. On the opposite side of the house there's the bedroom in the corner there, and the stairs leading down to the level below. There's a very useful storage area to this side of the house, Q16 it's the room next to the stairs. Then...next to the bedroom there are two adjoining rooms—the bathroom is the bigger one of these and the Q17 dressing room is the slightly smaller one. Apparently both of them have been completely refurbished recently, so they're in good condition. Then there's also an office on this level, it's Q18 opposite the bedroom, right next to the great room. Of course it could be used for something else if you wanted, but it's set up to take a large desk and computer hardware at the moment. Now you can see that there are two doors opening onto the deck...one of them gives access from the great room and the other Q19 gives access directly from the dining area, which is right next to the kitchen—there's no dividing wall, just a low partition, so light from the windows comes right through I guess. Oh yes, and there's a stove that burns wood, and heats the radiators. Q20 It's in the corner of the great room, so you can sit and look at it in winter. Very cosy! Then...here's the plan for the lower level. It's got two...[fade]

SECTION 3

(PRESENTER=P; MONICA=M)

P: Cheese is one of those foods that we tend to take for granted as always having been with us, and it's odd to think that someone somewhere must have discovered the process to make cheeses that takes place today. In the studio to tell us all about it is Monica Maxwell.

M: Today we all know that the process of making cheeses takes place when micro-organisms get into milk and bring about changes in its physical and biochemical structure. Well, obviously, we don't know who discovered the process, but it's thought that it came from Q21 southwest Asia about 8,000 years ago. In the early time, there were mainly two types of cheeses. One of them was rather tasteless and bland, in the case of the so-called Q22 "fresh cheeses", which are eaten immediately after the milk has coagulated, and another one was rough-tasting and salty, in the case of the Q22 "ripened cheeses", which are made by adding salt to the soft fresh cheese and allowing other biochemical processes to continue so that a stronger taste and a more solid texture results.

Q23 The ancient Romans changed all that. They were great pioneers in the art of cheese-making, and the different varieties of cheeses they invented and the techniques for producing them spread with them to the countries they invaded. This spread of new techniques took place between about Q24 60 BC and 300 AD. You can still trace their influence in the English word "cheese", which comes ultimately from the Latin word "caseus", that's C-A-S-E-U-S.

At this stage in history, people weren't aware in a scientific way of the role of different microorganisms and enzymes in producing different types of cheese. But they knew from experience that cheeses' tastes were relevant to something. If you kept your milk or your "pre-cheese" mixture at a certain Q25 temperature or in a certain Q25 environment, things would turn out in a certain way. In the 19th century, with the increasing knowledge about Q26 micro-organism, there came the next great step forward in cheese-making. Once it was known exactly which micro-organism were involved in the different stages of producing a cheese, and how the presence of different microorganisms affected the taste, it was possible to introduce them deliberately, and to Q27 industrialise the process.

Nowadays cheese has started being made on a large scale in Q28 factories, although the small producer working from his farm dairy continued to exist and still exists today. Cheese-making moved very much into the world of technology and industrial processes, although, because the aim is still to produce something that people like to eat, there's still an important role for Q29 human judgments. People still go round tasting the young cheese at different stages to see how it's getting on, and may add a bit of this or that to improve the final taste. Whatever the scale of production, there is still room for the development of Q30 art alongside the technology.

SECTION 4

Well, tonight I am going to talk something about one of the endangered species—penguins. In 1992, *the Implementing Regulation on Terrestrial Wild Animal Conservation* was issued by the State Council which was formulated according to *the Wild Animal Conservation Law of PRC*. This regulation has seven chapters and 46 Articles Q31 which provide specific regulations on protection of wild animals, management of wild animal hunting, wild animal domestication and reproduction and sales and utilisation of wild animals.

Experts say Q32–34 a shortage of fish and other food is threatening many of the world's penguins. They say as many as ten of the seventeen kinds of penguins may be in danger of disappearing.

For example, thousands of Magellanic penguins build their nests at Punta Tombo, Argentina. Wildlife Conservation Society researchers have studied these birds for eighteen years. They say the numbers of penguins have decreased by 30% since 1987.

Penguins are black and white birds that live in the southern half of the world. They are common to South America, New Zealand, Australia and South Africa. Many live near cold waters. But some live near warm waters in the Galapagos Islands, near the coast of Ecuador. Penguins cannot fly. But they are fine swimmers. Penguins eat fish. Some kinds of penguins eat a small shrimp-like crustacean called krill.

Many scientists blame global warming for the decrease in penguin populations. They believe

Q32–34 the heating of the atmosphere has caused ocean waters to become warmer. The scientists say higher water temperatures have reduced the supply of fish and krill.

Rising air and water temperatures may have especially harmed Galapagos penguins. Researchers say that these birds are completely unable to reproduce. In addition, Q35 many adult penguins die of hunger.

Widespread fishing, exploration for oil and oil leaks also threaten penguins. Poisonous organisms in ocean water are another danger. These toxic blooms result from changes in the ocean water. Some scientists believe the warming of the oceans is responsible.

In 1990, more than half the yellow-eyed penguins in New Zealand died suddenly. These endangered birds may have died of Q36 a mysterious disease.

Penguins also have natural enemies, including Q37–40 wild dogs, sharks, seals and sea lions.

News about penguins is not all bad, however. About a year ago, oil leaking from a ship threatened 40% of the penguins in South Africa. The penguins became covered with oil. But thousands of people helped clean and treat the birds. Then they returned the penguins to the wild. Now these South African penguins are reproducing in higher numbers than before the oil spill. Thank you.

Test 3

答案速查

LISTENING

Section 1, Questions 1–10

1 17th
2 2.30pm
3 (family) pet
4 2
5 3 and 6
6 (her) husband
7 722 4189
8 1.5 metres
9 mixed breed
10 6 years

Section 2, Questions 11–20

11&12 IN EITHER ORDER A E
13&14 IN EITHER ORDER B C
15 B
16 D
17 F
18 H
19 A
20 E

Section 3, Questions 21–30

21 C
22 H
23 F
24 E
25 B
26 Concentrate
27 Surf the Internet/Go to web
28 periodicals
29 final title
30 first draft

Section 4, Questions 31–40

31 overpopulation
32 South America
33 developed countries
34 middle classes
35 wealth gap
36 E
37 D
38 B
39 A
40 F

READING

Reading Passage 1, Questions 1–12

1 B
2 C
3 E
4 F
5 A
6 D
7 A
8 C
9 B
10 C
11 A
12 B

Reading Passage 2, Questions 13–26

13 owl solution
14 vertical steel pipes
15 to rotate
16 non-circular floors
17 solar panels
18 horizontal wind turbines
19 technological limitations
20 money
21 B
22 E
23 C
24 A
25 C
26 E

Reading Passage 3, Questions 27–40

27 F
28 D
29 H
30 C
31 E
32 A
33 B
34 G
35 NOT GIVEN
36 FALSE
37 TRUE
38 TRUE
39 C
40 A

名师解析

LISTENING

SECTION 1

主题场景	生活场景
主旨大意	一名申请者向动物保护协会(SPCA)申请养宠物
考查题型	表格填空题

名师解读

1 17th 题目要求填写申请者Helen Morgan向SPCA申请养宠物的日期，注意排除干扰信息18th，尤其是18th在录音中出现了两次，干扰性更强。

2 2.30pm Q2－Q8的大标题为Lifestyle Details，即生活方式的细节。本题考查的是工作时间表，Wednesday and Friday是关键词，注意填写to之后的时间2.30pm。

3 (family) pet 本空需填写领养狗的原因，因此as之后应填写用途，原文给出两个信息guard和family pet，注意转折词but之后的信息family pet为答案。

4 2 题干中permanently的意思为“长期地”，即题干考查的是家庭常住人口，though之后提到的信息为干扰信息，不是答案。

5 3 and 6 本空需填写定期拜访的孩子的年龄，注意ages和children均为复数，应填写两个年龄的数字，分别为3和6。

6 (her) husband carer为“看护人”，除了applicant即“申请人”，原文提到的另一个人husband应为答案。本题和Question 4对应。

7 722 4189 要求填写房东的联系电话，注意排除干扰。原文空格前已给出4位数字，补全即可。另外，题号为7，应填入的号码第一位亦为7，应避免漏写数字。

8 1.5 metres 填写fence的高度，原文只有一个数字1.5 metres出现，应为答案，注意一定要加单位metres，复数形式。

9 mixed breed Q9&Q10的大标题为Previous Ownership，即考查关于申领者之前养狗的信息。breed为关键词，即以前所养的狗的品种，之前的mixed为答案，同时注意答案的完整性。

10 6 years 由副标题Time owned可以确定应填写数字，排除之前说的5 years，答案为6 years。注意本题同第1题，说话者表述数字后，均作了修改，应确定正确数字后再填写答案。

SECTION 2

主题场景	旅行场景
主旨大意	介绍与出国旅行相关的借记卡、外币和旅行保险信息
考查题型	选择题、图表填空题

名师解读

11&12 IN EITHER ORDER A E 原文中的Text是选项E的重现，原文中的every time 与选项E中的whenever对应，原文中人称代词you由选项中的customers指代，原文中的any transaction与选项中的 is used对应。故选项E正确。原文中的charge在选项A中重现，one pound regardless of the price与选项中的a fixed charge for对应。

13&14 IN EITHER ORDER B C 原文中的have an account与选项C中的debit card对应，原文中的don't...a handling charge与选项C中的no administration charge对应。所以C项正确。原文中的order与选项B是重现，原文中的at whichever branch与选项B中的at any branch对应，原文中的following day与选项B中的

previous day对应，都是指要提前一天预约。所以B项也正确。

15　B　原文中的think与选项B中的Decide对应，而原文中whether...a single trip abroad...or whether...buying multi-trip insurance被选项B概括为type of cover。

16　D　原文中的insured 与选项D中的Check对应，原文中的existing policy为选项重现。考生需要注意表示顺序的连词then。

17　F　对于other account holders，要做的是visit our website，其中visit与选项F中的Go to对应，原文中的website为选项F的重现。

18　H　原文中的be asked与选项H中的Provide对应，原文中的journey与选项H中的travel对应，原文中的some information与选项H中的details对应。

19　A　原文中的supply与选项A中的Provide对应，原文中的you and your family—names, ages, passport numbers and so on在选项A中被概括为personal details。

20　E　题干中的关键词a discount 与原文中的20 percent reduction对应，故前面的pay online 就是答案，其中pay 与选项E中的payment为同根词，online为原文重现。

SECTION 3

主题场景	学术场景
主旨大意	介绍学生读论文著作的心得和迈克的论文计划
考查题型	配对题、笔记填空题

名师解读

21　C　根据题干关键词*The puzzling failure of economics*对答案进行定位，原文中quite odd和not what you'd expect与选项C中的uncommon对应。

22　H　原文中wouldn't have wanted to try and cope with与选项H中的not suitable for对应，原文中first year与选项H中的freshmen对应。

23　F　原文中easy to understand 与F中的easy to follow对应。本题又是对转折连词but后内容的考查。

24　E　原文中didn't put与选项E中的omits对应，原文中的the question of *New Deal*内容被概括为essential facts。

25　B　原文中index是选项B的重现，原文中的couldn't necessarily find what you wanted与选项B中的inadequate对应。

26　Concentrate　根据on IMF policies为原文重现，前面的动词concentrate为答案。考生注意此题的答案在关键词的前面出现，要求短时记忆的能力。

27　Surf the Internet/Go to web　题干中的useful为原文重现，而stuff和some good ones与题干中的information对应，这个词语与原文中的informative为同根词。考生要对第一个备选答案改写，否则超出题目要求字数。

28　periodicals　题干中的空格前后内容reference books和non-print materials均为原文重现。

29　final title　题干中的See Dr Forbes, to agree on the均为原文重现，故考生可以直接判定agree on the后的final title为答案。

30　first draft　题干中的work on为关键词，是原文重现，考生据此来对原文进行定位。本题的答案在定位词之后，相对简单，your后的first draft即为答案。

SECTION 4

主题场景	学术场景
主旨大意	环境问题的根本原因
考查题型	简答题、配对题

名师解读

31 overpopulation 题干中main environmental problem指出答案性质，原文提到first and foremost是开始预热，但之后的human beings不是“问题”，再往后听，强调this，之后的overpopulation为答案。

32 South America 答案应为一大陆的名称，听到South America，对应答案。

33 developed countries 答案为一类国家，听到US and Europe，应意识到这不是分类，但答案应该会马上出现，之后听到关键词group，答案为前面出现的developed ccuntries。

34 middle classes 答案应为某一类人，关键词是China，听到upper class，注意之前的连接词while表让步，答案为后面主句中的middle classes。

35 wealth gap 答案为某个术语，应注意原文call等这一类词，听到关键词rich, poor后，as people call it中提到wealth gap为答案。

36 E 题干中的energy为关键词，之后听到多个国家Spain, Germany and France，按照并列不选的原则，这几个都不是答案。之后听到一个单独的国家名Norway。

37 D 关键词recycling在原文后置，这样的重点场景词汇必须认识，从而能够判断同义替换。在之前原文提到another common option时就应意识到题目进入下一题，之后听到国家名England，虽然还没有听到recycling，但应有答题的意识。

38 B wastes为关键词，但接着听到Canada时注意may look like，不是肯定的信息，与同一句出现的British都不是答案。之后听到waste management其后的French是答案，选B项France。

39 A 此题干扰很大，多个国家名出现，一定要听清细节，American, English, French都是形容词，只有Canada是国家名，选A项。

40 F 与36题类似，前几个并列出现的不是答案，最后单独出现的Thailand为答案。泰国的法律仍然认为这是一个非常严重的罪行。

READING

READING PASSAGE 1

体　裁　　说明文
题　材　　社会科学类
主　题　　查尔斯·达尔文的自然选择学说
题　型　　配对题、选择题

Questions 1–6

题型 配对题(Matching Features)

注意 浏览文章，抓住各段的主题句和核心词（尤其是反复出现的核心词），重点关注段落首句、第二句与末句。

1	关键词	explaining the reason
	原文定位	第二段第二句There is an edited edition of his letters from his trip round the world on HMS Beagle...an attempt (surely redundant for supporters and futile for opponents) to explain "Why Evolution is True" ...
	题解	**答案B** The edition of Darwin's letters on HMS Beagle解释了"进化论为什么不可摇撼"。题干explaining the reason for the reality of evolution（解释进化论真实性的原因）对应原文to explain "Why Evolution is True"（解释"进化论为什么不可摇撼"）。
2	关键词	natural history
	原文定位	第三段第二句Instead, each chapter uses one of the naturalist's other books as a point of departure for a meandering, but ultimately enlightening, natural-history lesson.
	题解	**答案C** 注意，考官出这种题不是考查考生的细节阅读能力，而是考查考生对文章框架思路的把握能力。琼斯所著的《达翁之岛》对natural-history（自然史）的讨论发人深省。因此只要知道哪本书讲natural history就可以，并不需要了解具体内容。
3	关键词	problems, plants, animals
	原文定位	第三段第四句*The Movements and Habits of Climbing Plants* (also published in 1875) gives rise to an exploration of how similar the problems faced by plants are to those faced by animals...
	题解	**答案E** 首先浏览A–F选项，可以发现选项的6个editions中有4个(C–F)出现在第三段，因此要重视本段，提高正确率。出版于1875年的*The Movements and Habits of Climbing Plants*带领读者探索了植物和动物面临的问题。根据关键词即可确定答案。
4	关键词	human evolution
	原文定位	第三段末句And *The Descent of Man, and Selection in Relation to Sex* (1871) is the point of departure for the inevitable chapter on human evolution.
	题解	**答案F** *The Descent of Man, and Selection in Relation to Sex* (1871)对人类进化进行了讨论。浏览到关键词human evolution即可迅速做出选择。
5	关键词	races, starting points
	原文定位	第四段末句Their thesis is that, far from arriving at the idea of human evolution from his studies of natural history, Darwin took as one of his starting points the diversification of humanity into"races".
	题解	**答案A** evolution of humanity into "races"(人类演变成"种族")对应原文diversification of humanity into"races"（人类分化为"种族"）；题干的was considered as（被看作是……）为原文took as（把……当作是）的同义转述，即达尔文最初的起点之一是人类为何会分化出不同"种族"。

6	关键词	genetic
	原文定位	第三段第三句...*The Green Tyrannosaurs* that shows, using modern genetics, how insect ivory has evolved many times in unrelated groups of vegetables in response to a lack of nitrogen in the soil.
	题解	答案D *The Green Tyrannosaurs*这一章节，运用现代遗传学知识，告诉读者食人植物如何在土壤缺氮条件下，在不同种类植物中经历多次进化。题干genetic（遗传的）为原文genetics（遗传学）的形容词形式。注意，配对题题目数与选项数对应，最后一题如时间紧迫，可直接选择余下的最后一个答案，迅速将余下的题干同选项进行匹配，查看是否对应。

Questions 7–12

题型 选择题(Multiple Choice)

注意 答案在原文中是集中出现的，对应原文中的例举。确定一个答案，其余几个答案就在它的前后不远处。

7	关键词	“bottleneck”, Noah
	原文定位	第五段第三句Christians, at least, would have believed that everyone was descended from Adam and Eve, with what biologists would now refer to as a genetic“bottleneck”at the time of Noah.
	题解	答案A 三个选项中都含有human origins，因此可以推断出答案同人类起源相关。关键词“bottleneck”用双引号表示，显然为“高调词”，可以迅速定位。定位句大意为：至少基督徒会认为人类的祖先是亚当和夏娃——用现在生物学家的话说这就是诺亚时代一个遗传“瓶颈”。涉及亚当和夏娃，显然是从religious explanation（宗教的角度）讲述人类起源。注意用双引号或大写、黑体等表示的“高调词”，有利于在原文迅速定位。
8	关键词	different races, different origins
	原文定位	第五段倒数第二句The idea that the different races had different origins...began as a convenient piece of slave-traders' propaganda, intended to denigrate the humanity of Africans.
	题解	答案C 选择题中正确选项常常是原文相关词句的改写。该观点为奴贩们提供了宣传的便利。选项C（为奴贩们所利用）与此对应。这时可以直接选择不必看其他选项。这样既可以节省时间，同时也避免受干扰选项的误导。
9	关键词	geologists, literalist
	原文定位	第五段末句It rapidly became a matter of scientific debate, challenging the literalist interpretation of *the Bible* in a manner reminiscent of the questioning of the early geologists with their antediluvian fossils.
	题解	答案B 很多人一看到debate发现和第一个选项很相像，所以毫不犹豫地选A。其实选择题里最具有干扰性、迷惑性的就是选项和文中的句子长得相似，这样的答案多半是错误答案。看该句的后面，很快遇到了生词reminiscent（令人想起的），然后再往下看，看到了antediluvian（大洪水前的；远古的），因为生词不认识，导致内心紧张，影响了判断力。即使选项中也出现了生词，如archaeological（考古学的），也可采用排除法，排除干扰项A和D，及原文中未提及的选项C，正确答案为B。选项B将题干的antediluvian fossils（大洪水时代前的化石）总结为archaeological evidence（考古证明），与题意相符。

Test 3

10	关键词	Darwin, different races
	原文定位	第六段第二句He saw humanity as the product of common descent.
	题解	**答案C** 题干考查Darwin对于不同种族的观点。选项C They had the same origin（他们的起源是相同的）符合原文He saw humanity as the product of common descent（他认为人类源于共同的祖先）。
11	关键词	Why, Mr Desmond, Mr Moore
	原文定位	第六段末句According to Mr Desmond and Mr Moore, it was the unity he saw in humanity's diversity as much as that visible in the different breeds of domestic animals...which helped him understand what was going on.
	题解	**答案A** 本题可用排除法。首先看选项B、C，句子的差别在于compare和contrast。两者都表示比较，contrast侧重不同之处，而compare侧重强调两者的相同之处。由原文中的diversity（差异；多样性）可以看出比较的是不同，因此可把compare（选项B）优先排除。Mr Desmond和Mr Moore表示，达尔文在不同种族的人类和不同品种家养动物中看到了不同，受到启发，明白了生物进化是如何进行的。由此可见，二人的目的是为了揭示Darwin（达尔文）的灵感来源，故正确答案为A。
12	关键词	*Darwin's Sacred Cause*
	原文定位	末段首句Reader, beware: this book is as much about the anti-slavery movement as it is about the genesis of a scientific idea.
	题解	**答案B** 要注意这里的this book指的就是*Darwin's Sacred Cause*。对原句分析后会抓取出主要思想：这本书不仅仅讲述了genesis of a scientific idea（科学观点的起源），还描述了anti-slavery movement（反对奴隶制的运动）。选项B中体现了这两项，因此为正确答案。

READING PASSAGE 2

体　裁　说明文
题　材　科技
主　题　旋转建筑
题　型　摘要填空题、配对题

Questions 13–20

题型 摘要填空题(Summary Completion)

注意 观察空格前后是否有表示内容逻辑关系的连接词；观察空格前后词的词性及其数的形式；依据顺序原则，在空格前后找出关键词回原文定位。注意该题要求每个空格内所填单词的数量不超过三个。

13	关键词	solution
	原文定位	第二段首句The simplest approach to such a building is what might be called the owl solution—in other words, incomplete rotation.
	题解	**答案owl solution** 本题较为简单。观察空格前后内容，可以推测出空格内应填入名词。最简单的方法被称之为owl solution（猫头鹰方案），可以判断出owl solution即为正确答案。

14	关键词	Bill Butler, water, gas and sewage
	原文定位	第二段第三句Some years ago Bill Butler, an amateur architect, used this trick in a house in Snow Creek, California. 第四句Water and gas are delivered, and sewage removed, via vertical steel pipes in then on-rotating base.
	题解	答案vertical steel pipes 空格内应填入名词，做adopted的宾语，题干考查处理water, gas和sewage的方式。根据关键词定位，water（自来水）和gas（天然气）的传递，sewage（污水）的排放，都是通过一个在非旋转平面上的vertical steel pipes（垂直钢管）来完成的。注意确定答案的字数限制，绝对不要超字。
15	关键词	ability, restricted
	原文定位	第二段倒数第二句The house's ability to rotate is thus limited only by the length of the hoses at full stretch.
	题解	答案to rotate 题干restricted（限制）为原文limited（限制）的同义转述，被限制的是ability to rotate（旋转的能力），对应题意，故答案为to rotate（旋转）。
16	关键词	eighty, selfrotated
	原文定位	倒数第二段倒数第四句He wants to build a skyscraper called the Dynamic Tower in Dubai.和倒数第三句It would have 80 independently rotating, non-circular floors.
	题解	答案non-circular floors 空格前出现了数字eighty，可推断出空格内应填入名词，定位句中代词it指的就是The Dynamic Tower in Dubai，题干中的self rotating（自动旋转的）对应原文independently rotating（独立旋转的），因此，independently rotating后的内容应为空格内应填入的内容。
17 & 18	关键词	power, comes from
	原文定位	倒数第二段末句Solar panels and horizontal wind turbines between the floors would generate the power needed to turn it.
	题解	答案IN ORDER solar panels, holizontal wind turbines 17题与18题之间的距离非常近，由表示并列关系的词and连接，由此可以判断17题所对应的答案信息在原文中的位置应该与18题所对应的答案信息在原文中的位置非常近，且二者呈并列关系。题干以power（动力）作主语，为原文以Solar panels and horizontal wind turbines（太阳能板与水平风力涡轮机）作主语的同义转述，由此可以确定答案。
19	关键词	Antony Wood, confined
	原文定位	末段第二句But Antony Wood, head of the Council on Tall Building sand Urban Habitat, an industry association based in Chicago, says technological limitations no longer rule out such towers.
	题解	答案technological limitations 该空格前有一个介词by，由此推测出空格内应填入名词。Antony Wood说这样的建筑不会受到technological limitations（技术限制）。题干confine（限制）对应原文的rule out（排除；不考虑），not any more（不再）同no longer（不再）。

20	关键词	but, insufficiency
	原文定位	末段末句If the Dynamic Tower is not built, Mr Wood says, the explanation will not be an unavoidable lack of know-how, but an old-fashioned lack of money.
	题解	答案money 该空格前有一个介词of，由此推测出空格内应填入名词。伍德先生说，如果不建造动态大楼，原因不会是无法避免的技术缺口，而是一个老套的借口：资金匮乏。题干中的insufficiency of（缺乏）对应原文的lack of（缺乏），因此应填入of后的名词。

Questions 21–26

题型 配对题(Matching Features)

注意 识别配对的双方的类型以及各自的数量。

21	关键词	alter its appearance
	原文定位	倒数第二段第五句The most ambitious proposal yet comes from David Fisher, an architect based in Italy. 倒数第二句This would give the tower a continuously changing shape.
	题解	答案B 题干的alter its appearance（改变其外观）对应原文的changing shape（改变形状），即David Fisher设计的大楼能够不断地改变形状。
22	关键词	revolve at a certain frequency
	原文定位	第三段末句Their house, designed by 3 sixty Technology of Henderson, Nevada...and built in the aptly named neighbourhood of Mountain Helix, revolves completely, once an hour.
	题解	答案E Their house中的their指的是Al and Janet Johnstone，他们的房子一小时能完整地旋转一次。题干revolve at a certain frequency（以一定的频率旋转）与此对应。
23	关键词	rubber hoses
	原文定位	第二段倒数第三句Rubber hoses connect the uprights to their mates in the mobile part of the building.
	题解	答案C 题干指出用rubber hoses连接stationary（固定的）和moving（活动的）部分，stationary parts（固定的部分）其实就是对应原文的uprights（支柱），而moving parts（活动的部分）则对应their mates in the mobile part of the building（建筑中活动的部分）。注意题干using rubber hoses to connect the stationary and moving parts of the building（使用软管来连接建筑物的固定部分和活动部分）出现在第四段首句，只是用于比较，不要因此认定答案为Al and Janet Johnstone。

24	关键词	a great market
	原文定位	第六段末句Rogério Kffuri, Moro's head of sales, says the firm has signed contracts with developers in America, Canada, Japan, Portugal and the United Arab Emirates (UAE).
	题解	**答案A** Moro的销售主管Rogério Kffuri表示，公司已经与多个国家的开发商签订了合同。由此可以看出Rogério Kffuri所在的公司拥有广阔的市场。
25	关键词	rotating capability, limited
	原文定位	第二段倒数第二句The house's ability to rotate is thus limited only by the length of the hoses at full stretch.
	题解	**答案C** 经过15题的分析，很容易就能确定答案为Bill Butler。注意要先看题目说明，因为题目中有时候是一对一，有时候是一对多（即当出现NB时），导致有些选项会多次使用，有些根本不用，只是迷惑考生。所以仔细阅读题目说明，看清题目要求，再确定相应的答题方式。
26	关键词	clean energy
	原文定位	第五段末句The motor that moves Mr Butler's house consumes about 370 watts; the Johnstones'—which is solar-powered—a bit over a kilowatt.
	题解	**答案E** 驱动Johnstone住宅的是solar-powered（太阳能供电），太阳能即是clean energy（清洁能源）。

READING PASSAGE 3

体　裁　说明文
题　材　社会科学类
主　题　评论
题　型　判断题、配对题、选择题

Questions 27–34

题型 配对题(Matching Information)

注意 题干的信息并非完全地同义转换文中句子。

27	关键词	others read
	原文定位	F段末句Mr Shirk suggests that in many cases, writing a review is more like writing fan mail (or hate mail) for a product, and the people who post them do not really expect it to be read.
	题解	**答案F** F段末句指出，很多情况下发评论的人并不希望有人读它。符合题意。应该注意在去原文定位的过程中，一定要脑、眼和手并用。

28	关键词	more reviews, competitors
	原文定位	D段倒数第二句As a result there were more than ten reviews per product, compared with one or two for competitors' offerings.
	题解	**答案D** 该段指出，Kingston金士顿平均每个产品的评论要多于竞争对手的产品。题干所述与原文相对应。
29	关键词	long lifespan
	原文定位	H段末句Such discussion threads are more of a conversation...unlike the Amazon pages for the *Harry Potter* books, which continue to attract reviews even today, years after the books' publication.
	题解	**答案H** 该段指出有些新闻、博客的评论a limited lifespan（有效期限很短），并举了相反的例子，*Harry Potter*（《哈利·波特》）直到今天仍有很多评论。题干的a long lifespan（有效期限很长）对应原文中*Harry Potter*的例子。
30	关键词	rate of posting, increasing
	原文定位	C段末句But after about 20 reviews of a product are posted,"We start to see more reviews—it starts to accelerate," says Sam Decker, the chief marketing officer of Bazaar voice, a firm that powers review systems for online retailers.
	题解	**答案C** 该段中Sam Decker说，一个产品如果发了20条评论，评论就会越来越多。题干中的reach a certain number（达到一定数量）指的就是原文中的20；而题干中的increasing（越来越多）对应原文中的accelerate（增加）。
31	关键词	can't be stopped
	原文定位	E段首句Yet even when a product has attracted hundreds or even thousands of reviews, they keep coming in.
	题解	**答案E** E段主题句指出即使一个产品吸引到了成百上千的评论，还会有人不断地评论。题干中的can't be stopped（不会停止）对应原文的keep coming in（持续不断）。
32	关键词	value, discussed
	原文定位	A段首句If a book on *Amazon.com*, the leading online retailer, already has hundreds of reviews, is it worth bothering to add another? 第二句Evidently some people think it is.
	题解	**答案A** 该段指出如果一本书已经有了很多评论，是否有必要再添加新评论。并列举了Peter Hoflich的例子来说明这一现象。注意只要判断这个现象出现在A段即可，无需把整段都看完。

33	关键词	negative, effect, potential
	原文定位	B段末句So a small proportion of negative comments—"just enough to acknowledge that the product couldn't be perfect"—can actually make an item more attractive to prospective buyers.
	题解	答案B　B段认可了negative comments（负面评论）的价值。题干potential customers（潜在客户）对应原文prospective buyers（潜在的买家）。
34	关键词	Harriet Klausner
	原文定位	G段倒数第二句Now the"helpfulness"of reviews is taken into account, causing Harriet Klausner, the most prolific reviewer with over 18,000 reviews to her credit, to drop below 500th place in the rankings.
	题解	答案G　以人名为关键词，能够迅速找到信息所在句子。Harriet Klausner仅出现在了G段，即可确定G为答案。

Questions 35–38

题型　判断题(Identifying Information)

注意　正确的标准是唯一性的，只有在全部考点都正确的情况下，该命题才能被判断为TRUE。

35	关键词	Peter Hoflich, *Harry Potter and the Deathly Hallows*
	原文定位	A段第三句Peter Hoflich, a financial journalist based in Singapore, recently wrote the 3,250th review of *Harry Potter and the Deathly Hallows*, for example. 第四句"I wonder if anyone will benefit from my review, especially since there are so many," he muses.
	题解	答案NOT GIVEN　尽管题目和原文中有对应的词出现：Peter Hoflich和review等，但是题目中的因果关系在文章中并没有体现，也没有出现有关his own feelings（他自己的感觉）的相应表述。原文举Peter Hoflich的例子是为了说明网上的reviews（评论）非常多。
36	关键词	publishers and authours, negative
	原文定位	B段第二句Initially, publishers and authours were worried that allowing negative reviews would hurt sales.
	题解	答案FALSE　由于原文中的核心内容是were worried that allowing negative reviews would hurt sales（担心允许负面评论会影响销量），而题目中是supported allowing the negative reviews（支持允许负面评论）。因此，这就是False的第一种情况：命题与原文内容对立（相反）。注意题干中的at the beginning（开始时）为原文initially（最初）的同义转述。

37	关键词	buy something, amount
	原文定位	D段首句His company's research shows that visitors are more reluctant to buy until a product attracts a reasonable number of reviews and picks up momentum.
	题解	答案TRUE 从两个句子表达中不难看出，两句话都是针对visitors buy something（访客购买物品）的，并且在观点陈述中题干accumulate to a certain amount（积累到一定数量）对应原文attracts a reasonable number（吸引一定的数量），此处的attract表示“吸引（支持或资金等）”，picks up momentum表示“开始转旺”。要注意表达方式的理解。
38	关键词	past reviews
	原文定位	F段首句“Most people only look at the most recent—they don't go back and look at the first review,”says Mr McAteer.
	题解	答案TRUE 题干是对原文的同义转换，most people don't go（很多人不去……）转换成few people go（很少有人去……），否定变肯定；the first review（最初的评论）转换成the past reviews（过去的评论），同义转换。因此在判断题中要注意句型结构和同义词之间的转换。

Questions 39 and 40

题型 选择题(Multiple Choice)

注意 正确选项应是原文相关词句的改写，所以与原文特别一致的选项是正确选项的可能性不大。

39	关键词	balance
	原文定位	E段第三句、第四句Most retailers and comparison sites try to strike a balance between recent reviews and helpful ones. Allowing visitors to rate reviews allows the most informative to rise to the top.
	题解	答案C 题干考查的是零售商如何权衡最近的评论和有用的评论，E段指出他们采取的措施是允许访问者将最有帮助的评论置顶。选项C符合原文含义。
40	关键词	change, ranking system
	原文定位	G段第五句This prompts reviewers to focus on quantity, not quality, however, so Amazon recently changed its ranking system.
	题解	答案A 题干考查的是Amazon（亚马逊）更改其排序系统的原因，根据关键词进行定位，reviewers（评论者）重量不重质，Amazon（亚马逊）才更改了其排序系统。选项A符合原文。A项题干的rather than（而不是）对应原文的not。

WRITING

WRITING TASK 1

名师解读

本题为表格(table)题，表格展示：一项有关城市运动俱乐部的会员对俱乐部的活动、设施及营业时间看法的调查。注意：对于图表题来说，并非如实逐一描述图表中的数据就能够获得高分。

在图表题的写作当中，考生经常会遇到这种情况：看懂图表了，但因数据比较凌乱，找不出很明显的特征，或者找到了很多特征，却不知道应该用什么样的思路来把图表中的重要信息和规律特征有机、自然地联系、贯穿起来。考生应辅以适当的数据支持、段落划分和选用连接词。

最后考生要注意对极值进行描述。

高分范文

The table compares the opinions of male and female club members about the services provided by a city sports club.

We can see from the responses that the male members are generally happy or satisfied with the range of activities at the club, with only 5% dissatisfied. In contrast, however, only about two thirds of female members were positive about the activity range and almost a third were dissatisfied. The genders were more in agreement about the club facilities. Only 14% of women and 10% of men were unhappy with these, and the majority (64% and 63% respectively) were very positive. Finally, the female **respondents** were much happier with the club opening hours than their male **counterparts**. Almost three quarters of the women were very satisfied and only 3% were unhappy, whereas 37% of the men expressed their dissatisfaction.

Overall, the table indicates that female members are most unhappy with the range of activities, while male members feel that opening hours are the least satisfactory aspect of the club. (171 words)

WRITING TASK 2

文章结构

解释问题+建议

problem1+problem2+solutions
第一段：背景句+引出话题
第二段：问题1+问题2
第三段：建议+总结

思路点拨

步骤一：审题（<3分钟）

In recent years some countries have experienced very rapid economic development. This has resulted in much higher standards of living in urban areas but not in the countryside. This situation may bring some problems for the country as a whole. What are these problems? How might they be reduced?

→通读题目，了解大意。

近年来，某些国家的经济发展很快。导致城市地区的生活水平升高，而农村则没有。这种情况可能在整体上给国家带来问题。这种情况会对整个国家带来怎样的影响？会产生哪些问题？如何减少这些问题？

→再读题目，辨别关键词，区分主题词和限定词，推测考官的出题意图。

主题词：rapid economic development, urban areas, countryside

限定词：What, How

步骤二：列大纲（<3分钟）

英文提纲	Introduction: urban citizens have access to jobs and facilities that improve their living standards (topic) Body: Problem 1: more employment opportunities→increase in the urban population→pressure→slum areas→severe affects Problem 2: sense of inequality→more crime→civil unrest Suggestions + Conclusion: improving the standards of living and the facilities available in the countryside (incentives→road and rail networks→doctors and teachers)→requires investment and political will
中文提纲	引出话题：城市居民可以获得工作和设施，提高了他们的生活标准（话题） 主体段： 问题1：更多的就业机会→城市人口增加→压力→贫民窟→严重影响 问题2：不平等感→犯罪活动增加→国内动乱 建议和总结：提高农村的生活、设施标准（奖励措施→公路与铁路网→医生与教师）→需要投资和政治意愿

高分范文

From the evidence of developing countries all over the world, it seems **inevitable** that economic growth is generated in the business and industrial centres of the major cities. As a result, urban citizens have access to jobs and facilities that improve their living standards considerably.

However, it is usually the case that these are not equally enjoyed by people in the countryside and this generates several problems for the countries concerned. First of all, people from the countryside will try to move to the cities to get more employment opportunities and better access to the facilities available there. But this increase in the urban population puts great pressure on housing and services, and leads to the creation of massive **slum areas** where conditions may be poorer than in the rural villages. On the other hand, villages are often left under populated and this can impact on food production and can have severe affects for people in both urban and rural areas. Finally, as a country's economy develops, there may be an increasing sense of **inequality** as the towns get richer and the villages get poorer, and this may lead to more crime and even civil **unrest**.

The key to reducing these problems seems to lie in improving the standards of living and the facilities available in the countryside. Perhaps incentives can be offered to factories and companies to **relocate**; road and rail networks can be built to make such relocation possible; doctors and teachers could be required to spend part of their professional lives in rural areas, etc. In conclusion, however, improving rural living standards requires investment and political will that are sometimes not easy to generate. (279 words)

SPEAKING

名师解读

Part 1相对来说较为容易。注意根据问题的不同形式选择不同的立意方式，应该繁还是简答，考生需心中有数。

对于本Part 2，考生需注意描述what, who, when, why及how五个要素，且注意全文的时态。

Part 3要用例子来充实自己的话题，给出你的观点，亮出你的实际例子，给考官以直观的感受。

若你不知道如何回答问题，可以用一些间接法来回答。切记口语考试的控制权在于你自己，你可以把话题带到你想说的范围去，另外口语考试是一个互动的过程。

高分示例

PART 1

Collections

- Do you like to collect things?

I do have some things I like collecting, but they are mostly books and figurines for some **anime** that I enjoy. They are sometimes expensive, but worth it for my collection.

- What do Chinese people like to collect?

I've heard that some Chinese people collect **porcelain** fragments from around China in hopes of finding something valuable or rich in culture. Others might collect Jade figures or pendants.

- What did you collect when you were young?

When I was young, I liked to collect odd shaped stones and rocks. I also collected anything that looked really old.

- What can people get from their collections?

Collections are a private thing, and can mean different things to everyone. I know my current collection might not mean much to anyone else, but for me, some of those items are rare and one of a kind and mean a lot to me. Some people collect things in order to sell them off later at a high price. To me, these people are not true collectors.

PART 2

Next weekend is my grandmother's birthday. She is turning 98 years old but she is still moving around a lot and young at heart.

The party is being held at my childhood home, where she and my grandmother live with my mother. Both my brother, his family and I will travel to our hometown to celebrate this occasion.

Usually for birthdays in our family, my mother bakes a huge cake and each person brings the ingredients to make the birthday girl's or boy's favourite dish. Then we all cook it with love as a family.

I always look forward to birthdays in our family, but my grandmother's is very special to me as we are very close. I know she is old and might not be around for many more years, so I want to make this celebration a happy memory for everyone.

PART 3

Family celebrations

- What type of special occasions are generally celebrated in your country?

In China, we celebrate the Spring Festival and the Lantern Festival, just to name a few. We celebrate them with **fireworks** and visiting family members.

- How important is it for families to celebrate occasions together? Why?

For me it is very important to celebrate special occasions with family because it can bring us closer together. But for some people who do not have family, they celebrate with their friends who are like their family.

- Are family occasions as important today as they were for former generations?

I don't think family occasions are believed to be as important as they were in former generations, but this is wrong. The newer generations have little or no respect or interest in family occasions and so those who do **participate in** them hold them very dear.

Social changes

- How has the role of elderly people in the family changed in recent times?

The elderly used to be honoured and **revered** for their wisdom and guidance to the younger people, but in recent times, they have been pushed aside and held in little regard.

- Who has more power and influence in the family today, young people or grandparents?

In households today, unless they are very traditional, the parents usually have more influence over the household, and in some cases, the families **are dictated to** by the children.

- What impact have modern lifestyles had on neighbourhood communities? Why?

Modern lifestyles have severely impacted on neighbourhood communities because with all the technology, people are able to stay in contact with their friends faraway and have no need to meet and get to know the people around them. Because of this, there is little trust in communities barring small groups who do know each other well, perhaps from childhood.

重点词汇

LISTENING

dormouse	['dɔːmaʊs]	*n.*	榛睡鼠
hibernate	['haɪbəneɪt]	*v.*	过冬；冬眠
hazelnut	['heɪzlnʌt]	*n.*	榛子；榛树
vole	[vəʊl]	*n.*	野鼠
transaction	[træn'zækʃn]	*n.*	交易；事务；学报
reasonable	['riːznəbl]	*adj.*	合理的；通情达理的
fraud	[frɔːd]	*n.*	诈骗；骗子；诡计
regardless	[rɪ'gɑːdləs]	*adj.*	不管；不顾
minimum	['mɪnɪməm]	*n.*	最小值；最低限度
withdrawal	[wɪð'drɔːəl]	*n.*	提款；撤退；取消
take a certain amount of			需要花费定量
foreign currency			外币
competitive	[kəm'petətɪv]	*adj.*	竞争的；比赛的
branch	[brɑːntʃ]	*n.*	分支；分部；支流
otherwise	['ʌðəwaɪz]	*adv.*	否则；另外
convenient	[kən'viːnɪənt]	*adj.*	方便的
multi-trip insurance			多站旅行保险
premium	['priːmɪəm]	*n.*	保险费，额外费用
reduction	[rɪ'dʌkʃn]	*n.*	减少，下降
document	['dɒkjumənt]	*n.*	文件，公文
dissertation	[dɪsə'teɪʃn]	*n.*	论文，专题；学术演讲
assignment	[ə'saɪnmənt]	*n.*	分配；任务；功课
financial crisis			金融危机
macroeconomic policy			宏观经济政策
resolution	[ˌrezə'luːʃn]	*n.*	分辨率；决议；解决
bibliography	[ˌbɪblɪ'ɒgrəfi]	*n.*	参考书目；文献目录
illustration	[ˌɪlə'streɪʃn]	*n.*	说明；插图；例证
informative	[ɪn'fɔːmətɪv]	*adj.*	教育性的，有益的；情报的
reference	['refrəns]	*n.*	参考，参照；涉及
periodical	[ˌpɪərɪ'ɒdɪkl]	*n.*	期刊；杂志
predicament	[prɪ'dɪkəmənt]	*n.*	窘况，困境
sustain	[sə'steɪn]	*v.*	维持
staggering	['stægərɪŋ]	*adj.*	令人吃惊的
scarce	[skeəs]	*adj.*	缺乏的
devastate	[devəsteɪt]	*v.*	毁坏；毁灭
foreseeable	[fɔː'siːəbl]	*adj.*	可预知的
lucrative	['luːkrətɪv]	*adj.*	有利可图的
catastrophe	[kə'tæstrəfi]	*n.*	大灾难
culprit	['kʌlprɪt]	*n.*	犯人
stark	[stɑːk]	*adj.*	明显的
affluent	['æfluənt]	*adj.*	富裕的
legislation	[ˌledʒɪs'leɪʃn]	*n.*	立法；法律
gigantic	[dʒaɪ'gæntɪk]	*adj.*	巨大的
transferrable	[træns'fɜːrəbl]	*adj.*	可转让的

READING

origin	['ɒrɪdʒɪn]	*n.*	来源
avalanche	['ævəlɑːnʃ]	*n.*	雪崩
reviewer	[rɪ'vjuːə]	*n.*	评论家
redundant	[rɪ'dʌndənt]	*adj.*	不需要的，多余的
futile	['fjuːtaɪl]	*adj.*	无效的
treatise	['triːtɪs]	*n.*	专著
exhaustive	[ɪg'zɔːstɪv]	*adj.*	透彻的
diversification	[daɪˌvɜːsɪfɪ'keɪʃn]	*n.*	变化，多样性
take for granted			认为……是理所当然的
denigrate	['denɪgreɪt]	*v.*	诋毁
fossil	['fɒsl]	*n.*	化石
descent	[dɪ'sent]	*n.*	血统
revolve	[rɪ'vɒlv]	*v.*	旋转
intestine	[ɪn'testɪn]	*n.*	肠
rotation	[rəʊ'teɪʃn]	*n.*	旋转，转动
sewage	['suːɪdʒ]	*n.*	污物
stationary	['steɪʃənri]	*adj.*	静止的
ingenious	[ɪn'dʒiːnɪəs]	*adj.*	独特的；精巧的
horizontal	[ˌhɒrɪ'zɒntl]	*adj.*	水平的
friction	['frɪkʃn]	*n.*	摩擦力
dignified	['dɪgnɪfaɪd]	*adj.*	有尊严的
retailer	['riːteɪlə]	*n.*	零售商
prospective	[prə'spektɪv]	*adj.*	可能的；未来的
accelerate	[ək'seləreɪt]	*v.*	加速
reluctant	[rɪ'lʌktənt]	*adj.*	勉强的
momentum	[mə'mentəm]	*n.*	动力
drastically	['dræstɪkli]	*adv.*	彻底地；激烈地
chronological	[ˌkrɒnə'lɒdʒɪkl]	*adj.*	按时间顺序的
prolific	[prə'lɪfɪk]	*adj.*	多产的

WRITING

respondent	[rɪ'spɒndənt]	*n.*	被调查者
counterpart	['kaʊntəpɑːt]	*n.*	对应的人
inevitable	[ɪn'evɪtəbl]	*adj.*	必然的，不可避免的
slum areas			贫民区
inequality	[ˌɪnɪ'kwɒləti]	*n.*	不平等；不平均
unrest	[ʌn'rest]	*n.*	不安
relocate	[ˌriːləʊ'keɪt]	*v.*	重新安置

SPEAKING

anime	['ænɪmeɪ]	*n.*	日本动漫
porcelain	['pɔːsəlɪn]	*n.*	瓷器；瓷
firework	['faɪəwɜːk]	*n.*	烟火
participate in			参与
revere	[rɪ'vɪə]	*v.*	尊敬；敬畏
be dictated to			被……任意指挥

听力原文

SECTION 1

(SPCA REP=SR; APPLICANT=A)

SR: Hello, welcome to the SPCA. Thanks for coming for the interview. I know it must seem like quite a complicated process, when all you simply want to do is to give an unwanted dog a caring home. However, we need to be sure that the people we rehome dogs with are suitable owners. I hope you understand!

A: Yes, I do. Don't worry—it is really no problem.

SR: Great, well in this interview, we are just going to go over some details relevant to matching you with the right kind of dog and I'll put some details into the computer as we talk...So your name is *Example* Helen Morgan?

A: Yes, that's right.

SR: OK and today's date is September 18th, hmm oh no, it's the 18th tomorrow, so it's the Q1 17th. Now I have all the address details here from your first arranged interview, that's fine. 12 Towley Avenue, Meadow Lea, telephone number 443 5421, no problem with that, and I can see that you don't have any pets at the moment. Oh, there is no information here about your work schedule...we need to know how long the dog would be likely to be left on its own you see.

A: Well, I actually work full-time, but I run my own business at home. I am at home all day most of the week, apart from Wednesdays and Fridays when I work outside from Q2 10am to 2.30pm.

SR: OK, well, that sounds fine. We don't normally allow dogs to go to homes where no one would be at home all day every day.

A: I understand.

SR: Now I need to ask you, why you are interested in adopting a dog—I mean, people do for different reasons. Would you say that you want the dog to be a guard dog, for protection of your property I mean, or to be a family pet?

A: Well, it would be nice to have a dog that can tell us when someone is coming of course! But we don't want a big dog that would be a stereotypical guard dog, it would actually be a Q3 family pet for myself and my husband, but we do plan to have children in the near future, so it would need to have a temperament that would be good with children.

SR: Yes, OK. So how many people live in your house?

A: Just the Q4 two of us. Though my brother stays with us for summer holidays when he isn't at university.

SR: And do you have children who visit on a regular basis?

A: Yes my two nieces, they are Q5 3 and 6. They visit most weekends with my sister.

SR: OK, and is anyone living in the house allergic to animals?

A: My husband is allergic to cats but not dogs!

SR: So who will be responsible for the daily care of the pet?

A: Well Q6 my husband works at home too, so it would be a joint effort between myself and him.

SR: OK. Now, do you rent or own your home?

A: Actually we rent, but our landlord, Johnathon, has no problem with us having a dog, we've already checked with him and we are going to buy our own house in a few months anyway.

SR: Well, I hope you don't mind, but we do need to check everything is ok ourselves. Could you give me Johnathon's phone number so we can make a confirmation call?

A: Sure, I'll give you his mobile number. It's 0795 Q7 722 4189.

SR: 0795 722 4789?

A: No. 4189.

SR: OK. Now we need to be sure the animal would be safe from roads and traffic. Do you have a fenced yard or garden?

A: Yes, we do.

SR: And can you give me an idea how tall the fence is? Again it affects the type of dog that would be suitable as some can jump lower fences!

A: Actually, my friend adopted a dog last year and she told me that would be one of the questions, so I know exactly! It's Q8 1.5 metres tall.

SR: OK, now I just need to check your previous experience with dogs. Can you tell me if you have ever owned a dog before?

A: Yes, I have. We had dogs when I was a child but I have had only one myself as an adult.

SR: What breed was it?

A: It was Q9 mixed breed actually, a medium sized dog, I would say. He was really friendly.

SR: OK, and how long did you have him for?

A: Five, no wait a minute, Q10 six years.

SR: Do you mind telling me what happened to it?

A: Well, he was a rescue dog and wasn't young when I adopted him, so he died from age-related natural causes.

SR: OK, well thanks very much. You are welcome to go and have a look at the dogs that are here at the moment, but it will take three or four days to confirm approval of your application. I'll telephone you and let you know the outcome as soon as it has been processed.

A: OK, well thanks very much and I look forward to hearing from you.

SECTION 2

(FEMALE=F; MALE=M)

F: My family is planning a holiday in eastern Europe, so I'd like to know what's the best way of paying for things there?

M: Well if you have a debit card, that's probably the easiest way to pay for things like hotel bills, or meals, or shopping. You're going to eastern Europe, but the card is recognised and accepted in every country around the world, in millions of outlets. And in terms of security, debit cards are just as safe to use as they are here in the UK. When our customers go abroad we monitor their accounts and try to contact them if there's any activity that we think might be suspicious. Q11&Q12 In fact we have a system where you can register for free mobile phone text alerts, every time any transaction is made on your card abroad. And as long as we're happy that you've taken reasonable care of your card, we undertake to refund any money that you lose due to fraud, as long as you report it within 48 hours. So you're very well covered with a debit card. And it's not very expensive. Every time you buy something with your card, for example from a shop or restaurant, Q11&Q12 there's a charge of one pound regardless of the price. If you use the card to get cash from a machine or a bank, there's a fee of 1.5% with a minimum charge of £2 and a maximum of £4.50. So obviously it's best not to make too many small withdrawals when you're abroad.

We also advise our customers to take a certain amount of foreign currency with them as well, for small things, or to pay for a taxi from the airport, for example. The bank can get this for you — we always check the exchange rate at a UK post office and make sure that our charges are more competitive than theirs, and Q13&Q14 if customers have an account with us we don't impose a handling charge, as long as they use a debit card to buy it. You can get any amount, and a few of our branches keep Euros and US dollars all the time, so if your branch is one of those, there's no need to order your currency. Otherwise you just order it, and Q13&Q14 arrange to pick it up the following day at whichever branch is most convenient for you.

F: OK, thanks. And also, can you tell me about your travel insurance? What do I have to do to get cover?

M: Well first of all, before you go any further you need to think about whether you want insurance for a single trip abroad — this coming holiday for example — or whether you're likely to travel abroad again in the near future, in which case Q15 you might like to consider buying multi-trip insurance. Then for customers who have a premium account with this bank, they are actually already Q16 insured for foreign travel under their existing policy, so you only need to look at the details of that policy and see if it provides you with enough cover for what you're intending to do abroad. Otherwise, Q17 for all other account holders, it's easiest to visit our website. All the information you need is there, as well as a short questionnaire. Q18 You'll be asked for some information about the journey you're planning to make — how you're travelling and where you'll be staying, that kind of thing. It doesn't take more than ten minutes, and after that you'll get an instant quote for your insurance. Q19 If you decide to go ahead, you just have to supply information about you and your family — names, ages, passport numbers and so on. And then you can pay there and then. It's possible to pay by phone using a debit or credit card, Q20 but it's easiest to pay online and there's a 20% reduction for doing it that way. And you can just download your policy documents. It's very simple...

SECTION 3

(MICHAEL=M; JIM=J; JESSICA=JE)

M: So, Jim, did you manage to get all your reading done?

J: Yes, Michael, I did. What about you, Jessica?

JE: Me too, though it took much longer than I thought it would.

M: Yeah, some of those dissertations are really long, aren't they?

J: Mm, I'm not looking forward to having to write mine.

M: So, shall we compare thoughts about our reading? Let's start with *The puzzling failure of economics*. I thought it was pretty impressive.

J: There was quite a bit of detail.

JE: Yeah, all very relevant. I enjoyed the pictures, diagrams and photos.

J: Q21 Mm, they were quite odd, not what you'd expect to find in a dissertation, but very useful.

M: Whereas sometimes I couldn't really follow the arguments.

J: Yes—a bit of a mixed bag, really. While *Decay of the dismal science* was very serious and thorough, wasn't it?

JE: Indeed. Actually, it was rather dense—I didn't find it particularly easy to read, either.

M: The index was excellent, though, so I used that to guide me around.

J: Q22 I still think it was a bit high level. I certainly wouldn't have wanted to try and cope with it in the first year.

JE: No, that's not who it's aimed at, of course. What about *Economists and the Economy*? Not the world's most interesting title, of course.

M: Again, the index was helpful, though I think we could have done with more photos—there weren't really enough to support what he was saying in places.

JE: Q23 Yeah. But what he was saying was easy to follow, wasn't it? He takes you through step by step.

J: It was hard to believe it had been translated—seemed very natural.

M: Actually, it was better written than the next one, *History of Economic Thought*.

JE: But we're supposed to be thinking about economical ideas, not being history critics. I liked that one.

M: Really? I just didn't think it covered the whole situation.

J: Q24 Mm, it didn't put the question of *New Deal* into the context.

M: You mean how in The Great Depression of 1929, the *New Deal* created many government programmes to end the Depression, but government programmes alone could not end it?

J: Exactly.

JE: Again, I think you're asking too much of these dissertations.

M: Perhaps you're right. Well, I did like *The Evolution of Economic Ideas* anyway. Very focused.

J: Yes, although I did think it was oddly arranged in some ways. Q25 When you went to the index to track something down, you couldn't necessarily find what you wanted.

M: I know what you mean. But, I have to say, I'd be very proud if I'd written any of these.

JE: True.

J: And you will next year!

M: Never mind next year. It's this year that's the problem. I'm never going to get this assignment done.

JE: Yes, you are.

J: Come on. Let's make a plan for you.

M: Please. I'm just not sure where to go from here. I could look at the financial crisis of 2007—2009, you know, *causes of the crisis*, *IMF policies* and *debate on macroeconomic policy*, *lessons of the crisis for policy* and so on, but that's just too much information, I'm kind of being overwhelmed...

JE: I think you need a closer focus. You'd be better to Q26 concentrate on IMF policies, you know, capital, debt resolution, debt standstill proposals and so on.

M: OK. Though I don't know how much useful detail I'll be able to get from the basic bibliography.

J: It's true. They can be limited. But what you could do as a next stage is go on to the web. There's loads of useful stuff there.

M: More detailed plans you mean?

J: Well, I was thinking more of illustrations, that kind of thing. Q27 Surf the Internet, it's the most popular and informative source, I'm sure you'll find some good ones.

JE: I agree. And not just online. See what you do find there, and then, for your next step, check both campus libraries—I think you'll be able to get hold of books which will give you further information, for example, reference works, Q28 periodicals, and non-print materials.

M: This is all very helpful. Thanks guys. I'm beginning to think that, afterwards, I should see Dr Forbes as soon as possible to agree on the Q29 final title.

JE: Yeah. Once Dr Forbes has Okayed what you've done at that point, you could then work on your Q30 first draft.

M: That'd be really useful. Well, thanks again. Let me get you both another coffee.

SECTION 4

So, in this part I intend to address some of the root causes of environmental problems. Although I could offer countless suggestions, there are a couple which I believe warrant our immediate attention. First and foremost, the most pressing predicament is that of human beings. Whichever way you look at it, there are just too many people in the world today and this Q31 overpopulation will become even worse as time goes on. The planet cannot sustain this growth we are presently experiencing. Current figures project our population will reach seven billion by 2013 and a staggering eight billion in 2028. There is no sign of slowing up and as numbers swell, so does the resulting strain on the environment. Natural resources are already becoming scarce and companies are fighting over the last remaining oil fields in existence. Great acres of rainforests in Q32 South America have been devastated by intense logging to fuel developed countries' lust for energy, but at the expense of the extinction of wildlife and this is set to continue into the foreseeable future. Although, eventually we will have no other option but to opt for renewable power sources, the giant energy companies are intent on dragging our dependency out as long as possible, as financially it is extremely lucrative.

But who brought about this environmental catastrophe we may ask? Well, we can easily point the finger to the usual culprits such as the US and Europe. Statistics confirm that the group many refer to as the Q33 "developed countries" accounts for 20% of the world's population, yet rather surprisingly possesses an astonishing 85% of its wealth; they also consume 88% of the world's resources and as a result generate a practically identical amount of the world's waste. These are of course combined figures from all of those countries. I am not singling out just America as many do. If we now take a look at the alleged "developing countries" like say China and India, we can observe a stark contrast. They represent a staggering 80% of the population of the world but on the contrary only own 15% of its wealth. Unlike the previous group, India and China, the others account for a minute 12% of resource use. What must be taken into consideration is the reality that places like China are advancing at an alarming rate, so things are starting to change. While the upper class Chinese are still spending at high rates, the Q34 middle classes have experienced a substantial increase in spending power which has led to greater demands on resources. Actually, this can be said about countless countries but it goes without saying that it creates a greater strain on the environment. We also can not forget those on the other end of the scale, namely the less affluent members of society. Their predicament just worsens by the day. As the rich get richer, the poor certainly seem to look less well off. Although this Q35 "wealth gap" as people call it is not a new phenomenon, we are witnessing it on a more daily basis as it leads to serious social problems and as we saw all too often in the last financial crisis, it does not take much to go from one extreme to the other.

Now that we've gone over the causes of environment problems, let's move on to what countries are doing to remedy this situation, we all find ourselves in. Well, the main investment, from an international perspective, appears to be centred around pollution prevention and the ensuing debate over exactly how to reduce the amount of energy we all consume has become a bit of a hot issue. Politicians in Spain, Germany and France have all supported legislation over the past decade in order Q36 to follow Norway's continued improvement in this field. Some scientists claim that if every citizen takes action, we could curb quite substantially the results of energy consumption. Even just unplugging our TV sets, so they are not on standby, can help. There is another common option which I am sure most of you have come across at one point and that is the current fashion of turning one product into something else. As a matter of fact, you will find Q37 countless shops in England selling bags made out of books or other extremely imaginative uses for rubbish. So popular is recycling that these trendy products are even exported to America.

Nonetheless, there is still a gigantic amount of waste still out there. Landfills are overrun with what we throw away. One solution is to export your waste to another country, for instance Canada with its large expanses of land may look like an ideal home for the endless junk packed into British dumps. Incineration is another option. Nonetheless, the current initiative of choice is waste management which looks at sorting and reusing waste in all sorts of ways. Q38 I recently read about some award-winning French initiatives in this area, which put into practice a programme designed by a leading German research centre. On a people level, there are countries changing the way global citizens think about the environment. I recently saw Q39 an American style short film in Canada in English and French aimed at teaching kids how to protect the Earth. The overall goal of this kind of project is to nip the problem of waste and to resolve environmental catastrophes in the bud, as it were. Rather than fining people or incarcerating them for not protecting the Earth, we should educate them how to do it. After all you can't blame people for doing something which they may not actually know is bad. Those of you from Asia are probably familiar with the tough penalties or even imprisonment dealt out to people who throw rubbish in public places, whether they be Japanese, Brits or Norwegians, Q40 the law in Thailand still perceives it as a very serious offense. Sadly, for some such a response is not always possible due to different laws and regulations. What is acceptable in your country may not be transferrable to, say Germany or even France.

Test 4

答案速查

LISTENING

Section 1, Questions 1–10

1 (a) shared
2 *newhome.com*
3 employment
4 sheets, towels
5 90-day
6 two fitness classes
7 gold card
8 special routines
9 heated
10 by appointment

Section 2, Questions 11–20

11 B
12 B
13 C
14 A
15 B
16 B
17 room 34
18 $100
19 room service
20 $9

Section 3, Questions 21–30

21&22 IN EITHER ORDER D E
23&24 IN EITHER ORDER A D
25 A
26 A
27 C
28 B
29 B
30 C

Section 4, Questions 31–40

31 75 centimetres
32 70 eggs
33 drums
34 colour
35 5,000
36 licence
37 medicine
38 decades
39 mature
40 long

READING

Reading Passage 1, Questions 1–13

1 B
2 C
3 A
4 oldest female
5 (a) fungus
6 Parasites
7 infectious
8 mathematical model
9 existing chemicals
10 Spray
11 house walls
12 Reduce
13 life-threatening

Reading Passage 2, Questions 14–26

14 TRUE
15 FALSE
16 NOT GIVEN
17 FALSE
18 NOT GIVEN
19 B
20 C
21 A
22 C
23 D
24 E
25 A
26 C

Reading Passage 3, Questions 27–40

27 model fish farms
28 boreholes
29 rivers
30 DTU Aqua
31 inland
32 environmental restrictions
33 ammonia
34 nitrate
35 nitrogen
36 TRUE
37 NOT GIVEN
38 FALSE
39 TRUE
40 TRUE

名师解析

LISTENING

SECTION 1

主题场景	住宿场景
主旨大意	租房以及对住房周边设施的咨询
考查题型	笔记填空题、表格填空题

名师解读

1 (a) shared 题干要求是cheapest，因此注意听与价格有关的词汇，听到keep costs down之后预测答案可能会出现。注意much lower than后出现的a one-bedroom place是干扰信息。

2 *newhome.com* 读题时要理解题干的look on是查询的意思，本空要填写可以“查询”的名词，如网站、报纸等。注意原文new home—as in one word—dot com中，强调as in one word，因此newhome要写成一个单词。

3 employment 注意not just...but...的句型。这是典型的对话干扰方式，此空可能要填passport或employment，但注意题干中new requirement要求填“新的要求”，因此答案应为but之后的employment。

4 sheets, towels 题干中的check和included分别与原文中的know和provided相对应。根据背景知识，空格应填写与房租有关的费用，如水、电、煤气、电话及各种额外费用。听到if后应快速记录答案，注意towels的拼写。

5 90-day 通过上下文预测空格处需填写形容词。原文有多个信息出现，seven-day, 30-day, 90-day, one year，但要注意which引导的定语从句which would perhaps suit you most之前的90-day才是正确答案，因为题干限定了best。答案必须加连字符，否则不得分。

6 two fitness classes 6–10题为分类信息表格题，注意读题先横后纵，看清题目序号。此题可以将前一栏的guided tour作为关键词，而题干中的free是对原文no charge的同义替换，之前的名词two fitness classes为答案。注意Blooms和Good Life这两个名词的出现，弄清楚原文中与之相对应的描述。

7 gold card 注意此题是通过which引导的定语从句给出提示。这类题目答案出现在提示之前，要求考生具备较好的短暂记忆能力。此外，听到Blooms的名称时就应该意识到答案马上出现。

8 special routines so that表结果，其后通常引出答案。答案预测为名词，注意routine的单词拼写。

9 heated 根据上下文判断此空填写形容词，注意题干中表示时间的单词now，原文中it used to be rather chilly except in the summer是干扰信息，因为used to表过去。要注意原文but一词是典型的定位词，在but之后捕捉到的形容词heated才是答案。

10 by appointment 题目本身信息不全，比较难做预测，但是通过前几题的回答，可以发现此表格是对Blooms和Good Life相同设施或服务的对比，所以通过前一栏Personal trainers are always available的信息，可以猜测Good Life的培训师不是always available。同时注意关键词qualified的出现，后面即是答案，也就是会见培训师需要by appointment。

SECTION 2

主题场景	旅行场景
主旨大意	介绍预订房间的情况
考查题型	选择题、简答题

名师解读

11 B 题干中的has been to与原文中的stayed对应，据此定位答案。原文中的twice是选项B的重现，原文中的before与选项B中的previously为同义替换。

12 B 本题简单，根据Griffin和from准确定位，原文直接给出Mr Griffin来自Sydney。注意Griffin先生本人的肯定回答。

13 C 题干中的关键词passport number为原文重现，据此判定后面的一连串数字即为答案。考生注意听清数字即可。

14 A 考生注意原文中Barbara核实Griffin先生信息时的对话，原文提到的内容为a single room for two nights，对应选项A。

15 B 本题要求考生选出Griffin先生到达的时间，注意原文出现了多个时间：9.15pm, 20minutes, 10。题干中的arrive at与原文中的be at对应，所以真正到达的时间是最后的一个。考生注意不能急于作出判断，要听清楚再给出答案。

16 B 本题注意Barbara的回答，Barbara认为the fries会变凉，最后Griffin先生能够在房间找到的食物仅仅是the sandwich。

17 room 34 题干中的be与原文中的stick对应，原文中的him指代的是Griffin先生，故答案是后面的number 34，但注意题干问的是Which room...? 考生要对number 34进行改写。

18 $100 根据题干关键词How much判定本题要求考生填入的是房间的价格。原文中$150与the double对应，$100与the single对应，而Griffin先生要入住的就是the single。考生需要注意美元的符号，而且不能漏掉不写。

19 room service 题干中的take为原文重现，原文中的it指代的就是题干中的Mr Griffin's food，故原文句子的主语room service就是本题答案。

20 $9 根据题干关键词How much判定本题要求考生填入食物的价格。原文多处提到食物的价格：$10, $8, $9。考生要注意听完后再判定哪个是答案。

SECTION 3

主题场景	课业讨论场景
主旨大意	两个学生关于选课以及项目任务分配的讨论
考查题型	选择题、配对题

名师解读

21&22 IN EITHER ORDER D E 根据关键词course进行定位，关注so后面的内容，考生能听到although从句中architect（建筑师），archaeology（考古学）课程和主句的industrial side of design（工业设计）课程。考生要根据从句中的否定wasn't排除选项A和B，选项D为答案之一；接着考生能听到management, companies等信息词，但不要着急选答案，考生给出的想法是which I thought could be...（原来以为，其实不是）表达的是否定的意思，排除选项D。

23&24 IN EITHER ORDER A D 根据关键词student life...difficult与原文everything that's tricky for me对应定位答案。根据听力原文中...never decide...things are more important to get done first信息可以判定选项A正确；根据题干中find difficult与原文get into trouble对应进行定位，原文中的quiet与D项的silently相对应，the library为原文地点重现，判定选项D正确。注意原文中then一词，表明开始叙述下一件事。

25 A 题干中的design experiment为关键词，是对原文the design of the experiment名词短语的改写，原文中it was more in your territory一句中的your指的是Desmond，而且得到的答复don't mind也是肯定的。

26 A 关键词statistics tutor为原文重现，题干中get advice from与原文中的get some help from the statistics tutor对应，所以说这句的主语为Desmond。

27 C 根据previous与原文中that have been done对应定位答案的位置，Desmond对此项任务的意见是combine forces，而Jill的回答是肯定的。

28 B Jill提到I've got a friend there, so I could sound her out，与题干中possible support相对应。注意转折连词however后面的内容，经常为考点。

29 B Jill开始的提议是a pair, Desmond的回答是together，但马上转折but，说明这个任务由Jill自己来完成。

30 C 题干中的speak和presentation为关键词，分别与speaking和public对应，据此可以定位答案。Desmond前面说I have no ability in public speaking，但是Jill的建议是divide up the sections，最后Desmond的回答是肯定的。

SECTION 4

主题场景	学术主题讨论场景
主旨大意	关于河龟的讲座
考查题型	句子填空题

名师解读

31 75 centimetres 通过上下文判断应填写数字，表示长度。原文的第一个数字90 centimetres是干扰信息，指的是the holes的直径，之后的数字75 centimetres与length相连，为答案。

32 70 eggs 空格前的at least表示答案为数字，并且限定了填写最小的数字70，注意不能填写70 and 80 eggs。题干中的deposits与原文中laying相对应。

33 drums noise对应原文的sound，答案应为可以发出声音的名词，原文like与题干中similar to相对应，因此like后的名词drums为答案。

34 colour 题干中的heads和change均为原文重现，答案较直接，为colour。题干是对原文the colour changes to their oddly-shaped heads that take place的改写。

35 5,000 通过上下文判断空格处填写数字，注意原文有多个数字出现：25 bottles of oil, 200 eggs, 33 million eggs，但是一定要听到多少个jars。

36 licence 原文没有出现题干中的system，但是protect和egg collectors可以作为关键词。通过上下文判断应填写名词，听到egg collector时应马上回忆之前的名词licence。

37 medicine 通过空格前used in判断应填写表示目的、用途的名词，原文提供了很多相关信息，for pets in some countries, for food in others，但注意题干的地点状语in Asia，要听到Asia这个词，在这个词之前的就是答案。

38 decades 通过for判断此空格应填写一段时间，注意捕捉原文的时间词decades。题干中的reproduce与原文中reproducing是同根词，several与原文中a number of相对应；if they are unharmed是对原文的连词provided（假如；倘若）引导的从句的改写。

39 mature 通过上下文判断空格填写形容词。题干中until后面的are与原文中become相对应，因此become后的形容词mature就是答案。

40 long 通过空格后terms判断应填写形容词long或short。原文多处出现impossible...to know, probably fail这样不确定的语气，与题干中uncertain...successful相对应，因此题干应为“不确定在长远来看是否会成功”，此外原文也出现了in the long term。

Test 4

READING

READING PASSAGE 1

体　裁　说明文
题　材　科技生活
主　题　进化论可能帮助人们与致命的疟疾斗争
题　型　选择题、表格填空题

Questions 1–3

题型 选择题(Multiple Choice)

注意 选择题是阅读中的常规题型，答案在文中按顺序出现，每个题目在文中均可以利用选项定位。

1	关键词	AIDS
	原文定位	首段第二、三句For the past couple of decades AIDS has captured both the imagination and the research dollars. Recently, though, the focus has shifted towards malaria, which kills a million people a year...
	题解	**答案B** AIDS只在首段第二句出现，但作者叙述的重点是在though（尽管）后边：the focus has shifted towards malaria（关注点已经转向了疟疾），与B项对应；题干中的change（变化）与原文中的shifted（转移）对应，原文中the focus（关注点）指的是首段首句中出现的global health。
2	关键词	chemical insecticides, dreary pattern
	原文定位	第二段第二、三句They prove wonderfully effective at first, only to dwindle into uselessness. This is because evolution quickly throws up resistant strains.
	题解	**答案C** 本题的题干是对第二段首句的改写，两者的核心信息都为化学杀虫剂进入了同样的死循环。作者利用第三句This is because...对该现象产生的原因进行了解释；because（因为）后面就是答案，resistant strains是原文重现，quickly throws up（快速产生）和appear soon（很快出现）是同义替换，所以答案是C。
3	关键词	Andrew Read, focus on
	原文定位	第三段第三句They have rethought the logic of insecticides, putting evolutionary theory at the centre, instead of a simple desire to destroy the enemy.
	题解	**答案A** focus on（聚焦于）与原文中putting...at the centre（以……为中心）相对应。选项B与原文instead of a simple desire to destroy the enemy（而不是简单地想要消灭敌人）矛盾，故不对；选项C和D没有提及。

Questions 4–13

题型 表格填空题(Table Completion)

注意 答案可能是原文关键词的转换，也可能就是原文原字。

4	关键词	kill solely, mosquitoes
	原文定位	第四段第五句In theory, then, killing only the oldest female mosquitoes—those at significant risk of being infectious—could stop the transmission of the disease.
	题解	**答案oldest female** 此空填的名词或形容词修饰mosquitoes（蚊子），题干中kill solely（仅仅杀死）和原文killing only（只杀死）意思相同，原文mosquitoes前的修饰词the oldest female即为答案，由于答案单词数不得超过两个，所以去掉冠词the，填入oldest female。

5	关键词	more radical answer, method
	原文定位	末段首句A more radical answer, though, may be to use a completely different sort of insecticide: a fungus.
	题解	答案(a) fungus　根据上下文的信息和关键词a more radical answer（一个更激进的做法）定位到末段首句，答案可以是a completely different sort of insecticide: a fungus（完全不同的杀虫剂：真菌），但是要求填写不超过两个词，故答案取冒号后面的具体内容，即(a) fungus。
6	关键词	female mosquitoes, transmit the disease
	原文定位	第四段第二到四句Only females can transmit malaria...but they are not born with the parasites inside their bodies....whence they can be transmitted to another host when she next feeds.
	题解	答案Parasites　只有females（雌蚊）能传播疟疾，但是它们并不是一出生体内就有parasites（寄生虫）。相反，它们长期从携带疾病的人类那里沾染寄生虫。寄生虫会迁移到雌蚊的salivary glands（唾液腺）中，当雌蚊下次进食时，唾液腺里的寄生虫就能转移到另一个寄主身上。也就是说寄宿在雌蚊体内的寄生虫能够传染疾病。题干是对原文的概括，注意：此题答案的首字母要大写。
7	关键词	parasite-infected insects, before
	原文定位	末段第三句That is short enough to kill parasite-infected insects before they become infectious, but long enough to allow them to breed
	题解	答案infectious　题干中annihilate（消灭）与原文中的kill是同义替换，parasite-infected insects before they become infectious是原文重现，故答案为infectious（传染的）。
8	关键词	ways to practice, set up
	原文定位	第五段首句To test this insight, the researchers constructed a mathematical model of the mosquito’s lifecycle.
	题解	答案mathematical model　题干中的set up（建立）与原文中constructed（构建）对应，答案直接给出，就是mathematical model。
9	关键词	ways to practice, use
	原文定位	第六段第二句One option is to use existing chemicals, but at greater dilutions.
	题解	答案existing chemicals　这个数学模型的难题是要找到一种杀虫剂，能够只杀死那些年长的雌蚊虫。第六段第二句表明，一种方法是利用existing chemicals（现存的化学物质）。

Test 4

10	关键词	fungal spores
	原文定位	末段第四句A trial of this idea, spraying fungal spores on to bed nets and house walls in Tanzania, is being set up at the moment.
	题解	答案Spray　这个想法的验证性试验就是通过spraying（喷雾），这样fungal spores（真菌孢子）就被喷在了bed nets（蚊帐）和房屋的墙壁上。这个方法的实践方式就是spraying fungal spores（喷洒真菌孢子）。
11	关键词	fungal spores, bed nets
	原文定位	末段第四句A trial of this idea, spraying fungal spores on to bed nets and house walls in Tanzania, is being set up at the moment.
	题解	答案house walls　题干中的fungal spores（真菌孢子）和bed nets（蚊帐）均为原词重现，可以直接判定原文bed nets and后的house walls（房屋的墙壁）就是答案。
12	关键词	infectious bites
	原文定位	第五段末句 The model...reveals that selectively killing elderly mosquitoes would reduce the number of infectious bites by 95% and that resistance to such a tactic would spread very slowly...
	题解	答案Reduce　这句话很长，比较复杂，但考生只要抓住句子的主干，就能找出本题的答案。这个model（模式）揭示了有选择性地杀死年长的蚊虫能够减少95%的传染性叮咬。reduce the number of infectious bites（减少传染性叮咬）是原文重现，故答案为reduce（减少）。
13	关键词	bites
	原文定位	末段的末句People will still get bitten, but the bites will merely be irritating, not life-threatening.
	题解	答案life-threatening　注意but（但是）后的内容为答案，叮咬只会让人恼怒，不会life-threatening（对生命有威胁）。

READING PASSAGE 2

体　裁　　议论文
题　材　　生物科技
主　题　　生物学家针对世界范围内热带雨林中的物种灭绝的讨论
题　型　　判断题、配对题

Questions 14–18

题型　判断题(Identifying Information)

注意　题干常是对原文的改写，包括改写成与原文内容一致的题干(TRUE)，与原文不一致的题干(FALSE)或者改成原文中不存在或是不完整的内容(NOT GIVEN)。做题时根据题目的表述来确定出题人的考查点，找到与之相对应的原文。

14	关键词	analysis, the secondary forest
	原文定位	第三段首句This regrown “secondary” forest is crucial to the pair’s analysis.
	题解	**答案TRUE** 原文第二段后半部分描述了题干中生物学家的观点，他们认为在许多热带国家人口在减少，人们纷纷涌向城市，这样就使得热带雨林的树木得以再生长。第三段首句点明了This regrown “secondary” forest（雨林的再生长）在数据分析中的重要作用。secondary forest（二次雨林）是原文regrown “secondary” forest（雨林的再生长）的重现，plays an important part（起到重要作用）与原文中is crucial to（对……是关键的）相对应；pair’s analysis（两者的分析）指的就是题干中的the analysis of Joseph Wright and Helene Muller-Landau。题干与原文完全对应，答案是TRUE。
15	关键词	rate of extinction, forest cover
	原文定位	第四段末句Once forest cover does start increasing, the rate of extinction should dwindle.
	题解	**答案FALSE** 根据第四段末句可知the rate of extinction（物种灭绝的速度）随着forest cover（森林覆盖）的增加而减慢，题干是increase（增加）与原文相反，故此题错误。
16	关键词	big animals
	原文定位	第五段第二句The first questions whether the raw data about forest cover are a good indicator of biodiversity, at least for big animals.
	题解	**答案NOT GIVEN** 原文提到的是森林覆盖的原始数据是否能代表生物的多样性，尤其是哺乳动物的多样性，而没有提及森林是否能为大型动物提供栖息地。
17	关键词	climate change
	原文定位	末段首句What everyone agreed, though, was that climate change is a threat.
	题解	**答案FALSE** 本题只有一处提到关键词climate change（气候变化），题干是not everyone reaches the agreement（并不是每个人都达成了一致），这与原文what everyone agreed（每个人都同意）表达的意思相反，故本题错误。注意转折词though（但是）后面的内容，它们常常是考查点。
18	关键词	tropical species, 3°C
	原文定位	末段第三句He warned the meeting that because many tropical species evolved in an environment that has very little temperature variation, they are not equipped to cope with an increase of as little as 3°C...
	题解	**答案NOT GIVEN** 原文中的they指代上文的tropical species（热带物种），热带物种不能应对温度增加3°C的情况，但没有提及温度增加3°C，热带物种就会die out（灭绝）。

Test 4

Questions 19–26

题型 配对题(Matching Information)

注意 配对题的信息分散，通常具有归纳总结的特征，在阅读考试中有一定的难度。

19	关键词	tropical species, change their habitats
	原文定位	末段第四句Such species may thus have to migrate long distances if they are to survive.
	题解	**答案B** 原文中的Such species（这样的物种）与题干中Tropical species（热带物种）对应；原文中migrate long distances（长距离迁移）与题干中change their habitat对应。本句对应的段落都是Joseph Wright的观点。
20	关键词	the link, between a country's population and the rate of deforestation
	原文定位	倒数第二段首句The second criticism of Dr Wright's and Dr Muller-Landau's view questions their interpretation of the link between a country's population and its rate of deforestation. 和第二句Dr Laurance suggested this link may not be as strong in the future as it once was.
	题解	**答案C** 倒数第二段首句提到the link between a country's population and its rate of deforestation（一个国家的人口和森林采伐率之间的关系），接着后面就提到了Dr Laurance的观点，注意此句may not be（可能不），in the future（在未来），译为：将来两者之间的关联可能没有过去的那样紧密。题干把原文的间接表达转换成了直接表达。
21	关键词	the damage, an optimistic attitude
	原文定位	第二段第二句That was when Joseph Wright...and Helene Muller-Landau of the University of Minnesota first suggested that the damage might not be as grim as some feared.
	题解	**答案A** 题干中的have an optimistic attitude（持一种乐观的态度）与原文中not be as grim as some feared（并不像有些人所想的那么可怕）相对应。
22	关键词	The demand of land, increase
	原文定位	倒数第二段末句In particular, Dr Laurance is worried that the liberalisation of agricultural trade and the rise of biofuels could lead to a huge increase in demand for land in the tropics.
	题解	**答案C** 题干中的The demand on land（对土地的需求）是对原文in demand for land（对土地的需求）的改写，原文中的the liberalisation of agricultural trade（农业贸易的自由化）和the rise of biofuels（生物燃料的增加）被概括为some factors（一些因素），故本题答案为C。

23	关键词	healthy, satellite
	原文定位	第六段末句She said that although many forests look healthy when viewed from a satellite, they are actually falling silent because many of their large animals have been removed for subsistence or profit.
	题解	**答案D** 原文中使用了转折连词although（尽管），表达的重点在后面。many forests（许多雨林）看起来很健康，其实不是这样。此句中的she指的是前文中的Elizabeth Bennett。
24	关键词	insects, vulnerable
	原文定位	倒数第三段末句Most species, as Nigel Stork of the University of Melbourne pointed out, are insects—and these are more resilient and much less threatened.
	题解	**答案E** 题干中的are less vulnerable to（不易受攻击的）与原文中are more resilient and much less threatened（更有弹性和更不易受威胁）相对应。
25	关键词	tropical forests, natural range
	原文定位	第四段首句和第二句Dr Wright and Dr Muller-Landau therefore reckon that in 2003 reasonably unbroken tropical forest will still cover more than a third of its natural range...Much of this woodland will be secondary forest...
	题解	**答案A** 题干中的a certain proportion of（某一部分）与原文a third of（三分之一）和much of（许多）表达的是相同的含义；secondary forest（二次雨林）和natural range（自然范围）是原文重现。题干是对这两句的概括。
26	关键词	birds and mammals
	原文定位	第五段第三句William Laurance, a colleague of Dr Wright's, pointed out to the symposium that birds and mammals are more vulnerable to alterations in their habitat than are insects and other small animals.
	题解	**答案C** 题干中的harder...get used to（更难适应……）与原文more vulnerable to（更易受攻击的）表达的是相同的意思，原文是William Laurance的观点，故本题答案为C。要注意a colleague（同事）of Dr Wright's是William Laurance的同位语。

READING PASSAGE 3

体　　裁　　说明文
题　　材　　生态养殖
主　　题　　采用环保的模型鱼场养殖鲑鱼
题　　型　　摘要填空题、判断题

Questions 27–35

题型　摘要填空题(Summary Completion)

注意　该类题目涉及一小段文字，这段文字是对原文或原文中几个段落主要内容的缩写或改写。它遵从“顺序性”的原则，要求考生填写摘要中的空白部分。

27	关键词	fish farming, due to
	原文定位	第二段第二句Denmark has a long tradition of fish farming and today is among the world leaders in equipment for green production, thanks to the development of so-called model fish farms.
	题解	**答案model fish farms**　根据题目要求，需要填写的内容为一种环保技术的名称，因此答案可能为被定义的名词或加引号等特殊标点符号的专有名词。第二段第二句中出现了so-called（所谓的……），so-called后的名词恰好符合题意。题干中environmentally friendly field（环保领域）与原文中green production（绿色生产）相对应; due to（由于）与原文的thanks to（由于，多亏）是同义表达。
28	关键词	this practice, water from
	原文定位	第二段第三句The high-tech and environmentally friendly model fish farms use water from boreholes, rather than from rivers, and are based on water recirculation technology.
	题解	**答案boreholes**　题干中的this practice（这种做法）指的是前面的model fish farms（模型鱼场），题干中chooses...from（从……选择）与原文中use...from（从……使用）相对应，故此空应填入boreholes（地上凿洞）。
29	关键词	not
	原文定位	第二段第三句The high-tech and environmentally friendly model fish farms use water from boreholes, rather than from rivers, and are based on water recirculation technology.
	题解	**答案rivers**　此空承接上一个空而来，题干中的not（不是）与原文中rather than（而不是）是同义表达，故rather than from（而不是从……）后的rivers（河流）就是答案。
30	关键词	companies, stretch this high technology
	原文定位	第三段首句Now DTU Aqua and several of the key players in the industry are joining forces to take Danish fish farming a stage further.和第二句In order to put...take place inland.
	题解	**答案DTU Aqua**　由like可知，空格需要填写的内容为列举的实例，companies说明应该填写一个公司的名称。根据题目要求，回原文进行定位，得出答案。

31	关键词	somewhere, stretch this high technology
	原文定位	第三段第二句...the so-called model fish farms are to be expanded to include the breeding of saltwater fish as well as freshwater fish and it is to take place inland.
	题解	答案inland　此题应填写定语成份，根据空格前的somewhere可以了解到此空格应该填写表示地点的词语。回到原文可以发现，谈到将来的发展方向时，对于地点目标的描写只有一个词inland（内陆），即为答案。
32	关键词	output, because of
	原文定位	第四段第二句The production of fish in the aquaculture industry is increasing in several countries, but so far Denmark has not increased production significantly, mainly because of environmental restrictions.
	题解	答案environmental restrictions　根据题目要求，需要回答的内容为丹麦产量差强人意（没有明显增加）的原因，根据定位词可以锁定上面的句子，因果关系词because of（由于）在题干和原文中都出现了，because of 后面的environmental restrictions即为答案。
33	关键词	emitted from fish
	原文定位	第六段第二句This will be done partly through applying a known technique in freshwater farming, whereby bio-filters are used to convert the ammonia excreted by the fish into nitrate.
	题解	答案ammonia　根据题目要求，题目33至35三道题目之间都存在着“转换关系”。本题需填入“鱼排泄的”所修饰的成分本题题干中emitted from fish（鱼排泄出）与原文excreted by the fish（由鱼排泄）相对应。所以原文excreted by the fish所修饰的ammonia即为答案。
34	关键词	transferred into
	原文定位	第六段第二句This will be done partly through applying a known technique in freshwater farming, whereby bio-filters are used to convert the ammonia excreted by the fish into nitrate.
	题解	答案nitrate　题干中的be transferred into（被转化为……）与原文的convert...into对应，很明显into后的单词就是答案。
35	关键词	harmless
	原文定位	第六段第三句Now the goal is to develop the technology to do the same with salt water, in order to convert this nitrate into nitrogen which can be released as a harmless gas.
	题解	答案nitrogen　原文的which引导的定语从句which can be released as a harmless gas（作为无害气体被排放出来）修饰前面的名词nitrogen（氮气），也就是从句中指代的harmless gas（无害气体），故本空要填的是nitrogen。

Questions 36–40

题型 判断题(Identifying Information)

注意 判断题中画关键词要迅速，回原文定位要高效。一旦定位，就要认真阅读上下文，仔细比较原文和题目。遇到你认为答案是NOT GIVEN的题目时要冷静，清醒分析是“原文真的没有？”还是“我暂时没找到？”

36	关键词	GUDP, farmed inland
	原文定位	第七段首句In a four-year project supported by the Ministry of Food, Agriculture and Fisheries' Green Development and Demonstration Programme (GUDP), DTU Aqua...is to develop technology to enable large rainbow trout to be farmed inland in salt water.
	题解	答案TRUE 定位句大意为：DTU Aqua公司与其他合作伙伴通力协作开展了为期四年的项目研究，该项目由粮食部、农渔业绿色发展和示范工程资助，旨在研发技术使人们能够在内陆盐水中养殖大型虹鳟鱼。这一点和题目信息相同。
37	关键词	water quality parameters, cleaning technologies
	原文定位	第八段首句DTU Aqua is responsible for the professional management of the project...water quality parameters and the development and optimisation of cleaning technologies.
	题解	答案NOT GIVEN 原文提到了the environmental impact, water quality parameters和the development and optimisation of cleaning technologies，但并未指出两者在GUDP项目管理方面谁更重要。
38	关键词	long-term target, export market of saltwater fish
	原文定位	倒数第五段首句The goal in the long term is not only to create a basis for the Danish production and export of sustainably produced saltwater fish: the actual technology itself will have equally strong export potential...
	题解	答案FALSE 根据倒数第五段首句的内容，长期目标不仅是为丹麦的生产和大量输出咸水鱼奠定基础，更是要有强大的出口潜力。题干属于以偏概全，故错误。
39	关键词	dams, streams, wild fish stocks
	原文定位	倒数第二段第二句和第三句...the streams are now free of obstacles such as dams and barriers. This also provides free passage for the wild fish on their way to and from spawning grounds and the sea, which is beneficial for wild fish stocks.
	题解	答案TRUE 原文信息表明这些大坝的建造为野生鱼往返产卵地和海洋提供了便捷的通道，有利于野生鱼数量的增长。符合题目含义。
40	关键词	rapid progress of aquaculture industry
	原文定位	末段首句Today the aquaculture industry—both inland and sea-based fish farms—is the world's fastest growing food industry.
	题解	答案TRUE 此题目对应文章最后一句，根据上文的说明可以得出水产业的蓬勃发展是因为模型渔场在海水和内陆的采用。

WRITING

WRITING TASK 1

名师解读

本题为图表作文中的曲线图题型，属于对比说明型的文章，主要是让考生描述、对比使用和不使用治疗方法对这两种女性癌症的影响。

首先考生要花一分钟左右的时间来解析曲线图，先根据横轴分析变化，然后再进行比较。通过图内两条曲线以及两个图之间的对比找到使用和不使用治疗方法的差别以及治疗方法对两种癌症的不同影响。

首段介绍核心信息，一句话即可。第二、三段先分析第一种癌症，再分析后一种癌症。作答时，考生要灵活运用表示曲线图变化的单词和短语，比如slightly, rise, go down等。

高分范文

The two graphs show the situation with and without treatment for two types of cancer in women: cancer of the **alimentary tract** and **lymphosarcoma**.

For cancer of the alimentary tract, treatment can be **reasonably** effect ve. Whereas only 40% of patients **survive** one year after **diagnosis** without treatment; when treatment is applied about 65% of patients survive one year. Without treatment, fewer than 15% of patients survive for five years after diagnosis, but with treatment the survival rate after five years increases to nearly 40%.

For lymphosarcoma, however, treatment can have a **negative** effect compared with that of alimentary tract cancer. The survival rate two years after diagnosis is around 30%, whether treatment is applied or not. However, survival rate with treatment is lower than that without treatment beyond two years. After five years, 30% of untreated patients are still alive, whereas none of the cases studied who have received treatment survive for five years after diagnosis. (150 words)

WRITING TASK 2

文章结构

正反观点辩论+立场+原因+总结

viewpoint+standpoint+reason 1+reason 2+conclusion
首段：背景句+引出现象+正反两方面的观点+自己立场
第二段：立场+正面理由
第三段：立场+反面理由
第四段：总结+立场

思路点拨

步骤一：审题（<3分钟）

Some people think that old people should be taken care of at home, while others think they should be placed in old people's house. What is your opinion?

→通读题目，了解大意，判断题型。

本题的题型为论述型文章。题目的大意为：有人认为应该在家里照顾老人，而有些人则认为应该送老人到养老院。你的观点是什么?

→重审题目，辨别关键词，区分主题词和限定词，推测考官的出题意图。

主题词：old people, be taken care of at home, be placed in old people's house

限定词：your opinion

步骤二：列大纲（<3分钟）

英文提纲	Intro: development of medical science→increasing number of elderly people→some people, seniors, at home→as for me, to the nursing home Body: intensive medical care→a proper diet→regular medical check-ups→medical services, immediately available→more opportunities to communicate→not feel lonely, do things together→on the contrary, live at home, left alone→benefit for children's work and study→achieve more success Conclusion: Nursing homes benefit seniors, old people should be sent to nursing homes.
中文提纲	引出话题：医疗科学的发展→老龄人口增多→反方观点：老人待在家里→作者观点：送老人去养老院 主体段落：专业的医疗护理→合理的饮食→常规的医疗检查→即时的医疗救助→更多的交流机会→不会感到孤独，与大家一起做事情→相反：待在家里，老人感到孤独→有利于孩子的工作和学习→有利于孩子取得更大的成功 总结：养老院对老年人有利，老年人应该被送到养老院。

高分范文

Thanks to the development of medical science, there is an increasing number of elderly people in the world. Some people believe that the **seniors** should be looked after at home. Indeed, it is the children's **responsibility** and **obligation** to take care of their parents when they are old. However, as for me, a better way to ensure them a happy life is to send them to the **nursing home**.

First of all, in such **retirement** homes, aging people can receive intensive medical care from professional doctors. Besides, they can receive a proper diet prepared by **dieticians** to meet their individual requirements. This is especially good for those old people in poor health. Moreover, they could have regular medical check-ups so that any disease could be diagnosed at its early stage. What is the most beneficial is that if any disease strikes them, medical services are immediately available.

Living in nursing homes, they have more opportunities to communicate with their peers. They do not feel lonely and can do a great many things together, such as doing morning exercise, playing games, and exchanging memories and stories from their past. On the contrary, if they live at home, they are often left alone when their children and **grandchildren** are away working or studying. Some people may say that children have duties to take care of their aged parents. However, nowadays people are **confronted** with fierce competition and suffer from great pressure. They are too occupied to spare time for their parents. There are benefits for children's work and study when nursing homes take over the task of caring for the elderly. Children, free from care, can devote themselves to work or study and achieve more success.

Since nursing homes benefit seniors and other family members so much, I believe that old people should be sent to nursing homes. (310 words)

SPEAKING

名师解读

Part 1的题目属于朋友类，此类题目是口语考试当中最常见的一类。

Part 2在对电视节目进行描述时，首先要定位一档节目，然后介绍是在什么时间，哪个频道看到的。其次，可以说明一下节目的类别以及观众类型，接下来对主持人可以稍做描述，侧重说明主持人的主持风格，但不能偏离介绍节目内容的主题，如果想要说得生动，可以特别描述令自己印象最深刻的一期节目，描述内容包括节目涉及到的嘉宾以及节目中谈到的话题。最后总结说明自己为什么喜欢或者不喜欢该档节目。

Part 3中TV programme出现的频率非常高。在这个题目中，很多同学会错误地把电影之类内容作为题材来说，其实是不对的，该题目期待考生给的答案是电视节目，例如talk show, entertainment show, animal world等。Part 3是口语考试中最难的一部分。

高分示例

PART 1

Friends

- Do you often spend time with friends?

Yes. Since I live away from home, I spend most of my spare time with my friends. We often go to the movies and go shopping together.

- Did you meet most of your friends through school/work?

I' m still studying. So, yeah, I met most of them through school. We have classes together from Monday to Friday. I guess it's easier to be friends with someone you see on a regular basis.

- Do you and your friends have similar hobbies and interests?

Well, some of them share similar hobbies with me, hobbies like hiking, tennis, movies, Karaoke, etc. Some don' t, but we still manage to hang out.

- Do you spend more of your free time with friends or family?

With my friends, of course, since I live on campus. Being with friends keeps me away from homesickness.

PART 2

The programme I enjoyed most as a child was called *Pokémon*. It was about a boy and his friends who lived in a whole different world with creatures called Pokémon. He was on a quest to become the greatest Pokémon trainer in the world and the programme was all about his **adventures**.

It was on at 3.30pm, just in time for when I got home from school. It was a fight, but my mother finally allowed me to watch it before I did my homework every day.

Sometimes I would watch it in the living room with my brother, but if my mother was busy or my grandparents were at home, I would have to watch it in my parents' room.

I really enjoyed watching this programme when I was little because it was all about friendship and learning to work together. It showed friends using teamwork to get out of impossible situations. I still think of some of the better **episodes** today and use them in my day-to-day life.

PART 3

TV and radio in your country

- In your country, which do people prefer, watching TV or listening to radio? Why?

I think that most people prefer to watch TV, because they enjoy the programmes that are on. However, the older generation might prefer the radio because it is what most grew up with.

- What kind of programmes are most popular?

Programme **popularity** tends to differ between age groups and **gender boundaries**. Children would prefer the cartoons and teens the reality shows, while adults would enjoy the drama or historical programmes more.

- Do men and women tend to like the same kind of programmes? Why/Why not?

Also, women tend to watch more drama or romance programmes compared to men. Men seem to like action or sports programmes more, not always though. Some people prefer different things like cooking shows or game shows.

The effects of TV

- Some people think that watching TV can be a negative influence. Would you agree?

In some cases, yes, I would agree. At a young age when children's minds are still developing, watching too much TV could impair their imagination and creativity as well as keep them from developing their speech properly.

- What benefits can TV bring people?

TV does have many benefits, like informing people of news and weather and educating them on certain subjects. Some benefits are just to help people relax and learn about other cultures or their own.

- What priorities do you think TV stations should have?

TV stations should realise that the majority of the people who watch their programmes at certain times are children, and they should cater to their needs with not only fun shows but educational ones too.

重点词汇

LISTENING

accommodation	[əˌkɒmə'deɪʃn]	*n.*	住处，膳宿；调节
compromise	['kɒmprəmaɪz]	*n.*	妥协，和解
legislation	[ˌledʒɪs'leɪʃn]	*n.*	立法；法律
frequent	['friːkwənt]	*adj.*	频繁的，时常发生的
available	[ə'veɪləbl]	*adj.*	可利用的，可得的；有效的
refurbishment	[ˌriː'fɜːbɪʃmənt]	*n.*	整修；翻新
appointment	[ə'pɔɪntmənt]	*n.*	任命；约定
promptly	['prɒmptli]	*adv.*	迅速地，立即地；敏捷地
burger	['bɜːgə]	*n.*	汉堡包
blast	[blɑːst]	*v.*	爆炸；损害；使枯萎
fault	[fɔːlt]	*n.*	错误；缺点
ancient	['eɪnʃənt]	*adj.*	古代的；古老的
architect	['ɑːkɪtekt]	*n.*	建筑师，设计师
computerisation	[kəmˌpjuːtəraɪ'zeɪʃn]	*n.*	电子计算机化工作；电脑化
qualitative	['kwɒlɪtətɪv]	*adj.*	定性的；质的，性质上的
drum	[drʌm]	*n.*	鼓；鼓声
incredible	[ɪn'kredəbl]	*adj.*	难以置信的，惊人的
turtle	['tɜːtl]	*n.*	龟，甲鱼；海龟
appal	[ə'pɔːl]	*v.*	使惊骇，惊吓
terrapin	['terəpɪn]	*n.*	水龟
hatchling	['hætʃlɪŋ]	*n.*	刚孵化的小动物
optimism	['ɒptɪmɪzəm]	*n.*	乐观；乐观主义
sufficiently	[sə'fɪʃntli]	*adv.*	充分地，足够地

READING

malaria	[mə'leərɪə]	*n.*	[内科]疟疾；瘴气
debilitate	[dɪ'bɪlɪteɪt]	*v.*	使虚弱
insecticide	[ɪn'sektɪsaɪd]	*n.*	杀虫剂
bed net		*n.*	蚊帐
mosquito	[mə'skiːtəʊ]	*n.*	蚊子
makeover	['meɪkəʊvə]	*n.*	大转变；化妆美容
dwindle	['dwɪndl]	*v.*	减少；变小
progeny	['prɒdʒəni]	*n.*	子孙，后裔；成果
mutation	[mjuː'teɪʃn]	*n.*	突变；变化；元音变化
neutralise	['njuːtrəlaɪz]	*v.*	中和；中立化；变无效
upshot	[ʌpʃɒt]	*n.*	要点；结果，结局
rethink	[ˌriː'θɪŋk]	*v.*	重新考虑；再想
parasite	['pærəsaɪt]	*n.*	寄生虫；食客
plug	[plʌg]	*v.*	插入；塞住；接插头
tactic	['tæktɪk]	*n.*	策略，战略
vulnerable	['vʌlnərəbl]	*adj.*	易受攻击的，易受伤害的
extinction	[ɪk'stɪŋkʃn]	*n.*	消失；消灭；废止
biodiversity	[ˌbaɪəʊdaɪ'vɜːsəti]	*n.*	生物多样性
abandon	[ə'bændən]	*v.*	遗弃；放弃
reckon	['rekən]	*v.*	估计；计算；料想
tropical-forest		*n.*	热带森林，热带雨林

symposium	[sɪm'pəʊzɪəm]	*n.*	讨论会，座谈会
mammal	['mæml]	*n.*	[脊椎]哺乳动物
subsistence	[səb'sɪstəns]	*n.*	生存；生活；存在
resilient	[rɪ'zɪlɪənt]	*adj.*	弹回的，有弹力的
interpretation	[ɪnˌtɜːprɪ'teɪʃn]	*n.*	解释；翻译；演出
soya-bean		*n.*	大豆
borehole	['bɔːhəʊl]	*n.*	地上凿洞
salmon	['sæmən]	*n.*	鲑鱼；大马哈鱼
recirculation	[riːˌsɜːkju'leɪʃən]	*n.*	（信息）再循环
cross-disciplinary		*adj.*	跨学科的；交叉学科的
collaboration	[kəˌlæbə'reɪʃn]	*n.*	合作；勾结，通敌
complement	['kɒmplɪment]	*v.*	补足，补助
nitrogen	['naɪtrədʒən]	*n.*	[化学]氮
bio-filter		*n.*	（处理废水用）生物滤池
ammonia	[ə'məʊnɪə]	*n.*	[化学]氨
nitrate	['naɪtreɪt]	*n.*	硝酸盐
feasibility	[ˌfiːzə'bɪləti]	*n.*	可行性；可能性
responsible	[rɪ'spɒnsəbl]	*adj.*	负责的，有责任的；可靠的
optimisation	[ˌɒptɪmaɪ'zeɪʃən]	*n.*	最佳化，最优化
breeding	['briːdɪŋ]	*n.*	繁殖；饲养
composition	[ˌkɒmpə'zɪʃn]	*n.*	构成；合成物；成分
comprehensive	[ˌkɒmprɪ'hensɪv]	*adj.*	综合的；广泛的；有理解力的
documentation	[ˌdɒkjumen'teɪʃn]	*n.*	文件，证明文件
stream	[striːm]	*n.*	溪流；流动；潮流
spawn	[spɔːn]	*v.*	产卵；大量生产
aquaculture	['ækwəkʌltʃə]	*n.*	水产养殖，水产业

WRITING

alimentary tract			消化道
lymphosarcoma	[ˌlɪmfəʊsɑː'kəʊmə]	*n.*	淋巴肉瘤
reasonably	['riːznəbli]	*adv.*	相当地；合理地；适度地
survive	[sə'vaɪv]	*v.*	活下来；幸存
diagnosis	[ˌdaɪəg'nəʊsɪs]	*n.*	诊断
negative	['negətɪv]	*adj.*	消极的，否定的；阴性的
senior	['siːnɪə]	*n.*	年长者
responsibility	[rɪˌspɒnsə'bɪləti]	*n.*	义务，责任，职责
obligation	[ˌɒblɪ'geɪʃn]	*n.*	义务，职责；债务
nursing home			养老院
retirement	[rɪ'taɪəmənt]	*n.*	退休；退役
dietician	[ˌdaɪə'tɪʃən]	*n.*	营养学家，膳食学家
grandchildren	[ˌgræn'tʃɪldrən]	*n.*	孙子，孙（女），外孙（女）
confront	[kən'frʌnt]	*v.*	面对；遭遇；比较

SPEAKING

adventure	[əd'ventʃə]	*n.*	冒险活动，冒险经历，奇遇
episode	['epɪsəʊd]	*n.*	插曲，片断
popularity	[ˌpɒpju'lærəti]	*n.*	流行；普及
gender	['dʒendə]	*n.*	性别；性
boundary	['baʊndri]	*n.*	边界；范围

听力原文

SECTION 1

(FEMALE=F; MALE=M)

F: Easthill Town Hall, Tourism and City Life Office, Fiona speaking. How may I help you?

M: Yes, hello. I don't live in Easthill, but I've just been offered a job there for a few months. It means I need to arrange to move to Easthill for the summer.

F: Where would you like to start?

M: Perhaps with accommodation?

F: OK, Easthill's certainly not the easiest place to find accommodation in.

M: Oh, dear.

F: But I'm not saying it's impossible. It's not that big a town, and the centre, being historic, is quite small, so demand is very high and that's reflected in prices.

M: I only want a single place.

F: What I'd recommend, to keep costs down, is a Q1 shared flat. The rent would be much lower than a one-bedroom place, particularly in the centre.

M: Uh-huh. If I really wanted to maintain my privacy, and I'd get at least, say, a studio flat...

F: Well, that might be a compromise. I don't have any specific details. If you were already here, you could visit some of the local estate agents to get details of studio flats, but I do know that if you go onto Q2 newhome—as in one word—dot com, that site has quite a few places, and there are pictures and plans and so on.

M: OK, I'll just write that down. That's great, thanks.

F: One thing to be aware is a new piece of legislation which means that landlords are responsible for ensuring their tenants are who they say they are. So any landlord will ask you to provide documentary evidence, not just your passport etcetera as they always have, but now of your Q3 employment.

M: Right, thanks. And I guess I'll need to pay by standing order through my bank?

F: That's the normal way, yes. With the rent, do get clear what is and isn't part of the standard price. You'll need to know if Q4 sheets and towels are provided, or whether you'd have to allow extra. Bills such as electricity are always included, but I think the phone will always be an extra.

M: Right. Now, what about transport?

F: Easthill has really good bus services. They're frequent and they go everywhere, and they're how everyone gets around. But they are quite expensive if you pay for each trip, so it's better to get a pass.

M: OK.

F: They're available as seven-day, that's the shortest, 30-day, Q5 90-day, which would perhaps suit you the most, and one year, which works out the cheapest, but might be too long for you.

M: Yes, it definitely would be.

F: Is there anything else I can help you with?

M: Yes. I like to keep fit, so I'd like to know what health clubs there are in Easthill.

F: OK, well, there are two, Blooms Leisure Centre and also the Good Life Centre. I've got some information here about them.

M: Would I be able to try them before actually joining?

F: Let's see...yes, one of the staff at Blooms will show you around if you go along, and then you make your decision about joining. While at the Good Life, you can...well, OK, they offer Q6 two fitness classes at no charge, so you can get a taste of what they're like. This isn't for specialist classes, such as *tai chi*, it says.

M: It's something, anyway. I'd hope to meet new friends at a health club, you see.

F: Oh yes, and both clubs have cafés. If you do join Blooms, you can elect to be a Q7 gold card member, which means you'd be entitled to a discount of 10% in the café there. Actually, the café in the Good Life is shut at the moment for refurbishment, but I guess it might be open again by the time you move here.

M: Does it say much about the equipment available?

F: Blooms have a lot of different machines, so you can choose exactly what you want to do, while the Good Life doesn't have quite so many machines, but they're carefully sequenced, so that you follow Q8 special routines. It says that these get you really fit.

M: Sounds interesting. And I love swimming. Do they have pools?

F: Yes. The one at Blooms is full-size, and it's outdoor, so it used to be rather chilly except in the summer, but they've improved the situation by making it a Q9 heated one, so it feels as if you're indoors while you're swimming. The Good Life pool is just a small one, but they have covered tennis courts.

M: I don't play tennis. Maybe I should start! Are there trainers to help you?

F: Blooms, yes, at any time, but Good Life, no...well, the trainers are fully qualified, but you must see them Q10 by appointment, not just any time.

M: That seems fair enough. You've been very helpful, thank you.

F: Not at all. Now, would you like me to send you the information you asked about...

SECTION 2

(BARBARA=B; JOHN=J; MARK=MK)

B: Sunrise Hotel. Good Morning. Barbara speaking.

J: Hello. My name is John Griffin. I'd like to make a booking for tonight please. Are there any rooms still available?

B: Yes, there are a few left. What were you wanting?

J: Well, I'm on a business trip so I only need a single room.

B: I don't think that will be a problem. Let's look. Yes...There's one single room left. Shall I book it for you?

J: Yes please.That would be great.

B: Right then. Let me get a pen. So, what's your name again please?

J: That's J-O-H-N G-R-I-F-F-I-N.

B: OK. I've got that down. Wait a minute. You've been here before, haven't you?

J: Yes, that's right. I've stayed with you Q11 twice before .

B: Well, we should have your details already. Let's look at the cards. Here we are. So, John Griffin...from Q12 Sydney, right?

J: Yes, that's right.

B: So, tell me if I'm wrong. John Griffin, passport number Q13 87637489. Age 30.

J: Yes, that's right.

B: So, it's Q14 a single room for two nights. Is your credit card number the same to confirm the booking?

J: Yes, it's the same, but I'll want you to forward the bill to my company again, if that's OK.

B: Oh yes, Mr Griffin. That's no problem at all. Your company have always settled very promptly in the past. And, what time can we expect you tonight Mr Griffin?

J: Well, the plane lands Q15 at 9.15pm so by the time I get through the formalities...that should take about 20 minutes...I should be at your place at 10. Will the restaurant still be open at that time as I'll be hungry—I hate plane food!

B: I'm afraid it'll be closed by then Mr Griffin. Can I organise some snacks to be left in your room? A burger? Fries? Sandwiches?

J: Yes, that would be great. How about a cheese sandwich with fries?

B: No problem, sir. I'll see to that. Oh the fries might be cold when you get in.

J: Ah yes. Q16 Just the sandwich then.

B: No problem. Anything else Mr Griffin?

J: No, that's all.Thank you. See you tonight.

B: See you tonight, Mr Griffin. Goodbye.

J: Goodbye.

B: Oh, Mark, That was Mr Griffin. You know, that nice man from Sydney who's been here a couple of times before? He's booked a single room for two nights from tonight.

MK: Ah good. Wait a moment. Which room have you put him in?

B: Err...I put him in number 22. Is that OK?

MK: I think so. Let me check. Oh blast. There was a booking earlier this morning. All the singles are now gone.

B: Oh dear. I'm so sorry. I didn't realise.

MK: Don't worry, it's not a problem. We'll stick him in Q17 number 34. It's a double room but it shouldn't matter.

B: What about the price? The double is $150 a night and he's going to be expecting Q18 $100 a night for the single.

MK: Well, we don't want to upset him. We want him to come back. Make a note that we'll give him the single rate and he's got a free upgrade.

B: I'm so sorry Mark. I should have let him know that there weren't any singles left.

MK: No, it's not your fault. I took the booking earlier but the computers were down. I should have made a note of the booking so that everyone knew. It's my fault.

B: Mr Griffin has ordered a cheese sandwich to be left in his room too as the restaurant will be closed when he gets in.

MK: That's no problem. Just leave a message for my wife in the order book there. She'll make sure that it's prepared by the kitchen staff and then Q19 room service can take it to his room just before he arrives.

B: How much shall I charge him for the sandwich?

MK: What is it again? Ah yes cheese. Erm...well beef and chicken are both $10 and salad is $8. Just make it Q20 $9. That should be OK.

B: OK. Thanks Mark.

SECTION 3

(MALE=M; FEMALE=F)

M: Hi Jill, how are you?

F: Good, Desmond, good. We need to decide some things about our project, don't we?

M: Yes...By the way, Jill, I've been meaning to ask you. Did you always know you were going to do social sciences?

F: Well, to be honest, no. It took me quite a while to fix on it. Why, did you know from the start?

M: Not completely, no. I mean, I didn't do it at school, obviously.

F: No, nor did I. I was quite drawn to the, er, physical world, like how things are made, you know. There's a sort of ancient history to the industrial world we live in, isn't there, with the invention of the wheel, for example, through to high-spec computers today. So, although I wasn't drawn to being an architect, or doing archaeology, I wondered about the Q21 industrial side of design for some time.

M: That's surprising—I'd never have guessed.

F: And that's not all. There's a kind of earn-lots-of-money side to me, too, so I wondered if some kind of management role might suit me, and I spent quite a bit of time looking into diplomas and degrees in aspects of running companies, which I thought could be fascinating. But you know I'm quite allergic to much computerisation, and the Q22 information management aspects seemed to dominate those courses, and that's, really, how I've ended up where I am.

M: Well, I was just choosing between social sciences and psychology, and I thought that was tricky...!

F: But even having made the choice, I still find the course far from easy.

M: Yes, me, too. I mean, I've been making some great friends here—maybe too many, to be honest. And I'm glad I had a gap year before starting, so I got a bit of experience of the world, and learnt to deal with my finances, because I see a lot of students really struggling with that.

F: Including me!

M: It's planning everything that's tricky for me. Q23 I can never decide what to concentrate on in what order, which things are more important to get done first. So I go to lectures in the morning, and that's fine, but then I drift into the library, and I'm not sure what to do. Then I see some friends in there, Q24 and I get into trouble for trying to chat with them instead of keeping quiet and getting on with work. So I always seem a bit behind with the coursework.

F: Well, Desmond, that's not going to happen with this project we're doing together!

M: No, good. Right, now first up is the design of the experiment. Shall we work on that together?

F: Q25 I was thinking that it was more in your territory, that you're more the numbers man.

M: I don't mind doing it, certainly. I don't think it's going to be very easy. There are so many variables to take account of, aren't there? Q26 So I'll need to get some help from the

Test 4

statistics tutor, as I'm not as convinced of my powers as you seem to be.

F: You seem to get on with him quite well. If you deal with that, then Q27 I could be in the library, looking into the sorts of research projects that have been done in this area before. Or would you like to tack that onto what you're already doing?

M: I think your perspective would be more useful on this. Shall we say we'll combine forces for it?

F: OK, because there will be quite a heavy reading load.

M: Once the experiment's structure starts to become clear, we should check with the IT section if they'll be able to help us at all in setting it up. I don't know how easy it is to talk to them.

F: Not very, there. Q28 However, I've got a friend there, so I could sound her out. She's a helpful sort of person.

M: Good.

F: Now, we agreed that as well as the hard numerical data we'd set up some small focus groups to get qualitative data, didn't we? Shall we do that as a pair?

M: I agree that we'll conduct the group sessions together, but it's fairly straightforward to arrange the sessions, isn't it?

F: Q29 True. I'll take care of that, then. And then, finally, we need to think about the presentation.

M: Oh, you know I have no ability in public speaking. Whereas you...

F: We can divide up the sections.

M: I'll sort out the slides and the animations and the handouts, everything, if you do the talking. Q30 I mean, I agree that it should be a joint effort, it's just we should play to our strengths.

F: It's a deal!

M: OK, now we should go off and...

SECTION 4

Today on *Nature Focus* we're looking at the river turtle and the threats it's facing in today's world. The two main places we see the giant river turtle are South America and Southeast Asia. The best way to see the big rivers of South America, such as the Amazon and the Orinoco is probably by plane. But then you might miss the strange shallow craters that cover the sandbanks along these rivers. These are the nests of the arrau turtles, and at night thousands of turtles rise up out of the river water and scuttle into these holes. The holes are around 90 centimetres in diametre, so the turtles, whose shells are around Q31 75 centimetres in length, fit neatly.

Enormous numbers of eggs are laid on the beaches. Since hundreds of females each laying between Q32 70 and 80 eggs crowd together, it means that literally thousands of eggs fill the sandy nests, waiting to hatch. A similar story is played out in Asia, where the river terrapins also lay their eggs communally and in the open. The difference is that the terrapins, once they have used the nests, cover them over and then beat the sand down with their limbs, making an incredible sound, like Q33 drums. The noise at night of many terrapins doing this is incredible, and drowns out the sound of the river water. And the male terrapins are fascinating too. Throughout the breeding season, they are famous for the Q34 colour changes to their oddly-shaped heads that take place.

However, these wonderful creatures are under threat, and this has been the case for quite some time. As long ago as 1811, the scientist and explorer Alexander von Humboldt was a witness to the mass destruction of turtle eggs at the Orinoco river. The eggs made oil and the oil made money. He recorded that, "A jar contains 25 bottles of oil, each bottle being the production of 200 eggs, and allowing for the wastage of eggs damaged in the nest, 33 million eggs had been harvested to fill the Q35 5,000 jars"—and that was a sight and a calculation that appalled him.

And it appalled many others, too, so there have been, over the years, various initiatives designed to protect turtles and terrapins from such slaughter. For example, the Sultans of Perak in Asia ensured the safety, at least to some extent, of the beaches for terrapins when they issued Q36 licences to official egg collectors. These collectors would only collect eggs in numbers that were sustainable.

However, the scheme of course vanished with the Sultans. And despite efforts at protecting turtles, there are ever growing demands for them, for pets in some countries, and for food in others and also heavily in traditional Q37 medicine in various parts of Asia. These levels of exploitation unfortunately far exceeded their ability to reproduce and so replace their lost stock. It takes a turtle a long time—many years—to grow from a baby, or hatchling, to an adult that can reproduce, and so the survival of eggs and hatchlings is crucial to the survival of the species. But the threat never stops being acute. Once adult, a female turtle can continue reproducing for a number of Q38 decades, provided they are not killed or injured, so the loss of even a single adult can mean many years of reproduction are lost forever.

Is it all gloom? Well, there are some grounds for cautious optimism. There are some well thought out management systems in place which can help the stocks of threatened turtles and terrapins to rebuild. In Brazil, for example, the government has been encouraging and supporting the farming of river turtles, with the idea that this happens alongside the banning of the hunting of wild turtles. The idea of the scheme is to provide farmers with a one-off batch of hatchlings, which they are urged to keep until they become Q39 mature. This should mean that good quantities of turtles capable of reproducing come to the rescue of the species. Will it work? Let's hope so. The scheme has some doubters, who point out that, while the biology arguments for the scheme certainly do make sense, the farmers on the scheme of course have no experience of this kind of farming. That means it's impossible at this stage to know if the turtles they develop will be sufficiently marketable, and thus if the scheme will work well from an economic point of view. It may be that it has to rely on subsidies, and that would mean, in the Q40 long term, that it would probably fail. But it's certainly worth a try, and I hope to be back on this programme in a few years' time, reporting on its great success.

Test 5

答案速查

LISTENING

Section 1, Questions 1–10

1 18th–20th October
2 Pacific Hotel
3 0793332233
4 $60
5 Professor/Pr Catherine
6 last Friday
7 (an) interesting title
8 300 words
9 (a) brief CV
10 *admin@uniconf*

Section 2, Questions 11–20

11 central
12 British Museum
13 Twin
14 business centre/center
15 £50/fifty; 50/fifty pounds
16 receipts
17 entertainment
18 0800 777121
19 Brightwell
20 courier

Section 3, Questions 21–30

21 C
22 B
23 embossed letters
24 night writing
25 A
26 B
27 C
28–30 **IN ANY ORDER** A D E

Section 4, Questions 31–40

31 C
32 B
33 A
34 C
35 C
36–40 **IN ANY ORDER** A C F G J

READING

Reading Passage 1, Questions 1–13

1 grassland
2 carbon
3 wildfires
4 property
5 human health
6 temperate-forest
7 tropical forest
8 knee-high
9–11 **IN ANY ORDER** B C E
12 B
13 D

Reading Passage 2, Questions 14–25

14 NO
15 YES
16 NO
17 NOT GIVEN
18 YES
19 NOT GIVEN
20 A
21 C
22 B
23 D
24 A
25 E

Reading Passage 3, Questions 26–40

26 B
27 C
28 E
29 D
30 G
31 narrower
32 trait
33 health
34 low self-esteem
35 high self-esteem
36 NOT GIVEN
37 TRUE
38 FALSE
39 FALSE
40 TRUE

名师解析

LISTENING

SECTION 1

主题场景	会议咨询场景
主旨大意	关于会议咨询的对话
考查题型	笔记填空题

名师解读

1　18th–20th October　本题要求填入会议的时间。考生在听到three days时就要注意，预测后面可能会出现答案。原文的日期有两个，from...to，都要记录为答案。注意要将答案18th to the 20th of October改写为18th–20th October。

2　Pacific Hotel　本题要求填入会议的地点。否定词no排除了第一个提到的Paradise Hotel这个地点。解答本题的关键是定位actually词后的内容。注意单词的拼写和字母的大小写。

3　0793332233　本题需要填写电话号码，填写时要注意区号area code也要写上，不能漏掉，triple表示3个，double表示2个。

4　$60　本题要填入会费。原文中出现了多个价钱，$150 for the three days, $60 a day，注意原文与student相关的数字，钱和天数一定要对应上。

5　Professor /Pr Catherine　本题要填入人名。注意两个单词的拼写要正确，首字母均要大写，男士在后面的对话中给出了名字的拼写。

6　last Friday　本题要填入会议闭幕的时间。题干给出的关键词为day，答案处需要填入的是“周几”。注意在原文closing date后面的内容中就可以找到答案。

7　(an) interesting title　题干中的include为关键词，之后出现的内容an interesting title即为答案。

8　300 words　本题要填入outline的最大长度。原文先提到no more than 300 words（不超过300字），之后又提到可以控制在300–400字之间，但考生要注意400 words被否定了，答案为300 words。

9　(a) brief CV　题干中的send为关键词。CV大写，表示“个人简历”。

10　admin@uniconf　本题要填入邮箱地址。答案较长，注意邮箱地址的基本信息。dot表示“点”，注意对话中关于邮箱的拼写。

SECTION 2

主题场景	旅行场景
主旨大意	在伦敦机场中途停留、安排住宿的对话
考查题型	笔记填空题

名师解读

11　central　题干中的Hotel, Bedford是关键词，考生能够在原文中听到two of our partner hotels这样的信息。题干中的London为原文重现，故London前的central即为答案。注意本题的答案是在关键词Bedford前面出现，要求考生有一定的短时记忆能力。

12　British Museum　本题要求填入的是Family room的地点。题干中的Family room, special facilities均为关键词，均为原文重现。题干中的Close to与原文中的near to是同义替换，near to之后的地点British Museum即为答案。

13　Twin　题干中的very close to与原文中的very near为同义表达。题干空格后面的rooms为原文重现，故原文中room前的twin为答案。

14 business centre/centre 本题要求考生填入Premier Hotel具备的设施，该设施与a swimming pool构成并列关系。题干中的关键词a swimming pool为原文重现，在后面又提到了it also has a business centre，其中it指代的是Premier Hotel, also与题干中的and对应，has为原文重现。

15 £50/fifty, 50/fifty pounds 本题要求考生填入cash的数目。题干中的Airline与原文中的人称代词we对应，give, cash为原文重现，题干中的cover和incidental expenses分别与原文中的take care of和any minor expenses对应，故cash后的£50为答案。考生需要注意货币单位英镑的符号和拼写。

16 receipts 题干中的refund, other essential expenses, phone calls均为原文重现，据此对原文进行定位。题干中的must keep和need to obtain对应，obtain的宾语receipts即为答案。

17 entertainment 题干中的not reimburse, non-essential和expenses分别与原文中的don't refund, aren't strictly necessary和the costs of things对应，据此对原文进行定位。题干中的e.g.与原文中的like对应，shopping和refreshments均为原文重现，考生通过比较，可以直接判定like后的entertainment就是本题的答案。

18 0800 777121 题干中的free phone number为关键词，关键词为原文重现，它前面的一连串数字就是答案。注意听清楚数字。

19 Brightwell 根据题干判定，本题要求考生填入名字，题干中的Philip为关键词，此词后的Brightwell为答案。注意对话中对姓氏的拼读。

20 courier 题干中的the flight is cancelled again对应原文中的the worst comes to the worst。空格后的will为原文重现，drop与原文中的bring对应，原文中的them指代的是前面出现的more vouchers，与题干中的additional vouchers为同义表达。

SECTION 3

主题场景	学术主题讨论场景
主旨大意	介绍法国盲人教育家布莱叶发明的盲人用点字法
考查题型	选择题、句子填空题

名师解读

21 C 根据题干中的Where和选项确定本题要求考生选出地点。题干中的when...child与原文中的at the age of three对应，原文中的in his father's workshop与选项C是重现。

22 B 题干中的invent与原文中的invented为同根词，writing system为原文重现，故后面提到的时间1824就是答案。

23 embossed letters 题干中的early writing system指的是原文中的Frenchman提出的方法，题干中的used与原文中的printing对应。故后面的embossed letters为答案。注意答案的复数形式。

24 night writing 题干中的military system为关键词，为原文重现，据此定位答案。题干中的called与原文中的known as对应。

25 A 题干中的dots为原文重现，题干中的combined与原文中的combinations为同根词，故letters of the alphabet和based on the alphabet with each word都可以用dots表示。

26 B 本题要求考生选出时间。原文给出多个时间1854, two years, Braille's death，考生一定要耐心听到最后再做出选择。不要一听到two years就选A。

27 C 题干中的Hand written与原文中的hand, write对应，题干中的in reverse与原文中的backwards对应，也就是原文举的例子，from right to left...can be read like English from left to right。

28–30 IN ANY ORDER A D E 题干中的subjects为关键词。原文提到的subjects信息有mathematics, scientific notation, music notation，分别与选项A, D, E对应。

SECTION 4

主题场景	学术主题场景
主旨大意	大学介绍如何准备雅思考试
考查题型	选择题

名师解读

31 C 题干中的are adopting与原文中introduce对应，原文中的it指代的就是IELTS。据此判定as后的就是答案。答案为exit test，与选项C一致。

32 B band 6的解释是indicates a good competency of English, band 7的解释是you are doing very well and will be able to go and study for a Master's degree overseas，但注意题干要求的是competency，band 6提到了这个关键词。

33 A 注意题目要求选出在考试中需要重点考虑的the three main things，在听到three main things后，考生就要注意，后面就是对三件事的描述。答案不在同一句中出现，要注意分别记录，然后对应选项。

34 C 原文先提到了the courses and the workshops的内容，但根据题干关键词为时间Mondays 2.30 to 4.30与地点CILL，要求考生选出在这个时间段和这个地点可以参加的项目，而且注意此题的答案在关键词之前出现，为C项。

35 C 原文提到较多活动，the Speaking Assistance Programme, Writing Assistance Programme, books, CDs, tapes, videos and of course online materials。考生一定不能急于做出选择，要听到最后再选择，A、B项的内容都提到，应选C。

36–40 IN ANY ORDER A C F G J 36–40题要求选出在IELTS考试中"必须"要做的事情。也就是原文中的the most important thing，考生要注意听此后的内容。答案比较密集，如果不能及时在选项中寻找配对，要快速记录核心词，原文依次为format, asked or tested, test papers, speaking practice, start as early as possible，分别对应A、C、F、G、J项。

READING

READING PASSAGE 1

体　裁　说明文
题　材　生态环境
主　题　关于在亚马逊雨林燃起大火的一项新试验
题　型　摘要填空题、选择题

Questions 1–8

题型 摘要填空题(Summary Completion)

注意 利用关键词语与所给阅读文章的相关句子进行匹配。如果在填空题中所需填入的词为名词，要确定用其单数还是复数形式；如果所需填入的词为动词，要查看其动词的主语，根据主语来确定动词的形式。要确定填空所需单词在句中的作用，是肯定还是否定的。连接词通常会决定词意的性质。

1	关键词	landscape shift from one dominated by trees to one ruled
	原文定位	第二段第二句The first is: Will tropical forests survive the increasing occurrence of wildfires as the climate changes and people move in, or will the landscape shift from one ruled by trees to one dominated by grassland?
	题解	答案grassland　原文中trees对应的动词是ruled（由……统治），grassland（草原）对应的动词是dominated（由……控制），题干只不过是把两个动词互换了，故此空应填入grassland（草原）。

2	关键词	calculate, released into the environment
	原文定位	第二段末句The second is: How much carbon do such wildfires release into the atmosphere?
	题解	答案carbon　整个活动试图解释的第二个问题是：这样的山火会释放多少碳进入大气？题干中的the quantity（数量）和environment（环境）分别与原文how much（多少）和atmosphere（大气）相对应，故本题应填入carbon。
3	关键词	twice, between 1998 and 2005
	原文定位	第三段第二、三句During the droughts of 1997 and 1998...39,000 square kilometres of Amazonian forest were burned by such fires. That is twice the area deliberately cut down in Brazil each year between 1988 and 2005.
	题解	答案wildfires　关键词twice（两次）和between 1998 and 2005（在1998到2005年之间）都是原文重现，题干中的annually（每年）与原文each year（每一年）是同义替换。厄尔尼诺现象引起的干旱使亚马逊森林中3.9万平方千米的植被被烧为灰烬，是1988年到2005年巴西境内人为砍伐总面积的两倍，故本题的答案为wildfires。
4	关键词	through the loss of timber
	原文定位	第三段末句Similar fires occurred all over South-East Asia and Latin America, causing $19 billion–24 billion of damage through loss of timber, destruction of property and the effect of the smoke on human health.
	题解	答案property　题干是将原文destruction of property（财产的破坏）改写为主谓结构，将名词destruction改用动词形式，作谓语，而名词property作主语，故答案为property。
5	关键词	threatened
	原文定位	第三段末句Similar fires occurred all over South-East Asia and Latin America, causing $19 billion–24 billion of damage through loss of timber, destruction of property and the effect of the smoke on human health.
	题解	答案human health　此题承接上一题而来，也是将原文的名词短语the effect of the smoke on human health（烟雾对人类健康的影响）进行了改写，故此空应填入human health。
6	关键词	fires spread hot and fast
	原文定位	第四段第二句Temperate-forest fires burn hot and fast, and sometimes all the way up to the crown of a tree.
	题解	答案temperate-forest　题干中的spread（扩散）与原文burn（燃烧）相对应，fires...hot and fast（大火……灼热而迅速）是原文重现，可以直接判定此内容之前的名词temperate-forest就是答案。

7	关键词	humid
	原文定位	第四段第三句Tropical forest is wetter and usually supports only knee-high fires that spread slowly through the understory.
	题解	答案tropical forest　判定本题需填名词，再根据关键词humid（潮湿的）进行定位，与原文wetter（潮湿的）对应，所以wetter所属句子的主语即为答案。
8	关键词	fires
	原文定位	第四段第三句Tropical forest is wetter and usually supports only knee-high fires that spread slowly through the understory.
	题解	答案knee-high　本题需填形容fires的词，与原文比较，原文supports...fires（使大火不会熄灭）中间的形容词knee-high（高及膝盖的）就是答案。

Questions 9–11

题型　选择题(Multiple Choice)

注意　此种题型更侧重于对文章的理解，而非强调语法、词法的运用。本题一般按所给问题按顺序答题，同时要在问句中找出关键词语。

9-11	关键词	carbon dioxide, large-scale environmental change, degrade the tropical forests
	原文定位	第五段首句、第二句Tropical fires are, nevertheless, a significant source of carbon dioxide. And their increasing frequency is an important part of the degradation of the Amazon forest—and could be an indicator of large-scale environmental change.
	题解	答案IN ANY ORDER B C E　第五段首句提及热带树林的山火仍然是二氧化碳的一大来源，也就是选项B所说的山火导致二氧化碳增加这一说法是正确的。选项C就是原文an indicator of large-scale environmental change（重大环境变化的一个指标）的重现，C项中reveal（揭示）与原文中be an indicator of（……的指标）相对应。选项E中的degrade与原文中degradation是同根词，E项就是原文the degradation of the Amazon forest（亚马逊雨林的退化）的重现，故E项也正确。

Questions 12 and 13

题型　选择题(Multiple Choice)

注意　选择题的四个选项的意思通常差别较大，为考生排除选项设置了障碍。选项中有时会出现比较晦涩难懂的词和短语，增加了考生理解选项的困难。正确答案多为原文的同义替换。考生不仅要理解原文的意思，还要能快速识别选项中对原文同义替换的内容。

12	关键词	scientists, get
	原文定位	倒数第四段第四、五句Grasses, by contrast, are doing well. So far, they have invaded as far as 200 metres from the edge of the forest.
	题解	答案B　原文提到许多大树都可以历经多次大火幸存下来，但一些小的树种就没那么幸运了，这只是说小树比大树脆弱，并没有说小树就容易燃烧，故选项A错；原文提到科学家发现树苗物种只有一半数量留存了下来，但与此相反，草地却表现良好，它们已经从树林的边缘向外蔓生了200米之远。这说明草更容易适应山火。故选项B正确。选项C、D在原文中没有提及。

13	关键词	the attitudes of landowners, standing forests
	原文定位	倒数第二段末句But talk of financial incentives for forest-owners to preserve their trees is in the air, and a deal may be struck at the United Nations climate-change meeting being held in Copenhagen in December.
	题解	答案D 原文提到土地所有者都是为了盈利的，他们不想保护standing forests（现存的雨林），故A项错；原文提及了standing forest is of little commercial value（现存的雨林几乎没有商业价值），但这不是土地所有者认为的，这是事实，故B项错；C项原文没有提及；原文提到financial incentives for forest-owners to preserve their trees（对热带雨林所有者的金融激励促使人们保护他们的树木）在坊间流传，这说明土地所有者现在缺乏保护树木的财政鼓励措施。

READING PASSAGE 2

体　裁　　议论文
题　材　　食品保健
主　题　　功能性食品日趋流行
题　型　　判断题、配对题

Questions 14–19

题型 判断题(Identifying Writer's Views/Claims)

注意 判断题为若干陈述句，要求根据原文所给的信息，判断每个陈述句是对 (YES)、错 (NO)，还是未提及 (NOT GIVEN)。若题目为原文某句话的改写，那么题目与原文有明显对应信息。若对应信息较多，那么题目中真正设置的考点则要通过题目和原文的对比来判断。

14	关键词	over the past decade, customers, functional foods
	原文定位	首段首句、第二句Over the past decade...consumers in wealthier markets worldwide have demanded foods with minimal processing, in a state as close as possible to their natural one...
	题解	答案NO 在过去的几十年中，consumers（消费者）需要的食品是minimal processing（只需最小限度的加工），尽可能保持食物的自然状态。而消费者喜欢functional foods（功能性食物）是现在的事，时间不对。
15	关键词	multifunctional food giants, healthier or more nutritious
	原文定位	首段末句Ironically, this success is now prompting multinational food giants to accelerate investments in "functional" foods that are intentionally modified to make them healthier or more nutritious.
	题解	答案YES 题目是原文multinational food giants...are intentionally modified to make them healthier or more nutritious（多功能食品被有目的地改变，从而变得更健康或更有营养）的改写。

16	关键词	absorption of cholesterol, adding chemicals
	原文定位	第二段第四句Another is the addition of chemicals called sterols to margarines to impede the absorption of cholesterol.
	题解	答案NO 原文中的the addition of chemicals（化学剂的添加）与题干中adding chemicals（添加化学剂）是同义替换；the absorption of cholesterol（胆固醇的吸收）是原文替换，但对应的动词是impede（阻碍），而题干用的动词是improve（促进），意思相反，故本题错误。
17	关键词	on average, Japanese, spend, functional foods
	原文定位	第三段倒数第二句On average, the Japanese spend twice as much per person on functional foods as Americans and nearly three times as much as Europeans.
	题解	答案NOT GIVEN 原文提到的是日本人在functional foods（功能性食物）上花费的金钱是Americans（美国人）的两倍，是Europeans（欧洲人）的三倍，但并没有提及花费在functional foods（功能性食物）的金钱是最长的。
18	关键词	not all customers, happy
	原文定位	第五段首句All this sounds impressive, but there are two factors that could yet trip things up: consumer skepticism and regulatory disapproval.
	题解	答案YES 注意but后的内容，有的consumer（消费者）对functional foods（功能性食物）是持怀疑态度的，故本题正确。
19	关键词	consumers and regulators
	原文定位	末段末句If the only real function behind such labels is to bolster profits, consumers and regulators will eventually see through the hype.
	题解	答案NOT GIVEN 原文提到如果这样的标签背后唯一真正的功能是增加利润，那么consumers（消费者）和regulators（监管部门）最终会看穿广告宣传。题目中说的是：食品巨头能为其食品提供令人信服的医学证据时，消费者和监管部门才会相信宣传的内容。原文和题目的说法无明确关联，所以答案是NOT GIVEN。

Questions 20–25

题型 配对题(Matching Features)

注意 配对题是对考生的英语水平要求比较高的一类题目。此题平均花费时间要比一般的题目要长，所以要注意解题顺序，可以把配对题型放在最后做。

20	关键词	compensate, unhappy customers
	原文定位	第五段末句On September 18th the firm settled that case, admitting no wrongdoing but agreeing to set up a $35m fund to reimburse unhappy yogurt-eaters.
	题解	答案A 根据题干的关键词compensate定位到第五段末句，与原文中reimburse（偿还，赔偿）对应，原文中yogurt-eaters（吃酸奶酪的人）被题干中的customers（顾客）替换，agrees与原文中agreeing是同根词，此句的前一句的主语Danone就是答案。

Test 5

21	关键词	targets, Asian market
	原文定位	第三段末句When Coca-Cola wanted to experiment with a supposedly healthy green-tea-flavoured drink, it targeted young Japanese women first.
	题解	答案C　原文中的young Japanese women（日本的年轻女士）与题干中的Asian market（亚洲市场）相对应，本句的主语为Coca-Cola（可口可乐），故答案为C。
22	关键词	shorter history, yogurt, Japanese
	原文定位	第三段第六句Long before Activia came Yakult, a bioactive yogurt-like drink from Japan that is now available worldwide.
	题解	答案B　在Activia（达能碧悠）进入Yakult（益力多）很久以前，来自日本的生物活性yogurt（酸奶酪）饮料就已经有了，而且现在在全球范围内都可以见到。也就是题干所说的：Activia制作酸奶的历史比一些日本的竞争对手短。
23	关键词	adds some fiber, cater for customers
	原文定位	第四段第二句Firms selling everything...to artificial sweeteners (Splenda now comes with added fiber) are rushing to add miracle ingredients to their wares in the hope that the supposed benefits will entice customers.
	题解	答案D　注意括号里的内容，与题干一致。题干中的cater for（迎合）与原文中的entice（诱使）相对应；adds（增加），fiber（纤维），customers（顾客）均为原文重现。故本题题干中的it指代的就是括号句子的主语Splenda（三氯蔗糖）。
24	关键词	functional foods, a long history
	原文定位	第三段首句、第二句Functional foods are nothing new, observes Bernard Hours of Danone. He says that his firm, a French dairy giant, was selling yogurt in pharmacies in Barcelona as long ago as 1919.
	题解	答案A　Danone认为functional foods（功能性食物）并不是现在才有的，接着提到他的公司早在1919就有过这样的例子，也就是功能食品有很长的历史了。
25	关键词	common labeling, advertising standards
	原文定位	末段第三句More recently, the decision by the Smart Choices coalition to endorse sugary cereals such as Froot Loops has attracted criticism.
	题解	答案E　注意原文中endorse（认可，赞同）一词，也就是题干中agrees的同义词，题干中的functional foods对应原文中的sugary cereals such as Froot Loops，因此题干中的it指代的是Smart Choices。

READING PASSAGE 3

体　裁　议论文
题　材　社会生活
主　题　关于自尊的研究
题　型　配对题、摘要填空题、判断题

Questions 26–30

题型 配对题(Matching Information)

注意 配对题考查考生对细节信息的把握，这种题目难度不等，其中段落配信息题是雅思阅读考试所有类型题目中最难的一种，需要对各个段落有全面的把握。

26	关键词	varied aspects of self-esteem
	原文定位	B段第二句While some researchers have been particularly concerned with understanding the nuances of the self-esteem construct, others have focused on the adaptive and self-protective functions of self-esteem.
	题解	**答案B** 题干的关键词是varied aspects（各个方面），这与原文研究者研究自尊的nuances（细微差别），adaptive（适应的），self-protective functions（自我保护的功能）对应，故答案为B。
27	关键词	problematic drink behaviours
	原文定位	C段首句Low self-esteem is the universal common denominator among literally all people suffering from addictions to any and all mind altering substances such as alcohol—not genes.
	题解	**答案C** 定位句提到low self-esteem（自卑）与alcohol（酒精），addictions（成瘾）的关系。
28	关键词	violence, quality of self-esteem
	原文定位	E段末句And neither high nor low self-esteem is a direct cause of violence.
	题解	**答案E** 根据关键词violence（暴力）定位E段末句，这里提到了自尊心强和自卑都不是导致暴力的原因，这与本题题目中的描述一致。注意否定词neither（两个都不）。
29	关键词	scientists, results
	原文定位	D段第二句This conclusion is also shared by Andrew Keegan (1987), who maintains that low self-esteem either causes or contributes to neurosis, anxiety, defensiveness, and ultimately alcohol and drug abuse.
	题解	**答案D** D段提到Candito和Andrew Keegan两个专家的名字，与题干中scientists（科学家）对应；原文this conclusion（这个结论）指代前文Candito的研究结果，题干中的agreed with each other（彼此看法一致）与原文中shared（分享）对应；而且low self-esteem（自卑）为该段落高频词，故本题的答案为D。

30	关键词	inventions of methods, stimulated, increase the self-esteem
	原文定位	G段第三句Since then, there has been a nationwide proliferation of techniques to raise self-esteem—particularly in schools—and a proliferation of books marketed to people helping themselves.
	题解	答案G 定位句提到在全国范围内出现提高自尊的方法——特别是在学校——和大量上市的书籍，供人们自助使用。题干中methods（方法）与原文techniques（技术）是同义替换；题干中increase the self-esteem（增加自尊）与raise self-esteem（提高自尊）对应。

Questions 31–35

题型 摘要填空题(Summary Completion)

注意 该类题目是一小段文字，是原文或原文中的几个段落主要内容的缩写或改写。摘要中有几个空白部分要求考生填空。按照范围，摘要可分为两种：全文摘要和部分段落摘要。本题是部分段落摘要，其摘要信息来自原文某几个连续的段落，题目空格的数目较少。

31	关键词	broader sense
	原文定位	A段第二句While the construct is most often used to refer to a global sense of self-worth, narrower concepts such as self-confidence or body-esteem are used to imply a sense of self-esteem in more specific domains.
	题解	答案narrower 定位句提到global sense（总体意义），与题干中的broader sense（更广泛的意义）对应，接着说到narrower concepts（更狭义的概念），故此处填narrower。
32	关键词	on the other hand, people themselves
	原文定位	A段末句It is also widely assumed that self-esteem functions as a trait, that is, it is stable across time within individuals.
	题解	答案trait 题干中on the other hand重现于原文的also, people themselves对应于原文的self-esteem functions（自尊的作用），空格内需要填写一个单数名词，故答案为trait（品质）。
33	关键词	relationship, different
	原文定位	B段第三句Self-esteem has been related both to socioeconomic status and to various aspects of health and health-related behaviours, as has a related construct, self-efficacy.
	题解	答案health 题干中的different domains（不同的领域）是原句中various aspects of health（健康的各个方面）的重现，此处需填名词，故答案为health。
34	关键词	problematic behaviours, originated from
	原文定位	D段首句Candito comes to the conclusion that low self-esteem is the underlying origin of all problematic behaviours, and the true disease that plagues the world, resulting in alcohol abuse, drug abuse...
	题解	答案low self-esteem 题干中的most problematic behaviours originated from...（大多数问题行为是源于……）是对D段首句...is the underlying origin of all problematic behaviours（……是所有行为问题的起源）部分的改写。

35	关键词	brought about kinds of results positively
	原文定位	E段首句However, many of the positive outcomes attributed to high self-esteem are not substantiated by research...objective research studies on self-esteem at the invitation of the American Psychological Society.
	题解	答案high self-esteem brought about（引起）与原文中的attributed to（带来）形成重现关系，题干中的brought about kinds of results positively（积极地带来各种结果）与原文many of the positive outcomes attributed to...（许多积极结果归因于……）相对应，故本题答案就是attributed to（归因于……）后面的短语high self-esteem（自尊）。

Questions 36–40

题型 判断题(Identifying Information)

注意 题目是若干个陈述句，要求根据原文所给的信息，判断每个陈述句是对、错还是未提及。TRUE：题干和原文一致；FALSE：题干和原文矛盾，不能同时成立；NOT GIVEN：题干不能确定，有可能对，有可能错。

36	关键词	18 year olds, used drugs
	原文定位	C段第五句Studies have found that 18 year olds who used drugs frequently were using them as early as age seven, already more psychologically troubled than their peers.
	题解	答案NOT GIVEN 原文提到：研究发现18岁的长期吸毒者早在7岁时就开始吸毒了，他们比同龄人遭受着更多的心理问题的困扰，而题目说的是18岁使用毒品的人比其同龄人更容易心理消沉。而此信息在原文中未被提及。
37	关键词	unlikely, depression, under some conditions
	原文定位	F段第二句High self-esteem has a strong relationship to happiness and low self-esteem is more likely than high to lead to depression under some circumstances.
	题解	答案TRUE 原文high self-esteem（自尊心强）与happiness（高兴）是积极语义，而low self-esteem（自卑）会导致depression（沮丧），这与题干high self-esteem在某些情形下更不容易引起depression是一致的。故本题正确。
38	关键词	good qualities
	原文定位	F段第六句Those in the latter are characterised as narcissistic, defensive or conceited individuals.
	题解	答案FALSE 由定位句可知，属于第一类的人接受自己的好品质，而属于第二类的人却有自恋、自卫、自欺的性格特点，因此不是两类都有好品质。
39	关键词	campaign, California
	原文定位	G段首句The self-esteem movement began in California during the 1980s with the idea that many of society's problems were related to low self-esteem.
	题解	答案FALSE G段movement（运动）与题干中的campaign（活动）对应；started（起始）与题干中的began（开始）是同义替换；California（加利福尼亚州）是原文重现；但是考生要注意原文的时间为1980s，与题目中的1996年明显存在偷换概念。

Test 5

40	关键词	Krueger, would have, cure all kinds of difficulties
	原文定位	G段末句Yet, "...the high hopes of the self-esteem movement have not been realised, and customers of the self-help industry should not look to heightened self-esteem as a panacea," said Krueger.
	题解	答案TRUE 克鲁格的态度非常明显，self-esteem（自尊）没有达到可以当万灵药的高度。题目中用了虚拟语气，表示克鲁格认为self-esteem的高度是"应该达到而没有达到的"。

WRITING

WRITING TASK 1

名师解读

本题为图表作文中的表格题型。考生需要有"概括"性的句子，概括的是main features。通常来讲，与数字有关的特性有两项。第一项：随时间变化的数字就是趋势；第二项：有不同对象的数字就是比较。换句话讲，只要把题目中的这些特性概括出来，文章的最主要内容就完成了。接下来，就是用具体的数字作为例子来强调这种特性是存在的。

Make comparisons要求写作中要有切入点，其他的对象都要和它进行比较（或者相同，或者不同）。表格题的解题思路大致可以分为三步：

①先分类（横向，纵向，横竖交替）②挑出极值（最大值与最小值）③挑选剩余数值（倍数关系，两个数值，变化明显的数值）

在明确这些任务后，关于这种文章的语言问题应该注意的是：写简单而正确的句子，此外注意时态；用简单而词性正确的单词，此外注意避免重复。

高分范文

The table compares two sets of the **statistics** related to marriage in Australia in a 40-year period from 1970 to 2010. One of the two sets concerned whether the marriage bond was **religious** or civil; while the other involved the average age of the bride and the bridegroom.

Generally speaking, the number of religious marriage was always greater than that of the civil marriage during the first 3 decades, with the exception in the year 2010, when the latter exceeded the former by 6,000. **Specifically**, religious marriage rose from 22,000 in 1970. It doubled in 1980 and continued its gradually **ascending** trend across the next decade, standing at its peak of 50,000 in 1990. Then, it turned to decrease sharply by 18,000 in 2000 and staged a slight recovery to 34,000 in 2010.

However, civil marriage experienced an upward trend through all the years. It climbed from 8,000 in 1970 to 12,000 in 1980 and 16,000 in 1990, respectively. Till the year 1990, a doubling of the number can be found in 2000 to 30,000. The last decade witnessed another rise of 10,000 in this number.

Turning to the average ages of each gender in the marriage, the female part showed a generally upward trend from 21 in 1970 to 30 in 2010. After reaching 25 in 1980, the age declined to 23 in 1990 and kept increasing till 2010. The male part, however, showed a **consecutive** rise by 2 years old for each decade from 24 in 1970 to 32 in 2010.

To sum up, men are found to be older than women to step into the wedlock in all those five years. (281 words)

Test 5

WRITING TASK 2

文章结构

正反观点辩论+立场+理由+总结

viewpoint+standpoint+reason 1+reason 2+conclusion
第一段：背景句+引出现象+表明立场
第二段：正方观点+理由+自己立场
第三段：反方观点+理由+自己立场
第四段：总结立场

思路点拨

步骤一：审题（<3分钟）

Some people believe that personal happiness is directly related to economic success. Others believe there are other factors. What do you think?

通读题目，了解大意，判断题型。

本题的题型为论说型的作文。题目的大意为：一些人认为个人幸福指数与经济上的成功直接相关。其他人认为还有其他的因素。你怎么认为?

→再读题目，辨别关键词，区分主题词和限定词，推测考官的出题意图。

主题词：personal happiness, economic success

限定词：do you think

步骤二：列大纲（<3分钟）

英文提纲	Intro: the pursuit of happiness→What is happiness?→related to one's economic success?→financial success leads to happiness directly?→economic success, only prerequisite Pros: happiness→economic success, not completely→imagine an easy and simple life→able to afford a house→some people, feel happy basic demands→However, these people still need to be successful materialistically Cons: success in economy may not necessarily→money doesn't get you everything →the sacrifice of time, health and love→tasting loneliness alone, broken heart Conclusion: economic success, only one of the key factors→both spiritually and materially satisfied
中文提纲	引出话题：追求幸福→幸福是什么?→与经济成功有关吗?→经济成功直接与幸福度相关?→经济成功仅是先决条件 正方观点：幸福度→经济成功，不完全→想象简单的生活→能够负担得起房子等东西→有些人，感觉幸福，基本需求→然而，这些人仍然需要成功的物质生活 反方观点：经济成功可能不是必须的→钱不能买来一切→牺牲了时间、健康和爱→独尝寂寞，破碎的心 总结：经济成功，只是关键因素中的一个→需要精神和物质都能得到满足

高分范文

The pursuit of happiness has long been the dream of generations of human beings. They have always been puzzled by the essence of happiness. What is happiness? Is it closely related to one's economic success? Will one's financial success lead to happiness directly? Personally, I do not agree that one's economic success is the only prerequisite of one's happiness in life.

One's **materialistic** happiness is dependant on one's economic success, though not completely. Without a strong and steady economic background, one could never imagine an easy and simple life, let alone an affluent and luxurious one. If you are not able to afford a house, a car, or even a book, anybody would be **horrified** at the mere mention of this kind of life. **Definitely**, some people will feel happy right away if their basic demands for life are satisfied. However, we have to admit that these people still need to be successful materialistically to some degree.

On the other hand, one's success in economy may not necessarily lead to one's **spiritual** happiness. As we all know, money does not get you everything and some even say that money is the root of all evils. One's financial success may be built on the **sacrifice** of time, health and love, which are the three most essential elements of spiritual happiness. None of us are new to this picture: a successful businessman tasting loneliness alone with a broken heart.

In my point of view, one's economic success is only one of the key factors of happiness, but never the only one. To be happy, one needs to be both spiritually and materially satisfied to some extent. (274 words)

SPEAKING

名师解读

Part 1的题目属于媒体类。媒体在现代社会的地位是无可取代的。日常生活中考生接触和谈论最多的有电视、电影、书本、报刊、杂志和广播。这些媒介都起着举足轻重的作用，因此也成了雅思口语考试中必考的一个话题类别。

Part 2的话题为旅行。考生要注意句子前后的衔接性和词汇的多样性，所以要使用恰当丰富的连接词进行表述，以增强句子之间的紧密性。

Part 3是口语考试中最难的一部分，题目的性质已经超越了日常生活层面，进入到人的深层思维体系之中。它着重的是：world views（世界观）, belief systems（信仰体系）, values（价值观）, attitudes（态度）。

高分示例

PART 1

Media

- How do you get the latest news?

I get the latest news both on my phone and **laptop**, but sometimes I get the news from the newspaper. Also, every now and then, I will hear the radio or an **announcement** on the subway.

- Do many people in your country listen to the radio?

I do not know of the exact figure, but I would say a fair amount of the older generation would listen to the radio while they work or are having drinks with friends.

- Do you like to read newspapers?

I do enjoy reading the newspaper, but sometimes it gets too much to carry around with me everywhere. That's why I usually get the news on my phone.

PART 2

One day I plan to visit Japan. It is close to China, but still a completely different place. Japan is an island that has many natural **disasters**.

We learnt a little about Japan in school, but I really started learning after watching Anime. I can speak a few words in Japanese and know lots of different foods there.

When I get to Japan, I would like to visit Osaka, which is also the home of the Samurai. In Tokyo, I want to take a tour of Tokyo University and go to some of the comic convertions that take place there.

I've wanted to go to Japan to see the differences and **similarities** between our two cultures and maybe try to trace some common ancestors. Many foreigners get confused between Chinese and Japanese people so it would be interesting to see what differences we do have up close.

PART 3

Tourism

- Why do you think people want to visit other countries?

I think people like to visit other countries to experience cultures that are not their own. People also like to enjoy weather that is not their own, for example, people in the UK like to travel to warm places because their country is always cold, while those from warmer countries like to go to places that are colder so they can see things like snow.

- What makes some places very attractive to tourists?

Many different things **appeal** to tourists, from warm beaches to rich historical places. Most like to go to places that are beautiful while others like to explore the **underbelly** and the real places the locals would enjoy.

- Will international tourism increase or decrease in the future? Why?

I think it depends on the country and how its people interact with tourists. If tourists do not enjoy a country or have bad experiences there, it is likely they will tell friends who will spread the world. Then the tourism of that country might decrease.

The effects of tourism

- How can tourism benefit local people and places?

Tourism is a great way of boosting the economy of a country and its people. What some locals do not understand is that tourists bring lots of income to their areas, and more tourists usually means more money for them and their families.

- Are there any drawbacks of tourism?

There can be some **drawbacks** of tourism, such as over-running certain areas with so many tourists that it loses its appeal. Also, because areas with large tourist groups tend to raise their prices, the local populations tend to avoid the areas, not being able to see their own **landmarks**.

- Does tourism help to promote international understanding? Why/Why not?

Yes, I think that tourism does help to promote international understanding because once someone has actually been to a different country and seen how they live, they not only tend to appreciate their own country upon return, but have a better understanding of the people from the country they visited.

- How reliable is tourism as an industry?

Tourism as a whole **fluctuates** often, and is dependent on seasons and governments. Things change from year to year, even month to month and it causes **upheaval** amongst the locals and tourists alike.

重点词汇

LISTENING

forthcoming	[ˌfɔːθ'kʌmɪŋ]	*adj.*	即将来临的
facility	[fə'sɪləti]	*n.*	设施；设备
registration	[ˌredʒɪ'streɪʃn]	*n.*	登记；注册；挂号
proceeding	[prə'siːdɪŋ]	*n.*	进行；程序；诉讼；事项
administrative	[əd'mɪnɪstrətɪv]	*adj.*	管理的；行政的
inconvenience	[ˌɪnkən'viːnɪəns]	*n.*	不便；麻烦
reassure	[ˌriːə'ʃʊə]	*v.*	安心，消除疑虑
resume	[rɪ'zjuːm]	*v.*	重新开始；继续
vacancy	['veɪkənsi]	*n.*	空缺；空位
available	[ə'veɪləbl]	*adj.*	可得的，可利用的；有效的
suitable	['suːtəbl]	*adj.*	适当的，合适的
facility	[fə'sɪləti]	*n.*	设施，设备
accommodation	[əˌkɒmə'deɪʃn]	*n.*	住处，膳宿；调节
receipt	[rɪ'siːt]	*n.*	收据；收入
strictly	['strɪktli]	*adv.*	完全地；严格地
entertainment	[ˌentə'teɪnmənt]	*n.*	娱乐，消遣；款待
refreshment	[rɪ'freʃmənt]	*n.*	点心；起提神作用的东西
unfortunately	[ʌn'fɔːtʃənətli]	*adv.*	不幸地
definitely	['defɪnətli]	*adv.*	当然；清楚地
voucher	['vaʊtʃə]	*n.*	代金；收据；证人
reception	[rɪ'sepʃn]	*n.*	接待；接收；招待会
Braille	[breɪl]	*n.*	布莱叶（法国盲人教育家）；盲人用点字法
informal	[ɪn'fɔːml]	*adj.*	非正式的；不拘礼节的
institute	['ɪnstɪtjuːt]	*n.*	学会；学院
come up with			提出；想出；赶上
embossed	[ɪm'bɒsd]	*adj.*	上面有浮雕图案的
cumbersome	['kʌmbəsəm]	*adj.*	笨重的；难处理的
enterprising	['entəpraɪzɪŋ]	*adj.*	有事业心的；有进取心的
night writing			夜读
alphabet	['ælfəbet]	*n.*	字母表，字母系统
combination	[ˌkɒmbɪ'neɪʃn]	*n.*	结合；组合；联合
contraction	[kən'trækʃn]	*n.*	收缩，紧缩
adaptation	[ˌædæp'teɪʃn]	*n.*	适应；改编
backwards	['bækwədz]	*adv.*	倒；向后；逆
upwards	['ʌpwədz]	*adv.*	向上；在上部；向上游
notation	[nəʊ'teɪʃn]	*n.*	符号；乐谱
competency	['kɒmpɪtənsi]	*n.*	能力；资格

READING

prompt	[prɒmpt]	*v.*	促进；引起
deliberately	[dɪ'lɪbərɪtli]	*adv.*	故意地
timber	['tɪmbə]	*n.*	木材
degradation	[degrə'deɪʃən]	*n.*	下降
humidity	[hjuː'mɪdɪti]	*n.*	潮湿
inhale	[ɪn'heɪl]	*v.*	吸入

preserve	[prɪ'zɜːv]	*v.*	保护
in the air			悬而未决
intriguingly	[ɪn'triːgɪŋli]	*adv.*	令人感兴趣地
ironically	[aɪ'rɒnɪkli]	*adv.*	讽刺性地
nutritious	[njuː'trɪʃəs]	*adj.*	有营养的
cholesterol	[kə'lestərəʊl]	*n.*	胆固醇
sweetener	['swiːtnə]	*n.*	甜味剂
coalition	[ˌkəʊə'lɪʃən]	*n.*	同盟
reimburse	[ˌriːɪm'bɜːs]	*v.*	补偿
hype	[haɪp]	*n.*	天花乱坠的广告
integrity	[ɪn'tegrəti]	*n.*	正直，诚实
hamper	['hæmpə]	*v.*	妨碍，束缚
egotism	['egəʊɪzəm]	*n.*	自大
arrogance	['ærəgəns]	*n.*	傲慢，自大，自负
conceit	[kən'siːt]	*n.*	高傲，骄傲自大
narcissism	['nɑːsɪsɪzəm]	*n.*	自我陶醉，自恋
superiority	[suːˌpɪərɪ'ɒrəti]	*n.*	优越性，优势
trait	[treɪt]	*n.*	特点，特征
pseudo	['suːdəʊ]	*adj.*	假的，虚伪的；冒充的
contempt	[kən'tempt]	*n.*	藐视
component	[kəm'pəʊnənt]	*n.*	成分，部件，元件
rehabilitation	['riːhəˌbɪlɪ'teɪʃən]	*n.*	康复，修复；复兴
recidivism	[rɪ'sɪdɪvɪzəm]	*n.*	再犯，累犯
psychodynamic	[psaɪkəʊdaɪ'næmɪk]	*adj.*	心理动力的，精神动力的
cognitive	['kɒgnətɪv]	*adj.*	认知能力的
dimension	[daɪ'menʃn]	*n.*	尺寸，度量
discrepancy	[dɪs'krepənsi]	*n.*	差异，不一致之处
appraisal	[ə'preɪzl]	*n.*	估计，评价
manifest	['mænɪfest]	*v.*	清楚表示；显露
assertive	[ə'sɜːtɪv]	*adj.*	断言的，肯定的
resilience	[rɪ'zɪlɪəns]	*n.*	弹力；适应力
fluctuate	['flʌktʃʊeɪt]	*v.*	波动，起伏
disposition	[ˌdɪspə'zɪʃn]	*n.*	气质；天性；性格；性情
premise	['premɪs]	*n.*	前提，假定
commitment	[kə'mɪtmənt]	*n.*	承诺，保证
conviction	[kən'vɪkʃn]	*n.*	深信，坚信
pertain to			有关
authentic	[ɔː'θentɪk]	*adj.*	真的，真正的
conceited	[kən'siːtɪd]	*adj.*	自负的，自高自大的
brag	[bræg]	*v.*	吹牛
bully	['bʊli]	*v.*	恐吓
stem from			来自，起源于
heap	[hiːp]	*n.*	大量，许多
booster	['buːstə]	*n.*	辅助剂
inflate	[ɪn'fleɪt]	*v.*	膨胀
appraisal	[ə'preɪzl]	*n.*	估计，估量
adversity	[əd'vɜːsəti]	*n.*	逆境，窘境
engender	[ɪn'dʒendə]	*v.*	产生，造成
be equivalent to			相等，相当

WRITING

statistic	[stə'tɪstɪk]	*n.*	统计数值
religious	[rɪ'lɪdʒəs]	*adj.*	宗教的；虔诚的；严谨的
specifically	[spə'sɪfɪkli]	*adv.*	特别地；明确地
ascend	[ə'send]	*v.*	上升；登高；追溯
consecutive	[kən'sekjətɪv]	*adj.*	连贯的；连续不断的
materialistic	[məˌtɪərɪə'lɪstɪk]	*adj.*	唯物主义的；唯物论的，物质主义的
horrified	['hɒrɪfaɪd]	*adj.*	恐惧的；惊骇的；使极度厌恶的
definitely	['defɪnətli]	*adv.*	清楚地，当然；明确地，肯定地
spiritual	['spɪrɪtʃʊəl]	*adj.*	精神的，心灵的
sacrifice	['sækrɪfaɪs]	*n.*	牺牲；祭品；供奉

SPEAKING

laptop	['læptɒp]	*n.*	膝上型轻便电脑，笔记本电脑
announcement	[ə'naʊnsmənt]	*n.*	公告；宣告；通告
disaster	[dɪ'zɑːstə]	*n.*	灾难，灾祸；不幸
similarity	[ˌsɪmə'lærəti]	*n.*	类似；相似点
appeal	[ə'piːl]	*v.*	呼吁，恳求；上诉；诉诸
underbelly	['ʌndəbeli]	*n.*	下腹部；薄弱部分
drawback	['drɔːbæk]	*n.*	缺点，不利条件；退税
heighten	['haɪtn]	*v.*	提高；增高；加强
landmark	['lændmɑːk]	*n.*	地标；界标；里程碑
fluctuate	['flʌktʃʊeɪt]	*v.*	波动；涨落；动摇
upheaval	[ʌp'hiːvl]	*n.*	剧变；隆起；举起

听力原文

SECTION 1

(WOMAN 1=W1; WOMAN 2=W2; MAN=M; CATHERINE=C)

W1: University. Good morning.

M: Oh, good morning. Can you put me through to the School of Architecture, please?

W1: Certainly.

W2: School of Architecture. Professor Catherine's office.

M: Oh! Good morning. I was wondering if you could give some information about the forthcoming Architecture 21 Conference? Dates, enrollment procedures, costs...that sort of thing?

W2: Certainly.

M: When exactly is the conference?

W2: Well, the conference runs for three days from the Q1 18th to the 20th of October.

M: 18th to 20th of October...oh good. I'll still be here then and um...where exactly is it being held? Is it at the university as in previous years?

W2: No, it's actually being held at the Q2 Pacific Hotel—we've rather outgrown the university conference facilities so we've opted for this new venue.

M: Right—Paradise Hotel.

W2: No...Pacific Hotel.

M: Oh, right. And presumably we can get accommodation at the hotel?

W2: Yes, but you'll need to contact them direct to arrange that. I'll give you the number for hotel reservations. Have you got a pen ready?

M: Yeah, go ahead.

W2: It's area code Q3 07 and then nine triple three double two double three.

M: OK. And what's the registration fee?

W2: Individual fees are $300 for the 3 days, or $120 a day if you only want to attend for one day.

M: Are there any student concessions?

W2: Oh, sure. There's a 50% concession for students, and that's $150 for the three days, or Q4 $60 a day.

M: And am I too late to give a talk?

W2: Oh, I'm pretty sure you've missed the deadline for that.

M: Oh, really! But I've only just arrived here—is there any way I could have a paper accepted?

W2: Well, you need to talk to Q5 Professor Catherine. She's the person organising the conference this year. I can put you through, if you like.

M: Oh, yes please. That'd be great. Oh and can I just check the spelling of her name? Is that C-A-T-H-E-R-I-N-E?

W2: Yes, that's correct.

C: Professor Catherine speaking.

M: Oh, hello. My name is John Helstone. I'm an architecture student at London University. I'm here in Australia for 3 months, looking at energy saving house designs.

C: Right.

M: I'm interested in giving a talk on my research at the conference but I believe I may have missed the deadline.

C: Well, strictly speaking you have. The closing date was Q6 last Friday.

M: Oh, no!

C: But we may be able to include your paper if it fits into our programme...but you'll have to be quick.

M: OK. What do I need to do?

C: Send me an outline of your talk. And make sure you include Q7 an interesting title for the talk. Something to attract the delegates' attention.

M: OK. Interesting title. Right.

C: The outline should be no more than Q8 300 words, though.

M: OK. I should be able to keep it down to 300 words but would 400 be OK?

C: No, not really, because we have to print it in the proceedings and we just don't have the space.

M: Sure! I understand.

C: And also, you can send me a short CV—the usual stuff, name, age, and qualifications. That sort of thing.

M: OK. Include a Q9 brief CV.

C: Actually, you can e-mail it to me. That'd be quicker.

M: Sure. What's your e-mail address?

C: Well the best thing would be to send it to the conference administrative officer. The address is admin—in lower case. You know, in all small letters.

M: Right.

C: So that's Q10 A-D-M-I-N at uniconf, that's U-N-I-C-O-N-F, dot E-D-U dot A-U.

M: OK. I'll do that straight away. Thank you very much. You've been very helpful.

C: OK. Well, we hope to see you in October, then.

SECTION 2

(WOMAN=W; MAN=M)

M: Good morning madam. How can I help you?

W: I'm with my husband and two children, and we've just been informed that our flight to Detroit is cancelled. Your colleague told us to come and talk to you about what we do next.

M: OK...Well first let me apologise for your inconvenience. I'll be able to help you, and I'd like to reassure you that the airline will cover the cost of staying in London for one day. Hopefully you'll be able to resume your journey tomorrow.

W: I hope so too!

M: Now, you said there are four of you...?

W: That's right.

M: I'm just looking at some details on my computer and I see that there are vacancies at two of our partner hotels. The first one's in Q11 central London, that's the Bedford.

W: Oh, that sounds good!

M: The trouble is they only have one room available for tonight that might be suitable, and that's a family room. Could you all go in together?

W: It's possible, but not ideal. My kids are 12 and 14. Does the hotel have any special facilities for children?

M: No it doesn't. But it is situated very near to the Q12 British Museum, and I think your children would like going there. It's very popular with families.

W: OK...And...you said there are two hotels?

M: Yes. The other one is further out. It's in west London, very near this airport in fact. So you wouldn't have far to go and come back. And you could have Q13 twin rooms there; there are two of them available for tonight. No doubles I'm afraid.

W: I don't suppose it has a swimming pool, does it?

M: Let's see...It does actually. And in case you or your husband needs to touch base with the office, it also has a Q14 business centre. So it might suit all of you?

W: Yes. Both hotels have advantages I think. I'll just get a few more details from you and then I'll discuss the options with my husband over a cup of coffee. Is that OK?

M: Fine.

W: Can you tell me how the hotel will be paid for?

M: The airline will give you vouchers to cover the cost of accommodation, your evening meal and your breakfast. We'll also give you some cash—Q15 £50—to take care of any minor expenses. And we don't ask you to account for how you spend that.

W: What about things like taxi fares to and from the airport?

M: Yes, we'll refund those and any other essential expenses, like phone calls to your relatives or workplace. But in these cases you need to obtain Q16 receipts and submit them with your claim.

W: OK...That sounds very fair.

M: But the thing that we don't refund are the costs of things that aren't strictly necessary, like Q17 entertainment, or shopping, or light refreshments...

W: Well I think that's reasonable. We couldn't expect that.

M: Yes. Unfortunately not all of our clients see things like that!

W: Oh dear! And then what about tomorrow? How can we be sure that we'll definitely get a flight tomorrow? Is there a number we can ring to check?

M: Yes, here it is. It's Q18 0800 triple 7121. And that's a free phone number. Please call between 9 and 10am and I'll be able to update you.

W: And can you give me your name please?

M: Yes. It's Philip Q19 Brightwell, that's B-R-I-G-H-T-W-E-double L.

W: Thanks. One more thing, if the worst comes to

the worst, will we be given more vouchers to extend our stay?

M: You will, yes. A Q20 courier will bring them to your hotel and leave them with reception. But I sincerely hope it won't be necessary!

W: Well thanks. I'll just go off and have a chat with my husband and then I'll come back to tell you what we've decided.

M: You're welcome.

SECTION 3

(CHAIRMAN=C; DR MACDAVID=D; STUDENT=S)

C: We're very pleased to welcome to our special interest group today—Dr Cindy Macdavid who is from the City Institute for the Blind. Cindy is going to talk to us about the system of writing for the blind known as Braille. Cindy welcome.

D: Thank you.

C: Now we'd like to keep this meeting pretty informal, and I know Cindy would like to answer any questions whatever members of the group want to ask as we go along. Let's start with an obvious one. What is Braille and where does it get its name from?

D: Well, as you said, Braille is a system of writing used by and for people who cannot see. And it gets its name from the man who invented it, the Frenchman Louis Braille who lived in the early 19th century.

C: Was Louis Braille actually blind himself? I mean if he got the word "Braille" from his own experience.

D: Well...he wasn't born blind, but he lost his sight at the age of three as the result of an accident Q21 in his father's workshop. Louis Braille then went to Paris to the National Institute for Blind Children and that's where he invented his writing system at the age of only 15 Q22 in 1824 when he was at the Institute.

C: But he wasn't the first person to invent a system of touch reading for the blind, was he?

D: No, another Frenchman had already come up with the idea of printing Q23 embossed letters that stood out from the paper but this was very cumbersome and inefficient.

C: Did Louis Braille base his system on this first one?

D: No, not really. When he first went to Paris, he heard about a military system of writing using twelve dots. This was a system invented by an enterprising French army officer and it was known as Q24 "night writing". It wasn't meant for the blind, but rather...for battle communications at night.

C: That must've been fun!

D: Anyway, Braille took this system as a starting point but instead of using the twelve dots which "night writing" used, he cut the number of dots in half and developed a six-dot system.

C: Can you give us a little more information about how it works?

D: Well, it's a system of touch reading which uses an arrangement of raised dots called the "cell". Braille numbered the dot positions 1-2-3 downward on the left and 4-5-6 downward on the right. The Q25 letters of the alphabet are then formed by using different combinations of these dots.

S: Yes, so is the writing system based on the alphabet with each Q25 word being individually spelt out?

D: Well...it's not quite that simple, I'm afraid. For instance, the first 10 letters of the alphabet are formed using dots 1.2.4 and 5. But Braille also has its own short forms for common words. For example, "c" for the word "cat" and "a" for "apple", "b" for the word "bag", there are many other contractions like this.

C: So you spell out most words letter by letter, but you use short forms for common words.

D: Yes. Though, I think that makes it sound a little easier than it actually is!

C: And was it immediately accepted? I mean, did it catch on straight away?

D: Well, yes and no! Urn, it was immediately accepted and used by Braille's fellow students at the school but the system was not officially adopted until 1854, two years Q26 after Braille's death. So, the official acceptance was slow in coming!

S: I suppose it works for all languages which use

the roman alphabet?

D: Yes, it does, with adaptations, of course.

S: Can it be written by hand or do you need a machine to produce Braille?

D: Well. You can write it by hand on to paper with a device called a slate and stylus but the trick is that Q27 you have to write backwards, for example, from right to left so that then when you turn your sheet over, the dots face upwards and can be read like English from left to right.

S: Oh, I see,

D: But these days you'd probably use a Braille-writing machine, which is much easier!

C: And, er, tell us, Cindy. Is Braille used in other ways other than for reading text?

D: Yes, indeed. In addition to the literary Braille code, as it's known, which of course includes English and French, there are other codes. For instance, in 1965 they created a form of Braille for Q28 mathematics.

S: I can't imagine trying to do mathematics in Braille!

D: Yes. That doesn't sound easy, I agree. And there's also a version for Q29 scientific notation. Oh yes, I almost forgot, there is now a version for Q30 music notation as well.

C: Well. Thanks. Cindy. That was most interesting. Now, does anyone have any last questions...?

SECTION 4

Good morning. I'm going to talk about the IELTS preparation available for you at the Polytechnic University here in Hong Kong. First of all, I think it's important to say something about the background of the IELTS test in HK. The universities here decided to introduce it as Q31 an exit test in 2002. They are hoping that employers will consider the band score that students achieve. Basically, what students need to achieve is a band score of Q32 at least 6, which indicates a good competency of English. If you achieve a band score of seven, then you are doing very well and will be able to go and study for a Master's degree overseas.

There are three main things that you really need to consider about the test when you are preparing for it. Firstly, Q33 the timing. It's a very tight test as far as timing is concerned and you need to be well prepared so that you get through all of the sections that you need to complete.

You need to be well aware of Q33 the format of the test. If you do not understand how the test is put together, you will be disadvantaged. You also need to be aware of Q33 the type of test questions.

Now, the next thing I want to talk about is how you can prepare for this test. The English Language Centre at the Poly U offers you a variety of help. There are basically three things: courses and workshops, the Centre for Independent Language Learning and a variety of resources, both in hard copy and online, that you can use.

Firstly let me briefly mention the courses and the workshops. At present we are offering a two hour Q34 introductory workshop, which is on offer every Monday from 2.30 to 4.30 in AG301. If you want to join this course you can sign up at the CILL counter, it's based on "first come, first served". The workshop is free and you will also be given advice on how to do follow-up activities in the CILL. In the future, in the semester break and in the summer, we will be offering 10-hour IELTS courses which will take a more in-depth look at the exam/test and how you can prepare for it and give you lots of practice materials as well.

Now the second method to prepare for the test is to go to the CILL, where as well as studying by yourself, you can join Q35 the Speaking Assistance Programme (SAP) and the Writing Assistance Programme (WAP). It is essential that you get as much practice as possible and you can ask the teacher there anything about the test. Available within the CILL are Q35 a range of books, CDs, tapes, videos and of course online materials through which you can practise for the test.

Now, just to reiterate what the most important thing is about the test: you must Q36 understand the format, you must Q37 understand what you are being asked, what you are being tested on, you must

Test 5

do lots of practice, Q38 do as many test papers as possible, get feedback on your writing, Q39 do as much speaking practice as possible and finally, you must Q40 start as early as possible before your test date. Many students leave it until a few days before the test date to do any practice whatsoever. Of course, they cannot hope to get any higher than a band score 5 if they do this. Only you can make the difference if you want to get a higher band score and therefore have the possibility of getting a better job.

Test 6

答案速查

LISTENING

Section 1, Questions 1–10

1 two-week package
2 Susan Sharpe
3 Dover
4 MR47DT
5 03725943
6 Gold Star Policy
7 £660
8 back packs
9 bug spray
10 sunscreen

Section 2, Questions 11–20

11 B
12 B
13 B
14 I
15 P
16 F
17 F
18 P
19 68
20 techniques and materials

Section 3, Questions 21–30

21 C
22 A
23 A
24 B
25 C
26 D
27 B
28 A
29 C
30 B

Section 4, Questions 31–40

31 chemical
32 Eastern
33 free, effective
34 fifth/5th
35 Southeast Asia
36 sweet or bitter
37 4-6 servings
38 brain cells
39 1%-2%
40 economical

READING

Reading Passage 1, Questions 1–13

1 C
2 B
3 D
4 A
5 B
6 soil recomposition
7 natural processes
8 nitrogen
9 tree root system
10 G
11 E
12 B
13 D

Reading Passage 2, Questions 14–26

14 NO
15 NO
16 YES
17 YES
18 NOT GIVEN
19 NOT GIVEN
20 YES
21 clear
22 95%
23 mouth lining skin
24 10-20
25 neurotransmitters
26 D

Reading Passage 3, Questions 27–40

27 C
28 G
29 F
30 A
31 E
32 B
33 YES
34 NOT GIVEN
35 NOT GIVEN
36 YES
37 YES
38 NO
39 YES
40 NO

名师解析

LISTENING

SECTION 1

主题场景	旅行场景
主旨大意	咨询旅行信息及了解注意事项
考查题型	笔记填空题

名师解读

1　two-week package　题干中的Holiday booked与原文中的go for对应，for后的this one指代的就是two-week package，在前后文均提到过。并且题干中的in Egypt为原文重现，进一步说明in前面的two-week package为答案。考生注意不要忘记two和week之间的连字符。

2　Susan Sharpe　题干中的name为关键词，说明此处需要考生填入顾客的名字。注意姓氏和名字的拼写和首字母大写的问题。

3　Dover　题干中的关键词address为原文重现，据此定位原文。在关键词之后就提到了地址，并且题干中的Street，Melford原文重现也是对考生的提示。

4　MR47DT　题干中的关键词Postcode为原文重现，据此定位原文。考生须注意字母大写和数字的准确填写。

5　03725943　题干中的关键词Work number为原文重现，据此定位原文。考生只要注意听清原文中的数字和誊写无误即可。

6　Gold Star Policy　题干中的关键词Insurance为原文重现，据此定位原文。考生需注意在关键词后紧接着提到Policy一词，那就要注意下文中Policy前后的内容。注意首字母大写。

7　£660　题干中的tour price为原文重现，原文提到与价格相关的数字480和180，但考生要注意题干中的total一词，要求考生填入的是总共的价格，故是480加上180后的数字，即660。注意不要忘记填写单位“英镑”。

8　back packs　题干中的关键词recommend与原文中的suggest对应，bring为原文重现。题干中的Suitcases, Bags均为原文重现，故紧接着的内容back packs即为答案。

9　bug spray　原文提到了Comfortable shoes，这与题干一致，接着提到需要bring的东西有bug spray。

10　sunscreen　与第9题类似，在bug spray之后提到需要bring的东西有sunscreen，而后面提到的camera与题干一致。

SECTION 2

主题场景	课外活动场景
主旨大意	关于学校旅游活动的介绍
考查题型	选择题、配对题、表格填空题

名师解读

11　B　Mary Golding过去是a lecturer here at the college，但现在是student officer，注意题干的时态是一般现在时并注意原文转折词but后的内容，表转折关系连词后的内容常设置考点。

12　B　本题需选出与旅行有关的时间，听力原文用from...to...来表示旅行开始和结束的时间，故from后的内容为正确答案，即选项B，而选项A是结束的时间，为干扰项。

13　B　本题要选出旅行乘坐的交通工具。注意题干中的will，表示将来时。与此题相关的原文有两个信息：

Test 6

a medium-sized coach so there'll be 45 places和a minibus with only 16 places，但后者指的是last time，用的是过去时was。考生要注意听力原文和题干的时态。

14 I 题干中的关键词a boat ride与原文the boat cruise相对应，听清楚the boat cruise后面的included in the cost of the trip的内容就可以判断本题的答案。

15 P 根据but后的内容，have to pay to ride the "Eye"，可以判断答案。

16 F 题干中的关键词为Big Ben，注意听相关的内容...have a free visit up there，这里的there指的是前面的Big Ben。此题需要考生具备短暂记忆的能力。

17 F 题干中的关键词为Westminster Abbey，而原文的定位词为no admission charge，与free是同义表达。注意后面的need some money for those，这里的those是复数，指的是souvenir shops around，而不是Westminster Abbey。

18 P 考生要抓住have to pay to get in there，这里的there指的就是前面的British Museum，而且后面的but内容进一步说明这个地方不贵，基于以上两点可以判定答案。

19 68 题干中的million specimens, the Blue Whale exhibit, rainforest gallery都是原文重现。此题并不难，原文直接给出答案，听清楚原文的数字内容即可。

20 techniques and materials 题干中the same, the 16th century都是原文重现，与原文比较后，直接填入the same后的techniques and materials即可。

SECTION 3

主题场景	学业讨论场景
主旨大意	三个学生关于考试、学习方法的讨论
考查题型	选择题、配对题

名师解读

21 C 题干中的the last two questions为关键词，与原文中the last couple相对应，注意原文是否定，I didn't even manage read...对应有否定的选项C。不要将对话开始的人名弄混。

22 A 本题考查讲话人的态度。注意选项B的five minutes是干扰项，原文重读left，意为剩余时间。考生需理解a walk in the park相当于a piece of cake或a breeze，都是"非常容易"的意思。

23 A 原文John提到tough时就要注意，对应A项的challenging, Ken又补充说I didn't have a clue，都说明课程很难。其他的选项只有人名出现，细节不对应。注意本题的三个选项从不同角度讲，没有可比性，必须听细节。

24 B 原文出现了多个数字，如200，500，但考生应不急于选择，this was之后的数字450为答案。考查数字的选择题一定要注意题干条件，即in the exam。

25 C 题干中的effect与result对应，是表示结论的句子，原文lost its initial impact, immune等词与C项对应。A项干扰性很大，engage, advert等词在原文出现。记住慎选原文听力原词的原则，一定要继续听一两句再做决定。

26 D 最先提到Reread the course notes的是John，但最后补充了一句like Sarah，而Sarah也说me and Ken，所以应选D项，三人都采用了此方法。

27 B Ken提到了revision sites，但是要掌握should have的用法，表示"应做但没有做"，而之后Sarah表示赞同，故应选B项。

28 A John提到some other students, 与题目中的group对应，Sarah接着说never，所以只有John采用此方法，故选A。

29 C Ken提到some stuff（材料），last year，与题干past相对应，past exam为原文重现，而John对此表示了否定，故选C。

30 B 题干中support department为关键词, Sarah提到Students Help Desk，与题干中support相对应，故选B。

SECTION 4

主题场景	专题讲座场景
主旨大意	关于谷氨酸钠，即味精的讲座
考查题型	笔记填空题

名师解读

31 chemical 题干将结构重排，把commonly used前置，题干后面的to add flavours to food是原文重现，副词commonly修饰used。根据本题题干的语法结构，此空需填入名词。原文用过去分词used引导的过去分词短语后置修饰前面的名词chemical。考生应注意本讲座的开头部分有三个疑问句，But what is it? How long has it been used? How is it used?这说明后面的内容主要讲述这几个问题。

32 Eastern 根据题干的关键词1908定位答案。题干中的long before与原文中more than 1,200 years对应，所以此句的主语就是答案，即Eastern。注意答案首字母要大写。此题答案出自but后的内容，要注意。

33 free, effective 题干中的two forms为关键词，第一种是“bound”glutamate，后面跟了which引导的定语从句，连词and后的“free”glutamate是第二种形式，也就是答案，后面跟了that引导的定语从句。同时题干中的improving与原文中enhancing是同义替换，而the flavour of food是原文重现。

34 fifth/5th 提干中的it指的是MSG，题干中的关键词special taste与原文unique taste对应，同时原文中umami一词是用于形容MSG这种special taste的同义词，basic taste为原文重现，据此可以判定答案为basic taste前面的the fifth。

35 Southeast Asia 此题给出的信息点很多，原文中the bouillons对应Europe, the oyster sauce对应China, the soy and fish sauces 对应Southeast Asia, the pizza of Italy, the chowders and stews 对应America，考生要仔细辨别，一定要根据题干中的关键词soy sauces来确定答案。注意答案的首字母均要大写。

36 sweet or bitter 根据关键词salty and sour tastes定位，题干的转折连词despite对应原文中while这一句，题干中的否定表达less与little or nothing是同义替换，故后面的sweet or bitter就是要填入的内容。注意表示转折词后的内容，常常是考点。

37 4-6 servings 题干中的half a teaspoon of MSG为关键词，与原文中one-half teaspoon of MSG对应，题干中的a pound of meat or...vegetables为原文重现，据此得出答案。

38 brain cells 题干中的plenty of mild illness是对原文skin rashes to irregular heartbeat and depression的概括。题干中关键词kills后的brain cells就是答案。

39 1%-2% 听到关键词sensitive to MSG后，考生要注意后面关于数字的表述，one researcher的数字是30%，但与题干的主语food industry-sponsored studies不一致，不是答案，对应的数字1%-2%才是答案。注意要加percent符号。

40 economical 题干中的enhance the flavour为关键词，与原文simulating great taste对应，而way为原文重现，故way之前的economical就是答案。此题答案为but后的内容。

READING

READING PASSAGE 1

体　裁　说明文
题　材　生态环境
主　题　利用蚯蚓来再生旧钢铁厂中被污染的土壤
题　型　选择题、句子填空题、配对题

Questions 1–5

题型 选择题(Multiple Choice)

注意 选择题是阅读中的常规题型，答案在文中按顺序出现，每个题目在文中均可以利用选项定位。

1	关键词	Hallside site
	原文定位	C段首句Hallside's closure in 1979 put an end to more than 100 years of steel production.
	题解	**答案C** 注意题干的时态是现在完成时。A段提到earthworms（蚯蚓）将要帮助long-derelict site of a steelworks（长期被废弃的钢铁厂）转换成woodland（林地）和renewable energy park（可再生能源公园），是将来要完成的事情，而且没有提及Hallside site，故选项A和B错误；more than 100 years是一个很长的时间，选项D错误；选项C中的disused（滥用）与原文closure（关闭）和put an end（结束，终止）相对应，原文more than 100 years（超过100年）被替换为a long period of time（很长的时间）。
2	关键词	more than one hundred years of steel production, Hallside
	原文定位	C段首句Hallside's closure in 1979 put an end to more than 100 years of steel production.和末句The surrounding land had become heavily compacted and was too contaminated with heavy metals such as chromium, cadmium and led to support any kind of brick and mortar development.
	题解	**答案B** 选项A与原文to support any kind of brick and mortar development（使得砖块和灰浆得以开发）矛盾；选项D说得太绝对，错误；选项B和C是互为矛盾项，要依据原文的细节进行分析，关键是对build on的理解，意为"把……建立于……"，原文的意思是Hallside周围的土地被压得很实，而且污染严重，不能在土地上构建什么建筑物，但可以把土用于构建brick（砖块）和mortar（灰浆）。
3	关键词	plan, proposed
	原文定位	D段The site's 30 hectares...a rescue plan put together by local landscaping and earthmoving company, HL Banks, and the regional developer, Scottish Greenbelt, was approved by local authourities.
	题解	**答案D** 分析定位句子的结构，when 从句中句子的主干为a rescue plan was approved by local authourities（当地政府赞成一个营救计划）；过去分词put引导的过去分词短语修饰plan（计划）；HL Banks（HL银行）是local landscaping and earthmoving company（园林土方工程公司）的同位语；Scottish Greenbelt（苏格兰绿地公司）是the regional developer（地区开发者）的同位语，也是说这个计划是由HL Banks和Scottish Greenbelt提出来的，题干中的proposed（提议）与put（实施）相对应。
4	关键词	conversion of the soil
	原文定位	E段末句This will be converted into usable soil by about 21,000 Lumbricus terrestris (garden lobworms) and Aporrectodea longa (black headed worms) that have been let loose on the site.
	题解	**答案A** 题干中the conversion of the soil（土壤的转化）与原文be converted into usable soil（被转化为有用的土壤）相对应，括号里的garden lobworms（花园海蚯蚓）和black headed worms（黑头虫）就是土壤转化的worms。

5	关键词	soil regeneration
	原文定位	F段首句The specially raised hermaphrodites, which are self-impregnating, will spend the next five to ten years chewing their way through the topping layer to create a soil structure able to sustain long-term plant growth.
	题解	答案B 定位词soil regeneration（土壤翻新）是对原文create a soil structure able to sustain long-term plant growth（创造能够支持长期植物生长的土壤结构）的概括表达，同时题干中的take（花费）与原文中的spend（花费）是同义替换，故答案就是spend（花费）后面的时间。

Questions 6–9

题型 句子填空题(Sentence Completion)

注意 句子填空属于纯粹的填空题，答案均为原文原词。

6	关键词	Bell College
	原文定位	G段首句Researchers at Bell College of Technology...and found that even in the hostile mixture of coal-tip waste and partially treated sewage, earthworms were able to speed up the process of soil recomposition.
	题解	答案soil recomposition 题干中的worms（蠕虫）与原文earthworms（蚯蚓）对应，同时题干中的quicken（加快）与原文中的speed up（加速）是同义替换，答案应为speed up（加速）后面的内容the process of soil recomposition（土壤重构的过程），但题目要求不超过三个单词，故简化为soil recomposition（土壤重构）。
7	关键词	chose, convert
	原文定位	H段首句They selected different varieties of deeper burrowing earthworm species, whose bulk feeding and casting actions...would increase the rate of reformulation much faster than the natural processes.
	题解	答案natural processes 题干中的chose（选择）与原文中selected（选择）是同义替换，convert（转换）与原文中reformulation（再形成）相对应；比较级more rapidly（更快速地）与原文much faster（快得多）表达的是相同的意思，所以than后面的内容natural processes（自然过程）就是答案。
8	关键词	enriched, adding air
	原文定位	I段首句..."The idea is that earthworms will contribute in a cumulative way to further soil binding, and that they will aerate and add nitrogen to the soil covering the Hallside site."
	题解	答案nitrogen 题干中的be enriched by（被……丰富起来）与原文in a cumulative way（以积累的方式）相对应，题干中的adding air（增加空气）与原句中动词aerate（充气，让空气进入）是同义表达，也就是添加空气和nitrogen（氮气）使土壤丰富起来。

Test 6

9	关键词	contaminants
	原文定位	K段首句These will have the dual function of extracting contaminants from the soil through their root systems, and burning or chipboard manufacture.
	题解	答案tree root system　题干中Contaminants will be removed from the soil（污染物将从土壤中移除）是对原文extracting contaminants from the soil through（通过……将污染物从土壤中提取出来）的改写，故答案应为their root systems（它们的根系），这里的their指的是前面J段提到的trees，故本题答案为tree root system（树根系统）。

Questions 10–13

题型　配对题 (Matching Sentence)

注意　此题为句子配对题。根据在题目中划出的关键词，在原文中寻找信息点。

10	关键词	expected
	原文定位	L段首句By using the cash raised from wood harvesting, David Craven, director of Scottish Greenbelt, says he expects Hallside to be self-financing.
	题解	答案G　原文的he expects Hallside to（他希望Hallside……）改写为被动句the Hallside site is expected to（Hallside被希望……）；原文中的self-financing（自筹经费）与选项G对应。
11	关键词	bio-remediation
	原文定位	N段Craven says the cost of land bio-remediation—the labour intensive process of removing soil for chemical and bacterial cleansing—could have been more than £30m.
	题解	答案E　提取句子的主干为Craven says the cost of land bio-remediation could have been more than £30m (Craven说土地生物补救的成本可能超过£30m)。原文more than £30m与选项E的millions of pounds对应，题干中的bio-remediation（生物补救）是原文重现。
12	关键词	20 years
	原文定位	P段末句Within less than 20 years the land could be re-integrated into the community.
	题解	答案B　题干中的be re-integrated into（被重新整合为……）对应选项B中的be in use again by（被……再次使用），the community（生态群落）则是原文重现，故答案为B。
13	关键词	similar regeneration plans
	原文定位	Q段首句Hopes of a successful outcome at Hallside have paved the way for similar regeneration plans for the nearby Gartoosh steelworks and at Glengarnock in Ayrshire.
	题解	答案D　原文中the nearby Gartoosh steelworks and at Glengarnock in Ayrshire（附近的Gartoosh钢铁厂和埃尔郡的Glengarnock）与选项D的other steelworks（其他钢铁厂）对应，选项D是对原文内容的概括，故答案为D项。

Test 6

READING PASSAGE 2

体　裁　议论文
题　材　社会健康
主　题　介绍烟草中尼古丁使人上瘾的情况以及原因
题　型　判断题、简答题、选择题

Questions 14–20

题型 判断题(Identifying Writer’s Views/Claims)

注意 题干常是原文的改写，做题时根据题目的表述来确定出题人的侧重点，找到与之相对应的原文。

14	关键词	nicotine, changes
	原文定位	A段第三句Because of the more than 4,000 chemicals in tobacco smoke, nicotine is the primary one that acts on the brain, altering people's moods, appetites and alertness in ways they find pleasant and beneficial.
	题解	**答案NO** 本段说尼古丁是影响烟民的primary（最主要）物质，而题干主句中的表达是not necessarily the one（不是必要的一个），与原文矛盾。
15	关键词	35 million, give up
	原文定位	B段第二句、第三句Each year, nearly 35 million people make a concerted effort to quit smoking. Sadly, less than 7 percent succeed in abstaining for more than a year; most start smoking again within days.
	题解	**答案NO** 题干中的in spite of the difficulties（尽管有困难）是对B段首句Breaking nicotine addiction is not easy.（戒掉尼古丁上瘾是不容易的。）的改写，但后面的内容与B段第二、三句表达“35 million（3 500万）的人想戒烟，但只有less than 7 percent（不到7%）的人成功戒烟”这一内容相反。
16	关键词	quickly improve, perform
	原文定位	C段第二句、第三句One is enhancing performance. One study found that non-smokers given doses of nicotine typed about 5 percent faster than they did without it.
	题解	**答案YES** 本段前四句一直在说明尼古丁在某些方面有益处，还进一步说明它可快速提高人的表现。题干中improve（改善）与原文enhancing（提高）是同义替换；perform（动词，执行）与原文中performance（名词，执行）是同根词；比较级more quickly（更快地）与原文faster than（比……快）对应。
17	关键词	ammonia, inhale
	原文定位	E段第二句...they began adding substances such as ammonia to cigarette tobacco to release more nicotine和末句By inhaling smoke from a lighted cigarette, the average smoker takes 1 or 2 milligrams of vapourised nicotine per cigarette.
	题解	**答案YES** 根据题干的关键词定位到E段，本段有非常重要的定位词ammonia（氨），本段表示加入此物质会释放更多的尼古丁，与题干表述一致。

18	关键词	snorted, injected
	原文定位	F段倒数第五句Scientists have found that a smoked substance reaches the brain more quickly than one swallowed, snorted (such as cocaine powder) or even injected.
	题解	答案NOT GIVEN 原文提到关键词snorted（喷出）和injected（注射），但并没有把这两者做比较，原文相关处无比较级，而题目中有比较级。
19	关键词	nicotine, blood vessels
	原文定位	F段倒数第三句The nicotine travels through blood vessels, which branch out into capillaries within the brain.
	题解	答案NOT GIVEN 根据关键词blood vessels（血管）定位，但并没有说尼古丁可扩张血管。
20	关键词	electrical, neurones
	原文定位	H段末句With repeated smoking, the neurones adapt to this increased electrical activity, and the smoker becomes dependent on the nicotine.
	题解	答案YES 题干中的greater electrical charges（更大的电荷）与原文中increased electrical activity（增加电活动）对应，题干的谓语allow（允许）与原文adapt（适应）对应，也就是说神经细胞逐渐适应了这种不断增强的电流。故本题正确。

Questions 21–25

题型 简答题(Short-Answer Questions)

注意 绝大部分的答案来自原文原词，极少一部分需要考生改写答案。答案涉及数字的，最好写阿拉伯数字，以免发生拼写错误。所有的答案都不用大写，专有名词除外。

21	关键词	natural colour of nicotine
	原文定位	D段首句First isolated as a compound in 1828, in its pure form nicotine is a clear liquid that turns brown when burned and smells like tobacco when exposed to air.
	题解	答案clear 题干中的natural（自然）与原文pure（纯粹）对应，也是说天然的尼古丁的colour（颜色）是clear（无色的）。要注意答案为clear（无色的），不是clear liquid（无色的液体），因为问题问的是colour（颜色）。
22	关键词	prevent, addictive
	原文定位	F段第二句Research shows that manufacturers would have to cut nicotine levels in a typical cigarette by 95% to forestall its power to addict.
	题解	答案95% 题干的疑问词为how much（多少），所以本题的答案为数字。题干中的prevent（预防）与原文forestall（预先阻止）是同义替换，addictive（形容词，上瘾的）与原文addict（名词，有瘾的人）是同根词，原文的意思是只有降低95%才能不让人对尼古丁上瘾。故本题的答案为95%。

23	关键词	first
	原文定位	F段第四句The skin and lining of the mouth immediately absorb some nicotine, but the remainder flows straight down into the lungs, where it easily diffuses into the blood vessels lining the lung walls.
	题解	答案mouth lining skin　定位句说明了尼古丁在体内被吸收的顺序，原文中的immediately（立即地）与题干中的Name ONE thing（首要的事）对应，故本题的回答应为the skin and lining of the mouth（皮肤和嘴的内部），但题目要求不超过三个单词，所以需要改写，mouth lining skin（嘴和皮肤）首先将尼古丁带入体内。
24	关键词	heart rate
	原文定位	F段倒数第六句Studies have shown that a smoker's first cigarette of the day can increase his or her heart rate by 10 to 20 beats a minute.
	题解	答案10–20　题干中raise（增加）与原文中increase（增加）对应，题干把F段倒数第六句改成了疑问句，去掉了10 to 20，转换成how many（多少），也就是说可加速心跳10 to 20 beats（10到20次）。
25	关键词	cell, encloses neutrons
	原文定位	H段首句The neurotransmitters bind onto receptors on the surface of the recipient neurone.
	题解	答案neurotransmitters　第一句话很明显说出神经传递素将传感器凝固在能接受神经细胞的表面上。题干中的encloses（围绕）与原文recipient（接收）对应，故答案为neurotransmitters（神经递质）。

Question 26

题型　选择题(Multiple Choice)

注意　需要选择文章的主旨，不可以根据自己的理解或常识自行推断，而是要依据文中信息进行确定。

26	关键词	title
	原文定位	A段首句If it weren't for nicotine, people wouldn't smoke tobacco.
	题解	答案D　文章第一段开头开门见山地讲述了吸烟容易上瘾，之后的各段都围绕这一主题展开。

READING PASSAGE 3

体　裁　说明文
题　材　环境保护
主　题　介绍英国泰晤士河的清理工作的分工和监管情况
题　型　配对题、判断题

Questions 27–32

题型 配对题(Matching Features)

注意 以下题目为信息配对题，需根据题干中的关键词在原文准确定位，并进行比对。

27	关键词	The Environment Agency
	原文定位	E段第三句Although they will all still have their part to play, there is now a central department in the Environment Agency, which has the remit of monitoring the Thames.
	题解	答案C Environment Agency（环境部门）现在有central department（专门部门）负责监督清洁的工作，此句中的they（他们）指代该段首句提到的许多agencies（部门），包括British Waterways（英国排水部门），Port of London Authority（伦敦政府港口部门），the Environment Agency（环境部门），the Health and Safety Commission（健康和安全委员会），Thames Water（泰晤士河水处理部门），但考生要注意题目要求选出的是现在主要监督清洁工作的机构，而不是past，故该题目答案选C。
28	关键词	Transport for London
	原文定位	D段第五句For example, Transport for London—the agency responsible for transport in the capital—plays a role in regulating river use and river users.
	题解	答案G 定位句很明确地提到该机构负责管理交通工作，同时，在Transport for London（伦敦运输部门）一词的后面有明显的插入语the agency responsible for transport in the capital（负责首都运输的部门）。
29	关键词	The Greater London Council
	原文定位	B段末句In 1964 the Greater London Council (GLC) began work on greatly enlarged sewage works, which were completed in 1974.
	题解	答案F 本段最后一句说明此机构负责sewage（污水）处理的工作，而sewage（污水）一词与F选项形成对应。
30	关键词	Thames Water
	原文定位	D段倒数第五句...Thames Water now plans to introduce a new device to capture more rubbish floating down the river和末句This machine, known as the Rubbish Muncher, is hoped to be the first of many...
	题解	答案A 本段倒数第五句表明Thames Water（泰晤士河水处理部门）在引进一种新设备，而本段的末句说这一设备叫做Rubbish Muncher（垃圾咀嚼）。
31	关键词	Port of London
	原文定位	D段倒数第五句While the Port of London already collects up to 3,000 tons of solid waste from the tideway every year, Thames Water now plans to introduce a new device to capture more rubbish floating down the river.
	题解	答案E 本段倒数第五句的前半部分说Port of London（伦敦政府港口部门）负责collects up to 3,000 tons of solid waste（收集3 000吨固体垃圾）的工作。

32	关键词	Local Boroughs
	原文定位	C段倒数第二句The *2000 Local Government Act* requires each local borough to"prepare a community strategy for promoting or improving the economic, social and environmental well-being of their area."
	题解	答案B 本段第五句引号中的话证明Local Borough（当地的自治的市）负责community strategies（社区策略）的工作，选项B中的creating（创造）与原文prepare（准备）相对应，故答案选B。

Questions 33–40

题型 判断题(Identifying Writer's Views/claims)

注意 判断题一直是雅思阅读的最难的题型之一，难点就在于许多考生未能充分理解三个判断词的内在涵义及其区别。

33	关键词	Thames, cleaner
	原文定位	A段第二句The company says that thanks to major investment...the river that flows through the United Kingdom capital and the Thames Estuary into the North Sea is cleaner now than it has been for 130 years.
	题解	答案YES 定位句说泰晤士河现在是130年来最干净的，1900包含在距今130年内。故本题正确。
34	关键词	swimming, hazards
	原文定位	B段第四句Until the early 1970s, if you fell into the Thames you would have had to be rushed to hospital to get your stomach pumped.
	题解	答案NOT GIVEN 定位句虽然提到了20世纪70年代跳进河里应当立即去医院就医，但并没有说现在在泰晤士河里游泳是否对身体有害。考生应注意题干和原文中表示时间的词。
35	关键词	responsibility, pollute
	原文定位	B段倒数第二句Several Parliamentary Committees...legislation has been introduced that put the onus on polluters—effluent-producing premises and businesses—to dispose of waste responsibly.
	题解	答案NOT GIVEN 由本句内容可推出法律让污染者承担责任，但没有提到目前谁负mainly（最主要）的责任。
36	关键词	London boroughs, keeping the Thames clean
	原文定位	C段第三句In London's case, the urban and non-urban London boroughs that flank the river's course each has its own reasons for keeping "their" river nice.
	题解	答案YES 本段说明所有boroughs都有责任保持河水干净。故本题正确。

Test 6

37	关键词	River Police
	原文定位	D段第七句This is done by officers on official vessels regularly inspecting fling craft and doing spot checks.
	题解	答案YES 本句中this指代上文提到的controlling the effluents and rubbish coming from craft using the Thames（控制来自使用泰晤士河工艺产生的污水和垃圾），也就是题干中的enforce control of their regulations（加强他们规则的控制）部分；原文中officers（人员）与题干中a type of River Police（一种水上警察）对应。故本题正确。
38	关键词	Rubbish Munchers,various locations
	原文定位	D段末句This machine, known as the Rubbish Muncher, is hoped to be the first of many, as the TW is now looking for sponsors to pay for more cages elsewhere along the Thames.
	题解	答案NO 定位句末句说目前正在寻找投资人去投放更多的机器，这说明不是很多地方有很多机器，且沿着定位词Rubbish Munchers（垃圾咀嚼机器）向上看会发现此种机器现在只出现在Royal Naval College at Greenwich（在格林威治的皇家海军学院）附近。
39	关键词	previously, responsibility
	原文定位	E段首句Monitoring of the cleanliness of the River Thames in the past was the responsibility of a welter of agencies...as well as academic departments and national and local environment groups.
	题解	答案YES 注意题干中previously（以前）与原文past（过去）对应，定位句表明在过去，有很多的部门一起管，而不是由一个部门monitoring of the cleanliness of the River Thames（监管泰晤士河的清洁）。
40	关键词	British Waterways
	原文定位	E段第三句Although they will all still have their part to play, there is now a central department in the Environment Agency, which has the remit of monitoring the Thames.
	题解	答案NO 本句说以前的部门还part to play（部分参与清洁工作），故答案很显然为NO。

WRITING

WRITING TASK 1

名师解读

本题为地图题，属于地理变迁描述型文章，主要是想让学生对比说明Kelsbey村庄在1700年和2000年之间的发展变化。

首先考生需用1分钟的时间来解析图片，通过对比找到两个时间点的村庄各自的特征以及发生的变化。地图题描述的是一个地区的变化，那么必须掌握表示“变化”的词汇。变化包括两种：图中原有事物的改变，图中新添事物。此外，要注意正确运用时态。

要注意按方位顺序来描述，否则文章的逻辑方面会比较混乱，这就需要考生在考前对方位词进行总结。地图题的方位需描述为东、西、南、北，不用上、下、左、右表达。

高分范文

The village named Kelsbey saw a great change during the period of 1700 to 2000. In 1700, there was a castle near the river which ran across a bridge, while 300 years later, the previous castle was replaced by a school behind which a railway line was paved.

Moreover, another great change happened in the land utilization. The year 1700 could witness a large scale of grassland on both sides of the road which join together with the curve bridge, while the grassland was gone, followed by the built-up which even appeared close to the road on both boarders of the river. Another drastic change goes to the market place which existed in 1700 but completely disappeared in 2000 and was replaced by the built-up too. The woods which were in the east of the market place and west of the castle in 1700 seemed stable since they were right there in 2000.

All in all, the whole layout did not change while the specific constructions were established or removed. (169 words)

WRITING TASK 2

文章结构

正反观点辩论+立场+原因+总结

viewpoint +reason 1+reason2+standpoint+conclusion
第一段：背景句+引出现象
第二段：正方观点+理由
第三段：反方观点+理由
第四段：总结+立场+例证

思路点拨

步骤一：审题（<3分钟）

Nowadays, nurseries and kindergartens take care of children from an early age, so women can return to their work and children can get used to the society early. Is this a good thing? What's your opinion?

→通读题目，了解大意，判断题型。

本题为议论文。题目的大意为：早送孩子去幼儿园逐渐成为一种趋势，这样主妇们能够回归工作，孩子能较早地适应社会，这是好事吗？你的看法是什么？

→再读题目，辨别关键词，区分主题词和限定词，推测考官的出题意图。

主题词：nurseries and kindergartens take care of children from an early age

限定词：early age, your opinion

步骤二：列大纲（<3分钟）

英文提纲	Intro: a big issue→a growing tendency, send children earlier to nurseries and kindergartens →mothers, freed from child care→different attitudes Pro: some people, sent to nurseries earlier→reason 1→reason 2→reason 3→career success Opp：sending children earlier, demerits→opponent 1 →opponent 2→opponent 3 Conclusion：stand on the side of the opponents→reason 1→reason 2→reason 3

中文提纲	引出话题：大问题→早送孩子去幼儿园逐渐成为一种趋势→母亲不用照顾孩子→不同的人对此有不同的态度 正方观点：正方依据一→正方依据二→正方依据三→有利于母亲事业的成功 反方观点：反方依据一→反方依据二→反方依据三 总结：强烈支持反方观点→依据一→依据二→依据三

高分范文

Child care is a big issue in all families, and there is a heated debate on the best method of handling it. Nowadays there is a growing tendency for parents to send their children earlier to nurseries and **kindergartens**. Some even go to nurseries and kindergartens at age 2 or 3 so that mothers can free from child care and pursue their own careers. People from different backgrounds, however, hold different attitudes toward the matter in question.

Some people claim that children should be sent to nurseries earlier. First of all, psychologically speaking, the child needs more opportunities to communicate with his peers. The main task of the child care establishments is to **inculcate** honesty, courage, discipline, cooperation, friendliness, and good manners. Second, it is beneficial for them to receive systematic and scientific care and rudimentary knowledge from well-trained professionals. Last but not least, sending children earlier to nursery schools enables mothers to devote more time and energy to their jobs. In this way, career success becomes more possible, which is very beneficial to the whole family.

However, people rarely reach an absolute **consensus** on such a **controversial** issue. The opponents argue that sending children earlier to nursery schools has its **demerits**. In the first place, it may lead to poorer parent-child relationship for lack of emotional communication. In addition, with mother staying at home, children will be better cared for and given more attention. On the other hand, in nurseries and kindergartens, there is the possibility of lacking adequate care and attention because there are so many children in a class. Moreover, although the family may lose some income, its expenditure will also be greatly reduced. It will no longer be necessary to pay for attending nurseries and kindergartens.

Undeniably, there are points in both sides of the argument. But after a careful consideration of the above reasons, I stand on the side of the opponents. To start nursery schools too early is harmful for children mentally. Children who are sent earlier to nursery schools lack the affection of parents. Furthermore, mothers are the first teachers of their own children and exert profound impact on the child's future growth. (362 words)

SPEAKING

名师解读

Part 1为旅游话题。旅游话题是雅思几大必准备的话题之一，命题几率高。

Part 2属于口头作文，要求描述一位你钦佩的名人。

Part 3的内容为名人和成功。“名人”话题是一个非常经典的雅思口语话题，在很多次的考试中都出现过，也是大家口语考试的备考重点。有关于“成功”的话题比较难，其难点在于较为抽象，难以选材。如果能将“成功”具体化，灵活回答，其难度会大大降低。

高分示例

PART 1

Places of Interest

• Which places in your city or province would you suggest a tourist visit?

There are many sites that are worthwhile visiting such as Government (City Hall) Square with the Great Theatre alongside it, Zhong Shan Square, and the spectacular TV Tower which is the highest **architectural** attraction in Shenyang.

• Why are they significant?

Shenyang is rich in history. They are all important architects that bear unique historical meaning.

• Do you often visit such places?

Yes, I do. In fact, I often show my friends and schoolmates around the city.

PART 2

I think the most famous person I admire is Angelina Jolie.

She is a brilliant actress and has been in many different movies of all types.

Both her parents were in the film and media industry and so it was only logical that she would take the same step. She is very talented and has a certain appeal that draws crowds. This is what made her successful.

I admire her because of her down to Earth nature. She works hard with the United Nations to help countries and their people who are less **fortunate** than herself. She also has a large heart for children and has many of them, both adopted and **biological**.

PART 3

Fame

• Can you evaluate the pros and cons of being famous?

There are many ups and downs to be famous. While you get lots of money and many people looking up to you in admiration, you also don't get any privacy and are **scrutinized** for everything you do.

• Can you comment on whether the media should be allowed to report on the private lives of **celebrities**?

I don't think it should be completely stopped, it is human nature to want to know things about those we adore, but there should be serious boundaries around homes and families being exploited because of their fame.

• Can you outline the responsibilities celebrities have to our society?

Celebrities might seem "all that" to most people, but not many actually realise how much of an influence these people have on our lives and the lives of our children. They are role models, people who have succeeded in following and obtaining their dreams, but they also have the ability to destroy the people who look up to them.

Success

- Talk about which element is more important for success: luck or hard work?

I believe that it is a combination of both. Hard work will get you far, but if you are not lucky enough to be noticed by the right people, you will stay where you are. On the reverse side, you may be incredibly lucky and get noticed as a raw talent, but then will be cast aside if you do not work hard.

- Define how success is measured.

No one can define how success is measured as it is different for everyone. One person might see failure where another sees success and that is the fundamental argument to define how success is measured.

- How can success change a person?

Becoming successful can change even the most grounded of people, between lots of money and fame, many people become big headed and forget who their true friends and family are, and who are only around them to try and become famous too.

重点词汇

LISTENING

Ibiza	[iː'biːzə]	*n.*	伊比沙岛（位于地中海西部）
Pyramid	['pɪrəmɪd]	*n.*	金字塔；角锥体
insurance	[ɪn'ʃʊərəns]	*n.*	保险；保险费
cancellation	[ˌkænsə'leɪʃn]	*n.*	取消；删除
suitcase	['suːtkeɪs]	*n.*	手提箱；衣箱
back pack			背包
comfortable	['kʌmftəbl]	*adj.*	舒适的，舒服的
bug spray			喷雾杀虫剂
sunscreen	['sʌnskriːn]	*n.*	（防晒油中的）遮光剂
insufficient	[ˌɪnsə'fɪʃnt]	*adj.*	不足的，不充足的
souvenir	[ˌsuːvə'nɪə]	*n.*	纪念品；礼物
gallery	['gæləri]	*n.*	画廊；走廊
bunch	[bʌntʃ]	*n.*	群；串
ingredient	[ɪn'griːdɪənt]	*n.*	原料；要素
monosodium	[ˌmɒnəˌsəʊdɪəm]	*n.*	味精；谷氨酸钠
glutamate	['gluːtəmeɪt]	*n.*	[生化] 谷氨酸盐
fermentation	[ˌfɜːmen'teɪʃn]	*n.*	发酵
savory	['seɪvəri]	*adj.*	可口的；风味极佳的
meaty	['miːti]	*adj.*	肉的；多肉的
oyster	['ɒɪstə]	*n.*	牡蛎
sauce	[sɔːs]	*n.*	酱油；沙司
chowder	['tʃaʊdə]	*n.*	[美] 杂烩；海鲜杂烩浓汤
stew	[stjuː]	*n.*	炖，炖汤
harmonize	['hɑːmənaɪz]	*v.*	和谐；一致
ailment	['eɪlmənt]	*n.*	小病；不安

READING

appetite	['æpɪtaɪt]	*n.*	食欲
carcinogen	[kɑː'sɪnədʒən]	*n.*	[医] 致癌物（质），诱癌因素
concerted	[kən'sɜːtɪd]	*adj.*	协定的，商定的
abstain	[əb'steɪn]	*v.*	放弃；自制
insinuate	[ɪn'sɪnjueɪt]	*v.*	使潜入，缓慢地前进
deleterious	[ˌdelə'tɪərɪəs]	*adj.*	有害的，有毒的
susceptibility	[səˌseptə'bɪləti]	*n.*	感受性，易感性，敏感性
pharmacologically	[ˌfɑːməkə'lɒdʒɪkli]	*adv.*	药理学地
vapourize	['veɪpəraɪz]	*v.*	蒸发，汽化
miniscule	['mɪnɪskjuːl]	*adj.*	极小的
euphoria	[juː'fɔːrɪə]	*n.*	精神欢快，欣快
impulse	['ɪmpʌls]	*n.*	刺激
synaptic	[saɪ'næptɪk]	*adj.*	（染色体）联合的
latch	[lætʃ]	*v.*	闩上，抓住
vanquish	['væŋkwɪʃ]	*v.*	征服
metropolitan	[ˌmetrə'pɒlɪtən]	*adj.*	大城市的，大都会的；首府的；宗主国的
monitor	['mɒnɪtə]	*v.*	监控
cavort	[kə'vɔːt]	*v.*	跳跃

sewer	['suːə]	*n.*	阴沟，污水管，下水道
starve	[stɑːv]	*v.*	渴望；饿死
disparate	['dɪspərət]	*adj.*	（根本）不相同的；（种类）全异的
borough	['bʌrə]	*n.*	自治的市镇；区
flank	[flæŋk]	*v.*	侧面与……衔接
compelling	[kəm'pelɪŋ]	*adj.*	强制的
amenity	[ə'miːnəti]	*n.*	舒适；便利设施
accountability	[əˌkaʊntə'bɪləti]	*n.*	职能
enforcement	[ɪn'fɔːsmənt]	*n.*	实施，执行

WRITING

kindergarten	['kɪndəgɑːtn]	*n.*	幼儿园；幼稚园
inculcate	['ɪnkʌlkeɪt]	*v.*	教育；谆谆教诲
consensus	[kən'sensəs]	*n.*	一致；舆论；合意
controversial	[ˌkɒntrə'vɜːʃl]	*adj.*	有争议的；有争论的
demerit	[diː'merɪt]	*n.*	缺点，短处；过失
undeniably	[ˌʌndɪ'naɪəbli]	*adv.*	不可否认地；确凿无疑地

SPEAKING

fortunate	['fɔːtʃənət]	*adj.*	幸运的
biological	[ˌbaɪə'lɒdʒɪkl]	*adj.*	生物的；生物学的
scrutinize	['skruːtənaɪz]	*v.*	仔细检查；细看
celebrity	[sə'lebrəti]	*n.*	名人
architectural	[ˌɑːkɪ'tektʃərəl]	*adj.*	建筑学的；建筑上的

听力原文

SECTION 1

(Andrew=A; Travel Agent=TA)

A: Good afternoon.

TA: Good afternoon sir, how can I help you?

A: I'm looking for your best package holiday deal.

TA: Of course sir, please sit down and let me see what we have. Where were you thinking of going?

A: Well. I don't really know. I was thinking of somewhere sunny.

TA: How about Ibiza? I's the best place if you're looking for nightlife. We've got a good package deal for £349.

A: Mmm...That's not really my cup of tea.

TA: OK. Mmm...Well, we've got a two-week package in Egypt, based in Cairo. Actually, as well as the Pyramids of course, another little-known attraction in this city is that you can eat wonderful Arabian food, and it's very cheap. And that's a very good value package—one week for £480 and an extra week for only £180.

A: That sounds tempting...OK, I'll go for this one...

TA: Alright, Q1 two-week package in Egypt...Now, what I need to do is to take some information from you. Let me just get a form ready. First, the name, please.

A: Well, Q2 Susan Sharpe. Sharpe. S-H...

TA: Like a knife?

A: Yes, but with an E on the end.

TA: Fine. And what's your address?

A: It's 18, Q3 Dover Street, Melford, and the postcode is Q4 MR47DT.

TA: Thank you. And could I take a telephone number?

A: We're on 0372 5656 at home. Or, do you mean during the day?—Then my work number's Q5 03725943.

TA: I'll put the work one down, assuming that's normal office hours. Thank you. Are you in a position to pay cash, or would you need to pay by credit card?

A: Err...I prefer VISA.

TA: Fine, and...now, insurance. Do you need to get an insurance policy that came with your booking?

A: Well, no, I mean it came under our Q6 Gold Star Policy. So we didn't need extra.

TA: That's fine, it's just to check. Can I just mention that we require all bookings to be made at least fifteen days before you travel to avoid cancellation of tours? And if you cancel within seven days of departure you will have to pay 50% of your total booking.

A: OK. Q7 And the tour price is £480 for the first week, £180 for the second, right?

TA: Yeah, that's right.

A: Good. Oh, by the way, do I need to get some special preparation for the tour?

TA: I suggest you bring two suitcases, and three bags, e.g. hiking bags, Q8 back packs. And make sure to bring some comfortable shoes because we'll be beyond our feet for most of the days, and of course bring the Q9 bug spray, Q10 sunscreen, and a camera.

A: Right, I've got that. Thank you very much for all your help.

TA: You are very welcome. I hope you enjoy the trips.

SECTION 2

Hello. Can I just have your attention for a minute? Thank you. My name is Mary Golding, some of you may recognize me...I used to be a lecturer here at the college, but I changed my job last year, and I now work as the Q11 student officer. OK, well, I'm in today to tell you about a guided tour that we've got going to er...London. Well, this will be a good chance for those of you who haven't been to London before to have a look at this beautiful city. I think those of you who come will thoroughly enjoy it. The trip is going to be for five days, from the Q12 31st of March, which is a Saturday, to the 4th of April, the following Wednesday. We'll be taking Q13 a medium-sized coach so there'll be 45 places on that. Last time it was a minibus with only 16 places, which proved insufficient for students' need.

According to the London Development Agency, London has over 200 museums, 500 cinema screens, 108 music halls, and five symphony orchestras. Needless to say, we can't see it all in one day. Here are some major sights we are going to tackle on the first visit to London:

On the first day we're in London, we'll go on a boat trip, up the Thames River and up the London Eye. The "Eye" is a giant modern Ferris wheel which stands on the south of the river across from the Houses of Parliament. Q14 The boat cruise is included in the cost of the trip, so you won't need to worry about spending extra money. But Q15 you have to pay to ride the "Eye" to gaze out over the vast city.

After that we'll visit the Houses of Parliament. The Houses of Parliament, also known as Westminster Palace, was designed in the Gothic style. One of London's famous landmarks—Big Ben, the clock tower named for its 13-ton bell, is also found here. You can Q16 have a free visit up there. I think you all know Westminster Abbey, one of the most visited Christian churches in the world. Q17 There is no admission charge for this, but there are lots of souvenir shops around, so you might need some money for those!

On the second day, we'll go to the British Museum. The oldest museum in the world is also the most visited site in London. Q18 You have to pay to get in there, but it's not expensive. The museum's newly constructed £100 million Great Court—a two-acre square, enclosed by a glass roof—is the largest covered public square in Europe.

On the third day, you'll be free to do whatever you like. Personally I recommend the Natural History Museum. It has over Q19 68 million specimens. Fun exhibits include the Blue Whale exhibit, rainforest gallery, earthquake experience, and dinosaur displays. The Globe Theatre is a place worth visiting. The original Globe Theatre, where actors performed William Shakespeare's plays, burned down in 1613. The newly reconstructed Globe, however, copies original drawings of the 16th century building's details and uses many of the same Q20 techniques and materials. Theatre goers can see performances of Shakespeare's plays, such as *Romeo and Juliet* and *Much a Dc About Nothing.* If you'd like to go, can you sign up on this form on the student notice board by Friday? It'll be on "first come, first served" basis.

SECTION 3

(SARAH=S; JOHN=J; KEN=K)

S: Hi, John.

J: Oh, hi, Sarah. How did it go?

S: Well, it was really tough. Lots of hard questions I didn't know how to answer.

J: But you seemed so confident this morning. What is it really that bad?

S: I just ran out of time. I spent ages on the first questions so I didn't even manage to read Q21 the last couple. I'm sure Ken will say the same. There just wasn't enough time. Oh,there he is.

K: Hello, are you on about the exam?

J: Sarah was just complaining about the test and reckons that we could have done with extra time. To be honest, it was a bit of a race against the clock but I managed to do all the questions and even had five minutes left to go over what I'd written. Compared to the last class test, Q22 it was a walk in the park. And not half as hard as the management one.

K: Wow John, you must write quicker or maybe you weren't as nervous as us. I hardly slept last night because I was worried sick about this test, when it came to 9, I could hardly put pen to paper.

S: What about the first question though, the one on the development of marketing communication? We hadn't done that at all, had we?

J: Oh, yeah. Q23 That was a tough one alright. It completely threw me.

K: Me, too. I didn't have a clue about that and I attended every class, so I just scribbled down something about Cutler's theory of...

S: The theory of mass marketing from his book *Communication Tools in Marketing*. That's one of Professor Jones's favourites. He always quotes Cutler.

K: And what about the other one? In section 2, I think.

J: Section...

K: Rebranding. Yeah. I just about managed 200 words then I completely dried up.

J: Oh, no. That's terrible. You needed 500 at least.

S: Really? I thought it was 500 for the ethical marketing test.

J: No. The advertising exam was 500, Q24 this was 450 but the ethical marketing was 300. Anything more and you will get penalised. It's pretty confusing, isn't it?

K: The other one I got stuck on was question 6 about viral marketing.

J: Why? That was probably my best answer. I put down what we had discussed in the seminar about social media and the Internet generation and how viral adverts sent to prospective customers email accounts are cheap and really engage people.

S: I loved that subject. It's really cutting edge stuff. All the huge companies exploit it now.The result is that Q25 it's lost its initial impact. We're all immune I guess now, so they'll have to think of new ways to reach us.

K: Well, what's for sure is that none of us prepared enough. I did some last minute cramming. What about you, John?

J: What I did was Q26 go back over my notes from the lectures and seminars, highlighting all the major information. You know, like Sarah.

S: I always do that, I use loads of different colours, I remember things better that way. Q26 Ken and I ran out of pens because every time we looked at them, we found something important. Right, Ken?

K: Oh, yeah. There're loads on the net though. I should have gone on those revision sites Chris told us about.

S: They're fantastic. Everything from Chemistry to Maths. Q27 I couldn't survive without them.

J: Tell you what really helped me. Q28 I got together with some other students and recapped what we had done in class. We met up at the café, just for an hour at a time. Sarah, you fancied organising your own study group, didn't you?

S: What? It never got off the ground. Shame really. Revision groups can be very productive.

K: Tom gave me some stuff he had from the course last year. There was Q29 a whole bunch of past exams. I really got to grips with the style and format by going through them. It really helped a lot.

J: This exam was pretty different though I heard. They must have changed examiners.

S: Tell you what? Q30 After speaking to Paul at the Students Help Desk, I booked an appointment at that new office where they help students with study problems. I was there about an hour in the end. The woman, er, Shirley, her name was, gave me loads of tips.

J: Shirley, I know her. I used to see her all the time when she managed the library.

SECTION 4

You've probably noticed that MSG appears regularly among the ingredients of your favourite foods. But what is it? How long has it been used? How is it used?

MSG, or monosodium glutamate, is a Q31 chemical commonly used to add flavour to salty or sour tasting foods. The average person knows almost nothing about it, but today MSG is found in everything from potato chips to soup.

Its principal component is an amino acid called glutamic acid or glutamate. It was identified by Professor Kikunae Ikeda in 1908. But Q32 Eastern cooks have been using glutamate-rich sea weed as flavouring for more than 1,200 years. Glutamate is found in two forms: "bound" glutamate, which is linked to other amino acids forming a protein molecule and Q33 "free" glutamate that has no link to protein. Only free glutamate is Q33 effective in enhancing the flavour of food. Foods often used for their flavouring qualities, such as tomatoes and mushrooms, they have high levels of naturally occurring free glutamate.

MSG is usually produced through fermentation of corn, sugar beets or sugar cane. The finished

Test 6

product is a pure, white crystal which dissolves easily and blends well in many foods. Monosodium glutamate enhances the basic flavour of many foods. New studies also show that MSG elicits a unique taste that is known as "umami" in Japan, and often described by Americans as a savory, broth-like or meaty taste. "Umami" may be the Q34 fifth basic taste, beyond salty, sweet, sour and bitter. As an integral part of cuisines around the world, this savory taste is common to the bouillons of Europe, the oyster sauce of China, the soy and fish sauces of Q35 Southeast Asia, the pizza of Italy, and the chowders and stews of America.

MSG helps bring out the best natural flavours in a variety of foods such as meat, poultry, seafood and vegetables. While MSG harmonizes well with salty and sour tastes, it contributes little or nothing to Q36 sweet or bitter foods. Results of taste panel studies indicate that a level of 0.1% to 0.8% MSG by weight in food provides optimum enhancement of the food's natural flavour. This is within the range of glutamate that naturally occurs in foods. Approximately one-half teaspoon of MSG is an effective amount to enhance the flavour of a pound of meat or Q37 4–6 servings of vegetables or soup.

MSG is a self-limiting substance—once the proper amount is used, adding more contributes little to food flavour. Overuse of MSG, as with many other seasonings and spices, may cause some foods to have an undesirable taste. There is simply no substitute for wholesome, quality food and good cooking techniques. MSG makes good-quality food taste better, but it will not improve the flavour of poor-quality food.

Disturbingly, scientists have known since the 1960s that MSG kills Q38 brain cells in young animals. Further research suggested that MSG may also be responsible for ailments ranging from skin rashes to irregular heartbeat and depression. Reports vary on just what percentage of the population is sensitive to MSG. One researcher puts the figure as high as 30%, but food industry-sponsoured studies have suggested it is as low as Q39 1%–2%.

Baby food manufacturers agreed to take MSG out of their products in the 1970s, but it is still widely used in other foods. This is because MSG is an Q40 economical way of simulating great taste. If you're making a chicken stew but can't afford a whole chicken, why not use a little chicken and a lot of MSG? Consumer groups in the USA campaign regularly against its use, but for many of us, MSG will continue to be a part of everyday life. Food, it seems, will always be a matter of personal taste.

Test 7

答案速查

LISTENING

Section 1, Questions 1–10

1 student
2 9/nine weeks
3 reliable
4 18/eighteen years
5 safe
6 culture
7 friends
8 insurance
9 resume/CV
10 visa

Section 2, Questions 11–20

11 B
12 F
13 D
14 A
15&16 IN EITHER ORDER B D
17 fully booked
18 guided tour
19 2.15pm
20 local farm

Section 3, Questions21–30

21 PTF78196
22 May 26th
23 5
24 (an) additional class
25 (individual or personal) feedback
26 Good
27 Excellent
28 shampoo
29 Rarely
30 expand (the) menu

Section 4, Questions 31–40

31 A
32 A
33 C
34 B
35 C
36 C
37 D
38 B
39 A
40 D

READING

Reading Passage 1 Questions 1–12

1 G
2 C
3 D
4 I
5 F
6 H
7 B
8 E
9 B
10 A
11 C
12 A

Reading Passage 2, Questions 13–25

13 NO
14 YES
15 NO
16 NOT GIVEN
17 NO
18 NO
19 YES
20 twice
21 tiny share
22 cash
23 noticeable
24 fair rate
25 B

Reading Passage 3, Questions 26–40

26 C
27 B
28 C
29 A
30 B
31 official documents
32 reads or buys
33 phone conversations
34 dates
35 a friend's name
36–38 IN ANY ORDER C E F
39 B
40 D

名师解析

LISTENING

SECTION 1

主题场景	校园场景
主旨大意	介绍夏令营的相关情况
考查题型	笔记填空题

名师解读

1 student 题干中的关键词a full time为原文重现，题干中的must 与原文中的have to为同义替换。题干中的系动词be为原文重现。本题的答案在关键词前出现，需要考生具有短时记忆的能力。考生应注意转折连词but后的内容常常是考点。

2 9/nine weeks 题干中的minimum与原文中的at least为同义替换，故least后的时间名词nine weeks即为答案。

3 reliable 题干中的形容词outgoing与原文中的sociable对应，题干中的flexible与原文中的flexibility为同根词。原文接着在后面提到了reliable，即答案。

4 18/eighteen years 题干中的be at least与原文中的have to be对应，题干中的age与原文中的years old对应。考生应注意year要用复数形式。

5 safe 题干中的environment为关键词，与原文中的place对应，同时题干中的work为原文重现，故place前面的safe即为答案。

6 culture 题干中的become和familiar with分别与原文中的get和know对应，题干中的American又为原文重现，故American后的culture即为答案。

7 friends 题干的内容是将原文中make...from the international community内容进行改写，题干将介词from后的内容改写为定语。故make和 from之间的friends就是答案。

8 insurance 题干中的up to 30 days, travel均为原文重现，CCUSA负责insurance的费用，也就是说这个insurance是免费的。

9 resume/CV 题干中的enhances与原文中的add是同义替换。考生应注意resume的同义词为大写的两个字母CV。

10 visa 本题要求考生填入申请流程的第三步。题干中的apply与原文中的application为同根词，故前面的visa即为答案。

SECTION 2

主题场景	旅游场景
主旨大意	关于一个度假旅馆的介绍
考查题型	地图题、选择题、笔记填空题

名师解读

11 B 注意第一个方位词rear of the hotel（旅馆后门），之后听到nearest, swimming pool，与图中Q11的位置相符。

12 F 此题有干扰信息，先说第二个路口右转，又改为第一个，对应图中Q12位置，因此，Q12答案应为之后提到的sports centre。

13 D 听到图中的Zen spa，继续向前向海的方向行走到达Q13位置，对应原文continue, towards，因此答案应为family rooms。

14　A　注意14题的位置，在图的右下角，在停车场的对面。再由本段的介绍可知这里为restaurant。

15&16 IN EITHER ORDER B D　aquarium为关键词，听到kids，对应选项B的children，同义词必选；之后swimming被否定，是干扰项。最后的afternoon tea不在水族馆，为干扰信息。而原文中的feed the tea lions与D项意思吻合，指“喂动物”。

17　fully booked　注意前几栏信息的出现均可作为关键词，最后听到but，转折词之后的fully booked为答案。

18　guided tour　此题填写景点或活动，听到lake, wood, maze等词时因同为并列信息，暂不选，之后听到guided tour为答案。

19　2.15pm　填写时间，注意quarter past two是2.15不是1.45。要注意时间之间的换算。

20　local farm　与18题类似，本题也需填写景点名称。只要注意时间与景点的对应即可。

SECTION 3

主题场景	市场调查场景
主旨大意	关于休闲中心的访谈调查
考查题型	表格填空题

名师解读

21　PTF78196　题干考查会员号。填写号码，注意字母和数字组合的号码字母必须大写。

22　May 26th　填写日期，注意排除之前的干扰信息。会员卡的开卡日期为5月26日。

23　5　注意题干此栏的提示，应填写从1至5的数字表示优劣。此题有definitely表强调的词，数字five/5为答案。

24　(an) additional class　此题中run为“开设”之意，后面应填写课程之类的名词，即俱乐部在晚上开设的课程。答案为(an) additional class。

25　(individual or personal) feedback　注意原文关键词的替换，原文中的chance与题干中的opportunity为同义替换，答案为名词(individual or personal) feedback。

26　Good　此题答案范围为四个形容词，注意排除干扰，一定要听到最后讲话人最终的观点是good。

27　Excellent　答案性质同上，听到定位词关键词as时应注意，后面的excellent为答案。

28　shampoo　通过空格后的body cream判断，空格填写同样性质的名词，答案为shampoo。

29　Rarely　填写频率副词，如often, rarely等，考生应提前预热相关词汇。

30　expand (the) menu　根据and前后词性相同的原则，应填写动词词组，关键词waiting time后出现答案。

SECTION 4

主题场景	校园设施讨论场景
主旨大意	关于学习辅导中心的介绍
考查题型	选择题、配对题

名师解读

31　A　三个选项都很长，如果没有足够的时间阅读选项，要通过题干中的purpose定位答案位置，之后重点听原文的信息。原文的not only...but also...是重要信息，主要包括general procedure, familiar等词，应选择A项。B项的内容在下一句被否定，C项的内容不全面。

32　A　首先注意原文的强调词in fact，之后的newest, all kinds of与A项中的关键词对应。

33　C　题干考查原因，注意原文表原因的连接词as的出现，as之后为正确信息，对应选项C。选项A应划出否定词not required，选项B划出重点词汇change，原文均未出现相关词汇。

34 B 题干中的limited and short-term为关键词，之后听到independently，按照同根词必选原则，选择B项。

35 C 题干关键词flexible在原文中以同根词flexibility的形式出现，flexibility之后为答案信息，强调not your particular specialty，对应C项。

36 C 此题为配对题，关键词较明显，注意排除干扰。原文会提到多个选项，但否定与题干无关的内容，最后通常用转折词but, however或归纳词so等引出答案。注意此题中的while从句之后的主句为答案，听到faculty，对应选项C的department。

37 D 原文中的exemption是很重要的场景词汇，要明白其意为“免试”，听到direct them之后出现的academic office应为答案，选择D项。

38 B library resource是关键词，注意原文中的强调句it is the learning center...答案应为此信息。

39 A 此题与上题位置很接近，通过on occasions判断题目进入下一题，之后听到关键词及library。

40 D 注意题干关键词是student ID card而不是library card，找准关键词，对应原文academic office，应选D项。

READING

READING PASSAGE 1

体　裁　　说明文
题　材　　社会科学类
主　题　　人的面相（欲知心，先知面）
题　型　　选择题、配对题

Questions 1–8

题型 配对题(Matching Information)

注意 题目是文章句子的高度同义替换，很少出现与文中重复的字眼。

1	关键词	a large scale of samples
	原文定位	G段首句The researchers looked at 6,821 loan applications, 733 of which were successful.
	题解	答案G　原文F段及G段描述了研究小组进行的大众调查。G段中出现6 821例贷款申请和申请成功的733例。上述两个数字对应题干a large scale of samples（大规模的样本）。
2	关键词	web-site, borrowing money from strangers
	原文定位	C段第三句Now it is possible to do business directly with a stranger, using a peer-to-peer lending site.
	题解	答案C　快速浏览文字，掌握段落大意，可知本段主要讲的是在过去，如果你想借钱，你要么去银行，要么去找有钱的朋友或亲戚。现在通过使用借贷网站就可以直接和陌生人做生意了。题干中的borrowing money from strangers（从陌生人那里借钱）对应原文do business directly with a stranger（直接和陌生人做生意）。

Test 7

3	关键词	process of loaning, public
	原文定位	D段末句And the process is an open auction, which means that all offers, acceptances and rejections are in the public domain.
	题解	答案D　带着关键词浏览文章。浏览文章时不需要明白每句话的意思，主要是寻找与所划关键词为同义替换的词句。D段这个过程是一个公开的竞拍，题干中的public field（公共领域）对应原文中的public domain（公共领域）。
4	关键词	trustworthiness, unknown
	原文定位	I段第二句Unfortunately, Dr Duarte's method was not designed to find out which features label someone as trustworthy.
	题解	答案I　带着关键词trustworthiness浏览文章，确定该词只出现在G段和I段，即可缩小排查范围。如果能确定第4题的答案为G，则可直接确定本题答案为I。定位句的大意为：遗憾的是，Duarte所用的方法没有试图去确认具体是哪些面部特征标明人的可信度。本句的意思对应题干中的unknown（未知）。
5	关键词	forecast, creditworthiness
	原文定位	F段第二句In particular, they were asked to rate, on a scale of one to five, how trustworthy these people looked, and to estimate the percentage probability that each individual would repay a $100 loan.
	题解	答案F　工作人员被要求给这些借款人打可靠度的分数，并评估其偿还贷款的概率。题干中的forecast（预测）对应原文中的estimate（估计），creditworthiness（信誉）对应trustworthy（可靠的）。
6	关键词	untrustworthy, higher interest rates
	原文定位	H段末句To have the same chance of getting one as those deemed most trustworthy they were required to pay an interest rate that was, on average, 1.82 percentage points higher...
	题解	答案H　H段指出，这些不可靠的人要想得到和那些被认为最值得信赖的人相同的贷款几率，他们也要pay an interest rate that was, on average, 1.82 percentage points higher（支付平均高出1.82个百分点的利率）。题干中have to pay for higher interest rates为原文的同义简化。
7	关键词	women, men, appearance
	原文定位	本段第三句Testosterone levels are reflected in the face, and who is seen as a one-night stand and who as a potential husband depends in part on this physical feature.
	题解	答案B　B段指出外表的重要性，并以女人以相貌评判男人作为例子。who is seen as a one-night stand（谁看起来是做一夜情的情人），who as a potential husband（谁看起来是将来的老公）都可以从外表看出来。

8	关键词	prejudice, physiognomy
	原文定位	E段第二句His intention was twofold: to see if physiognomy-based prejudices about creditworthiness existed and, if they did, whether they were justified.
	题解	**答案E** Duarte的研究有两重目的：一、看一下基于面相学的对信誉的偏见是否存在；二、如果确实存在，又是否公正。题干中的prejudice based on physiognomy（基于面相学的偏见）等同于原文中的physiognomy-based prejudices（以面相学为基础的偏见）；而reasonable（合理的）对应justified（正当的）。

Questions 9–11

题型 选择题(Multiple Choice)

注意 有些题目能先定位到原文中的一个段落，这必将大大加快解题速度，并提高准确率。

9	关键词	mad relatives in a Victorian novel
	原文定位	A段第三句The errors are often regarded with embarrassment by subsequent generations, and locked away in attic rooms of the subject's mansion like mad relatives in a Victorian novel.
	题解	**答案B** 作者举出mad relatives in a Victorian novel（维多利亚时代小说中的疯癫的亲戚）的例子是为了说明人们对待错误的方式，如同维多利亚时代小说中的疯癫的亲戚（被锁在阁楼里）一样，错误被锁在科学领域宏伟大厦的阁楼里。故答案为B项。选项A是根据原文relatives（亲戚）做出的干扰项。
10	关键词	physiognomy
	原文定位	A段倒数第二句For years physiognomy—the idea that a person's face is a reflection of his character—was sneered at.
	题解	**答案A** 由sneer at可以看出，人们过去对physiognomy（面相学）是嗤之以鼻的。故正确答案为A，题干中的didn't take it seriously（没有认真对待）对应原文的was sneered at（蔑视）。
11	关键词	Jefferson Duarte
	原文定位	B段末句For Jefferson Duarte of Rice University in Houston, Texas, and his colleagues are suggesting that one of a person's most telling moral features, his creditworthiness, can also be seen in his face.
	题解	**答案C** Jefferson Duarte和他的同事们指出：一个人最为显著的品性特征之一——credit-worthiness（信誉），可以从其脸上看出来。A项可以看出一个人的外表和内心是否一样，不符；B项可以看出一个人是否说谎，不符；D项可以看出一个人是否有进取心，不符；C项（可以看出一个人是否值得被信任）符合题意。

Question 12

题型 选择题(Multiple Choice)

注意 当不能直接找出主题句时，通常文章中作者给予叙述较多或强调较多的某一事物或某一观点即是文章的中心。

12	关键词	suitable title
	原文定位	B段末句For Jefferson Duarte of Rice University in Houston, Texas, and his colleagues are suggesting that one of a person's most telling moral features, his creditworthiness, can also be seen in his face.
	题解	答案A　题干考查文章的主旨大意。四个选项中，关键词分别是：Creditworthiness, Self-discipline, Marital Status和Happiness。文章中反复提及的词就是creditworthiness（信誉）及trustworthiness（信用），文章所讲的主题就是一个人的信誉好坏似乎可以从面相上看出来，故正确答案为A。

READING PASSAGE 2

体　裁　　说明文
题　材　　经济类
主　题　　农作物咖啡
题　型　　判断题、句子填空题、选择题

Questions 13–19

题型 判断题(Identifying writer's views/claims)

注意 所谓YES，并不意味着题目和原文百分之百的相等，只要两者的表述是在同一个方向上的便可。

13	关键词	coca leaf
	原文定位	B段第二句In other parts of the same area, some families have turned to growing drugs in order to survive; higher prices are paid for coca leaf (the raw material for cocaine). 和末句The Menzas have stayed loyal to the coffee crop but not without great personal sacrifices.
	题解	答案NO　此定位句可知：coca leaf的价格更高，很多家庭为了生存改种coca leaf（可卡叶）；但尽管有很大的损失，Menza一家还是坚持种植咖啡作物，题干与原文相反。
14	关键词	trade, oil
	原文定位	D段首句Coffee is the second most valuable commodity after oil.
	题解	答案YES　在贸易领域，咖啡是在价值上仅次于石油的一种商品。即石油第一，咖啡第二，所以答案是YES。

15	关键词	50% of the supermarket price
	原文定位	F段末句An examination of the price paid to a farmer like Menza and the cost to a shopper in the supermarket reveals that both have lost out while many of the players in between have still managed to make gains.
	题解	答案NO 1989年至1993年期间，咖啡的世界市场价格降低了50%。一项对于Menza收入和超市购买者支出的研究表明，他们都受到了损失，而仍有很多中间商设法赚到了钱。题干属于偷换50%的概念，与原文矛盾。
16	关键词	cocoa, less exploitative
	原文定位	D段第三句Its total value— $8,000 million per year—is twice the value of exports of tea and cocoa put together.
	题解	答案NOT GIVEN 咖啡的价格是tea和cocoa的出口价格总额的twice（两倍），而题目中所说的cocoa（可可豆）的产量比咖啡的产量小并未提及。所以答案是NOT GIVEN。注意若根据关键词，如less exploitative（剥削性较低的）在文章中无法定位，则看有无同义转换，若无同义转换，那么确定答案是NOT GIVEN。
17	关键词	1989, dropped
	原文定位	G段首句When the world price fell by 50% during 1989, farmers suffered an immediate fall in their incomes yet there was no noticeable reduction in the supermarket price of coffee.
	题解	答案NO 1989年世界价格降了50%，而超市价格却no noticeable reduction（无明显降低），这显然与题目中“两者价格都下降”不符。在判断题中尤其要注意否定词的出现。
18	关键词	setting up a co-operative
	原文定位	J段第二句、第三句Many farmers have got together to set up cooperative marketing ventures which enable them to bypass the middlemen. All too often however, even the coop cannot get finance to buy the crop, and members still sell to local traders for cash.
	题解	答案NO 比较题目和原文，甚至农民合作社也无法帮助他们获得资金，这显然与题目中“对于农民来说建立农民合作社是有效解决方式’不符。
19	关键词	money to spend families
	原文定位	J段倒数第二句Evidence of low and declining living standards is clear. 末句The Fairtrade Foundation's research shows that reduced spending on housing, children's education, health and food.
	题解	答案YES 农民的生活水平在下降，他们花在各个方面的钱都在减少，与题目意思吻合，题干为原文的同义表达。

Test 7

Questions 20–24

题型 句子填空题(Sentence Completion)

注意 答案的字数必须服从于题目要求中答案的字数限制，至于是否需要达到字数的上限需要根据原文内容来决定，切不可盲目“凑字”，否则极易导致答案超字或答案词性发生变化从而失分。

20	关键词	as much value as
	原文定位	D段第三句Its total value—$8,000 million per year—is twice the value of exports of tea and cocoa put together.
	题解	答案twice 做题前要理解整个句子的含义并判断空格所缺词的词性，并确定关键词，然后回原文找重现。根据空格前后的内容可以推测，空格应填入的为表示倍数的副词，回原文定位可以确定为twice。
21	关键词	keep, final retail value
	原文定位	E段From tree to supermarket shelf it has been estimated the Menzas' coffee beans can change hands as many as 150 times, whilst the Menzas, like millions of other coffee growers, retain only a tiny share of the price consumers pay for the crop.
	题解	答案tiny share 由空格前的冠词a可以确定，空格应填入的为名词。题干中的keep（保持）对应原文中的retain（保留）；而the final retail value（最终零售价）对应原文中的the price consumers pay for the crop（消费者支付的价格），因此原文retain（保留）后的宾语tiny share（小部分）应为答案。
22	关键词	coffee crop, harvest
	原文定位	I段倒数第二句With only one major harvest a year, farmers are desperate for cash by the time their crop is ripe and are keen to sell at whatever price they can get.
	题解	答案cash 由空格前的little可知，空格应填入的为名词。Desperate for cash（迫切需要现金）表明他们手中的cash（现金）很少，农民们急需现金，故答案为cash。
23	关键词	1989
	原文定位	G段首句When the world price fell by 50% during 1989, farmers suffered an immediate fall in their incomes yet there was no noticeable reduction in the supermarket price of coffee.
	题解	答案noticeable 由空格前后的内容可知，空格应填入的为形容词。题干中的drop（下降）对应原文中的reduction（减少），故原文中修饰reduction（减少）的形容词noticeable（明显的）为本题答案。注意noticeable的拼写。
24	关键词	borrow money
	原文定位	J段首句The farmers' need for a quick sale is a symptom of their inability to get loans at a fair rate from banks, pushing them into the arms of loan sharks to pay for fertilizers...
	题解	答案fair rate 由空格前的冠词可知，空格应填入的为名词。题干中的impossible（不可能的）对应原文中的inability（没有……的能力）；borrow money（借钱）对应get loans（贷款）。农民们想要快点儿出售他们的作物表示他们不能borrow money at a fair rate（从银行以公平的费率贷款）。

Question 25

题型 选择题(Multiple Choice)

注意 若要避免落入选择题所设置的陷阱以及干扰项中，就要从学会判断考官的出题意图这点出发。

25	关键词	purpose
	原文定位	E段From tree to supermarket shelf it has been estimated the Menzas' coffee beans can change hands as many as 150 times, whilst the Menzas, like millions of other coffee growers, retain only a tiny share of the price consumers pay for the crop.
	题解	**答案B** 本文客观地描述解释了种植咖啡的农民如何在国际大环境中受到盘剥，获益微薄，难以为生的一种现象，并没有流露出作者主观的看法，没有建议或激励读者的意图。

READING PASSAGE 3

体　裁　说明文
题　材　科技类
主　题　软件与您的生活
题　型　分类题、摘要填空题、选择题

Questions 26–30

题型 分类题(Classification)

注意 注意先读文章后面的问题，找到分类的标准，看题目要求按照什么标准来分类，再去阅读找答案。题目的问题是按照四个人物来分类的，那么阅读时就要有意识地将与这四个人物有关的关键句子和内容用不同的符号标出来。

26	关键词	save most of what we see and hear
	原文定位	J段第三句"Users will eventually be able to keep every document they read, every picture they view, all the audio they hear and a good portion of what they see," says Gemmell.
	题解	**答案C** 根据题干四个人物的分类我们来阅读文章，并且用不同的记号将关于上述人物的描述标出来。先明确各个人物具体出现在哪一段。然后我们来看第一题：In the future we will be able to save most of what we see and hear. 从J段中我们看到be able to keep（能够保留），the audio they hear（他们听到的声音）和a good portion of what they see（他们看到的大部分）等短语，与题干的意思相符，因此应该选C。
27	关键词	MyLifeBits, memories
	原文定位	J段第四句Bell believes that for some people, especially those with memory problems, MyLifeBits will become a surrogate memory that is able to recall past experiences...
	题解	**答案B** 在本题中，题干中的especially helpful for people whose memories are not very good（对于那些记忆力不是很好的人格外有用）与定位句的especially those with memory problems（尤其是那些有记忆问题的人）对应，因此应该选B。

28	关键词	aren't all kept in one place
	原文定位	D段第二句、第三句"In a giant shoebox full of photos, it's hard to find what you are looking for,"says Microsoft's Jim Gemmell. Add to this the reels of home movies, videotapes, bundles of letters and documents we file away, and remembering what we have, let alone finding it, becomes a major headache.
	题解	答案C 本题的关键是要把握住a giant shoebox full of photos, the reels of home movies, videotapes, bundles of letters and documents we file away的意思，即一般情况下我们存放相片、一盘一盘的家庭电影和录像带的胶片以及成捆的信件和文件的地方，即为一种传统的保存相片的方式与题干的conventional ways对应。
29	关键词	descendants, system
	原文定位	K段末句Doug de Groot...says Bell's system could eventually form the basis for "meet the ancestor" style educational tools, where people will quiz their ancestors on what happened in their lifetimes.
	题解	答案A Doug de Groot指出通过Bell的系统，人们可以用它考察他们祖先的一生曾经发生过什么。此处的system（系统）指的就是MyLifeBits。
30	关键词	storing information, go down in the near future
	原文定位	G段第二句But Bell calculates that within five years, a 1,000-gigabyte hard drive will cost less than ＄300 and that is enough to store four hours of video every day for a year.
	题解	答案B Bell小组的计算表示a 1,000-gigabyte hard drive（一个1 000千兆字节的硬盘）将会花费不到300美元。这就说明信息存储的价格下降了，符合题干的go down（下降），因此应该选B。

Questions 31–35

题型 摘要填空题(Summary Completion)

注意 在题干中（即空格周围）寻找合适的定位词，根据定位词回原文寻找正确答案。本题空格周围的关键词较少，这增加了本题的难度。

31	关键词	letters, photos
	原文定位	F段首句Apart from official documents like his passport, he is hoping to post everything from letters and photos, to home videos and work documents.
	题解	答案official documents 首先，根据空格前后的内容可以确定，空格应填入的为名词；原文中like是一种解释关系，而题干中的冒号也是一种解释关系，所以本题应该填写like（如同）前面的核心词，即official documents（官方文件）。

Test 7

32	关键词	online and on audio
	原文定位	F段第二句All his email is automatically saved on the system, as is anything he reads or buys online.
	题解	答案reads or buys　首先，根据空格前后的内容可以确定，空格应填入的为动词；然后利用关键词语online and on audio（在线、听音频）与所给阅读文章的相关句子进行匹配，此处应该填上online（在线）前面的动词reads or buys（阅读或购买）。
33	关键词	saving, meetings
	原文定位	F段第三句He has also started recording phone conversations and meetings to store as audio files.
	题解	答案phone conversations　以空格前后的saving和meetings作为关键词回原文定位答案信息。因空格后为and，表并列，可以确定空格应填入的为与meetings（会议）并列的名词，即phone conversations（电话会议）；另外，回原文定位时要留意同义替换表达，题干中的saving（保存）对应原文中的recording（记录）。
34	关键词	keying in
	原文定位	H段首句To recall a period in his past, Bell just types in the dates he is interested in.
	题解	答案dates　空格前为定冠词the，可以确定空格应填入的为名词；题干中的keying in（键控输入）为原文types in（输入）的同义替换，故可以确定其共同的宾语dates（日期）为答案。
35	关键词	look for
	原文定位	I段末句Searching for a friend's name would bring together a chronological set of files describing when you both did things together, for instance.
	题解	答案a friend's name　题干中的look for（寻找）对应原文的searching for（搜索），故其共同宾语a friend's name（朋友的名字）为本题答案。注意要求从原文选词，有字数要求，如Use NO MORE THAN THREE WORDS等，答案必须满足这个要求。

Questions 36–38

题型 选择题(Multiple Choice)

注意 任何一个题干中其实都隐藏着很多的细节，而这些细节能够极大地帮助考生去缩小阅读范围，集中精力来寻找题目关键词。

36–38	关键词	difficult, where accidentally throw away, too much stuff
	原文定位	D段第二句、第三句“In a giant shoebox full of photos, it's hard to find what you are looking for,” says Microsoft's Jim Gemmell. Add to this the reels of home movies, videotapes, bundles of letters and documents we file away, and remembering what we have, let alone finding it, becomes a major headache.
	题解	答案IN ANY ORDER C E F　看到conventional ways（传统的方式），即可反射到之前回答的Q28题。在对Q28进行分析后，可以确定“在庞大的装满相片的鞋盒中，很难发现你想找的东西”。C项与此相符合。接下来可以采用排除法。首先，A项忘记事情发生的时间为设计MyLifeBits的动机之一，即对应experiences get exaggerated, we muddle the timing of events and simply forget stuff中的muddle the timing of events（混淆了事情发生的时间），而不是problems（问题），故排除；B项很难找到一个合适的鞋盒来装照片和信件等，原文未提及，另外根据常识亦可排除；D项We forget what records of our past we have（我们忘记了我们有什么样的历史记录），为原文remembering what we have（记得我们有的）的干扰项，题干以偏概全，原文未特指records（记录），故排除。可确定答案为E、F。

Questions 39 and 40

题型 选择题(Multiple Choice)

注意 读下面的五个选项，并留意它们的核心意义和彼此之间的区别，以利于接下来的判断，然后再到文章中寻找对应的内容。

39	关键词	not secure
	原文定位	F段末句The privacy and corporate security risks are clear.
	题解	答案B　题干考查possible disadvantages of the MyLifeBits。F段最后指出，显然，这样做容易暴露隐私和公司安全。注意避免干扰项A项，unreliable表示不可靠的，而本段强调的是不安全，即not secure（不安全）。
40	关键词	large, computer memory
	原文定位	G段首句Of course the system takes up a huge amount of memory.
	题解	答案D　系统占据了极大的储存空间。题干a large amount（大量）为原文a huge amount的同义替换。

WRITING

WRITING TASK 1

名师解读

本题为曲线图(graph)和柱形图(bar chart)的结合，展示的是东非某地区的月均降雨量和温度。柱形图代表降雨量，而曲线代表温度。写作时直接把柱状图和条形图看成复杂版的曲线图、表格图、扇形图即可，同样是描述极值、拐点值、趋势等。

在看组合图时，先思考以下问题：

* 柱形图和曲线图各自展示了什么数据？在某个时间点或段的变化特征是什么？

* 柱形图有何特征？是否以时间为轴？各个柱形所占百分比是多少？百分比从大到小如何排列的？谁最大？谁最小？

* 曲线图有何特征？根据特征，曲线可以分成几段来描述？起点值、终点值、峰值、谷值各是多少？各自对应的时间点又是什么？

高分范文

The graph shows the average weather conditions in one region of East Africa. It shows that there are significant differences in the average monthly **precipitation** and some variation in temperature. The range of rainfall figures is very large across the year (from approximately five to 280 millimetres) whereas the temperature only fluctuates by three degrees, from 20.5°C to 23.5°C.

Broadly speaking, in this region periods of high rainfall tend also to be periods of slightly hotter weather, with three noticeable peaks in the year. Temperatures are fairly high in March and April, which coincides with a time of very heavy rainfall (with a top figure of 280mm in April) and October (just over 23°C). Both rainfall and temperature figures fall in the middle of the year (to a yearly low of 20.5°C, and just 5mm of rain in July).

The exception to this pattern—of warmer weather being damper—is January/February and September where there are relatively high temperatures (22°C–23°C) but low rainfall (less than 20mm). (165 words)

WRITING TASK 2

文章结构

观点+措施+影响

viewpoint+measure 1+measure 2+problems
第一段：背景句+强调观点
第二段：措施1
第三段：措施2
第四段：影响+建议

思路点拨

步骤一：审题（<3分钟）

Meat production requires relatively more land than crop production. Some people think that as land is becoming scarce, the world's meat consumption should be reduced. What measures could be taken to reduce the world's meat consumption? What kinds of problem might such measures cause?

→通读题目，了解大意。

肉类生产比农作物生产需要相对更多的土地。有些人认为，随着土地越来越稀缺，世界应该减少肉类消费。可以采取什么措施来减少世界上的肉类消费吗？这样的措施会导致什么样的问题？

→再读题目，辨别关键词，区分主题词和限定词，推测考官的出题意图。

主题词：Meat production, reduced

限定词：measures, problem

步骤二：列大纲（<3分钟）

英文提纲	Introduction: Agree (opinion)→strongly agree with the suggestion that human kind should consume less meat (topic) Body: Measure 1: education → change of lifestyle → cheaper and more environmentally sound → figures → children should also be taught → shift from meat to vegetables Measure 2: financial →taxes →a luxury item Problem: a danger → ignoring + suggestion: a compromise position → encourage less wastage in food
中文提纲	引出话题：同意（观点）→强烈赞同人类应该少吃肉（话题） 主体段： 措施 1：教育→生活方式的改变→更便宜、更环保→用数字说话→教育孩子→肉类到蔬菜的转换 措施 2：财政的→税收→奢侈品 影响：危害→ 忽视+建议：折中的方式→鼓励减少食物浪费

高分范文

I strongly agree with the suggestion that humankind should **consume** less meat and instead have more vegetables in their diet, and I believe that a number of steps can be taken to persuade people to do this.

Firstly, I feel that education has a major role to play in bringing about this change of lifestyle. A well-informed minority of the world's population may be fully aware of the fact that it is much cheaper and more environmentally sound to eat vegetables, thereby cutting out a whole stage of production, rather than consuming the animals which **graze** on vegetation. However, I believe that the majority are not conscious of this. Figures should be made widely available showing the savings to be made from this option, both financial and ecological. From a young age, children should also be taught this as an essential part of the **curriculum** and to set an example, school meals should be **redesigned** to reflect a shift from meat to vegetables.

A second measure would be financial. Taxes can be put on meat to make it a luxury item to be eaten fairly rarely, at most three or four times a week, rather than two or three times a day as is the practice in many parts of the developed world.

There is, however, a danger in too much interference in people's choice. It is often the case that resistance builds up against lecturing and **fiscal penalties**, meaning that people will react by ignoring all the advice. Perhaps a compromise position would be to encourage less wastage in food production and retail, particularly in the developed world. Huge amounts of perfectly usable food are thrown away by households, restaurants and supermarkets. Less wastage would mean less food production in the first place. (299 words)

SPEAKING

名师解读

Part 1的话题为交通，考生应对这个话题所能涉及的所有素材及答题方法有所积累。另外，本组问题均为特殊疑问句，则需考生先确定主题，再展开问答。

对于Part 2的叙述不必都说事实，因为由于文化差异，有时我们所说的经历和话题可能与考官的理解不尽相同。但真实的故事往往更具有说服力，更容易连贯。因此，在雅思口语考试中，最好还是有真实的故事陈述。

Part 3是要和考官互动的，有点类似于讨论、辩论之类的，可以尽量说长一点。示例中的题目多为一般疑问句，考生一定要避免中式固定思维的错误回答，即只答yes，无下文。注意如何规避由只答yes而出现的误用时态问题。

高分示例

PART1

- What form of transport do you prefer to use? Why?

I prefer to use the subway, even though it can get crowded and I then have to walk to my destination. I feel it is safer than driving a car or bike on the roads. The people do not know how to drive safely and so **endanger** everyone and themselves each time they go on the roads.

- What's the most common means of/form of transport in your hometown?

In my hometown, bicycles and walking are the most common forms of transport. The town is pretty small, so everything is close together. There is no need to have cars or trucks.

- What do you think of the transport conditions in your hometown?

I think they could make the walkways easier for the older generations that cannot **manoeuvre** too well in rain or mud by maybe paving or making a pathway through the town.

- How has the transport system in your hometown changed in the past few decades?

The transport system has not changed much besides from the one or two cars or trucks that pass through towards the farms. They only come out once or twice per month to check crops or collect them.

PART 2

One of the problems in Beijing is the rules of the road. Simply, there are none, and no one has any **inclination** to change it anytime soon. Everybody drives the way they want with next to no consideration for the other motorists or **pedestrians** on the road or even the sidewalks. This isn't just about the drivers of cars though, it's for everyone; motorbikes, truck, buses, and even bicycles need to start driving properly.

The problem is caused by people being too impatient and believing they have right of way or the ability to drive how they want. It is a huge problem because it puts everyone at risk, the drivers, the children walking back from school, and of course, everyone in the area.

I think one of the ways this can start to get better is by forming a traffic police unit, such as you see in many other countries. Their job is to make sure that the population is following the rules of the road, like keeping the scooters and bikes of the sidewalk and in the **lane** meant for them, as well as keeping cars from driving across three lanes to the left when they were in the far right lane. Being caught doing these things should get you a fine or even prison time if you have been caught more than once.

PART 3

The development of cities

- Can you discuss the causes of urbanization?

Urbanization is caused when a country's population increases. Due to the growing number of people, the government needs to construct more homes, and production areas. This causes the loss of rural, farm and forest areas.

- Can you explain how the overcrowding of cities affects our lives?

Overcrowding is caused when there is little space for the amount of people living in a city or town. It has **drastic** effects on everything in our lives, even if we do not realise it at times, from driving up prices to the pollution and garbage overflowing around the city.

- Can you predict how cities will develop in the future?

As much as I want to believe that with everyone becoming more ecologically friendly, that things will get better, the truth is it isn't. Even if companies are trying to be green, the majority of the population is still used to doing things the easy way and saying it isn't their problem. By the time the general population realises that they need to change, plant more tree, and living "green", it will be too late.

Global issues

- Can you evaluate the problem of overpopulation in your country?

I believe the overpopulation here has to do with many different issues. Years ago, the people were told to have big families, and then were told later that there was a one child per family law. I do not know how the law is enforced or if it is **enforced** at all, but if the population keeps growing, the country will not be able to support itself.

- How obvious is the gap between rich and poor in your country?

There is quite a gap between the wealthy and the poor, but you cannot see it unless you go into the real living areas of China. Tourists will not see such a big gap, but those who know of it, know where to find it.

- Can you talk about how worried you are about rising world temperatures?

Global warming is a huge thing, but not everyone is worried, and some people still believe it's "not real". No one can see what will happen in the future, but from most studies, it is known that if global warming carries on at its current pace, many cities and towns, even islands will be covered in water in 50 years or so. I am worried that people do not take the destruction of our only planet so **casually**.

重点词汇

LISTENING

enquiry	[ɪn'kwaɪəri]	*n.*	问，询盘
sociable	['səʊʃəbl]	*adj.*	社交的；好交际的
non-resident		*n.*	非居民
basically	['beɪsɪkli]	*adv.*	主要地，基本上
participant	[pɑː'tɪsɪpənt]	*n.*	参与者；关系者
requirement	[rɪ'kwaɪəmənt]	*n.*	要求；必要条件
flexibility	[ˌfleksə'bɪləti]	*n.*	灵活性；弹性
unpredictable	[ˌʌnprɪ'dɪktəbl]	*adj.*	不可预知的；不定的
especially	[ɪ'speʃəli]	*adv.*	特别；尤其；格外
probably	['prɒbəbli]	*adv.*	大概；或许；很可能
accommodation	[əˌkɒmə'deɪʃn]	*n.*	住处，膳宿；调节
opportunity	[ˌɒpə'tjuːnəti]	*n.*	时机，机会
community	[kə'mjuːnəti]	*n.*	社区；共同体；团体
presumably	[prɪ'zjuːməbli]	*adv.*	大概；推测起来
suitable	['sjuːtəbl]	*adj.*	适当的；相配的
orientation	[ˌɔːrɪən'teɪʃn]	*n.*	方向；适应
complex	['kɒmpleks]	*n.*	综合设施
pamper	['pæmpə]	*v.*	纵容；使……过量
jacuzzi	[dʒə'kuːzi]	*n.*	极可意水流按摩浴缸
aquarium	[ə'kweərɪəm]	*n.*	水族馆；养鱼池
excursion	[ɪk'skɜːʃn]	*n.*	远足；短程旅行
encompass	[ɪn'kʌmpəs]	*v.*	包含
wander	['wɒndə]	*v.*	漫步；迷路
savour	['seɪvə]	*v.*	品尝；尽情享受
expire	[ɪk'spaɪə]	*v.*	期满；终止
aerobics	[eə'rəʊbɪks]	*n.*	有氧运动
hygienic	[haɪ'dʒiːnɪk]	*adj.*	卫生的，保健的
polytechnic	[ˌpɒlɪ'teknɪk]	*n.*	工艺学校
literacy	['lɪtərəsi]	*n.*	读写能力
numeracy	['njuːmərəsi]	*n.*	计算能力
jurisdiction	[ˌdʒʊərɪs'dɪkʃn]	*n.*	权限
orientation	[ˌɔːrɪən'teɪʃn]	*n.*	情况介绍

READING

craniology	[ˌkreɪnɪ'ɒlədʒi]	*n.*	头骨学；头盖学
phrenology	[frə'nɒlədʒi]	*n.*	骨相学
eugenics	[juː'dʒenɪks]	*n.*	优生学
rehabilitate	[ˌriːə'bɪlɪteɪt]	*v.*	恢复
testosterone	[te'stɒstərəʊn]	*n.*	睾丸素
business acumen			商业头脑
creditworthiness	['kredɪtwɜːðɪnəs]	*n.*	信誉，商誉
open auction			开放式拍卖
physiognomy	[ˌfɪzɪ'ɒnəmi]	*n.*	面相学
at stake			在危险中，在危急关头
fluctuate	['flʌktʃʊeɪt]	*v.*	波动

malnutrition	[ˌmælnjuːˈtrɪʃn]	*n.*	营养失调，营养不良
tortuous	[ˈtɔːtʃʊəs]	*adj.*	曲折的
devastating	[ˈdevəsteɪtɪŋ]	*adj.*	毁灭性的
precarious	[prɪˈkeərɪəs]	*adj.*	岌岌可危的
vicious circle			恶性循环
desperate	[ˈdespərət]	*adj.*	极度渴望的
surrogate	[ˈsʌrəgət]	*adj.*	代理的
chronicle	[ˈkrɒnɪkl]	*v.*	记录
muddle	[ˈmʌdl]	*v.*	混淆
chronological	[ˌkrɒnəˈlɒdʒɪkl]	*adj.*	按年代顺序排列的
scrapbook	[ˈskræpbʊk]	*n.*	剪贴本
avatar	[ˈævətɑː]	*n.*	化身
farsighted	[fɑːˈsaɪtɪd]	*adj.*	有远见的

WRITING

precipitation	[prɪˌsɪpɪˈteɪʃn]	*n.*	冰雹；沉淀
consume	[kənˈsjuːm]	*v.*	消耗，消费
graze	[greɪz]	*v.*	吃草；放牧
curriculum	[kəˈrɪkjələm]	*n.*	课程
redesign	[ˌriːdɪˈzaɪn]	*v.*	重新设计
fiscal	[ˈfɪskl]	*adj.*	财政的
penalty	[ˈpenəlti]	*n.*	处罚；罚款

SPEAKING

endanger	[ɪnˈdeɪndʒə]	*v.*	危及
manoeuvre	[məˈnuːvə]	*v.*	移动
inclination	[ˌɪnklɪˈneɪʃn]	*n.*	倾向
pedestrian	[pəˈdestrɪən]	*n.*	行人；步行者
lane	[leɪn]	*n.*	车道
urbanization	[ˌɜːbənaɪˈzeɪʃn]	*n.*	都市化
drastic	[ˈdræstɪk]	*adj.*	激烈的
enforce	[ɪnˈfɔːs]	*v.*	实施，执行
casually	[ˈkæʒʊəli]	*adv.*	随便地

听力原文

SECTION 1

(MAN=M; WOMAN=W)

M: Hello, this is the volunteer enquiry line. How may I help?

W: Oh hi...A Japanese friend of mine is interested in getting some work experience here in the US, and I said I'd get some information for her.

M: And is your friend sociable?

W: Very.

M: Then I'd suggest the summer camp programme—CCUSA is the name of the organisation that runs it.

W: OK. And can you tell me a little bit about the programme?

M: Well, it's not open to people living here, it's only for non-residents. And basically there are two types of work—participants can either work with the children, that's organising and running activities, or they can apply to work as support staff. But in that case they have to be a Q1 student on a full time course. I don't know about your friend?

W: Well she would qualify for support work, but I guess she'd rather work with the children anyway.

M: And CCUSA only accept people who are able to work for at least Q2 nine weeks, even though most of the summer camp programmes last for twelve weeks, even longer in some cases. They start in either May or June and go on till August.

W: I think that'll be OK. And what sort of people get accepted onto programmes? What are the people requirements?

M: The most important one is a liking for children...

W: Sure...

M: People need to be quite sociable, as I said. Then...flexibility's important, because sometimes unpredictable things happen. And it's really important to be Q3 reliable—I know there's been some problems in the past with participants turning up late, or forgetting to be somewhere...And that really messes things up for the leaders.

W: Yes, I can see that. But my friend would be a model employee, I'm sure!

M: You also have to be Q4 18 years old to participate in a camp programme, though you can make an application when you're still only 17.

W: That's fine My friend's already 19 years old.

M: Fine...I'm sure your friend would get a lot out of doing a CCUSA programme.

W: Yes, I think there'd be a lot of benefits. For one thing, I think a summer camp would be a Q5 safe place to work, and that's important, especially when you're in a strange country.

M: That's right. And she'd be able to get to know American Q6 culture. It's probably quite different here in many ways compared to Japan.

W: Right. And...Would she have to pay for her accommodation?

M: That's free, and so are meals. And your friend would get the opportunity to Q7 make friends from the international community, not just Americans. These camps are very mixed.

W: Yes, she'd love that I'm sure.

M: And at the end of the volunteer programme the US government allows participants to Q8 travel independently for up to 30 days, and CCUSA covers their insurance for that. So people often go places together with some of the people they met at summer camp.

W: It sounds ideal. And another thing is, I know that it's useful to be able to add that kind of work experience to your Q9 resume. Future employers really like it.

M: Correct.

W: I'll pass all that information on. And presumably my friend can apply online for a position?

M: That's right. And if she's considered suitable she'll be asked to attend an interview in Japan.

W: And if she's accepted, does CCUSA help with her Q10 visa application?

M: No, she has to do that herself.

W: Right. And is that everything?

M: The final stage is an orientation programme, and again that'd be in Japan. Most people say that's very useful and they...[fade]

SECTION 2

Good afternoon, I'd like to welcome you all to the Palm Leaf Holiday Park. My name is Kate Green and I'm your tour guide. So, first of all I want to explain where all the main facilities are so that you can enjoy everything the hotel complex has to offer during your holiday. I'm sure you're all going to have a great stay.

Well, from the rear of the hotel you can access all of the facilities as they are all connected via small walkways. The nearest is of course the newly renovated outdoor Q11 swimming pool. This has great views of the sea and is directly in front of you as you exit the hotel, it even has a pool side bar. For those more interested in keeping fit, if you turn left out of the hotel and take the second right, no sorry, the first right and follow the path round, you will come to the fully equipped Q12 sports centre which offers tennis, football, basketball and also has a hi-tech gym. Regular classes are on offer and you can sign up at the reception which is just facing us now.

Another great facility is the Zen relaxation spa. There you can pamper yourself with massages and enjoy a dip in the medicinal jacuzz or have an alternative body treatment. Again, please sign up at the front desk. From the spa you can continue towards the sea to the Q13 family rooms which offer a fantastic view of the southern coast. Those of you who have booked the luxury rooms will be pleased to know that they have direct access to our private beach, one of the best in the country. For other guests beach access can be gained by crossing the swimming pool bridge, passing the entertainment centre on your right and you can't miss the sea.

After a day on the beach you'll probably be hungry so why not try the newly opened and award winning Q14 cafe restaurant called the Blue Dolphin. Whether you just want a coffee, snack or a meal, that's the place to head to. You can get to it from the beach if you're sunbathing and hungry or from the hotel's front desk as it's on the opposite side of the complex to the car park. However, please bear in mind that main meals are only served at meal times. If you would like something between those times, there is a food menu at the bar.

As you know Cornwall has plenty of local attractions. It's one of the most popular tourist destinations in England because of the beautiful natural coastline and the pleasant scenery, and not to mention the great attractions, many of which aren't far from the hotel.

Perhaps the most interesting place in this area is, the old Carryman Castle built by the Normans which many believe is the original site of King Arthur's round table, so it's certainly not to be missed. Whether you believe it or not, I highly recommend it for a nice morning out. This county also has its our own answer to Disneyland, Paradise Park, which is a great family day out and within walking distance of the hotel. It has a full range of rides, games and even a circus to keep everyone amused.

For those more interested in souvenirs, the best place may be the hotel shop where you can pick up some local handmade gifts. As the region boasts some of the best beaches in England, it's no surprise that there's an aquarium in town which has a huge range of sea life from all corners of the world. Q15 Their hourly kids shows are not to be missed. The trained dolphins and whales perform amazing tricks, so don't forget to bring your cameras. Entrance is included in the ticket price but you can't swim with the animals. Between shows there's the chance to Q16 feed and touch the sea lions which can be great fun. Last but not least is the famous Lanterey house, a fine example of a classic Cornish country mansion, previously owned by a distant member of the royal family. Left to the council for safe keeping, now open to the public twice a week. It's a nice place to enjoy afternoon tea.

Full details of excursions can be obtained from the hotel's reception desk. Next week on Monday at 8am there's a full day trip to Land's End but it's already Q17 fully booked. There are still a few tickets for the next day's trip but it's an early one. Breakfast starts at 7 so you have about half an hour to get something to eat before the bus leaves at 7.30 for a grand Elizabethan manor.

Anthony Place has been lovingly restored, as to have

the 20 acre grounds which encompass a lake, a great wood and a large maze for kids. After a short Q18 guided tour by a local historian, you will be free to wander the entire premises. Please note that lunch is included at the orangery restaurant where, you can savour local delicacies.

Then on Wednesday after lunch Q19 at a quarter past 2, you can ride the Smithson steam train from the local train station along the coast to a quaint little village named Bowman, famed for its delicious cider. You'll have plenty of time to try some as the train back doesn't leave until half past 6.

The Friday excursion to the lighthouse at Hell's Mouth has been cancelled. As a replacement, there's a 25 to 2 afternoon trip to see an active Q20 local farm. Kids of all ages will love it as they can get close to pigs and sheep. It's named after the owner Victoria Brown, hence the name Vicky's farm. Don't miss the shop, they have the county's best range of Cornish biscuits. Perfect gifts for friends and family.

SECTION 3

(Interviewer=I; Customer=C)

I: Hello, I am carrying out some market research for the leisure centre, asking customers about how they feel about the facilities and service, would you be able to spare a few minutes to answer a few questions?

C: Sure as long as it doesn't take more than about five minutes, I have an appointment I need to get to soon.

I: OK, well first of all, would you mind giving me your membership number? You don't have to if you would rather not, you can just do the survey without identifying who you are if you prefer.

C: No, I don't mind. Hang on a minute. Let me just get my card. It's PTF7 something I think—here it is. It's PTF78196.

I: OK, so that's PTF7896. That's right, isn't it?

C: No—It's Q21 PTF78196.

I: OK, and could you tell me when your membership started?

C: Yes, I joined in May, around the 20th I think...oh no, it was on Q22 May 26th and it's due to expire, pretty soon now actually, I've been coming now for almost six months. Yes, that's right. It finishes on October 28th.

I: And are you planning to renew your membership?

C: Yes, I am.

I: OK, now I want to ask you some questions relating to a number of aspects of the leisure club. First of all, the instructors, would you say that you are happy with their classes?

C: Erm, yes, I would. I really enjoy all of the classes and I think the instructors are extremely professional and supportive. I attend aerobics and yoga, though I don't go to the pilates class, I might try it next month. My favourite instructor is Janet—she's great.

I: So, on a scale of 1–5, 5 being the best, how would you rate the instructors for the yoga class?

C: Oh, I would say the top score—Q23 5, definitely. I really enjoy the class.

I: Do you have any suggestions for improvement?

C: Well, the only thing I would say is that evening classes can get very busy, I prefer coming in the mornings as there are fewer people in the class, but it's not always possible. Maybe the club could think about running an Q24 additional class in the evening, you know, so that the room's less crowded.

I: And how about the aerobics class?

C: I would rate it one point lower at four. I still think that it is really good too, but I don't enjoy it quite as much as yoga.

I: So how could it be improved do you think?

C: Well, it's just that with the yoga class, the teachers really seem to give you personal feedback on how well you do and how you can improve. Aerobics isn't quite as personal and there is never really any chance to get any individual Q25 feedback.

I: OK, well, thanks very much for that, we'll now move on to talking about the facilities.
So with regards to the facilities, I need to ask a few questions about your impressions of the changing rooms, swimming pool and café. First, the swimming pool. Would you say that it is of an excellent, good, average or poor standard?

C: It is a few years old now and so may need repainting and freshening up a little bit, especially as the new club down the road has excellent swimming pool facilities, but I wouldn't say it is poor. You know it is very clean and hygienic, so I would rate it as Q26 good but it could be improved a bit I guess.

I: OK, thanks for that, and how about the changing rooms?

C: Well again, the level of cleanliness is very good and they are quite spacious, so unless the club is exceptionally busy there is room for everyone. I would rate them overall as Q27 excellent really. Maybe a way to improve would be to offer complementary items for customers to use, you know, like Q28 shampoo and body creams—they have started to do that in quite a few places now.

I: Great, OK, well the final part of the questionnaire relates to the café. Could you tell me how often you tend to use it? Every visit, often, sometimes, rarely or never?

C: Well, you know to be honest, I would only rate the café as average, so I don't really use it very often, Q29 "rarely" I would have to say.

I: Can you tell me why?

C: Well, I think that there is too much competition from the café around the corner. They serve an excellent range of fresh and healthy food and very good coffee too, though actually the coffee in the leisure centre is very good. The range in the leisure centre café is quite limited and you often have to wait quite a long time if you order anything.

I: So what could we do to make it better?

C: In my opinion, maybe you should be decreasing waiting time for orders and Q30 expand the menu choice so it can appeal to more people.

I: Well, thanks very much for taking the time to answer the questions, we take the views of our customers very seriously and I am sure you will see some exciting developments in the near future.

SECTION 4

OK, well thank you for coming to our Staff Orientation Day, all eight of you are new members of the Learning Support Centre team and today will be an opportunity, not only Q31 to learn more about the general procedures of the centre but it will also give you an opportunity to get to know each other and the existing members of the team. Health and Safety issues will not be covered in today's session, however, a seminar will be held to cover issues relevant to that in the first week of the new semester.

Now, as I am sure you were informed during your interviews, the Learning Centre is a relatively new department within the polytechnic, in fact, the newest of all departments. It was established two years ago as part of an initiative Q32 to strengthen the support systems available to our students and its aim is to offer all kinds of academic support to a wide variety of students who may be finding it difficult to study completely independently. Your clients will be from a variety of backgrounds and may come to you for all kinds of issues, for example, a non-native English speaker may be having problems with their course because of language and may come to you for extra practice, or someone may be able to cope well with the language content of the course, but have problems with academic skills, such as being able to reference work correctly. We also offer literacy and numeracy support to many of our mature students who are returning to education after many years.

As you can appreciate, the needs of the students who visit you are very individual to that person. It is difficult, if not impossible, to plan sessions in advance, even though appointments are not run on a drop in basis but by pre-arrangement only, Q33 as you will not be completely aware of the student's needs until you meet with them face to face for the counseling session. Occasionally students return for a second or third appointment and you are therefore aware of their requirements; however, many students will visit only once with specific questions. The Learning Support Centre is open to all students and they can arrange counselling sessions as many times as they need, despite our busy schedule. The greatest success, however, is offering support for a limited period of time Q34 which equips clients with the skills to progress independently through the rest of their course.

Within the Learning Support Centre team, there are

a variety of strengths; some staffs have particular areas of skill in mathematics, science, business or English language, for example. The receptionist, who is responsible for booking appointments, will match a student's needs to the background of the tutor, though be aware that flexibility is important as in extremely busy periods Q35 you may need to help a student in an area that is not your particular specialty. We do try to avoid this as much as possible and this should be a situation you are faced with only very occasionally. The Learning Centre is open during usual business hours and there is no requirement for evening or weekend work.

The student learning centre works closely with all other departments within the university. One thing to be aware is that students may come to you with a variety of questions that are out of the Learning Centre's jurisdiction. If this situation occurs, please advise the students as to which department they are supposed to see.

Often students are referred to us by lecturers if they have failed an assignment. Our role is to offer support while they are writing their next assignment to try to ensure that they perform better in their next assessment. On occasion, students may bring marked assignments to you to ask why they have failed and whether they can appeal their mark. While we can work through the student's work and show them where they went wrong and give suggestions for improvement, Q36 all requests for appeals are dealt with by the Head of the Faculty the student is studying with. In this situation, please instruct students to see the administrator for the relevant school.

A number of our students have studied diplomas and other certificates in other institutions. Many are able to apply for credit points into their current course. From their previous studies, Q37 should students request information on such exemptions, please direct them to the academic office who will liaise with the appropriate academic department on the student's behalf. Please remind them that they must submit all relevant documentation before such requests can be processed.

As I am sure you are aware, the learning centre is situated on the floor below the library. Q38 It is the learning centre advisors' responsibility to assist students with finding relevant information for assignments in the library resources, should they request help. Q39 While there is a wide range of academic sources available there, on occasion, students may request a copy of a journal or book which is unavailable. Members of the library staff are on hand to take bookings for such sources which may need to be ordered in from our other campus. Please remind students that they need their student identification card prior to being able to apply for a library card. The former needs to be issued Q40 by the academic office and library staff are able to issue library cards if the required identification is provided.

OK, well I think we should take a short break and when we return, in say 10 minutes time, we can give you an orientation of the centre's resources.

Test 8

答案速查

LISTENING

Section 1, Questions 1–10

1 Rigby White
2 134 Church
3 6
4 3422576
5 May 15th
6 Central Park
7 wedding(party)
8 AQ469 ZY
9 5 film rolls
10 Yes

Section 2, Questions 11–20

11 B
12 E
13 F
14 D
15 quality of life
16 80
17 add value
18 1,400
19&20 IN EITHER ORDER will cause congestion, will affect nature

Section 3, Questions 21–30

21 across the world
22 pound coins
23 picture
24 farmland
25 E
26 A
27 B
28 record
29 container
30 label

Section 4, Questions 31–40

31 Negative
32 pleasure
33 poverty
34 Active
35 success
36 B
37 A
38 C
39 A
40 B

READING

Reading Passage 1, Questions 1–14

1 E
2 H
3 I
4 D
5 G
6 yeast
7 bacteria
8 protein
9 chemical solvents
10 (small) holes
11 (solid) fibre
12 FALSE
13 TRUE
14 NOT GIVEN

Reading Passage 2, Questions 15–27

15 TRUE
16 FALSE
17 FALSE
18 TRUE
19 FALSE
20 NOT GIVEN
21 influenza
22 rubber
23 powdered carbolic acid
24 tube
25 B
26 D
27 E

Reading Passage 3, Questions 28–40

28 v
29 vi
30 ii
31 YES
32 YES
33 NOT GIVEN
34 NO
35 C
36 F
37 A
38 E
39 D
40 B

名师解析

LISTENING

SECTION 1

主题场景	购物场景
主旨大意	客户对柯达胶卷进行投诉
考查题型	笔记填空题

名师解读

1 Rigby White 题干中的Name为关键词。注意名字的拼写和首字母大写。

2 134 Church 答案在Road的前面。本题需要考生具有短时记忆的能力，并要注意首字母大写和数字的拼写。

3 6 题干中的Flat为关键词，为原文重现。依据第2题的信息就可直接判定本题答案。

4 3422576 题干中的telephone number为关键词，本题为原文重现。考生注意数字的书写。

5 May 15th 此空要求考生填入日期。注意月份和时间的拼写。

6 Central Park 此空要求考生填入地点名词或名词短语。题干中的taken与原文中的took为同根词。故此句中的地点名词Central Park即为答案。

7 wedding (party) 此空要求考生填入表示场合的名词或名词短语。根据第6题的信息，此句中的wedding (party)即为答案。

8 AQ469ZY 题干中的Serial number为关键词，为原文重现。注意字母和数字的拼写。

9 5 film rolls 题干中的Compensation为关键词，为原文重现。故five rolls of film为答案，但题目要求不超过三个单词，需要考生对答案进行改写，将of后的名词改写为ro ls的定语即可。

10 Yes 本题的题干是一般疑问句，答案非Yes即No。根据原文中I appreciate your effort. 的信息判定答案为Yes，也就是客户对此次的解决意见是满意的。

SECTION 2

主题场景	会议场景
主旨大意	向斯托克顿市居民发布某一地区的发展计划的会议
考查题型	地图题、摘要填空题、简答题

名师解读

11 B 第一遍读题时快速浏览所有题干，划出关键词。这四道题要求考生根据地图进行选择。首先位置11处有一个关键标注A53，根据原文the main road at the A53可以定位，但答案在此句的前面，即for a new housing estate。

12 E 根据关键词Edgefield Ln, Moss Hill，定位到原文be located where Edgefield Lane meets Moss Hill，可知开发的目的是为了建a second and more convenient school。

13 F 根据between Bunts Lane and the waterway可知，在13这个位置要开发成a newer and larger recreation centre。

14 D 图中14这个位置比较空旷，并且在绿化位置，根据原文，可知此处要开发成一个conservation area。

15 quality of life 根据关键词maintained可以定位到原文conservation and preservation of our residents' quality of life，其中maintained和conservation and preservation为同义替换。

16 80 根据空格后面的名词4-bedroomed houses可知需要填写一个修饰词或定语，根据原文allow building of 80 new homes，可知应填写80。

17 add value 做听力题时要在读完题目的同时对句子中的空缺处进行预测，预测出该空的内容大意和词性。此处缺动词，且根据关键词high quality可定位原文，直接找到add value to the local area。

18 1,400 数字听写题很容易失分，要避免失分就需要做专项数字练习以提高听写的准确度。根据Stockton's projected population可以直接确定答案为1,400。

19&20 IN EITHER ORDER will cause congestion, will affect nature 根据关键词worried about可以在原文中找到对应的同义词组are concerned，在其后的the plans will cause congestion and will affect nature中即可找到答案。

SECTION 3

主题场景	学术演讲
主旨大意	认识并保护睡鼠
考查题型	句子填空题、配对题、摘要填空题

名师解读

21 across the world 根据空格后as well as判断，应填写与in the UK形式相同的短语，答案为地点，听到原文declined，对应题干fallen，之后的地点词across the world为答案。

22 pound coins 通过上下文判断空格处应填写一个名词，与睡鼠重量相当的物品，要注意原文weight之后的as a couple of pound coins（两三个英镑硬币）那么重，a couple of与two基本上是同义替换。

23 picture 通过题目判断介词in后填写地点名词，听到probably与题干中的likely为同义替换，定位probably all seen a picture of a dormouse之后有picture dormice出现，即为答案。

24 farmland 题目中next to后需填写地点词汇，hedges和woods为关键词，之后一个地点词farmland为答案。

25 E woodmice（小林姬鼠）为关键词, parallel为原词重现，根据原文Woodmice make a hole in the shell too, but...on the inner rim of the shell，可知parallel marks on the inner rim符合题意。

26 A vole（野鼠）为关键词，根据原文leave tooth marks on the inner rim of the hole与a hole in the shell with an even and regular edge意思同，其中an even and regular edge（平整规则的痕迹）与tooth marks意思同。

27 B dormice为关键词，和野鼠田鼠区别的是has a smooth inner edge对应orderly，两者也是同义替换。

28 record 题目空格处应填写动词，听到关键词nuts opened by dormice后注意动词record的出现。原文their location as与题干where you found them为同义替换。

29 container 应填写可以把nut shells放进去的物品，如瓶子等，应该是一个容器，nut shells之后出现in a small container，其中的container为答案。

30 label 空格处需要填写一个动词，根据括号里的name, address，应为做“标签”之意，听到give them a label，应意识到label可作动词为答案。

SECTION 4

主题场景	学术场景
主旨大意	有关个人时间观念的讲座
考查题型	表格填空题、选择题

Test 8

名师解读

31 Negative 根据关键词disappointments, failures, bad decisions可以在原文中找到同义词regrets, failures, poor decisions，由此可从原文People living in the past negative time zone中找到对应的答案。

32 pleasure 根据填空的其他部分可知空格里面要填写的是一个和sensation并列的词语，根据原文Present hedonists are driven by pleasure and immediate sensation可知，driven by后面的pleasure即为答案。

33 poverty 根据关键词religious beliefs, social conditions可定位到原文whether it's poverty, religion or society itself，可知与religious beliefs并列的词语是poverty。

34 Active 题干采用一个Prefer...Don't give in to...结构，指出宁愿工作也不娱乐，不屈服于诱惑。所以这是一个积极的人生态度。定位的原文为as future active are the planners and go-getters。

35 success 题干中的a strong belief in life after death和importance of...in life分别与原文how virtuously they have lived 和 what success they have had in their lives相对应，答案一目了然。

36 B 根据题干中的关键词present hedonists可定位到原文Everyone is brought into this world as a present hedonist，可知答案为is brought into this world，与选项B at birth对应。

37 A 根据题干中的关键词American boys和drop out of school定位到原文these boys require a situation...可知其真正原因是他们想要一种这样的环境：they have the ability to manage their own learning environment.

38 C 注意特殊定位词是指在听力材料中起到转折连接的连词，原文中的although是一个特殊关键词，后面的understand the potentially negative consequences of their actions不是考点，而逗号后面的才是考点，即they persist with the behaviour，与C项对应，本题难度比较大。

39 A 通过题干中的关键词an extra day per week定位到原文中的an eight-day week，可知They would spend that time labouring away to achieve more. 这里注意：听力材料中的more很容易成为考点，本题的more与harder相对应。

40 B 通过题干中的关键词can help us定位到原文can facilitate more effective cooperation，该表述与选项B work together better意义相同。

READING

READING PASSAGE 1

体　裁　说明文

题　材　科学研究

主　题　根据提取蜘蛛基因制造强韧、有弹性且轻质的生物材料

题　型　配对题、流程图填空题、判断题

Questions 1–5

题型 配对题 (Matching Information)

注意 本题属于段落信息配对题，建议考生通读该题型的所有问题，找出要点，画出关键词。注意关键词主要是以名词和动词为主，概括整个句子的单词或短语。

1	关键词	two materials
	原文定位	E段首句At DuPont, researchers have used both yeast and bacteria as hosts to grow the raw material, which they have spun into fibres.
	题解	**答案E** 根据题干中所说的two materials（两种材料）定位到原文后得到：研究人员利用酵母和细菌栽培原材料，并将其纺成纤维。这两种材料正是原文所说的yeast and bacteria（酵母和细菌）。

2	关键词	predictions
	原文定位	H段首句At DuPont's laboratories, Dorsch is excited by the prospect of new super-strong materials but he warns they are many years away.
	题解	答案H　该段大意为：新型超强材料的前景非常可观，但理论预测告诉我们，最终会创造出比传统的材料更结实的材料。prospect（前景，预期）与题干中的 prediction（预测）相对应。注意but之后的内容才是本句的主要意图。
3	关键词	on-going research
	原文定位	I段首句、第二句The spider is not the only creature that has aroused the interest of material scientists.They have also become envious of the natural adhesive secreted by the sea mussel.
	题解	答案I　原文的"他们也非常羡慕海贻贝产生的天然胶黏剂"表明研究人员要研究其他的材料，这对应题干中的on-going research into other synthetic materials（对其他合成材料的持续研究）。
4	关键词	spider, manufactures silk
	原文定位	D段第二句"We took out the glands that produce the silk and looked at the coding for the protein material they make, which is spun into a web. We then went looking for clones with the right DNA," he says.
	题解	答案D　该段大意为：科学家研究蜘蛛是如何产丝的，这对应题干中的the research into the part of the spider that manufactures silk（研究蜘蛛产丝这一部分）。
5	关键词	application, engineering
	原文定位	G段首句Researchers at DuPont say they envisage many possible uses for a new biosilk material.
	题解	答案G　该段指出研究人员为新材料设想了很多可行的用途，并举例说明抗震悬挂桥的使用，这对应题干中的the possible application of the silk in civil engineering（在土木工程方面，新材料的可行性应用）。

Questions 6–11

题型　流程图填空题(Flow-Chart Completion)

注意　流程图填空题可以进一步划分为单句填空题、总结填空题和提纲式填空题。类型的不同使得干有长有短，难度上也有一定的差别，但是本质上都是填空，因此一些基本的步骤方法在它们之间都是可以通用的。

6	关键词	Synthetic gene
	原文定位	E段首句At DuPont, researchers have used both yeast and bacteria as hosts to grow the raw material, which they have spun into fibres.
	题解	答案yeast　题干问合成基因在哪里生长，由E段首句可知，研究者已经采用both yeast and bacteria（酵母和细菌）作为寄主来栽培已经被纺成纤维的原料。

7	关键词	Synthetic gene
	原文定位	E段首句At DuPont, researchers have used both yeast and bacteria as hosts to grow the raw material, which they have spun into fibres或I段末句It is tedious and expensive to extract the protein from the mussel, so researchers have already produced a synthetic gene for use in surrogate bacteria.
	题解	答案bacteria 此答案可以通过E段首句得到，题解司上一题。也可以通过I段末句来验证，即从贻贝中提取蛋白质时间长且花费高，因此研究者已经生产出供替代细菌使用的合成纤维，此句包含定位词synthetic gene。
8	关键词	globules
	原文定位	E段第二句Robert Dorsch, Dupont's director of biochemical development, says the globules of protein, comparable with marbles in an egg, are harvested and processed.
	题解	答案protein 生化系主任罗比特·杜什指出，蛋白质小球体可以和一个经过加工处理的大理石鸡蛋相媲美。
9	关键词	dissolved
	原文定位	F段末句Since we are not as clever as the spider and we are not using such sophisticated organisms, we substituted man-made approaches and dissolved the protein in chemical solvents...to form the solid fibre.
	题解	答案chemical solvents 原文指出：“虽然我们不像蜘蛛那样聪明可以使用一个如此复杂的生物体，但是我们可以用人造的方法和用化学溶剂溶解蛋白质，然后纺成材料通过小孔形成纤维”。所以dissolved in后面应该是chemical solvents（化学溶剂）。
10	关键词	passed through
	原文定位	F段末句...which are then spun to push the material through small holes to form the solid fibre.
	题解	答案(small) holes 根据F段末句，可以看出passed through的是一些(small) holes（小孔）。对所填词的词性进行预判断，有助于提高考生对正确答案的敏感性，帮助考生精确锁定答案，个别词性的判断甚至能直接帮助考生找到答案。
11	关键词	produce
	原文定位	F段末句...which are then spun to push the material through small holes to form the solid fibre.
	题解	答案(solid) fibre 根据第9题对F段末句的解释，可以看出to produce的是一些solid fibre（固态纤维）。从命题特点看，流程图填空题都是对原文的一句话或者几句话进行的同义改写，并不是对原文彻底的替换，一些词仍然会保留它的原形，因此被称为关键词。关键词一般是名词，包括专有名词、大写字母缩写、数字、斜体字等。

Questions 12–14

题型 判断题(Identifying Information)

注意 判断题一直是阅读中最难的题型之一。可以根据段落首句快速看一下文章整体方向来做出判断。

12	关键词	parachute
	原文定位	B段末句Army scientists are already looking at the possibilities of using it for lightweight, bullet-proof vests and parachutes.
	题解	答案FALSE 通过定位原文可知：军事科学家已经考虑可能在减轻重量、防弹背心和降落伞方面使用这种合成材料，但科学家只是有可能去使用，而非题干所述这种材料已经替换了尼龙，所以不正确。
13	关键词	varying strengths
	原文定位	B段首句The attraction of the silk spun by the spider is a combination of great strength and enormous elasticity, which man-made fibres have been unable to replicate.
	题解	答案TRUE 原文阐述的“蜘蛛吐出来的丝很有力量且极具弹性，这是人造纤维所不能复制的”，与题干所说varying strengths（不同的强度）相对应。
14	关键词	Lewis and Dorsch
	原文定位	G段第四句Biochemists such as Lewis see the potential range of uses of biosilk as almost limitless.和H段首句At DuPont's laboratories, Dorsch is excited by the prospect of new super-strong materials but he warns they are many years away.
	题解	答案NOT GIVEN 原文只是说Lewis认为生化丝的潜在使用范围是无限的，Dorsch认为这种合成材料的前景是可观的，但并没有提及二人合作制作合成丝。

READING PASSAGE 2

体　裁　说明文
题　材　科学研究
主　题　关于碳酸烟球的介绍
题　型　判断题、摘要填空题、配对题

Questions 15–20

题型 判断题(Identifying Information)

注意 判断题难点就在于这种题型不仅要求考生根据原文信息判断题干正确与否，而且还需要判断另外一个模棱两可的可能性：NOT GIVEN。NOT GIVEN题目的麻烦就在于它有双重标准。阅读题目的所有答案都能在原文中找到，最多换个同义词，而且看到生词千万不要怕，越是生僻的词越是关键词，越是不可能换。

15	关键词	the relationship between customers and companies
	原文定位	第二段第二句It is also seen by some as the birth of modern consumer protection as it helped to define in law the trading relationship between a company and its customers.
	题解	**答案TRUE** 原文中的“碳酸烟球案作为现代消费者保护的案例，在法律上有助于定义公司与消费者间的交易关系”为本题提供了答案。题干中the relationship between customers and companies（顾客与公司的关系）与原文所述的the trading relationship between a company and its customers相对应。文中的it即指代Carbolic smoke ball case（碳酸烟球案）。
16	关键词	advertisement
	原文定位	第四段首句The company making the ball advertised it in the *Pall Mall Gazette* offering a £100 reward to anyone using it correctly who then contracted influenza.
	题解	**答案FALSE** 原文说该公司在《波迈宪报》上刊登广告，称正确使用碳酸烟球而感染流感的人可获得100英镑，而题干所述为正确使用碳酸烟球，并能感染流感的人可获得the deposited money（银行活期存款），并不是原文所说的100英镑。
17	关键词	turned down, request
	原文定位	第七段第一、二句Mrs Carlill sued, claiming there was a contract between her and the company. The company denied there was one.
	题解	**答案FALSE** 原文表明公司否认了自己与Carlill的契约，即不承认当初答应给Carlill的报酬，这与题干所述公司turned down Mrs Carlill's request（拒绝Carlill的要求）且for no reason（无端地）不相对应。
18	关键词	won, High Court
	原文定位	第七段第三句She won her case in the High Court.
	题解	**答案TRUE** 定位句指出：她在高等法院胜诉了，won her case（赢得案件）与题干所述won her suit（赢得诉讼）相对应，属于同义词替换。
19	关键词	toothpaste company, marketing strategy
	原文定位	第七段第七句Claims like these are not meant to have any legal consequences and are understood not to by the public.
	题解	**答案FALSE** 定位句指出：像这类的说法并不具有任何法律后果，不为市民所理解，而题干所述为public should understand it（市民应该理解这类广告），与原文所述不相对应。
20	关键词	Thalidomide scandal, *Medicines Act*
	原文定位	倒数第四段第二句However, it was not until the Thalidomide scandal in 1961, which led to the *Medicines Act* of 1968...
	题解	**答案NOT GIVEN** 答案 原文只说直到1961年的沙利度胺丑闻事件，才导致1968年的“药品法案”，该段并未说明何为具体原因，所以题干because the customer won the case again（因为消费者再次赢得诉讼）属于没有提及的内容。

Questions 21–24

题型 摘要填空题(Summary Completion)

注意 利用题干中的信息确定答案在文章中的位置，从而缩小了搜索答案的范围，而不必通篇阅读。查看空格前后的词语及该空格所在句子，并理解其含义。

21	关键词	cure for, diseases
	原文定位	第三段首句The carbolic smoke ball was a peculiar device marketed as a cure for various ailments including influenza.
	题解	答案influenza 摘要填空可分为三种：定位句指出：原文原词、从多个选项中选词和自己填词。根据定位词cure for可定位到第三段首句，碳酸烟球是治愈各种疾病（包括流感在内）的一种特殊装备。题干和原文相比只是把various ailments （不同的疾病）和influenza（流行性感冒）换了顺序，且ailments（疾病，小病）和diseases（疾病）为同义词替换，由此可找到答案influenza。
22	关键词	ball, filled with
	原文定位	第三段第二句It consisted of a rubber ball, filled with powdered carbolic acid.
	题解	答案rubber 根据filled with定位到文中第三段第二句可直接找到答案：它由橡胶球组成，并填满了石碳酸。原文中的it指代烟球，与题干中的smoke ball（烟球）相对应，题干所述为原文的同义转换。
23	关键词	ball, filled with
	原文定位	第三段第二句It consisted of a rubber ball, filled with powdered carbolic acid.
	题解	答案powered carbolic acid 本题关键词及定位句与23题同。本题所在的句子为非限定性定语从句。本题仍为原词重现。
24	关键词	inserted, user’s nose
	原文定位	第三段第三句You squeezed the ball sending a puff of acidic smoke right up a tube inserted into your nose.
	题解	答案tube 题干中所述的inserted into the user’s nose（插入使用者鼻子内），根据原文可知是tube（试管）被插入鼻子内。

Questions 25–27

题型 配对题(Matching Endings)

注意 配对类题型难度相对较大，对考生能力要求相对较高，且占了非常大的比重。

25	关键词	Carlill’s husband
	原文定位	第六段首句The manufacturers ignored two letters from her husband who had trained as a solicitor.
	题解	答案B 根据Carlill’s husband（卡利尔的丈夫）找到第六段首句：厂商忽视了她丈夫的两封信。与B选项sent letters to the carbolic smoke ball company（寄信给碳酸烟球公司）相对应。

26	关键词	Mr Frederick Rowe
	原文定位	第七段第四句、第五句The company and its proprietor, Mr Frederick Rowe, appealed. He raised almost every conceivable reason why there was no contract between themselves and Mrs Carlill.
	题解	答案D 由定位句可知Frederick Rowe进行上诉，他们提出几乎所有可能的原因解释为什么他们和Carlill间没有契约。这与D选项appealed and put forward several reasons to prove his ideas（上诉并提出几种原因来证明他的观点）相对应。
27	关键词	Lord Bowen
	原文定位	倒数第五段首句...If I advertise to the world that my dog is lost, and that anybody who brings the dog to a particular place will be paid some money...
	题解	答案E 该段主题为Lord Bowen用丢失的狗来举例贬低碳酸烟球公司。而选项E指出quoted an example to turn the company down（举例贬低公司），其中公司代指碳酸烟球公司，正与原文对应。

READING PASSAGE 3

体　　裁　　说明文
题　　材　　风土人情介绍
主　　题　　日本种植大米的历史
题　　型　　配对题、判断题

Questions 28–30

题型 配对题(Matching Headings)

注意 段落标题配对题不但要求掌握所读段落的主旨大意、中心思想，而且要求掌握文章中的详细事实与细节。并且，不但要求对于具体事实情节的理解，而且要求对其抽象含义的理解，既要理解字面意思，又要理解其深层含义，包括作者的态度、观点、意图等。

28	关键词	dilemma
	原文定位	Section A第三段末句If they take rice's rich heritage to the grave, what will that do to Japan?
	题解	答案v 该部分主要讲述了日本人种植的大米质量好、味道佳、黏性大， 他们对此引以为傲。但同时令人困扰的是，大米反映了自己本身的瑕疵。若他们把大米的文化遗产埋葬，日本将如何是好？而选项the dilemma the country confronts（该国面临的进退两难的境地）与原文相对应。
29	关键词	symptoms
	原文定位	Section B第二段首句The shortage of children is symptomatic of chronic affliction: young families have abandoned places like Tochikubo, unable to make a living.
	题解	答案vi Section B的整篇主题为：Tochikubo村的表面景色虽好，但学校却令人担忧。为何令人担忧？Tochikubo村缺少儿童。更糟糕的是，Tochikubo村的村民不知道该如何来解决这种现状。而选项vi the reasons for the symptoms in the village Tochibuko（Tochibuko村这种症状的原因）与原文相对应。

30	关键词	heart of rice
	原文定位	Section C整段
	题解	**答案ii** 通读Section C发现本部分主题为即便现在种植水稻，但吃大米的人越来越少。同时日本老百姓反对进口大米，对农业有一种特别的保护主义。虽然瘫痪的日本农业可能会使农民永远失去稻田，但农民们还是共同努力来出售大米。而选项ii the existence of heart of rice（大米存在的核心地位）与原文相对应。

Questions 31–34

题型 判断题(Identifying Writer's View/Claims)

注意 看到一个判断题题目，可以直接把它假设为正确的，也就是把它当作样板。同时再思考一下题干的逆命题，也就是与题干相反的镜像。然后回原文中带着题干的原样和镜像一起去找。找到原样的话，那么这个题干就是正确的；如果找到的是镜像，那么这个题干就是错误的。如果原样和镜像都找不到的话，那么这个题目就是NG。这样子我们就可以有效地将烦人的NG情况绕过去。

31	关键词	pilgrimage, harvest
	原文定位	Section A的首段首句In early autumn a pilgrimage takes place in Japan和第三句They travel to see the harvest, which takes place as the leaves on the trees are turning red.
	题解	**答案YES** 题干所述包括pilgrimage（朝圣之行）和see the scene of harvest分别与原文这两句相对应。
32	关键词	schedule, self-awareness
	原文定位	Section A的第二段第二句This awareness of time is closely associated with a rice-growing calendar that has helped to shape Japan's identity since 2,400 years ago.
	题解	**答案YES** 通过题干schedule（时间表）及self-awareness（自我意识）定位到Section A的第二段第二句，大意为：这个时间与种植水稻的时间紧密相连，在2 400年以前就对促成日本自我意识起了作用。题干所述的schedule of agriculture in rice（耕种水稻的时间表）与原文with a rice-growing calendar（水稻生长日历）相对应。
33	关键词	grade
	原文定位	Section A的第二段末句Anything below grade two is considered unfit for the table and the price plummets accordingly.
	题解	**答案NOT GIVEN** 定位句指出：任何低于二级的大米都被认为不适于食用，因此价格也会骤降。但关于题干中的此类大米能否适用于living stock（家禽）在本文中并未提到。
34	关键词	abandon, Tochikubo, physical exhaustion
	原文定位	Section B的第四段首句、第二句It is not just the physical effort that is discouraging. The economics are too.
	题解	**答案NO** 定位句指出：令人沮丧的不仅仅是体力上艰辛的付出，还有经济方面。题干所述的年轻家庭放弃Tochikubo村，仅仅是因为身体的疲劳，与原文表述不符。

Questions 35–40

题型　配对题(Matching Features)

注意　绝大多数的英语文章均采用演绎法来写，也就是先说出中心句，然后再写支持中心句的细节。这个时候，判断的标准就是看第二句话是否是支持细节。支持细节经常会有以下特征：a. 有举例信号词，如For example, for instance, sometimes, often等。b. 有专有名词，如人名、地名等。c. 有直接引语。d. 数字。中心句在第二句或后半句的情况往往是由于首句是让步句、过渡句或介绍句。

35	关键词	policy, consumption, mount
	原文定位	C段第二句The irony is that if the government did not protect farmers quite so assiduously, then lower prices might encourage people to eat more rice.
	题解	**答案C**　该段主题为：日本老百姓反对进口大米，讽刺的是：若政府不保护农民，低价格会鼓励人们食用更多的稻米。题干中所述若没有适当的政策，大米的消费就会增多，这与原文C段相对应。
36	关键词	elderly people
	原文定位	F段首句"It's rare to find people in their 60s and 70s, trying to be entrepreneurs. But there's only us left." said Mr Fueki, the co-operative president.
	题解	**答案F**　F段首句指出：几乎没有人在其60或70岁的时候想成为企业家。其中in their 60s and 70s与题干所说的elderly people（老年人）相对应，It's rare to...there's only us left与there are still hope相对应。寻找主题句往往是做好此类题的关键。要注意每段的主题句往往为首句，本题就是一个例子。
37	关键词	cut the productivity
	原文定位	A段倒数第二句Self-sufficiency in rice quickly turned to surplus, and from the 1970s onwards the government has paid people not to produce.
	题解	**答案A**　从20世纪70年代开始，政府不断补偿老百姓，使他们减少产量，其中not to produce与题干所说的cut the productivity（减少产量）相对应。
38	关键词	Farmers, efforts
	原文定位	E段末句But there was a sense of purpose to the shared endeavour, and the farmers sold their rice to the visitors for good prices.
	题解	**答案E**　定位句指出：对于共同的努力，有一种目的感，那就是把大米以令人满意的价格卖给游客。此描述与题干基本一致，并且题干中的efforts（努力）与原文中的endeavour（努力）对应，属于同义词替换。
39	关键词	personally-owned firms
	原文定位	D段第三句Hearteingly, in villages such as Tockikubo, a small flame of private enterprises is being lit.
	题解	**答案D**　题干指出personally-owned firms（私有企业）会采取一些行动，这与原文所说的private enterprises（私有企业）"被点燃"相对应。

Test 8

40	关键词	nationally-produced rice
	原文定位	B段首句For all the lyricism, many Japanese are also disturbingly nationalistic over the food stuff.
	题解	**答案B** 题干所说的nationally-produced rice（国内生产的大米），这与原文所说的nationalistic（国家的）相对应，也属于同义词替换。

WRITING

WRITING TASK 1

名师解读

本题考查的是通过两个饼状图分析相关问题。饼状图写作思路：归纳最大值、归纳最小值、分析变化趋势（增长趋势，下降趋势，波动趋势）。首先概述背景信息+概述整体变化趋势；其次，突出关键特征；最后，归纳总结。写作时也要注意语法问题。这篇作文是关于低收入和高收入两个群体的消费情况比对的饼状图。

高分范文

The two pie charts show that low and high income groups spend their **disposable** income (earnings excluding house rent or purchase) on similar items but in different proportions.

Regarding the low income group, the highest proportion of their money is spent on food and drink—29 percent, compared to just 15 percent for the high income group. This is closely followed by 24 percent paid out on fuel bills, which **contrasts** with a much lower figure for this item for the high income group (only 7 percent).

The most popular item for the high earners is recreation and cultural activities—21 percent compared with 11 percent by the low earning group. The higher group also spends a much higher proportion than the lower income group on restaurants and hotels (12 percent and 4 percent **respectively**) and on transportation (16 percent and 9 percent respectively). The proportion of expenditure on clothing for the two groups is very similar, with only one percent difference between the two (6 percent for high income group and 5 percent for the low). (300 words)

WRITING TASK 2

文章结构

提出问题+举例论证（正面）+举例论证（负面）+结论

problem+reason 1+reason 2+ conclusion
第一段：背景句+引出话题
第二段：有利+列举
第三段：不利+列举
第四段：结论+建议

思路点拨

步骤一：审题（<3分钟）

What do you imagine are the advantages and disadvantages of working abroad, as far as individuals and countries are concerned?

→通读题目，了解大意。

请你想象一下出国工作的利弊，从对个人和对国家两个方面来论述。

要把握题目中的句子间逻辑关系，关键首先需要给出一个明确的个人观点，觉得利多还是弊多，可以分析完两个方面，最后给出结论。

→再读题目，辨别关键词，区分主题词和限定词，推测考官的出题意图。

主题词：the advantages and disadvantages of working abroad

限定词：individuals and countries

步骤二：列大纲（<3分钟）

英文提纲	Introduction: an inevitable trend→still keeps rising→What does this tendency imply? Body: advantages: such an experience→broaden one's horizons; a more objective attitude; more tolerant→promote peace; overpopulation and high unemployment are concerned disadvantages: encountering language barriers and culture shock→weakens family ties→become overcrowded with high-calibre experts Conclusion: the advantages of working overseas far outweigh its disadvantages
中文提纲	引出话题： 当今社会的现状（出国工作成为一种潮流）→潮流有扩大趋势→到底有利还是不利呢? 主体段： 有利方面：丰富经历→视野更宽，看问题更客观，更宽容→促进和平；缓解人口压力和高失业率 不利方面：语言障碍和文化冲击→弱化家庭关系→高水平专家过度集中 总结： 有利方面远远大于不利方面

高分范文

In an era of economic globalisation, working abroad is emerging as an **inevitable** trend. A recent study has revealed that the number of people who are employed overseas across the world still keeps rising. What does this tendency imply for individuals and nations?

Advantages can be expected from such an experience. Being exposed to different cultures, individuals can get a clear picture of the way other people live. Work experience overseas can also broaden one's horizons about the world and lead one to a more objective attitude toward it. This results from being able to view things in different ways and from different cultural angles. **Ultimately**, one could also become more tolerant. When this is the case for a great number of individuals, the collective impact may even produce less conflict and promote peace between countries. As far as nations suffering from overpopulation and high unemployment are concerned, another benefit from the trend of working abroad can be perceived, as it may ease employment pressure there. For countries that receive employees, the influx might satisfy the demand for labour.

However, in some cases, overseas employment may bring some **undesirable** consequences for individuals as well as nations involved. There is a likelihood of encountering language barriers and culture shock, when one finds oneself try to adapt to local customs and culture. Living overseas also means being away from one's family and, as a consequence, this weakens family ties. A good case in point is that a couple who live apart often ends up divorcing. In addition, because talented people prefer developed areas as their **destinations**, these places are more liable to become overcrowded with high-calibre experts. At the same time, the underdeveloped countries are in urgent need of such people.

On the whole, I would say that the advantages of working overseas far outweigh its disadvantages. (309 words)

SPEAKING

名师解读

Part 1的题目属于个人类的话题，第一部分的这类题目一般都是固定的，考官会问考生一些关于他/她自己，关于他/她的家庭、他/她的工作、学习和一些类似的问题。这类题目的回答要符合道德标准，关注个人特色。但这个关注噪音的问题相对较难，有一些不太常见的词汇会出现。

Part 2属于口头作文，只有1分钟的考虑时间，然后做1–2分钟的陈述。表达的内容在围绕考点，也尽量包括小的要点的同时，有自己的重点。这次是描述一个你的电子设备。

Part 3一般是对Part 2提示卡内容的深化和拓展。但这个话题离得稍微有一点远，虽然都是电子科技的范畴，但是有很多词汇要重新考量。希望考生根据自己的词汇量完成好这个口语考核最难的部分。

高分示例

PART 1

Noise

- Do you mind noises?/Do any noises bother you?

Sometimes some of the noises around me do bother me, but sometimes they don't. I suppose it all depends on where I am and what time it is. If it's noisy early in the morning or really late at night, it does bother me, but during the day at a market or at a party, it doesn't bother me too much.

- What types of noise do you come across in your daily life?

There are lots of different noises every day. In the mornings, I hear the children from the school near my home and the shop keepers getting ready for the day. When I get to the subway, there are the voices of lots of people, advertisements and the trains whistling through the station. It's quieter when I get to work, small chatter and phones ringing and then again at night when I get home, the sounds of the people around me, shopping and preparing food for their families. Every day is different, and yet, still the same.

- Are cities becoming noisier?

Yes, I believe that with the growth of the population, it is becoming noisier. The more people there are in the area, the more noise there is. With large cities, there are more people, more cars and more shops. This raises the noise levels.

- Would you like to work in a noisy place? Why?/Why not?

I prefer to work in a quieter place when I am writing or preparing my lessons, but during the classes, I prefer the students to enjoy the lesson and talk a lot with each other. It tends to make a noisy class, but it is well worthy in the end.

PART 2

I own a Samsung laptop. It's not hugely big or expensive but it is mine and I do so much work with it. It has quite a bit of space for work and play things too.

My laptop is silver and shiny. It has a full sized keyboard and a track pad...which I do not really use. I don't use it because I have a USB mouse that attaches to it through the USB port. It makes it easier to use.

The laptop has one of the newer Operating Systems called Windows 8. It allows me to connect my laptop with any Samsung product and even use Samsung Apps on it instead of my phone. It is not incredibly user friendly and takes someone who really knows their way around a computer to use it to its full possibilities.

I do love my laptop and the help it gives me, but I do not really enjoy the Windows 8 version of the Operating System. While I am good with computers, the system has some flaws which make general use a little tricky. On that note though, I do enjoy the layout of the laptop and the speed in which it works.

PART 3

The Internet

- Is online shopping popular in your country?

Yes, I believe that online shopping is very popular in my country and lots of other countries. It makes it easier to compare prices from different shops easier, not to mention being able to shop at thousands of different stores all from your home or office.

- Can you suggest several ways to make the Internet safer for children?

I think that one of the **fundamental** things about the Internet is that it is open and free for everyone, but that also **poses danger for** children. One way to keep them safe is to keep locks on certain sites as well as keeping them informed of the dangers of the Internet. If they are too young to understand, "Do not give personal information or meet anyone in person," then there is no reason for them to be online at all. The Internet is a huge "space" and it is pretty much impossible to make it safer from the inside. Keeping our children safe is something that we have to **enforce**.

- Can you summarise **the pros and cons of** e-learning?

I believe that until children reach a certain age, they can do most, if not all their research for school projects in the library, just like we used too. However, the time has come when younger and younger students are taking to the Internet to pretend to be older. The Internet is an amazing thing and our world would be a lot slower without it, but just like all things, there are amazing dangers on there too.

Information technology

- Has technology made our lives simpler or more complex?

It is hard to answer this question when our lives have been made easier and at the same time more **complex**. While technology has made many things a lot easier, it has also made some things more difficult, like finding **criminals** or **keeping track of** our children and their habits or the people they interact with.

- Can you predict how technology will change our daily lives?

The more advanced technology becomes, the more it influences our daily lives. Hopefully, it will influence it in a good and positive way and not create problems. I would like to think that technology will find a way to reverse the effects of global warming and wipe out pollution and make the world a better place, not just use it for selfish reasons.

- **Can you justify the amount of money spent on developing technology?**

  I think it depends on what branch of technology is being developed. Using large funds to develop weapons is a poor way to spend so much money, when it could, and should be used to develop ways of saving our world and the people in it.

重点词汇

LISTENING

complicated	['kɒmplɪkeɪtɪd]	*adj.*	复杂的
stereotypical	[ˌsterɪə'tɪpɪkl]	*adj.*	老一套的
be allergic to			对……过敏
perspective	[pə'spektɪv]	*n.*	观点；远景
psychologist	[saɪ'kɒlədʒɪst]	*n.*	心理学家；心理学者
sensation	[sen'seɪʃn]	*n.*	感觉；轰动
temptation	[temp'teɪʃn]	*n.*	引诱；诱惑物
fatalistic	[ˌfeɪtə'lɪstɪk]	*adj.*	宿命论的
hedonist	['hiːdənɪst]	*n.*	快乐主义者；享乐主义者
potentially	[pə'tenʃəli]	*adv.*	潜在地；可能地
constantly	['kɒnstəntli]	*adv.*	不断地，时常地

READING

spider	['spaɪdə]	*n.*	蜘蛛；三脚架
synthetic	[sɪn'θetɪk]	*adj.*	合成的；人造的
generation	[ˌdʒenə'reɪʃn]	*n.*	一代；产生
spin	[spɪn]	*v.*	纺
enormous	[ɪ'nɔːməs]	*adj.*	巨大的；庞大的
parachute	['pærəʃuːt]	*n.*	降落伞
biochemist	[ˌbaɪəʊ'kemɪst]	*n.*	生物化学家
synthesise	['sɪnθəsaɪz]	*v.*	综合处理；人工合成
University of Wyoming			美国怀俄明州立大学
usher	['ʌʃə]	*v.*	引导；迎接
bacteria	[bæk'tɪərɪə]	*n.*	细菌
globule	['glɒbjuːl]	*n.*	药丸；血球
excrete	[ɪk'skriːt]	*v.*	排泄；分泌
protein	['prəʊtiːn]	*n.*	蛋白质
yeast	[jiːst]	*n.*	酵母；泡沫
sophisticated	[sə'fɪstɪkeɪtɪd]	*adj.*	复杂的；精致的
organism	['ɔːgənɪzəm]	*n.*	有机体；微生物
solvent	['sɒlvənt]	*n.*	溶剂；解决办法
suspension	[sə'spenʃn]	*n.*	悬浮；暂停
petrochemical	[ˌpetrəʊ'kemɪkl]	*n.*	石油化工产品；石油化学产品
adhesive	[əd'hiːsɪv]	*n.*	黏合剂；胶黏剂
mussel	['mʌsl]	*n.*	贻贝；蚌；淡菜
surrogate	['sʌrəgət]	*n.*	代理；代用品
backdrop	['bækdrɒp]	*n.*	背景
swirling	[swɜːlɪŋ]	*n.*	漩涡；涡流
pandemic	[pæn'demɪk]	*n.*	流行性疾病
peculiar	[pɪ'kjuːlɪə]	*adj.*	特殊的；罕见的
ailment	['eɪlmənt]	*n.*	疾病；小病
influenza	[ˌɪnflʊ'enzə]	*n.*	流行性感冒
testimonial	[ˌtestɪ'məʊnɪəl]	*n.*	客户评价；证明书
aristocrat	['ærɪstəkræt]	*n.*	贵族
equivalent	[ɪ'kwɪvələnt]	*n.*	等价物；相等物

Test 8

promptly	['prɒmptli]	*adv.*	迅速地；立即地
fraudulent	['frɔːdjələnt]	*adj.*	欺骗性的，不正的
conceivable	[kən'siːvəbl]	*adj.*	可能的；可以想象的
statutory	['stætʃətri]	*adj.*	法定的；法令的
carbolic	[kɑː'bɒlɪk]	*adj.*	碳的；煤焦油的
pilgrimage	['pɪlgrɪmɪdʒ]	*n.*	漫游；朝圣之行
bucolic	[bjuː'kɒlɪk]	*n.*	田园诗；农夫
plummet	['plʌmɪt]	*v.*	骤然下跌；垂直落下
accordingly	[ə'kɔːdɪŋli]	*adv.*	相应地
obsession	[əb'seʃn]	*n.*	困扰；痴迷
blemish	['blemɪʃ]	*n.*	污点；缺点
heritage	['herɪtɪdʒ]	*n.*	遗产；继承物
prosperous	['prɒspərəs]	*adj.*	繁荣的，兴旺的
symptomatic	[ˌsɪmptə'mætɪk]	*adj.*	有症状的；症候的
chronic	['krɒnɪk]	*adj.*	慢性的；长期的
hectare	['hekteə]	*n.*	公顷
renaissance	[rɪ'neɪsns]	*n.*	新生；再生
superfluous	[suː'pɜːflʊəs]	*adj.*	多余的；不必要的
extraordinary	[ɪk'strɔːdnri]	*adj.*	非凡的；特别的
protectionism	[prə'tekʃənɪzəm]	*n.*	保护主义；贸易保护主义
endeavor	[ɪn'devə]	*n.*	努力；尽力
depressingly	[dɪ'presɪŋli]	*adv.*	郁闷地；压抑地

WRITING

percentage	[pə'sentɪdʒ]	*n.*	百分比，百分数
comparison	[kəm'pærɪsn]	*n.*	比较，对照
relevant	['reləvənt]	*adj.*	相关的；有意义的
disposable	[dɪ'spəʊzəbl]	*adj.*	可自由使用的；用完即可丢弃的
contrast	['kɒntrɑːst]	*v.*	对比；形成对照
respectively	[rɪ'spektɪvli]	*adv.*	分别地，各自地
imagine	[ɪ'mædʒɪn]	*v.*	想象，猜想
individual	[ˌɪndɪ'vɪdʒʊəl]	*n.*	个人，个体
inevitable	[ɪn'evɪtəbl]	*adj.*	必然的；不可避免的
ultimately	['ʌltɪmətli]	*adv.*	最后，根本
undesirable	[ˌʌndɪ'zaɪərəbl]	*adj.*	不良的，不受欢迎的
destination	[ˌdestɪ'neɪʃn]	*n.*	目的地，终点

SPEAKING

fundamental	[ˌfʌndə'mentl]	*adj.*	基本的，根本的
pose danger for			对……造成危险
enforce	[ɪn'fɔːs]	*v.*	实施，执行
the pros and cons of...			……的利与弊
complex	['kɒmpleks]	*adj.*	复杂的
criminal	['krɪmɪnl]	*n.*	罪犯
keep track of...			记录……

听力原文

SECTION 1

(CLERK=C; RIGBY=R)

C: Hello, Kodak customer service. Can I help you?

R: Good morning, madam. I have a complaint. I bought some Kodak films at your store last week. There was nothing wrong with the film, but after I dropped the film off to have it developed by you, the shop assistant told me to pick the pictures up yesterday. When I went in, they told me all my pictures are lost. Now, these pictures have a strong emotional value; and I would like to get a compensation of some sort.

C: I am so sorry this happened. And of course we will compensate you. I need some personal information, though.

R: All right.

C: Hold on a second. I need to get a pen and paper. OK, what is your name sir?

R: Q1 Rigby White.

C: Could you spell that, please?

R: R-I-G-B-Y, White as the colour "white".

C: And your address?

R: Q2 134 Church Road, Flat Q3 6.

C: Which road was it on did you say?

R: Church Road.

C: So, 134 Church Road, Flat 6. That's pretty close to our store, isn't it?

R: Yes, it is. That is why I bought the film at your store.

C: Can I also have your telephone number?

R: Q4 342 2576.

C: 3-4-2 2-5-7-6. Could you tell me when and where you took your pictures? I will first try to locate them. Maybe somebody just misplaced them.

R: I took them on Q5 May 15th in Q6 Central Park at a Q7 wedding party. You see, this was just a one-day event and I would really regret it if they were lost.

C: I understand. Do you remember your film's serial number by any chance?

R: Yes, I do. I wrote it down. The number was Q8 AQ 469 ZY.

C: A-Q-4-6-9-Z-Y. Is that what you said?

R: Yes, that's right.

C: Well, Mr Rigby. I will do my best to find your pictures. In case, we can't find them, we will give you Q9 five rolls of film for free as compensation. Is that all right with you?

R: Q10 I appreciate your effort. Thank you.

C: We will call you as soon as possible. And again, we're sorry for the mess-up.

R: That's all right. Good-bye.

C: Good-bye.

SECTION 2

Thank you to all the local residents who have taken the time to attend this evening's meeting. As you know this is an information session arranged with the purpose of keeping you informed of council plans for development of certain areas of Stockton Village.

Now, if we look at the map of the area here on the projector screen we can see that the areas planned for development have been marked. First, I'll start by talking about the planned location for a Q11 new housing estate. The area chosen for this is to the right of the main road at the A53 junction. This part of Stockton is currently underdeveloped and has been chosen as it is the least likely to cause disruption to existing residents and has existing road links in place. Other locations, including the area near Wilfield Lane were originally considered, but rejected as they would cause too much disruption to local residents.

In order that the area will be able to sustain an increase in population, there are associated plans to build Q12 a new primary school. The current school, as you know, is situated in the neighbouring village; however, a second and more convenient school will be located where Edgefield Lane meets Moss Hill. The site is currently used as a recreation centre, but development of the primary school is scheduled for the end of the year.

Q13 A newer and larger recreation centre will be

built between Bunts Lane and the waterway. Its development is being funded by both council subsidiaries and funding from local investors; all financial arrangements are already in place. There has also been an application to build a new family restaurant, but the location and application itself are still under discussion.

I would like to assure you that the Stockton area will retain its greenery and countryside feel; the Woodland Park area which begins at the top of Edgefield Lane and extends down to the river will remain a green-belted Q14 conservation area and will not be affected at all by the development plan.

While it is necessary for us to accommodate the growing population of the district, I would like to assure you that conservation and preservation of our resident's Q15 quality of life has been considered throughout the planning process.

I'll now move on to specific details related to the housing development. As you know, it is necessary for extended provision of housing throughout the county and similar developments are planned in a number of areas. In Stockton, the council plans to allow building of Q16 80 new homes. These houses have been designed to be in-keeping with properties already in existence in the village. They will be 4-bedroomed properties and will be developed by Stone Construction. They are intended to be high quality homes which will Q17 add value to the local area.

Building is planned to commence in two months time and the estimated completion date is July of next year. Taking into account new arrivals, Stockton's projected population will be approximately, Q18 1,400.

Now as you know, the area is classified as semi-rural and has green-belt protection against over development, I know that some of you are concerned that the plans Q19 & Q20 will cause congestion and will affect nature; however, I hope that the information given in this meeting has helped to put your minds at rest and has clarified the situation.

I believe I have covered the main points and I'd now like to invite any questions you may have about the development plan that were not clarified completely in the presentation.

SECTION 3

(PRESENTER=P; LECTURER=L)

P: Good morning, and welcome to our weekly programme about countryside matters. With me today I have Jacky Lamerton. Jacky works for the nature organization Action for Wildlife, and he's appealing for volunteers for a project he's organizing, so if you think you might be willing to help, please listen carefully. Jacky...

L: Thank you. Yes...as you've just heard, I represent a charity called Action for Wildlife, which works to protect plants and animals. And I'm here today to talk about a project to save a type of mouse known as a dormouse. We can still find the dormouse in this area, but in the last few decades the number of dormice has seriously declined, not just in this country but Q21 across the world. There are several reasons for this—loss of habitat, climate change, competition for food—and this area of the UK is now regarded as one of the last strongholds. So naturally, we want to help the creature to survive here as much as we can. The aim of the first stage of our project is simply to identify specific locations where dormice are still to be found, and estimate the number we have here. So I'll just tell you a little bit about the creature, in case you don't already know. The dormouse is a very attractive, very small mammal—it only weighs about the same as a couple of Q22 pound coins. It's bright golden in colour, and it has a thick furry tail and big black eyes. Now, you've probably all seen a Q23 picture of a dormouse, but you're very unlikely to have seen a real one because they're strictly nocturnal. Also, they hibernate from October to April, so it's not around at all for about half the year.

So where is the dormouse to be found? Well, dormice need to be near a variety of trees and plants, so they can be sure of a continuous supply of food throughout the spring and summer. They feed on flowers, pollen, fruit, insects, ripe nuts—things that are available in turn as the summer progresses. Here in the UK the dormouse is most likely to live in places like hedgerows, or woods, or at the edges of Q24 farmland.

So how do we find out exactly where dormice are? Well, as they're hard to spot, as I said, we have to use indirect methods. Instead of trying to see dormice ourselves, we look for evidence of dormouse activity. Dormice eat hazelnuts, so we'll be looking for the shells that dormice have opened to get at the nut inside.

A lot of wildlife species eat hazelnuts—it's not just dormouse. But it's usually possible to tell which particular animal has opened a nut by looking at the marks on the shells. So now, for those of you who would like to help us carry out this survey, let me tell you exactly what to do.

You'll need to get an identification sheet like this form, then you should spend time looking for hazelnut shells in the bottom of hedgerows, or on the ground in woodlands.

If you find one, use the identification sheet to try and establish what kind of creature has opened it. You'll see from the pictures on the sheet that different creatures do it in different ways. For example, you'll see that insects make a small hole in the shell, less than two millimetres across. Then there's another type of mouse called a woodmouse. Woodmice make a hole in the shell too, but they leave Q25 parallel tooth marks on the inner rim of the shell, as well as rough scratches on the surface. Thirdly there are little mammals called voles. These creatures don't leave any marks on the surface, but they leave Q26 tooth marks on the inner rim of the hole. And these marks are neat and consistent. So they're fairly easy to identify. Then there are squirrels and birds. They both open the nuts, leaving half shells that have got jagged edges. And finally we have our dormice. They make Q27 a hole in the shell that has a smooth inner edge. And the tooth marks they leave are on the surface, at an angle to the hole. And these are the ones we're looking for of course.

Firstly, if you do find any nuts which you think have been opened by dormice, you need to Q28 record their location as precisely as possible. You can use the grid references on a map, or you can sketch your own map, but if you do, be sure to include landmarks or road names. It's very important that we know exactly where the shells came from. Then put the nut shells in a small Q29 container. Any kind will do, a film box or a match box, anything that prevents them from being crushed in the post. And then finally, give them a Q30 label —just your name and contact details—and send them to Action for Wildlife. When we receive them, an expert will look at the shells to confirm your identification—the address to send them to.

SECTION 4

Today, I'm going to be talking about time. Specifically I'll be looking at how people think about time, and how these time perspectives structure our lives. According to social psychologists, there are six ways of thinking about time, which are called personal time zones.

The first two are based in the past. Past positive thinkers spend most of their time on a state of nostalgia, fondly remembering moments such as birthdays, marriages and important achievements in their life. These are the kinds of people who keep family records, books and photo albums. People living in the past Q31 negative time zone are also absorbed by earlier times, but they focus on all the bad things—regrets, failures, poor decisions. They spend a lot of time thinking about how life could have been.

Then, we have people who live in the present. Present hedonists are driven by Q32 pleasure and immediate sensation. Their life motto is to have a good time and avoid pain. Present fatalists live in the moment too, but they believe this moment is the product of circumstances entirely beyond their control; it's their fate. Whether it's Q33 poverty, religion or society itself, something stops these people from believing they can play a role in changing their outcomes in life. Life simply "is" and that's that.

Looking at the future time zone, we can see that people classified as future Q34 active are the planners and go-getters. They work rather than play and resist temptation. Decisions are made based on potential consequences, not on the experience itself. A second future-orientated perspective, future fatalistic, is driven by the certainty of life after death and some kind of a judgment day when they will be assessed on how virtuously they have lived and what Q35 success they have had in their lives.

Okay, let's move on. You might ask "How do these time zones affect our lives?" Well, let's start at the beginning. Q36 Everyone is brought into this world as a present hedonist. No exceptions. Our initial needs and demands—to be warm, secure, fed and watered—all stem from the present moments. But things change when we enter formal education—we're taught to stop existing in the moment and to begin thinking about future outcomes.

But, did you know that every nine seconds a child in the USA drops out of school? For boys, the rate is much higher than for girls. We could easily say "Ah, well, boys just aren't as bright as girls", but the evidence doesn't support this. A recent study states that boys in America, by the age of 21, have spent 10,000 hours playing video games. The research suggests that they'll never fit in the traditional classroom Q37 because these boys require a situation where they have the ability to manage their own learning environment.

Now, let's look at the way we do prevention education. All prevention education is aimed at a future time zone. We say "Don't smoke or you'll get cancer", "Get good grades or you won't get a good job". But with present-orientated kids, that just doesn't work. Although Q38 they understand the potentially negative consequences of their actions, they persist with the behaviour because they're not living for the future; they're in the moment right now. We can't use logic and it's no use reminding them of potential fall-out from their decisions or previous errors of judgment—we've got to get in their minds just as they're about to make a choice.

Time perspectives make a big difference in how we value and use our time. When Americans are asked how busy they are, the vast majority report being busier than ever before. They admit to sacrifice their relationships, personal time and a good night's sleep for their success. Twenty years ago, 60% of Americans had sit-down dinners with their families, and now only 20% do. But when they're asked what they would do with an eight-day week, they say "Oh that'd be great". They would Q39 spend that time labouring away to achieve more. They're constantly trying to get ahead, to get toward a future point of happiness.

So, it's really important to be aware of how other people think about time. We tend to think: "Oh, that person's really irresponsible" or "That guy's power hungry" but often what we're looking at is not fundamental differences of personality, but really just different ways of thinking about time. Seeing these conflicts as differences in time perspective, rather than distinctions of character, can Q40 facilitate more effective cooperation between people and get the most out of each person's individual strengths.

Test 9

答案速查

LISTENING

Section 1, Questions 1–10

1 Meldrum
2 16 Ocean
3 AB 864653
4 Singapore
5 (A) backpack
6 purple
7 35 centimetres/cms/cm
8 giraffe
9 strap
10 Camera

Section 2, Questions 11–20

11&12 IN EITHER ORDER A C
13&14 IN EITHER ORDER B E
15 G
16 I
17 C
18 D
19 B
20 A

Section 3, Questions 21–30

21 B
22 C
23 C
24 B
25 no trains
26 convenient public transportation
27 attractive bay
28 polluted bay/pollution
29 airport
30 many insects

Section 4, Questions 31–40

31 secure locks
32 burglar alarm
33 valuables
34 delivery
35 milk and bread
36 property
37 suspicious
38 personal documents
39 ignition key
40 handy wall chart

READING

Reading Passage 1, Questions 1–13

1 iii
2 i
3 v
4 ii
5 ix
6 vii
7 NO
8 NOT GIVEN
9 YES
10 NO
11 YES
12 YES
13 NOT GIVEN

Reading Passage 2, Questions 14–26

14 iv
15 v
16 x
17 i
18 vi
19 ii
20 xi
21 TRUE
22 FALSE
23 FALSE
24 TRUE
25 TRUE
26 NOT GIVEN

Reading Passage 3, Questions 27–40

27 F
28 C
29 B
30 A
31 wind/solar/wave
32 tide table
33 tide direction
34 control mechanisms
35 large credits
36 FALSE
37 FALSE
38 FALSE
39 NOT GIVEN
40 TRUE

名师解析

LISTENING

SECTION 1

主题场景	旅行场景
主旨大意	关于机场丢失包裹的对话
考查题型	笔记填空题

名师解读

1 Meldrum 题干中的Name为关键词，是原文重现，要求考生填入失主的名字。考生应注意后面对名字的拼读是正确填入答案的关键，同时应注意首字母大写的问题。

2 16 Ocean 题干中的View为关键词，是原文重现，故View前面的16 Ocean为答案。考生应注意Ocean的拼写在后面有提示，同时注意首字母大写的问题。

3 AB 864653 题干中的Passport number为关键词，是原文重现。考生只要听清楚字母和数字即可填对答案。

4 Singapore 题干中的Stopover与原文中的stops over对应，据此考生可以判断本题要求考生填入的是飞机经停的地点，故后面的地点名词Singapore为答案。

5 (A) backpack 题干中的description与原文中的describe为同根词。原文中，女士提到了suitcase, holdall，但要注意男士的回答，女士提到的都不是答案，只有男士提到的a backpack才是答案。注意首字母大写的问题。

6 purple 要求考生填入丢失包裹的颜色。题干中的Blue为原文重现，后面又提到的purple为答案。

7 35 centimetres/cms/cm 题干中的60为关键词，题干中的乘号“x”与原文中的by对应，故by后面的35 centimetres即为答案。注意centimetres可以简写为cms或cm。

8 giraffe 题干中的picture, on the front均为原文重现，后面提到的giraffe为答案。本题要求考生填入旅行包的突出特征，注意对话中男士的回答。

9 strap 根据题干中的形容词Striped可知，本题要求考生填入的是名词或名词短语。Striped与原文中的stripes为同根词，对应put round的宾语，strap即为答案。

10 Camera 题干中的Contents与原文中的What was inside it? 对应，据此定位答案。后面紧接着提到了clothing, a couple of books, money，最后男士重点强调了main thing是camera。

SECTION 2

主题场景	体育运动场景
主旨大意	介绍城市一年一度的慈善赛跑以及赛跑的路线问题
考查题型	选择题、地图题

名师解读

11&12 IN EITHER ORDER A C 原文提到charity race仅仅向女士和12岁及以下的男孩开放，选项C正确；接着原文提到了不同的预订方式，可以do it online, by phone, 亦可以do it at various retail outlets in the city, various retail outlets对应选项A中的at certain shops，选项A正确。

13&14 IN EITHER ORDER B E 题干中的must说明，本题要选出参与者“必须”要穿的东西，与原文中的no-one is allowed to race without wearing these prominently对应，其中these指代的是前文中的a personal running number和a sign to pin onto their back，分别与选项B和E对应。

15 G 考生应注意图上已经给出the starting point, also the finishing point和yacht club的位置，原文提到它在ferry stop和yacht club之间，据此直接判定ferry stop的位置为G。考生在做地图题时，要仔细看图上已经给出的信息。

16 I 原文提到route是沿着Fleet Road向西，与sea平行，在road的拐弯处就是children's playground，也就是图中I的位置。注意听力原文中的参照物和表示方向的词westward。

17 C 原文提到route进入Mount Street，这个street已在图上标出，它的一侧是the park，另一侧是Grand Hotel，也就是图中C的位置。

18 D 题干中的关键词swimming pool为原文重现，据此对原文进行定位。它的位置是在park和St George's Road的交界处，且在park的east corner，也就是图中的D处。注意St是Saint的缩写。

19 B 原文提到library的位置是在St George's Road的北面，紧挨图中两个roundabouts中相对较小的那个，即可确定就是图中B的位置。

20 A 题干中的关键词police station为原文重现，据此对原文进行定位。police station的位置为Fleet Road和St George's Road的交叉进口，从图上的信息看，只有A位置是两者的交叉点。

SECTION 3

主题场景	专题讲座场景
主旨大意	关于澳大利亚某个区域的房产介绍
考查题型	选择题、表格填空题

名师解读

21 B 原文提到three areas，之后又提到表示地点的名词短语the northern part，紧接着考生能够听到low end, the cheapest housing等短语，这两个短语与价格有联系，而且出现了cheapest一词。答案为the north。

22 C 根据题干中的because of，可以判断本题是考查原因的选择题，注意原文表示原因的连词后面的内容。题干中表示地点的名词短语the east为关键词，在听到原文the eastern part后，考生就要注意其后的内容。后面的一句就出现了because of，其后面的all the hills and parks就是答案。

23 C 同22题类似，根据题干中的because，可以判断本题是考查原因的选择题。注意题干中的关键词为$1,100，考生听到这个价格以后就要预测后面可能会出现答案。后面提到了on the hills, run through the east, the best views of the city，但考生要注意前两个是现象，不是原因。

24 B 本题需选择与价格有关的数字，选择最低的价格。原文中有多个数字出现，$650, $350, $170，但是对应the west, the south, north三个不同地点的价格。题目要求选出north地区的the lowest price，注意排除干扰。根据原文的关键词the cheapest flats定位，start from...up to，那么start from后面的价格就是答案。

25 no trains 分类信息表格，考查各处的优缺点，注意讲话人语气的变化，及表示转折关系的连词，如but, however等。另注意题号的排列顺序。此题前面听到lots of parks和lots of trees是优点，与pretty scenes对应，之后提到缺点there aren't any trains，故答案为no trains。

26 convenient public transportation south之后提到convenient，之后的public transport为答案。

27 attractive bay 在听到quite attractive in that sense后，考生需要判断出前面的内容就是the west的优点。此题答案在两句中出现，要结合两句得出答案attractive bay。

28 polluted bay/pollution 注意原文a couple of problems，就是两个问题，这后面的内容对应着28、29题的答案。两个答案在原文并列出现，有明确的表并列的词，one...the other，填写名词或形容词作为答案。One指代其中的一个问题，其后的表语从句the bay is polluted改写后就是答案。

29 airport 原文中的the other指代另一个问题，其后的表语从句it is where the airport is改写后就是答案。

30 many insects 答案在转折词之后出现，注意but后的重读。原文中的amount of同many替换。

SECTION 4

主题场景	讲座场景
主旨大意	介绍与家庭安全相关的防范措施
考查题型	表格填空题、句子填空题

名师解读

31 secure locks　题干中的关键词windows为原文重现，在关键词之后紧接着提到与它相反的建议，fit为原文重现，其后的secure locks需要考生填入空格中。

32 burglar alarm　题干中的关键词doors为原文重现，据此定位答案所在的位置。题干中的a good quality为原文重现，并且提到两次，第一次提到的后面是lock，但lock是essential故并不是答案；第二次提到的后面是burglar alarm，在描述burglar alarm时原文用了good investment, 为主观建议，故其为答案。

33 valuables　题干中的locked away in a safe为原文重现，原文此前提到的valuables即为答案。

34 delivery　题干中的newspaper为关键词，cancel the为原文重现，考生可以直接判定后面的delivery为答案。

35 milk and bread　35题由34题而来，需要取消递送服务的除了题干中提到的newspaper外，与newspaper构成并列关系且属于同类性质的milk和bread即为答案。

36 property　题干中的Inform, go分别与原文中的tell, be away对应，keep an eye为原文重现，与后文的look out for同义，题干中的your与each other's对应，look out for的宾语即为答案。

37 suspicious　题干中的showing和others'分别与原文中的taking和someone's对应，call the police station, a particular interest, property均为原文重现。本题的考点是but后的内容。

38 personal documents　Don't leave与原文中的never keep是同义替换，in your car为原文重现。接着后文提到了一系列不能放在车里的东西，包括mobile phones, laptop computers, cash，它们均为原文重现，最后提到的personal documents即为答案。

39 ignition key　题干中的when you leave your car为原文重现，据此进行定位，题干与原文中的always remove the...and lock all doors为一一对应，考生经过比对就可得出答案。

40 handy wall chart　题干中的contains与原文中的gives对应，gives的宾语是all the details和a handy wall chart，根据题干中的不定冠词a，可以判定答案为handy wall chart。考生应注意不要被定语从句干扰。

READING

READING PASSAGE 1

体　裁　议论文
题　材　网络媒体
主　题　网络欺凌的出现与蔓延
题　型　配对题、判断题

Questions 1–6

题型　配对题(Matching Headings)

注意　配对题是雅思阅读中的一种重要题型。段落标题配对题的出题形式为先给出题目，再给出阅读文章：先给出选项，即若干标题，标题序号为罗马数字（如i、ii、iii等）；选项下方是有待匹配标题的段落符号（如Paragraph A, Paragraph B等），接下来是考生需要阅读的文章。该题型要求考生根据阅读文章从标题列表中为指定的段落选出恰当的标题。

1	关键词	example, cyber-bullying
	原文定位	A段第三句This is extreme but far from unique example of the devastation wrought by cyber-bullying和末句Meanwhile...bullying occurs are becoming both more central to young people's lives, and more public.
	题解	**答案iii** A段开头列举了盖尔·琼斯遭受网络暴力后自杀的例子。本题定位句点明了主题——网络暴力并总结其危害性——由网络暴力引发的灾难不止这一起。A段的末句引出了这种危害性随着网络的日益普及可能会扩大化的担忧，对应iii。
2	关键词	effects of cyber-bullying
	原文定位	B段首句Research into the causes and effects of cyber-bullying is still in its infancy.
	题解	**答案i** B段首句为主题句，原句中的effects of cyber-bullying（网络暴力行为的影响）与i项中的impact of cyber-bullying（网络暴力行为的影响）表达的意思一致。
3	关键词	relentlessness, cruelty
	原文定位	C段首句"Another reason why cyber-bullying is so harmful is its relentlessness"，第三句、第四句"With cyber-bullying it is 24/7, 365 days a year. There is no escape."
	题解	**答案v** C段提到网络暴力危害如此巨大的另一个原因是它永无休止(relentlessness)，而且网络暴力行为是一年365天，一周7天，一天24小时地存在，无处可逃。这些事实都说明很难阻止网络暴力行为。此外，与现实中的暴力行为相比，永无休止也是网络暴力的一大特点，因此它更难消除。
4	关键词	developed role-playing software, taken legislative action
	原文定位	D段首句Led by Ruth Aylett of Heriot-Watt University in Edinburgh, UK...recently developed role-playing software called Fear Not!...和第四句Meanwhile, some governments have taken legislative action.
	题解	**答案ii** 英国爱丁堡赫瑞瓦特大学的露丝·艾莱特领导的欧洲研究联盟开发了"不要怕！"角色扮演软件……同时，一些国家也采取了立法行动。这些都是为应对网络暴力行为而提出的方法。
5	关键词	teens, cyber-bullying, adults
	原文定位	E段首句Known best as a problem facing teens, cyber-bullying affects adults too.
	题解	**答案ix** 定位句为E段的主题句。cyber-bullying（网络暴力行为）不仅对青少年(teens)产生影响，对成年人(adults)也有很大的影响。原文中的adults与ix项中的grown-ups（成人）是同义表达。
6	关键词	teachers, victims, celebrities
	原文定位	F段首句Teachers have also been victims.和末句Meanwhile in South Korea, celebrities have been the high-profile victims of anonymous cyber-bullying attacks, reportedly including TV star Jeong Da-Bin and pop singer Yuni...
	题解	**答案vii** F段介绍了teachers（老师），celebrities（名人）也都是cyber-bullying（网络暴力行为）的受害者。

Questions 7–13

题型 判断题(Identifying Information)

注意 考生要理解FALSE/NO的含义。它包含三种矛盾对立状况：命题与原文内容对立（相反）；命题与原文对立（相反），因为命题否定原文内容；命题信息既不对立（相反）也不否定，但是和原文内容矛盾。

7	关键词	reasons and impacts of cyber-bullying
	原文定位	B段首句Research into the causes and effects of cyber-bullying is still in its infancy.
	题解	答案NO　题干中的the reasons and impacts（理由和影响）与原文中的the causes and effects（原因和影响）相对应；cyber-bullying（网络暴力行为）属于原文重现，但题干中的well-researched by scientists（科学家对此已开展了比较深入的研究），与原文中的still in its infancy（仍处于起步阶段）表达的意思在程度上不符。
8	关键词	2003, classmates, put his video online
	原文定位	B段倒数第四句、倒数第三句When his classmates found the video in 2003, they posted it online as a joke. Raza was so upset he finished the school year from a psychiatric ward.
	题解	答案NOT GIVEN　原文提到拉兹的同学在2003年找到了这段录像，并放到网上当笑料。拉兹受到极大刺激，以致在精神病院度过了那一学年。但没有提及最后是否因为这个事情而自杀。
9	关键词	playground bullying, happens all the time
	原文定位	C段第二句、第三句、第四句When I was a kid, playground bullying stopped when the bell rang and you went back inside or... With cyber-bullying it is 24/7, 365 days a year. There is no escape.
	题解	答案YES　C段提到约翰·卡尔的观点“在我小的时候，操场上的欺辱行为会随着铃声响起、走进教室或是放学回家而停止，而网络暴力行为却是一年365天，一周7天，一天24小时地存在，无处可逃。”题干中的all the time（一直）是对原文24/7, 365 days a year（一年365天，一周7天，一天24小时）的同义替换。
10	关键词	restrain, playground bullying
	原文定位	C段倒数第五句“On the playground, seeing the stress and pain of the victim face to face can act as an inhibitor to some degree,” explains Carr.
	题解	答案NO　C段提到了卡尔声称在操场上亲眼看到被侵害者的痛苦，一定程度上(to some degree)会阻止侵害进一步升级，并不是什么都不能做。
11	关键词	authourities, law
	原文定位	D段第四句Meanwhile, some governments have taken legislative action.
	题解	答案YES　题干中的authourities（官方）和law（法律）分别与原文中的governments（政府）和legislative action（立法行为）对应。

12	关键词	mortals, influenced by cyber-bullying
	原文定位	E段首句Known best as a problem facing teens, cyber-bullying affects adults too. F段首句Teachers have also been victims和F段末句...anonymous cyber-bullying attacks...
	题解	答案YES 题干中的mortals from all walks of life（来自各行各业的人）是对原文teens, adults, teachers, celebrities的概括。
13	关键词	bullied, students
	原文定位	F段第二句Tired of insults from students on websites...this year that it is ready to go to court in support of teachers who have been libelled online.
	题解	答案NOT GIVEN F段提到老师受到网上的libelled（诽谤），但并没有提及老师是否是受自己班级学生的威胁。

READING PASSAGE 2

体　裁　议论文
题　材　社会生活
主　题　介绍噪音带来的危害以及原因
题　型　配对题、判断题

Questions 14–20

题型 配对题(Matching Headings)

注意 在段落标题配对题中，标题选项的数量远多于出题段落的数量。但是，一个段落只有一个标题，一个标题也只能选择一次。因此，标题选项中会存在大量的干扰选项。

14	关键词	ill effects of noise pollution
	原文定位	A段末句The ill effects of noise pollution are of two kinds: acute-exposure to an individual instance of a very loud noise...too much noise over an extended period of time.
	题解	答案iv 定位句为A段的主题句，主要讲的是noise pollution（噪音污染）的ill effects（不良影响），由此可以判断iv项为本段的标题，其中ill effects（不良影响）与选项中的harmful（有害的）对应。
15	关键词	city and urban dwellers, almost impossible
	原文定位	B段首句City and urban dwellers exist in an increasingly noise-ridden environment, and it is now almost impossible to escape exposure to high noise levels.
	题解	答案v 定位句为B段主题句。原句中city and urban dwellers（城镇居民），almost impossible to escape（几乎不可能逃过……）都与选项v中的everywhere（到处）对应，也就是噪音无处不在。

16	关键词	hearing problems
	原文定位	C段首句Our noise level acceptance threshold is rising in step with the number of persons developing hearing problems.
	题解	**答案x** C段首句提出有听力问题的人的数量逐渐增多，接着就列举了一系列的数据来说明存在的问题，此外，考生也可借助本段中频繁出现的百分比数据推测答案，这些数据正是x中的statistical evidence的具体化。
17	关键词	damage, earphones
	原文定位	D段首句Of current concern to acoustical engineers and psychologists...caused by the transmission of loud sound through earphones placed directly into the ear canal.
	题解	**答案i** D段首句为本段的主题句。根据首句中的关键词damage（损害），earphones（耳机）可以判定答案为i。
18	关键词	one danger, another danger, finally
	原文定位	E段首句One danger posed to young ears is that the peak sound level from these radio-cassette players is often far too great; at high volume it is all too easy to receive Dose 1 in a short period of time.
	题解	**答案vi** E段用One danger...Another danger...Finally...（一个危险……另一个危险……最终……）的形式，解释了earphones（耳机）对人造成危害的原因。
19	关键词	most alarming
	原文定位	F段首句But perhaps the most alarming potential for danger caused by insertable earphones is the ease with which the listener can exceed the safe time length of exposure to noise.
	题解	**答案ii** 定位句为F段的主题句，由其中的关键词the most alarming potential for danger（令人最为吃惊的潜在危险），insertable earphones（可插入式耳机）可以直接判定ii为本题答案, the most alarming danger为原文重现。
20	关键词	varying degrees of hearing loss, chronic and irreversible disability
	原文定位	G段首句、第二句Noise abuse soon leads to varying degrees of hearing loss. What may begin as an acute temporary condition, in time becomes a chronic and irreversible disability.
	题解	**答案xi** 通过阅读题目信息，发现原文hearing loss（听力能力的丧失），chronic（慢性的）与选项xi一致，同时，根据首句及第二句也可以判定答案就是xi。

Questions 21–26

题型 判断题(Identifying Information)

注意 NOT GIVEN的情况有：题目中有比较结构，在文章中出现此结构，但是比较的对象不同；题目中用情态动词表示对未来的预测或者展望，而在文章中没有提及；题目中有的修饰词（即考点词）在文章中没有与之相对应的同义词表达；在文章中出现过题目中的定位词，但是对比定位词所在的句法结构，两者之间没有关系。

21	关键词	not easy, in the past
	原文定位	A段首句It is by old saying that the virtue of silence by claiming it is golden, yet experience tells us that silence is as hard to come by as the precious metal itself.
	题解	答案TRUE 题干中的not easy（不容易的）与原文中的hard（困难的）是同义表达，考生要特别注意转折词yet（然而）后面的内容。
22	关键词	one category of
	原文定位	A段末句The ill effects of noise pollution are of two kinds...such as a gunshot or explosion; and chronic—the experience of too much noise over an extended period of time.
	题解	答案FALSE 题干中的one category of （一个种类）与原文of...kinds（……种类）对应；但gunshot or explosion（枪击和爆炸）属于instance of a very loud noise（瞬间爆发的巨大声响），不属于an extended period of time（延续时间较长的声音）。
23	关键词	“Layering”sound, masking
	原文定位	B段倒数第二句The popular practice of “layering” sound, by adding a louder source of noise to that which already exists in order to mask it, merely compounds the problem.
	题解	答案FALSE 原文提到的是用a louder source of noise（一个更大的噪声来源）来掩盖“layering” sound（分层声音），题干的意思与此相反。
24	关键词	Australian Bureau of Statistics, 20 percent, 14 years old
	原文定位	C段第二句、第三句Data...the Australian Bureau of Statistics show that 7.4% of people over 14 years of age...either at work, in the everyday living environment...
	题解	答案TRUE 题干中的less than 20 percent（少于20%）与原文中的7.4%对应；over 14 years old（大于14岁）与原文over 14 years of age（大于14岁）对应；constant barrage of noise at work or in the everyday living environment（在工作或日常的居住环境里持续的噪声阻塞）是原文重现。
25	关键词	achieve Dose 1 in 4 hours
	原文定位	D段末句For instance, to achieve Dose 1 in four hours, it is necessary to raise the decibel exposure level by a mere three decibels.
	题解	答案TRUE 定位句提到为了在四小时内达到Dose 1（剂量1），需要在90 decibel（90分贝）的基础上提高three decibels（三分贝），也就是93 decibels（93分贝）。

Test 9

26	关键词	Beethoven, tinnitus
	原文定位	G段倒数第二句It is believed the composer Beethoven was particularly aggravated by this malady.
	题解	答案NOT GIVEN　G段提到了Beethoven（贝多芬），但没有提及Beethoven（贝多芬）是否认为tinnitus（耳鸣）威胁他的音乐创作。

READING PASSAGE 3

体　裁　　说明文
题　材　　能源
主　题　　由一种新的潮汐涡轮机的发明而引发的对各种新能源的介绍
题　型　　摘要填空题、段落信息配对题、判断题

Questions 27–30

题型　配对题(Matching Information)

注意　在段落信息配对题中，题干中的信息虽然陈述的都是文章中的细节，但其内容基本都是围绕文章主题或是某一段落的主题进行描述的。通过快速阅读题干中的若干条细节信息，考生可以迅速了解原文的主旨大意，从而能够返回去阅读原文时加快阅读速度，节省定位时间。

27	关键词	new plan, a new factor, tidal power
	原文定位	F段第四句To build an effective surface tidal turbine, Johnston realised that both tidal and wave power should be taken into account.
	题解	答案F　原文中的both tidal and wave power（潮汐能和波浪能）为并列关系(both... and...)，它对应题干中的关键词besides（除……之外，还有），而定位词tidal power（潮汐能）在原文中重现，故判断题干中提到的new factor（新的因素）一定与原文中的wave power（波浪能）有关。
28	关键词	damages, in the past years
	原文定位	C段倒数第二句Some of the prototypes that have been tested in the decades are quickly destroyed by rushing tides.
	题解	答案C　原文中的destroy（破坏）与题干中damages（损坏）为同义转换，而原文中的in the decades（几十年）与题干中的in the past years（过去的几十年）为同义转换。
29	关键词	detailed structure of a model
	原文定位	B段末句It looks like a model rocket with two fins with propellers attached to the ends of the fins.
	题解	答案B　该段详细阐述了模型的构造，末句中又有model的重现。

30	关键词	immature model, at the beginning of the 21st century
	原文定位	A段第二句The 8-metre-long prototype, ideally, will go into the water at the European Marine Energy Centre (EMEC) Tidal Test Site that sits just down the road from ScotRenewables in 2010.
	题解	答案A 原文中的prototype（原型）与题干中的model（模型）为同义转换，原文中的2010与题干中的at the beginning of the 21st century（开始于21世纪的初期）在时间上对应。

Questions 31–35

题型 摘要填空题(Summary Completion)

注意 该类题目是一小段文字，它是对原文或原文中几个段落主要内容的缩写或改写。摘要中有几个空白部分要求考生填空。

31	关键词	such as
	原文定位	C段第三句You can't do that with intermittent, variable sources like wind, solar or wave.
	题解	答案wind/solar/wave 题干中的such as（例如）和原文中的like（像……）是同义表达，故答案是wind/solar/wave（风能/太阳能/波浪能）三者选一个即可。
32	关键词	turbine output, counted
	原文定位	C段第二句With a tide table and computer, ScotRenewables can calculate the power output of a turbine decades in advance.
	题解	答案tide table with在句中表使用，原文中的and computer和题干中的as well as computer（以及电脑），原文中的calculate（计算）和题干中的count（计算）为同义表达。
33	关键词	hard, pointed to
	原文定位	D段第三句The difficulty has been keeping the turbine pointed in the direction of the tide.
	题解	答案tide direction 题干中的hard（困难的）与原文中的difficulty（困难）为同义表达。
34	关键词	ScotRenewables, building up, advanced hydrodynamics
	原文定位	D段末句ScotRenewables says it will come up with control mechanisms and advanced hydrodynamics (i.e., aerodynamics in water) to keep the turbines pointed in the right direction.
	题解	答案control mechanisms 题干中的building up（建立）和原文中的come up with（提出）为同义表达，ScotRenewables, advanced hydrodynamics, in water均为原文重现。

35	关键词	EMEC, government, put tidal and wave power on the grid
	原文定位	E段倒数第四句The government has also passed exceptionally large credits for power providers that put tidal and wave power on the grid.
	题解	答案large credits 题干用被动将原文的主动表现出来，将原句的主语the government（政府）转换为宾语，故答案是原句的宾语large credits（大的信誉）。

Questions 36–40

题型 判断题(Identifying Information)

注意 判断题的设题模式基本上可分为两大类：细节的对应和观点的对应（两者又可合并称为信息点对应），考查考生简单的推理、总结和归纳能力。雅思考试是一种语言能力的测试，所以它不考查专业知识，也不考查阅读文章以外的背景知识（除基本常识以外，如简单的地理知识）。

36	关键词	Floating turbine, be anchored, forever
	原文定位	B段第三句Rather than anchoring a permanent turbine on the ocean floor, ScotRenewables will build a floating turbine that is slack moored with chains to an anchor on the sea floor.
	题解	答案FALSE 题干中的forever（永远）与原文中的permanent（永久的）为同义转换，B段第三句话后面的内容均对floating turbine（漂浮的涡轮机）持正面评价，题干中的not good enough（不够好）与此相悖。
37	关键词	forecasted, renewable energy
	原文定位	C段首句Tidal is the potentially most predictable, reliable form of renewable energy.
	题解	答案FALSE 定位句出现了关键词forecast（预测）的同义表达predictable（可预测的），但原文讲潮汐能很可能是可预测的能源，而题干则说已经证明了，属于偷换概念。
38	关键词	ScotRenewables model, easier
	原文定位	C段末句Taking the ScotRenewables turbine in for repairs should be easy: maintenance workers would just have to take a boat out, unhook it, and put another in its place while the first is being entangled.
	题解	答案FALSE 由定位句可知ScotRenewables turbine（ScotRenewables的涡轮机）维修起来简单的原因在于其操作流程很简单，而并不是题干所说的因为花费时间少。
39	关键词	prototype, commercial use
	原文定位	F段首句Talking about the prototype and commercial power production, however, is easier said than done.
	题解	答案NOT GIVEN 题干中的关键词prototype（原型），commercial（商业的）均为原文重现，但原文提及的是is easier said than done（说比做容易），没有提及有足够的经验使其投入商业使用。

40	关键词	Booking time, EMEC wave tank, more difficult
	原文定位	F段倒数第三句It was easier than trying to book time at an EMEC wave tank.
	题解	答案TRUE　题干中的book time（预定时间）为原文重现，原文中的it指代的是ScotRenewables，原文表达的是ScotRenewables比trying to book time at an EMEC wave tank（试图在EMEC波能容器内预定时间）容易，而题干是把比较的事物反过来，用了more difficult than（比……更难），由此可知本题答案为TRUE。

WRITING

WRITING TASK 1

名师解读

小作文主要以图表为主，而在这些图表中曲线图是最常见的一种形式。在曲线图这一题型中，考生要对图表的内容加以描述和分析。本题主要是让考生描述和对比1992年某一天英国4岁以上的人在不同时间段使用收音机和电视机的情况。

首先考生要花一分钟左右的时间来分析曲线图，先根据横轴分析变化，然后再进行比较。对于以时间为横轴的题，描写趋势的时候就必须用increase, decline这些来写，不仅仅是曲线图，对于任何一种图（流程图例外）都要这么写。通过图内两条曲线对比找到收听电视和收音机人数的异同。

在解析了曲线图以后，就进入到写作的实际操作阶段。既然是描述和对比型文章，描述的逻辑性和重点性就应该受到重视。注意，数据少的时候，就把数据都写上，但是数据多的话，对于曲线图，一定要描述起点值、终点值、峰值、谷值和交点值。

高分范文

TV and radio **audiences** in the UK differ sharply throughout the day. **Predictably**, TV attracts larger audiences than radio, but in the early morning hours, the radio get by far the largest share while, in the evening, TV viewers are most active.

Looking at the course of a day from the early hours in the morning, we see that the **index** for radio listeners grows **sharply** from 15% to a peak of over 30% just between 6 and 7.30am.

From that point on, the number of listeners **declines** at a gradual rate to eventually return to the original value with the exception of a non-significant slight surge in the late afternoon and at bed time. While radio listening starts rising in the early morning, the TV watching level is close to zero.

As the day proceeds, we see a constant upward fluctuation that comes to a peak of 45% around 6pm. From 8pm on, a steady decline to about 38% is followed by a drop to, again, almost zero in the next few hours. (174 words)

WRITING TASK 2

文章结构

正反观点辩论+立场+原因+总结

viewpoint +reason 1+ reason 2+conclusion
第一段：背景句+引出现象+反方的观点+表明立场
第二段：立场+理由
第三段：总结+立场

思路点拨

步骤一：审题（<3分钟）

Some people argue that national governments should use large projects to provide jobs and economic growth. Others argue that this wastes money and leads to corruption. Discuss both these views and give your own opinion.

→通读题目，了解大意，判断题型。

本题的题型为论说型作文。题目的大意为：有人认为政府应搞一些大型项目以提高就业率，促进经济增长，而有些人则认为政府这样做不仅浪费金钱还会导致腐败。讨论双方观点并表明你的立场。

→再读题目，辨别关键词，区分主题词和限定词，推测考官的出题意图。

主题词：national governments, large projects, jobs and economic growth, wastes money, corruption

限定词：both these views, your own opinion

步骤二：列大纲（<3分钟）

英文提纲	Intro: governments influence employment and economic growth→implement and carry out massive public works→critics, wasteful→personally, justified Body: several conditions→the first, necessary and ultimately beneficial→ second point, projects, carefully thought out→prevent corruption Conclusion: projects themselves, beneficial, the country's culture
中文提纲	引出话题：政府影响就业率和经济增长→大力发展公共事业工程→批评者认为这是浪费→个人认为这是正确的做法 主体段落：发展公共事业工程需要注意的问题→首先：必要性、益处→其次：需要全盘考虑→预防腐败 总结：政府应考虑工程本身、益处、国家文化

高分范文

When the economy is weak, citizens often turn to their governments for help. They believe that governments can directly influence employment and economic growth. One thing national governments can do is to **implement** and carry out **massive** public works. Critics point out that this is wasteful. Personally, I believe that there are times when government involvement in huge public projects, such as **freeways** and bridges, are justified.

There are several conditions governments must meet before they spend the public's money on large projects. The first is that the project should actually be necessary and **ultimately beneficial**. Building roads in poor countries can **dramatically** improve the economy by encouraging trade. Road-building is also **labour-intensive**, which means that many people are directly employed. As a result, most of the money spent is **injected back into** the economy. This brings me to my second point. Projects that transfer large amounts of money out of the country must be carefully thought out. In many cases, projects like power plants and hydroelectric dams must be financed by debt. In other words, the country must borrow the money. Because this money is mostly spent **overseas**, the country must clearly gain

Test 9

in the long term. Generally, this is not a viable option for boosting employment. Moreover, even if all the projects are judged to be beneficial, there is still the criticism of government waste. Critics rightly ask how necessary it is for the government to actually do the work. They point out that private companies could do the work instead. While this is a good point, I do not agree that private companies are less susceptible to corruption. In reality, the likelihood of millions of dollars being lost depends on the culture of the country, and not whether private **corporations** or the government spends it.

In conclusion, whether government spending on large public projects is appropriate depends on the projects themselves, how beneficial they are, and the country's culture. (327 words)

SPEAKING

名师解读

Part 1的题目属于购物话题。网购的出现让很多人的购物方式变得多样化，于是对购物这类话题的讨论也成了近些年来考官经常考的题目。

Part 2属于口头作文，考查考生对话题的理解力和表达流畅度，切记要听清楚题，不要因为着急回答而词不达意，在2分钟的陈述时间内，要尽量表达出自己的观点，充分展现自己的口语表达能力。

Part 3比起Part 1和Part 2更加学术、抽象，考生要随时准备对问题进行评价与预测。但如果仅仅是将简单的ideas堆砌在一起，并不能取得高分。在Part 3，考官最关心的是考生有没有抓住机会展示其驾驭高级词汇、语法以及连贯上下文的能力。

高分示例

PART 1

Shops

- Do you enjoy going shopping? Why?

Shopping is something everyone has to do, and while I know it is **stereotypical** that a woman should like shopping, I only do certain shopping when I absolutely have to. For instance, I will only go shopping for clothes if I need something new, or grocery shopping if I am having guests over.

- In your country, what time do shops generally open?

The time shops open and close is **seasonal**. In spring and summer, these shops open earlier and close later because there is good weather and lots of people around, but in autumn and winter, the shops tend to open later and close earlier because it is so cold.

- What would you recommend visitors to your country to buy? Why?

I think it would depend on which season they are coming to China; for example, I would recommend they buy a big, thick jacket, **scarf,** ear **muffs** and some thinner underwears before arriving in winter. During summer, I might suggest that they bring sun block and drink lots of water to stay **hydrated** in the hot weather.

- How are shops changing in your country? Why?

Shops are changing all the time, they change **ownership** or get passed down to family members who change different things to either change the "look" of the shop or the **clientele**. I have noticed lately that there are a lot more shops owned by people in the last five years, as with the economy, everyone is opening their own business to get by. It is almost like there are four of the same types of shops on the same stretch of road and then another four across from them.

PART 2

I ran into an old friend from school last Wednesday. I was just going into a restaurant close to my office building for lunch when I saw her waiting inside for her food.

Lucy was one of my best friends at school, but after finishing high school, we went to different colleges and then she went abroad. We lost contact after a while.

I had not seen Lucy for almost six years when we ran into each other in the restaurant.

It was a happy moment as well as a sad moment for me. I was able to get back in touch with an old friend, but at the same time, hearing about all she has done and all the places she has travelled made me a little **jealous** about what she had accomplished that I had not.

PART 3

Keeping in contact

- In what different ways can people keep in touch with each other?

Nowadays there are lots of ways for people to keep in contact. There are more out-dated methods, like sending a letter via the post office and then there are more reliable ways that we have all become accustomed to in recent years—email, texting, instant messaging, phone calls, Skype calls, video chat, social media and networking sites. Nowadays, it's easier than ever to maintain connections to people, no matter where they are.

- How important do you think it is to keep in touch with friends? Why/Why not?

I think it is very important to keep in touch with friends. The connections you make at school, or have with family are important to everyone's mental health. Most people are incredibly social creatures and so require certain amounts of interaction with other people. Maintaining your contact with friends gives us some of that contact.

- Which way of keeping in touch do you think is most popular with young people?

Most young people use texting or instant messaging systems to keep in contact with each other. Another thing they do to keep in contact is video chat if the people have good enough phones.

Long-term relationships

- How valuable do you think long-term friendships are compared with new relationships? Why/Why not?

Having a long standing, **long-term friendship** with someone is an **amazing** feeling. The thought that there is someone or a group of people that know you so well that they will know when you are unhappy or scared and be there for you is amazing. A new friendship is also good. Getting to know new people can influence your outlook, but the level of trust will need to be built up still.

- Do you agree that maintaining long-term relationships sometimes requires effort? Why/Why not?

Maintaining a long-term relationship requires a lot of effort, especially with a large group of friends that have known each other for many years. People are jealous by nature, and ensuring friends that you are all close friends and one is not closer than the other requires certain balance. Also, you cannot expect to be taken seriously if you make no effort to help them with their problems and **celebrate** in their **victories**.

重点词汇

LISTENING

backpack	['bækpæk]	*n.*	双肩背包，背包；远足用的背包
plastic	['plæstɪk]	*n.*	塑料制品
reasonably	['riːznəbli]	*adv.*	合理地；相当地；适度地
inconvenience	[ˌɪnkən'viːnɪəns]	*n.*	不便；麻烦
reassure	[ˌriːə'ʃʊə]	*v.*	安心，消除疑虑
resume	[rɪ'zjuːm]	*v.*	重新开始；继续
vacancy	['veɪkənsi]	*n.*	空缺；空位
available	[ə'veɪləbl]	*adj.*	可得的，可利用的；有效的
suitable	['suːtəbl]	*adj.*	适当的，合适的
facility	[fə'sɪləti]	*n.*	设施，设备
accommodation	[əˌkɒmə'deɪʃn]	*n.*	住处，膳宿；调节
receipt	[rɪ'siːt]	*n.*	收据；收入
strictly	['strɪktli]	*adv.*	完全地；严格地
entertainment	[ˌentə'teɪnmənt]	*n.*	娱乐，消遣；款待
refreshment	[rɪ'freʃmənt]	*n.*	点心；起提神作用的东西
unfortunately	[ʌn'fɔːtʃənətli]	*adv.*	不幸地
definitely	['defɪnətli]	*adv.*	当然；清楚地
voucher	['vaʊtʃə]	*n.*	代金；收据；证人
reception	[rɪ'sepʃn]	*n.*	接待；接收；招待会
burglar	['bɜːglə]	*n.*	夜贼，窃贼
professional	[prə'feʃənl]	*adj.*	专业的；职业性的
electrician	[ɪˌlek'trɪʃn]	*n.*	电工；电气技师
prevention	[prɪ'venʃn]	*n.*	预防；阻止；妨碍
deposit	[dɪ'pɒzɪt]	*n.*	存款；保证金；沉淀物
precaution	[prɪ'kɔːʃn]	*n.*	预防，警惕
delivery	[dɪ'lɪvəri]	*n.*	递送
permission	[pə'mɪʃn]	*n.*	允许，许可
suspicious	[sə'spɪʃəs]	*adj.*	可疑的，怀疑的
possession	[pə'zeʃn]	*n.*	财产；拥有
particularly	[pə'tɪkjələli]	*adv.*	特别地，独特地
satellite navigation systems			卫星导航系统

READING

cyber-bullying		*n.*	网络暴力；网路霸凌；暴力
devastation	[ˌdevə'steɪʃn]	*n.*	破坏，毁坏；荒废
embarrassing	[ɪm'bærəsɪŋ]	*adj.*	使人尴尬的；令人为难的
chatroom	['tʃætˌruːm]	*n.*	聊天室
infancy	['ɪnfənsi]	*n.*	初期；婴儿期；幼年
aggressively	[ə'gresɪvli]	*adv.*	侵略性地，好斗地；有进取心地
detrimental	[ˌdetrɪ'mentl]	*adj.*	不利的，有害的
conventional	[kən'venʃənl]	*adj.*	符合习俗的，传统的；常见的，惯例的
criminologist	[ˌkrɪmɪ'nɒlədʒɪst]	*n.*	犯罪学者；刑事学家
pretend	[prɪ'tend]	*adj.*	假装的
sabre	['seɪbə]	*n.*	军刀；马刀；击剑或决斗用的长剑
psychiatric	[ˌsaɪkɪ'ætrɪk]	*adj.*	精神病治疗的；精神病学的

ward	[wɔːd]	*n.*	病房；保卫；监视
amusing	[ə'mjuːzɪŋ]	*adj.*	有趣的，好玩的，引人发笑的
relentlessness	[rɪ'lentlɪsnəs]	*n.*	无止境
amplify	['æmplɪfaɪ]	*v.*	放大，扩大；增强；详述
anonymous	[ə'nɒnɪməs]	*adj.*	匿名的，无名的；无个性特征的
anonymity	[ˌænə'nɪməti]	*n.*	匿名；匿名者；无名之辈
ramification	[ˌræmɪfɪ'keɪʃn]	*n.*	分枝，分叉
sibling	['sɪblɪŋ]	*n.*	兄弟姐妹；民族成员
immediacy	[ɪ'miːdɪəsi]	*n.*	目前；直接
consortium	[kən'sɔːtɪəm]	*n.*	联盟；财团；联合；合伙
animation	[ˌænɪ'meɪʃn]	*n.*	活泼，生气；激动；卡通片绘制
legislative	['ledʒɪslətɪv]	*adj.*	立法的；有立法权的
harass	['hærəs]	*v.*	使困扰，使烦恼；反复袭击
portal	['pɔːtl]	*n.*	门户网站；入口；大门
libel	['laɪbl]	*v.*	诽谤，中伤
infringment	[ɪn'frɪndʒmənt]	*n.*	侵犯，违反；破坏
jurisdiction	[ˌdʒʊərɪs'dɪkʃn]	*n.*	司法权，审判权；权限
advocacy	['ædvəkəsi]	*n.*	主张；拥护；辩护
recount	[rɪ'kaʊnt]	*v.*	叙述；重新计算
virtual	['vɜːtʃʊəl]	*adj.*	虚拟的；有效的；实质上的
abuse	[ə'bjuːs]	*n.*	滥用；虐待；辱骂
hassle	['hæsl]	*v.*	找麻烦，扰乱；与……争辩
disparaging	[dɪ'spærɪdʒɪŋ]	*adj.*	诽谤的；轻蔑的
suicide	['suːɪsaɪd]	*v.*	自杀
scientifically	[ˌsaɪən'tɪfɪkli]	*adv.*	系统地；合乎科学地；学问上
demonstrable	[dɪ'mɒnstrəbl]	*adj.*	可论证的；显而易见的
commodity	[kə'mɒdəti]	*n.*	商品，货物，日用品
gunshot	['gʌnʃɒt]	*n.*	射击；射程；炮击
chronic	['krɒnɪk]	*adj.*	慢性的，长期的；习惯性的
suburban	[sə'bɜːbən]	*adj.*	郊区的，城郊的；土气的
endurance	[ɪn'djuərəns]	*n.*	忍耐力，忍耐；持久，耐久
merely	['mɪəli]	*adv.*	仅仅，只不过；只是
intersperse	[ˌɪntə'spɜːs]	*v.*	点缀；散布
acceptance	[ək'septəns]	*n.*	接纳；赞同；容忍
threshold	['θreʃhəʊld]	*n.*	入口，门槛；开始
discernible	[dɪ'sɜːnɪbl]	*adj.*	可辨别的；可识别的
barrage	['bærɑːʒ]	*n.*	阻塞；弹幕；齐射式攻击
acoustical	[ə'kuːstɪkəl]	*adj.*	听觉的；声学的；音响的
dosage	['dəʊsɪdʒ]	*n.*	剂量，用量
slightly	['slaɪtli]	*adv.*	稍微，轻微地；纤细地
decibel	['desɪbel]	*n.*	分贝
earphone	['ɪəfəʊn]	*n.*	耳机
canal	[kə'næl]	*n.*	运河；水道
insertable	[ɪn'sɜːteɪbl]	*adj.*	可插入的
accumulation	[əkjuːmju'leɪʃn]	*n.*	积聚，累积；堆积物
madness	['mædnəs]	*n.*	疯狂；愚蠢的行为
temporary	['temprəri]	*adj.*	暂时的，临时的
ailing	['eɪlɪŋ]	*adj.*	生病的，身体不舒服的；体衰的
prototype	['prəʊtətaɪp]	*n.*	原型；标准，模范
version	['vɜːʃn]	*n.*	版本；译文；倒转术
megawatt	['megəwɒt]	*n.*	兆瓦特，百万瓦特

turbine	['tɜːbaɪn]	*n.*	涡轮；涡轮机
moor	[mɔː]	*v.*	停泊
predictable	[prɪ'dɪktəbl]	*adj.*	可预言的
entangle	[ɪn'tæŋgl]	*v.*	使纠缠；卷入；使混乱
notorious	[nəʊ'tɔːrɪəs]	*adj.*	声名狼藉的，臭名昭著的
hydroelectric	[ˌhaɪdrəʊɪ'lektrɪk]	*adj.*	水力发电的；水电治疗的
terawatt	['terəwɒt]	*n.*	瓦；兆兆瓦
validate	['vælɪdeɪt]	*v.*	证实，验证；确认；使生效
grid	[grɪd]	*n.*	网格；格子，栅格；输电网
vessel	['vesl]	*n.*	船，舰

WRITING

audience	['ɔːdɪəns]	*n.*	观众，受众
predictably	[prɪ'dɪktəbli]	*adv.*	可预言地，可预测地
index	['ɪndeks]	*n.*	指标，指数；索引；指针
sharply	['ʃɑːpli]	*adv.*	急剧地；锐利地
decline	[dɪ'klaɪn]	*v.*	下降；衰落；谢绝
implement	['ɪmplɪment]	*v.*	贯彻，执行
massive	['mæsɪv]	*adj.*	巨大的；厚重的；魁伟的
freeway	['friːweɪ]	*n.*	高速公路
ultimately	['ʌltɪmətli]	*adv.*	最后；根本；基本上
beneficial	[ˌbenɪ'fɪʃl]	*adj.*	有益的，有利的；可享利益的
dramatically	[drə'mætɪkəli]	*adv.*	戏剧地；引人注目地
labour-intensive		*adj.*	劳动密集型的
inject back into			注射回
overseas	[ˌəʊvə'siːz]	*adv.*	在海外，海外
corporation	[ˌkɔːpə'reɪʃn]	*n.*	公司，企业

SPEAKING

stereotypical	[ˌsterɪə'tɪpɪkl]	*adj.*	老一套的，陈旧的
weakness	['wiːknəs]	*n.*	劣势，弱点
seasonal	['siːzənl]	*adj.*	季节的，依照季节的，周期性的
scarf	[skɑːf]	*n.*	围巾；嵌接，嵌接处
muff	[mʌf]	*n.*	暖手筒；接球失误
hydrated	['haɪdreɪtɪd]	*adj.*	水润的
ownership	['əʊnəʃɪp]	*n.*	所有权，物主身份
clientele	[ˌkliːən'tel]	*n.*	客户；诉讼委托人
jealous	['dʒeləs]	*adj.*	妒忌的；猜疑的；唯恐失去的；戒备的
long-term friendship			长久以来形成的友谊
amazing	[ə'meɪzɪŋ]	*adj.*	非常棒的
celebrate	['selɪbreɪt]	*v.*	庆祝；举行；赞美；祝贺
victory	['vɪktəri]	*n.*	胜利，成功

听力原文

SECTION 1

(WOMAN=W; MAN=M)

W: Good afternoon sir. How can I help you?

M: I've just arrived on a flight from Indonesia, and my hold luggage wasn't on the conveyor belt. I mean it's missing.

W: Oh dear, I'm sorry to hear that. I'll just need to take a few details from you, and then I'll see what I can do. So you flew in today... that's the 5th of August...

M: That's right.

W: OK. And may I have your full name please sir?

M: It's John Q1 Meldrum , that's M-E-L-D-R-U-M.

W: Right. And your home address?

M: It's Q2 16 Ocean View.

W: "Ocean" as in "Pacific"?

M: Right.

W: Sounds lovely!

M: It is, yes...And that's in Takapuna, Auckland.

W: OK. Right. And I need a telephone number please. The one you use most often.

M: My landline number's 9712170. And you can always leave a message if I'm out.

W: Yes of course. And your passport number? Do you have it there?

M: It's Q3 AB 864653.

W: Thank you. And now I need your flight details. Do you have the number of your flight?

M: It was PA980 from Medan.

W: OK. And I believe that flight stops over in Q4 Singapore. Is that right?

M: That's right, it does. But I'd checked my luggage through to Auckland when I boarded in Indonesia.

W: Yes, well I'm going to make some enquiries in a minute, just as soon as I've completed this form. It is possible that your luggage was taken off the plane early, by mistake.

W: Now about your luggage, was it one item only?

M: Yes. I was carrying my other bag with me on the plane.

W: And how would you describe it? I mean is it a suitcase, or a holdall, or...?

M: Q5 A backpack. And it had my name and flight details on a label inside the pocket.

W: Oh, that'll help, good. And what colour is it?

M: It's mainly blue, but it's got a Q6 purple trim and pocket.

W: Do you know what it's made of? Is it made of canvas? Or plastic?

M: I'm not sure really. Canvas I suppose.

W: OK. That'll do. And can you give me a rough indication of how big it is?

M: I'm not very good at estimating, but I'd say it's about 60 centimetres by Q7 35 centimetres.

W: That'll do. It only has to be a rough guide. And does it have any distinctive features at all?

M: Well yes, there's a small picture on the front, a Q8 giraffe. I ve never seen another one like that. It's probably the brand image.

W: I should think that's likely, yes. And it'll help to identify it. And is there anything else?

M: Well I'd put a Q9 strap round the whole thing, so it'd be easier to recognise, and that's got red and yellow stripes.

W: OK. One last thing, sorry to take up your time but we've nearly finished. What was inside it?

M: Mainly clothing, and a couple of books.

W: Was there any money?

M: Well yes, I can't remember how much, but it wasn't a lot The main thing is my Q10 camera. It's quite an expensive one.

W: Mmm. Well I'm reasonably confident you're going to get it back. What would you say the total value of the luggage is? Very roughly?

M: I'd say something like...eight hundred New Zealand dollars.

W: Fine. I'll just make a phone call if you wouldn't mind waiting there. It won't...

SECTION 2

(Podcast=P)

P: The city's annual charity race will take place on 3rd June. As usual it is approximately five kilometres in length, and is Q11&Q12 only open to females of any age or boys of 12 years and under. Participants can choose to run or walk, and there is no time limit for completing the course. There are different ways to book—Q11&Q12 you can do it online or by phone, and it's also possible to do it at various retail outlets in the city. Check the race website for more details. Booking ahead is essential: it isn't possible to enter on the day itself as organisers need to know exact numbers in advance so that they can make adequate arrangements for supervision, as well as being sure there are the right number of medals to give out. Children are welcome, and the under 5s go free of charge, while there's a reduction of 20% for those under 12. The race registration fees only cover the costs involved in holding the event, and participants have to obtain their own sponsorship to raise donations for charity.

On the day of the race itself participants are requested to come well prepared. Sun hats and sunglasses are advisable if the weather is hot, and trainers or other comfortable shoes are recommended. Barefoot walking is definitely discouraged. In the registration pack, participants will receive Q13&Q14 a personal running number and a sign to pin onto their back, and no-one is allowed to race without wearing these prominently, so don't forget to bring them. You'll need to bring the necessary safety pins too! If you've taken part in previous years you will also know that many runners like to wear fancy dress—favourites are a fairy suit or a rabbit costume—to make the event more fun. The more imaginative, the better.You can look on the website to see what some of last year's contestants had on.

P: Now I'll just mention some of the landmarks along the route of this year's race. The route is a circular one, so the starting point is also the finishing point. Q15 This is on Fleet Road, between the ferry stop and the yacht club. It's a fairly simple route, it goes westward along Fleet Road, running parallel to the sea at first, Q16 before turning inland as the road goes around the edge of the children's playground. When it reaches the junction with St George's Road, it turns right. Q17 Then the route turns left into Mount Street, and follows this road around, passing between the park on one side and the Grand Hotel on the other. At the roundabout on the east end of Mount Street the route heads towards the sea front again, and eventually joins Fleet Road and goes on to the finish. Then...there are two stops on the route for refreshments—Q18 the main one is in front of the swimming pool. This is situated on St George's Road in the east corner of the park. Stewards will be on hand here to give out water or fruit to the runners. There are also voluntary first-aiders here who can give help with minor injuries or any other health problems if necessary. The other refreshment stop is in front of Q19 the library, which is on the north side of St George's Road, next to the smaller of the two roundabouts...So...we're hoping the race will be great fun for everyone, and we expect the event to run very smoothly, as the organisers are very experienced. But in case of lost property or any other problem not relating directly to the race, we advise you to go to the Q20 police station. This is situated at the junction of Fleet Road and St George's Road...Well all that remains is to urge you to pick up the phone or go online now, and arrange to take part. It's in a very good cause!

SECTION 3

Hi, I'm Gavin Murray. I'm the Rental Manager for the Central Chapmanville Real Estate Agency. I'm a real estate agent much like any other in that I help people buy and sell houses, but about half of my time is spent working to assist people in renting houses and flats. I've been in this business for a dozen years now, and I know the city very well—in terms of which areas are the better places to live and how much it costs to rent in these areas.

Now, I normally divide Chapmanville into three areas in terms of rental prices. Generally speaking, the area in Q21 the northern part of the city is the low end of the spectrum, the cheapest housing. So if you're looking to spend as little as possible on rent, I suggest you look there. The most expensive area would be the eastern part of Chapmanville. Most people think it's the prettiest part of the metropolitan area because of all Q22 the hills and parks. As so many people desire to live there, housing prices tend to be quite high. The middle market in terms of price for accommodation is found in the city's western and southern areas.

Now, let me give some examples of how much it will cost you to rent in these areas. Let's imagine you're a single person looking for a one-bedroom flat. In eastern Chapmanville, you would be paying no less than $650 a month for such a flat. You won't find anything for less than that. But a lot of people pay as much as $1,100 per month or more. The higher-priced flats are usually the ones on the hills, which run through the east. Q23 They've got the best views of the city.

A similarly sized flat in the west of the city—and in the south, too, for that matter—would cost you at most $650, but there are many flats going for less, and if you look around a bit, you find one for as little as $350. That's quite a reasonable rental price for most people. If you find that too expensive, I suggest you head to Chapmanville's north, where the cheapest flats are to be found. One-bedroom flats there start Q24 from about $170 a month up to about $400.

Now, for those of you who want something bigger, you'll have to be prepared to pay about double those prices for a small two or three-bedroom house. That goes for any of the areas I mentioned.

OK, so much for prices. What are the advantages and disadvantages of these areas? Well, I told you that the eastern part of Chapmanville is the prettiest. There are lots of parks and lots of trees all around there. Oh, I should mention that the only public transport in the east is bus; Q25 there aren't any trains. So, it's not that convenient, as you can imagine, even though it's the richer part of the city.

In the south, you've also got the river, but you won't find too many parks there, because of all the factories alongside the river. In fact, there's quite a bit of industry in the south, which makes it a less desirable place to live in. Still, the south is Q26 convenient because of public transport. The south has very good train services to the city centre as well as buses, and that's why a lot of people choose to live there.

I said earlier that western and southern parts of Chapmanville are about the same in terms of the price you pay for accommodation. They also have the same sort of public transport services. But, the two areas are quite different in other ways. Q27 The west is next to the bay, so it's quite attractive in that sense. But there are a couple of problems with the west. Q28 One is that the bay is polluted. So polluted, in fact, that you wouldn't want to swim there. I used to take my family there about ten years ago, but now I wouldn't go near it. The other disadvantage of the west is that it is where the Q29 airport is, the Chapmanville International Airport. The noise can be quite annoying.

Lastly, the north. In northern Chapmanville, as I said before, housing is cheap. Quite cheap, in fact. But you pay in other ways. For example, the area is very low and is made up entirely of wetlands. It's beautiful in a way, but it attracts an incredible Q30 amount of insects for most of the year: the mosquitoes there are really bad. This makes things quite unpleasant, and so few people have any real wish to live there. But, if money's a problem, that's the place to go. Just bring your insect repellent.

Let me just finish by again welcoming you all to Chapmanville and wishing you good luck in finding accommodation and settling down in whichever part of the city which suits you best.

SECTION 4

Good morning ladies and gentlemen. My name's Brian Jones and I've been invited here today to talk to you about home security.

Home security, of course, refers to making sure that no one can enter your home without your permission. Now the most common time for burglaries to occur is when you are away, even if only for a short time, such as when you are out at work. Therefore, I've put together a list of do's and don'ts that you should follow. But first of all I'd like you to take a look at this slide I've prepared, that outlines the main points of my talk.

Now if we take a look at this table here we see that one of the least secure points in any home, and the place that burglars most often use to gain entry to your home, is the windows. Therefore, make sure you fit Q31 secure locks to all the windows in your home. And don't forget the small ones either. You know the sort, those small windows you often find in kitchens and bathrooms.

Now the main point of entry into any home is, of course, the front door. Therefore, a good, stout wooden door is essential, as well as a good quality lock that can be locked from the outside by the means of a key. But avoid doors with glass in them. Glass can easily be broken allowing a burglar access to the main lock. And a good quality Q32 burglar alarm is also a good investment. But do make sure you get it fitted by a professional electrician because they run off the main electricity supply and can be a fire hazard if they are not fitted correctly.

Prevention, of course, is better than cure. Therefore, don't, and I repeat don't, leave valuables lying around your home. You know the sort of thing, jewelry, money, even passports, which can be a tempting item for any would-be thief. Instead, keep Q33 valuables locked away in a safe. Or better still hire a safe deposit box in your local bank.

Of course, most people generally take a holiday once a year. Therefore, when you do go away for any length of time, even if it's only for a few days, there are certain precautions that you should take. For instance, if you have a newspaper delivered in a morning, make sure you cancel the Q34 delivery for the time that you are away. And the same for other items such as Q35 milk and bread. Also contact the post office. Tell them that you will be away and ask them to leave your mail with a neighbour. But do ask your neighbour's permission first!

And this brings me on to my next point. Neighbours. Do get to know your neighbours, and tell them when you will be away. That way they can keep an eye open for any strangers. And of course do the same for them when they go away. This way everyone in the neighbourhood can look out for each other's Q36 property, and the area where you live will be a much safer place to live.

Now, of course, what to do if you see a stranger? Of course, strangers come and go all the time. Often they will be perfectly innocent. Maybe just passing through or visiting a friend. But if they seem Q37 suspicious, or seem to be taking a particular interest in someone's property, then call the police station. Even if it turns out that the stranger is, in fact, innocent, we'd much prefer questioning an innocent person than having to spend time and resources investigating a burglary. In short, if you have any doubts about strangers call the police station, and let us handle the matter.

So far this morning I've been talking about burglaries. That is someone breaking into your home to steal your possessions. However, a far more common type of crime, and, I may add, one that takes a lot of time and effort to investigate is car crime. So it's car crime that I'd like to come onto next.

Cars are an easy target for thieves. They are easy to break into and are often parked in places where everyone is a stranger. Car parks, that sort of thing. Now the most important thing is never to keep valuable items in your car. Ladies and gentlemen, never leave any of the following on display in your car, as they are all particularly attractive to car thieves. You know, mobile phones, laptop computers, satellite navigation systems. Remember to remove the suction cap from the vehicle as well and think "Do I need to take this today?" Take your cash, however a small amount! And your Q38 personal documents.

However, most car thefts occur because people simply forget to lock their doors when they leave their car. Therefore, when you leave your car, always remove the Q39 ignition key and lock all doors—it only takes a few seconds for a thief to jump into your car and drive away. Follow this routine all the time, even when filling up with petrol or just popping into the shop.

Remember, it takes a thief less than ten seconds to steal something from your car and only about 20 seconds to steal the car itself! So even if you leave your car for half a minute make sure you lock all the doors and windows.

Well, that's all for helpful hints for today. But I have put together an information pack that you can take away with you. The information pack gives all the details that I have talked about today as well as a Q40 handy wall chart that you can easily and quickly use as a reference point whenever you leave home. In the meantime stay safe and secure.

Test 10

答案速查

LISTENING

Section 1, Questions 1–10

1 catering
2 Minimum
3 weekends
4 Horbeck
5 76 Church
6 07975183224
7 cookery
8 Spanish
9 Waitress
10 text

Section 2, Questions 11–20

11 D
12 B
13 E
14 F
15 C
16 G
17 A
18 C
19 F
20 H

Section 3, Questions 21–30

21 A
22&23 IN ANY ORDER B D
24 easier reviewing
25 abbreviations and symbols
26 Definitions
27 Enumerations
28 digital voice recorder
29 Transcribe/Re-writing/Re-typing
30 Review

Section 4, Questions 31–40

31 general joint
32 surgery
33 ache, feel stiff
34 trouble spots
35 chronic overuse
36 injection
37 side effects
38–40 IN ANY ORDER B D E

READING

Reading Passage 1 Questions 1–14

1 D
2 H
3 D
4 H
5 NI
6 NI
7 B
8 H
9 nostrils
10 eight weeks
11 cool temperature
12 muddy
13 B
14 C

Reading Passage 2, Questions 15–27

15 ii
16 vii
17 ix
18 v
19 iv
20 "911" emergency system
21 police computer systems
22 YES
23 YES
24 YES
25 NOT GIVEN
26 NO
27 YES

Reading Passage 3, Questions 28–40

28–30 IN ANY ORDER A D F
31 cartoons, serials
32 (slapstick) comedy/slapstick
33 (the) avant-garde [film(s)]
34 A
35 C
36 H
37 C
38 A
39 F
40 D

名师解析

LISTENING

SECTION 1

主题场景	工作场景
主旨大意	应聘人员对兼职工作的要求及个人信息
考查题型	表格填空题

名师解读

1 catering 题干中的Job sector是关键词，为原文重现，与原文中的work in对应，题干中的Retail 与原文中的a shop of some kind对应，or为原文重现，故work in后的catering为答案。

2 Minimum 题干中的wage是关键词，答案为原文重现。注意答案首字母需要大写。

3 weekends 题干中的关键词daytimes or evenings为原文重现，题干中的no与原文中的否定词don't对应，故后面的名词weekends为答案。注意要填入复数形式。

4 Horbeck 原文后面对名字的拼读是对填写本题的提示，考生一定要听清，同时要注意首字母大写。

5 76 Church 题干中的Address为关键词，是原文重现。本题要求考生填入地址。注意数字和地址的单词的拼写以及首字母大写的问题。

6 07975183224 题干中的Phone number为关键词，是原文重现。听清楚数字是本题的关键。

7 cookery 题干中的basic为原文重现，题干对原文...learnt cookery, but only to a basic level进行了改写，专业是基础级的cookery。

8 Spanish 题干中的Fluent为关键词，与原文中的fluently为同根词，本词通常用于形容语言技能，接着后文提到了Spanish。

9 Waitress 题干中的Previous与原文中的in the past对应，work, experience均为原文重现，并与下文的had a job对应。考生应注意与本题相关的信息的原文时态为过去完成时。注意答案首字母需要大写。

10 text 题干中的contacted与原文中的contacts为同一动词的不同形式，并与原文中的send对应。原文提到很多联系方式，包括text, phone, emails，但后两个均为否定的。

SECTION 2

主题场景	旅行场景
主旨大意	介绍港口周边饭店的信息和城镇的景点布局
考查题型	配对题、地图题

名师解读

11 D 原文中对Benidentes的描述提到overlooks the whole of the bay，与选项D中的a very good view对应，并且后面提到worth going there，这里的there指的就是Benidentes。考生应注意题目要求选出每个地方对应的characteristic。

12 B 原文中reserve...in advance与选项B中的book为同义表达，原文中的won't unless...与选项B中的necessary对应，a table为原文重现。

13 E 原文中的everything与选项E中的All the ingredients对应，from与选项E中的are produced对应，surrounding area, nothing's imported与选项E中的locally对应，并且前面提到了tour manager推荐这个地方的the food的信息，其中原文中的this place 指代的就是Paul and Lenny's。

14 F 原文中的help themselves 与选项F中的self-service 是同义表达，原文中的presented 与选项F中的operates对应。

15 C 根据题干中的关键词Torreminos对原文进行定位，原文中的at the very upper end of the price range与选项C中的expensive对应，原文此句的主语是This restaurant，指代的就是前面提到的Torreminos。

16 G 考生注意图上已经给出from the quay, Marine Way, plaza的位置。原文提到cathedral在plaza的the east side，据此直接判定cathedral的位置为G。考生在做地图题时，要仔细看图上已经给出的信息。同时注意表示方位的词east。

17 A 原文提到museum的位置在Plaza 的the west side，那有可能是A或B的位置，接着原文提到museum在右侧，那就是图中A位置，最后原文提到就是在第一个转弯处，至此考生可以完全判定museum的位置就是图中的A。

18 C 题干中的tour bus为原文重现，据此定位答案，原文中的The office指的就是tour bus office。原问提到the office在Marine Way上，那有可能是C或D的位置，但最后提到它在路的尽头，所以不是D，而是C位置。

19 F 题干中的bike, hire company均为原文重现。bike hire company也在Marine Way上，但是是从quay进来后右转，那有可能是E或F。接着提到的关键点是从mini roundabout左转，在左手边上，那就是F位置。注意本题对bike hire company位置的描述比较复杂，考生要仔细定位位置。

20 H 根据题干关键词market对原文进行定位，与本题相关的信息是以Plaza为参照物，根据提到的straight across it, the road heading north, first turning，一步一步定位位置后，考生就可以找到在路右侧的H就是market。

SECTION 3

主题场景	学习技巧介绍场景
主旨大意	老师与学生关于如何做课堂笔记的讨论
考查题型	选择题、笔记题

名师解读

21 A 根据题干中的When判断，本题要求考生选出时间。题干中的appointment为关键词，为原文重现，故appointment后的时间ten o'clock即为答案。注意题干中的appointment的信息，听力原文中虽然也出现了thirty minutes, twelve的信息，但不是题目要求的时间。

22&23 IN ANY ORDER B D 题干中的recommend为关键词，与原文中You'd better use, figure...need to相对应，在其后面，原文分别直接给出了答案a three-ring binder, highlighters。针对本题，考生只需注意关键词的定位即可。

24 easier reviewing 题干中的关键词为Developing a note taking method，与原文中develop a note taking method相对应。据此定位原文的位置。本题干中的Set them out side-by-side for为原文重现，故for后的easier reviewing即为答案。

25 abbreviations and symbols 题干中的Develop a system of为关键词，为原文重现，故of后的abbreviations and symbols即为答案。

26 definitions 题干中的关键词included in notes与原文中include in my notes相对应，据此定位答案的位置。根据题干后面提供的Details, facts, or explanations信息，可以判定本空要填入的是名词。紧跟着关键词后Johnson提到了the most important可能是definitions。注意Johnson的回答内容和首字母大写。

27 Enumerations 题干中的关键词or lists of things that are discussed与原文一一对应，故or前面的enumerations即为答案。注意首字母大写。

28 digital voice recorder 关键词前面的that所指代的内容即为答案，根据对话内容，指代上面的Use a后的digital voice recorder。本题需要考生具有短时记忆的能力，并注意单词拼写。

29 Transcribe/Re-writing/Re-typing 题干中your notes为原文重现，right away 与原文中的as soon as possible为同义替换，when与原文中的while对应, they替换原文中的the subject, still fresh为原文重现，故your notes前的transcribe即为答案。在关键词出现的下一句，by后的re-writing or re-typing也可以作为答案。注意首字母大写。

30 Review 题干中的关键词your note, within 24 hours均为原文重现，故原文your note前的review为答案。注意首字母大写的问题。

SECTION 4

主题场景	讲座场景
主旨大意	一位医师做的有关关节损伤的起因、避免办法及类型的演讲
考查题型	句子填空题、笔记填空题、选择题

名师解读

31 general joint　这篇文章涉及的生僻词汇较多，要求考生不仅听力好，还要掌握大量词汇，才能很好地完成题目，所以要求考生完全听懂文章语义难度较大，这就要求考生抓住关键词。通过题干关键词sporting injuries定位答案，but转折词后出现答案general joints。

32 surgery　在include, such as, like等词后的填空题中，已出现的信息一般是关键词。因此workouts与instant care可以帮助考生定位，接下来听到surgery一词即为答案。

33 ache, feel stiff　注意阅读小标题或黑体字部分，此题应先把标题中的 bones, muscles, ligaments划为关键词。通过上下文判断，空格处应填动词。

34 trouble spots　空格处应填名词，根据X-rays定位This includes X-rays to identify potential trouble spots，可知potential为原词重现，之后的名词短语trouble spots应为答案。

35 chronic overuse　标题joints为关键词，定位句为may lead to chronic overuse of the soft tissue connecting bones at the joints，本空应填名词，题干中的cause与原文的lead to均为导致（骨折），暗示答案为chronic overuse（长期的过度使用）。

36 injection　根据标题new treatment可以定位到The injured joint then receives an injection of the mixture，接下来听到healing protein和blood，答案在之后的句子中出现。

37 side effects　convenience之后与其并列的单词或词组应为答案，其中without与原文lack of对应。

38–40 IN ANY ORDER B D E　多选题通常是原文并列的事实，注意每一项的关键词，错误的选项往往以否定形式出现，或用只言片语干扰。正确的选项与原文通常是同义替换，如B项的constant和原文的regular对应，D项的preparatory与原文的warming-up对应，E项的don’t feel well与原文的feel sick对应。

READING

READING PASSAGE 1

体　裁　　说明文
题　材　　自然科学类
主　题　　通过养鸭子和鸭蛋与养母鸡和鸡蛋的对比，分析养鸭子的好处
题　型　　分类题、摘要填空题、选择题

Questions 1–8

题型　分类题 (Classification)

注意　分类题要求将一些项目分别归入几个类别之中。在文章中，一般会讲述两种不同的事物A和B。一类是与A类事物有关的项目，一类是与B类事物有关的项目，另一类是与A和B都有关的项目，本题多了一个第四类——文章没有提及的项目。

1	关键词	laying period
	原文定位	首段末句In addition, ducks lay eggs over a longer season than hens do.
	题解	**答案D**　定位句指出母鸭的产蛋期比母鸡的长，其中lengthier period（较长的期间）和a longer season（较长的时期）为同义词替换。

2	关键词	mothers
	原文定位	第六段第二句、第三句、第四句If the aim is to hatch duckling, keepers should be aware that not all ducks make good mothers, and that certain breeds of duck appear to be worse than others. The poor mothers abandon their eggs a few days after laying them. A sure way of making sure the rejected eggs hatch is to place them next to chicken eggs under a hen.
	题解	**答案H** 通过原文可以看出not all ducks make good mothers即不是所有的鸭子都是好母亲，为了保持能量他们甚至会遗弃鸭蛋。但如果把这些鸭蛋混在鸡蛋里母鸡就会孵化，由此可见母鸡是更好的母亲。
3	关键词	uproot plants
	原文定位	第二段首句Poultry keepers with gardens have less to worry about if they keep ducks rather than hens because the former are less apt to dig up plants and destroy roots.
	题解	**答案D** 文章指出：家禽养殖者如果有花园，那么养鸭比养殖母鸡更让人省心。因为比起母鸡，母鸭不大可能将植物连根拔起并毁坏根部。uproot plants（连根拔起）与原文的dig up plants and destroy roots为同义转换。
4	关键词	grass
	原文定位	第二段第二句While both hens and ducks benefit the garden by eating pests, hens are known to damage herb and grass beds.
	题解	**答案H** 母鸡和鸭子在消灭花园里的害虫方面都有功，可是众所周知，母鸡会破坏草本植物和草坪，也就是对草本植物和草坪都构成威胁。题干中的dangerous（危险的）与文中的damage（破坏）对应，但词性不同。
5	关键词	more eggs
	原文定位	首段末句In addition, ducks lay eggs over a longer season than hens do.
	题解	**答案NI** 原文中虽然在两处分别提到产蛋和孵蛋的内容，但没有明确提到鸭和鸡每周产蛋量的多少，所以无从比较。
6	关键词	eat, grain
	原文定位	第五段第三句If the ducks...to find for themselves approximately 70% of their daily dietary. 和末句Therefore, it is important that they are fed enough food, such as grain, every day.
	题解	**答案NI** 原文指出：每天给它们喂足食物（如谷物）是很重要的，不能说一定吃谷物。而且，母鸭是吃得多，但可以靠自己找到很多吃的东西，所以不能比较母鸭和母鸡哪个吃更多的谷物。

7	关键词	garden
	原文定位	第二段第二句While both hens and ducks benefit the garden by eating pests, hens are known to damage herb and grass beds.
	题解	答案B 母鸡和鸭子都可吃掉花园里的害虫，都对花园有利，beneficial（有利的）与benefit对应，by eliminating pests（消除害虫）与by eating pests（吃掉害虫）对应。
8	关键词	illness
	原文定位	首段第二句Ducks are immune to some common diseases found in hens and are less vulnerable to others.
	题解	答案H 母鸭对一些母鸡常得的疾病更有免疫力，也更加不易患上其他疾病。more vulnerable to illness（易受疾病攻击）与鸭子的immune to...（对……有免疫力）是反义词，所以答案是hen（母鸡）。

Questions 9–12

题型 摘要填空题(Summary Completion)

注意 本题要求考生根据空格前后的关键词去文中定位，同时一定要提前预测空格处应填的词性。

9	关键词	getting dirty
	原文定位	第三段第二句Something this large is not absolutely necessary; however, ducks need only to be able to dip their heads in the water to keep their nostrils clean.
	题解	答案nostrils 题干中的prevent...from getting dirty与原文中的 keep...clean为同义转换。
10	关键词	pond, age
	原文定位	第三段末句If a pond is provided...old enough to withstand the cool temperature of the water—about eight weeks.
	题解	答案eight weeks 由定位句中的until they are old enough可知八周以后小鸭子的身体才能抵挡住冷的水温，在这之前，必须防止小鸭子进入池塘。
11	关键词	prevented from entering
	原文定位	第三段末句If a pond is provided...old enough to withstand the cool temperature of the water—about eight weeks.
	题解	答案cool temperature keep...away from（防止）和prevented from（阻止）为同义转换，是说小鸭子彻底长大前，要远离cool temperature（低温）的水。

12	关键词	soil
	原文定位	第四段第三句If more than this proportion is introduced, there is a risk of compacting the soil, which can lead to muddy conditions for long periods as the rain is not easily absorbed into the ground.
	题解	答案muddy　题干中的空格处需填一个形容词来修饰soil（土壤）, lead to muddy conditions（导致泥泞的状况）与become muddy（变得泥泞）对应。

Questions 13 and 14

题型　选择题(Multiple Choice)

注意　有些题目比较简单，可以直接选择。对于难题，可以用排除法确定正确答案。有些选项中所讲的内容在原文中根本不存在，或找不到语言依据。要注意，答题的唯一依据就是原文，不能凭借自己的知识或主观想象做选择。

13	关键词	Salmonella
	原文定位	倒数第二段第二句、第三句This is because of a number of cases of salmonella food poisoning in Europe in the 1970s. Although it was never conclusively shown that duck eggs were to blame, the egg-eating public stopped buying and many duck egg producers went bankrupt.
	题解	答案B　虽然没有最后确定是不是鸭蛋的原因，但是沙门氏菌食物中毒导致鸭蛋产业的困难，stopped buying and...went bankrupt（不再购买，从而破产）与created difficulties（产生很多困难）对应。
14	关键词	eggs
	原文定位	倒数第二段第四句Indeed, there is a risk of salmonella poisoning when ducks lay their eggs in damp conditions, such as on ground that is constantly wet...
	题解	答案C　题干中的be contaminated（被污染）与原文中a risk of salmonella poisoning（存在染上沙门氏菌的风险）意思相同。

READING PASSAGE 2

体　裁　　说明文
题　材　　社会科学类
主　题　　讲述警察快速反应会带来的好处及反应成功的影响
题　型　　配对题、简答题、判断题

Questions 15–19

题型　配对题 (Matching Headings)

注意　段落标题配对题的标题选项数量多于段落数量，存在大量的干扰项。可以先找到段落的主题句的关键词，然后看题目有无此关键词，再根据题目的替换词，确定是不是这个段落。

15	关键词	advantages
	原文定位	B段首句An important part of police strategy, rapid police response is seen by police officers and the public alike as offering tremendous benefits.
	题解	**答案ii** 本段讲述了警察快速反应带来了诸如帮助受害者、抓住嫌疑犯、找到证人、提高警察的声望和预防犯罪等好处。选项中的perceived（感知）与原文的seen（理解）同义，advantages（优点）与原文的benefits（收益）意思相同。
16	关键词	time and success
	原文定位	C段第二句For example, it has been...by the police. 和第四句Similarly, in...a call for help.
	题解	**答案vii** 定位句内容主要是关于Rapid response time and success of rapid response（反应时间和反应成功之间的关系），即如果快速反应的时间短，快速反应就会成功，否则快速反应成功的可能性就不大。
17	关键词	not quickly contacting the police
	原文定位	D段首句、第二句Should police assume all the responsibility for ensuring a rapid response? Studies have shown that people tend to delay after an incident occurs before contacting the police.
	题解	**答案ix** 定位句提到警方应该对确保快速反应承担所有的责任吗？第二句是主题句：研究表明人们在事件发生之后一般会延迟一会儿再联系警方。接下来进行举例论证，人们不及时报警导致警察快速反应的效率降低，而段落的末句与主题句相互呼应，为 Not quickly contacting the police（没有立即联系警方）。
18	关键词	when
	原文定位	E段首句The effectiveness of rapid response alsc needs to be seen in light of the nature of the crime.
	题解	**答案v** 本句为主题句，大意为：快速反应是否有效还和罪行的性质有关。全段说明快速反应对于抢劫等罪行是有效的，而快速反应对于偷窃等罪行没有什么效果，即主题为When rapid response is and is not necessary（快速反应何时需要，何时不需要）。
19	关键词	communicating response
	原文定位	F段第三句Studies have shown, however, that while the public wants quick response, more important is the information given by the police to the person asking for help.
	题解	**答案iv** 本句是主题句，虽然公众需要快速反应，但是更重要的是警察传递给求助人的信息。show后面的从句是重点，为正确选项的改写，为Communicating response time to people requesting help（公众需要警方快速反应以获得帮助）。

Questions 20 and 21

题型 简答题 (Short-Answer Questions)

注意 简答题比其他题型要稍微简单。主要原因有两点：一是题干的指令比较明确，容易定位到原文；二是答案通常简短而直接。大部分简答题的暗示比较明显，考生应该在预览问题或格式的同时便预测答案的相关信息。

20	关键词	latest technological developments
	原文定位	A段第四句In more recent times there has been the introduction of the "911" emergency system, which allows the public easier and faster contact with police...
	题解	答案"911" emergency system 如果先根据A段中的The telephone and police radio，容易做出错误回答，注意题目中黑体大写的TWO LATEST，并且文章指出The telephone and police radio（电话和警用收音机）已经使用很久(already long in use)了，所以需要继续往后阅读。通过第四句可知答案。
21	关键词	reduce police response time
	原文定位	A段第四句...and the use of police computer systems, which assist police in planning patrols and assigning emergency requests to...
	题解	答案police computer systems the use of police computer systems（警务计算机系统的使用）帮助planning patrols and assigning emergency requests（警察规划巡逻和安排紧急任务）。原文在这两个短语后面都有一个解释说明它们的定语从句。

Questions 22–27

题型 判断题 (Identifying Writer's Views/Claims)

注意 找出题目中的关键词，最好先定位到原文中的一个段落。快速阅读该段落，根据题目中的关键词，在原文中找出与题目相关的一句或几句话，确定正确答案。要注意顺序性，即题目的顺序和原文的顺序基本一致。

22	关键词	witnesses
	原文定位	B段第三句It aids in identifying those who witnessed an emergency or crime, as well as in collecting evidence.
	题解	答案YES 警察快速反应可用来帮助确认那些目击了紧急突发情况和犯罪的人，题干是对原文的改写，finding witnesses（找到证人）与identifying those who witnessed（确定谁是目击证人）为同义替换。
23	关键词	1–2 minutes
	原文定位	C段第二句For example, it has been demonstrated that rapid response leads to a greater likelihood of arrest only if responses are in the order of 1–2 minutes after a call is received by the police.
	题解	答案YES 题目"反应慢了1–2分钟对于是否能抓捕罪犯可能产生很大的影响"，这与原文大意完全吻合。不同之处就是原文用了if从句的形式来表示，而题目用whether or not。

24	关键词	The public and the police, the amount of time
	原文定位	C段末句Yet both police officers and the public define "rapid response" as responding up to 10–12 minutes after calling the police for help.
	题解	答案YES 公众和警方对于一个正常的快速反应的时间有一个普遍的共识，与题干同义。generally agree on the amount of time（一般对快速反应时间取得一致意见）与both police officers and the public define "rapid response"（警察和公众都明确什么是"快速反应"）意思相同。
25	关键词	Physical barriers
	原文定位	D段第四句Often, however, there is no such physica barrier to calling the police.
	题解	答案NOT GIVEN 文中的"没有这种导致无法报警的身体上的障碍"，也就是说有这种身体上的障碍的概率是非常小的。而题目的意思是身体上的障碍是最大的原因，但实际上小概率事件也可能是最大概率事件，所以答案未曾提及。
26	关键词	burglary
	原文定位	E段第三句It is common in such burglary or theft cases that the victim discovers the crime hours, days, even weeks after it has occurred.
	题解	答案NO 通过"被害人在几小时、几天甚至几周后才发现被盗窃的案例很常见"可知，原文中的there is little point（几乎没有意义）和题目中的desirable（有利的）意思相反，不正确。
27	关键词	75%
	原文定位	E段末句Based on statistics comparing crimes that are discovered and those in which the victim is directly involved, Spelman and Brown (1981) suggest that three in four calls to police need not be met with rapid response.
	题解	答案YES 原文说明对比的是后来被发现的案件和受害者在现场的案件的数据，结果表明3/4的求助电话不需做出快速回应，说明这3/4的案件是受害者发现的，确实如此。

READING PASSAGE 3

体　裁　说明文
题　材　媒体
主　题　介绍电影的发展历史
题　型　选择题、简答题、配对题

Questions 28–30

题型 选择题(Multiple Choice)

注意 可用排除法确定正确答案。答题的唯一依据就是原文，不能根据自己的猜测选择。有些选项明显与原文不符，有些选项在原文中找不到依据。

28–30	关键词	American dominance of the film industry
	原文定位	第四段Hollywood took the lead artistically as well as industrially. Hollywood films appealed because they had better-constructed narratives...
	题解	**答案IN ANY ORDER A D F** 原文中的better-constructed（构建较好的）与选项D中的well-written（写得好的）对应，同时narratives（故事）为原文重现，故选项D正确；原文中的special effects were more impressive（特效给人深刻印象的）与F项中的excellent special effects（良好的特效）意思相同，故选项F正确；原文中的a great deal of（大量）与题干中的plenty of（许多）是同义替换，原文中的money（钱）与题干中的capital（资金）是同义替换，原文中的buy up（购买）与题干中的purchase（购买）是同义替换，原文中的artists and technical innovations from Europe（来自欧洲的艺术家和技术革新）被题干概括为what it didn't have（他们，即美国人所没有的），故选项A正确。

Questions 31–33

题型 简答题(Short-Answer Questions)

注意 简答题，看起来很难，实际很简单。答案多选自原文原句，基本是原文原词。注意：答案必须对应问题中的特殊疑问词；答案都有字数限制。

31	关键词	not generally made, major studios
	原文定位	第六段倒数第三句The making of cartoons became a separate branch of film-making, generally practiced outside the major studios, and the same was true of serials.
	题解	**答案cartoons, serials** 题干中的not generally made in major studios（一般不会在主要的工作室做）与原文的generally practiced outside the major studios（一般在主要的工作室以外实践）表达的是同一个意思，因此此句的主语cartoons（卡通动画）就是答案之一。原句中的the same was true（……具有相同的情况）指代前面的generally practiced outside the major studios（一般在主要的工作室以外实践），故serials（电视连续剧）也是答案。
32	关键词	both short and feature films
	原文定位	倒数第三段首句From early cinema, it was only American slapstick comedy that successfully developed in both short and feature format.
	题解	**答案(slapstick) comedy/slapstick** 题干中的both short and feature films（短片和故事片）与原文both short and feature format同义，develop是原词重现。本句的主语slapstick comedy（低级喜剧）即为答案。
33	关键词	profitable, "silent" period
	原文定位	倒数第三段末句It was also at this time that the avant-garde film first achieved commercial success, this time thanks almost exclusively to the French and the occasional German film.
	题解	**答案(the) avant-garde [film(s)]** 注意题目要求答出started to become profitable（开始变得有利可图），因此答案在后面一句中，倒数第三段末句中的first achieved commercial success（首次获得商业成功）与题干中started to become profitable（开始变得有利可图）对应。

Questions 34–40

题型 配对题(Matching Information)

注意 本题是要求考生将相关信息与选项中的国家名配对。注意题目要求给出的是You may use any letter more than once这样的提示。此外，由于这种题型一般都是跨全文出的，因此跟前面或后面的题目不可避免地会出现交叉，有可能根据其他的题目也能推断出细节所在的位置。

34	关键词	helped other countries, develop, film industry
	原文定位	倒数第二段首句、第二句Of the countries...developed and maintained distinctive national cinemas...were France, Germany and the Soviet Union. Of these, the French displayed the most continuity...
	题解	**答案A** 倒数第二段第二句中的代词those（那些）指代的是上一句中的France（法国），Germany（德国）and the Soviet Union（苏联），而在这些国家中，法国起到了最重要的作用。答案为A。
35	关键词	biggest producer of films
	原文定位	第三段首句In the end, it was the United States that was to become, and remain, the largest single market for films.
	题解	**答案C** 题干中的biggest producer（最大的制造商）与原文中的the largest single market（最大的市场）相对应，题干中的films（电影）是原文重现，故本句的主语the United States（美国）就是答案。
36	关键词	the “feature” film
	原文定位	第三段第五句The Italian industry, which had pioneered the feature film with spectacular films like *Quo Vadis* (1913) and *Cabiria* (1914) almost collapsed.
	题解	**答案H** 题干中的first to develop（首先发展起来）与原文中的pioneered（开辟）对应；the “feature” film（故事片）是原文重现，所以答案为Italy（意大利）。
37	关键词	creating stars
	原文定位	第四段第二句Hollywood films appealed because they had better-constructed narratives, their special effects were more impressive, and the star system added a new dimension to screen acting.
	题解	**答案C** 题干中的creating（创造）与原文中的added a new dimension（增加了新的维度）相对应；题干中的stars（明星）与原文中star（明星）是同根词，又因为Hollywood（好莱坞）在此处代表了America（美国），故本题的答案为C。
38	关键词	“avant-garde” films
	原文定位	倒数第三段末句It was also at this time that the avant-garde film first achieved commercial success, this time thanks almost exclusively to the French and the occasional German film.
	题解	**答案A** 题干中的made the most money（最赚钱）与原文achieved commercial success（取得了商业成功）对应，故本题的答案为French（法国）。注意本题答案是本段前面提到的French而不是German（德国）。

39	关键词	own culture, outside influences
	原文定位	末段...Japan, where a cinema developed based primarily on traditional theatrical and, to a lesser extent, other art forms and only gradually adapted to Western influence.
	题解	答案F 题干中的own culture（自己的文化）与原文中traditional theatrical（传统的戏剧）对应；based more on（更多是基于……）与原文based primarily on（主要基于……）对应；outside influences（外部影响）与原文Western influence（西方影响）是同义替换。答案是Japan。
40	关键词	It had a great influence on silent movies, despite its size
	原文定位	末段...the Scandinavian countries, particularly Denmark, which played a role in the development of silent cinema quite out of proportion to their small population...
	题解	答案D 题干中had a great influence on...（对……产生重要影响）与原文played a role in...（在……起到重要作用）对应，movies（电影）与原文cinema（电影）是同义替换，despite its size（尽管它很小）与原文quite out of proportion to their small population（与它们较少的人口不成比例）对应，silent（无声的）是原文重现。答案为D。

WRITING

WRITING TASK 1

名师解读

本题为流程图题，该图向考生展示了整个皮革的加工生产过程。步骤较多，若对每一个环节都详细说明会使文章显得冗长，所以要把可以合并的步骤一同说明，才不会使文章看起来像记“流水账”。

在具体写作的过程中，要注意开头总览全文，中间井然有序，结尾概括总结。

高分范文

The diagram shows the different stages in the process of converting an animal hide into leather goods. The first stage is to hang out the hide on a line, in the open air to dry. After this, it is **transported** by lorry to the factory for processing. On arrival, it is **submerged** in vats of soap and water, washed and then transferred to another vat where it is soaked in lime. Having been cleaned in this way, the hide is then sent to a large rolling machine where it is smoothed and flattened. In the next stage it is submerged in a liquid called tannin, which is a **mixture** of vegetable matter and water. This is followed by the polishing stage where small rollers are moved over the surface to produce a shine. The leather is then transported to a different factory where it is manufactured into the leather products we see in the shops, for example, shoes, handbags and sports equipment. (162 words)

WRITING TASK 2

文章结构

提出问题+原因1+原因2+建议

problem + reason 1 + reason 2 + suggestions
第一段：背景句+引出话题
第二段：原因1+举例
第三段：原因2+举例
第四段：建议和总结

思路点拨

步骤一：审题（<3分钟）

Some people think that parents should spend more time with their children. To what extent do you agree or disagree?

→通读题目，了解大意。

有些人认为父母应该花更多的时间与孩子相处，你是否同意这种观点?

→再读题目，辨别关键词，区分主题词和限定词，推测考官的出题意图。

主题词：parents should spend more time with their children

限定词：more, agree or disagree

步骤二：列大纲（<3分钟）

英文提纲	Introduction: they seldom have time to stay with their children→agree (opinion)→no matter how busy they are, they should make the best use of their time to stay with their children (topic) Body: Reason 1: the relationship between children and adults changes→feel parents' affection→become treasure in their memories Reason 2: children need the direction→some wrong behaviours→parents' instructions→good behaviours influence their children Conclusion: some disadvantages→educate and instruct their children appropriately in their spare time
中文提纲	引出话题： 当今社会的现状（父母很少有时间陪孩子，只注重他们的物质生活）→同意（观点）→无论多忙，都应该多陪孩子（主题） 主体段： 原因1：改善父母与孩子的关系→孩子感受父爱和母爱→成为记忆里最大的财富 原因2：孩子需要由父母指明未来的方向→一些错的行为→父母的教导→好的行为可以影响孩子 总结： 和孩子在一起时间太长的不利因素→应该协调好和孩子相处的时间

高分范文

In China, the parents both have their jobs. With the development of economy, people tend to pursue high quality living conditions. Most of the parents try their best to offer their children comfortable circumstances, but they seldom have time to stay with their children. In my point of view, no matter how busy they are, they should make the best use of their time to stay with their children.

First, the relationship between children and adults will be enhanced with parents'spending more time on their children. Children could feel parents' affection through the genial conversation and sharing their pleasure with them. Every time when parents take them to the **amusement** park, help them to prepare their birthday parties, applaud for them when they are competing in the sports meeting, the time they spend with children will become treasure in their memories.

Second, children need the direction from their parents. There are some wrong behaviours in our society such as dishonesty, corruption, violence, eroticism and so on. Children have weak resistance in defending this **detrimental** influence. In this case, parents' instructions seem to be very important to children's growth. Parents should sit down and talk with them about what they should and should not do. In addition, if parents often spend time in staying with their children, adults' good behaviours will greatly influence their children.

Here I do not deny that there are some disadvantages in spending too much time on children. Some parents restrict their children, and give them little freedom to develop their interests. Therefore, I emphasize that parents should educate and instruct their children **appropriately** in their spare time apart from their busy works. (285 words)

SPEAKING

名师解读

Part 1的题目属于家庭类的话题，这类题目一直都是口语考试当中最常见的一类，经常以变化不大的形式出现，主要问题是关于考生与家人、朋友的交流，一般都与考生有关。

Part 2属于口头作文，陈述的内容应围绕考点，并包括全部考点，但不能面面俱到，要有重点。

Part 3一般是对Part 2的深化和拓展。这部分最难，但也最容易展现自己的观点，也是考生有可能得到较高分数的一个部分，希望考生把握好这个机会。

高分示例

PART 1

Communication

- How do you usually keep in touch with members of your family?

I mostly keep in touch with my family by phone, and I' ve started using the Internet to make video calls. I also try to visit members of my family in person as often as I can.

- Do you prefer to speak to people by phone or by writing emails?

It depends on the situation. I use email and text messages to communicate with friends, but my parents prefer it if I phone them. I prefer phone to email. A phone is something I can carry around all the time, and it gives priority and it seems more personal if you call someone. It is more expensive, but it is nevertheless worth it.

- Do you ever write letters by hand? Why/Why not?

Yes, I still send birthday cards through the mail, and Christmas cards as well. I think it's nice to get cards in the mail and hand written messages. It shows you' re willing to make the effort rather than just by sending a Facebook birthday wish or e-card.

PART 2

I would say that I like my bedroom the most. It is near the back of the apartment, but gets the most light in the whole floor.

I mostly use the room to sleep in, of course, but there are times when I want to just relax and take it easy. My room is perfect for that. I can open the curtains and get an amazing view of the city and the late evening glow and just soak it all in.

I did my room in my favourite colours, green, black and silver. All the woodwork and **furniture** is black with the **accessories** and covers being either a dark emerald green or silver.

My room is my place, the place where I can go when I want to feel safe and **comfortable**. Even when my friends and family come over, they know that unless invited in, my room is off-limits to everyone. My room is my haven and I love it there.

PART 3

Rooms in general

- Which room do families usually spend most time in? Why?

The larger room of a house is usually the lounge or living room, although some families have dining rooms as well for meals. My family spent most of our time together in the kitchen, as it was open with the living area, cooking and chatting about our day or doing homework. Usually, families gather around where most of the movement is in order to gather and share information from their days.

- What types of thing do people usually put on the walls of their rooms?

House **decorations** vary from family to family, but paintings and photos of **ancestors** and living or recently deceased relatives tend to be popular. I have some pictures of my family around the living room, but most of my wall decorations are posters from movies and shows I enjoy.

- Is it more important for a room to look nice, or to be comfortable? Why?

I enjoy a room to be comfortable over looking good, but it is possible to have both if you buy properly. Making sure you have at least one comfortable sofa is a must. People like to be comfortable, but having a good looking room will also set them at ease.

Interior design

- How can different room colours affect the way people feel?

We are raised with beliefs in the vastly different feelings associated with colours. Putting someone in a light blue or green room will make them feel calm and settled, where on the other hand, a bold red or purple room will bring excitement. It does change from culture to culture as some colours represent different meaning to different people and countries.

- What is modern furniture like compared to older styles of furniture?

While modern furniture can look amazing, I tend to feel that it is just not as comfortable as the older furniture that was hand made with love, or even the shop made ones that were designed for comfort. Modern furniture tends to have very sharp edges and is usually—"shiny". They tend to be for the younger generation who feel everything—"modern"—should be almost space age in design.

- Do you think women are more interested than men in the way rooms are decorated? Why/Why not?

It would depend on the woman and on the man, in general though, women tend to be more interested in the presentation of a room than the men are. It has something to do with the long age of women being at home while the men worked. The home was our office at that point and we made it as perfect as we wanted it. Nowadays though, with more women working, their interior decorations are more about prestige and what they have to show off. Men generally don't care what they have as long as they are comfortable, warm and have a meal in front of them.

重点词汇

LISTENING

definitely	['defɪnətli]	*adv.*	清楚地，当然；明确地
postcode	['pəʊstkəʊd]	*n.*	邮政编码
cookery	['kʊkəri]	*n.*	烹调术；烹调业
fluently	['fluːəntli]	*adv.*	流利地；通畅地
briefing	['briːfɪŋ]	*n.*	简报；作战指示
mention	['menʃn]	*v.*	提到，谈到；提及
comparatively	[kəm'pærətɪvli]	*adv.*	比较地；相当地
surrounding	[sə'raʊndɪŋ]	*adj.*	周围的，附近的
normally	['nɔːməli]	*adv.*	正常地；通常地，一般地
energetic	[ˌenə'dʒetɪk]	*adj.*	精力充沛的；有力的
attractive	[ə'træktɪv]	*adj.*	吸引人的；有魅力的
qua	[kweɪ]	*prep.*	作为；以……身份或资格
landmark	['lændmaːk]	*n.*	路标，地标
silverware	['sɪlvəweə]	*n.*	银器；镀银餐具
pottery	['pɒtəri]	*n.*	陶器；陶器厂
donation	[dəʊ'neɪʃn]	*n.*	捐款，捐赠物
subscription	[səb'skrɪpʃn]	*n.*	捐献；订阅
photocopy	['fəʊtəʊkɒpi]	*n.*	复印件；影印
grant	[graːnt]	*n.*	拨款；授予
scholarship	['skɒləʃɪp]	*n.*	奖学金；学识
award	[ə'wɔːd]	*v.*	授予；判定
inspect	[ɪn'spekt]	*v.*	检查；视察
verify	['verɪfaɪ]	*v.*	核实；查证
maximum	['mæksɪməm]	*adj.*	最高的；最大极限的
validate	['vælɪdeɪt]	*v.*	证实，验证
authenticate	[ɔː'θentɪkeɪt]	*v.*	鉴定；证明……是真实的
identity	[aɪ'dentəti]	*n.*	身份；同一性
specialty	['speʃəlti]	*n.*	专业；专长
orthopedic	[ˌɔːθə'piːdɪk]	*adj.*	整形外科的
cartilage	['kaːtɪlɪdʒ]	*n.*	软骨
ligament	['lɪgəmənt]	*n.*	韧带
therapeutic	[ˌθerə'pjuːtɪk]	*adj.*	治疗的；治疗学的
degenerate	[dɪ'dʒenəreɪt]	*adj.*	退化的；堕落的

READING

immune	[ɪ'mjuːn]	*adj.*	有免疫力的
vulnerable	['vʌlnərəbl]	*adj.*	易受伤的，脆弱的
poultry	['pəʊltri]	*n.*	家禽
insect	['ɪnsekt]	*n.*	昆虫
snail	[sneɪl]	*n.*	蜗牛
delicate	['delɪkət]	*adj.*	娇弱的
nostril	[nɒstrɪl]	*n.*	鼻孔
withstand	[wɪð'stænd]	*v.*	经受得住
compact	[kəm'pækt]	*v.*	压缩
absorb	[əb'sɔːb]	*v.*	吸收
salmonella	[ˌsælmə'nelə]	*n.*	沙门氏菌

patrol	[pə'trəʊl]	*n.*	巡逻，侦察
assign	[ə'saɪn]	*v.*	分配
tremendous	[trə'mendəs]	*adj.*	巨大的，极大的
arrest	[ə'rest]	*n.&v.*	逮捕
participate	[pɑː'tɪsɪpeɪt]	*v.*	参与
identify	[aɪ'dentɪfaɪ]	*v.*	确认
enhance	[ɪn'hɑːns]	*v.*	改进
consequence	['kɒnsɪkwəns]	*n.*	结果，后果
demonstrate	['demənstreɪt]	*v.*	展示
substantially	[səb'stænʃəli]	*adv.*	相当多地，大大地
incident	['ɪnsɪdənt]	*n.*	意外
diminish	[dɪ'mɪnɪʃ]	*v.*	降低，减少
in light of			根据，按照
burglary	['bɜːgləri]	*n.*	破门盗窃；抢劫
frustrating	[frʌ'streɪtɪŋ]	*adj.*	沮丧的
odd	[ɒd]	*adj.*	（用在数字后）有零数的，……以上的
synaesthesia	[ˌsɪnəs'θiːzɪə]	*n.*	通感
interpretation	[ɪnˌtɜːprɪ'teɪʃn]	*n.*	诠释
stimulate	['stɪmjuleɪt]	*v.*	刺激
evoke	[ɪ'vəʊk]	*v.*	引起
simultaneously	[ˌsɪml'teɪnɪəsli]	*adv.*	同时地
ophthalmologist	[ˌɒfθæl'mɒlədʒɪst]	*n.*	眼科医师
scepticism	['skeptɪsɪzəm]	*n.*	怀疑
involuntary	[ɪn'vɒləntri]	*adj.*	本能的，不知不觉的
arbitrary	['ɑːbɪtrəri]	*adj.*	随意的
abstract	['æbstrækt]	*adj.*	抽象的
compose	[kəm'pəʊz]	*v.*	编写，作曲
revelation	[ˌrevə'leɪʃn]	*n.*	出乎意料的事；揭露；显示
unwittingly	[ʌn'wɪtɪŋli]	*adv.*	不经意地；不知不觉地
hamper	['hæmpə]	*v.*	阻碍
drawback	['drɔːbæk]	*n.*	缺点

WRITING

leather	['leðə]	*n.*	皮革；皮革制品
comparison	[kəm'pærɪsn]	*n.*	比较；对照
transport	['trænspɔːt]	*v.*	运输
submerge	[səb'mɜːdʒ]	*v.*	淹没；侵入
mixture	['mɪkstʃə]	*n.*	混合物；混合剂
amusement	[ə'mjuːzmənt]	*n.*	消遣；娱乐
detrimental	[ˌdetrɪ'mentl]	*adj.*	不利的；有害的
appropriately	[ə'prəʊprɪətli]	*adv.*	适当地；相称地

SPEAKING

furniture	['fɜːnɪtʃə]	*n.*	家具；设备
accessory	[ək'sesəri]	*n.*	配件；附件
comfortable	['kʌmftəbl]	*adj.*	舒适的，舒服的
decoration	['dekəreɪtʃn]	*n.*	装饰品
ancestor	['ænsestə]	*n.*	祖先；被继承人

听力原文

SECTION 1

(MAN=M; WOMAN=W)

M: Workfit Employment. Good afternoon?

W: Oh hello. I'd like to register for work please.

M: Right. I'll just get you to answer a few questions for our records, if you don't mind.

W: That's fine.

M: First of all, are you looking for temporary or permanent employment?

W: Temporary. I want to get a job for about six months. Because in October I'm planning to do some travelling.

M: OK. And have you any idea which job sector you want to work in? I mean do you want to work in business or in...

W: I'd either like to work in a shop of some kind, or I'd like to work in the Q1 catering industry. I don't really mind which.

M: Fine. I'll put both of those down. And I see that you're calling from a London number. Is that the area where you'd like to get the job?

W: Yes, I'm in north London, so preferably in this area so that I don't have to travel too far.

M: Fine. And about wages, some employers only offer the Q2 minimum that is required by law, especially for temporary work. Would you be willing to accept that?

W: If necessary yes. Obviously if it were more than that I'd prefer it, but...

M: Of course. And what sort of hours would you accept?

W: I don't mind whether it's daytimes or evenings, I could do either, but I definitely don't want to do Q3 weekends, because I have to help my father. He's got a small chicken farm and I manage the orders once a week.

M: OK, got that. And presumably you'd be ready to start more or less straight away? Shall we say 1st of March as that's next Monday?

W: The sooner the better, yes.

M: Fine. Well, now I'll get your personal details if I may. Starting with your full name please.

W: It's Alison Q4 Horbeck , that's H-O-R-B-E-C-K.

M: Fine. And your date of birth please?

W: The 8th of October, 1992.

M: And your address?

W: It's Q5 76 Church Street.

M: I don't suppose you have the postcode, do you?

W: I'm afraid I can never remember it, but...

M: That's not a problem, I can look it up later. Don't worry. But can I take a phone number as well please?

W: Yes. It's Q6 07975 183 double 2 4

M: Thanks.

M: And now, if you don't mind I'll just get a few other details. First of all, about your education. Can you just tell me what your most recent qualification is?

W: I did a college diploma, I learnt Q7 cookery, but only to a basic level.

M: Well, that could be useful, you never know. And what about general skills. You know, for example can you speak any foreign languages reasonably fluently?

W: Only Q8 Spanish really. I studied French when I was younger but I've forgotten it all now.

M: Right. And do you drive?

W: Yes, I've got a full driving licence.

M: OK. That can be useful, I'll note that too. And another thing, have you done other work in the past? What type of experience do you have, if any?

W: Oh yes. It was only temporary work, but I had a job as a Q9 waitress last year, and I've also worked in a shop before—Selling clothes.

M: OK. That's all fine, thanks. We'll post your details, and as soon as an employer contacts us we'll let you know. Is it ok if we send you a Q10 text? We have your number.

W: That'd be best actually. I don't always answer my phone, but I do check for messages regularly. More often than I look at emails too.

M: Fine. And is there anything you'd like us to know?

W: Only that I can't make interviews on Wednesdays. Any other day would be fine, but I'm taking care of my nephew one day a week till I get a job.

M: No problem, I'll pass that information on if we...[fade]

SECTION 2

(Tour manager =T)

T: Good morning everyone! In about half an hour the ship will be docking, and you'll have the rest of the day to visit the area around the port. In your briefing pack, you'll find a map and an information sheet, but some of you have been asking me about places to eat, so I just thought I'd mention one or two restaurants that I know of. Benidentes has been around for a long time, it's well established, and you often find local people eating there, which is always a good sign. Q11 It overlooks the whole of the bay, and it's worth going there for that reason alone, but the food is good too...Then there's Jingjing. This is a popular place too, and Q12 you definitely won't get a table unless you reserve one in advance because it's comparatively small. It specialises in fish dishes, so there isn't much meat on the menu, which could put some people off...Then there's Paul and Lenny's. Q13 Why I'd recommend the food at this place is that it gets everything from the surrounding area, nothing's imported. That means the food is fresh and also reasonably priced, but you only get what's in season so the menu isn't very wide. Then...Primera. This restaurant serves good quality food, and Q14 because it's presented as a buffet and customers help themselves, there are fewer staff, so prices tend to be on the low side. It's not in a particularly attractive location, but the internal decor is smart and very original. And then the last one to mention is Torreminos. Q15 This restaurant's at the very upper end of the price range, and it only serves a small number of dishes on any one day. But what there is delicious. The service is also excellent and very quick...So there's something for everyone really, and wherever you choose to eat I hope you'll give me your feedback tomorrow. It's always useful.

T: OK. Well have a quick look at the map of the town. You'll be coming into town from the quay, and there'll be a main road straight ahead of you called Marine Way. Now the most well-known landmark in the town is the cathedral, built in the fifteenth century. I expect most of you'll want to see that, so cross over Marine Way and keep going straight ahead till you get to the plaza, which is the main public space. Q16 The cathedral is on the east side of this. On weekdays it's open for tourists, apart from between six and seven o'clock when there's normally a service. Then...Some of you have asked about the museum already. If you take the road that Q17 leads from the Plaza on the west side, the museum's on the right, just before the first turning. It's very interesting—there are a lot of artefacts there from an archaeological dig just outside the town in the 1990s. Now for those of you who aren't keen on walking, there is a tour bus which can take you around the town on a circular route, and it drops you off at various places of interest. Q18 The office where you can get a ticket and board the bus is on Marine Way. Turn left as you come from the quay, and it's facing you at the end of the road. Tickets cost about ten dollars and last for the whole day. For those who are more energetic, it's possible to get around by bicycle. You can get one for a few hours from a hire company. Q19 When you get to Marine Way from the quay, turn right. Then at the mini roundabout turn left and walk a short distance. You'll see the hire company on your left... Then one last thing...If you want to buy local crafts to take home as gifts, a very good place to go is the market. Q20 If you go to the Plaza and then go straight across it, and walk along the road heading north, the market is on the right, just after the first turning. You can find textiles there, and silverware, and some very attractive pottery. And the things there are often cheaper than you find them in the shops...Well, I'll leave you now, and hope you have a very enjoyable day ashore!

SECTION 3

(Angela=A; Dr Johnson=DJ)

A: Dr Johnson? I'm sorry I'm late. Do you still have time to see me?

DJ: Oh, Angela. I thought our appointment was at Q21 ten o'clock.

A: Yes, I'm sorry. I forgot. I had a lecture then.

DJ: Well, I'm free for thirty minutes now, but I have to leave at twelve. What did you want to see me about?

A: Well, actually I wanted to talk about note taking. You know, it's hard to keep up the lectures, especially the two-hour ones. Sometimes I just seem to zone out, and write down nothing. It's really frustrating!

DJ: Mmm. You are certainly not the only person in that position, I'm afraid. It all comes down to preparing before you go to class. So, firstly, tell me, what kind of note book are you using right now?

A: I use a hard-cover notebook. Is that OK?

DJ: You'd better use a Q22 & Q23 three-ring binder instead of a spiral or bound book. Pages can be easily removed for reviewing. Handouts can be inserted into your notes for cross-referencing. You can insert your own out-of-class notes in the correct order.

A: All right, I got that. Anything else do I need to pay attention to? You know, stationery like pens, pencils that kind of thing...

DJ: Oh, I figure you need to bring Q22 & Q23 highlighters to class. Instructors will frequently make comments like, "This is an important concept.", or "Make sure you understand this." These are direct clues that this will more than likely be on an exam. Highlighting these notes will help remind you later that this is definitely something you need to know.

A: OK, highlighters. No problem.

DJ: Another thing I want to stress here is that—always go to class prepared. You know, read assigned material and previous class notes before class. Make notations about material or concepts you don't understand. If you look up vocabulary words that are unfamiliar to you beforehand, you will have a better understanding about what the instructor is lecturing about and that will allow you to better decipher the more important points of the lecture.

A: OK, I see. My tutor also tells me to always have a plan and believe in it. Nothing good happens by accident. But Dr Johnson, I still find it difficult to fine-tune the structure and organization of my notes as well as increase my note taking speed. Do you have any good suggestions?

DJ: Well, basically, you should develop a note-taking method that works for you! First of all, start each new lecture on a new page, and date and number each page. The sequence of material is important. Then, write on one side of the paper only. You can set them out side-by-side for Q24 easier reviewing when studying for an exam. Also, remember to leave blank spaces. This allows you to add comments or note questions later. Besides, make your notes as brief as possible. You know, never use a sentence when you can use a phrase, or a phrase when you can use a word. You may develop a system of Q25 abbreviations and symbols that you can use wherever possible. Last but not least, try to note all unfamiliar vocabulary or concepts you don't understand. This reminds you to look them up later.

A: Wow, that sounds a little bit complicated. OK, I think I'll try to use the abbreviations and symbols. But Dr Johnson, to be frank, I'm tired of struggling to keep up with a lecture, sometimes, I just don't know what and how much to write down, I'm so confused, can you be more specific about what to include in my notes?

DJ: Hmm, let me see. There's quite a wide range of things, but I guess the most important could possibly be Q26 definitions, and you have to make sure to write down word for word. A subsequent category would be something like details, facts, or explanations that expand or explain the main points that are mentioned. And of course there are the usual things like Q27 enumerations or lists of things that are discussed.

A: Um, I've made a note of that...oh by the way, Dr Johnson, do you think it's a good idea to use a Q28 digital voice recorder?

DJ: Of course you can. Actually that's the secrets to taking better notes. Now, not many people can write fast enough to capture everything their professor says in class, so they would record the lecture. That way you won't miss something while you write, and you can double-check the tape for accuracy. Ask professors who lecture too fast if you can tape record their lecture. You'll generally find that many professors are willing to assist you in your efforts to gain as much from their lecture as possible.

A: OK, I see, I will ask the professors whether they mind me recording their lectures.

DJ: Whether you use a recorder or not, it's important to transcribe your notes as soon as possible while the subject is still fresh in your mind. By Q29 re-writing or re-typing your notes, you become more familiar with the material. You mentally reinforce what was said in class. And you get practice writing the information, making it easier to write the material a second time whether it be for a test or a term paper. And it is extremely important to Q30 review your notes within 24 hours. Few people realize how fast memory fades. Studies on memory have shown that, without review, 47% of what a person has just learnt is forgotten in the first twenty minutes and 62% is forgotten after the first day.

A: Yes, I will. Well that's very helpful. Thanks a lot, Dr Johnson!

DJ: My pleasure! Now all you need to do is get started.

SECTION 4

(Presenter=P; Mr David=M)

P: Morning, everyone, and welcome to our regular lecture on health issues. This series of lectures are organized by the Students' Union. It's a great pleasure for me to welcome Mr David Greenbaum, a physician in sports medicine, to come along and talk to us today.

M: Thank you. You may doubt what good sports medicine can do to non-athletes like you, college students. According to public assumptions, sports medicine doctors deal only with sporting injuries. But actually we treat Q31 general joint problems experienced by an average person more than treating people who hurt themselves by playing sports. So whether you're an athlete or not, a sports medicine physician can help you start off every day on the right foot.

If you are a college athlete or a sporty person, you must stay at the top of your game. But how do you maintain best physical fitness? You should be under the watchful eye of your sports team physician. Sports medicine doctors offer "total care" treatment, such as customized workouts, immediate care of injuries and Q32 surgery when needed. A sports medicine doctor's training falls within the specialty of orthopedic surgery. At such, it focuses on the cartilage, ligaments and muscles involved in your body's movement.

So how do injuries happen? Most of us take for granted the intricate interactions of our bones, muscles and ligaments—until they are damaged. When injured, these tissues can degenerate, causing your joints to Q33 ache and feel stiff. Even ordinary daily movements such as walking and bending may cause a "sports injury" through overuse. Furthermore, the normal wear and tear on your body's tissue may become more taxing as you age.

To prevent such problems, especially as you begin a fitness exercise, your sports medicine doctor offers total care. This includes X-rays to identify potential Q34 trouble spots. Afterwards, he helps you set an exercise routine that fits your body's present condition. Do you know your joints? The body's most complex structural feature is its joints. Your joints allow you to grasp, twist, sit and even feed yourself. Repetitive motions, however, may lead to Q35 chronic overuse of the soft tissue connecting bones at the joints. This overuse can result in injuries, such as tennis elbow or even carpal tunnel syndrome.

A more severe type of injury occurs when you lose your balance, thereby putting a joint under abnormal stress. Worse still, you could suffer a bone fracture. When a traumatic injury happens, effective medical care is crucial. Improper treatment of any joint injury can cause permanent loss of flexibility and reoccurring joint pain. As quickly as possible, the doctor applies ice packs to your injury. Ice deters swelling and inflammation, so you feel less pain. After keeping it iced for the first 48 hours after injury, the doctor begins therapeutic exercise of your wounded joint.

Recently a new treatment for degenerating joints has been developed, which is a product called orthokin. This treatment involves combining healing proteins with a sample of the patient's own blood. The injured joint then receives an Q36 injection of the mixture. This new technology stimulates our own white blood cells to produce large quantities of a protective protein. Our cells make this protein naturally, but not in sufficient amounts to protect the damaged cartilage in our joints. It also has the advantage of convenience and lack of Q37 side effects.

Here are some suggestions on how to prevent sports injury.

- Use appropriate protective equipment. Maintain proper lighting in the training area.
- Have adequate rest; avoid alcohol and drugs in order to prevent injuries.
- Follow Q38 a regular fitness-training programme to improve overall coordination and endurance. Better endurance will absorb pressure and prevent injury.
- Q39 Perform adequate warm-up exercises before training or performance.
- Q40 Avoid performing sports or work when you are sick. Most injuries happen when one is fatigued.
- Avoid treatment by dubious health practitioners. Use of inappropriate massage, adjustment and homemade medicine (often with steroids or other non-tested drugs) can cause more damage to the injury.

General Training Reading and Writing TEST A

答案速查

READING

Section 1, Questions 1–14

1 **IN EITHER ORDER** A C
2 **IN ANY ORDER** A C D
3 **IN EITHER ORDER** B C
4 C
5 **IN EITHER ORDER** C D
6 D
7 **IN EITHER ORDER** A D
8 TRUE
9 NOT GIVEN
10 TRUE
11 TRUE
12 NOT GIVEN
13 FALSE
14 FALSE

Section 2, Questions 15–27

15 2/two children
16 no
17 Southeast England
18 valid
19 discount
20 London area
21 £3.61
22 B
23 D
24 C
25 A
26 B
27 A

Section 3, Questions 28–40

28 FALSE
29 TRUE
30 TRUE
31 NOT GIVEN
32 TRUE
33 Japan
34 Holland
35 England
36 Teashops
37 B
38 A
39 E
40 D

名师解析

READING

Section 1

体　裁　　应用文
题　材　　广告、通知
主　题　　公司招聘合适的工作人员、公司政策调整
题　型　　选择题、判断题

Questions 1–7

题型 选择题(Multiple Choice)

注意 应仔细阅读题目的要求以弄清实际需要的答案的特点。

1	关键词	travel
	原文定位	A篇Desirable：中末句Willingness to travel和C篇第三段末句Some travelling may be required within the Greater Manchester area.
	题解	答案IN EITHER ORDER A C　根据题目的关键词travel（旅行）定位，A篇出现travel；有时找到的是该词的变形形式，例如C篇出现的名词形式travelling。
2	关键词	studied the subject
	原文定位	A篇Desirable：中首句A university degree in business or a related subject. C篇第三段首句A GNVQ level IV in nursing is desirable although training will be given. D篇首段A qualified and experienced teacher of psychology required for a prestigious boys schools in the West of England.
	题解	答案IN ANY ORDER A C D　题目要求require you to have studied the subject（要求你学习过该专业）的THREE jobs（三份工作），四选三，可采用排除法。理解题目要求后，看ABCD的标题，可知ACD分别招聘专业的bookkeeper（簿记员），a nursing assistant（护工助理）以及teacher of psychology（心理学老师），同时浏览B篇查看是否需要专业要求，根据B篇前两段，可知没有专业要求，答案为A C D。
3	关键词	a team
	原文定位	B篇首段、第二段中Are you a team player? If the answer to the above questions is “Yes” then you may be the person we are looking for. C篇第二段末句You need to be an excellent communicator with a patient and caring disposition, willing to work with other members of staff and be prepared to work unsociable hours.
	题解	答案IN EITHER ORDER B C　题目的关键词为team，B篇列出的三点要求第一点就是team player（具有团队精神的人），符合题目要求；C篇指出willing to work with other members of staff（愿意同其他成员合作），符合题目要求，故答案为B C。

4	关键词	work evenings
	原文定位	C篇第二段末句You need to be an excellent communicator with a patient and caring disposition, willing to work with other members of staff and be prepared to work unsociable hours.
	题解	答案C　本题稍有难度，因为浏览全文可以发现，四篇文章中均未提及工作时间。但仔细阅读C篇后看到be prepared to work unsociable hours. work unsociable hours意思为"非正常工作时间"，故答案为C。
5	关键词	offer specialised training
	原文定位	C篇第三段首句A GNVQ level IV in nursing is desirable although training will be given. D篇第二段末句Although a qualification in teaching basic skills is desirable, it is not necessary...Basic Skills will be provided.
	题解	答案IN EITHER ORDER C D　由C篇的A GNVQ level IV in nursing is desirable；D篇的the opportunity to work towards a City and Guilds in the Teaching of Basic Skills will be provided（有机会边工作边考取城市行业协会教师资格）可知答案为C D。
6	关键词	how much, earn
	原文定位	D篇第三段Salary is paid in accordance to the national scale.
	题解	答案D　D篇指出salary（工资）依照国际标准进行支付；注意干扰项为B篇，B篇首段首句Successful members of our sales team earn in excess of £35,000 per year. 其销售团体成功的成员每年收入超过£35,000，但注意限定词是Successful members（成功的成员），与题目要求的how much you will earn（你将挣多少钱）不符。
7	关键词	experience
	原文定位	A篇Essential中首句、第二句3 years experience in a multi-national company. Experience of computerised accounting. Desirable:中第二句5 years work experience. D篇首段A qualified and experienced teacher of psychology required for a prestigious boys schools in the West of England.
	题解	答案IN EITHER ORDER A D　带着关键词experience浏览四篇文章可以发现，A篇中该词出现了三次，可确定为正确答案；D篇experienced（经验丰富的）为experience的形容词形式，故答案为A D。

Questions 8–14

题型　判断题(Identifying Information)

注意　对于此类题，要注意细节，进行信息之间的比较。

8	关键词	two days, issued
	原文定位	通知起始The management hereby gives notice of a change in smoking policy to take effect from Monday July 1st, 2002.和结尾Issued: Friday June 28th, 2002
	题解	答案TRUE　文章为公司政策变动的通知，首先看通知的发布时间，Issued: Friday June 28th, 2002（2002年6月28日，星期五）；再看通知的生效时间，take effect from Monday July 1st, 2002（2002年7月1日，星期一），故仍有两天的时间容许在公司吸烟，题目符合原文。

9	关键词	outside of the building
	原文定位	第二段首句、第二句Smoking is now prohibited throughout the building, including all office space, adjoining corridors as well as toilets. Smoking is allowed in the work's canteen but only in the area designated for this purpose.
	题解	答案NOT GIVEN 文第二段指出在整个办公楼，包括所有的办公地点、走廊及洗手间都禁止吸烟。在餐厅允许吸烟，但仅限于指定的地点。文中未提及办公楼外的区域，因此题目Areas outside of the building have been designated for smoking（指定办公楼外的区域用于吸烟）未提及，答案为NOT GIVEN。
10	关键词	smoke
	原文定位	第二段首句Smoking is now prohibited throughout the building, including all office space, adjoining corridors as well as toilets.
	题解	答案TRUE 整个办公楼，包括所有的办公地点、走廊及洗手间都禁止吸烟。这说明同过去相比，现在允许吸烟的地方少了很多。故题目是正确的。
11	关键词	complained
	原文定位	首段Due to in-house complaints and changes in social acceptance of smoking in general...led to a revision in our smoking policy.
	题解	答案TRUE 公司发布吸烟政策的变动就是因为in-house complaints（内部的抱怨）及changes in social acceptance of smoking in general（总体上社会对吸烟接受程度的变化），因此可以确定人们抱怨在办公室吸烟的行为，故题目是正确的。
12	关键词	only, lunch times
	原文定位	第二段末句Smoking is allowed in the work's canteen but only in the area designated for this purpose.
	题解	答案NOT GIVEN 同样，由Q9可知，原文只是提到在餐厅允许吸烟，但仅限于指定的地点。文中未提及允许吸烟的时间。即题目所说的Smoking is only allowed in the company restaurant during lunch times（公司餐厅只有在午餐时间允许吸烟），故答案为NOT GIVEN。注意，判断题中NOT GIVEN选项最简单的答题方法就是：题目中涉及的内容原文没有提到。
13	关键词	smoking rooms, each floor
	原文定位	第三段首句、第二句Following complaints from smokers, it has been decided that a smoking room is going to be built on each floor. Construction of the smoking rooms is due to begin next month.
	题解	答案FALSE 如果完全禁止吸烟，那么吸烟的人也会有怨言。于是将在每一楼层都建吸烟室，计划下个月开建。注意文中的is going to及next month都表示了这是将来的动作。因此题目中的have been built（表示完成时的动作）则与原文矛盾，故答案为FALSE 。

14	关键词	loss of one's job
	原文定位	末段The management will take any infringement of this regulation seriously, and any member of staff seen to be smoking on work premises, outside of the designated smoking areas, will receive a written warning that may lead to dismissal.
	题解	答案FALSE 文中指出对于在指定区域外吸烟的人，将收到书面警告，may lead to dismissal（可能会被解雇）；而题目表达的是will result in the loss of one's job（导致失去工作）。注意，区分FALSE和NOT GIVEN的关键在于：FALSE的题目可以根据原文逻辑推理明确地断定题目与原文矛盾，并且在语气上或者说是程度上差别较大（一个是符合说明文严谨的语气，表示约数的副词较多；一个是比较武断的个人主观臆断，表示绝对化的词语较多），如原文的may被改为题目中的will；而NOT GIVEN的题目和原文的语气几乎没有差别，只是范围上不同罢了，根据原文的线索无法判断出题目的对错，也就是说，题目给出的内容可能发生也可能不会发生。

Section 2

体　裁　说明文
题　材　介绍类文章
主　题　交通卡介绍、门户网站介绍
题　型　句子填空题、选择题

Questions 15–21

题型 句子填空题(Sentence Completion)

注意 句子填空题可以看成是摘要填空题和简答题两者的结合，在解题思路和技巧上都可以互相借鉴。

15	关键词	Family Saver Card
	原文定位	第三段首句A variety of cards are available from our Singles Travel Card...which can be used by up to four people travelling in a group*.
	题解	答案2/two children 第三段分别说明了单人、双人及家庭交通卡的使用范围。Family Saver Card（家庭优惠卡）可用于四人组家庭，根据星号注释可知，家庭组中的两个成员must be children under the age of 16（必须是年龄在16岁以下的儿童），因此答案为2/two children。注意阅读中的注释内容常为考点出处。
16	关键词	restrictions
	原文定位	第二段第二句Unlike many other travel cards that restrict you to travelling between the hours of 10am and 4pm, a Capital Travel Card has no time restrictions: you are free to travel where and when you wish, even during peak times, saving you £30 on travel expenses.
	题解	答案no 题干考查Capital Travel Card的限制条件。文中第二段指出了Capital Travel Card（首都交通卡）的好处，它不像其他交通卡那样限制了出行的时间，这种卡没有时间限制，可以在任何时间去任何地方，因此答案为no。

17	关键词	Capital Travel Extra
	原文定位	第四段For travel outside of London our Capital Travel Extra allows you to travel on any train service in the Southeast of England and provides you with a 10% discount on Train-travel to other parts of the country.
	题解	答案Southeast England 根据关键词Capital Travel Extra定位到第四段，可知使用Capital Travel Extra（首都超值交通卡），可以在Southeast of England（英格兰东南部）乘火车旅行。注意题目对答案字数的限制。
18	关键词	cost
	原文定位	第五段首句The price of the cards vary according to the time for which they are valid (see table below), and can be purchased for one day, a weekend or seven days.
	题解	答案valid 根据卡的有效时间，卡的价格有所不同，分为一天卡、周末卡和七天卡。题干The cost of the cards（卡的价格）对应原文中的The price of the cards（卡的价格）；而depends on（取决于）对应vary according to（根据……而变化），故其共同宾语为答案。
19	关键词	students
	原文定位	第三段第二句In addition, there is our Student Traveller which is available at a discounted price for students with a valid student union card but which comes with the same restrictions as a Singles Card.
	题解	答案discount 根据空格前的冠词a，可以确定空格应填入名词。根据核心词定位到原文，学生可以a discounted price（折扣价格）购买Student Traveller（学生交通卡），discounted（打折扣的）为形容词，空格应填入其名词形式，即discount。
20	关键词	only be purchased
	原文定位	第五段第二句Cards can be purchased from any train or tube station in the London area.
	题解	答案London area 本题较为简单。根据关键词进行定位，可在London area（伦敦地区）的任何火车站或地铁站购买交通卡，因此答案为London area。
21	关键词	Student Traveller, spend
	原文定位	定位至第三段下面的表格
	题解	答案￡3.61 题干考查的是如果学生使用学生交通卡，在伦敦旅行，一天会花多少钱，根据表格中的信息可知答案为￡3.61。

Questions 22–27

题型 选择题(Multiple Choice)

注意 下面题目中有些比较简单，从原文很快找到对应答案。这时可以直接选择不必看其他选项。

22	关键词	Secondary Online Science, ability
	原文定位	第二段第三句Children of all abilities can enjoy the games.
	题解	答案B 选项A, B和C分别出现了low ability, mixed ability和high ability，可见答案与ability相关。根据关键词ability定位到第二段，选项mixed ability（各种能力）对应原文的all abilities（所有能力）。注意正确选项常常是对原文相关词句的改写。
23	关键词	designed to be
	原文定位	第二段末句The style of SOS is motivational and supportive for individual learners.
	题解	答案D 浏览Q22–Q27，可以发现题干的结构基本相同，无法从题干中确定关键词，因此可以浏览各个选项，从选项中寻找线索进行定位。由定位句发现选项D motivating and educational为原文重现，因此答案为D。
24	关键词	designed as
	原文定位	首段首句Learning has joined up with the Institute of Physics and the Royal Society of Chemistry to create a new science web portal, Secondary Online Science (SOS).
	题解	答案C 定位句中的Web portal（门户网站）与Secondary Online Science为同位语，由此可知SOS即为网站，其中Web portal与题目选项中的Web site对应。
25	关键词	mainly
	原文定位	第二段第三句Children of all abilities can enjoy the games.
	题解	答案A 由定位句中children一词，可确定答案。
26	关键词	improve, understanding
	原文定位	第二段第二句The games are complex and challenge the students' game-playing skills, at the same time testing their understanding of science.
	题解	答案B 首先，选项C improve students, understanding of fabrics and music（提高学生对纺织品和音乐的理解）指的是游戏Fashion Victim（时尚牺牲品）和Sound Park（声音乐园）的作用，可排除。第二段指出，游戏challenge the students' game-playing skills（挑战学生玩游戏的技巧），而不是选项D的improve（提高），可排除。根据文章题目及全文大意可知，SOS网站是为了提高学生们的understanding of science（对科学的理解），即B项。
27	关键词	used by
	原文定位	第二段末句The style of SOS is motivational and supportive for individual learners.
	题解	答案A 根据定位句的individual learners可知，SOS为单人游戏，因此答案为A。注意如果题目中的关键词难以确定答案的位置，选项中的关键词也可以作为定位的参考依据。

Section 3

体　　裁　　说明文
题　　材　　社会科学类
主　　题　　茶的历史
题　　型　　判断题、流程图题、摘要填空题

Questions 28–32

题型 判断题(Identifying Information)

注意 在题目中划出定位词，在文章中定位。若定位词在文章中无法定位，则看有无同义转换，若无同义转换，那么确定答案是NOT GIVEN。

28	关键词	legend, accidentally poisoned
	原文定位	A段第三句Indeed, legend has it that China's father of agriculture and medicine, Shen Nong Shi, ...recovered from a serious bout of accidental poisoning after eating tealeaves.
	题解	答案FALSE　题干中的the founder of Chinese agriculture指的就是神农氏，他亲自品尝百草，发明药物及治病教人。原文中指出神农氏中毒后吃茶叶解毒，而题干中accidentally poisoned after eating tealeaves（吃茶叶后意外中毒）不符合原文，因此答案为FALSE。
29	关键词	medicine
	原文定位	A段倒数第二句、末句From that time on tea was administered as a remedy for illnesses ranging from poisoning and digestive problems to common fatigue. And even today, tea is believed to help prevent certain types of cancer.
	题解	答案TRUE　文中指出茶叶可以用来治疗疾病、解毒、助消化及缓解疲惫等，时至今日，人们也认为茶可以预防某些癌症。因此题干是正确的。
30	关键词	demise of the Mongol empire
	原文定位	C段末句Many of the traditional arts of tea preparation...some one hundred years later, albeit in a modified form.
	题解	答案TRUE　在题干中发现大写的Mongol，是明显的"高调词"，便于迅速地回文中定位。发现Mongol后迅速通读整个句子，很多制茶的传统艺术在Mongol Empire期间都失传了。题干表示：加工和制茶的方式在蒙古帝国灭亡后发生了改变，符合原文，因此答案为TRUE。
31	关键词	international trade routes
	原文定位	D段首句Tea eventually reached Western countries by way of the great trading routes, such as the Silk Road, and first became established as a national drink in Holland, and later England...
	题解	答案NOT GIVEN　确定题目中的关键词international trade routes, Chinese economy; great trading routes出现在D段首句。但是原文中无法定位任何表示因果关系的词组。而且通过浏览原文也无法搜索到有关Chinese economy的信息。因此，可以判断本题的答案是NOT GIVEN。

32	关键词	Glasgow, Scotland
	原文定位	D段第二句The demand for tea became so great that ships known as tea clippers were specially designed and built for the sole purpose of transporting tea, stimulating the ship building industry in Glasgow, Scotland...
	题解	**答案TRUE** 题干中的专有名词Glasgow和Scotland，是明显的“高调词”，容易定位。原文中指出tea clippers...stimulating the ship building industry in Glasgow, Scotland（运茶帆船促进了苏格兰格拉斯哥的造船行业），则判断题干是正确的。

Questions 33–36

题型 流程图题(Flow-Chart Completion)

注意 本题需要考生注意顺序性，即题目的顺序和原文的顺序一致。

33	关键词	exported to
	原文定位	C段倒数第三句Moreover, during the Song Dynasty tea was exported to Japan and sparked off a tea drinking culture there.
	题解	**答案Japan** 浏览整个流程图，查看空格的位置，Q33–Q35的空格位于介词之后，空格应填入的为表示地点的名词。Q33考查中国茶叶exported（出口）的地点。原文C段指出宋代期间，tea was exported to Japan（茶被出口到日本）。因此答案为Japan（日本）。
34	关键词	popular
	原文定位	D段首句Tea eventually reached Western countries by way of the great trading routes, such as the Silk Road, and first became established as a national drink in Holland...
	题解	**答案Holland** 题目的顺序和原文的顺序一致。因此，继Q33之后寻找Q34的答案。茶出口日本之后，最后通过丝绸之路等商路到达西方国家成为Holland（荷兰）的a national drink（国饮），可见其受欢迎的程度。因此答案为Holland。
35	关键词	a tea culture
	原文定位	D段倒数第二句Tea became so popular, in fact, that during the Victorian period...engaged in conversation and tea drinking, out of which grew numerous teashops.
	题解	**答案England** 维多利亚时期，女士们喝茶度过下午的闲暇时光，她们边喝茶边聊天，茶文化逐渐盛行。注意此处的the Victorian period（维多利亚时期）暗示为英国。
36	关键词	popular
	原文定位	D段倒数第二句Tea became so popular, in fact, that during the Victorian period...engaged in conversation and tea drinking, out of which grew numerous teashops.
	题解	**答案Teashop** 通过对定位句的分析，可以看出英国出现茶文化之后，开始专船运茶，继而出现了众多的teashops（茶室）。注意题目对于答案字数的限制。

Questions 37–40

题型 摘要填空题(Summary Completion)

注意 对所填词的词性进行预判断，有助于提高对正确答案的敏感性，精确锁定答案。

37	关键词	tea, drinking
	原文定位	A段第二句Even so, when man first began drinking tea is unclear, although it is thought to have been first used as a medicine.
	题解	答案medicinal 根据空格前后内容可以确定，空格内应填入的为形容词。A段以神农氏的传说为例，指出了茶的药用。备选项中的medicinal（药用的）对应原文的medicine。因此答案为medicinal。
38	关键词	Eastern and Western
	原文定位	C段倒数第三句Moreover, during the Song Dynasty tea was exported to Japan and sparked off a tea drinking culture there. 和D段首句Tea eventually reached Western countries by way of the great trading routes...
	题解	答案tea culture 由空格前的冠词可以确定，空格内应填入单数可数名词，词库中符合条件的单数可数名词有tea culture（茶文化）、trade rcute（贸易路线）和drink（饮料）。注意词库中的poison为集合名词，不符合条件。根据Q33–Q36的流程图可以看出，在东西方国家，茶文化风靡，因此可从三个备选项中确定答案为tea culture（茶文化）。
39	关键词	different
	原文定位	C段第二句This in turn spurred on the ceramic industry...D段第二句...stimulating the ship building industry in Glasgow, Scotland...
	题解	答案industries 由空格前的形容词different可以确定，空格内应填入名词。茶叶受到欢迎，器皿成为必需品，因此促进了ceramic industry（陶瓷业）；同时运茶又促进了ship building industry（造船业）。可见茶叶种植、精制、备茶等促进了不同行业的兴起。因此，答案为industries。
40	关键词	second only to water
	原文定位	F段末句And although tea has less commercial value than coffee, it still remains second only to water in being the world's most popular beverage.
	题解	答案drink 空格内应填入名词，根据关键词second only to water回原文定位，可在结尾发现it still remains second only to water in being the world's most popular beverage（在世界上最受欢迎的饮品中，茶仅次于水）。如无词库，可确定答案为beverage（饮品），在备选答案中只有drink符合词义，因此答案为drink。

WRITING

WRITING TASK 1

名师解读

书信的通用结构：称呼语、主体和结束语三部分。

称呼语：如果是给熟悉的人写信可以直呼其名或用他们的昵称，比如：Sonic或Kitty等；如果与对方不是很熟悉可以使用Dear Mr Lee或Dear Sir or Madam等。

主体：首段应该说明信的主旨，然后在后续的段落里提供细节，清楚说明你希望收信人该如何做。

结束语：在结束语中总结心境或写信的目的。在写信人的名字前加上sincerely yours, thankful或obedient。这种总结语没有什么真正的目的，但确是应有的礼节。

无论遇到哪种类型的书信或是题目中有任何的具体要求，都要谨记下列的三要素：

1. 明确地指出自己写信的目的；
2. 清晰、准确地陈述事实；
3. 使用坚定但礼貌的语言。

高分范文

Dear Alice,

I hope you are well and enjoying being back at university after the holiday. I wonder if you could do me a favour. Would it be possible to buy some books suitable for a 14-year-old boy?

My friend (Jasmine) has a son who is not doing particularly well in his English classes at school. His English is actually quite good, but he has lost motivation and Jasmine wondered whether it might help if he could be persuaded to do some more reading in the language. As you know, it is very difficult to **get hold of** English books here and the ones in the bookshops are rather boring for a teenage boy. As you have two younger brothers, I thought you might have some suggestions about what he would enjoy. If you could choose a couple of books, Jasmine would be very happy to send money to cover the cost of the books and **postage**.

I hope you do not mind my asking you to do this and do let me know if there is anything I can send you from here to say thank you.

Best wishes,

Sasha (190 Words)

WRITING TASK 2

文章结构

双方观点+双方论据+自己观点

both views+both arguments+opinion

首段：背景句+引出话题+一方观点+另一方观点

第二段：一方论据+另一方论据

第三段：自己的观点

思路点拨

步骤一：审题

Housing shortage in big cities can cause severe consequences. Only government action can solve this problem. To what extent do you agree or disagree?

→通读题目，了解大意。

大城市住房紧张引起严重后果。只有政府行动能够解决这个问题。你在多大程度上同意或不同意这种说法?

→再读题目，辨别关键词，区分主题词和限定词，推测考官的出题意图。

主题词：Housing shortage, Only government action

限定词：agree or disagree

步骤二：列大纲

英文提纲	Introduction: housing shortage in metropolitan cities has already become an extremely serious problem (topic)→Some people claim that proper actions shculd be taken by the government (one view)→but others...both individuals and big enterprises should also take on the responsibilities (the other view) Body: Former opinion: obligation and ability to make out po icies→provide sufficient fund and necessary facilities Latter viewpoint: joint efforts→professional insights→the government has a lot more issues to address→overpopulation Conclusion: the government, enterprises and individuals should join their efforts
中文提纲	引出话题：大都市的住房紧张问题已经成为非常严重的问题（话题）→一些人主张政府应当采取适当的行动（一方观点）→另一些人表示个人和大企业也应该承担责任（另一方观点） 主体段： 前者观点：制定政策的义务和能力→提供充足的资金和必要的设施 后者观点：共同努力→专业的洞察力→政府有很多事情需要处理→人口过剩 总结：政府、企业和个人三方共同努力

高分范文

There is no denying that housing shortage in **metropolitan cities** has already become an extremely serious problem over the last decades. The severe consequences caused by housing shortage have also become an issue that has drawn wide public concerns. Some people **claim** that proper actions should be taken by the government without any delay in view of the severity of the problem, but others are in high favour that, in addition to the government, both individuals and big enterprises should also take on the responsibilities to deal with this problem.

Thus, a **controversial** discussion has arisen on this issue. People who **side with** the former opinion point out that only the government has the obligation and ability to make out policies to standardize the behaviours in house construction and purchasing. In addition, only the government can provide sufficient fund and necessary facilities in the process of problem solving. People who agree with the latter viewpoint believe that joint efforts from both the government and big enterprises are needed to better solve this problem. For one thing, big enterprises, especially real estate companies, have more professional **insights** into this issue. For another, it is impossible for the government to focus only on solving housing problems because it has a lot more issues to address. Besides, housing problem is closely related to the overpopulation in big cities and the problem of cverpopulation can not be solved in the short term.

Based on the foregoing discussion, I would argue that the government, enterprises and individuals should join their efforts in order to effectively cope with this problem. (264 words)

重点词汇

READING

motivation	[ˌməʊtɪ'veɪʃn]	*n.*	动机；积极性
disposition	[ˌdɪspə'zɪʃn]	*n.*	性情；处置
psychology	[saɪ'kɒlədʒi]	*n.*	心理学
prestigious	[pre'stɪdʒəs]	*adj.*	有名望的
curriculum	[kə'rɪkjələm]	*n.*	课程
in accordance to			根据
take effect			生效，起作用
consultation	[ˌkɒnsl'teɪʃn]	*n.*	磋商；咨询
prohibit	[prə'hɪbɪt]	*v.*	阻止，禁止
canteen	[kæn'tiːn]	*n.*	餐厅，食堂
infringement	[ɪn'frɪndʒmənt]	*n.*	违反
premise	['premɪs]	*n.*	前提
dismissal	[dɪs'mɪsl]	*n.*	解雇，免职
facilitate	[fə'sɪlɪteɪt]	*v.*	促进，使容易
tram	[træm]	*n.*	有轨电车
discounted	['dɪskaʊntɪtd]	*adj.*	折扣的
web portal			门户网站
games console			游戏控制台
innovative	['ɪnəveɪtɪv]	*adj.*	革新的，创新的
appeal to			对……有吸引力；呼吁
originate in			起源于……
recede	[rɪ'siːd]	*v.*	减弱
bout	[baʊt]	*n.*	发作
remedy	['remədi]	*n.*	补救
digestive	[daɪ'dʒestɪv]	*adj.*	消化的
Tibetan plateau			青藏高原
utensil	[juː'tensl]	*n.*	器皿
ceramic	[sə'ræmɪk]	*adj.*	陶瓷的
spark off			引起；导致
predominate	[prɪ'dɒmɪneɪt]	*v.*	支配
albeit	[ˌɔːl'biːɪt]	*conj.*	虽然
unfermented	[ˌʌnfə'mentɪd]	*adj.*	未发酵的
monopoly	[mə'nɒpəli]	*n.*	垄断
botanist	['bɒtənɪst]	*n.*	植物学家
oxidation	[ˌɒksɪ'dzeɪʃn]	*n.*	氧化

WRITING

get hold of			得到；抓住
postage	['pəʊstɪdʒ]	*n.*	邮资，邮费
there is no denying			不可否认
metropolitan city			大都市
claim	[kleɪm]	*v.*	声称
controversial	[ˌkɒntrə'vɜːʃl]	*adj.*	有争议的
side with			支持，站在……的一边
insight	['ɪnsaɪt]	*n.*	洞察力

General Training Reading and Writing TEST B

答案速查

READING

Section 1, Questions 1–14

1 TRUE
2 FALSE
3 FALSE
4 TRUE
5 NOT GIVEN
6 FALSE
7 TRUE
8 TRUE
9 NOT GIVEN
10 iv
11 iii
12 vi
13 i
14 ii

Section 2, Questions 15–27

15 B
16 C
17 B
18 B
19 B
20 B
21 A
22 A
23 B
24 C
25 D
26 TRUE
27 NOT GIVEN

Section 3, Questions 28–40

28 FALSE
29 TRUE
30 NOT GIVEN
31 TRUE
32 TRUE
33 TRUE
34 FALSE
35 TRUE
36 insect control
37 (unwanted) weeds
38 dry weather
39 food
40 humidity

TEST B

名师解析

READING

Section 1

体　裁　　应用文
题　材　　宣传品、产品使用手册
主　题　　关于全市电力公司(Citywide Power Company)的宣传和如何使用弗莱明斯电熨板的手册
题　型　　判断题、配对题

Questions 1–9

题型 判断题(Identifying Information)

注意 题目会提供一组陈述。如果是意见或看法，考生需回答这些陈述是否符合或反映了作者的观点或看法。

1	关键词	Calls, Citywide Customer Service, billed
	原文定位	Welcome段第三句If you need to call us for any reason, freephone Customer Service on 1900 12 55 12.
	题解	答案TRUE　题干中的Calls（电话）与原文中的call对应，原文中的us指的就是题干中的Citywide Customer Service（全市电力公司），题干中的not billed （不开账单）与原文中的freephone（免费电话）对应。答案为TRUE。
2	关键词	a 15% discount
	原文定位	Payment Options段首句Choose the option that suits your preference and rest assured that we offer everyone a 15% discount if the entire bill is paid before the due date.
	题解	答案FALSE　题干中的Every Citywide customer与原文中的everyone对应，receives与原文中的offer对应，a 15% discount为原文重现；但不是随便就有15%折扣，是有条件的，即the entire bill is paid before the due date（整个账单到期之前支付）。答案为FALSE。
3	关键词	have enough money, direct debit, bank account, 2%
	原文定位	Direct Debit段首句、第二句Set up a direct debit...(as long as you have sufficient funds in your chosen bank account). You qualify for a further 2% Prompt Pay Discount if you choose this method.
	题解	答案FALSE　根据题干中的关键词direct debit（直接借记），bank account（银行账户）在原文进行定位。题干中的have enough money（有足够的钱）与原文中的have sufficient funds（有充足的资金）对应。但原文提到的是有足够的钱才有2%的折扣，而题干表述的是没有足够的钱就要面临2%的罚金。答案为FALSE。
4	关键词	Internet banking, transfer
	原文定位	Internet Banking段首句Add Citywide Power to your bill payment options; receive your bill online; transfer the full amount owing before the due date and get a 2% Prompt Pay Discount.
	题解	答案TRUE　采用Internet Banking（网上银行）方式的流程是Add Citywide Power（添加全市电力公司账户），然后是receive your bill online（在线接收你的账单），最后才是transfer the full amount owing（按账单金额全额转账）。答案为TRUE。

5	关键词	Automatic payment
	原文定位	Automatic Payment段末句This option is more suitable for customers with regular energy usage, although you can change the amount and the interval at any time.
	题解	答案NOT GIVEN 题干中的suits（适合）与原文的suitable（合适的）为同根词，原文中的This option（这个选择）指代题干中的Automatic Payment（自动支付）；people与原文中customers对应，原文提到的是具有regular energy usage（常规能源使用）的人，并没有提及low incomes（低收入者）。答案为NOT GIVEN。
6	关键词	telephone transfer
	原文定位	Telephone Transfer段第二句Make Citywide Power one of your telephone transfer options at the bank and you can just pick up the phone and pay straight from your bank account when you receive your energy bill.
	题解	答案FALSE 根据题干中的关键词telephone transfer（电话转账）在原文进行定位。原文提及的pay your bill（支付账单）的方式是straight from your bank account（直接从你的银行账户中扣除），题干与此不符。答案为FALSE。
7	关键词	does not accept all, credit cards
	原文定位	Credit Card段末句We accept most credit cards—all the major ones anyway.
	题解	答案TRUE 题干中的Citywide（全市电力公司）用来具体指代原文中的we（我们），does not accept all（不全接受）与原文中的accept most（接收大多数）是同义表达。答案为TRUE。
8	关键词	a cheque, mail
	原文定位	Cheque段第二句If this is the case, simply write the cheque—being sure to note your account number on the back—and mail it in your pre-paid, reusable envelope in which you received your bill.
	题解	答案TRUE 题干中的sending...in the mail（通过邮件发送）与原文中的动词mail（邮寄）对应；cheque（支票）为原文重现；题干中的no postage costs（没有邮资的费用）与原文pre-paid（预支付的）相对应。答案为TRUE。
9	关键词	in person
	原文定位	In Person段末句Then pop into any branch of Citywide with your bill and the means to pay it.
	题解	答案NOT GIVEN 根据题干关键词in person在原文进行定位，原文只是提及了可以到Citywide（全市电力公司）任何的branch（分支），采用任何的means（方法）支付账单，但没有提及题干中的use cash to pay（用现金支付）。

Questions 10—14

题型 配对题(Matching Headings)

注意 段落标题配对题是阅读考试中比较特殊的题型，因为大部分的题型都是考查考生对细节的理解，而段落标题配对题考查的是考生对段落主旨的把握能力。

10	关键词	heat-protective, stop...from
	原文定位	A段Make sure to coat strands with a heat-protective spray before use. This will stop the straightening irons from causing excessive dehydration and frizz, which can sap the integrity of the hair shaft.
	题解	答案iv　A段首句为主题句。原文关键词heat-protective（隔热保护的）和stop...from（阻止）与iv中的prevent（阻止）对应，而causing excessive dehydration and frizz（造成过度脱水和卷发），integrity of the hair shaft（毛干的完整性）被概括为damage（破坏）。
11	关键词	blow-dry
	原文定位	B段Part hair into four or five large sections, and blow-dry each section using a paddle brush.
	题解	答案iii　原文中的dry（干的）与iii中的wetness表达的是相反的意思，blow-dry each section（用吹风机吹干每个部分）的目的就是Avoid excessive wetness（避免过度潮湿）。
12	关键词	clamp...down, pull...down
	原文定位	C段首句、第二句Take a one or two inch section of hair and clamp the iron down as close to the roots as possible. Pull the iron down towards the tips with a firm, steady hand.
	题解	答案vi　原文中的动词clamp...down（施加压力）和pull...down（拉下来）与vi中的move（移动）对应，the iron（直发器）为原词重现；a one or two inch section of hair（一两英寸的头发）被概括为the hair（头发）。
13	关键词	a slightly reflective sheen
	原文定位	D段末句This creates a slightly reflective sheen, which gives a polished and healthy appearance to your hair.
	题解	答案i　原文中的关键词a slightly reflective sheen（有点反射光泽）与i中的shine（闪耀）对应，而动词creates（创造）与i中的add（增加）是同义替换。
14	关键词	return to
	原文定位	E段末句This will counteract the effect of the straightening, and the hair will return to its natural curly or wavy state.
	题解	答案ii　原文中的关键词return to（回到）与ii中的内容为原词重现；natural（自然的）与ii中的original（原始的）对应；state（状态）与ii中的condition（情况）对应。

Section 2

体　裁　　说明文
题　材　　工作、计划
主　题　　介绍雇主、员工和承包商之间的差别及关系和带薪育婴假的计划
题　型　　配对题、选择题、判断题

Questions 15–23

题型 配对题(Matching Information)

注意 此种题型是雅思阅读中比较普遍的题型，题目中会出现某些选项不被选择作为答案的情况，还会出现有些选项会被选择两次或两次以上的情况。

15	关键词	wages or salary, profit
	原文定位	第三段首句Payment—employees are usually paid on the basis of an hourly rate or a salary. 第五段首句Risk—employees generally do not bear in a direct way the risk of financial loss incurred by the business for which they work.
	题解	答案B 题干中的work for（为……工作）与原文中的paid on the basis of（基于……支付）对应；wages or salary（工资或薪水）与原文中的an hourly rate or a salary（每小时工资或薪水）对应；rather than（而不是）与原文do not （不能）对应；profit（利润）与原文financial（财政的）对应，故本题描述的对象就是employees（雇员）。
16	关键词	pay tax on behalf of others
	原文定位	末段首句Income tax and superannuation—employers usually pay these for their employees whereas contractors make their own arrangements.
	题解	答案C 题干中的pay为原文重现；pay后的these指代的是tax（税）；题干中的on behalf of（代表）与原文中的for对应；题干中的others用来指代原文中的their employees（他们的雇员），故本题描述的对象就是原文的主语employers（雇主）。
17	关键词	the way in which, a job
	原文定位	第二段末句Control over work—generally an employee works as directed by the employer whereas a contractor has a greater say in how the work is to be done.
	题解	答案B 题干中的the way in which与原文中的how对应；题干中的have less responsibility for（对……有较少的责任）与原文中的as directed by the employer（直接由雇主……）对应；题干中的is carried out（被实施）与原文中的be done（被做）对应。故本题描述的对象就是employee（雇员）。
18	关键词	gear
	原文定位	倒数第二段段首句Tools and equipment—contractors may supply special equipment or tools to do the job.
	题解	答案B 题干中的gear（工具）与原文中的special equipment or tools（特种设备或工具）对应，contractors（承包商）需要提供特殊的设备或工具，言外之意就是employees（雇员）不用提供，这与题干中的do not provide（不提供）对应。

19	关键词	pay by the hour
	原文定位	第三段首句Payment—employees are usually paid on the basis of an hourly rate or a salary.
	题解	**答案B** 题干中的hour（小时）与原文中的hourly（每小时）为同根词；题干中的pay为原文重现，故本题描述的对象就是原文的主语employee（雇员）。
20	关键词	do not have, pay other people
	原文定位	倒数第三段首句Sub-contracting—an employee cannot assign or delegate the work to others whereas a contractor is typically permitted to do so.
	题解	**答案B** 题干中的do not与原文中的cannot对应；have the freedom to pay...do（可以自由支付……做……）与原文中的Sub-contracting（转包）对应；do与原文中的assign or delegate（指定或委托）对应；their job与原文中的the work对应，故本题描述的对象就是原文的主语employee（雇员）。
21	关键词	a trade union
	原文定位	首段第五句Only an “employee” can be covered by an award: something (e.g. a pay rise) given as a result of arbitration (process of resolving a dispute e.g. between employers and a trade union) or make a workplace agreement.
	题解	**答案A** 根据题干中的a trade union在原文进行定位。题干中的benefit（利益）与原文中的award（奖励）对应，从a trade union（一个工会）得到利益的是employee（雇员），不包括contractors（承包商）。
22	关键词	are paid for, the end result
	原文定位	第三段Payment—employees are usually paid on the basis of an hourly rate or a salary. Contractors are more often paid for a required outcome, with less regard for time.
	题解	**答案A** 题干中的are paid for为原文重现；题干中的the end result（最终的结果）与原文中的a required outcome（需要的结果）对应；题干中的hours recorded（记录时间）与原文中的an hourly rate（小时费）对应，但小时计费描述的是employee（雇员），不是contractors（承包商）。
23	关键词	sign, an employment contract
	原文定位	首段首句An employee is someone who performs work under a contract of employment.
	题解	**答案B** 题干中的sign an... contract（签署）与原文中的under a contract（按合同）对应perform work（执行工作），故本题描述的对象就是原文的主语employee（雇员）。

Questions 24 and 25

题型 多项选择题 (Multiple Choice)

注意 多项选择题是一项比较难而且比较另类的题型，因为其他题型只会有一个答案，而多选题往往要从选项中选出2–3个答案。

24	关键词	is entitled to Paid Parental Leave
	原文定位	第三段Eligible working parents of children born or adopted on or after 1st August may get 18 weeks government-funded pay at the National Minimum Wage to help them care for a new baby.
	题解	答案C 原文中的working parents（双职工父母）与选项C中的A couple（一对夫妇）对应；原文中的adopted（领养）与选项C中的adopts（领养）的原形为同一动词；原文中的a new baby（新生儿）与选项C中的a child（一个孩子）对应。
25	关键词	is entitled to Paid Parental Leave
	原文定位	第四段末句You can earn up to $100, 000 a year (individual salary) and still be eligible.
	题解	答案D 根据题干中的$100, 000定位。原文中的up to（多达……）与选项D中的less than（少于）对应；原文中的人称代词you指代的是mother或father。

Questions 26 and 27

题型 判断题(Identifying Information)

注意 判断题在出题时一般只考查题目中一个信息的是非对错，不会同时考查多个信息，那么考查的这个成分就是设置的考点。

26	关键词	12 months
	原文定位	第六段第二句It will be paid in one continous period from the start date and must all be taken with the first year after the birth or adoption.
	题解	答案TRUE 题干中的the age of 12 months与原文中的the first year after the birth or adoption对应；题干中的will be paid与原文中的receive the benefit对应，即只有在孩子出生一年内，其父母才能享受这种优待。
27	关键词	make a claim
	原文定位	第六段首句You can claim up to three months in advance, and your pay can start any time you choose from when your child is born or adopted.
	题解	答案NOT GIVEN 题干中的make a claim（对……提出要求）与原文中的claim up（对……的要求）对应，但原文提及的是提前three months（3个月）申请，没有提及如果不早点申请就会错过的信息。

Section 3

体　裁　　说明文
题　材　　社会生活
主　题　　介绍与鸡相关的信息
题　型　　判断题、句子填空题

Questions 28–35

题型 判断题(Identifying Information)
注意 这种题型考查考生进行跳读、扫读和对细节进行理解的能力。

28	关键词	keeping chickens, some cities, practice
	原文定位	首段第二句Regulations vary from region to region and, although some cities still allow residents to keep chickens, the practice is far from usual today.
	题解	**答案FALSE** 题干中的some cities（一些城市），Keeping chickens（饲养鸡），practice（惯例）均为原文重现，但考生需要注意原文中的转折连词although（尽管）强调的内容是：一些城市虽然允许居民养鸡，但养鸡这种行为如今并不常见。答案为FALSE。
29	关键词	male chickens, noise.
	原文定位	首段第三句Some communities prohibit roosters because of their early morning crowing and only allow the much quieter hens.
	题解	**答案TRUE** 题干中的Male chickens（公鸡）与原文中的roosters（公鸡）对应；题干中的noise（噪音）与原文中的crowing（啼叫）对应。由此可知答案。
30	关键词	keep chickens
	原文定位	首段末句However, in most rural areas, there are generally no restrictions on keeping chickens either as ornamental or practical birds.
	题解	**答案NOT GIVEN** 题干中的keep chickens（饲养鸡）为原文重现；但原文提到的是在rural areas（农村地区）饲养鸡no restrictions（没有限制），并没有提及many people（许多人）养鸡。答案是NOT GIVEN。
31	关键词	some species, beautiful feathers
	原文定位	第二段首句There are some Asian ornamental varieties with eye-catching plumage: the Cochin and Silkie from China have distinctive feathery feet and the Peacock from Sri Lanka has a strikingly long tail.
	题解	**答案TRUE** 题干中的Some species（一些种类）与原文中的varieties（种类）对应；题干中的beautiful（漂亮的）与原文中的eye-catching（耀眼的）对应；题干中的feathers（羽毛）与原文中的plumage（鸟类羽毛）对应。答案为TRUE。
32	关键词	threat to chickens
	原文定位	第三段第二句The main concern is protection from predators—both domestic predators such as dogs and wild predators such as stoats and weasels.
	题解	**答案TRUE** 题干中的tame, household animals（驯服的家养动物）与原文中的domestic predators（家养的捕食者）对应；题干中的pose a threat（形成一种威胁）与原文中的protection from predators（采取免受其他捕食者骚扰的保护措施）对应。答案为TRUE。

33	关键词	at night, straw, the hen house
	原文定位	第三段第三句、第四句、第五句Backyard poultry need a secure place to roost at night, A cage or other structure...will suffice. Straw or non-toxic wood shavings can be spread on the floor and in the nesting boxes.
	题解	答案TRUE 题干中的at night（在晚上），straw（稻草）为原文重现，据此定位原文。题干中的other bedding（其他铺盖）与原文中的non-toxic wood shavings（无毒的木屑）对应，后面的定语从句被题干替换为后置定语scattered on the floor of the hen house（散落在鸡舍的地板上），其中题干中的scattered（散落）与原文中的spread（散布）对应；题干中的hen house（母鸡舍）与原文中的nesting boxes（巢箱）对应。
34	关键词	fly out of harm's way
	原文定位	第三段第六句Nocturnal predators are a danger and most chickens cannot flap their wings well enough to escape from peril.
	题解	答案FALSE 题干中的fly（飞）与原文中的flap（振翅而飞）对应；题干中的out of harm's way（脱离危险地带）与原文中的escape from peril（逃离危险）对应，但题干中的will manage to（能做到）与原文的否定cannot（不能）表达的意思相反。
35	关键词	Free-range chickens, a large hen house.
	原文定位	第三段末句If the birds are expected to stay in the chicken coop all day, a much larger structure is called for.
	题解	答案TRUE 题干中的Free-range chickens（自由放养的鸡）不需要a large hen house（一个大的鸡舍），原文中的stay in the chicken coop all day（整天待在鸡笼）需要much larger structure（更大的结构），题干与原文对应。

Questions 36–40

题型 句子填空题(Sentence Completion)

注意 句子填空题的题目要求中有字数限制。这种题型有两种形式：1）第一种是考生需按照要求的字数完成一个从文章中抽取出来的句子；2）第二种是题目中给出了前半个句子（该句与文章内容有关），考生需从若干个选项中选取合适的内容完成这个句子。考生有时需要多次使用某一个选项作答。

36	关键词	chickens, a good form of
	原文定位	第四段首句Chickens which are allowed to roam around the back garden during the day will prove to be safe, natural and effective methods of insect control.
	题解	答案insect control 题干中的Chickens, garden为原文重现，据此定位原文。题干中的good（好的）与原文中的effective（有效的）对应；题干中的form（形式）与原文中的methods（方法）对应，故原文of后的insect control（病虫害防治）即为答案。

37	关键词	scratching, soil, get rid of
	原文定位	第四段第二句Not only that, but their constant scratching in search of insects will take care of unwanted weeds under bushes and other plants and even provide some beneficial soil cultivation.
	题解	答案(unwanted) weeds　题干中的scratching（扒拉，刨），soil（土壤）为原文重现；题干中的not only...but...also（不但……而且……）与原文中的and对应；题干中的helps（帮助）与原文中的provide beneficial（提供有益的……）对应；题干中的get rid of（摆脱）与原文中的take care of（照顾）对应。
38	关键词	hens prefer, rain
	原文定位	第四段第七句、第八句This may include...in a clean, dry pen in times of extremely rainy weather. In dry weather, there is nothing more luxurious for a hen than a good dust bath to take care of mites and other problems.
	题解	答案dry weather　题干中的hen（母鸡）为原文重现；原文中的nothing more luxurious...than...用比较级形式表示最高级含义，意思是"没有比……更奢侈的了"，与题干中的prefer（喜欢）对应；题干中的rain（雨）与原文中的rainy（多雨的）为同根词。
39	关键词	chickens, make a connection, people
	原文定位	第四段倒数第四句、倒数第五句Older hens also respond well to being fed by hand...In both these cases, human presence is undoubtedly associated with food and will not only be tolerated but welcomed.
	题解	答案food　题干中的hand-reared（一手养大的）与原文中的fed by hand（亲手喂食）对应；题干中的connection（关系）与原文中的associated with...（与……相联系）对应；题干中的people（人）与原文中的human（人类）对应。题干是对原文两句的概括。
40	关键词	incubating eggs, consistent, warmth
	原文定位	倒数第二段首句、第二句When a hen goes "broody", she stops laying eggs and sits on the nest to incubate the clutch of eggs under her....because she must keep the eggs at a constant temperature and humidity.
	题解	答案humidity　题干中的Incubating（孵）与原文中的incubate（孵）为同根词；题干中的have（有）与原文中的keep（保持）对应；题干中的consistent（始终如一的）与原文中的constant（不变的）对应；题干中的warmth（温暖）与原文中的temperature（温度）对应，故and后的humidity（湿度）即为答案。

WRITING

WRITING TASK 1

名师解读

本题为投诉信。投诉信一直是移民类小作文常考的话题，其内容要点主要是：所要投诉或抱怨的事情是什么；将时间、地点及事情的经过及问题所在说清楚；你对解决问题的建议等。

本题的投诉理由为服务不周，一般在结构上可分为以下三个部分：

1. 自我介绍，表明投诉内容以及与收信人的相关性；

2. 陈述投诉内容，本题题目没有指明具体投诉内容，因此考生选择余地较大，一般来说，建议考生可以考虑卫生条件差、服务员的服务态度不好等。

3. 提出建议或者希望得到对方的赔偿或补偿。

高分范文

I am writing to **complain** about the meal I had in your restaurant in the evening last Saturday (Sept. 10th).

It is said that your restaurant offers excellent service in our area. So my family and I went to your restaurant to **celebrate** my wife's birthday last Saturday. However, the experience shocked me. At first, the sanitary condition was **unexpectedly bad** in your restaurant. The dirty water was flooding on the ground, which made our shoes wet. Secondly, the waiters and waitresses were wearing long faces all the time. One of the waiters just turned a **deaf** ear when I asked for some hot water. I could not believe my eyes that you were offering the best service in our area! What's more, the birthday cake offered by your restaurant was stale. My son and I were suffering diarrhea after coming back home. I was so disappointed at the service you provided last week.

I suggest that you should improve your management as soon as possible. And you'd better train your waiters and waitresses to level up their service **consciousness**. I am looking forward to enjoying the dinner in your restaurant some day.

Yours sincerely,

Loren (202 words)

WRITING TASK 2

文章结构

问题+原因+解决方案+结论

problem+reason1+reason2+reason3+solutions+conclusion
首段：背景句+引出现象
第二段：现象+原因1+原因2+原因3
第三段：解决方案
第四段：总结

思路点拨

步骤一：审题（<3分钟）

Research suggests that the majority of criminals who are sent to prison would commit crimes when set free. Why do you think this is the case? What can be done to solve this problem?

通读题目，了解大意，判断题型。

本题的题型为论说性的作文。题目的大意为：研究表明，大多数的罪犯被送进监狱，释放后将持续犯罪。你认为背后原因是什么？能做些什么来解决这个问题呢？

→再读题目，辨别关键词，区分主题词和限定词，推测考官的出题意图。

主题词：criminals, commit crimes, set free

限定词：do you think, solve this problem

步骤二：列大纲（<3分钟）

英文提纲	Introduction: recommit crimes after prison terms→negative and ceaseless damage Body: deal with this serious issue→three things should be mentioned→difficult to settle down→without any supervision→run after revenge→living problem→reinforce the guidance→treat them as equal as others Conclusion: have no right to impose our ideas on others
中文提纲	引出话题：重复犯罪→消极和不断的破坏 主体段落：处理这个问题→需要注意三个方面→不容易安定下来→没有监管→报复行为→生活问题→加强监管→平等对待 总结：没有权利把我们的想法强加给别人

高分范文

It is weird that some criminals, not all of them, will **recommit** crimes after prison terms. Obviously, this brings about negative and **ceaseless** damage in many aspects.

To deal with this serious issue, the priority of all is to seek the very reasons. When it comes to the motives of recommitting crimes, three things should be mentioned. Firstly, after their prison lives, usually, it is difficult to settle down in the city with a stable pay check and a life **insurance**, which may force them to reunite with the crew before in order to make a living. Namely, for criminals, committing crimes is a way to feed their own. Secondly, it should never be neglected that the governmental **supervision** is so vital that it will ensure all used-to-be criminals worry about the penalty if they did once more. Without any supervision, there is no security for city dwellers. Lastly, the worst situation is that some **lawbreakers** commit crimes only because they suffer ill treatment from others. In other words, they run after **revenge**.

The so-called purposeless crime poses huge menace to social peace. According to the reasons above, some solutions will show up: The living odds can be resolved through supplying more subsidies, because the living problem is the very basic thing the government should guarantee. In addition, the government and the local communities should also reinforce the guidance for those people, which will benefit both the residents and criminals as well. Finally, to cure criminals' mental **anxiety**, the whole society should, at least, treat them as equal as others, and then, we should care about their living conditions, materially and spiritually. All in all, criminals are a group of people who made some mistakes, intentionally or **accidentally**.

According to the law, we may punish them, but please remember that we have no right to impose our ideas on others. (315 words)

重点词汇

READING

payment	['peɪmənt]	*n.*	付款，支付；报酬
special	['speʃl]	*adj.*	特别的；专门的，专用的
discount	['dɪskaʊnt]	*n.*	折扣；贴现率
automatically	[ˌɔːtə'mætɪkli]	*adv.*	自动地；机械地；无意识地
sufficient	[sə'fɪʃnt]	*adj.*	足够的，充分的
instalment	[ɪn'stɔːlmənt]	*n.*	分期付款；装设；就职
fortnightly	['fɔːtnaɪtli]	*adv.*	隔周地；每两星期一次地
fingertip	['fɪŋgətɪp]	*n.*	指尖；指套
cheque	[tʃek]	*n.*	支票
flat iron			熨斗；烙铁
heat-protective		*adj.*	隔热保护的
hair shaft			毛干
blow-dry			吹干头发
serum	['sɪərəm]	*n.*	乳清；树液
gloss	[glɒs]	*n.*	光彩
mid-shaft		*n.*	中间水平
reflective	[rɪ'flektɪv]	*adj.*	反射的；反映的；沉思的
sheen	[ʃiːn]	*n.*	光彩，光辉，光泽
hairdo	['headuː]	*n.*	发型；发式
counteract	[ˌkaʊntər'ækt]	*v.*	抵消；中和；阻碍
contractor	[kən'træktə]	*n.*	承包人；立契约者
sub-contractor		*n.*	分包商
award	[ə'wɔːd]	*v.*	授予；判定
dispute	[dɪ'spjuːt]	*v.*	辩论；怀疑
obligation	[ˌɒblɪ'geɪʃn]	*n.*	义务；职责；债务
distinguish	[dɪ'stɪŋgwɪʃ]	*v.*	区别，区分；辨别
whereas	[ˌweər'æz]	*conj.*	然而；鉴于；反之
paid Parental Leave			带薪育婴假
eligible	['elɪdʒɪbl]	*adj.*	符合条件的；合格的，合适的
adoption	[ə'dɒpʃn]	*n.*	收养
entitlement	[ɪn'taɪtlmənt]	*n.*	权利；津贴
convenient	[kən'viːnɪənt]	*adj.*	方便的
egg-layer		*n.*	生育机器
council	['kaʊnsl]	*n.*	委员会；会议
regulation	[ˌregju'leɪʃn]	*n.*	管理；规则
rooster	['ruːstə]	*n.*	公鸡；狂妄自负的人
restriction	[rɪ'strɪkʃn]	*n.*	限制；约束；束缚
ornamental	[ɔːnə'mentl]	*adj.*	装饰的，装饰性的
eye-catching		*adj.*	引人注目的；耀眼的；显著的
plumage	['pluːmɪdʒ]	*n.*	翅膀；鸟类羽毛
distinctive	[dɪ'stɪŋktɪv]	*adj.*	有特色的，与众不同的
feathery	['feðəri]	*adj.*	柔软如羽毛的；生有羽毛的
strikingly	['straɪkɪŋli]	*adv.*	显著地；突出地，引人注目地
tail	[teɪl]	*n.*	尾巴；踪迹
exhibition	[ˌeksɪ'bɪʃn]	*n.*	展览，显示
domestic	[də'mestɪk]	*adj.*	家庭的；驯养的；国内的

predator	['predətə]	*n.*	捕食者
boost	[buːst]	*v.*	促进；增加
well-being	[ˌwel'biːɪŋ]	*n.*	幸福；康乐
fowl	[faʊl]	*n.*	家禽；鸟；飞禽
extremely	[ɪk'striːmli]	*adv.*	非常，极其；极端地
luxurious	[lʌg'ʒʊərɪəs]	*adj.*	奢侈的；丰富的；放纵的
intelligent	[ɪn'telɪdʒənt]	*adj.*	智能的；聪明的；理解力强的
incubate	['ɪnkjubeɪt]	*v.*	孵化；培养
nourishing	['nʌrɪʃɪŋ]	*adj.*	有营养的；滋养多的

WRITING

complain	[kəm'pleɪn]	*v.*	投诉；发牢骚；诉说
celebrate	['selɪbreɪt]	*v.*	庆祝；举行；赞美；祝贺
sanitary	['sænətri]	*n.*	公共厕所
unexpectedly	[ˌʌnɪk'spektɪdli]	*adv.*	出乎意料地，意外地
deaf	[def]	*adj.*	聋的
consciousness	['kɒnʃəsnəs]	*n.*	意识；知觉；觉悟；感觉
recommit	[riːkə'mɪt]	*v.*	再犯；再关进监狱
crime	[kraɪm]	*n.*	犯罪
ceaseless	['siːsləs]	*adj.*	不断的；不停的
insurance	[ɪn'ʃʊərəns]	*n.*	保险；保险费；保险契约；赔偿金
supervision	[ˌsuːpə'vɪʒn]	*n.*	监督，管理
lawbreaker	['lɔːbreɪkə]	*n.*	犯法者
revenge	[rɪ'vendʒ]	*n.*	报复；复仇
anxiety	[æŋ'zaɪəti]	*n.*	焦虑；渴望；挂念；令人焦虑的事
accidentally	[æksɪ'dentəli]	*adv.*	意外地；偶然地

General Training Reading and Writing TEST C

答案速查

READING

Section 1, Questions 1–14

1 C
2 F
3 C
4 E
5 D
6 A
7 E
8 A
9 TRUE
10 FALSE
11 NOT GIVEN
12 FALSE
13 FALSE
14 NOT GIVEN

Section 2, Questions 15–27

15 80 or higher
16 March 15
17 $30
18 13
19 international student
20 non-degree admission
21 complete academic information
22 Mortgage Loan Officer
23 innovative solutions
24 AVON Sales Representative
25 over 5 million
26 The Restaurant Manager
27 Quiznos Restaurant Manager

Section 3, Questions 28–40

28 FALSE
29 TRUE
30 FALSE
31 TRUE
32 NOT GIVEN
33 TRUE
34 FALSE
35 B
36 C
37 C
38 A
39 B
40 A

名师解析

READING

Section 1

体　裁　说明文
题　材　校园生活类
主　题　学生住宿指南、NIS课外活动
题　型　配对题、判断题

Questions 1–8

题型 配对题 (Matching Information)

注意 出现这样的提示：NB You may use any letter more than once.则说明某些选项可以重复选用。

1	关键词	tenancy, ended, landlord
	原文定位	C部分第二段Resident landlords have greater freedom to bring your tenancy to an end because it is acknowledged that, should the relationship between the landlord and tenant break down...
	题解	**答案C** 题干Your tenancy could be ended easily by the resident landlord.（房东可以轻易地结束你的租期。）符合原文Resident landlords have greater freedom to bring your tenancy to an end...（房东有较大的自由结束你的租期……），由原文的主动形式转换为被动形式。题干和原文的说法一致。
2	关键词	representative of the landlord
	原文定位	F部分首段第五句Your fellow tenants will see you as the landlord's representative on the ground.
	题解	**答案F** 题干的consider（视为）对应原文的see...as（将……看作……）; the representative of the landlord（房东的代表）也是the landlord's representative（房东的代表）的同义改写，因此答案为F。
3	关键词	squalid shared houses, a reasonable rent
	原文定位	C部分首段首句、第二句This may not be the type of accommodation that you had in mind when you imagined your wild student days ahead, but if you have left it later it may be preferable to some of the more squalid shared houses. At least with this type of accommodation you are generally guaranteed a well maintained property at a reasonable rent and no additional bills.
	题解	**答案C** 两个句子较长，如果从始至终看一遍，不仅会花很多时间，而且很可能读完之后，没有什么印象，也抓不住什么关键词。可以只关注含有关键词的部分并将关键词标示出来，如it may be preferable to some of the more squalid shared houses（它可能比一些脏乱的合租房要好一些），...at a reasonable rent...（租金合理）即可确定答案为C。

4	关键词	facilities, hotel
	原文定位	E部分第二段首句They are generally new build multi-storey blocks and are fitted out to a similar standard of a three star hotel with en-suite bathrooms and large communal areas.
	题解	**答案E** 正确答案常常是原文词句的改写。E段中指出...fitted out to a similar standard of a three star hotel with en-suite bathrooms and large communal areas（为三星级宾馆的相似标准，配有套房浴室及大型公共区域）。而题干somewhat like those of a hotel（类似宾馆的设施）是对原文含义的归纳。因此答案为E。
5	关键词	most expensive kind
	原文定位	D部分第二句The trouble is that it's expensive and therefore out of reach for most students.
	题解	**答案D** 题干考查的是最贵的住宿地点。D段指出Private Flat（私人公寓）的问题就是expensive（昂贵的），因此很多学生负担不起。
6	关键词	freshmen only
	原文定位	A部分首段第二句Due to their limited availability "halls" are generally only available to first year students.
	题解	**答案A** A部分指出generally only available to first year students（一般只有大一新生可以入住）。题干中的freshmen（大一新生）为原文first year students（一年级新生）的同义替换。
7	关键词	single room, a shared kitchen
	原文定位	E部分首段第三句These properties tend to be designed around the principles of a shared house with four or five single rooms grouped around a communal kitchen/diner.
	题解	**答案E** E段出现了a shared house with four or five single rooms（合租屋，带有四或五个单人房）和grouped around a communal kitchen/diner（周围是公用厨房/餐厅），由此可见可以住a single room（单间）但是只有a shared kitchen（公用厨房）。
8	关键词	a cleaner living environment, convenient for college life
	原文定位	A部分第二段第二句、第三句They are generally located on campus or within easy reach of the university. Other benefits include having your linen washed once a week and the bathrooms cleaned regularly.
	题解	**答案A** 题目中的观点与原文中的对应观点在句子形式上变化较大，造成对应困难。可将题干和原文的关键词摘取出来进行对比。题干have a cleaner living environment（生活环境较为整洁）对应原文the bathrooms cleaned regularly（浴室定期清理）；而is convenient for college life（方便大学生活）对应within easy reach of the university（在学校附近）。

Questions 9–14

题型 判断题(Identifying Information)

注意 使用句子对句子，词对词这种点对点的做题方法，多对照题目和原文。

9	关键词	life in China
	原文定位	A部分第三句Our programme aims to provide students with opportunities to cultivate and enrich existing skills, explore new areas of interest and to grow physically, socially and cognitively, and adjust to life in China.
	题解	答案TRUE　文中A部分指出了programme的若干目的，其中之一就是adjust to life in China（适应在中国的生活），题干get more familiar with their life in China（更加熟悉在中国的生活）与此对应，表达的意思完全吻合。
10	关键词	Ya Dong community
	原文定位	B部分首段第三句Local members of the Ya Dong community are encouraged to contact NIS to discuss the possibility of developing joint activities with NIS or for utilising NIS facilities outside regular school hours.
	题解	答案FALSE　注意坚持句子对句子，词对词这种点对点的做题方法，保证每个题目的正确定位，精读对照并验证题目和原文的替换和转化。能够发现题目中的at any time（在任何时候）与原文中的outside regular school hours（课余时间）矛盾，所以答案为FALSE。
11	关键词	2006
	原文定位	B部分第二段末句Since NIS initiated this programme in 2006 the programme has developed and we look forward to offering more exciting activities this year.
	题解	答案NOT GIVEN　题干中的begins（开始）对应原文的initiated（开始），因此题干中并列句的前半部分是正确的，但是complex（复合的）是原文未提到的新概念，所以答案为NOT GIVEN。
12	关键词	2009, English arts
	原文定位	B部分第二段末句Since NIS initiated this programme in 2006 the programme has developed and we look forward to offering more exciting activities this year.
	题解	答案FALSE　原文中列出了more exciting activities this year（今年更激动人心的活动），第一项列出的是Chinese arts（中国艺术），并没有English arts（英国艺术），所以答案为FALSE。
13	关键词	ACAMIS and CISSA
	原文定位	C部分第三句ACAMIS offers competitions in a range of sports for senior students as well as cultural activities and academic competitions, while CISSA provides sporting and cultural opportunities for Primary and Middle Year students within the Shanghai–Suzhou–Nanjing region.
	题解	答案FALSE　原文表明ACAMIS针对senior students（高中生），CISSA针对Primary and Middle Year students（小学生和初中生），而题目提及ACAMIS和CISSA针对students of any grade（所有年级），与原文矛盾。所以本题答案为FALSE。

14	关键词	representatives
	原文定位	D部分第三段首句Each house has a male and female house captain in MYP/DP and two representatives from Grade. House captains are elected by the students each year.
	题解	答案NOT GIVEN　文中并没提到representative（代表）的选举问题，所以答案为NOT GIVEN。

Section 2

体　裁　说明文
题　材　校园生活类
主　题　ADAMS大学录取条件、职位描述
题　型　句子填空题、简答题

Questions 15–21

题型 句子填空题(Sentence Completion)

注意 从形式上来看，句子填空题其实就是“迷你”的摘要填空题。可以将句子填空题看成是分解断裂开的摘要填空题。

15	关键词	Colorado Commission on Higher Education Admission Index, Index Score
	原文定位	首段第二句Students should have an Index Score of 80 or higher, based on the Colorado Commission on Higher Education Admission Index.
	题解	答案80 or higher　题干中的Colorado Commission on Higher Education Admission Index（科罗拉多高等教育入学指标委员会）是明显的定位词，主要是在首段出现。而在题目中，Index Score又是一个关键词，所以再次缩小范围定位到首段第二句。答案是80 or higher。
16	关键词	scholarship
	原文定位	第三段NOTE: If applying for scholarships or financ al aid, prospective students must be admitted by March 15.
	题解	答案March 15　由题干中的scholarship可知问题是与奖学金方面有关系。而文中第三段主要讲scholarships or financial aid（奖学金或助学金）方面的问题，那么就能判定此处必有答案。原文must be admitted by后的内容则是空格内应填入的内容，因此答案是March 15。
17	关键词	freshman, application fee
	原文定位	第四段的条目1　Send a completed application for admission, including the $30 application fee or complete our online application.
	题解	答案$30　题干的关键词为freshman，在原文中以黑体表示，可以迅速定位。再根据application fee可以确定空格内应填入的为表示钱数的数字。第1条中列出$30 application fee，因此答案为$30。

18	关键词	transfer students, 23 cumulative GPA
	原文定位	第五段Transfer students entering from an accredited college or university are required to submit official transcripts with a minimum of 13 transferable credit hours and a 23 cumulative GPA or higher.
	题解	**答案13** 同Q17，题干中的关键词transfer student在原文中以黑体表示，可以迅速定位。题干中的transferable credit hours 在原文重现，题干中的at least（至少）对应原文的a minimum of（至少），因此答案为13。
19	关键词	English proficiency
	原文定位	第八段首句A score of 550 or better on the TOEFL exam or successful completion of level 109 in an ESL programme will satisfy the English proficiency requirement.
	题解	**答案international student** 本题的关键词为English proficiency（英语水平），第八段出现了明显标志如TOEFL、ESL等，第八段的标题为International student Admission（留学生录取），因此答案为international student。
20	关键词	don't have financial aid, taking class only
	原文定位	倒数第四段首句、第十段首句A student who is interested in taking classes, but is not interested in a degree programme, may be accepted to Adams State College on a non-degree status. 和第十段首句Non-degree students are not eligible for financial aid.
	题解	**答案non-degree admission** 根据financial aid和taking class在原文定位，其中financial aid（经济援助）是原词再现，题干中的taking class（上课）与原文的taking classes是同义表达，因此non-degree admission即为答案。
21	关键词	non-degree student, test scores
	原文定位	倒数第三段第二句If a non-degree student wishes to change his/her status to degree seeking, the student must provide complete academic information, test scores, and other required information to the Office of Admissions.
	题解	**答案complete academic information** provide后的宾语即为空格应填入的内容，而所有宾语中只差一个complete academic information（完整的学业信息）。因此答案为complete academic information。

Questions 22–27

题型 简答题(Short-Answer Questions)

注意 简答题，相对于填空题会容易些，因为它有所指向。考生只要根据题目里疑问代词或副词来定位即可。

22	关键词	finance and funds processing
	原文定位	A部分第二句PNC is an established, growing and successful financial services company, with businesses organised around retail and commercial banking, asset management, and funds processing.
	题解	答案Mortgage Loan Officer 一般来讲，阅读题型中多数题型都具备“顺序性”特点，即出题者根据原文信息顺序依次出题，这样就便于定位。根据题干中的finance和fund processing进行原文定位，定位至A部分，该部分形容的job是Mortgage Loan Officer（抵押信贷员），因此答案是Mortgage Loan Officer。
23	关键词	IBM, most complex and technical issues
	原文定位	B部分第二段星号*1Develop innovative solutions to solve our clients' most complex business and technical issues.
	题解	答案innovative solutions 根据题干中的关键词IBM很容易定位至B部分。再根据另外的关键词most complex and technical issues寻找具体信息，可确定答案为innovative solutions（创新的解决方案）。
24	关键词	working at home
	原文定位	C部分Location: Work from home; work online
	题解	答案AVON Sales Representative 本题的关键词为working at home，浏览C部分Location: Work from home; work online与此对应；由此可知答案应为C部分对应的AVON Independent Sales Representative，但题目要求已限定NO MORE THAN THREE WORDS，故将答案缩略为AVON Sales Representative。
25	关键词	Avon Representatives, worldwide
	原文定位	C部分第三段Over 5 million Avon Representatives worldwide are enjoying these advantages...
	题解	答案over 5 million 根据题干里疑问代词How many确定答案与数字相关，再根据关键词AVON Representatives确定答案在C部分，因此查找C部分中的数字来定位，可以看出全世界有500多万的销售代表在为AVON工作，因此答案为over 5 million。
26	关键词	Quiznos Restaurant
	原文定位	D部分第二段The Restaurant Manager is responsible for the execution of internal systems, training of operational procedures and managerial functions such as: customer experience, speed of service...
	题解	答案The Restaurant Manager 根据题干中的关键词Quiznos Restaurant可迅速定位到D部分，题目为原文原句，较为容易。故答案为the Restaurant Manager。

27	关键词	relatively long work hours
	原文定位	D部分Requirements的第一条Ability to work extensive hours during openings including nights and weekends
	题解	答案Quiznos Restaurant Manager　D部分对manager的要求之一就是Ability to work extensive hours during openings including nights and weekends（能够加班，包括晚上和周末），对应题干的relatively long work hours（较长时间的工作），因此答案为Quiznos Restaurant Manager。此处仍需注意题目对字数的限制要求。

Section 3

体　　裁　　说明文
题　　材　　社会科学类
主　　题　　人类噪音会干扰鲸鱼的“情歌”
题　　型　　判断题、选择题、配对题

Questions 28–34

题型 判断题(Identifying Information)

注意 雅思阅读考查的是考生对于所考文章的理解，而不是考生的知识面或是对于某个问题的见解。切忌不依照文章内容判断而凭生活常识或个人感觉来答题，尤其是针对TRUE/FALSE/NOT GIVEN题。

28	关键词	20 hertz
	原文定位	第五段The whales belt out their songs at a frequency of about 20hertz—just below the range of human hearing—and at an intensity equivalent to sitting in the front row of a rock concert.
	题解	答案FALSE　根据题干中的20hertz迅速定位，原文为just below the range of human hearing（鲸鱼发出的声音人类根本听不到），而题干表示they can be heard by human（鲸鱼发出的声音人类能听到），与原文相反。答案为FALSE。
29	关键词	Low frequency sounds
	原文定位	第六段Since the human contribution to ocean noise is also dominated by the low frequency sounds produced by shipping vessels, oil and gas exploration, and military activities...
	题解	答案TRUE　题干中的mainly（主要地）和原文中的dominated（占主导地位）为同义关系，即题干为原文的同义转述。答案为TRUE。
30	关键词	hydrophone
	原文定位	第七段第二句The hydrophone fed into a converter box crafted by Clark to shift the whale songs to a higher pitch that humans could hear. 和末句 A computer also analysed the sounds and allowed the researchers to pinpoint the location of the individual making the noise.
	题解	答案FALSE　定位句指出hydrophone的作用是shift the whale songs to a higher pitch that humans could hear（将鲸鱼之歌转换为高音，使得人类能够听到），末句指出the location of the individual making the noise（发出声音的个体的位置）的是a computer，而不是hydrophone。

31	关键词	rhythm and pitch of the song
	原文定位	第八段第四句Only when the composition is played at about 60 times its actual speed is the rhythm and pitch variation apparent.
	题解	答案TRUE　题干将原文原句的倒装句式only when转换为普通句式，题干的at a higher speed（以较高的速度）对应原文的at about 60 times its actual speed（约为其实际速度的60倍）；而changes clearly（变化明显）对应variation apparent（明显的变化），即题干与原文一致。答案为TRUE。
32	关键词	eight to ten minutes
	原文定位	第八段第二句、第三句Then there is a 14-second pause before the fin whale hits the next note. The entire song lasts about eight to ten minutes.
	题解	答案NOT GIVEN　题干并列句的前半部分为原文原句，是正确的；但针对后半部分，原文只说到上个音符和下个音符之间间隔为14秒，并未提到停顿几次。答案为NOT GIVEN。
33	关键词	nine whales analysed
	原文定位	第九段末句In all nine cases the singers were male.
	题解	答案TRUE　题干All of the nine whales analysed（分析的九条鲸鱼）对应原文的In all nine cases（所有的九个案例中）；另外，原文的male为形容词，而题干的males为名词。题干与原文所述一致。答案为TRUE。
34	关键词	signals
	原文定位	倒数第四段首句But like people chatting in a crowded room, whales must have the ability to pick out signals from the rest of the noise, said Payne.
	题解	答案FALSE　通过原文和题目比较我们发现：原文表示whales must have the ability to pick out signals from the rest of the noise（鲸鱼肯定拥有从其余的噪音中辨认出信号的能力），而题干表示impossible for whales to pick out signals from others（鲸鱼无法从其余的噪音中辨认出信号），题目否定原文内容。答案为FALSE。

Questions 35–37

题型　选择题(Multiple Choice)

注意　选择题的答案常常是原文相关词句的改写。

35	关键词	cacophony
	原文定位	第六段Since the human contribution to ocean noise is also dominated by the low frequency sounds produced by shipping vessels, oil and gas exploration, and military activities...
	题解	答案B　研究者担忧的真正原因是人类制造了很多low frequency sounds（低频率的噪音）会对鲸鱼产生影响。

36	关键词	hydrophone
	原文定位	第七段第二句The hydrophone fed into a converter box crafted by Clark to shift the whale songs to a higher pitch that humans could hear.
	题解	**答案C** 题干考查关于hydrophone的错误陈述，因此定位到描述hydrophone的第七段。A、B、D三个选项的表述均可从原文中找到。用排除法可知应选C项。而且通过本段第二句的表述可知人类利用hydrophone是可以听到鲸鱼的歌声的。答案是C项。
37	关键词	attract females
	原文定位	第十一段首句Clark's team also surveyed all the fin whales in the area and found there were equal numbers of males and females—further supporting the idea that the singing was to attract females to the area.
	题解	**答案C** 题干为原文破折号后的原句further supporting the idea that the singing was to attract females to the area（进一步支持了歌声是用来吸引该区域的雌性鲸鱼的观点），因此破折号前的部分there were equal numbers of males and females（雄性鲸鱼和雌性鲸鱼的数量是一样的）应为正确答案，因此答案为C。

Questions 38–40

题型 配对题(Matching Information)

注意 题貌似是全篇文章的考查，其实考查的就是这些人所说的几句话。在之前的题目中涉及到的内容有助于确定答案。

38	关键词	a higher pitch
	原文定位	第七段首句、第二句Clark and his colleagues towed a hydrophone—an underwater microphone originally developed by the Navy to look for submarines—behind the research vessel to detect whale songs. The hydrophone fed into a converter box crafted by Clark to shift the whale songs to a higher pitch that humans could hear.
	题解	**答案A** 在看到本题题干时，就能够确定题干内容已多次出现过，通过对Q30和Q36的分析，可直接定位到第七段，继而锁定段首出现的Clark and his colleagues（克拉克和他的同事们）。
39	关键词	signals
	原文定位	倒数第四段首句But like people chatting in a crowded room, whales must have the ability to pick out signals from the rest of the noise, said Payne.
	题解	**答案B** 同Q38一样，本题的题干也出现过，由Q34的分析可以确定，Payne表示whales must have the ability to pick out signals from the rest of the noise（鲸鱼肯定拥有从其余的噪音中辨认出信号的能力）。

40	关键词	*Nature*
	原文定位	第十一段Clark's team also surveyed all the fin whales in the area and found there were equal numbers of males and females—further supporting the idea that the singing was to attract females to the area. The research is published in the June 20th issue of the journal *Nature*.
	题解	**答案A** 以*Nature*为关键词，可以迅速定位到第十一段，The research is published in the June 20th issue of the journal *Nature*. 此处的the research（研究）指的是前面Clark's team（克拉克的团队）的研究。

WRITING

WRITING TASK 1

名师解读

书信写作一定要记得：以完成任务为中心。题目中所有的细节必须涉及，所有的问题必须回答。TASK1中列出的三点，都必须回答。

书信的基本点：在考试中，无论遇到哪种类型的书信又或是题目中有任何的具体要求，都要谨记下列的三要素：

1. 明确地指出自己写信的目的
2. 清晰、准确地陈述事实
3. 使用坚定但礼貌的语言

高分范文

Dear Sir or Madam,

I am applying for a job overseas as a music edition, which not only **amuses** myself but also make the audience enjoy themselves. I am confident I can be **competent** for this job. As to the company, I expect being hired by the broadcasting station which I have been dreaming of for years. I am **definitely** sure that I can have the chance to learn many new techniques and then create more excellent works.

The reason why I am eager to work abroad can be summarised as follows: First I have learnt that American broadcasting companies enjoy a long history and a high **prestige** and are equipped with much advanced equipment. So working there can enable me to make great progress and put my potential into full play. Moreover, I would like a working atmosphere in which people there are all energetic, **motivated** and full of passion. To go to work abroad is just one little step toward my dream, and I still have a long way to go.

I really **appreciate** if you can offer such a superb job as I wish. Thank you in advance for considering my application. I hope to hear from you soon.

Yours sincerely,

Mandy Ya (208 words)

WRITING TASK 2

文章结构

提出问题+好处+坏处+自己观点

topic+advantage+disadvantage+opinion
首段：背景句+引出话题+正方观点+反方观点
第二段：好处
第三段：坏处
第四段：总结

思路点拨

步骤一：审题

Some people think the recent increase in cheap air travel brings benefits, while other people think it has drawbacks to the environment and the world's resources. Discuss both views and give your own opinion.

→通读题目，了解大意。

一些人认为当前廉价空中旅行的增加带来了好处，而另一些人认为对环境和世界资源有影响。讨论双方观点并提出自己的观点。

→再读题目，辨别关键词，区分主题词和限定词，推测考官的出题意图。

主题词：cheap air travel, benefits, drawbacks

限定词：discuss both views and give your opinion

步骤二：列大纲

英文提纲	Introduction: The most expensive and comfortable way to travel around the globe is by jet obviously (topic)→good for the global communication (one view)→bad for the global environment (the other view) Body: Advantages: without any regional limit→the global communication and understanding improves Disadvantages: fuels costing→pollution→risk and danger Conclusion: a must for international business and cultural exchanges→use it soundly
中文提纲	引出话题：在世界各地旅行最贵、最舒适的方式就是乘坐飞机（话题）→有利于全球交流（一方观点）→不利于全球环境（另一方观点） 主体段： 好处：没有区域限制→提高全球交流及理解 坏处：燃料消耗→污染→风险与危险 总结：是国际商务和文化交流的必需条件→合理利用

高分范文

The most expensive and comfortable way to travel around the globe is by jet obviously. However, since the invention of air flight, the debate over air flight never stops. The focus is that it is good for the global communication but it is bad for the global environment. Personally, both sides of the issue should be **taken into consideration** as follows.

When it comes to the benefits of air travelling, two sections should be mentioned: For one thing, nothing can compare with the jet which takes people to anywhere they want without any regional limit but only with courage and imagination. In other words, the air flight enables people to broaden their **horizons**. For another, modern transportation helps the world become smaller and more effective.

Thanks to air travel, the global communication and understanding improves day by day. In the morning, you stay in China, but at night you may drink coffee beside the Seine.

However, the drawbacks it has should also be focused. Firstly, it costs a huge amount of fuel like oil for a single flight. Taking automobiles for example, an air flight uses about 1,500 times as much fuel as a private car for the same distance. Secondly, using too much energy naturally results in **discharging** too much pollution. Besides, air pollution that we have learnt for ages, soil, water and noise pollution are also caused during the flying. Lastly, this most advanced transportation exists with high risk and danger. Every time when an air crash happens, there are rare **survivors**.

In conclusion, air travel is a must for international business and cultural exchanges. To use it soundly, we should try our best to reduce pollution and the use of fuel, and most importantly, keep it taking off and landing safely. (294 words)

重点词汇

READING

accommodation	[əˌkɒmə'deɪʃn]	*n.*	住宿
availability	[əˌveɪlə'bɪləti]	*n.*	可用性
abide by			遵守
hurdle	['hɜːdl]	*n.*	障碍
squalid	['skwɒlɪd]	*adj.*	肮脏的
guarantee	[ˌgærən'tiː]	*v.*	保证
vulnerable	['vʌlnərəbl]	*adj.*	易受攻击的
landlord	['lændlɔːd]	*n.*	房东
acknowledged	[ək'nɒlɪdʒd]	*adj.*	公认的
camaraderie	[ˌkæmə'rɑːdəri]	*n.*	友情
solidarity	[ˌsɒlɪ'dærəti]	*n.*	团结
exclusive	[ɪk'skluːsɪv]	*adj.*	唯一的；专用的
representative	[ˌreprɪ'zentətɪv]	*n.*	代表
extra-curricular		*adj.*	课外的
integral	['ɪntɪgrəl]	*adj.*	完整的，整体的
cultivate	['kʌltɪveɪt]	*v.*	培养
enrich	[ɪn'rɪtʃ]	*v.*	使富足，丰富
existing skills			生存技巧
cater to			迎合
adjust to			适应，调整
facility	[fə'sɪləti]	*n.*	设施
incorporate	[ɪn'kɔːpəreɪt]	*v.*	合并
tournament	['tɜːnəmənt]	*n.*	比赛，竞赛
presentation	[ˌprezn'teɪʃn]	*n.*	陈述
application	[ˌæplɪ'keɪʃn]	*n.*	申请
admission	[əd'mɪʃn]	*n.*	允许进入；入学
combine	[kəm'baɪn]	*v.*	使联合
scholarship	['skɒləʃɪp]	*n.*	奖学金
financial	[faɪ'nænʃl]	*adj.*	财政的
prospective	[prə'spektɪv]	*adj.*	预期的
clarification	[ˌklærəfɪ'keɪʃn]	*n.*	澄清；净化
authourity	[ɔː'θɒrəti]	*n.*	权威
transcript	['trænskrɪpt]	*n.*	手抄本
cumulative	['kjuːmjələtɪv]	*adj.*	积累的
proficiency	[prə'fɪʃnsi]	*n.*	熟练
accredit	[ə'kredɪt]	*v.*	信任，授权
association	[əˌsəʊʃɪ'eɪʃn]	*n.*	联合
eligible	['elɪdʒəbl]	*adj.*	符合条件的，合格的
veteran	['vetərən]	*n.*	退伍军人
establish	[ɪ'stæblɪʃ]	*v.*	建立
retail	['riːteɪl]	*v.*	零售
asset management			资产管理
innovative	['ɪnəveɪtɪv]	*adj.*	创新的
integrated	['ɪntɪgreɪtɪd]	*adj.*	综合的，完整的
potential	[pə'tenʃl]	*adj.*	潜在的
incentive	[ɪn'sentɪv]	*n.*	动机

coordinate	[kəʊ'ɔːdɪneɪt]	*adj.*	同等的，并列的
contractor	[kən'træktə]	*n.*	订约人，承包人
utility	[juː'tɪləti]	*n.*	效用，功用
certificate	[sə'tɪfɪkət]	*n.*	证书
sanitation	[ˌsænɪ'teɪʃn]	*n.*	卫生
operational	[ˌɒpə'reɪʃənl]	*adj.*	操作的
serenade	[ˌserə'neɪd]	*v.*	为……唱小夜曲
bassist	['beɪsɪst]	*n.*	低音歌手
sonar	['səʊnaː]	*n.*	声波定位仪
vessel	['vesl]	*n.*	船
courtship	['kɔːtʃɪp]	*n.*	求爱
equivalent	[ɪ'kwɪvələnt]	*adj.*	相等的
dominate	['dɒmɪneɪt]	*v.*	支配，占优势
frequency	['friːkwənsi]	*n.*	频率
cacophony	[kə'kɒfəni]	*n.*	刺耳的音调，杂音
submarine	[ˌsʌbmə'riːn]	*n.*	潜水艇
hydrophone	['haɪdrəfəʊn]	*n.*	水中听音器
pinpoint	['pɪnpɔɪnt]	*v.*	查明
ambiguity	[ˌæmbɪ'gjuːəti]	*n.*	含糊
sample	['saːmpl]	*n.*	取样，抽取
grinding	['graɪndɪŋ]	*adj.*	摩擦的
elusive	[ɪ'luːsɪv]	*adj.*	难懂的

WRITING

amuse	[ə'mjuːz]	*v.*	娱乐
competent	['kɒmpɪtənt]	*adj.*	胜任的；有能力的
definitely	['defɪnətli]	*adv.*	清楚地；明确地
prestige	[pre'stiːʒ]	*n.*	威望，声望
motivated	['məʊtɪvetɪd]	*adj.*	有动机的
appreciate	[ə'priːʃɪeɪt]	*v.*	感激
take...into consideration			考虑到……
when it comes to...			当谈到……
horizon	[hə'raɪzn]	*n.*	视野
discharge	[dɪs'tʃaːdʒ]	*v.*	排放
survivor	[sə'vaɪvə]	*n.*	幸存者

General Training Reading and Writing TEST D

答案速查

READING

Section 1, Questions 1–14

1 NO
2 NOT GIVEN
3 YES
4 NO
5 YES
6 on December 1
7 2
8 permanent residents
9 any other credentials
10 (a) mnemonics
11 key concepts
12 goals to achieve
13 Thursdays
14 5mg

Section 2, Questions 15–27

15 collect personal information
16 maturity
17 parental control features
18 age
19 Administrator account
20 Internet Explorer
21 anonymity
22 a first name
23 FALSE
24 FALSE
25 TRUE
26 NOT GIVEN
27 TRUE

Section 3, Questions 28–40

28 B
29 C
30 D
31 D
32 insecurities and anxiety
33 problems
34 the scrutiny
35 NO
36 NO
37 NO
38 YES
39 NOT GIVEN
40 YES

名师解析

READING

Section 1

体　裁　　说明文
题　材　　校园生活类
主　题　　有关新生入学需提交的内容和入学程序、关于大学课程学习技巧的指导
题　型　　判断题、简答题、句子填空题

Questions 1–5

题型 判断题 (Identifying Writer's Views/Claims)

注意 G类阅读短文通常选自通知、广告、活页、指导手册、书籍、报纸、杂志等。第一部分多考查考生基本的“社会生存”英语，短文内容包括广告、时间表、通知等。本篇文章为一则通知。

1	关键词	earliest date, summer application
	原文定位	表格中第二栏中第二句The online summer/fall application opens on August 1.
	题解	**答案NO** 原文提到夏季/秋季在线申请系统于8月1号开放。题干中的October 1（10月1日）与原文August 1（8月1日）表述不符。
2	关键词	scholarship applicants
	原文定位	表格中第二栏中第二项Scholarship applicants must apply for admission using the online Apply Texas Application for Admission.
	题解	**答案NOT GIVEN** 奖学金申请人必须通过Texas入学申请来提交申请。而题干的前半部分表述与原文一致，但是题干中后半部却说申请人only when apply for admission（只有在申请入学时）才能使用这个系统，文章没有提及。
3	关键词	official transcript
	原文定位	第四栏中第一项An official transcript includes...usually through the end of the junior year.
	题解	**答案YES** 题干中的includes the signature of a school official, the size of the class, and high school coursework（包括校方领导签名、班级规模及中学所学课程）与原文定位处的信息点相对应。
4	关键词	pay $60
	原文定位	表格第七栏中左栏中标题Non-refundable $60 application processing fee ($90 for international applicants)
	题解	**答案NO** 不可退款的60美元的申请手续费（90美元是国际申请的费用）。题干中的will be returned in the future（将来退款）与原文Non-refundable（不可退款）不符。

5	关键词	copy of the Residency Affidavit
	原文定位	表格中第八栏中第二项International students who qualify for Texas residency (under HB 1403): submit a complete copy of the Residency Affidavit.
	题解	答案YES　国际生有资格申请德克萨斯州的住所，需要提交一份完整的居住的宣誓书副本。题干和原文完全对应，只是句子的结构发生了变化。

Questions 6–9

题型　简答题 (Short-Answer Questions)

注意　简答题通常是用“5W+H”的疑问词进行提问。

6	关键词	the online summer/fall application
	原文定位	第二段第二行Summer/Fall Deadline: December 1
	题解	答案on December 1　原文指出夏季/秋季在线申请系统于12月1号结束。其中原文中的Deadline（截止期限）与题干中的end是同义替换。
7	关键词	essays
	原文定位	表格中第三栏首句Include two admissions essays; the easiest way to submit your essays is with your Apply Texas online application.
	题解	答案2　题干询问所需文章的数量，根据关键词essays定位到原文，可知必须提交两篇论文，其中一个最方便的提交方式是通过“Texas入学申请系统”在线提交。
8	关键词	photocopy
	原文定位	表格中第八栏中第三项Permanent residents: submit a photocopy of the front of your permanent resident card.
	题解	答案permanent residents　永久居民需要提交一个永久居民卡的正面复印件，所以答案为permanent residents（永久居民）。
9	关键词	home-schooled
	原文定位	表格中第八栏中第四项Home-schooled students: submit any other credentials that reflect your academic potential (such as SAT Subject Test scores or dual credit coursework).
	题解	答案any other credentials　在校生需提交任何能反映自己学术能力的证书（比如美国高考成绩或双学分课程），注意题干的字数限制。

Questions 10–14

题型 句子填空题(Sentence Completion)

注意 句子填空题的题目多是长陈述句。从形式上来看，句子填空题其实就是“迷你”的摘要填空题。从内容上来看，句子填空题常是给出一个空（也有两到三个，但所需填写的空的内容多是相并列成份）来让考生填补相对重要的信息。

10	关键词	Aunt Sally
	原文定位	第二段第二句A really basic example of a mnemonic is “Please excuse my dear Aunt Sally” which stands for parenthesis, exponents, multiplication, division, addition, and subtraction.
	题解	**答案 (a) mnemonics** 根据题干中的Please excuse my dear Aunt Sally（请原谅我亲爱的莎莉姑妈），在原文进行定位。题干中的illustrate（解释）与原文中的basic example（基本的例子）对应，importance of（……的重要性）与原文中的really basic（最基本的）对应。所以答案是(a) mnemonics。
11	关键词	Flash cards, vocabulary, formulas
	原文定位	第四段首句Making flash cards can be a bit time-consuming, but flash cards are helpful tools in remembering vocabulary, formulas, and key concepts.
	题解	**答案key concepts** 根据题干中的关键词Flash cards（抽认卡）定位答案，题干中的Flash cards（抽认卡），helpful tools（有力工具），remembering（记忆），vocabulary（词汇），formulas（公式）均为原文重现，与题干进行对比，直接得出答案。
12	关键词	productivity, possibly
	原文定位	第五段第二句You' re more likely to be productive if you have goals to achieve.
	题解	**答案goals to achieve** 题干中的productivity（效率）与原文中的productive（多产的）为同根词，题干中的possibly（可能）与原文中的likely to（可能）为同义替换；题干的主语One（任何人）指代的是原句的主语you（你）。同时通过对比，题干与原文的句型一致。
13	关键词	notorious, college nights
	原文定位	第七段倒数第三句Thursdays are notorious for being college nights, so don't plan on studying late that night.
	题解	**答案Thursdays** 根据关键词college nights进行答案定位，与原句对比，题干中的notorious（臭名昭著的），college（大学），nights（晚上），so don't plan to study late that night（不要计划在那一天学得太晚）均为原文重现，所以句首的时间名词Thursdays即为答案。

TEST D

14	关键词	Ritalin and Adderall, at first
	原文定位	末段倒数第二句If you choose to go that route and try it (not recommended), be sure to try small doses at first (5mg or 10mg) so you can see its effects.
	题解	答案5mg 根据关键词Ritalin and Adderall（盐酸哌醋甲酯和阿德拉药物）定位答案所在的段落。题干中的主语students（学生）替换原文中的主语you（你）；题干中的want to use Ritalin and Adderall（想要使用药物）与原文中的choose to go that route（选择使用药物）对应；原文中it（它）指代前文的Ritalin and Adderall；题干中的at first（首先），doses（剂量）均为原文重现，所以括号内的内容即为答案。

Section 2

体　裁　说明文

题　材　家庭生活、校园生活

主　题　如何提高家庭的网络安全、关于奖学金的介绍

题　型　摘要填空题、判断题

Questions 15–22

题型 摘要填空题(Summary Completion)

注意 考生需按照要求的字数完成从文章中抽取出来的段落，题目的指示中会说明考生最多可以使用多少个单词。本类题一般遵循“顺序原则”。

15	关键词	particularly, sites
	原文定位	Step1首段第二句Pay particular interest to sites that collect personal information.
	题解	答案collect personal information 题干particularly attention should be paid（特别注意）与原文pay particular interest（特别注意）为同义替换，题干中的Web sites（网站）与原文中的sites（网站）对应，故that引导的定语从句后的内容即为答案。
16	关键词	appropriate
	原文定位	Step1第二段首句As a parent you have a unique opinion on what kind of content is appropriate for your child depending on his age, maturity, and your personal beliefs.
	题解	答案maturity 题干中的is approriate for chibren（适合孩子）与原文is appropriate for your child是同义替换，题干中的child's age（孩子的年龄），personla beliefs（个人信仰）均为原文再现，所以原文所列的第二项内容maturity即为答案。
17	关键词	Windows Vista
	原文定位	Step1第二段第二句Windows Vista introduces a rich and powerful set of parental control features to help parents monitor, manage, and administer their children's computer use and help keep them safe.
	题解	答案parental control features 根据关键词Windows Vista（微软的Vista系统）定位答案，与原句对比，题干的结构和词语均为原文重现。考生只需简单对比，即可得出答案。

18	关键词	software, filter information
	原文定位	Step1第三段首句Software that helps you filter information based on each child's age to help protect them from content you don't want them to see.
	题解	答案age　题干中的Software（软件），filter information（过滤信息），help protect them from（使他们远离），content（内容）均为原文重现；be used to（被用来）与原文helps（帮助）对应，故based on each child's （基于每个孩子的不同）后的age（年龄）即为答案。
19	关键词	with full control over the computer
	原文定位	Step2首段第三句As a parent you can give yourself an Administrator account with full control over the computer, and give your children Limited User accounts, with restricted controls.
	题解	答案Administrator account　题干中的Parents（父母）为原文重现，指代原句的主语you；themselves与原句中的yourself对应；题干中的give（给予），with full control over the computer（完全控制计算机），limited user accounts（被控制的使用者账户）均为原文重现。
20	关键词	assign security levels
	原文定位	Step2第二段第二句Internet Explorer helps you control your security and privacy preferences by allowing you to assign security levels to Web sites.
	题解	答案Internet Explorer　本题只需根据关键词assign security levels（确定安全等级）进行定位，与原句对比，题干的句子的结构和词语均为原文重现。
21	关键词	imposters and predators
	原文定位	Step3首段第二句But the anonymity of the Internet can also put children at risk of falling victim to imposters and predators.
	题解	答案anonymity　本题根据关键词imposters and predators（冒名顶替者和江湖骗子）进行定位，与原句对比，题干的句子的结构和词语均为原文重现。of the Internet（网络的）前的anonymity（匿名者）为答案，原词重现。
22	关键词	to help minimise your children's vulnerability, nickname
	原文定位	Step3 首段末句To help minimise your children's vulnerability, teach them to take precautions such as；第一星号首句Using only a first name or nickname to identify themselves.
	题解	答案a first name　题干关键词help minimize your children's vulnerability（为了将孩子受攻击的可能性降至最低）为原文重现，根据其进行定位。题干中的or nickname（或昵称），identify themselves（表明他们自己的身份）均为原文重现，题干中的be used to（被用来）与原文Using（用）对应，题干将动名词短语改写为that引导的宾语从句，故原句中Using（用）的宾语即为题干的主语。

TEST D

Questions 23–27

题型 判断题(Identifying Information)

注意 题目会提供一组陈述。陈述涉及事实性信息，考生需回答这些陈述是否与文章中的信息一致。答案的形式有TRUE, FALSE或NOT GIVEN。这种题型考查考生跳读、扫读和对细节进行阅读理解的能力。

23	关键词	type, scholarship
	原文定位	Types of scholarships项下首句Truth is there are scholarships designed for almost every type of student.
	题解	**答案FALSE** 原文说奖学金几乎为所有类型的学生设置，而题干说奖学金为每个类型的学生设置，与原文不符，注意副词almost（几乎，差不多）与every（每个）不可视为对应词汇。
24	关键词	GPA, performance
	原文定位	Types of scholarships项下第一星号首句Academic scholarships abound and are based on GPA and performance in school.
	题解	**答案FALSE** 学术奖学金是基于学校提供的平均分数的，而题干则用了All scholarships，原文补充到Other scholarships are based on athletics, skills or extra-curricular activities（其他奖学金基于体育、技巧或课外活动），所以All scholarships的说法不正确。
25	关键词	merit, need-based
	原文定位	Scholarship Providers项第一星号首句Institution specific scholarships, or academic scholarships, come directly from the college to which you are applying and often include both merit and need-based Programmes.
	题解	**答案TRUE** 题干中的academic scholarships（学术奖学金），come from（来自），often include（通常包括），both merit and need-based Programmes（优等和基本奖学金项目）均为原文重现，所以本句描述是正确的。
26	关键词	charitable organisations
	原文定位	Scholarship Providers项第三星号首句Charitable organizations nationally and locally based.
	题解	**答案NOT GIVEN** 原文说国家和当地的慈善组织都提供奖学金，但题干所说的慈善组织与大学相比提供more scholarships（更多的奖学金）的内容在原文中并没有提到。
27	关键词	guidance, career counselor
	原文定位	末段第二句A good resource should be your high school guidance or career counselor, local teen centre or community centre.
	题解	**答案TRUE** 题干中的High school guidance or career counselor（高中或职业顾问指导）为原文重现，are（是）与原文中be（是）对应，the best sources（最好来源）与原文中good resource（好的资源）对应，题干表明其中的一个机构是奖学金的最好来源，并无错误。

Section 3

体　裁　说明文
题　材　科学研究
主　题　揭示做梦的机理
题　型　选择题

Questions 28–31

题型 选择题(Multiple Choice)

注意 选择题看似简单，但实际上比较难。它的特点是：四个选项，哪个都像正确选项。好像在原文中都提到了，但又都和原文的叙述有差异，所以很容易选错。这种题型应该先找出题干中的关键词，最好先定位到原文中的一个段落。然后从头到尾快速阅读该段落，根据题干中的其他关键词及选项确定正确答案。

28	关键词	deepest sleep
	原文定位	第三段第四句Our brain activity throughout these stages is gradually slowing down so that by deep sleep, we experience nothing but delta brain waves—the slowest brain waves.
	题解	**答案B** A项所说第二阶段应该为a slightly deeper sleep，与原文“在这些阶段我们大脑的活动逐渐减慢，以便进入只存在最慢的脑波（delta脑波）的深睡眠状态”不符。C项提到的REM sleep应该在深度睡眠之后，D项入睡数分钟就进入了REM sleep也与原文不符。
29	关键词	distinguished characteristic, REM
	原文定位	第三段末句REM sleep is primarily characterised by movements of the eyes and is the fifth stage of sleep.
	题解	**答案C** 快速眼动睡眠最主要的特点就是眼部运动，这是the fifth stage of sleep（睡眠的第五个阶段）。
30	关键词	the content of dreams, more easily
	原文定位	How to Improve Your Dream Recall项中第二段提到Set your alarm to go off every hour and half so you' ll wake up around the times that you leave REM sleep when you' re most likely to remember your dreams.
	题解	**答案D** 原文说设置一个或半个小时的闹钟，在这个时间醒来离开眼动睡眠状态，这时你更可能记住你的梦。B项属于偷换概念，文章原意为“提醒自己remember（记住）你的梦”，而题干却为have a dream（做个梦）。
31	关键词	flying dreams
	原文定位	Flying项末句If you are afraid while flying, you may have challenges that you don't feel up to.
	题解	**答案D** A项与Flying项第三句和第四句对应...flying means you are on top of things. You are in control of the things that matter to you.（飞翔表示你处在事物的顶端，能掌控任何对你重要的事情），属原形重现。B项与Flying项中第六句It may also mean you are strong-willed and feel like no one and nothing can defeat you.（这个梦也可能意味着你很有毅力，感觉所向披靡）一致。C项同Flying项中第五句Or, maybe you' ve just gained a new perspective on things.（也许你对某些事情获得了一个新视野）。只有D项与原文不符，文章只说如果飞翔时感到害怕，就说明可能你挑战的是一个你不能胜任的工作，并没有如题干所说的作者害怕飞翔。

Questions 32–34

题型 句子填空题(Sentence Completion)

注意 首先详细阅读答题指引，获取必要的答题信息，利用语法知识确定句子缺失的部分。然后仔细查看所给句子的含义，并找出关键词语，利用所给部分的关键词语在文章中找出相关句子后，在文章中的相关句子里，选取缺失部分（即答案）。

32	关键词	falling
	原文定位	Being naked in public项第四条You're falling, falling, falling...and then you wake up. This is a very common dream and is said to symbolise insecurities and anxiety.
	题解	答案insecurities and anxiety 题干中which is said to（这是说）与原文中的and is said to（并说）为同义转换，所以symbolise的宾语即为答案。
33	关键词	chased
	原文定位	Being chased 项第二句What it usually symbolises is that you' re running away from your problems.
	题解	答案problems 这通常表明你在逃避一些问题。 题干running away from“逃离于……”， means（意味着）与symbolises（象征着）为同义词替换，所以从symbolise后的宾语从句中便可找到答案。
34	关键词	an examine means
	原文定位	Taking an exam 项倒数第二句You don't feel prepared or able to hold up to the scrutiny.
	题解	答案the scrutiny 题干don't feel prepared for（没做好准备）后面需要名词形式，原文don't feel prepared or able to hold up to（没有做好准备或者不能经得起）与其对应，应填写the scrutiny（严格检查）。

Questions 35–40

题型 判断题(Identifying Writer's Views/Claims)

注意 题目会给出一组信息，考生需在文章中找到出现这些信息的段落。需要寻找的信息包括：特定信息、某种事情/事物的例子、事件等发生的原因、一个描述、一个总结、一个解释等。考生有可能需要在同一个段落里寻找不止一个信息。

35	关键词	early theories
	原文定位	首段第二句Early civilisations thought dream worlds were real, physical worlds that they could enter only from their dream state.
	题解	答案NO 文章提到早期的理论认为梦的世界是真实的物质世界，并且只能从睡梦状态进入，并没有指出题干中的the reflection（反思）之意，所以错误。

36	关键词	physiological theories
	原文定位	第二段第二句Psychological theories are based on the idea that dreaming allows us to sort through problems, events of the day or things that are requiring a lot of our attention.
	题解	答案NO 题干中的prevent...from与原文的allow...to do意思相反，导致题干所述信息与原文信息相悖，所以答案是NO。
37	关键词	REM, primarily
	原文定位	第四段末句REM sleep is primarily characterised by movements of the eyes and is the fifth stage of sleep.
	题解	答案NO 快速眼动睡眠最主要的特点就是眼部运动，这发生在the fifth stage of sleep（睡眠的第五个阶段）。题干REM occurs at the third and fourth stage与原文不符。答案是NO。
38	关键词	dreams，remember
	原文定位	How to Improve Your Dream Recall 项首段末句The fact that they are so hard to remember makes their importance seem less.
	题解	答案YES 作者指出：由于梦很难被记住，所以看起来不太重要。题干difficult与原文hard是同义词替换，importance seem less与not seem important对应。答案是YES。
39	关键词	increase your dream recall
	原文定位	How to Improve Your Dream Recall中第二段Here are some steps you can take to increase your dream recall.
	题解	答案NOT GIVEN 原文所述加强梦境记忆的五种方式没有包括题干的Trying to get recorded what you said or did（尝试记录梦中的所说、所做）。答案是NOT GIVEN。
40	关键词	naked
	原文定位	Being naked in public中第三项If we don't care that we' re naked, the interpretation is that we' re comfortable with whom we are.
	题解	答案YES 原文是说在梦境中如果我们不介意自己处于裸体状态，那么可解释为我们满足于自己的身份、地位等。这与题干中的满意现状是一个意思。答案为YES。

WRITING

WRITING TASK 1

名师解读

本题要求考生给校方写一封信，内容包括未来一个月将缺课的原因和这个月如何补习功课。

首先，称呼要注意格式，称呼后面的标点一般只能用逗号。其次，点名信件主题：解释将缺课的原因。第三段征求建议，最后信尾为客套语 ，即写信人在信的左（或右）下角，写上谦称。一般有Sincerely, Sincerely yours, Yours sincerely, Friendly yours, Truly yours, Yours truly, Cordially yours, Yours cordially等，别忘了信尾签名。

高分范文

Dear Mr Smith,

I am writing to explain my absence from last week's classes.

On November 20, 2013, I was involved in a serious motor vehicle accident. I was transported to the hospital in an **ambulance**, where I was treated for a broken ankle, **fractured collarbone**, and 3 **bruised** ribs. My doctor advised me to have a complete bed rest for 6 weeks, and as a result, I will be unable to attend classes in the coming one month.

I am concerned about keeping up with my studies, and have been doing the required readings, as assigned by my professors. My biggest concern is whether I will be **eligible** to write the final exams in June. Would you please advise me regarding my courses and exams, **specifically** if there will be any special consideration given to me in light of my current situation?

Thank you for your kind assistance. I look forward to hearing from you soon.

Sincerely,

Richard Jiang (162 words)

WRITING TASK 2

文章结构

提出问题+分析原因+总结

problem+reason 1+reason 2+conclusion
第一段：背景句+引出话题
第二段：原因1+影响
第三段：原因2+影响
第四段：总结+建议

思路点拨

步骤一：审题（<3分钟）

Surveys show that in many countries, people are living longer but increased life expectancy has many implications for the aging individuals and for society as a whole. What are the possible effects of longer living for individuals and society?

→通读题目，了解大意。

调查显示，许多国家的人民都很长寿，但是预期寿命增长对个体老龄化和整个社会分别有怎样的影响呢?

→细读题目，分析句子间的逻辑关系。

题目先指出现状：调查显示许多国家的人民都很长寿。而后用but话锋一转，这个现象到底对the aging individuals（个体老龄化）和 society as a whole（整个社会）有什么影响呢? 这是需要我们重点分析的地方。

→再读题目，辨别关键词，区分主题词和限定词，推测考官的出题意图。

主题词：effects, longer living

限定词：individuals, society

步骤二：列大纲（<3分钟）

英文提纲	Introduction: old age boom → the effects for both individual & public Body: for individuals: the generation gap→ pressing pressure for the families especially the next generation for the society: loss of labour force→ diminish the range of society → unemployment Conclusion: the government and individuals cooperate and collaborate
中文提纲	引出话题： 老龄化 → 对于个人的影响和社会的影响 主体段： 对个人的影响：代沟→对于下一代产生了巨大的家庭压力 对社会的影响：缺少劳动力→社会规模减小→失业问题 总结： 政府和个人齐心协力

高分范文

Benefiting from the **demographic bonus**, China is confronting an **unremarkable** old age boom crisis that many developed countries have already **encountered**. With the number of the old generation increasing, the pressure has become more and more irresistible. The following sections will analyse the effects from both individual and public aspects.

What the old age boom brings about to individuals can be divided into two parts. For one thing, it is impossible for all the old generations to follow the new trends of society; therefore a generation gap will appear between the old and the young. For another, if a family consists of more old people and fewer young ones, it will face a pressing economic burden of living and health care.

In addition, to a society, the old age boom is not a good sign for the modernisation as well. Firstly, each society whose **vigour** is endless demands more and more people to work as labour force for a certain period of time. However, with the number of old people growing, the loss and lack of labour force will be a huge crisis for those nations. Secondly, with a certain number of residents, the nation will develop and maintain a certain number of companies and factories **in accordance with** the demands of society. With a high **mortality** rate but a low birth rate, the local government has no other choices but to **diminish** the local scale of production, which will cause unemployment at the same time.

In conclusion, the old age boom is a huge social problem for both developing and developed countries. To deal with this problem, governments and individuals should **collaborate** as much as possible. (278 words)

重点词汇

READING

prompt	[prɒmpt]	*n.*	提示，提示符
signature	['sɪgnətʃə]	*n.*	署名；信号
transcript	['trænskrɪpt]	*n.*	成绩单；改写本
principal	['prɪnsəpl]	*n.*	校长；资本
permanent	['pɜːmənənt]	*adj.*	永久的，不变的
credential	[krə'denʃl]	*n.*	证书，文凭
recommendation	[ˌrekəmen'deɪʃn]	*n.*	推荐信；建议
mnemonics	[nɪ'mɒnɪks]	*n.*	记忆术
parenthesis	[pə'renθəsɪs]	*n.*	插入语；圆括号
exponent	[ɪk'spəʊnənt]	*n.*	指数
productive	[prə'dʌktɪv]	*adj.*	多产的；富有成效的
convince	[kən'vɪns]	*v.*	说服，使确信
hungover	[ˌhʌŋ'əʊvə]	*adj.*	心里难受的
prescribed	[prɪ'skraɪbd]	*adj.*	规定的
inappropriate	[ˌɪnə'prəʊprɪət]	*adj.*	不恰当的；不相称的
imposter	[ɪm'pɒstə]	*n.*	骗子；冒名顶替者
predator	['predətə]	*n.*	食肉动物；捕食者
vulnerability	[ˌvʌlnərə'bɪləti]	*n.*	易损性；弱点
supervision	[ˌsuːpə'vɪʒn]	*n.*	监督；管理
substitute	['sʌbstɪtjuːt]	*v.*	代替，取代
strings attached			附加条件
tinfoil	['tɪnfɔɪl]	*n.*	锡箔，锡纸
essentially	[ɪ'senʃəli]	*adv.*	本质上；本来
physiological	[ˌfɪzɪ'ɒlədʒɪkəl]	*adj.*	生理学的；生理的
presentation	[ˌprezn'teɪʃn]	*n.*	展示；描述
variation	[ˌveərɪ'eɪʃn]	*n.*	变奏曲；变更

WRITING

expectancy	[ɪk'spektənsi]	*n.*	期望，期待
implication	[ˌɪmplɪ'keɪʃn]	*n.*	含义；暗示
ambulance	['æmbjuləns]	*n.*	救护车
fracture	['fræktʃə]	*v.*	破裂；折断
bruise	[bruːz]	*v.*	擦伤；挫伤
collarbone	['kɒləbəʊn]	*n.*	锁骨
eligible	['elɪdʒəbl]	*adj.*	合格的；合适的
specifically	[spə'sɪfɪkli]	*adv.*	特别地；明确地
demographic bonus			人口红利
unremarkable	[ˌʌnrɪ'mɑːkəbl]	*adj.*	平凡的，不显著的
encounter	[ɪn'kaʊntə]	*v.*	遭遇，偶然碰见
vigour	['vɪgə]	*n.*	活力，精力
in accordance with			依照；与……一致
mortality	[mɔː'tæləti]	*n.*	死亡数，死亡率
diminish	[dɪ'mɪnɪʃ]	*v.*	使减少；变小
collaborate	[kə'læbəreɪt]	*v.*	合作

General Training Reading and Writing TEST E

答案速查

READING

Section 1, Questions 1–14

1 B
2 A
3 E
4 C
5 A
6 C
7 D
8 B
9 B
10 E
11 D
12 A
13 B
14 D

Section 2, Questions 15–27

15 TRUE
16 FALSE
17 NOT GIVEN
18 TRUE
19 NOT GIVEN
20 NOT GIVEN
21 F
22 A
23 G
24 B
25 E
26 H
27 C

Section 3, Questions 28–40

28 NOT GIVEN
29 TRUE
30 FALSE
31 TRUE
32 FALSE
33 D
34 C
35 C
36 A
37 A
38 C
39 E
40 F

名师解析

READING

Section 1

体　裁　　广告、公告
题　材　　社会生活、校园生活
主　题　　关于饭店和校园活动的信息
题　型　　配对题

Questions 1–5

题型　配对题(Matching Information)

注意　本题是段落细节配对题，这种题目的具体做题步骤是：先读题目；然后，阅读每个段落，看是否有对应的答案。

1	关键词	can't eat, Monday evenings
	原文定位	B部分末行Evening Wednesday–Saturday
	题解	**答案B**　这里提到晚饭的时间是周三到周六的晚上，所以不包括周一晚上。
2	关键词	peaceful country surroundings
	原文定位	A部分set in 40 acres of scenic woodland, view over beautiful landscaped gardens
	题解	**答案A**　根据A中的关键词scenic woodland（风景林地）和view over beautiful landscaped gardens（观赏美丽的园林花园）可推测出人们在该饭店可以在安静的乡村环境下享用美餐。
3	关键词	eat, Sunday night
	原文定位	E部分Restaurant and takeaway　Sunday　Closed　5–11pm
	题解	**答案E**　这个饭店在周日的下午5–11点营业，也就是可以在周日的晚上在此吃饭。
4	关键词	order delivered, an extra fee
	原文定位	C部分home delivery service wihtin a 4-mile radius of our takeaway—small charge
	题解	**答案C**　周围四公里直径范围内有送货上门服务，收取少量的服务费。题干中的order delivered（预订送货）和extra fee（额外的费用）分别与原文中的home delivery service（送货上门）和takeaway—small charge（收取一点儿费用）相对应。
5	关键词	have dinner, stay the night
	原文定位	A部分Luxury Accommodation Available
	题解	**答案A**　A提到这里有豪华住宿，言外之意吃完饭可以在这里过夜。

Questions 6—14

题型 配对题(Matching Information)

注意 这种题型考查考生进行跳读和扫读的能力，以及阅读并理解文中某一部分要点的能力。

6	关键词	friendly greeting
	原文定位	C部分末句We guarantee you a warm welcome.
	题解	答案C　根据题干中的关键词friendly（友好的），greeting（欢迎）可以定位到C部分，分别与原文的warm（热情的），welcome（欢迎）对应。
7	关键词	relevant skills, preferred
	原文定位	D部分末句An ability to sight-read and previous experience in choral singing in desirable, although not essential.
	题解	答案D　题干中的关键词relevant skills（相关的技能）是对原文an ability to sight-read and previous experience in choral singing（即兴演奏的能力和在唱诗班唱歌的先前经验）的概括，题干中的preferred（首选的）与desirable（令人满意的）相对应。
8	关键词	cheer you up
	原文定位	B部分首句Samba percussion workshop. Lift your spirits with the taste of carnival!
	题解	答案B　题干中的关键词cheer you up（使你高兴起来）与原文中的lift your spirits（提起你的精神）相对应。
9	关键词	suitable for a variety of ages
	原文定位	B部分末句An event for all the family.
	题解	答案B　B部分末句提到这个活动适合所有的家人，与题干表达的内容一致。
10	关键词	individual guidance, provided
	原文定位	E部分中The small class (12 students) assures maximum attention for each student.
	题解	答案E　题干中的individual（个人）与原文中each student（每个学生）对应；题干中的guidance（指导）与原文的attention（关心）对应；题干中的provided（提供）与原文assures（保证）对应。
11	关键词	take part in, public performance
	原文定位	D部分第四句And this term we are rehearsing for a special concert with audience participation on Saturday 1st December.
	题解	答案D　原文中a special concert with audience participation（有观众参加的特别音乐会）就是题干概括的public performance（公开演出）。

TEST E

12	关键词	help someone, overcome shyness
	原文定位	A段末句 The atmosphere is relaxed and unthreatening and great emphasis is placed on developing the confidence and abilities of people who may initially be a little apprehensive!
	题解	答案A 题干中的overcome shyness（克服害羞）与原文中的developing the...apprehensive（培养焦虑的人的自信和能力）意思相同，所以答案为A。
13	关键词	promises rapid progress
	原文定位	B部分第二句It doesn't matter whether you' re an experienced musician or a complete beginner, you' ll be creating complex exotic rhythms in no time.
	题解	答案B 题干中的promises rapid progress（承诺快速进步）是对原文be creating complex exotic rhythms in no time（立刻能够创造出复杂的具有异域风格的韵律）的改写，其中题干中的rapid（快速的）与原文中的in no time（立刻）对应。
14	关键词	not held during the day
	原文定位	D部分第二句We meet every Wednesday evening from 7.30pm to 9.30pm.
	题解	答案D 此题考查的点为时间。其他活动都没有提及时间，只有D的活动提到时间在7.30–9.30pm.（晚上7点半到9点半），也就是活动不在白天举行。

Section 2

体　裁　　公告
题　材　　校园生活
主　题　　介绍大学校园里的学生生活和课程情况
题　型　　判断题、配对题

Questions 15–20

题型 判断题(Identifying Information)

注意 判断题在出题时一般只考查题目中一个信息的是非对错，不会同时考查多个信息，那么考查的这个就是考点，考生要特别留意这个信息的要点是什么。

15	关键词	allocated, job experience, abroad
	原文定位	第三段末句...as a result, many students have the opportunity of visiting and working in a European country in the course of their studies.
	题解	答案TRUE 题干中的allocated（分派）与原文中have the opportunity of...in the course of their studies（学习过程中有参观、工作的机会）相对应；题干中的abroad（国外）与原文中in a European country（在欧洲国家）对应。答案为TRUE。

16	关键词	elections, Union President and Executive Committee
	原文定位	第四段第二、三句The Union...is run by an Executive Committee elected by students in the Autumn Term. The President is elected every Summer Term to provided continuity for the next academic year.
	题解	答案FALSE 从原文可知Executive Committee（执行委员会）的选举在Autumn Term（秋季），而President（主席）的选举在every Summer Term（每个夏季），两个选举不是在同一个季节进行，题干说法有误。答案为FALSE。
17	关键词	staff, LRC, facilities
	原文定位	第五段首句The Carey learning resources centre provides easy access to a wide range of printed and audiovisual learning materials which can help students with coursework.
	题解	答案NOT GIVEN 原文提到LRC会给学生提供printed（打印的）和audiovisual（视听的）学习材料，但没有提及有没有staff（员工）来帮助学生使用设备。答案为NOT GIVEN。
18	关键词	nursery care, a first-come, first-served basis
	原文定位	第七段末句Places are limited, so, if you are interested, apply early to reserve a place by contacting Linda Baker on the college telephone number.
	题解	答案TRUE 题干中a first-come, first-served basis（先到先得）与原文Places are limited...apply early to reserve a place（地方是有限的……早预订最好）表达的意思是一致的。答案为TRUE。
19	关键词	Refectory serves
	原文定位	第八段首句This provides refreshments between 08.30 and 19.00 with hot meals served three times a day.
	题解	答案NOT GIVEN 原文提到Refectory（食堂）是在早8点半到晚7点之间提供一日三餐，没有提及fast-food（快餐）服务。
20	关键词	Chapel View Restaurant, students only
	原文定位	末段首句This is another training restaurant that is set up as a quick-service facility which offers a selection of snacks and main courses at a modest price.
	题解	答案NOT GIVEN Chapel View Restaurant（教堂视图餐厅）提供快速服务的设施，这些设施提供零食和主食，价格合理，没有说for students only（仅为学生）。

Questions 21–27

题型 配对题(Matching Information)

注意 题目会出现某些选项不被选择作为答案的可能，或者有些选项会被用到不止一次。

21	关键词	advertising
	原文定位	F段末句Students complete units in picture composition and photographic design, and gain hands-on experience of desktop publishing and presentations.
	题解	**答案F** F课程学习之后，学生可以获得picture composition（图片构成）、photographic design（摄影设计）、desktop publishing（桌面出版系统）和presentations（演示）的经验，这说明此门课程为advertising（广告）。
22	关键词	TV production
	原文定位	A段首句This course will enable students to experience performing arts and the media at a basic level.
	题解	**答案A** A课程学习之后，学生能够获得基础级的performing arts（表演艺术）和media（媒体）知识，这说明此门课程为TV production（电视制作）。
23	关键词	architecture
	原文定位	G段首句This course is designed to provide an introduction to the construction industry.
	题解	**答案G** G课程能够提供construction（建筑）行业的介绍，这里construction（建筑）与题目的architecture（建筑）是一致的。
24	关键词	company management
	原文定位	B段首句The aim of this course is to provide a thorough grounding in business-related skills and a comprehensive knowledge of business practice.
	题解	**答案B** B课程传授的是与商业相关的技能和完整的商业实践知识，根据business-related（与商业相关的），business practice（商业实践）的提示，可以判定指的是company management（公司管理）课程。
25	关键词	working with the disabled
	原文定位	E段首句This course gives a foundation for a career in caring for children, the elderly or people with special needs.
	题解	**答案E** E课程是为children（儿童），the elderly（老人），people with special needs（有特殊需要的人）这些人提供照顾而设置的，题干中the disabled（残疾人）是原文中people with special needs（有特殊需要的人）的具体化。

TEST E

26	关键词	secretarial tasks
	原文定位	H段首句、第二句...this course...employment in office work. In addition to word processing, the course also covers spreadsheets, computerized accounting, databases and desktop publishing.
	题解	答案H　H段首句中的office work（办公室工作），第二句中提到课程教授的word processing（文字处理），spreadsheets（电子表格），computerized accounting（电脑会计），databases（数据库），desktop publishing（桌面出版系统）内容都是说明这门课程是为secretarial tasks（秘书工作）而设置的。
27	关键词	beauty therapy
	原文定位	C段第二句Units will include maintaining employment standards, salon management duties, providing facial massage and skin care, instruction on make-up.
	题解	答案C　C课程提供facial massage（面部按摩）和skin care（皮肤护理），这都是beauty therapy（美容护理）课程的内容。

Section 3

体　裁　说明文
题　材　社会科学类
主　题　关于通感的说明文章
题　型　判断题、选择题

Questions 28–32

题型　判断题 (Identifying Information)

注意　判断题型会提供一组陈述，这种题型考查考生进行跳读、扫读和对细节进行阅读理解的能力。

28	关键词	Newspaper articles and TV news
	原文定位	首段第二句...when by chance I came across an article in a newspaper on research into synaesthesia at a London hospital.
	题解	答案NOT GIVEN　原文中只在首段提到作者偶然在报纸上看到一篇伦敦一家医院关于通感的研究文章，目的是为了引出下文，文章中没有出现关于 monotonous regularity（无变化的规则）的说明。
29	关键词	at the same time
	原文定位	第二段末句Or, to put it simply, synaesthetes, i.e. people with synaesthesia, have their senses held together, so that they experience several senses simultaneously.
	题解	答案TRUE　原文指出：简言之，有通感的人，他们的感官是集中在一起的，他们能同时体验不同的感觉。而题干中的at the same time同义替换原句中的simultaneously。

TEST E

30	关键词	new phenomenon
	原文定位	第三段首句To those not already aware of it, synaesthesia seems a new phenomenon.
	题解	答案FALSE 那些还没有意识到通感存在的人，把通感看做一个新的现象。接下来说Yet, it is far from new（是的，它不是一个新鲜事物），并进行举例说明，最后得出结论：So, synaesthesia has a respectable history（通感有一段明晰的历史），即通感并不是新鲜事物，所以原文和题干意思相反，错误。
31	关键词	the 17th century
	原文定位	第三段第三句In 1690, John Locke, the philosopher, wrote of a blind man with synaesthetic capabilities.
	题解	答案TRUE 早在1690年哲学家约翰·洛克就曾写过一个具有通感能力的盲人，题干说对于通感的描述最早可追溯到17世纪，1690年属于17世纪。
32	关键词	strange
	原文定位	第四段首句Synaesthesia is understandably met with a certain degree of scepticism, since it is something beyond the comprehension of the vast majority of people.
	题解	答案FALSE 人们对通感有某种程度的怀疑也是可以理解的，就是说这种怀疑并不足为奇， Understandably（可理解地）与It is strange that...sceptical（它是奇怪的……怀疑的）意思相反，错误。

TEST E

Questions 33–36

题型 选择题 (Multiple Choice)

注意 由于选择题考查细节，所以题干或选项中的词往往能够提供定位线索，方便考生在文章中把所对应的句子或段落找出来。

33	关键词	Son et lumiere shows
	原文定位	第四段第二句Son et lumiere shows in the 19th century were an attempt at combining the senses in a public display, but such displays were not capable of conveying the sensations experienced by involuntary synaesthesia...
	题解	答案D 19世纪的声光演出就试图将各种感觉融合展示给公众，但是这样的展示不能传递本能地产生通感的感觉，所以did not reproduce符合题意。
34	关键词	Alexander Scriabin, Rimsy-Korsako
	原文定位	第四段第四句、第五句Alexander Scriabin, the Russian composer (1871–1915), tried to express his own synaesthetic abilities in his symphony Prometheus, *the Poem of Fire* (1992)和第五句And another Russian, Rimsky-Korsakov, noted the colour associations musical keys possessed.
	题解	答案C 原文指出亚历山大·斯克里亚宾和里姆斯基–柯萨科夫在音乐作品中表达他们的通感能力，所以linked music to colour（联系音乐和颜色）符合题意。

35	关键词	Wassily Kandinsky
	原文定位	第五段In the field of the visual arts...credited with being the founder of abstract painting,和第三句He did not see colours solely in terms of objects, but associated them with sounds.
	题解	**答案C** 原文指出瓦斯里·康定斯基是抽象画派的鼻祖，在一次瓦格纳的音乐会上经历了感觉的融合，音乐带来了不同的颜色，第五段第三句指出他也创作音乐，他创作的歌剧是色彩、灯光和音乐的结合，故答案为composed music（结合的音乐）。
36	关键词	sufferers
	原文定位	第六段第二句Initially, they often feel that there is something wrong psychologically or mentally, or that everyone feels that way.
	题解	**答案A** 起初，那些人认为自己心理或者精神上有问题，原文的initially（最初）就是题干中at first的重现，即something wrong with them（他们存在一些错误）。

Questions 37–40

题型 选择题 (Multiple Choice)

注意 在多项选择题中，指示语中会提示正确选项的数量。在誊写答题卡的时候，一定要注意多项选择题的题号，一个正确选项占用一个题号。

37	关键词	disoriented
	原文定位	第六段第五句While the condition of synaesthesia may hamper many people because of its disorienting effects, it can also open up a range of new skills.
	题解	**答案A** 通过原文可知：一些通感者被他们的能力弄得不知所措，disoriented（无判断的）符合题意，这是选项之一。
38	关键词	memory
	原文定位	第六段倒数第二句Synaesthetes find they are able to remember certain things with great ease.
	题解	**答案C** 原文指出通感能增强记忆力，memory（记忆）与to remember certain things（记得某些事情）为同义转换，这是选项之二。
39	关键词	use their ability to help themselves
	原文定位	第六段第四句Suppression is an option, but unwittingly some people have managed to make use of the ability to their advantage.
	题解	**答案E** 第六段指出有的通感者会利用这种能力并让它成为一种优势，这里make use of the ability to their advantage（利用能力使之成为一种优势）与use their ability to help themselves（用他们的能力去帮助他们自己）为同义转换。

40	关键词	obstacle
	原文定位	第六段第五句While the condition of synaesthesia may hamper many people because of its disorienting effects.
	题解	答案F 原文可知通感的能力在通感失效后，有可能成为一种障碍，be an obstacle与may hamper属于同义词替换。

WRITING

WRITING TASK 1

名师解读

书信写作一定要记得以完成任务为中心。题目中所有的细节必须涉及，所有的问题必须回答。本题G类小作文是写一封投诉信。投诉信中投诉产品质量问题是经常会考到的话题。

投诉信的内容要点：

1 所要投诉或抱怨的事情是什么；

2 将时间、地点、事情的经过及问题说清楚；

3 解决问题的建议。

投诉信的注意事项：

1 言语要平和，不要用太过激的言语；

2 对解决问题的建议要合理；

3 一封信只写一件事；

4 事情的来龙去脉要写清楚。

高分范文

Dear Sir or Madam,

I' m writing to **complain** about the recent purchase of a woolen sweater from your **department** store on Philip Street, on August 25, 2013.

I recently washed the sweater in cool water, as per the **instructions** on the label. However, when I removed it from the machine, the garment was stretched out of shape and no longer fit.

I phoned the store last Tuesday (June 21) and spoke to the department manager, a Mr. Morris, who was rather rude on the phone and informed me that I could not get a replacement as it was purchased at a reduced price. I felt really **upset**, for I have been a loyal customer of your store for many years and until this incident, never had made any complaints. I, therefore, feel disappointed to be treated in such a manner.

I would, however, be perfectly satisfied if you would kindly replace the sweater or **refund** my money, whichever is more **convenient**.

I look forward to hearing from you soon.

Yours truly,

Kenny Gao (177 words)

WRITING TASK 2

文章结构

问题+影响因素1+影响因素2+总结

problem + reason 1 + reason 2 + conclusion
第一段：背景句+引出话题+解释
第二段：影响因素1+理由
第三段：影响因素2+理由
第四段：总结+理由

思路点拨

步骤一：审题（<3分钟）

When we seek a future career, what factors should we consider? Whose suggestions should we consider?

通读题目，了解大意，判断题型。

本题的题型为论说性的作文。题目的大意为：进行职业选择时，需要考虑哪些因素，需要考虑谁的建议？

→再读题目，辨别关键词，区分主题词和限定词，推测考官的出题意图。

主题词：future career, factors, suggestions

限定词：what factors, whose suggestions, your answer, relevant examples

步骤二：列大纲（<3分钟）

英文提纲	Introduction: choosing the right career→cannot afford to make a single mistake→not easy→in dilemmas→factors, be taken into consideration Body: first factor, salary should not be too low→another factor, have an objective understanding of your ability and interest Conclusion：keep in mind the old saying→seek advice from the career advisory office
中文提纲	引出话题：选择合适的事业→不能出一点差错→做出选择不容易→处于两难的境地→需要考虑的因素 主体段落：第一个因素，薪水不能太低→第二个因素，对自己的能力和兴趣要有客观的了解 总结：记住这句俗语→咨询职业顾问

高分范文

Choosing the right career is regarded as a turning point in one's life. It is so crucial that we cannot afford to make a single mistake. However, it is always not easy to make a satisfying choice. Sometimes we find ourselves involved in dilemmas. To my mind, when we seek a job, the following factors need to be **taken into consideration.**

The first factor that can be seen by every person is that the **salary** should not be too low. Most of us will get married and have children. Consequently we need a stable income because of our family **responsibilities** even if they are not satisfied with our job. In addition, to live a more comfortable life is a part of human nature. All these things need a certain amount of money.

Another factor we must consider is that we should have an objective understanding of our ability as well as interest so that we will know which **occupation** is **suitable** for us. In other words, the job should allow us to live a balanced life. It should not be so time-consuming that we have no time for family, friends and personal interests. Nor should it give us so much pressure that we cannot relax in our free time.

As the proverb goes, two heads are better than one. When we choose a job, always remember to talk with parents, teachers or anyone we trust. They possess rich experience and knowledge from which we are sure to benefit. They know us best and can offer us most sincere advice. Keep in mind the old saying that it is good to learn at another man's cost. Furthermore, we may also seek advice from the career **advisory** office that is always ready to provide professional suggestion. (302 words)